BUSN

4th Edition

Kelly | McGowen

Australia • Brazil • Japan • Korea • Mexico • Singapore • Spain • United Kingdom • United States

BUSN: 4th Edition

BUSN4
Marce Kelly | Jim McGowen

© 2012, 2011 South-Western, Cengage Learning. All rights reserved.

Planning Your Career
Julie Griffin Levitt

© 2008, 2006 South-Western, Cengage Learning. All rights reserved.

Executive Editors:
 Maureen Staudt
 Michael Stranz

Senior Project Development Manager:
 Linda deStefano

Marketing Specialist:
 Courtney Sheldon

Senior Production/Manufacturing Manager:
 Donna M. Brown

PreMedia Manager:
 Joel Brennecke

Sr. Rights Acquisition Account Manager:
 Todd Osborne

Cover Image:
Getty Images*

*Unless otherwise noted, all cover images used by Custom Solutions, a part of Cengage Learning, have been supplied courtesy of Getty Images with the exception of the Earthview cover image, which has been supplied by the National Aeronautics and Space Administration (NASA).

For product information and technology assistance, contact us at
Cengage Learning Customer & Sales Support, 1-800-354-9706

For permission to use material from this text or product, submit all requests online at **cengage.com/permissions**
Further permissions questions can be emailed to
permissionrequest@cengage.com

This book contains select works from existing Cengage Learning resources and was produced by Cengage Learning Custom Solutions for collegiate use. As such, those adopting and/or contributing to this work are responsible for editorial content accuracy, continuity and completeness.

Compilation © 2011 Cengage Learning
ISBN-13: 978-1-133-36160-2

ISBN-10: 1-133-36160-9

Cengage Learning
5191 Natorp Boulevard
Mason, Ohio 45040
USA
Cengage Learning is a leading provider of customized learning solutions with office locations around the globe, including Singapore, the United Kingdom, Australia, Mexico, Brazil, and Japan. Locate your local office at:
international.cengage.com/region.

Cengage Learning products are represented in Canada by Nelson Education, Ltd.
For your lifelong learning solutions, visit **www.cengage.com/custom.**
Visit our corporate website at **www.cengage.com.**

Printed in the United States of America

Brief Custom Contents

BUSN, 4th Edition
Marce Kelly | Jim McGowan

with

Planning Your Career
Julie Griffin Levitt
(located after the blue divider)

Visit www.cengagebrain.com to see the online
appendices.

Online Appendix 1:
Labor Union
and Collective
Bargaining

Online Appendix 2:
Business Law

Online Appendix 3:
Personal Finance

© IMAGE SOURCE BLACK/IMAGE SOURCE

CHAPTER 5

Business Communication: Creating and Delivering Messages that Matter 60

PART 2 CREATING A BUSINESS

CHAPTER 6

Business Formation: Choosing the Form that Fits 72

CHAPTER 7

© DANNY MOLOSHOK/REUTERS/LANDOV

© VASILIY YAKOBCHUK/ISTOCKPHOTO.COM

PART 3 FINANCING A BUSINESS

CHAPTER 8

AP IMAGES/DAVID KARP; © TETRA IMAGES/JUPITERIMAGES

AP IMAGES/JASON DECROW; © CREATAS IMAGES/JUPITERIMAGES

CHAPTER 13

CHAPTER 15

CHAPTER 16

Managing Information and Technology: Finding New Ways to Learn and Link 236

© PHOTOLINK/PHOTODISC/GETTY IMAGES

CHAPTER 17

Operations Management: Putting It All Together 252

To my family—
Scot, Justin, Lauren,
Allison, Cathy, and Shel.
You are my greatest blessing.

—Marce Kelly

To my wife, Judy.
Your patience,
encouragement and
love made this
possible.

—Jim McGowen

The idea for this book—a whole new way of learning—began with students like you across the country. We paid attention to students who wanted to learn about business without slogging through endless pages of dry text. We listened to students who wanted to sit through class without craving a triple espresso. We responded to students who wanted to use their favorite gadgets to prepare for tests.

So we are confident that BUSN will meet your needs. The short, lively text covers all the key concepts without the fluff. The examples are relevant and engaging, and the visual style makes the book fun to read. But the text is only part of the package. You can access a rich variety of study tools via computer or iPod—the choice is yours.

We did one other thing we hope you'll like. We paid a lot of attention to students' concerns about the high price of college textbooks. We made it our mission to ensure that our package not only meets your needs but does so without busting your budget!

This innovative, student-focused package was developed by the authors—Marce Kelly and Jim McGowen—and the experienced Cengage Learning publishers. The Cengage team contributed a deep understanding of students and professors across the nation, and the authors brought years of teaching and business experience.

Marce Kelly, who earned her MBA from UCLA's Anderson School of Management, spent the first 14 years of her career in marketing, building brands for Neutrogena and The Walt Disney Corporation. But her true love is teaching, so in 2000 she accepted a full-time teaching position at Santa Monica College. Professor Kelly has received seven Outstanding Instructor awards from the International Education Center and has been named four times to *Who's Who Among American Teachers*.

Jim McGowen is professor emeritus in the Business Division at Southwestern Illinois College. He has taught Introduction to Business for over a quarter of a century, and continues to teach several sections of the course each year. Professor McGowen chaired the Business Transfer Department at Southwestern Illinois College for twelve years, giving him the opportunity to work with faculty teaching a wide range of business courses. This experience gave him a deep appreciation for role the Introduction to Business course plays in a business curriculum. Professor McGowen has a bachelor's degree in business administration and a master's degree in economics, both from Auburn University. He has received the Emerson Prize for Teaching Excellence and been recognized for teaching excellence by the Illinois Community College Trustees Association. He was named Faculty Member of the Year at Southwestern Illinois College in 2007.

We would appreciate any comments or suggestions you want to offer about this package. You can reach Jim McGowen at jmcgowen4@gmail.com and Marce Kelly at marcella.kelly@gmail.com. We wish you a fun, positive, productive term, and look forward to your feedback!

Marce Kelly

Jim McGowen

1

BUSINESS NOW:

CHANGE IS THE ONLY CONSTANT

LEARNING OBJECTIVES

After studying this chapter, you will be able to:

LO1 Define business and discuss the role of business in the economy

LO2 Explain the evolution of modern business

LO3 Discuss the role of nonprofit organizations in the economy

LO4 Outline the core factors of production and how they affect the economy

LO5 Describe today's business environment and discuss each key dimension

LO6 Explain how current business trends might affect your career choices

Visit CourseMate at **www.cengagebrain.com.**

> # Success is simply a matter of luck—ask any failure!
>
> *Earl Wilson, U.S. Baseball Player*

LO1 Business Now: Moving at Breakneck Speed

Day by day, the business world simply spins faster. Industries rise—and sometimes fall—in the course of a few short months. Technologies forge instant connections across the globe. And powerful new trends surface and submerge, sometimes within less than a year. In this fast-paced, fluid environment, change is the only constant.

Successful firms lean forward and embrace the change. They seek the opportunities and avoid the pitfalls. They carefully evaluate risks. They completely understand their market. And they adhere to ethical practices. Their core goal: to generate long-term profits by delivering unsurpassed **value** to their customers.

Business Basics: Some Key Definitions

While you can certainly recognize a business when you see one, more formal definitions may help as you read through this book. A **business** is any activity that provides goods and services in an effort to earn a profit. **Profit** is the financial reward that comes from starting and running a business. More specifically, a profit is the money that a business earns in sales (or revenue), minus expenses such as the cost of goods and the cost of salaries. But clearly, not every business earns a profit all the time. When a business brings in less money than it needs to cover expenses, it incurs a **loss**. If you launch a music label, for instance, you'll need to pay your artists, buy or lease a studio, and purchase equipment, among other expenses. If your label generates hits, you'll earn more than enough to cover all your expenses and make yourself rich. But a series of duds could leave you holding the bag.

Just the possibility of earning a profit provides a powerful incentive for people of all backgrounds to launch their own enterprise. Despite the economic meltdown of 2008, nearly 19% of American adults were engaged in entrepreneurial activity—either launching or managing their own

businesses.[1] The numbers among your peers are probably even higher, since more than two-thirds of college students plan to launch their own business at some point in their career. People who risk their time, money, and other resources to start and manage a business are called **entrepreneurs**.

The *Forbes* list of the richest Americans highlights the astounding ability of the entrepreneurial spirit to build wealth. The top ten—featured in Exhibit 1.1—includes multiple members of the Walton family who were not themselves entrepreneurs: their money comes from retail powerhouse Walmart, founded by brilliant, eccentric entrepreneur Sam Walton.

Interestingly, as entrepreneurs create wealth for themselves, they produce a ripple effect that enriches everyone around them. For instance, if your new website becomes the next Facebook, who will benefit? Clearly, *you* will. And you'll probably spend at least some of that money enriching

EXHIBIT 1.1 The Richest Americans 2009, *Forbes* Magazine[2]

Name	Net Worth	Source of Wealth
Bill Gates	$50,000,000,000	Microsoft
Warren Buffet	$40,000,000,000	Berkshire Hathaway
Lawrence Ellison	$27,000,000,000	Oracle
Christy Walton and family	$21,500,000,000	Walmart
Jim C. Walton	$19,600,000,000	Walmart
Alice Walton	$19,300,000,000	Walmart
S. Robson Walton	$19,000,000,000	Walmart
Michael Bloomberg	$17,500,000,000	Bloomberg
Charles Koch	$16,000,000,000	manufacturing, energy
David Koch	$16,000,000,000	manufacturing, energy

value The relationship between the price of a good or a service and the benefits that it offers its customers.

business Any activity that provides goods and services in an effort to earn a profit.

profit The money that a business earns in sales (or revenue), minus expenses, such as the cost of goods, and the cost of salaries. Revenue – Expenses = Profit (or Loss)

loss When a business incurs expenses that are greater than its revenue.

entrepreneurs People who risk their time, money, and other resources to start and manage a business.

© MIKE POWELL/STONE+/GETTY IMAGES

Oops! what were they THINKING?!

Not Every Dumb Move Is an Utter Disaster...

In the wake of disastrous mistakes and outrageous mismanagement across our economy, it might be tough to remember that some mistakes are actually pretty amusing. But *Fortune* magazine and *Business 2.0* have collected a number of examples that might help remind you.[3] A sampling:

- *Too much to bear...* Disneyland temporarily closed the "It's a Small World" attraction to deepen its water channel after the ride's boats started getting stuck under loads of overweight passengers. Employees asked larger passengers to disembark—and compensated them with coupons for free food!

- *Clicking without thinking.* To test Google's ability to block harmful advertising, Belgian IT security consultant Didier Stevens posted an ad that read, "Is your PC virus-free? Get it infected here!" It was accepted by Google and displayed 259,723 times; 409 Web surfers actually clicked on the ad.

- *Must sleep now...* During a routine service call, a Comcast cable repairman fell asleep on customer Brian Finkelstein's couch. Finkelstein's ensuing video, complete with commentary on the company's poor equipment, high prices, and lousy customer service, quickly became a viral hit on the Web. Comcast apologized and fired the nodding worker—who, incidentally, had been stuck on hold for more than an hour while calling in to the company for assistance.

- *Insecurity alert!* Diebold Corporation tightened security after learning that a simple virus could hack its electronic voting machines. Months later a hacker used a picture of a key from the company website to make a real key that could open the company's machines.

- *We just needed a Guy...* The BBC recently invited IT expert Guy Kewney to its studios for an interview about Apple's iTunes Music Store. But when the cameras started rolling, the BBC correspondent found herself talking to the wrong Guy—namely, Guy Goma, a computer technician who was waiting in the lobby for a job interview. Goma gamely tried his best in the TV interview, but failed to land the gig.

---

your local clubs, clothing stores, and car dealerships. But others will benefit, too, including your members, advertisers on your site and the staff who supports them, contractors who build your facilities, and the government that collects your taxes. The impact of one successful entrepreneur can extend to the far reaches of the economy. Multiply the impact by thousands of entrepreneurs—each working in his or her own self-interest—and you can see how the profit motive benefits virtually everyone.

From a bigger picture perspective, business drives up the **standard of living** for people worldwide, contributing to a higher **quality of life**. Not only do businesses provide the products and services that people enjoy, but they also provide the jobs that people need. Beyond the obvious, business contributes to society through innovation—think cars, TVs, and personal computers. Business also helps raise the standard of living through taxes, which the government spends on projects that range from streetlights to environmental cleanup. And socially responsible firms contribute even more, actively advocating for the well-being of the society that feeds their success.

LO2 The History of Business: Putting It All in Context

You may be surprised to learn that—unlike today—business hasn't always been focused on what the customer wants. In fact, business in the United States has changed rather dramatically over the past 200–300 years. Most business historians divide the history of American business into five distinct eras, which overlap during the periods of transition:

- **The Industrial Revolution:** Technological advances fueled a period of rapid industrialization in America from the mid-1700s to the mid-1800s. As mass production took hold, huge factories replaced skilled artisan workshops. The factories hired large numbers of semiskilled workers, who specialized in a limited number of tasks. The result was

Chapter 1   Business Now: Change Is the Only Constant

unprecedented production efficiency, but also a loss of individual ownership and personal pride in the production process.

- **The Entrepreneurship Era:** Building on the foundation of the industrial revolution, large-scale entrepreneurs emerged in the second half of the 1800s, building business empires. These industrial titans created enormous wealth, raising the overall standard of living across the country. But many also dominated their markets, forcing out competitors, manipulating prices, exploiting workers, and decimating the environment. Toward the end of the 1800s, the government stepped into the business realm, passing laws to regulate business and protect consumers and workers, creating more balance in the economy.

- **The Production Era:** In the early part of the 1900s, major businesses focused on further refining the production process and creating greater efficiencies. Jobs became even more specialized, increasing productivity and lowering costs and prices. In 1913, Henry Ford introduced the assembly line, which quickly became standard across major manufacturing industries. With managers focused on efficiency, the customer was an afterthought. But when customers tightened their belts during the Great Depression and World War II, businesses took notice. The "hard sell" emerged: aggressive persuasion designed to separate consumers from their cash.

- **The Marketing Era:** After WWII, the balance of power shifted away from producers and toward consumers, flooding the market with enticing choices. To differentiate themselves from their competitors, businesses began to develop brands, or distinctive identities, to help consumers understand the differences among various products. The *marketing concept* emerged: a consumer focus that permeates successful companies in every department, at every level. This approach continues to influence business decisions today as global competition heats up to unprecedented levels.

- **The Relationship Era:** Building on the marketing concept, today, leading-edge firms look beyond each immediate transaction with a customer and aim to build long-term relationships. Satisfied customers can become advocates for a business, spreading the word with more speed and credibility than even the best promotional campaign. And cultivating current customers is more profitable than constantly seeking new ones. A key tool is technology. Using the Web and other digital resources, businesses gather detailed information about their customers and use this data to serve them better.

standard of living The quality and quantity of goods and services available to a population.

quality of life The overall sense of well-being experienced by either an individual or a group.

WITHOUT A MAP...

CHARTING AN ETHICAL COURSE

When in doubt, we usually don't!

Most of us can probably think of a time when we should have taken some action, but instead we did nothing, because doing nothing was easier. . . . Enter the choice architects, behavioral scientists, who claim that businesses, governments, and other institutions can engineer our options to "nudge" us into making choices that are (ideally) more socially desirable, or (from a business standpoint) more profitable than the choices that we'd make on our own. A couple of examples:

- ***Better Aim:*** As most women who share toilets with men can attest, even the best-intentioned men don't seem to, uh, aim well when it comes to toilet hygiene. In busy restrooms, this is more than just a gross annoyance; dirty bathrooms increase cleaning costs and undermine brand image. Aad Kiedboom, an economist who worked for the Schiphol International Airport in Amsterdam, tackled this issue by etching the image of a black housefly onto the bowls of the airport's urinals, just to the left of the drain. As a result, "spillage" decreased 80%.

- ***Musical Stairs:*** In response to rising obesity rates the city of Stockholm has retrofitted a staircase in their Odenplan subway station to resemble giant piano keys, which produce real sound, to encourage commuters to climb the stairs rather than ride the escalator. Hidden video footage suggests that so far it's been a resounding success—well used and fun for everyone.

Advocates argue that choice architects work for the good of society, encouraging—but never coercing—people to make positive choices. Critics argue that choice architects are manipulative—shoving rather than nudging, which interferes with peoples' freedom of choice. In the wrong hands, that can be dangerous. What is your perspective? In the hands of business, will choice architecture ultimately be positive or negative?[4]

LO3 Nonprofits and the Economy: The Business of Doing Good

Nonprofit organizations play a critical role in the economy, often working hand-in-hand with businesses to improve the quality of life in our society. Focusing on areas such as health, human services, education, art, religion, and culture, **nonprofits** are business-*like* establishments, but their primary goals do not include profits. Chuck Bean, Executive Director of the Nonprofit Roundtable, explains: "By definition, nonprofits are not in the business of financial gain. We're in the business of doing good. However, nonprofits are still businesses in every other sense—they employ people, they take in revenue, they produce goods and services and contribute in significant ways to our region's economic stability and growth." Nationwide, nonprofits employ about one in ten workers, accounting for more paid workers than the entire construction industry and more than the finance, insurance, and real-estate sectors combined. And nonprofit museums, schools, theaters, and orchestras have become economic magnets for many communities, drawing additional investment.[5]

LO4 Factors of Production: The Basic Building Blocks

Both businesses and nonprofits rely on **factors of production**—four fundamental resources—to achieve their objectives. Some combination of these factors is crucial for an economic system to work and create wealth. As you read through the factors, keep in mind that they don't come free of charge. Human resources, for instance, require wages, while entrepreneurs need a profit incentive.

- **Natural resources:** This factor includes all inputs that offer value in their natural state, such as land, fresh water, wind, and mineral deposits. Most natural resources must be extracted, purified, or harnessed; people cannot actually create them. (Note that agricultural products, which people do create through planting and tending, are not a natural resource.) The value of all natural resources tends to rise with high demand, low supply, or both.

- **Capital:** This factor includes machines, tools, buildings, information, and technology—the synthetic resources that a business needs to produce goods or services. Computers and telecommunications capability have become pivotal elements of capital across a surprising range of industries, from financial

Many businesses work with nonprofits to boost their impact in the community.

© JIM BOURG/REUTERS/LANDOV

services to professional sports. You may be surprised to learn that in this context, capital does not include money, but clearly, businesses use money to acquire, maintain, and upgrade their capital.

- **Human Resources:** This factor encompasses the physical, intellectual, and creative contributions of everyone who works within an economy. As technology replaces a growing number of manual labor jobs, education and motivation have become increasingly important to human resource development. Given the importance of knowledge to workforce effectiveness, some business experts, such as management guru Peter Drucker, break out knowledge as its own category, separate from human resources.

- **Entrepreneurship:** Entrepreneurs are people who take the risk of launching and operating their own businesses, largely in response to the profit incentive. They tend to see opportunities where others don't, and they use their own resources to capitalize on that potential. Entrepreneurial enterprises can kick-start an economy, creating a tidal wave of opportunity by harnessing the other factors of production. But entrepreneurs don't thrive in an environment that doesn't support them. The key ingredient is economic freedom: freedom of choice (who to hire, for instance, or what to produce), freedom from excess regulation, and freedom from too much taxation. Protection from corruption and unfair competition is another entrepreneurial "must."

Clearly, all of these factors must be in place for an economy to thrive. But which factor is *most* important? One way to answer that question is to examine current economies around the world. Russia and China are both rich in natural resources and human resources.

And both countries have a solid level of capital (growing in China, and deteriorating in Russia). Yet neither country is wealthy; both rank relatively low in terms of gross national income per person. The missing ingredient seems to be entrepreneurship, limited in Russia largely through corruption and in China through government interference and taxes. Contrast those examples with, say, Hong Kong. The population is small and the natural resources are severely limited, yet Hong Kong has consistently ranked among the richest regions in Asia. The reason: operating for many years under the British legal and economic system, the government actively encouraged entrepreneurship, which fueled the creation of wealth. Recognizing the potential of entrepreneurship, China has recently done more to relax regulations and support free enterprise. The result has been tremendous growth, which may yet bring China into the ranks of the wealthier nations.[6]

LO5 The Business Environment: The Context for Success

No business operates in a vacuum. Outside factors play a vital role in determining whether each individual business succeeds or fails. Likewise, the broader **business environment** can make the critical difference in whether an overall economy thrives or disintegrates. The five key dimensions of the business environment are the economic environment, the competitive environment, the technological environment, the social environment, and the global environment, as shown in Exhibit 1.2.

EXHIBIT 1.2 The Business Environment

Each dimension of the business environment affects both individual businesses and the economy in general.

The Economic Environment

In September 2008 the U.S. economy plunged into the worst fiscal crisis since the Great Depression. Huge, venerable financial institutions faced collapse, spurring unprecedented bailouts by the Federal government and the Federal Reserve. By the end of the year, the stock market had lost more than a third of its value, and 11.1 million Americans were out of work. Housing prices fell precipitously, and foreclosure rates reached record levels. As fear swept through the banking industry, neither businesses nor individuals could borrow money to meet their needs. Economic turmoil in the United States spread quickly around the world, fueling a global economic crisis.

But through 2009 the U.S. economy began to recover, although unemployment remained high. The Federal Reserve—the U.S. central banking system—took unprecedented, proactive steps to encourage an economic turnaround. And President Barack Obama spearheaded passage of a massive economic stimulus package, designed not only to create jobs, but also to build infrastructure—with a focus on renewable

business environment The setting in which business operates. The five key components are: economic environment, competitive environment, technological environment, social environment, and global environment.

The bank bailout was about as popular as a root canal.

Barack Obama, State of the Union address, January 2010

energy—to position the U.S. economy for stability and growth in the decades to come. (The price, of course, will be more national debt, which could counterbalance some of the benefits.)

The government also takes active steps on an ongoing basis to reduce the risks of starting and running a business. The result: free enterprise and fair competition flourish. Despite the economic crisis, research suggests that most budding entrepreneurs still plan to launch their firms in the next three years. One of the government policies that support business is the relatively low Federal tax rate, both for individuals and businesses. And President Obama has proposed lowering the tax rate even further for a large swath of individual taxpayers and businesses. A number of states—from Alabama to Nevada—make their local economies even more appealing by providing special tax deals to attract new firms. The Federal government also runs entire agencies that support business, such as the Small Business Administration. Other branches of the government, such as the Federal Trade Commission, actively promote fair competitive practices, which help give every enterprise a chance to succeed.

Another key element of the U.S. economic environment is legislation that supports enforceable contracts.

For instance, if you contract a company to supply your silk screening business with 1,000 blank tee shirts at $4.00 per piece, that firm must comply or face legal consequences. The firm can't wait until a day before delivery and jack up the price to $8.00 per piece, because you would almost certainly respond with a successful lawsuit. Many U.S. business people take enforceable contracts for granted, but in a number of developing countries—which offer some of today's largest business opportunities—contracts are often not enforceable (at least not in day-to-day practice).

Corruption also affects the economic environment. A low level of corruption and bribery dramatically reduces the risk of running a business by ensuring that everyone plays by the same set of rules—rules that are clearly visible to every player. Fortunately, U.S. laws keep domestic corruption mostly—but not completely—at bay. Other ethical lapses such as shady accounting can also increase the cost of doing business for everyone involved. But in the wake of ethical meltdowns at major corporations such as Enron and WorldCom, the Federal

AP IMAGES/RON EDMONDS

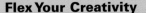

Flex Your Creativity

As the second decade of the 21st century begins, our nation stands at a crossroads. The day he took office, President Obama declared, "*Today I say to you that the challenges we face are real, they are serious and they are many. They will not be met easily or in a short span of time. But know this, America: They will be met.*"

We will meet these challenges with hard work and sacrifice. But we also will count on the basic creativity that underpins the American economy. How can you prepare to contribute? The first step is to debunk some common misconceptions about creativity:

- *Myth: Lone geniuses drive creativity.* Virtually anyone is capable of doing at least some creative work. And the process doesn't happen in a vacuum—collaboration is crucial. (So yes, hanging out with your buddies at the coffee shop can be highly productive!)
- *Myth: The best ideas come in bursts of brilliant insight.* If you wait for the magic, opportunity may pass you by. But if you keep plugging away at a problem, the answer may arrive in an "aha!" moment, when you least expect it.
- *Myth: Nothing matters more than the idea itself.* Ideas clearly do matter. But insight and execution are inextricably bound. Execution can spark insight that sparks execution that can ultimately build a breakthrough product.
- *Myth: Time pressure fuels creativity.* According to a recent study, people are *least* creative under severe time pressure. Not only that, their creativity drops for the two days following the crunch—a "time pressure hangover" of sorts.
- *Myth: Slacking never pays.* For some of you, this may be the best news of all: doing nothing—some of the time—gets better results than always doing something. In fact, researchers recently confirmed that boredom may have the "power to exert pressure on individuals to stretch their inventive capacity."[7]

Chapter 1 Business Now: Change Is the Only Constant

government has passed tough-minded new regulations to increase corporate accountability. If the new legislation effectively curbs illegal and unethical practices, every business will have a fair chance at success.

Upcoming chapters on economics and ethics will address these economic challenges and their significance in more depth. But bottom line, we have reason for cautious (some would say *very* cautious) optimism. The American economy has a proven track record of flexibility and resilience, which will surely help us navigate this crisis and uncover new opportunity.

The Competitive Environment

As global competition intensifies yet further, leading-edge companies have focused on customer satisfaction like never before. The goal: to develop long-term, mutually beneficial relationships with customers. Getting current customers to buy more of your product is a lot less expensive than convincing potential customers to try your product for the first time. And if you transform your current customers into loyal advocates—vocal promoters of your product or service—they'll get those new customers for you more effectively than any advertising or discount program. Companies such as Coca-Cola, Nordstrom, and Google lead their industries in customer satisfaction, which translates into higher profits even when the competition is tough.[8]

Customer satisfaction comes in large part from delivering unsurpassed value. The best measure of value is the size of the gap between product benefits and price. A product has value when its benefits to the customer are equal to or greater than the price that the customer pays. Keep in mind that the cheapest product doesn't necessarily represent the best value. If a 99-cent toy from Big Lots breaks in a day, customers may be willing to pay several dollars more for a similar

EXHIBIT 1.3 2009 Global Brand Champions and the Ones to Watch, *BusinessWeek* and Interbrand[9]

MOST VALUABLE BRANDS	BIGGEST GAINERS / PERCENTAGE GAIN	
1. Coca-Cola	1. Google	+25%
2. IBM	2. Amazon	+22%
3. Microsoft	3. Zara	+14%
4. GE	4. Nestlé	+13%
5. Nokia	5. Apple	+12%
6. McDonald's		
7. Google		
8. Toyota		
9. Intel		
10. Disney		

toy from somewhere else. But if that 99-cent toy lasts all year, customers will be delighted by the value and will likely encourage their friends and family to shop at Big Lots. The key to value is quality, and virtually all successful firms offer top-quality products relative to their direct competitors.

Jack Trout, author, consultant, and 40-year veteran of marketing wars, sums up the current competitive environment by pointing out that markets he used to think were intensely competitive look like a tea party by today's standards. He recommends that companies cope by following four basic principles:

1. Avoid your competitors' strength, and exploit their weakness. Don't even try to beat them at their own game—instead, start a new one.
2. Always be a little bit paranoid about competition. This means never, ever underestimating your competitors.
3. Remember that competitors will usually get better if pushed. So don't assume that they won't fix their problems.
4. Don't forget that competitors are sometimes irrational when threatened. They may sacrifice their own profits to drive you out of business.[10]

A recent ranking study by *BusinessWeek* magazine and Interbrand consulting firm highlights brands that use imagination and innovation to deliver value to their customer. Exhibit 1.3 shows the winners and the up-and-comers in the race to capture the hearts, minds, and dollars of consumers around the world.

Leading Edge versus Bleeding Edge Speed-to-market—the rate at which a firm transforms concepts into actual products—can be another key source of competitive advantage. And the pace of change just keeps getting faster. In this tumultuous setting, companies that stay ahead of the pack often enjoy a distinct advantage. But keep in mind that there's a difference between leading edge and bleeding edge. Bleeding-edge firms launch products that fail because they're too far ahead of the market. During the late 1990s, for example, in the heart of the dot.com boom, WebVan, a grocery delivery service, launched to huge fanfare. But the firm went bankrupt just a few years later in 2001, partly because customers weren't yet ready to dump traditional grocery stores in favor of cyber-shopping. Leading-edge firms, on the other hand, offer products just as the market becomes ready to embrace them.[11]

Apple computer provides an excellent example of leading edge. You may be surprised to learn that Apple—which owns about 70%[12] of the digital music player market—did not offer the first MP3 player. Instead, they surveyed the existing market to help develop a new product, the iPod, which was far superior in terms of design and ease-of-use. But Apple didn't stop with one successful MP3 player. Racing to stay ahead, they soon introduced the colorful, more affordable iPod mini. And before sales reached their peak, they launched the iPod Nano, which essentially pulled the rug from under the blockbuster iPod mini just a few short months before the holiday selling season. Why? If they didn't do it, someone else may well have done it instead. And Apple is almost maniacally focused on maintaining its competitive lead.[13]

Motivated Apple employees help create satisfied Apple customers.

© DAVID BUTOW/BLOOMBERG VIA GETTY IMAGES

The Workforce Advantage

Employees can contribute another key dimension to a firm's competitive edge. Recent research suggests that investing in worker satisfaction yields tangible, bottom-line results. The researchers evaluated the stock price of *Fortune* magazine's annual list of the "100 Best Companies to Work for in America" over a seven-year period. As a whole, the firms with the highest employee satisfaction gained an average return on investment of 14% per year, compared to 6% a year for the overall market—a difference of more than 130%! The three crucial sources of employee satisfaction seemed to be a sense of fairness, a chance for achievement, and a team-oriented atmosphere (but other factors—such as superb top management—likely *also* played a role in both employee satisfaction and stock performance).[14]

Innovation: For Better or for Worse

Creativity matters, not just for individual businesses, but also for the overall economy. And with global competition, the stakes are high. The editors of *Encyclopedia Britannica* recently explored creativity over time and across countries, compiling a list of the 100 greatest inventions of all time. The editors chose the winners—which they did not rank—based on how profoundly the innovations have affected human life—for better or for worse. Before you read further, consider which inventions you would place on the list. How have they affected human life? What inventions would you expect to find on the list in the future?

© JOHN MUTRUX/MCT/LANDOV

Many of the citations are not surprising, such as the computer, eyeglasses, gunpowder, candles, vaccinations, and the atomic bomb. Others are somewhat amusing, including disposable diapers (which *have* improved the quality of life for millions of parents worldwide!), cat litter, Astroturf (artificial grass), and Post-It notes. A few citations, such as Muzak (generic "elevator music"), the Monopoly board game, Kool-Aid (powdered drink mix for kids), and bikinis, are somewhat puzzling, although they have clearly permeated contemporary culture.

While most of the inventions on this top 100 list are fairly recent, some are older than you might think. Flush toilets, for instance, have been around since the 1500s (thank you, Sir Harrington of England!), although toilet tissue wasn't invented until 1857. Vending machines were invented in Egypt sometime between 200 and 100 BC. And the construction nail was invented by the Sumerians in about 3300 BC.

Interestingly, over the last century, corporations rather than individuals have been responsible for a growing number of key innovations. Examples include the Camcorder (Sony), the laptop computer (Radio Shack), and Viagra (Pfizer). This trend is only likely to build momentum as global competition intensifies.

The United States, despite our relatively short history, dominates the list of greatest inventions, with 162 of 325 mentions, or just under 50%. One reason may be that our nation celebrates individuality, creativity, and, of course, the profit incentive. If we continue to flex our creative muscles, we could find ourselves with a competitive edge far into the 21st century.[15]

Finding and holding the best talent will likely become a crucial competitive issue in the next decade, as the baby boom generation begins to retire. The 500 largest U.S. companies anticipate losing about half of their senior managers over the next five to six years. Replacing them will be tough: baby boomers include about 77 million people, while the generation that follows includes only 46 million. Firms that cultivate human resources now will find themselves better able to compete as the market for top talent tightens.[16]

Technological Environment

The broad definition of **business technology** includes any tools that businesses can use to become more efficient and effective. But more specifically, in today's world, business technology usually refers to computers, telecommunications, and other digital tools. Over the past few decades, the impact of digital technology on business has been utterly transformative. New industries have emerged, while others have disappeared. And some fields—such as travel, banking, and music—have changed dramatically. Even in categories with relatively unchanged products, companies have leveraged technology to streamline production and create new efficiencies. Examples include new processes such as computerized billing, digital animation, and robotic manufacturing. For fast-moving firms, the technological environment represents a rich source of competitive advantage, but it can clearly be a major threat for companies that are slow to adopt or to integrate new approaches.

The creation of the **World Wide Web** has transformed not only business, but also people's lives. Anyone, anywhere, anytime can use the Web to send and receive images and data (as long as access is available). One result is the rise of **e-commerce** or online sales, which allow businesses to tap into a worldwide community of poten-

tial customers. In the wake of the global economic crisis, e-commerce has slowed from the breakneck 20%+ growth rates of the last five years, but even so, analysts predict that solid single-digit growth will continue. Business-to-business selling comprises the vast majority of total e-commerce sales (and an even larger share of the profits). A growing number of businesses have also connected their digital networks with suppliers and distributors to create a more seamless flow of goods and services.[17]

Alternative selling strategies thrive on the Internet, giving rise to a more individualized buying experience. If you've browsed seller reviews on eBay or received shopping recommendations from Amazon, you'll have a sense of how personal Web marketing can feel. Online technology also allows leading-edge firms to offer customized products at prices that are comparable to standardized products. On the Scion website, for instance, customers can build their own car and "see it inside and out, with full rotation and zooming" while sitting at home in their pajamas.

As technology continues to evolve at breakneck speed, the scope of change—both in everyday life and business operations—is almost unimaginable. In this environment, companies that welcome change and manage it well will clearly be the winners.

The Social Environment

The social environment embodies the values, attitudes, customs, and beliefs shared by groups of people. It also covers **demographics**, or the measurable characteristics of a population.

© RADIUS IMAGES/JUPITERIMAGES

business technology Any tools—especially computers, telecommunications, and other digital products—that businesses can use to become more efficient and effective.

World Wide Web The service that allows computer users to easily access and share information on the Internet in the form of text, graphics, video, and animation.

e-commerce Business transactions conducted online, typically via the Internet.

demographics The measurable characteristics of a population. Demographic factors include population size and density and specific traits such as age, gender, and race.

Demographic factors include population size and density and specific traits such as age, gender, race, education, and income. Clearly, given all these influences, the social environment changes dramatically from country to country. And a nation as diverse as the United States features a number of different social environments. Rather than cover the full spectrum, this section will focus instead on the broad social trends that have the strongest impact on American business. Understanding the various dimensions of the social environment is crucial, since successful businesses must offer goods and services that respond to it.

Diversity While the American population has always included an array of different cultures, the United States has become more ethnically diverse in recent years. Caucasians continue to represent the largest chunk of the population at 66%, but the Hispanic and Asian populations are growing faster than any other ethnic groups. Looking ahead, the U.S. Census Bureau projects that those two groups will nearly double their size by 2050, while the Caucasian population will drop to less than half of the U.S. population by 2042. Exhibit 1.4 demonstrates the shifting population breakdown.

EXHIBIT 1.4 U.S. Population Estimates [18]

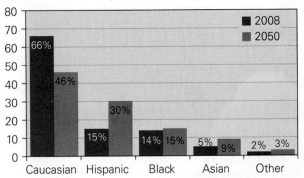

But the national statistics are somewhat misleading, since ethnic groups tend to cluster together. African Americans, for example, currently comprise about 38% of the Mississippi population, Asians comprise about 55% of the Hawaii population, and Hispanics comprise about 45% of the New Mexico population.[19]

So what does this mean for business? Growing ethnic populations offer robust profit potential for firms that pursue them. For instance, a number of major corporations such as AutoZone, Kellogg, Anheuser-Busch, PepsiCo, and Procter & Gamble have invested heavily in the Hispanic market over the past five years. A recent study shows that these heavy-hitters have realized an impressive $4 return on each $1 that they invested in Hispanic marketing. Targeting an ethnic market can also yield remarkable

results for products that cross over into mainstream culture. Music mogul and entrepreneur Russell Simmons, for example, initially targeted his music and clothing to the black market, but his success quickly spilled over to mainstream culture, helping him build a hip-hop empire.[20]

Growing diversity also affects the workforce. A diverse staff—one that reflects an increasingly diverse marketplace—can yield a powerful competitive advantage in terms of both innovation and ability to reach a broad customer base. From global behemoths such as General Electric to local corner stores, companies have taken proactive steps to hire and nurture people from a broad range of backgrounds. And that doesn't just reflect racial or ethnic roots. True diversity also includes differences in gender, age, religion, and nationality, among others. Leading-edge firms have also taken proactive steps to train their entire workforce to manage diversity for top performance.[21]

Effectively managing diversity should only become easier as time goes by. Multiple studies demonstrate that young American adults are the most tolerant age group, and they are moving in a more tolerant direction than earlier generations regarding racial differences, immigrants, and homosexuality. As this generation gathers influence and experience in the workforce, they are likely to leverage diversity in their organizations to hone their edge in a fiercely competitive marketplace.[22]

Aging Population As life spans increase and birthrates decrease, the American population is rapidly aging. Its current median age is 36.7 years, and it's increasing month by month. Over the next 20 years, the size of our working population will shrink, while the number of retirees will explode. And the United States isn't alone in this trend. The population is aging across the developed world, from Western Europe to Japan. China faces the same issue, magnified by its huge population. Demographers estimate that by the middle of the 21st century, China will be home to more than 330 million people age 65 or older.[23]

The rapidly aging population brings opportunities and threats for business. Companies in fields that cater to the elderly—such as healthcare, pharmaceuticals, travel, recreation, and financial management—will clearly boom. But creative companies in other fields will capitalize on the trend as well by reimagining their current products to serve older clients. Possibilities include books, movies—maybe even video games—with mature characters, low-impact fitness programs such as water aerobics, and cell phones and PDAs with more readable screens. Again, the potential payoff of age diversity is clear: companies with older employees are more likely to find innovative ways to reach the aging consumer market.

But surging retirement rates also pose significant threats to overall business success. With a smaller labor pool, companies will need to compete even harder for top talent, driving up recruitment and payroll costs. As state and Federal governments stretch to serve the aging population, taxes may increase, putting an additional burden on business. And as mid-career workers spend more on elder care, they may find themselves with less to spend on other goods and services, shrinking the size of the consumer market.

Rising Worker Expectations Workers of all ages continue to seek flexibility from their employers. Moreover, following massive corporate layoffs in the early 2000s, employees are much less apt to be loyal to their firms. A recent survey shows that only 59% of employees say they are loyal to their companies, and only 26% believe that their companies are loyal to them. As young people today enter the workforce, they bring higher expectations for their employers in terms of salary, job responsibility, and flexibility—and less willingness to pay dues by working extra-long hours or doing a high volume of "grunt work." Smart firms are responding to the change in worker expectations by forging a new partnership with their employees. The goal is a greater level of mutual respect through open communication, information sharing, and training. And the not-so-hidden agenda, of course, is stronger, long-term performance.[24]

Ethics and Social Responsibility With high-profile ethical meltdowns dominating the headlines in the past few years, workers, consumers, and government alike have begun to hold businesses—and the people who run them—to a higher standard. Recent Federal legislation, passed in the wake of the Enron fiasco, demands transparent financial management and more accountability from senior executives. And recognizing their key role in business success, a growing number

Sorting Through Shades of Green

Green is everywhere. Firm after firm—including Whole Foods, Toyota, and Clorox, among many others—have staked their future on green marketing, trumpeting claims that range from "locally grown" to "fully recyclable." But if you can't figure out which to believe and which to blow off, you have plenty of company. In a recent Boston College survey, only 47% of consumers said they trusted corporate green claims.

To help guide confused consumers, TerraChoice, an environmental marketing agency, has laid out *The Six Sins of Greenwashing*, defined as false or misleading green claims. The Sins:

- *Sin of the Hidden Trade-Off:* Green claims based on a single environmental attribute, without attention to more important issues.
    Example: A paper company that promotes recycled products but doesn't mention how it impacts global warming.
- *Sin of No Proof:* Environmental claims without evidence or reliable certification.
    Example: Lightbulb manufacturers that promote energy efficiency without documentation to support this claim.
- *Sin of Vagueness:* Green claims that are so broad or poorly defined that consumers are likely to misunderstand their real meaning.
    Example: Anything labeled "All Natural." Natural substances—such as arsenic—can be toxic, too.
- *Sin of Irrelevance:* Environmental claims that may be truthful but just don't matter.
    Example: Anything labeled "Chlorofluorocarbon (CFC) Free" is a bit silly, since CFCs have been banned in the U.S. for more than 20 years. *No* product should contain them.
- *Sin of Lesser of Two Evils:* Green claims that may be true but distract consumers from the greater negative environmental impacts of the category as a whole.
    Example: Organic cigarettes. Enough said.
- *Sin of Fibbing:* Green claims that are out-and-out lies.
    Example: Some dishwashing detergents claim to be "Energy Star" registered, even though the official Energy Star website excludes them.

Finding products that meet the rigorous TerraChoice standards can be almost impossible, but you can still be a reasonably green consumer. First, recognize that green comes in many shades. A somewhat green product certainly beats a product that isn't green at all. And you can always encourage the companies you buy from to be honest and clear about just how green they actually are.[25]

free trade An international economic and political movement designed to help goods and services flow more freely across international boundaries.

General Agreement on Tariffs and Trade (GATT) An international trade agreement that has taken bold steps to lower tariffs and promote free trade worldwide.

of consumers and workers have begun to insist that companies play a proactive role in making their communities—and often the world community—better places. Sustainability—doing business today without harming the ability of future generations to meet their needs—has become a core issue in the marketplace, driving business policies, investment decisions, and consumer purchases on an unprecedented scale.[26]

> { **"There need not be any conflict between the environment and the economy."**
>
> *Al Gore, Nobel Peace Prize winner* }

The Global Environment

The U.S. economy operates within the context of the global environment, interacting continually with other economies. In fact, over the last two decades, technology and free trade have blurred the lines between individual economies around the world. Technology has forged unprecedented links among countries, making it cost effective—even efficient—to establish computer help centers in Bombay to service customers in Boston, or to hire programmers in Buenos Aires to make websites for companies in Stockholm. Not surprisingly, jobs have migrated to the lowest bidder with the highest quality—regardless of where that bidder is based.

Often, the lowest bidder is based in China or India. Both economies are growing at breakneck speed, largely because they attract enormous foreign investment. China has been a magnet for manufacturing

Global trade has forged unprecedented links among nations.

> **In Asia, the average person's living standards are currently set to rise by 10,000% in one lifetime!**
> *Newsweek*

jobs because of the high population and low wages—an average of 72 cents per hour versus $22.86 per hour in the United States. And India has been especially adept at attracting high-tech jobs, in part because of their world-class, English-speaking university graduates who are willing to work for less than their counterparts around the globe.[27]

The migration of jobs relates closely to the global movement toward **free trade**. In 1995, a re-negotiation of the **General Agreement on Tariffs and Trade (GATT)**—signed by 125 countries—took bold steps to lower tariffs (taxes on imports) and to reduce trade restrictions worldwide. The result: goods move more freely than ever across international boundaries. Individual groups of countries have gone even further, creating blocs of nations with virtually unrestricted trade. Mexico, Canada, and the United States have laid the groundwork for a free-trade mega-market through the North American Free Trade Agreement (NAFTA), and 25 European countries have created a powerful free-trading bloc through the European Union. The free-trade movement has lowered prices and increased quality across virtually every product category, as competition becomes truly global. We'll discuss these issues and their implications in more depth in Chapter 3.

A Multi-Pronged Threat In the past decade alone, war, terrorism, disease, and natural disasters have taken a horrific toll in human lives across the globe. The economic toll has been devastating as well, affecting businesses around the world. The 9/11 terrorist attacks in New York and Washington, D.C. decimated the travel industry and led to multibillion-dollar government outlays for Homeland Security. In 2002 a terrorist bombing at an Indonesian nightclub killed nearly 200 people, destroying tourism on the holiday island of Bali. The 2003 deadly epidemic of the SARS flu dealt a powerful blow to the economies of Hong Kong, Beijing, and Toronto. Less than two years later, the Indian Ocean tsunami wiped out the fishing industry on long swaths of the Indian and Sri Lankan coastlines and crippled the booming Thai tourism industry. That same year, in 2005, Hurricane Katrina destroyed homes and businesses alike and brought the Gulf Coast oil industry to a virtual standstill. And the war in Iraq—while a boon to the defense industry—has dampened the economic potential of the Middle East. With nationalism on the rise, and growing religious and ethnic tensions around the world, the global economy may continue to suffer collateral damage.[28]

LO6 Business and You: Making It Personal

Whatever your career choice—from video game developer, to real estate agent, to Web designer—business will affect your life. Both the broader economy and your own business skills will influence the level of your personal financial success. In light of these factors, making the right career choice can be a bit scary. But the good news is that experts advise graduating students to "Do what you love." And this is a hardheaded strategy, not softhearted puffery. Following your passion makes dollars and sense in today's environment, which values less routine abilities such as creativity, com-munication, and caring. These abilities tend to be more rewarding for most people than routine, programmable skills that computers can easily emulate. Following your passion doesn't guarantee a fat paycheck, but it does boost your chances of both financial and personal success.[29]

The Big Picture

Business today is complex, global, and faster moving than ever before. Looking forward, the rate of change seems likely to accelerate yet further. While the full impact of the global economic crisis is still unclear, China and India seem poised to gain economic clout, raising worldwide competition to a whole new level. Technology will continue to change the business landscape. And a new focus on ethics and social responsibility will likely transform the role of business in society. This book will focus on the impact of change in every facet of business, from management to marketing to money, with an emphasis on how the elements of business relate to each other, and how business as a whole relates to you.

WHAT ELSE? *RIP & REVIEW* CARDS IN THE BACK

2

ECONOMICS:

FRAMEWORK
FOR BUSINESS

LEARNING
OBJECTIVES

LEARNING
OBJECTIVES

After studying this chapter, you will be able to:

LO1 Define economics and discuss the global economic crisis

LO2 Analyze the impact of fiscal and monetary policy on the economy

LO3 Explain and evaluate the free market system and supply and demand

LO4 Explain and evaluate planned market systems

LO5 Describe the trend toward mixed market systems

LO6 Discuss key terms and tools to evaluate economic performance

Visit CourseMate at **www.cengagebrain.com.**

LO1 Economics: Navigating a Crisis

In September 2008, the United States economy plunged into a deep economic crisis. The banking system hovered on the edge of collapse. Property values plummeted and home foreclosure rates soared. Massive layoffs put more than a million Americans out of work. By the end of the year, the stock market had lost more than a third of its value, and financial turmoil in the United States had sparked sequential economic shocks from Europe, to South America, to Asia, and beyond. The outlook was grim.

How did this happen? Why? How could the economy get back on track?

Understanding these issues—and how the government responded to them—requires understanding some basic definitions: The **economy** is essentially a financial and social system. It represents the flow of resources through society, from production, to distribution, to consumption. **Economics** is the study of the choices that people, companies, and governments make in allocating those resources. The field of economics falls into two core categories: macroeconomics and microeconomics. **Macroeconomics** is the study of a country's overall economic issues, such as the employment rate, the gross domestic product, and taxation policies. While macroeconomic issues may seem abstract, they directly affect your day-to-day life, influencing key variables such as what jobs will be available for you, how much cash you'll actually take home after taxes, or how much you can buy with that cash in any given month. **Microeconomics** focuses on smaller economic units such as individual consumers, families, and individual businesses. Both macroeconomics and microeconomics have played an integral role in the global economic crisis.

Global Economic Crisis: How Did this Happen?

The seeds of the crisis were planted more than a decade ago, during a time of prosperity. Through the last half of the 1990s, America enjoyed unprecedented growth. Unemployment was low, productivity was high, inflation was low, and the real standard of living for the average American rose significantly. The American economy grew by more than $2.4 trillion, a jump of nearly 33% in just five years. But the scene changed for the worse when the dot.com bubble burst in 2000, followed by the 9/11 terrorist attacks in 2001. As the stock market dropped and unemployment rose, economic experts feared that the country was hovering on the brink of a full-blown recession.[1]

In an effort to avert recession by increasing the money supply and encouraging investment, the Federal Reserve—the nation's central bank—decreased interest rates from 6.5% in mid-2000 to 1.25% by the end of 2002. As a result, the

economy A financial and social system of how resources flow through society, from production, to distribution, to consumption.

economics The study of the choices that people, companies, and governments make in allocating society's resources.

macroeconomics The study of a country's overall economic issues, such as the employment rate, the gross domestic product, and taxation policies.

microeconomics The study of smaller economic units such as individual consumers, families, and individual businesses.

© CREATAS IMAGES/JUPITERIMAGES

© PAMELA MOORE/ISTOCKPHOTO.COM

economy was awash with money, but opportunities to invest yielded paltry returns. This is when *subprime mortgage loans* came into play. Most experts define subprime mortgages as loans to borrowers with low credit scores, high debt-to-income ratios, or other signs of a reduced ability to repay the money they borrow.

These subprime mortgage loans were attractive to borrowers and lenders alike. For the borrowers, getting a loan suddenly became a cinch, and for the first time ever, hundreds of thousands of people could afford homes. The lenders were all too willing to give them mortgage loans, sometimes with little or no documentation (such as proof of income), and sometimes with little or no money down. As demand for homes skyrocketed, prices continued to rise year after year. Borrowers took on adjustable rate loans assuming that when their loans adjusted up—usually sharply up—they could simply refinance their now-more-valuable homes for a new low starter rate and maybe even pull out some cash.

Subprime loans were attractive to lenders because they provided a higher return than many other investments, and—given the growth in housing prices—they seemed relatively low-risk. Banks and investment houses invented a range of stunningly complex financial instruments to slice up and resell the mortgages as specialized securities. Hedge funds swapped the new securities, convinced that they were virtually risk-free. With a lack of regulation—or any other government oversight—financial institutions did *not* maintain sufficient reserves in case those mortgage-backed funds lost value.

And they did indeed lose value. In 2006, housing prices peaked, and in the months that followed, prices began falling precipitously (see Exhibit 2.1). Increasing numbers of subprime borrowers found themselves "upside down"—they owed their lenders more than the value of their homes. Once this happened, they couldn't refinance

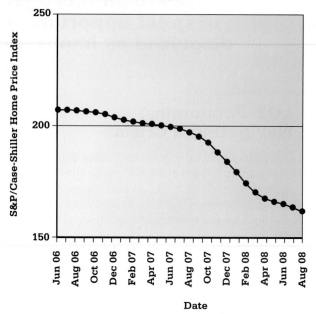

EXHIBIT 2.1 House Price Index

to lower their payments. Foreclosure rates climbed at an increasing pace. RealtyTrac, a leading online marketplace for foreclosure properties, reported that foreclosure rates were 21% higher in 2009 than they were in all of 2008. Looking forward, RealtyTrac noted that "in the long term a massive supply of delinquent loans continues to loom over the housing market, and many of those delinquencies will end up in the foreclosure process in 2010 and beyond as lenders gradually work their way through the backlog."[2]

As mortgage values dropped, financial institutions began to feel the pressure—especially firms such as Bear Stearns that specialized in trading mortgage-backed securities, and firms such as Washington Mutual that focused on selling subprime mortgages. When financial institutions actually began to face collapse, a wave of fear washed

A *trillion* dollars? Say *what??*

Between stimulating the economy and bailing out the banking system, "a trillion dollars" is a figure you may have heard a lot lately. But getting your mind around what that actually means may be a little tricky, since it's just so much money. To understand the true magnitude of a trillion dollars, consider this:

- If you had started spending a million dollars a day—every day, without fail—at the start of the Roman Empire, you still wouldn't have spent a trillion dollars by 2010; in fact, you'd have more than $250 billion left over.
- One trillion dollars, laid end-to-end, would stretch farther than the distance from the earth to the sun. You could also wrap your chain of bills more than 12,000 times around the earth's equator.
- If you flew a jet at the speed of sound, spooling out a roll of dollar bills behind you, it would take you more than 14 years to release a trillion dollars. But your plane probably couldn't carry the roll, since it would weigh more than one million tons.

Turning the economy around may take even more than a trillion dollars, but make no mistake when you hear those numbers thrown around on the news—a trillion dollars is an awful lot of money!

over the entire banking industry. Banks became unwilling to lend money to each other or to clients, which meant that funds were not available for businesses to finance either day-to-day operations or longer-term growth. Company after company—from General Motors, to Yahoo!, to American Express, to countless small employers—began to announce layoffs. The December 2008 unemployment rate hit 7.2%. Nearly two million Americans lost their jobs in the last four months of 2008 alone.

{
A billion here and a billion there, and pretty soon you're talking real money.
}

U.S. Senator Everett Dirksen

Moving in a Better Direction

Although the benefits were not immediately obvious in the face of a downward trend, the Federal Government and the Federal Reserve—known as "the Fed"—intervened in the economy at an unprecedented level to prevent total financial disaster. In March 2008, the Fed staved off bankruptcy at Bear Stearns. In early September 2008, the Federal Treasury Department seized Fannie Mae and Freddie Mac, which owned about half of the U.S. mortgage market. A week later, the Fed bailed out tottering global insurance giant AIG with an $85 billion loan. But the bleeding continued.

The negative spiral spurred Congress to pass a $700 billion economic bailout plan in early October 2008. By the end of the year, the Treasury Department had spent the first half of that money investing in banks, although early results were imperceptible for the economy. No sooner had the Treasury begun to release funds to the banks than GM and Chrysler, two of the Big Three U.S. automakers, announced they also desperately needed a bailout. Both firms suggested that bankruptcy was imminent without government assistance. (Ford, the other member of the Big Three, also admitted to financial problems but claimed that it was not in the dire straits faced by its domestic competitors.) Facing the loss of more than 2.5 million auto industry-related jobs, the Treasury Department agreed to spend a portion of what remained of the $700 billion in a partial auto industry bailout.[3]

As the new administration began, President Obama proposed an $825 billion economic stimulus package, called the American Recovery and Reinvestment Act, designed to turn the economy around over the next two years. The plan included cutting taxes, building infrastructure, and investing $150 billion in green energy. By early 2010, the economy had begun to turn around at a very slow pace, although unemployment remained high, and economists predicted that the jobless rate would remain painfully high through the middle of the decade.[4]

All of these moves by the Federal Government and the Federal Reserve are part of fiscal and monetary policy.

fiscal policy Government efforts to influence the economy through taxation and spending.

LO2 Managing the Economy Through Fiscal and Monetary Policy

While the free market drives performance in the American economy, the national government and the Federal Reserve can help *shape* performance. During the recent crisis, both the government and the Fed have taken proactive roles to mitigate this economic contraction. The overarching goal is controlled, sustained growth, and both fiscal and monetary policy can help achieve this objective.

Fiscal Policy

Fiscal policy refers to government efforts to influence the economy through taxation and spending decisions that are designed to encourage growth, boost employment, and curb inflation. Clearly, fiscal strategies are closely tied to political philosophy. But regardless of politics, most economists agree that lower taxes can boost the economy by leaving more money in people's pockets for them to spend or invest. Most also agree that government spending can boost the economy in the short term by providing jobs, such as mail carrier or park ranger, and in the long term by investing in critical public assets, such as a national renewable energy

© DNY59/ISTOCKPHOTO.COM

grid. Done well, both taxation and spending can offer economic benefits. The tricky part is finding the right balance between the two approaches.

Every year, the government must create a budget, or a financial plan that outlines expected revenue from taxes and fees, and expected spending. If revenue is higher than spending, the government incurs a **budget surplus** (rare in recent years, but usually quite welcome!). If spending is higher than revenue, the government incurs a **budget deficit**, and must borrow money to cover the shortfall. The sum of all the money borrowed over the years and not yet repaid is the total **federal debt**. Exhibit 2.2 shows key sources of revenue and key expenses for the Federal Government in 2009. Note that spending significantly outstrips receipts, creating a one-year budget deficit of more than

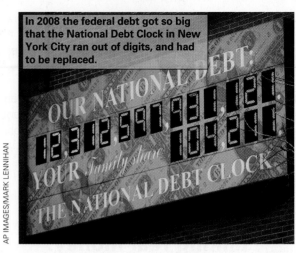

In 2008 the federal debt got so big that the National Debt Clock in New York City ran out of digits, and had to be replaced.

AP IMAGES/MARK LENNIHAN

a trillion dollars. Clearly, any additional spending without corresponding tax increases could dramatically increase the shortfall.

As of April 2010, the total U.S. federal debt stood at more than $12.8 trillion, a staggering $41,770 for every U.S. citizen (see an online national debt clock at http://brillig.com/debt_clock/ for the latest figures).

Recession Successes

Even in the worst of times a few bright lights still manage to shine, and the Great Recession of 2009 was no exception. Here are some notable examples of strong businesses that thrived during economic contractions:

- *Redbox DVD Rental kiosks:* In 2009, when businesses across the economy were struggling simply to survive, Redbox added one new location per hour for a total of more than 22,000 kiosks, generating twice as much in revenue in 2009 as it did in 2008. Redbox even rattled movie-rental innovator Reed Hastings, founder of Netflix, who characterized Redbox as "really scary."
- *FedEx:* The shipping behemoth launched just before the oil crisis in 1973, which thrust the country into prolonged economic turmoil. FedEx has continued to thrive, despite ongoing turmoil in the oil industry, which directly affects FedEx's bottom line.
- *Hewlett-Packard:* The technology giant that ranks #9 on the Fortune 500 list, launched in 1939, at the end of the Great Depression, with $538 and a used drill press.

Today, in fact, Hewlett-Packard and FedEx are working together to pioneer on-demand printing, a transformative service based on cloud computing technology. So, a Great Idea and a Great Recession can sometimes give birth to a Great Success, which can yield other Great Ideas throughout its life span.[5]

© RICK WILKING/REUTERS/LANDOV

The debt has only grown bigger every year since 1957, and the pace of growth will likely increase further in the wake of the economic crisis. This matters to each taxpayer because as the government repays the debt—not to mention paying the skyrocketing interest to finance this debt—less and less money will be available for other uses; services may be eliminated (e.g., student loans, veterans' benefits, housing subsidies), or taxes will soar, or perhaps even both.

Monetary Policy

Monetary policy refers to actions that shape the economy by influencing interest rates and the supply of money. The Federal Reserve—essentially the central bank of the United States—manages U.S. monetary policy. For the first time in its history, the Fed has also taken an activist role in bailing out and propping up staggering financial firms during the economic crisis. Other Fed functions include banking services for member banks and the Federal Government.

The Fed is headed by a seven-member Board of Governors. The President appoints each member of the Board to serve a single 14-year term—though a member can also complete a former member's unexpired term and still be appointed to a full term of his or her own. These terms are staggered, with one expiring every two years, so that no single President can appoint all of the members. This structure helps ensure that the Fed can act independently of political pressure.

In addition to setting monetary policy, the Board of Governors oversees the operation of the 12 Federal Reserve Banks that carry out Fed policies and perform banking services for commercial banks in their districts. Interestingly, the Federal Government does not own these Federal Reserve Banks. Instead, they're owned by the member commercial banks in their individual districts.

The President appoints one of the seven members of the Board of Governors to serve as its Chairman—a position so powerful that many consider him the second most powerful person on Earth. For nearly 19 years, the Chairman was Alan Greenspan. When Greenspan retired in early 2006, President Bush appointed economist Ben Bernanke to the Chairman role. Bernanke has led the Fed's proactive efforts to turn the ailing economy around.

The core purpose of the Fed is to influence the size of the **money supply**—or the total amount of money within the overall economy. The two most commonly used definitions of the money supply are M1 and M2:

- **M1**: All currency—paper bills and metal coins—plus checking accounts and traveler's checks.
- **M2**: All of M1 plus most savings accounts, money market accounts, and certificates of deposit (low-risk savings vehicles with a fixed term, typically less than one year).

As of April 2010, the M1 money supply totaled about $1.7 trillion, and the M2 version of the money supply totaled about $8.5 trillion. In practice, the term "money supply" most often refers to M2. (Note that credit cards are not part of the money supply, although they do have an unmistakable impact on the flow of money through the economy.)[6]

When the economy contracts, the Fed typically increases the money supply. If more money is available, interest rates usually drop, encouraging businesses to expand and consumers to spend. But when prices begin to rise, the Fed attempts to reduce the money supply. Ideally, if less money is available, interest rates will rise. This will reduce spending, which should bring inflation under control. Specifically, the Fed uses three key tools to expand and contract the money supply: open market operations, discount rate changes, and reserve requirement changes.

monetary policy Federal Reserve decisions that shape the economy by influencing interest rates and the supply of money.

money supply The total amount of money within the overall economy.

M1 money supply Includes all currency plus checking accounts and traveler's checks.

M2 money supply Includes all of M1 money supply plus most savings accounts, money market accounts, and certificates of deposit.

EXHIBIT 2.2 Federal Government Revenue and Expenses[7]

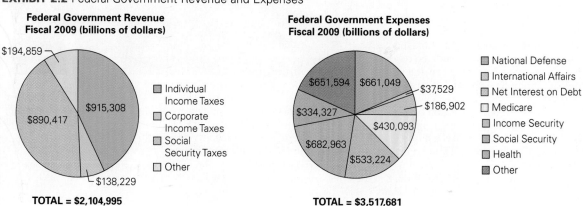

Federal Government Revenue Fiscal 2009 (billions of dollars)

$194,859
$915,308
$890,417
$138,229

- Individual Income Taxes
- Corporate Income Taxes
- Social Security Taxes
- Other

TOTAL = $2,104,995

Federal Government Expenses Fiscal 2009 (billions of dollars)

$651,594 $661,049 $37,529
$334,327 $186,902
$682,963 $430,093
$533,224

- National Defense
- International Affairs
- Net Interest on Debt
- Medicare
- Income Security
- Social Security
- Health
- Other

TOTAL = $3,517,681

Open Market Operations This is the Fed's most frequently used tool. **Open market operations** involve buying and selling government securities, which include treasury bonds, notes, and bills. These securities are the IOUs the government issues to finance its deficit spending.

How do open market operations work? When the economy is weak, the Fed *buys* government securities on the open market. When the Fed pays the sellers of these securities, money previously held by the Fed is put into circulation. This directly stimulates spending. In addition, any of the additional funds supplied by the Fed that are deposited in banks will allow banks to make more loans, making credit more readily available. This encourages even more spending and further stimulates the economy.

When inflation is a concern, the Fed *sells* securities. Buyers of the securities write checks to the Fed to pay for securities they bought, and the Fed withdraws these funds from banks. With fewer funds, banks must cut back on the loans they make, credit becomes tighter, and the money supply shrinks. This reduces spending and cools off the inflationary pressures in the economy.

Open market operations are set by the aptly named Federal Open Market Committee, which consists of the seven members of the Board of Governors and five of the twelve presidents of the Federal Reserve district banks. Each year, the Federal Open Market Committee holds eight regularly scheduled meetings to make decisions about open market operations, although they do hold additional meetings when the need arises.

Discount Rate Changes Just as you can borrow money from your bank, your bank can borrow funds from the Fed. And, just as you must pay interest on your loan, your bank must pay interest on loans from the Fed. The **discount rate** is the interest rate the Fed charges on its loans to commercial banks. When the Fed reduces the discount rate, banks can obtain funds at a lower cost and use these funds to make more loans to their own customers. With the cost of acquiring funds from the Fed lower, interest rates on bank loans also tend to fall. The result: businesses and individuals are more likely to borrow money and spend it, which stimulates the economy. Clearly, the Fed is most likely to reduce the discount rate during recessions. In fact, during the early months of the financial crisis, the Fed cut the rate to less than 1%. But in response to inflation—usually a sign of a rapidly expanding economy—the Fed usually increases the discount rate. In response, banks raise the interest rates they charge their customers. Fewer businesses and individuals are willing to take loans, which ultimately slows down the economy and reduces inflation.[8]

Reserve Requirement Changes The Fed requires that all of its member banks hold funds called "reserves,"

Looking to Multiply Your Money? Look No Further Than Your Local Bank!

Everyone knows that banks help people save money, but most people don't realize that banks actually create money. While the process is complex, a simplified example illustrates the point: Say you deposit $5,000 in the bank. How much money do you have? Obviously, $5,000. Now imagine that your neighbor Anne goes to the bank for a loan. In line with Federal Reserve requirements, the bank must hold onto about 10% of its funds, so it loans Anne $4,500. She uses the money to buy a used car from your neighbor Jake, who deposits the $4,500 in the bank. How much money does Jake have? Clearly, $4,500. How much money do you have? Still, $5,000. Thanks to the banking system, our "money supply" has increased from $5,000 to $9,500. Multiply this phenomenon times millions of banking transactions, and you can see why cold, hard cash accounts for only about 10% of the total U.S. M2 money supply.[9]

© KEITH BROFSKY/PHOTODISC/GETTY IMAGES

But what happens if everyone goes to the bank at once to withdraw their money? The banking system would clearly collapse. And in fact, in 1930 and 1931, a run on the banks caused wave after wave of devastating bank failures. Panicked customers lost all their savings, ushering in the worst years of the Great Depression. To restore public confidence in the banking system, in 1933 Congress established the **Federal Deposit Insurance Corporation (FDIC)**. The FDIC insures deposits in banks and thrift institutions for up to $100,000 per customer, per bank. In the wake of the banking crisis, the FDIC temporarily increased its coverage to $250,000 per depositor at the end of 2008. Since the FDIC began operations on January 1, 1934, no depositor has lost a single cent of insured funds as a result of a bank failure.[10]

Chapter 2 Economics: The Framework for Business

equal to a stated percentage of the deposits held by their customers. This percentage is called the **reserve requirement** (or required reserve ratio). The reserve requirement helps protect depositors who may want to withdraw their money without notice. Currently, the reserve requirement stands at about 10%, depending on the size and type of a bank's deposits. If the Fed increases the reserve requirement, banks must hold more funds, meaning they will have fewer funds available to make loans. This makes credit tighter and causes interest rates to rise. If the Fed decreases the reserve requirement, some of the funds that banks were required to hold become available for loans. This increases the availability of credit and causes interest rates to drop. Since changes in the reserve requirement can have a dramatic impact on both the economy and the financial health of individual banks, the Fed uses this tool quite infrequently.

Other Fed Functions In addition to monetary policy, the Fed has several other core functions, including regulating financial institutions and providing banking services both for the government and for banks. In its role as a regulator, the Fed sets and enforces rules of conduct for banks and oversees mergers and acquisitions to ensure fairness and compliance with government policy. The Fed will likely become even more proactive regarding regulation in the wake of the financial crisis. In its role as a banker for banks, the Fed coordinates the check-clearing process for checks on behalf of any banks that are willing to pay its fees. And as the government's bank, the Fed maintains the Federal Government's checking account and keeps the U.S. currency supply in good condition.

LO3 Capitalism: The Free Market System

It's a simple fact, more clear now than ever before: no one can get everything they want all of the time. We live in a world of finite resources, which means that societies must determine how to distribute resources among their members. An **economic system** is a structure for allocating limited resources. Over time and around the globe, nations have instituted different economic systems. But a careful analysis suggests that no system is perfect, which may explain why there isn't one standard approach. The next sections of this chapter examine each basic type of

economic system and explore the trend toward mixed economies.

The economic system of the United States is called **capitalism**, also known as a "private enterprise system" or a "free market system." Brought to prominence by Adam Smith in the 1700s, capitalism is based on private ownership, economic freedom, and fair competition. A core capitalist principle is the paramount importance of individuals, innovation, and hard work. In a capitalist economy, individuals, businesses, or nonprofit organizations privately own the vast majority of enterprises (only a small fraction are owned by the government). These private sector businesses are free to make their own choices regarding everything from what they will produce, to how much they will charge, to whom they will hire and fire. Correspondingly, individuals are free to choose what they will buy, how much they are willing to pay, and where they will work.

To thrive in a free enterprise system, companies must offer value to their customers—otherwise, their customers will choose to go elsewhere. Businesses must also offer value to their employees and suppliers in order to attract top-quality talent and supplies. As companies compete to attract the best resources and offer the best values, quality goes up, prices remain reasonable, and choices proliferate, raising the standard of living in the economy as a whole.

The Fundamental Rights of Capitalism

For capitalism to succeed, the system must ensure some fundamental rights—or freedoms—to all of the people who live within the economy.

- *The right to own a business and keep after-tax profits:* Remember that capitalism doesn't guarantee that anyone will actually *earn* profits. Nor does it promise that there won't be taxes. But if you do earn profits, you get to keep your after-tax income and spend it however you see fit (within the limits of the law, of course). This right acts as a powerful motivator for business owners in a capitalist economy; the lower the tax rate, the higher the motivation. The U.S. government strives to maintain low tax rates to preserve the after-tax profit incentive that

© INTERFOTO PRESSEBILDAGENTUR/ALAMY

reserve requirement A rule set by the Fed, which specifies the minimum amount of reserves (or funds) a bank must hold, expressed as a percentage of the bank's deposits.

economic system A structure for allocating limited resources.

capitalism An economic system—also known as the private enterprise or free market system—based on private ownership, economic freedom, and fair competition.

plays such a pivotal role in the free enterprise system.

- *The right to private property:*
This means that individuals and private businesses can buy, sell, and use property—which includes land, machines, and buildings—in any way that makes sense to them. This right also includes the right to will property to family members. The only exceptions to private property rights are minimal government restrictions designed to protect the greater good. You can't, for instance, use your home or business to produce cocaine, abuse children, or spew toxic smoke into the air.

- *The right to free choice:* Capitalism relies on economic freedom. People and businesses must be free to buy (or not buy) according to their wishes. They must be free to choose where to work (or not work) and where to live (or not live). Freedom of choice directly feeds competition, creating a compelling incentive for business owners to offer the best goods and services at the lowest prices. U.S. government trade policies boost freedom of choice by encouraging a wide array of both domestic and foreign producers to compete freely for our dollars.

- *The right to fair competition:* A capitalist system depends on fair competition among businesses to drive higher quality, lower prices, and more choices. Capitalism can't achieve its potential if unfair practices—such as deceptive advertising, predatory pricing, and broken contracts—mar the free competitive environment. The government's role is to create a level playing field by establishing regulations and monitoring the competition to ensure compliance.

Four Degrees of Competition

While competition is essential for the free market system to function, not all competition works the same. Different industries experience different degrees of competition, ranging from pure competition to monopolies.

- **Pure competition** is a market structure with many competitors selling virtually identical products. Since customers can't (or won't) distinguish one product from another, no single producer has any control over the price. And new producers can easily enter and leave purely competitive markets. In today's U.S. economy, examples of pure competition have virtually disappeared. Agriculture probably comes closest—corn is basically corn, for example—but with the dramatic growth of huge corporate farms and the success of major cooperatives such as Sunkist, the number of competitors in agriculture has dwindled, and new farmers have trouble entering the market. Not only that, segments of the

© HEMERA TECHNOLOGIES/PHOTOS.COM/JUPITERIMAGES

Going Green: Good for the Bottom Line

As demand for goods and services has dropped and consumers have tightened their purse strings, businesses have begun to go green, not just to do right by the planet, but also to cut costs. In fact, some argue that the staggering economy has actually pushed forward the environmental agenda more than any other factor, because it has forced business owners to acknowledge the connection between going green and the bottom line.

In 2008, Walmart, for example, began selling only concentrated liquid laundry detergent at all of its stores (a pretty big deal, since Walmart sells about 25% of all liquid detergent in the United States). From an environmental standpoint, the projected payoff over a three-year timeframe is huge:

- Saving over 95 million pounds of plastic resin
- Conserving over 520,000 gallons of diesel gasoline
- Preserving more than 400 million gallons of water
- Reducing more than 125 million pounds of cardboard

But the economic payoff is big, too, since costs drop for each member of the supply chain. Other industry titans have gone green to cut costs, too. Google, Microsoft, and Yahoo!, for instance, have all built giant data centers along the northwest's Columbia River to tap into cheap hydroelectric power. In fact, overall technology-industry spending on green initiatives will likely keep growing, even as the recession deepens. One reason may be that it now costs nearly as much money to power a server for three years—the typical life span—as it does to buy the hardware itself. That equation just doesn't make dollars and sense.

Looking forward, Zachary Karabell, a senior advisor to the nonprofit organization *Business for Social Responsibility*, points out that environmental concerns have become a dominant driver of global corporations. When the impulse to save the planet fuses with the need to make money, we could see "a brand new world of business practices and investment opportunities."[11]

agriculture market—such as organic farms and hormone-free dairies—have emerged with hit products that command much higher prices than the competition.

- **Monopolistic competition** is a market structure with many competitors selling differentiated products. Producers have some control over the price of their wares, depending on the value that they offer their customers. And new producers can fairly easily enter categories marked by monopolistic competition. In fact, in monopolistic competition a successful product usually attracts new suppliers quite quickly. Examples of monopolistic competition include the clothing industry and the restaurant business. Think about the clothing business, for a moment, in local terms. How many firms do you know that sell tee shirts? You could probably think of at least 50 without too much trouble. And the quality and price are all over the board: designer tee shirts can sell for well over $100, but plenty of options go for less than $10. How hard would it be to start your own tee shirt business? Probably not hard at all. In fact, chances are strong that you know at least one person who sells tee shirts on the side. In terms of product and price variation, number of firms, and ease of entry, the tee shirt business clearly demonstrates the characteristics of monopolistic competition.

- **Oligopoly** is a market structure with only a handful of competitors selling products that are either similar or different. The retail gasoline business and the car manufacturing industry, for instance, are both oligopolies, even though gas stations offer very similar products, and car companies offer quite different models and features. Other examples of oligopoly include the soft drink industry, the computer business, and network television. Breaking into a market characterized by oligopoly can be tough because it typically requires a huge upfront investment. You could start making tee shirts in your kitchen, for instance, but you'd need a pretty expensive facility to start manufacturing cars. Oligopolies typically avoid intense price competition, since they have nothing to gain—every competitor simply makes less money. When price wars do flare up, the results can be devastating for entire industries.

- **Monopoly** is a market structure with just a single producer completely dominating the industry, leaving no room for any significant competitors. Monopolies usually aren't good for anyone but the company that has control, since without competition there isn't any incentive to hold down prices or increase quality and choices. Because monopolies can harm the economy, most are illegal according to federal legislation, such as the Sherman Antitrust Act of 1890 and the Clayton Antitrust Act of 1914. Microsoft is the latest example of an industry giant that ran afoul of anti-monopoly laws due to its position and policies in the software business. Even though Microsoft is not an actual monopoly, it was convicted of "monopolistic practices" that undermined fair competition.

However, in a few instances, the government not only allows monopolies, but actually encourages them. This usually occurs when it would be too inefficient for each competitor to build its own infrastructure to serve the public. A **natural monopoly** arises. Cable television offers a clear example. Would it really make sense for even a handful of competitors to wire neighborhoods separately for cable? Clearly, that's not practical. Just imagine the chaos! Instead, the government has granted cable franchises—or monopolies—to individual companies and then regulated them (with mixed results) to ensure that they don't abuse the privilege. In addition to natural monopolies, the government grants patents and copyrights, which create artificial monopoly situations (at least temporarily) in order to encourage innovation.

monopolistic competition A market structure with many competitors selling differentiated products. Barriers to entry are low.

oligopoly A market structure with only a handful of competitors selling products that are either similar or different. Barriers to entry are typically high.

monopoly A market structure with one producer completely dominating the industry, leaving no room for any significant competitors. Barriers to entry tend to be virtually insurmountable.

natural monopoly A market structure with one company as the supplier of a product because the nature of that product makes a single supplier more efficient than multiple, competing ones. Most natural monopolies are government sanctioned and regulated.

Supply and Demand: Fundamental Principles of a Free Market System

In a free market system, the continual interplay between buyers and sellers determines the selection of products and prices available in the economy. If a business makes something that few people actually want, sales will be low, and the firm will typically yank the product from the market. Similarly, if the price of a product is too high, low sales will dictate a price cut. But if a new good or service becomes a hit, you can bet that similar offerings from other firms will pop up almost immediately (unless barriers—such as government-granted patents—prevent new entrants). The concepts of demand and supply explain how the dynamic interaction between buyers and sellers directly affects the range of products and prices in the free market.

Supply Supply refers to the quantity of products that producers are willing to offer for sale at different market prices. Since businesses seek to make as much profit as possible, they are likely to produce more of a product that commands a higher market price and less of a product that commands a lower price. Think about it in terms of pizza: Assume it costs a local restaurant about $5 to make a pizza. If the market price for pizza hits, say, $20, you can bet that restaurant will start cranking out pizza. But if the price drops to $6, the restaurant has

EXHIBIT 2.3 Supply Curve

much less incentive to focus on pizza and will probably invest its limited resources in cooking other, more pricy, dishes.

The relationship between price and quantity from a supplier standpoint can be shown on a graph called the **supply curve**. The supply curve maps quantity on the x-axis (or horizontal axis) and price on the y-axis (or vertical axis). In most categories, as the price rises, the quantity produced rises correspondingly, yielding a graph that curves up as it moves to the right. Exhibit 2.3 shows a possible supply curve for pizza.

Demand Demand refers to the quantity of products that consumers are willing to buy at different market prices. Since consumers generally seek to get the products they need (or want) at the lowest possible prices, they tend to buy more of products with lower prices and less of products with higher prices. Pizza and tacos, for instance, are both popular meals. But if pizza costs a lot less than tacos, most people will get pizza more often than tacos. Likewise, if the price of pizza were out of hand, people would probably order tacos (or some other option) more often, reserving their pizza-eating for special occasions.

The relationship between price and quantity from a demand standpoint can be shown on a graph called the **demand curve**. Like the supply curve, the demand curve maps quantity on the x-axis and price on the y-axis. But different from the supply curve, the demand curve for most goods and services slopes downward as it moves to the right, since quantity demanded tends to drop as prices rise. Exhibit 2.4 shows how a demand curve for pizza could look.

Chapter 2   Economics: The Framework for Business

EXHIBIT 2.4 Demand Curve

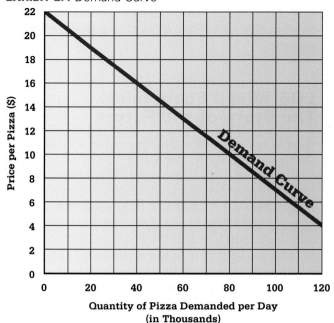

EXHIBIT 2.5 Equilibrium

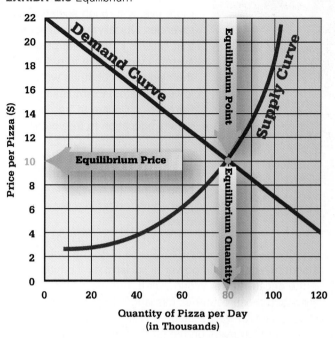

Equilibrium Price It's important to remember that supply and demand don't operate in a vacuum. The constant interaction between the two forces helps determine the market price in any given category. In theory, market prices adjust toward the point where the supply curve and the demand curve intersect (see Exhibit 2.5). The price associated with this point of intersection—the point where the quantity demanded equals the quantity supplied—is called the **equilibrium price**, and the quantity associated with this point is called the "equilibrium quantity."

LO4 Planned Economies: Socialism and Communism

In capitalist economies, private ownership is paramount. Individuals own businesses, and their personal fortunes depend on their success in the free market. But in planned economies, the government plays a more heavy-handed role in controlling the economy. The two key categories of planned economies are socialism and communism.

Socialism

Socialism is an economic system based on the principle that the government should own and operate key enterprises that directly affect public welfare, such as utilities, telecommunications, and healthcare. Although the official government goal is to run these enterprises in the best interest of the overall public, inefficiencies and corruption often interfere with effectiveness. Socialist economies also tend to have higher taxes, which are

Coca-Cola Gets the Cold Shoulder

Most of us are used to the idea that a matinee costs a whole lot less than an evening at the movies. And even if we don't like it, we've accepted that the same airplane seat costs more if you buy it right before you fly. But in 1999, Coca-Cola took the laws of supply and demand just a little too far. The beverage behemoth announced its intention to install thermometers in its vending machines so it could charge more for a cold Coke on a hot day. But consumers were outraged at the very idea, forcing Coca-Cola to backpedal almost immediately. Tim Manners of *Reveries* marketing magazine suggests that Coca-Cola should have considered *lowering* their prices on hot days. Even if they didn't sell enough extra sodas to boost their profits, the bump in goodwill would have probably more than made up for the few lost cents per bottle.

designed to distribute wealth more evenly through society. Tax revenues typically fund services that citizens in free enterprise systems would have to pay for themselves in countries with lower tax rates. Examples range from free childcare to free university education to free public healthcare systems. Critics of the recent government intervention in the U.S. economy believe that the new moves have pushed us too far in a socialist direction.

Most Western European countries—from Sweden, to Germany, to the United Kingdom—developed powerful socialist economies in the decades after World War II. But more recently, growth in these countries has languished. Although many factors have contributed to the slowdown, the impact of high taxes on the profit incentive and lavish social programs on the work incentive has clearly played a role. Potential entrepreneurs may migrate to countries that let them keep more of their profits, and workers with abundant benefits may find themselves losing motivation.

Communism

Communism is an economic and political system that calls for public ownership of virtually all enterprises, under the direction of a strong central government. The communist concept was the brainchild of political philosopher Karl Marx, who outlined its core principles in his 1848 *Communist Manifesto*. The communism that Marx envisioned was supposed to dramatically improve the lot of the worker at the expense of the super rich.

But countries that adopted communism in the 1900s—most notably the former Soviet Union, China, Cuba, North Korea, and Vietnam—did not thrive. Most imposed authoritarian governments that suspended individual rights and choices. People were unable to make even basic choices such as where to work or what to buy. Without the free market to establish what to produce, crippling shortages and surpluses developed. Corruption infected every level of government. Under enormous pressure from their own people and the rest of the world, communism began to collapse across the Soviet Union and its satellite nations at the end of the 1980s, replaced with democracy and the free market. Over the past two decades, China has also introduced significant free market reforms across much of the country, fueling its torrid growth rate. And in the 1990s, Vietnam launched free market reforms, stimulating

rapid, sustained growth. The remaining communist economic systems—North Korea and Cuba—continue to falter, their people facing drastic shortages and even starvation.

LO5 Mixed Economies: The Story of the Future

In today's world, pure economies—either market or planned—are practically nonexistent, since each would fall far short of meeting the needs of its citizens. A pure market economy would make insufficient provision for the old, the young, the sick, and the environment. A pure planned economy would not create enough value to support its people over the long term. Instead, most of today's nations have **mixed economies**, falling somewhere along a spectrum that ranges from pure planned at one extreme to pure market at the other.

Even the United States—one of the most market-oriented economies in the world—does not have a *pure* market economy. The various departments of the government own a number of major enterprises, including the postal service, schools, parks, libraries, entire systems of universities, and the military. In fact, the Federal Government is the nation's largest employer, providing jobs for more than 4 million Americans. And—although the government does not directly *operate* firms in the financial sector—the Federal Government has become part owner in a number of financial institutions as part of the recent bailouts. The government also intervenes extensively in the free market by creating regulations that stimulate competition and protect both consumers and workers. Regulations are likely to become stronger in the wake of the economic crisis.[12]

Over the past 30 years, most economies of the world have begun moving toward the market end of the spectrum. Government-owned businesses have converted to private ownership via a process called **privatization**. Socialist governments have reduced red tape, cracked down on corruption, and created new laws to protect economic rights. Extravagant human services—from free healthcare to education subsidies—have shrunk. And far-reaching tax reform has created new incentives for both domestic and foreign investment in once-stagnant planned economies.[13]

Unfortunately, the price of economic restructuring has been a fair amount of social turmoil in many nations undergoing market reforms. Countries from France to China have experienced sometimes violent demonstrations in response to social and employment program cutbacks. Change is challenging, especially when it redefines economic winners and losers. But countries that have taken strides toward the market end of the spectrum—from small players like the Czech Republic, to large players like China—have seen the payoff in rejuvenated growth rates that have raised the standard of living for millions of people.

LO6 Evaluating Economic Performance: What's Working?

Clearly, economic systems are complex—very complex. So you probably won't be surprised to learn that no single measure captures all the dimensions of economic performance. To get the full picture, you need to understand a range of terms and measures, including gross domestic product, employment level, the business cycle, inflation rate, and productivity.

> **Raising a child from birth to age 17 costs anywhere from $148,300 to $298,700 (not including college!).**
>
> *U.S. Department of Agriculture*

Gross Domestic Product

Real **gross domestic product**, or GDP, measures the total value of all final goods and services produced within a nation's physical boundaries over a given period of time, adjusted for inflation. (Nominal GDP does not include an inflation adjustment.) All domestic production is included in the GDP, even when the producer is foreign-owned. The U.S. GDP, for instance, includes the value of Toyota pickup trucks built in Texas, even though Toyota is a Japanese firm. Likewise, the Mexican GDP includes the value of Whirlpool appliances built in Mexican factories, even though Whirlpool is an American firm.

GDP is a vital measure of economic health. Business people, economists, and political leaders use GDP to measure the economic performance of individual nations and to compare the growth among nations. Interestingly, GDP levels tend to be somewhat understated, since they don't include any illegal activities—such as paying undocumented nannies and gardeners, or selling illegal drugs—which can represent a significant portion of some countries' production. The GDP also ignores legal goods that are not reported to avoid taxation, plus output produced within households. In 2008 the GDP of the United States was just over $14.6 trillion, reflecting a tepid .3% growth rate versus 2007.[14] Check out Chapter 3 for a survey of the world's key economies according to total GDP and GDP growth rate.

Employment Level

The overall level of employment is another key element of economic health. When people have jobs, they have money, which allows them to spend and invest, fueling economic growth. Most nations track employment levels largely through the **unemployment rate**, which includes everyone age 16 and older who doesn't have a job and is actively seeking one. The U.S. unemployment rate climbed precipitously through the Great Recession, rising from 5.8% in 2008 to 9.3% in 2009, to 9.5% by March 2010. As the economy began its glacially slow turnaround, competition for new positions was fierce, since the recession wiped out 8.2 million jobs, leaving five or six applicants to compete for each new position.[15]

Interestingly, some unemployment is actually good—it reflects your freedom to change jobs. If you have an awful boss, for instance, you may just quit. Are you unemployed? Of course you are. Are you glad? You probably are, and the chances are good that you'll find another position that's a better fit for you. This type of job loss is called *frictional unemployment*, and it tends to be ultimately positive. *Structural unemployment*, on the other hand, is usually longer term. This category encompasses people who don't have jobs because the economy no longer needs their skills. In the United States, growing numbers of workers in the past decade have found themselves victims of structural unemployment as manufacturing jobs have moved overseas. Often their only option is expensive retraining. Two other categories of unemployment are *cyclical*, which involves layoffs during recessions, and *seasonal*, which involves job loss related to the time of year. In some areas of the country, construction and agricultural workers are seasonally unemployed, but the best example may be the department store Santa who has a job only during the holiday season!

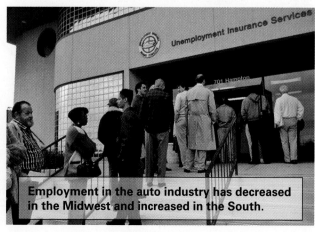

Employment in the auto industry has decreased in the Midwest and increased in the South.

© FRITZ HOFFMANN/THE IMAGE WORKS

The Business Cycle

The **business cycle** is the periodic contraction and expansion that occurs over time in virtually every economy. But the word "cycle" may be a little misleading, since it implies that the economy contracts and expands in a predictable pattern. In reality, the phases of the cycle are different each time they happen, and—despite the efforts of countless experts—no one can accurately predict when changes will occur or how long they will last. Those who make the best guesses stand to make fortunes, but bad bets can be financially devastating. The two key phases of the business cycle are contraction and expansion, shown in Exhibit 2.6.

- **Contraction** is a period of economic downturn, marked by rising unemployment. Businesses cut back on production, and consumers shift their buying patterns to more basic products and fewer luxuries. The economic "feel-good factor" simply disappears. Economists declare an official **recession** when GDP decreases for two consecutive quarters. A **depression** is an especially deep and long-lasting recession. Fortunately, economies seldom spiral into full-blown depressions, thanks

in large part to proactive intervention from the government. The last depression in the United States was the Great Depression of the 1930s. Whether a downturn is mild or severe, the very bottom of the contraction is called "the trough," as shown in Exhibit 2.6.

> { It's a recession when your neighbor loses his job; it's a depression when you lose yours. }
>
> *Harry Truman*

- **Recovery** is a period of rising economic growth and increasing employment, following a contraction. Businesses begin to expand. Consumers start to regain confidence, and spending begins to rise. The recovery is essentially the transition period between contraction and expansion.

- **Expansion** is a period of robust economic growth and high employment. Businesses expand to capitalize on emerging opportunities. Consumers are optimistic and confident, which fuels purchasing, which fuels production, which fuels further hiring. As Exhibit 2.6 demonstrates, the height of economic growth is called the peak of the expansion. The U.S. economy had the longest growth spurt on record during the 10-year period from 1991 to 2001. After a relatively mild slowdown in 2001–2002, the U.S. economy again expanded for several years before it plunged into a full-blown recession in 2008.[16]

Price Levels

The rate of price changes across the economy is another basic measure of economic well-being. **Inflation** means that prices on average are rising. Similar to unemployment, a low level of inflation is not so bad. It reflects a healthy economy—people have money, and they are willing to spend it. But when the Federal Reserve—the nation's central bank—manages the economy poorly, inflation can spiral out of control, which can lead to **hyperinflation**, when average prices increase more than 50% per month. In Hungary, for example, inflation

EXHIBIT 2.6 Business Cycle

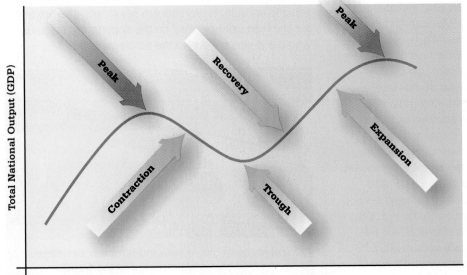

Total National Output (GDP)

Time (Years)

in its unstable, post–World War II economy climbed so quickly that prices doubled every 15 hours from 1945 to 1946. More recently, prices in the war-torn former Yugoslavia doubled every 16 hours between October 1993 and January 1994.

When the rate of price increases slows down, the economy is experiencing **disinflation**, which was the situation in the United States in the mid-1990s and more recently in the second half of 2008. But when prices actually decrease, the economy is experiencing **deflation**, typically a sign of economic trouble that goes hand-in-hand with very high unemployment. People don't have money and simply won't spend unless prices drop. During the Great Depression in the 1930s, the U.S. economy experienced deflation, with prices dropping 9% in 1931 and nearly 10% in 1932. Despite some economic turmoil, inflation in the United States was relatively low from 2000 to 2007, hovering at around 3%. But inflation picked up in the first half of 2008, only to fall during the first months of the economic crisis.

The government uses two major price indexes to evaluate inflation: the **consumer price index (CPI)** and the **producer price index (PPI)**. The CPI measures the change in weighted-average price over time in a consumer "market basket" of goods and services that the average person buys each month. The U.S. Bureau of Labor Statistics creates the basket—which includes hundreds of items such as housing, transportation, haircuts, wine, and pet care—using data from more than 30,000 consumers. While the market basket is meant to represent the average consumer, keep in mind that the "average" includes a lot of variation, so the CPI may not reflect your personal experience. For example, as a college student, you may be painfully sensitive to increases in tuition and the price of textbooks—a fact the authors of this particular textbook fully realize! But tuition and textbook prices aren't a big part of the "average" consumer's budget, so increases in these prices have a relatively small impact on the CPI.

The PPI measures the change over time in weighted-average wholesale prices, or the prices that businesses pay each other for goods and services. Changes in the PPI can sometimes predict changes in the CPI because producers tend to pass on price increases (and sometimes also price decreases) to consumers within a month or two of the changes.

Productivity

Productivity refers to the relationship between the goods and services that an economy produces and the resources needed to produce them. The amount of output—goods and services—divided by the amount of input (e.g., hours worked) equals productivity. The goal, of course, is to produce more goods and services, using fewer hours and other inputs. A high level of productivity typically correlates with healthy GDP growth, while low productivity tends to correlate with a more stagnant economy.

Over the past couple of decades, the United States has experienced strong productivity growth, due largely to infusions of technology that help workers produce more output, more quickly. But keep in mind that that productivity doesn't measure quality. That's why it's so important to examine multiple measures of economic health, rather than relying on simply one or two dimensions.

The Big Picture

From a business standpoint, a key goal of economics is to guide your decision-making by offering a deeper understanding of the broad forces that affect both your business and your personal life. Knowing even basic economic principles can help you make better business decisions in virtually every area—from production, to marketing, to accounting, to name just a few—regardless of your specific function or level within an organization. But you won't find an economics department within many (if any) businesses—rather you'll find people across the organization applying economic theories and trends to their work, even in the face of continual economic flux. As you read through the other chapters in this book, take a moment to consider both the macroeconomic and microeconomic forces that affect each area you study. You're likely to find a surprising number of examples.

WHAT ELSE? *RIP & REVIEW* **CARDS IN THE BACK**

disinflation A period of slowing average price increases across the economy.

deflation A period of falling average prices across the economy.

consumer price index (CPI) A measure of inflation that evaluates the change in the weighted-average price of goods and services that the average consumer buys each month.

producer price index (PPI) A measure of inflation that evaluates the change over time in the weighted-average wholesale prices.

productivity The basic relationship between the production of goods and services (output) and the resources needed to produce them (input) calculated via the following equation: output/input = productivity.

3

THE WORLD MARKETPLACE:

BUSINESS WITHOUT BORDERS

LEARNING OBJECTIVES

After studying this chapter, you will be able to...

LO1 Discuss business opportunities in the world economy

LO2 Explain the key reasons for international trade

LO3 Describe the tools for measuring international trade

LO4 Analyze strategies for reaching global markets

LO5 Discuss barriers to international trade and strategies to surmount them

LO6 Describe the free-trade movement and discuss key benefits and criticisms

Visit CourseMate at **www.cengagebrain.com.**

ATLANTIC

LO1 An Unprecedented Opportunity

As access to technology skyrockets and barriers to trade continue to fall, individual economies around the world have become more interdependent than ever before. The result is a tightly woven global economy marked by intense competition and huge, shifting opportunities. The long-term potential for U.S. business is enormous. Although the global economic crisis caused the world GDP to contract in 2009 for the first time since World War II, compared with average increases of about 3.5% per year since 1946, economists anticipated that the world GDP growth trend would turn positive again by 2010, led by emerging markets and developing countries such as China, India, Indonesia, Vietnam, and Brazil.[1]

A quick look at population trends validates the global business opportunity, especially in developing nations. With more than 300 million people, the United States accounts for less than 4.6% of the world's total population. More than 6.3 billion people live beyond our borders, representing more than 95% of potential customers for U.S. firms. But even though the growth rates in many high-population countries are strong, most of these nations remain behind the United States in terms of development and prosperity, posing considerable challenges for foreign firms.

AP IMAGES/RICHARD VOGEL

(In other words, most of their populations may not have the resources to buy even basic goods and services.) The issue is likely to become even more severe in the wake of the global economic crisis. Exhibit 3.1, a comparison of population, GDP growth rate, and per capita GDP for the world's five largest nations, highlights some of the discrepancies. Note that even though U.S. consumers clearly have money, China and India represent a much bigger opportunity in terms of both sheer size and economic growth.

The growing number of people with cell phones offers an interesting indicator of economic growth. A recent study by consulting firm McKinsey & Co. found that if a country increases cell phone penetration by 10 percentage points, GDP will likely increase by about .5%. That may

EXHIBIT 3.1 Selected Population and GDP Figures[2]

Nation	Population*	Per Capita GDP (U.S. Dollars)**	GDP Growth Rate***
China	1,338,612,968	$6,600	+8.70%
India	1,156,897,766	$3,100	+6.50%
United States	307,212,123	$46,400	−2.40%
Indonesia	240,271,522	$4,000	+4.50%
Brazil	198,739,269	$10,200	−0.20%

*CIA World Factbook, 2009 Population Estimate, updated April 2010.
**CIA World Factbook, 2009 GDP Estimates, updated April 2010.
***CIA World Factbook, 2009 GDP Growth Estimates, updated April 2010.

© PAUL TEARLE/STOCKBYTE/JUPITERIMAGES

seem small, but it equates to about $12 billion for an economy the size of China. In other words, when the percentage of the population with cell phones goes up, the entire economy benefits.

Not surprisingly, cell phone penetration in India and China is skyrocketing. China currently boasts the world's largest base of cell phone users—about 766 million—and the growth will likely continue. India's current subscriber base is more than 584 million; it has grown explosively over the last 5 years and seems likely to follow suit in the next decade. In the United States, Europe, and Japan, cell phones followed landlines, but large swaths of developing nations aren't bothering to build conventional phone service. Rather, they're moving directly to cell phone networks. David Knapp, general director of Motorola Vietnam, points out that "they can leapfrog technology." And Vietnamese micro-entrepreneur Nguyen Huu Truc says, "It's no longer something that only the rich can afford. Now, it's a basic means of communication." As more people get the chance to get connected, better communication will likely feed economic growth. The upshot is that millions of people worldwide will have a higher standard of living.[3]

> ## The developing world boasts nearly double the cell phone subscriptions in advanced economies.
> *Washington Post*

LO2 Key Reasons for International Trade

Companies engage in global trade for a range of reasons beyond the obvious opportunity to tap into huge and growing new markets. The benefits include better access to factors of production, reduced risk, and an inflow of new ideas.

- *Access to factors of production:* International trade offers a valuable opportunity for individual firms to capitalize on factors of production that simply aren't present in the right amount for the right price in each individual country. India, China, and the Philippines, for example, attract multibillion-dollar investments because of their large cohort of technically skilled university graduates who work for about one-fifth the pay of comparable American workers. Russia and the OPEC nations offer a rich supply of oil, and Canada, like other forested nations, boasts an abundant supply of timber. The United States offers plentiful capital, which is less available in other parts of the world. International trade helps even out some of the resource imbalances among nations.

- *Reduced risk:* Global trade reduces dependence on one economy, lowering the economic risk for multinational firms. When the Japanese economy entered a deep, sustained slump in the 1990s, for instance, Sony and Toyota thrived through their focus on other, healthier markets around the world. But a word of caution is key: as national economies continue to integrate, an economic meltdown in one part of the world can have far-reaching impact. Major

Global Branding

Every year *BusinessWeek* magazine and Interbrand branding consultancy rank the best brands in the world. Their methodology ensures that only truly global companies are eligible. To appear on the list, a brand must derive at least one third of its earnings from outside its home country, be recognizable beyond its base of customers, and have publicly available marketing and financial data. The top ten global brands in 2009 were:

1. Coca-Cola
2. IBM
3. Microsoft
4. GE
5. Nokia
6. McDonald's
7. Google
8. Toyota
9. Intel
10. Disney

In the wake of the Great Recession, top global brands are laser-focused on building and in some cases *re*building the trust of their consumers. According to respected branding consultant Larry Light, "Trust is what drives profit margin and share price." Since today's consumers have access to so much information, transparency and openness are critical components of trust. Marketing executive Randall Beard commented that "consumers are telling companies in a thousand ways that if you aren't open with me, then I won't trust you." Brands that succeed at building trust may well top the *BusinessWeek* list in years to come.[4]

foreign banks, for example, were badly burned by the U.S. subprime market mess, due to heavy investments in U.S. mortgage markets.

- *Inflow of innovation:* International trade can also offer companies an invaluable source of new ideas. Japan, for instance, is far ahead of the curve regarding cell phone service. Japanese cell phone "extras," including games, ringtones, videos, and stylish new accessories, set the standard for cell service around the world. In Europe, meanwhile, consumers are seeking to bring a top-quality pub experience into their homes with professional-quality home beer taps. Companies with a presence in foreign markets experience budding trends like these firsthand, giving them a jump in other markets around the world.[5]

Competitive Advantage

Beyond individual companies, industries tend to succeed on a worldwide basis in countries that enjoy a competitive advantage. But to understand competitive advantage, you need to first understand how **opportunity cost** relates to international trade. When a country produces more of one good, it must produce less of another good (assuming that resources are finite). The value of the second-best choice—the value of the production that a country gives up in order to produce the first product—represents the opportunity cost of producing the first product.

A country has an **absolute advantage** when it can produce more of a good than other nations, using the same amount of resources. China, for example, has an absolute advantage in terms of clothing production, relative to the United States. But having an absolute advantage isn't always enough. Unless they face major trade barriers, the industries in any country tend to produce products for which they have a **comparative advantage**—meaning that they tend to turn out those goods that have the lowest opportunity cost compared to other countries. The United States, for instance, boasts a comparative advantage versus most countries in movie and television program production; Germany has a comparative advantage in the production of high-performance cars; and South Korea enjoys a comparative advantage in electronics.

But keep in mind that comparative advantage seldom remains static. As technology changes and the workforce evolves (through factors such as education and experience), nations may gain or lose comparative advantage in various industries. China and India, for example, are both seeking to build a comparative advantage versus other nations in technology production by investing in their infrastructure and their institutions of higher education.

LO3 Global Trade: Taking Measure

After a decade of robust growth, global trade began slowing in 2007, due largely to turbulence in the worldwide financial markets. In 2008, the rate of growth in world trade slid below 5%, as the global recession tightened its grip. In 2009, global trade plummeted nearly 25% from 2008's level, the largest single-year drop since World War II. Global gross fixed investment fell about 4% year-over-year, or by roughly $800 billion. Measuring the impact of international trade on individual nations requires a clear understanding of balance of trade, balance of payments, and exchange rates.[6]

Balance of Trade

The **balance of trade** is a basic measure of the difference between a nation's exports and imports. If the total value of exports is higher than the total value of imports, the country has a **trade surplus**. If the total value of imports is higher than the total value of exports, the country has a trade deficit. Balance of trade includes the value of both goods and services, and it incorporates trade with all foreign nations. Although a **trade deficit** signals the wealth of an economy that can afford to buy huge amounts of foreign products, a large deficit can be destabilizing. It indicates, after all, that as goods and services flow into a nation, money flows out—a challenge with regard to long-term economic health. The United States has had an overall trade deficit since 1976, and as the American appetite for foreign goods has grown, the trade deficit has ballooned. But that growth may slow over the next few years as demand falls in response to the global economic crisis.

Balance of Payments

Balance of payments is a measure of the total flow of money into or out of a country. Clearly, the balance of trade plays a central role in determining the balance

opportunity cost The opportunity of giving up the second-best choice when making a decision.

absolute advantage The benefit a country has in a given industry when it can produce more of a product than other nations using the same amount of resources.

comparative advantage The benefit a country has in a given industry if it can make products at a lower opportunity cost than other countries.

balance of trade A basic measure of the difference in value between a nation's exports and imports, including both goods and services.

trade surplus Overage that occurs when the total value of a nation's exports is higher than the total value of its imports.

trade deficit Shortfall that occurs when the total value of a nation's imports is higher than the total value of its exports.

balance of payments A measure of the total flow of money into or out of a country.

of payments. But the balance of payments also includes other financial flows such as foreign borrowing and lending, foreign aid payments and receipts, and foreign investments. A **balance of payments surplus** means that more money flows in than out, while a **balance of payments deficit** means that more money flows out than in. Keep in mind that the balance of payments typically corresponds to the balance of trade, since trade is, in general, the largest component.

Exchange Rates

Exchange rates measure the value of one nation's currency relative to the currency of other nations. While the exchange rate does not directly measure global commerce, it certainly has a powerful influence on how global trade affects individual nations and their trading partners. The exchange rate of a given currency must be expressed in terms of another currency. Here are some examples of how the exchange rate can influence the economy, using the dollar and the euro.

Strong Dollar versus Euro: Who Benefits? (Example: $1.00 = 1.20 euros)	Weak Dollar versus Euro: Who Benefits? (Example: $1.00 = .60 euros)
U.S. travelers to Europe: Their dollars can buy more European goods and services.	*European travelers to the United States:* Their dollars buy more American goods and services.
American firms with European operations: Operating costs—from buying products to paying workers—are lower.	*European firms with American operations:* Operating costs—from buying products to paying workers—are lower.
European exporters: Their products are less expensive in the United States, so Europe exports more and we import more.	*American exporters:* Their products are less expensive in Europe, so we export more and Europe imports more.

Countertrade

A complete evaluation of global trade must also consider exchanges that don't actually involve money. A surprisingly large chunk of international commerce—as much as 20%—involves the barter of products for products rather than for currency. Companies typically engage in **countertrade** to meet the needs of customers that don't have access to hard currency or credit, usually in developing countries. Individual countertrade agreements range from simple barter to a complex web of exchanges that end up meeting the needs of multiple parties. Done poorly, countertrading can be a confusing nightmare for everyone involved. But done well, countertrading is a powerful tool for gaining customers and products that would not otherwise be available.[7]

LO4 Seizing the Opportunity: Strategies for Reaching Global Markets

There is no one right way to seize the opportunity in global markets. In fact, the opportunity may not even make sense for every firm. While international trade can offer new profit streams and lower costs, it also introduces a higher level of risk and complexity to running a business. Being ready to take on the challenge can mean the difference between success and failure.

Firms ready to tap the opportunity have a number of options for how to move forward. One way is to seek foreign suppliers through outsourcing and importing. Another possibility is to seek foreign customers through exporting, licensing, franchising, and direct investment. These market development options fall in a spectrum from low cost–low control to high cost–high control, as shown in Exhibit 3.2. In other words, companies that choose to export products to a foreign country spend less to enter that market than companies that choose to build their own factories. But companies that build their own factories have a lot more control than exporters over how their business unfolds. Keep in mind that profit opportunity and risk—which vary along with cost and control—also play a critical role in how firms approach international markets.

Smaller firms tend to begin with exporting and move along the spectrum as the business develops. But larger firms may jump straight to the strategies that give them more control over their operations. Large firms are also likely to use a number of different approaches in different countries, depending on the goals of the firm and the structure of the foreign market. Regardless of the specific strategy, most large companies—such as General Electric, Nike, and Disney—both outsource with foreign suppliers and sell their products to foreign markets.

EXHIBIT 3.2 Market Development Options

LOWER Risk — Exporting · Licensing · Franchising · Direct Investment — HIGHER Risk

LESS Control — MORE Control

Most of the clothing you're wearing right now was probably produced in another country.

© LUCIOPIX/ALAMY

Foreign Outsourcing and Importing

Foreign outsourcing means contracting with foreign suppliers to produce products, usually at a fraction of the cost of domestic production. Gap, for instance, relies on a network of manufacturers in 50 different countries, mostly in less-developed parts of the world, from Asia, to Africa, to Central America. Apple depends on firms in China and Taiwan to produce the iPod. And countless small companies contract with foreign manufacturers as well. The key benefit, of course, is dramatically lower wages, which drive down the cost of production.

But while foreign outsourcing lowers costs, it also involves significant risk. Quality control typically requires very detailed specifications to ensure that a company gets what it actually needs. Another key risk of foreign outsourcing involves social responsibility. A firm that contracts with foreign producers has an obligation to ensure that those factories adhere to ethical standards. Deciding what those standards should be is often quite tricky,

given different cultures, expectations, and laws in different countries. And policing the factories on an ongoing basis can be even harder than determining the standards. But companies that don't get it right face the threat of significant consumer backlash in the United States and Europe. This has been a particular issue with products produced in China. In the last few years, for instance, product defects forced U.S. firms to recall a host of Chinese-produced toys, including Thomas the Tank Engine trains that were coated with toxic lead paint, ghoulish fake eyeballs that were filled with kerosene, and an infant wrist rattle that posed a choking hazard.[8]

Importing means buying products from overseas that have already been produced, rather than contracting with overseas manufacturers to produce special orders. Imported products, of course, don't carry the brand name of the importer, but they also don't carry as much risk. Pier 1 Imports, a large retail chain, has built a powerful brand around the importing concept, creating stores that give the customer the sense of a global shopping trip without the cost or hassle of actually leaving the country.

Exporting

Exporting is the most basic level of international market development. It simply means producing products domestically and selling them abroad. Exporting represents an especially strong opportunity for small and midsized companies. Ernest Joshua, for instance,

foreign outsourcing (also contract manufacturing) Contracting with foreign suppliers to produce products, usually at a fraction of the cost of domestic production.

importing Buying products domestically that have been produced or grown in foreign nations.

exporting Selling products in foreign nations that have been produced or grown domestically.

Unleashing Consumer Demand in China

© DESIGN56/ISTOCKPHOTO.COM

For decades, Chinese consumers have been savers rather than spenders, feeding global economic expansion by producing and exporting everything from cheap clothing to pricey electronic toys, prompting Dong Tao, a top economist at UBS in Hong Kong, to observe, "A Barbie doll costs $20, but China only gets about 35 cents of that."

In an attempt to shift their economic model away from reliance on exports, and to keep more money in China, Chinese officials are attempting to unleash domestic consumer demand via tax incentives and stimulus programs. Results to date have been mixed. But if the strategy succeeds, the long-term opportunity could be huge for American businesses, given that the Chinese population is more than 1.3 billion strong. In mid-2009, *Advertising Age* magazine published a guide for multinational marketers, pointing out that "China's size doesn't guarantee success." Following are some of the top *AdAge* tips:

- **Don't think of China as a single country.** Two hundred seventy-three of China's cities are home to more than 1 million people, compared to fewer than ten in the U.S. And China's landmass covers five different time zones. There is no typical Chinese consumer.
- **Despite the popularity of some Western brands, do not assume that Chinese want to become Westernized.** While many Chinese are interested in joining the modern, global community, most do not want to abandon their ancient traditions, beliefs, and culture.
- **Underestimate local brands at your peril.** Local manufacturer Haier, for example, dominates the home appliance market, while homegrown search engine Baidu has clobbered Goggle in terms of market share.

If China does indeed unleash consumer demand, they may find themselves dealing with a whole new set of social problems that go hand in hand with a more materialistic society.[9]

---

developed a thriving Arkansas-based hair care company that specializes in products for African Americans. Recognizing opportunity abroad, his firm now exports products to Africa and the Caribbean.[10]

Even though exporting is relatively basic, it still isn't easy. Exporters must negotiate their way through documentation requirements, shipping standards, content regulations, packaging requirements, and more. Finding the right distributor represents another key challenge. The good news is that the U.S. Commercial Service, a wing of the Department of Commerce, offers companies guidance through the entire export process, providing invaluable advice and connections. The government is clearly quite motivated to provide export assistance, because higher exports can help lower the trade deficit, strengthening the economy by keeping more money in the country.

Foreign Licensing and Foreign Franchising

Foreign licensing and foreign franchising, the next level of commitment to international markets, are quite similar. **Foreign licensing** involves a domestic firm granting a foreign firm the rights to produce and market its product or to use its trademark/patent rights in a defined geographical area. The company that offers the rights, or the *licensor*, receives a fee from the company that buys the rights, or the *licensee*. This approach allows firms to expand into foreign markets with little or no investment, and it also helps circumvent government restrictions on importing in closed markets. But maintaining control of licensees can be a significant challenge. Licensors also run the risk that unethical licensees may become their competitors, using information that they gained from the licensing agreement. Foreign licensing is especially common in the food and beverage industry. The most high-profile examples include Coke and Pepsi, which grant licenses to foreign bottlers all over the world.

Foreign franchising is a specialized type of licensing. A firm that expands through foreign franchising, called a *franchisor*, offers other businesses, or *franchisees*, the right to produce and market its products if the franchisee agrees to specific operating requirements—a complete package of how to do business. Franchisors also often offer their franchisees management guidance, marketing support, and even financing. In return, franchisees pay both a start-up fee and an ongoing percentage of sales to the franchisor. A key difference between franchising and licensing is that franchisees assume the identity of the franchisor. A McDonald's franchise in Paris, for instance, is clearly a McDonald's, not, say, a Pierre's Baguette outlet that also carries McDonald's products.

Foreign Direct Investment

Direct investment in foreign production and marketing facilities represents the deepest level of global involvement. The cost is high, but companies with direct investments have more control over how their business operates in a given country. The high dollar commitment also represents significant risk if the business doesn't go well. Most direct investment takes the form of either acquiring foreign firms, or developing new facilities from the ground up. Another increasingly popular approach is strategic alliances or partnerships that allow multiple firms to share risks and resources for mutual benefit.

Foreign acquisitions enable companies to gain a foothold quickly in new markets. In 2005, for instance, eBay purchased Skype Technologies, a Luxembourg-based communications company. The acquisition brought them an instant presence in the Internet telephone business in 225 countries. A number of other global giants such as Microsoft, General Electric, and Nestlé tend to follow a foreign acquisition strategy.[11]

Developing new facilities from scratch—or "offshoring"—is the most costly form of direct investment. It also involves significant risk. But the benefits include complete control over how the facility develops and the potential for high profits, which makes the approach attractive for corporations that can afford it. Intel, for instance, plans to build a $2.5 billion specialized computer chip manufacturing plant in northeastern China. And foreign car companies, from German Mercedes-Benz, to Korean Hyundai, to Japanese Toyota, have built factories in the southern United States.[12]

> # Obstacles are those frightful things you see when you take your eyes off your goal.
>
> *Henry Ford, founder of Ford Motor Company*

Joint ventures involve two or more companies joining forces—sharing resources, risks, and profits, but not merging companies—to pursue specific opportunities. A formal, long-term agreement is usually called a **partnership**, while a less formal, less encompassing agreement is usually called a **strategic alliance**. Joint ventures are a popular, though controversial, means of entering foreign markets. Often a foreign company connects with a local firm to ease its way into the market. In fact, some countries, such as Malaysia, require that foreign investors have local partners. But research from Harvard finance professor Mihir Desai finds that joint ventures between multinational firms and domestic partners can be more costly and less rewarding than they initially appear. He and his team suggest that they make sense only in countries that require local political and cultural knowledge as a core element of doing business.[13]

LO5 Barriers to International Trade

Every business faces challenges, but international firms face more hurdles than domestic firms. Understanding

© AGE FOTOSTOCK/SUPERSTOCK

and surmounting those hurdles is the key to success in global markets. Most barriers to trade fall into the following categories: sociocultural differences, economic differences, and legal/political differences. As you think about these barriers, keep in mind that each country has a different mix of barriers. Often countries with the highest barriers have the least competition, which can be a real opportunity for the first international firms to break through.

Sociocultural Differences

Sociocultural differences include differences among countries in language, attitudes, and values. Some specific and perhaps surprising elements that affect business include nonverbal communication, forms of address, attitudes toward punctuality, religious celebrations and customs, business practices, and expectations regarding meals and gifts. Understanding and responding to sociocultural factors are vital for firms that operate in multiple countries. But since the differences often operate at a subtle level, they can undermine relationships before anyone is aware that it's happening. The best way to jump over sociocultural barriers is to conduct thorough consumer research, cultivate firsthand knowledge, and practice extreme sensitivity. The payoff can be a sharp competitive edge. Hyundai, for instance, enjoys a whopping 17% share of the

partnership A voluntary agreement under which two or more people act as co-owners of a business for profit.

strategic alliance An agreement between two or more firms to jointly pursue a specific opportunity without actually merging their businesses. Strategic alliances typically involve less formal, less encompassing agreements than partnerships.

sociocultural differences Differences among cultures in language, attitudes, and values.

Veggie Surprise, Anyone?

AP IMAGES/VINCENT THIAN

Travel around the world, and you're likely to see American fast food franchisees in virtually every city. Although you'll surely recognize the names of these fast food behemoths, you may not be as familiar with the food that they serve, since many of the dishes have been completely changed in response to local culture.

Some favorites from the Domino's international menus:

- Japan: squid pizza
- England: tuna and sweet corn pizza
- South Korea: broccoli and potato pizza
- Netherlands: grilled lamb pizza

Pizza Hut:

- Japan: crust stuffed with shrimp nuggets and injected with mayonnaise
- South Korea: crust filled with sweet potato mousse

McDonald's:

- India: Paneer Salsa Wrap (cottage cheese with Mexican-Cajun coating)
- Australia: Bacon and Egg Roll ("Rashers of quality bacon and fried egg")
- Kuwait: Veggie Surprise Burger (no detailed description...yikes!)
- United Kingdom: Five "Toasted Deli" sandwich options[14]

infrastructure A country's physical facilities that support economic activity.

passenger car market in India. They beat the competition with custom features that reflect Indian culture, such as elevated rooflines to provide more headroom for turban-wearing motorists.[15]

Economic Differences

Before entering a foreign market, it's critical to understand and evaluate the local economic conditions. Key factors to consider include population, per capita income, economic growth rate, currency exchange rate, and stage of economic development. But keep in mind that low scores for any of these measures don't necessarily equal a lack of opportunity. In fact, some of today's biggest opportunities are in countries with low per capita income. For example, the Indian division of global giant Unilever gets 50% of its sales from rural India by selling products to individual consumers in tiny quantities, such as two-cent sachets of shampoo. And Hewlett-Packard has recently joined forces with Unilever to give microdistributors in rural India the ability to check prices and place orders online from "what are now distinctively offline villages and regions."

Effectively serving less-developed markets requires innovation and efficiency. Emerging consumers often need different product features, and they almost always need lower costs. C. K. Prahalad, an influential business scholar, believed that forward-thinking companies can make a profit in developing countries if they make advanced technology affordable. Many markets are simply so large that high-volume sales can make up for low-profit margins.

Foreign markets can differ dramatically in terms of infrastructure development.

© MAO SIQIAN/XINHUA/XINHUA PRESS/CORBIS

Overall, the profit potential is clear and growing. And as consumers in developing countries continue to gain income—although at a much slower pace in the wake of the economic crisis—companies that established their brands early will have a critical edge over firms that enter the market after them.[16]

Infrastructure should be another key economic consideration when entering a foreign market. Infrastructure refers to a country's physical facilities that support economic activity. It includes basic systems in each of the following areas:

*   Transportation (e.g., roads, airports, railroads, and ports)
*   Communication (e.g., TV, radio, Internet, and cell phone coverage)

Global Greening?

The consensus is nearly complete: the world community must take dramatic steps to combat global warming and mitigate environmental destruction. According to the International Energy Agency, the future of human prosperity depends on it.

Clearly, change won't be easy, and coordinated action is vital. But encouraging signs are out there. A recent Pew Environmental Group report found that the clean energy sector experienced investment growth of 230 percent between 2005 and 2009. "Demonstrating its strength, the clean energy sector declined only 6.6 percent in 2009, despite the worst financial downturn in over half a century. In 2009, $162 billion was invested in clean energy around the world. In an encouraging sign for the future, many governments prioritized clean energy within economic recovery funding." More than 66 countries have specific renewable energy policies.

At the end of 2009, the United Nations sponsored an international Climate Change Conference in Copenhagen. The goal was to forge a binding global climate agreement. Although a binding treaty did not emerge, 107 nations signed up to support the nonbinding Copenhagen Accord, which calls for limiting the rise in global temperatures mostly by helping emerging nations adapt to climate change, and protecting tropical forests from deforestation. Negotiators are trying to craft an enforceable global climate treaty, but national environmental leaders believe that the first real opportunity to reach such an agreement will come in 2011 at a United Nations conference in South Africa. Perhaps we should simply change the questions:

*   Do you think the U.S. has done enough to promote global greening? If not, what more would you recommend? Support your answer, and be sure to consider the cost/benefit trade-offs.
*   Would you accept a high-paying job at a company with environmental policies that offend you?
*   Are you willing to pay more money to buy products that are produced in countries with sound environmental policies? If so, how can you research where the products are produced and what the environmental policies are?[17]

© BRENDON DE SUZA/ISTOCKPHOTO.COM

- Energy (e.g., utilities and power plants)
- Finance (e.g., banking, checking, and credit)

The level of infrastructure can vary dramatically among countries. In Africa, for instance, only 5% of the population has Internet access, compared to 74% in North America. In Vietnam and Thailand, many consumers buy products directly from vendors in small boats, compared to firmly grounded stores in Europe. And as of 2007, Indian consumers made just 1% of their total purchases through credit cards, compared to 20% for Koreans, and a world average of 9%.[18]

Political and Legal Differences

Political regimes obviously differ around the world, and their policies have a dramatic impact on business. The specific laws and regulations that governments create around business are often less obvious, yet they can still represent a significant barrier to international trade. To compete effectively—and to reduce risk—managers must carefully evaluate these factors and make plans to respond to them both now and as they change.

Laws and Regulations International businesses must comply with international legal standards, the laws of their own countries, and the laws of their host countries. This can be a real challenge, since many developing countries change business regulations with little notice and less publicity. The justice system can pose another key challenge, particularly with regard to legal enforcement of ownership and contract rights. A look at the World Bank "Doing Business" rankings reveals that some high-growth markets have plenty of room to improve in this area. In 2009 India ranked #180—resolving a contractual issue took an average of 46 procedures and 1,420 days. China did much better at #18—resolving an issue took an average of 34 procedures and 406 days. As a point of comparison, the United States (the top high-population nation on the list) ranked #6—resolving an issue took an average of 30 procedures and 300 days. The key benefit of an effective legal system is that it reduces risk for both domestic and foreign businesses.[19]

Bribery, the payment of money for favorable treatment, and corruption, the solicitation of money for favorable treatment, are also major issues throughout the world. While bribery and corruption are technically illegal in virtually every major country, they are often accepted as a standard way of doing business. Regardless, U.S. corporations and American citizens are subject to prosecution by U.S. authorities for offering bribes in any nation. See Chapter 4 for more details.

Political Climate The political climate of any country deeply influences whether that nation is attractive to foreign business. Stability is crucial. A country subject to strife from civil war, riots, or other violence creates huge additional risk for foreign business. Yet figuring out how to operate in an unstable environment such as Russia, Bolivia, or the Middle East can give early movers a real advantage. Grant Winterton, Coca-Cola's regional manager for Russia, commented to *Time* magazine that "the politics do concern us." But having snagged 50% of the $1.9 billion carbonated-soft-drink market, he concludes that "the opportunity far outweighs the risk." Poor enforcement of intellectual property rights across international borders is another tough issue for business. The Business Software Alliance piracy tracking study found that worldwide piracy rates increased three percentage points to 41% in 2008, and dollar losses from piracy broke the $50 billion level for the first time ever. The highest-piracy countries are Armenia, Bangladesh, Georgia, and Zimbabwe, all over 90 percent.[20]

International Trade Restrictions National governments also have the power to erect barriers to international business through a variety of international trade restrictions. The arguments for and against trade restrictions—also called **protectionism**—are summarized below. As you read, note that most economists find the reasons to eliminate trade restrictions much more compelling than the reasons to create them.

Just as trade restrictions have a range of motivations, they can take a number of different forms. The most common trade restrictions are tariffs, quotas, voluntary export restraints, and embargos.

- **Tariffs** are taxes levied against imports. Governments tend to use protective tariffs either to shelter fledgling industries that couldn't compete without help, or to shelter industries that are crucial to the domestic economy. In 2002, for instance, the United States imposed tariffs of 8% to 30% on a variety of imported steel products for a period of three years, in order to give some relief to the large, but ailing, U.S. steel industry.

- **Quotas** are limitations on the amount of specific products that may be imported from certain countries during a given time period. Russia, for instance, has specific quotas for U.S. meat imports.

- **Voluntary Export Restraints (VERs)** are limitations on the amount of specific products that one nation will export to another nation. Although the government of the exporting country typically imposes VERs, they usually do so out of fear that the importing country would impose even more onerous restrictions. As a result, VERs often aren't

protectionism
National policies designed to restrict international trade, usually with the goal of protecting domestic businesses.

tariffs Taxes levied against imports.

quotas Limitations on the amount of specific products that may be imported from certain countries during a given time period.

voluntary export restraints (VERs) Limitations on the amount of specific products that one nation will export to another nation.

embargo A complete ban on international trade of a certain item, or a total halt in trade with a particular nation.

free trade The unrestricted movement of goods and services across international borders.

General Agreement on Tariffs and Trade (GATT) An international trade treaty designed to encourage worldwide trade among its members.

World Trade Organization (WTO) A permanent global institution to promote international trade and to settle international trade disputes.

World Bank An international cooperative of 186 member countries, working together to reduce poverty in the developing world.

as "voluntary" as the name suggests. The United States, for instance, insisted on VERs with Japanese auto exports in the early '80s (which many economists believe ultimately precipitated the decline of the U.S. auto industry).

- An **embargo** is a total ban on the international trade of a certain item, or a total halt in trade with a particular nation. The intention of most embargoes is to pressure the targeted country to change political policies or to protect national security. The U.S. embargo against trade with Cuba offers a high-profile example.

Quotas, VERs, and embargoes are relatively rare compared to tariffs, and tariffs are falling to new lows. But as tariffs decrease, some nations are seeking to control imports through nontariff barriers such as:

- Requiring red-tape-intensive import licenses for certain categories

- Establishing nonstandard packaging requirements for certain products

- Offering less-favorable exchange rates to certain importers

- Establishing standards on how certain products are produced or grown

- Promoting a "buy national" consumer attitude among local people

Nontariff barriers tend to be fairly effective because complaints about them can be hard to prove and easy to counter.[21]

LO6 Free Trade: The Movement Gains Momentum

Perhaps the most dramatic change in the world economy has been the global move toward **free trade**—the unrestricted movement of goods and services across international borders. Even though *complete* free trade is not a reality, the emergence of regional trading blocks, common markets, and international trade agreements has moved the world economy much closer to that goal.

Reasons to *Create* Trade Restrictions	Reasons to *Eliminate* Trade Restrictions
Protect domestic industry (e.g., the U.S. steel industry)	Reduce prices and increase choices for consumers by encouraging competition from around the world
Protect domestic jobs in key industries (but perhaps at the cost of domestic jobs in other industries)	Increase domestic jobs in industries with a comparative advantage versus other countries
Protect national security interests	Increase jobs—both at home and abroad—from foreign companies
Retaliate against countries who have engaged in unfair trade practices	Build exporting opportunities through better relationships with other countries
Pressure other countries to change their policies and practices	Use resources more efficiently on a worldwide basis

GATT and the World Trade Organization

The **General Agreement on Tariffs and Trade (GATT)** is an international trade accord designed to encourage worldwide trade among its members. Established in 1948 by 23 nations, GATT has undergone a number of revisions. The most significant changes stemmed from the 1986–1994 Uruguay Round of negotiations, which took bold steps to slash average tariffs by about 30% and to reduce other trade barriers among the 125 nations that signed.

The Uruguay Round also created the **World Trade Organization (WTO)**, a permanent global institution to

© STEPHEN JAFFE/GETTY IMAGES NEWS/GETTY IMAGES

promote international trade and to settle international trade disputes. The WTO monitors provisions of the GATT agreements, promotes further reduction of trade barriers, and mediates disputes among members. The decisions of the WTO are binding, which means that all parties involved in disputes must comply to maintain good standing in the organization.

Ministers of the WTO meet every two years to address current world trade issues. As the world economy has shifted toward services rather than goods, the emphasis of WTO meetings has followed suit. Controlling rampant piracy of intellectual property is a key concern for developed countries. For less-developed countries, a central issue is U.S. and European agricultural subsidies, which may unfairly distort agricultural prices worldwide.

In fact, both the broader agenda and the individual decisions of the WTO have become increasingly controversial over the past 10 years. Advocates for less-developed nations are deeply concerned that free trade clears the path for major multinational corporations to push local businesses into economic failure. A local food stand, for instance, probably won't have the resources to compete with a global giant such as McDonald's. If the food stand closes, the community has gained inexpensive hamburgers, but the entrepreneur has lost his livelihood and the community has lost the local flavor that contributes to its unique culture. Other opponents of the WTO worry that the acceleration of global trade encourages developing countries to fight laws that protect the environment and workers' rights, for fear of losing their low-cost advantage on the world market. The concerns have sparked significant protests during the past few meetings of the WTO ministers, and the outcry may well grow louder as developing nations gain economic clout.

> # World peace through international trade and commerce.
> *Hilton Hotel's corporate motto*

The World Bank

Established in the aftermath of World War II, the **World Bank** is an international cooperative of 186 member countries, working together to reduce poverty in the developing world. The World Bank influences the global economy by providing financial and technical advice to the governments of developing countries for projects in a range of areas including infrastructure, communications, health, and education. The financial assistance usually comes in the form of low interest loans. But to secure a loan, the borrowing nation must often agree to conditions that can involve rather arduous economic reform.

The World Bank sees international trade as a vital tool for decreasing poverty. It actively encourages aid

WITHOUT A MAP... CHARTING AN ETHICAL COURSE

Farm Support: Fair or Foul?

It's tough farming cotton in Africa. And the United States makes it tougher still by using subsidies to guarantee American farmers a set price for their cotton—currently 72 cents per pound—that is well above the going global rate. With such a rich pledge, American cotton farmers have flooded the world market with so much cotton that the actual price in world markets has plummeted. As a result, farmers in Africa, who produce top-quality cotton for about half the cost of production in the United States, sometimes end up getting so little for their crop that they struggle simply to feed their families.

Oxfam, a respected nonprofit organization that promotes fair trade, notes a sad irony: U.S. aid to West African cotton-producing countries is comparable to the export losses that those countries incur from American cotton subsidies. And support for cotton is only a fraction of the $12+ billion that the United States doles out each year in farm subsidies.

Not surprisingly, developing nations protest that farm subsidies in America and Europe unfairly distort the world agricultural market. And the United States has claimed willingness to reduce them, but only in return for greater access to service industries, such as insurance and banking, in developing countries. This solution could improve the health of the agricultural business in countries such as Benin and Mali, but it could also decimate their fledgling service industries.

From a U.S. perspective, the reluctance to eliminate farm subsidies is not surprising. American farmers feel singled out, since European farmers receive over $50 billion in farm subsidies, more than four times the U.S. level. In fact, to highlight the inequity, World Bank chief economist Nicholas Stern estimates that a European cow receives $2.50 a day in government subsidies, while 75% of Africans live on less than $2 a day.

The U.S. cotton industry feels particularly targeted and has agreed to submit to subsidy cuts only if other sectors get hit as well. But beyond these specific issues lies a broader concern that U.S. farm subsidies help maintain a strong agricultural industry in the United States. A drastic decline in American farming would not be in the best long-term interest of American citizens and could even represent a threat.

In light of the heated debate, the World Trade Organization has given particular attention to farm subsidies—especially cotton—but negotiations have been painfully slow. As the trade talks drag on, African farmers continue to handpick their cotton, hoping that this year it will help them earn enough to survive.[22]

© ALEXEY IVANOV/ISTOCKPHOTO.COM

International Monetary Fund (IMF) An international organization of 186 member nations that promotes international economic cooperation and stable growth.

trading bloc A group of countries that have reduced or even eliminated tariffs, allowing for the free flow of goods among the member nations.

common market A group of countries that have eliminated tariffs and harmonized trading rules to facilitate the free flow of goods among the member nations.

North American Free Trade Agreement (NAFTA) The treaty among the United States, Mexico, and Canada that eliminated trade barriers and investment restrictions over a 15-year period starting in 1994.

recipients to reduce trade barriers. The World Bank also promotes trade by working with aid recipient governments to strengthen court systems, build financial services, and fight corruption. But over the last decade the World Bank has become controversial as well. Critics suggest that in actual practice, the World Bank—contrary to its mission—undermines local economies by introducing deep-pocketed, global competitors who drive smaller firms out of business. They claim that the ultimate result is a lower standard of living for impoverished citizens. Critics have also accused the World Bank of inadvertently lining the pockets of corrupt officials and their cronies. Other key concerns involve the impact of World Bank projects on the environment and on local working conditions.

The International Monetary Fund

Like the World Bank, the **International Monetary Fund (IMF)** is an international organization accountable to the governments of its 186 member nations. The basic mission of the IMF is to promote international economic cooperation and stable growth. Funding comes from the member nations, with the United States contributing more than twice as much as any other country. To achieve these goals, the IMF:

- Supports stable exchange rates
- Facilitates a smooth system of international payments
- Encourages member nations to adopt sound economic policies
- Promotes international trade
- Lends money to member nations to address economic problems.

Although all of its functions are important, the IMF is best known as a lender of last resort to nations in financial trouble. This policy has come under fire in the past few years. Critics accuse the IMF of encouraging poor countries to borrow more money than they can ever hope to repay, which actually cripples their economies over the long term, creating even deeper poverty.

At the end of 2005, the IMF responded to its critics by implementing a historic debt relief program for poor countries. Under this program, the IMF has extended

> **Over the past 40 years, life expectancy in developing countries has risen by 20 years —about as much as was achieved in all of human history prior to the mid-20th century.**
> *World Bank FAQs*

100% debt forgiveness to 34 poor countries, erasing about $51 billion in debt. The managing director of the IMF pointed out that the canceled debt will allow these countries to increase spending in priority areas to reduce poverty and promote growth (although some experts worry that debt cancellation sets a troubling precedent for future lending). The result should be a higher standard of living for some of the poorest people in the world.[23]

Trading Blocs and Common Markets

Another major development in the last decade is the emergence of regional **trading blocs**, or groups of countries that have reduced or even eliminated all tariffs, allowing the free flow of goods among the member nations. A **common market** goes even further than a trading bloc by attempting to harmonize all trading rules. The United States, Mexico, and Canada have formed the largest trading bloc in the world, and the 27 countries of the European Union have formed the largest common market.

NAFTA The **North American Free Trade Agreement (NAFTA)** is the treaty that created the free-trading zone among the United States, Mexico, and Canada. The

Economic growth in India continues to boom.

© ADNAN ABIDI/REUTERS/LANDOV

agreement took effect in 1994, gradually eliminating trade barriers and investment restrictions over a 15-year period. Despite dire predictions of American jobs flowing to Mexico, the U.S. economy has grown significantly since the implementation of NAFTA. The Canadian and Mexican economies have thrived as well (although all three economies have slowed significantly during the global economic crisis).

But NAFTA critics point out that the U.S. trade deficit with both Mexico and Canada has skyrocketed. While exports to both nations have increased, imports have grown far faster, accounting for more than 32% of the total U.S. trade deficit, and threatening the long-term health of the American economy. Other criticisms of NAFTA include increased pollution and worker abuse. Companies that move their factories to Mexico to capitalize on lower costs also take advantage of looser environmental and worker protection laws, creating major ethical concerns. But the full impact of NAFTA—for better or for worse—is tough to evaluate, since so many other variables affect all three economies.[24]

economic power. To help make this happen, the EU has removed all trade restrictions among member nations and unified internal trade rules, allowing goods and people to move freely among EU countries. The EU has also created standardized policies for import and export between EU countries and the rest of the world, giving the member nations more clout as a bloc than each would have had on its own. Perhaps the EU's most economically significant move was the introduction of a single currency, the euro, in 2002. Of the 15 EU members at the time, 12 adopted the euro (exceptions were the United Kingdom, Sweden, and Denmark). Most economists anticipate that the holdouts plus the 12 newest members of the EU will eventually adopt the euro, creating an even bolder presence on the world market. The EU also affects the global economy with its leading-edge approach to environmental protection, quality production, and human rights.

European Union (EU) The world's largest common market, composed of 27 European nations.

EXHIBIT 3.3 European Union 2010

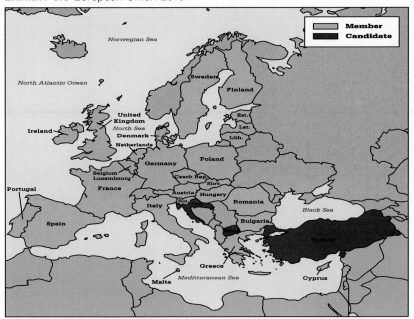

The Big Picture

The last decade has been marked by extraordinary changes in the world economy. The boundaries between individual countries have fallen lower than ever before, creating a new level of economic connectedness. The growing integration has created huge opportunities for visionary companies of every size. But integration also means risk. The dangers became clear in 2008, when the economic crisis in the United States rapidly reverberated around the globe, fueling a deep, worldwide recession.

To succeed abroad—especially in tough economic times—individual firms must make the right choices about how to structure their operations, surmount barriers to trade, meet diverse customer needs, manage a global workforce, and handle complex logistics. Human rights and environmental protection continue to be especially critical for international businesses. Both are vital components of social responsibility and will only gain importance as advocates raise awareness around the world. In the face of economic, political, and social flux, effective global business leaders must master both strategy and implementation at a deeper level than ever before.

European Union Composed of 27 nations and nearly half a billion people, and boasting a combined GDP of nearly $15 trillion, the **European Union (EU)** is the world's largest common market. Exhibit 3.3 shows a map of the 2010 EU countries plus the three countries that have applied to join.[25]

The overarching goal of the EU is to bolster Europe's trade position and to increase its international political and

WHAT ELSE? *RIP & REVIEW* **CARDS IN THE BACK**

4

BUSINESS ETHICS AND SOCIAL RESPONSIBILITY: DOING WELL BY DOING GOOD

LEARNING OBJECTIVES

After studying this chapter, you will be able to:

LO1 Define ethics and explain the concept of universal ethical standards

LO2 Describe business ethics and ethical dilemmas

LO3 Discuss how ethics relates to both the individual and the organization

LO4 Define social responsibility and examine the impact on stakeholder groups

LO5 Explain the role of social responsibility in the global arena

LO6 Describe how companies evaluate their efforts to be socially responsible

Visit CourseMate at www.cengagebrain.com

> ## Your moral compass counts far more than any bank balance, any résumé, and any diploma.
>
> *Elizabeth Dole, U.S. Senator*

LO1 Ethics and Social Responsibility: A Close Relationship

Ethics and social responsibility—often discussed in the same breath—are closely related, but they are definitely not the same. Ethics are a set of beliefs about right and wrong, good and bad; business ethics involve the application of these issues in the workplace. Clearly, ethics relate to individuals and their day-to-day decision making. Just as clearly, the decisions of each individual can affect the entire organization.

Social responsibility is the obligation of a business to contribute to society. The most socially responsible firms feature proactive policies that focus on meeting the needs of all their stakeholders—not just investors but also employees, customers, the broader community, and the environment. The stance of a company regarding social responsibility sets the tone for the organization and clearly influences the decisions of individual employees.

While this chapter discusses ethics and social responsibility separately, keep in mind that the two areas have a dynamic, interactive relationship that plays a vital role in building both profitable businesses and a vibrant community.

Defining Ethics: Murkier Than You'd Think

In the most general sense, **ethics** are a set of beliefs about right and wrong, good and bad. While your individual ethics stem from who you are as a human being, your family, your social group, and your culture also play a significant role in shaping your ethics. And therein lies the challenge: in the United States, people come from such diverse backgrounds that establishing broad agreement on specific ethical standards can be daunting. The global arena only amplifies the challenge.

A given country's legal system provides a solid starting point for examining ethical standards. The function of laws in the United States (and

elsewhere) is to establish and enforce ethical norms that apply to everyone within our society. Laws provide basic standards of behavior. But truly ethical behavior goes beyond the basics. In other words, your actions can be completely legal, yet still unethical. But since the legal system is far from perfect, in rare instances your actions can be illegal, yet still ethical. Exhibit 4.1 shows some examples of how business conduct can fall within legal and ethical dimensions. Clearly, legal and ethical actions should be your goal. Legality should be the floor—not the ceiling—for how to behave in business and elsewhere.

Do all actions have ethical implications? Clearly not. Some decisions fall within the realm of free choice with no direct link to right and wrong, good and bad. Examples might include where you buy your morning coffee, what features your company includes on its new MP3 players, or what new machines your gym decides to purchase.

EXHIBIT 4.1 Legal – Ethical Matrix

Legal and Unethical	Legal and Ethical
Promoting R-rated movies to young teens	Producing high-quality products
Producing products that you know will break before their time	Rewarding integrity
	Leading by example
Paying non-living wages to workers in developing countries	Treating employees fairly
	Contributing to the community
	Respecting the environment
Illegal and Unethical	**Illegal and Ethical**
Embezzling money	Providing rock-bottom prices *only* to distributors in underserved areas
Engaging in sexual harassment	
Practicing collusion with competitors	Collaborating with other medical clinics to guarantee low prices in low-income countries (collusion)
Encouraging fraudulent accounting	

universal ethical standards Ethical norms that apply to all people across a broad spectrum of situations.

business ethics The application of right and wrong, good and bad in a business setting.

ethical dilemma A decision that involves a conflict of values; every potential course of action has some significant negative consequences.

Universal Ethical Standards: A Reasonable Goal or Wishful Thinking?

Too many people view ethics as relative. In other words, their ethical standards shift depending on the situation and how it relates to them. Here are a few examples:

- "It's not okay to steal paper clips from the stationery store… *but* it's perfectly fine to 'borrow' supplies from the storage closet at work. Why? The company owes me a bigger salary."

- "It's wrong to lie…*but* it's okay to call in sick when I have personal business to take care of. Why? I don't want to burn through my limited vacation days."

- "Everyone should have a level playing field…*but* it's fine to give my brother the first shot at my company's contract. Why? I know he really needs the work."

This kind of two-faced thinking is dangerous because it can help people rationalize bigger and bigger ethical deviations. But the problem can be fixed by identifying **universal ethical standards** that apply to everyone across a broad spectrum of situations. Some people argue that we could never find universal standards for a country as diverse as the United States. But the nonprofit, nonpartisan Character Counts organization has worked with a diverse group of educators, community leaders, and ethicists to identify six core values, listed in

Ethical dilemmas tend to arise when values are in conflict.

© STOCKBYTE/GETTY IMAGES

Exhibit 4.2, that transcend political, religious, class, and ethnic divisions.

LO2 Business Ethics: Not an Oxymoron

Quite simply, **business ethics** is the application of right and wrong, good and bad in a business setting. But this isn't as straightforward as it may initially seem. The most challenging business decisions seem to arise when values are in conflict…when whatever you do will have negative consequences, forcing you to choose among bad options. These are true **ethical dilemmas**. (Keep in mind that ethical *dilemmas* differ from ethical *lapses*, which involve clear misconduct.) Here are a couple of hypothetical examples of ethical dilemmas:

- You've just done a great job on a recent project at your company. Your boss has been very vocal about acknowledging your work and the increased revenue that resulted from it. Privately, she said that you clearly earned a bonus of at least 10%, but due to company politics, she was unable to secure the bonus for you. She also implied that if you were to submit inflated expense reports for the next few months, she would look the other way, and you could pocket the extra cash as well-deserved compensation for your contributions.

- One of the engineers on your staff has an excellent job offer from another company and asks your advice on whether or not to accept the position. You need him to complete

© BANANASTOCK/JUPITERIMAGES

EXHIBIT 4.2 Universal Ethical Standards[1]

Trustworthiness	Be honest. Don't deceive, cheat, or steal. Do what you say you'll do.
Respect	Treat others how you'd like to be treated. Be considerate. Be tolerant of differences.
Responsibility	Persevere. Be self-controlled and self-disciplined. Be accountable for your choices.
Fairness	Provide equal opportunity. Be open-minded. Don't take advantage of others.
Caring	Be kind. Be compassionate. Express gratitude.
Citizenship	Contribute to the community. Protect the environment. Cooperate whenever feasible.

a project that is crucial to your company (and to your own career). You also have been told—in strictest confidence by senior management—that when this project is complete, the company will lay off all internal engineers. If you advise him to stay, he would lose the opportunity (and end up without a job), but if you advise him to go, you would violate the company's trust (and jeopardize your own career).

LO3 Ethics: Multiple Touchpoints

Although each person must make his or her own ethical choices, the organization can have a significant influence on the quality of those decisions. The next two sections discuss the impact of both the individual and the organization on ethical decision making, but as you read them, keep in mind that the interaction between the two is dynamic: sometimes it's hard to tell where one stops and the other starts.

Ethics and the Individual: The Power of One

Ethical choices begin with ethical individuals. Your personal needs, your family, your culture, and your religion all influence your value system. Your personality traits—self-esteem, self-confidence, independence, and sense of humor—play a significant role as well. These factors all come into play as you face ethical dilemmas. The challenge can be overwhelming, which has led a range of experts to develop frameworks for reaching ethical decisions. While the specifics vary, the key principles of most decision guides are very similar:

- Do you fully understand each dimension of the problem?
- Who would benefit? Who would suffer?

Bad News Today—Worse News Tomorrow!

In 2008 the Josephson Institute Center for Youth Ethics produced a Report Card on the Ethics of American Youth, based on a survey of nearly 30,000 students in high schools across the United States. The results suggest that students are disturbingly willing to lie, cheat, and steal, despite a sky-high opinion of their own personal character. Some highlights (or perhaps we should call them lowlights):

- 64% admitted that they cheated on a test at school within the past 12 months (38% admitted doing so two or more times).
- 62% admitted that they copied another's homework two or more times within the past 12 months.
- 19% admitted that they stole something from a friend within the past 12 months.
- 30% admitted that they stole something from a store within the past 12 months.

Sadly, the actual rates of bad behavior are probably understated, since 26% admitted that they lied on one or two questions, and experts agree that dishonesty on surveys usually reflects an attempt to conceal misconduct.

Despite rampant lying, cheating, and stealing, 98% of respondents agreed that it's important to be a person of good character, and 77% would rate their own character higher than that of their peers. Furthermore, 93% said they were satisfied with their personal character.

A number of analysts find it easy to dismiss the long-term implications of these findings, claiming that as teenagers mature, their judgment and morals will mature as well and their conduct will reflect stronger values. A more recent large-scale study by the Josephson Institute of Ethics found unequivocally that high school attitudes and behaviors and actions are a clear predictor of adult behavior across a range of situations. Cheaters in high school are far more likely as adults to lie to their spouses, customers, bosses, and employers and to cheat on expense reports, taxes, and insurance claims.

Clearly, now is the time for smart companies to clarify their standards and establish safeguards to head off costly ethical meltdowns in their future workforce.[2]

© DIGITAL VISION/GETTY IMAGES

- Are the alternative solutions legal? Are they fair?
- Does your decision make you comfortable at a "gut feel" level?
- Could you defend your decision on the nightly TV news?
- Have you considered and reconsidered your responses to each question?

The approach seems simple, but in practice, it really isn't. Workers—and managers, too—often face enormous pressure to do what's right for the company or right for their career, rather than simply what's right. And keep in mind that it's completely possible for two people to follow the framework and arrive at completely different decisions, each feeling confident that he or she has made the right choice.

Ethics and the Organization: It Takes a Village

Although each person is clearly responsible for his or her own actions, the organization can influence those actions to a startling degree. Not surprisingly, that influence starts at the top, and actions matter far more than words. The president of the Ethics Resource Center states, "CEOs in particular must communicate their personal commitment to high ethical standards and consistently drive the message down to employees through their actions." Any other approach—even just the *appearance* of shaky ethics—can be deeply damaging to a company's ethical climate. Here are a couple of examples from the news:

- High Flyers: When the CEOs of the Big Three automakers—hovering on the edge of bankruptcy—went to Washington to request a $25 billion bailout package, they flew in three separate corporate jets at an estimated cost of $20,000 per round-trip flight. All three were operating in line with official corporate travel policies, but it just didn't look right. One lawmaker pointedly asked, "Couldn't you all have downgraded to first class or jet-pooled or something to get here? It would have at least sent a message that you do get it." Not surprisingly, the execs left empty-handed.[3]
- Retirement Perks: When Jack Welch retired from his post as CEO of General Electric, the Board awarded him a generous financial package, and an eye-popping collection of perks. His perks ranged from use of an $80,000 per month apartment, to country club fees, to corporate jet privileges. These perks did not represent an ethical breach—Welch negotiated them in good faith—but when the list surfaced in the press a year after his retirement, he voluntarily gave up his perks to mitigate a public relations problem that could tarnish his reputation as a tough, ethical, and highly successful CEO.[4]

- Gross Excess: In the mid-1990s, Disney CEO Michael Eisner hired his friend Michael Ovitz as Disney's president. Fourteen months later, Disney fired Ovitz for incompetence, and he walked away with a $140 million settlement. Disgruntled stockholders sued the Disney Board for mismanagement, which led to the release of Ovitz's Disney expense account documents. In 14 months he spent $4.8 million (that's about $80,000 per week!). Specifics included $54,330 for Lakers tickets, a $946 gun for Robert Zemeckis, and $319 for breakfast. Was he stealing? *No.* Was he unethical? You decide.[5] How do you feel about the business decisions described in Exhibit 4.3?

Creating and Maintaining an Ethical Organization

Research from the Ethics Resource Center (ERC) suggests that organizational culture has more influence than any other variable on the ethical conduct of individual employees. According to the ERC, key elements of a strong culture include displays of ethics-related actions at all levels of an organization and accountability for actions. The impact of these elements can be dramatic. Consider, for example, the following research results:

- A 61 percentage point favorable difference in the level of observed misconduct when employees say they work in a strong ethical culture.
- When employees felt that the great recession negatively impacted the ethical culture of their company, misconduct rose by 16 percentage points.
- If an accountable business is defined as one that confronts misconduct and establishes a rigorous system to prevent a recurrence, nearly 80% of employees said they work in a firm where, in practice, employees at all levels are held accountable to company standards [6]

A strong organizational culture works in tandem with formal ethics programs to create and maintain

Pierre Omidyar eBay creator Omidyar has contributed $100 million to the Tufts University Micro Finance Fund. His goal is to give economic power to poor people around the world through small business loans. Ultimately, he hopes to create entrepreneurial self-sufficiency as eBay has done for so many avid users.

Sherron Watkins Despite intense pressure and high personal stakes, Watkins, a former vice president of Enron, reported the accounting irregularities that led to the discovery of staggering corporate fraud.

Stanley O'Neal As investment house Merrill Lynch began racking up losses that led to its collapse, CEO O'Neal announced his "retirement" and walked away with a compensation package worth more than $160 million.

John A. Thain Thain, the ousted Merrill Lynch executive, under pressure from President Obama, agreed to reimburse Federal bailout recipient Bank of America for an expensive renovation of his office that included an $87,000 area rug and a $35,000 commode.

Bill Gates As Microsoft CEO, Bill Gates made some ethically shaky moves, but he and his wife also established the Bill and Melinda Gates Foundation, by far the largest U.S. charity. Working for the foundation, Gates applies his famous problem-solving skills to global health, global development, and American education.

John Mackey From 1999 until 2006, Whole Foods CEO John Mackey posted thousands of anonymous comments on Yahoo! Finance, hyping his company and occasionally attacking rival Wild Oats, which he hoped to purchase for an advantageous price.

code of ethics
A formal, written document that defines the ethical standards of an organization and gives employees the information they need to make ethical decisions across a range of situations.

whistle-blowers
Employees who report their employer's illegal or unethical behavior to either the authorities or the media.

social responsibility
The obligation of a business to contribute to society.

ethical work environments. A written **code of ethics** is the cornerstone of any formal ethics program. The purpose of a written code is to give employees the information they need to make ethical decisions across a range of situations. Clearly, an ethics code becomes even more important for multinational companies, since it lays out unifying values and priorities for divisions that are rooted in different cultures. But a written code is worthless if it doesn't reflect living principles. An effective code of ethics flows directly from ethical corporate values and leads directly to ongoing communication, training, and action.

Specific codes of ethics vary greatly among organizations. Perhaps the best-known code is the Johnson & Johnson Credo, which has guided the company profitably—with a soaring reputation—through a number of crises that would have sunk lesser organizations. One of the striking elements of the Credo is the firm focus on fairness. It carefully refrains from overpromising financial rewards, committing instead to a "fair return" for stockholders.

To bring a code of ethics to life, experts advocate a forceful, integrated approach to ethics that virtually always includes the following steps:

1. Get executive buy-in and commitment to follow-through. Top managers need to communicate—even overcommunicate—about the importance of ethics. But talking works only when it's backed up by action: senior management must give priority to keeping promises and leading by example.

2. Establish expectations for ethical behavior at all levels of the organization, from the CEO to the nighttime cleaning crew. Be sure that outside parties such as suppliers, distributors, and customers understand the standards.

3. Integrate ethics into mandatory staff training. From new employee orientation to ongoing training, ethics must play a role. Additional, more specialized training helps for employees who face more temptation (e.g., purchasing agents, overseas sales reps).

4. Ensure that your ethics code is both global and local in scope. Employees in every country should understand both the general principles and the specific applications. Be sure to translate it into as many languages as necessary.

5. Build and maintain a clear, trusted reporting structure for ethical concerns and violations. The structure should allow employees to seek anonymous guidance for ethical concerns and to anonymously report ethics violations.

6. Establish protection for **whistle-blowers**, people who report illegal or unethical behavior. Be sure that no retaliation occurs, in compliance with both ethics and the recently passed Sarbanes-Oxley Act (see discussion later in the chapter). Some have even suggested that whistle-blowers should receive a portion of the penalties levied against firms that violate the law.

7. Enforce the code of ethics. When people violate ethical norms, companies must respond immediately and—whenever appropriate—publicly to retain employee trust. Without enforcement, the code of ethics becomes meaningless.

LO4 Defining Social Responsibility: Making the World a Better Place

Social responsibility is the obligation of a business to contribute to society. Similar to ethics, the broad definition is clear, but specific implementation can be complex. Obviously, the number-one goal of any business is long-term profits; without profits, other contributions are impossible. But once a firm achieves a reasonable return, the balancing act begins: how can a company balance the need to contribute against the need to boost profits, especially when the two conflict? The answer depends on the business's values, mission, resources, and management philosophy, which lead in turn to its position on social responsibility. Business approaches fall across the spectrum from no contribution to proactive contributions, as shown in Exhibit 4.4.

The Stakeholder Approach: Responsibility to Whom?

Stakeholders are any groups that have a stake—or a personal interest—in the performance and actions of an organization. Different stakeholders have different needs, expectations, and levels of interest. The federal government, for instance, is a key stakeholder in pharmaceutical companies but a very minor stakeholder in local art studios. The community at large is a key stakeholder for a coffee shop chain but a minor stakeholder for a Web design firm. Enlightened organizations identify key stakeholders for their business and consider stakeholder priorities in their decision making. The goal is to balance their needs and priorities as effectively as possible, with an eye toward building their business

> **Nearly 80% of Americans consider corporate citizenship when making investment and purchasing decisions.**
> *Community Wealth Ventures/Cone Research*

over the long term. Core stakeholder groups for most businesses are employees, customers, investors, and the broader community.

Responsibility to Employees: Creating Jobs That Work Jobs alone aren't enough. The starting point for socially responsible employers is to meet legal standards, and the requirements are significant. How would you judge the social responsibility of the firms listed in Exhibit 4.5? Employers must comply with laws that include equal opportunity, workplace safety, minimum wage and overtime requirements, protection from sexual harassment, and family and medical unpaid leaves. We will discuss these legal requirements (and others) in Chapter 16 on Human Resource Management.

But socially responsible employers go far beyond the law. They create a workplace environment that respects the dignity and value of each employee. They ensure that hard work, commitment, and talent pay off. They move beyond minimal safety requirements to establish proactive protections, such as ergonomically

Capitalism with a Conscience

Since its inception, capitalism has fueled the creation of great wealth. But the gains in wealth, healthcare, education, and technology have not been evenly spread—far from it. In fact, about half of the world's population lives on less than $2 per day.

Moved by the magnitude of the need, software tycoon Bill Gates called for a new approach to economics: "creative capitalism." He challenged leaders at the 2008 World Economic Forum to work with him to harness market forces against the devastating problems of the needy. But he doesn't advocate giving up profits. For creative capitalism to succeed, he believes that the profit incentive must be tightly fused to the goal of "improving lives for those who don't fully benefit from market forces."

Nobel Peace Prize winner Muhammad Yunus also recognizes the power of business to solve pressing societal issues. Yunus, who built a profitable banking network to offer collateral-free credit to poor entrepreneurs, has pioneered the idea of "Social Business." He advocates using the creative vibrancy of business to tackle problems ranging from poverty to pollution. To make this happen, he calls for entrepreneurs to set up enterprises that generate personal gain, but also pursue specific social goals.

Can capitalism with a conscience really work on a broadscale basis? Early results suggest that it can. Gary Hirshberg, co-founder of Stonyfield Farm Yogurt, explains by telling his story. As a young environmentalist, Hirshberg was convinced that business was "the source of all things evil." But recognizing the power of enterprise, he eventually launched Stonyfield Farm, an attempt to harness commerce for the benefit of the environment. He and his partner challenged themselves to answer a basic question: "Is it possible to run a commercial enterprise that doesn't hurt the planet—and still be highly profitable?" Twenty years later he answers from experience: absolutely![7]

EXHIBIT 4.4 The Spectrum of Social Responsibility

LESS Responsible

No Contribution

Some businesses do not recognize an obligation to society and do only what's legally required.

Responsive Contributions

Some businesses choose to respond on a case-by-case basis to market requests for contributions.

Proactive Contributions

Some businesses choose to integrate social responsibility into their strategic plans, contributing as part of their business goals.

MORE Responsible

consumerism
A social movement that focuses on four key consumer rights: (1) the right to be safe, (2) the right to be informed, (3) the right to choose, and (4) the right to be heard.

correct chairs and computer screens that reduce eyestrain. And the best employers respond to the ongoing employee search for a balance between work and personal life. With an increasing number of workers facing challenges, such as raising kids and caring for elderly parents, responsible companies are stepping in with programs such as on-site day care, company-sponsored day camp, and referral services for elder care.

Responsibility to Customers: Value, Honesty, and Communication A core responsibility of business is to deliver consumer value by providing quality products at fair prices. Honesty and communication are critical components of this equation. **Consumerism**—a widely accepted social movement—suggests that consumer rights

© PURESTOCK/JUPITERIMAGES

Socially responsible employers provide safe workspaces for all of their employees.

EXHIBIT 4.5 Social Responsibility at Work

How would you judge the actions of these firms?	
The Clorox Company	**Enron/Arthur Andersen (now defunct)**
In early 2008, Clorox introduced a line of "99% natural" cleaning products called Green Works. This is the first such effort from a major consumer products company, and also the first time that the Sierra Club has endorsed a product line by allowing the use of its logo on the labels. In return, Clorox makes an annual contribution to the Sierra Club, the amount based on total Green Works sales.	Enron, once hailed as a shining example of corporate excellence, collapsed in late 2001 due to massive accounting fraud, which bilked employees and other small investors out of millions of dollars. Arthur Andersen, hired to audit Enron's accountings, participated in the scandal by masking the issues and shredding documents containing potential evidence.
MTV	**Bank of America**
Tapping the potential of its fans, MTV has drawn millions of young people to the polls through its Choose or Lose campaign during the last four presidential elections. Its tactics include MTV specials, on-air promotion, concert tours, and voter registration drives. Due in large part to MTV's efforts, a record number of young people flooded the polls in the 2008 presidential election.	After receiving $45 billion in taxpayer bailout funds, Bank of America sponsored a five-day carnival-like event outside the 2009 Super Bowl stadium called the NFL Experience. The high-profile attraction included 850,000 square feet of sports games, plus marketing solicitations for football-themed B of A banking products. The bank defended the event as an effective growth strategy, while critics blasted it as an abuse of taxpayer dollars.
Kraft	**Toyota**
As obesity among kids spirals out of control, Kraft has taken a brave stand: a pledge to stop advertising unhealthy—yet highly profitable—foods to young children. Kraft also plans to eliminate in-school marketing and drop some unhealthy snacks from school vending machines. As the king of the food business, Kraft has chosen what's right for kids over what's right for its own short-term profits.	In 2009 Toyota stonewalled for months before admitting to a defect in some of its most popular cars that appeared to cause fatal accidents due to unintended acceleration. Even after announcing a large-scale recall, Toyota waited five days before halting new sales on models affected by the recall. Some analysts believe that Toyota knew about the defects long before the problems began and opted to do nothing.

should be the starting point. In the early 1960s, President Kennedy defined these rights, which most businesses respect in response to both consumer expectations and legal requirements:

- **The Right to Be Safe:** Businesses are legally responsible for injuries and damages caused by their products—even if they have no reason to suspect that their products might cause harm. This makes it easy for consumers to file suits. In some cases, the drive to avert lawsuits has led to absurdities such as the warning on some coffee cups: "Caution! Hot coffee is hot!" (No kidding...)

- **The Right to Be Informed:** The law requires firms in a range of industries—from mutual funds, to groceries, to pharmaceuticals—to provide the public with extensive information. The Food and Drug Administration, for instance, mandates that most grocery foods feature a very specific "Nutrition Facts" label. Beyond legal requirements, many firms use the Web to provide a wealth of extra information about their products. KFC, for example, offers an interactive Nutrition Calculator that works with all of their menu items (and it's fun to use, too).

- **The Right to Choose:** Freedom of choice is a fundamental element of the capitalist U.S. economy. Our economic system works largely because consumers freely choose to purchase the products that best meet their needs. As businesses compete, consumer value increases. Socially responsible firms support consumer choice by following the laws that prevent anticompetitive behavior such as predatory pricing, collusion, and monopolies.

- **The Right to Be Heard:** Socially responsible companies make it easy for consumers to express legitimate complaints. They also develop highly trained customer service people to respond to complaints. In fact, smart businesses view customer complaints as an opportunity to create better products and stronger relationships. Statistics suggest that 1 in 50 dissatisfied customers takes the time to complain. The other 49 quietly switch brands. By soliciting feedback, you're not only being responsible, but also building your business.[9]

Delivering quality products is another key component of social responsibility to consumers. **Planned obsolescence**—deliberately designing products to fail in order to shorten the time between consumer repurchases—represents a clear violation of social responsibility. In the long term, the market itself weeds out offenders. After all, who would repurchase a product that meets a premature end? But in the short term, planned obsolescence thins consumer wallets and abuses consumer trust.

TechNotes

Virtual Intruder Alert!

As wireless networks become more mainstream, wireless intruders stalk them closely. In 2006 there were 286 million wireless subscribers in the United States alone—up from 213 million in 2005. That same year the number of mobile wireless devices with high-speed Internet increased more than 600%. Many wireless networks operate in homes, but businesses of every size are going wireless at a rapid pace. Vulnerability to hackers, viruses, and unwanted snooping increases with each new wireless network. Some examples:

- In mid-2008, 11 people were charged with hacking wireless systems to steal 41 million credit and debit card numbers from multiple retailers, including Boston Market, Barnes and Noble, Sports Authority, and Forever 21.
- In 2003, two young men hacked a Michigan Lowe's store through the airwaves. From a car in the parking lot, they hooked into the store's wireless network of bar code readers, capturing credit card information as shoppers checked out. Today, the thieves wouldn't even need to be in the parking lot – wireless cybercriminals use telescope antennas to attack their targets from up to 45 miles away.
- Demonstrating overzealous ambition, salespeople have been known to hack into business networks from company lobbies, scanning emails to get the inside scoop on how to tailor their pitches.
- *The Wall Street Journal* reports that IBM consultants tracked the source of a virus that shut down a company's network to a passing car that connected by accident and transmitted the bug.

How can you protect yourself and your business? The first step is encryption, which means sending your transmissions in code. But remote hacking often starts with face-to-face communication, which can be an easy starting point for intruders. Low-level IT workers and chatty support staff can unwittingly share too much information with potential hackers who don't fit the outdated computer nerd stereotype. And too many forgetful people post their passwords on or near their computers, assuming that no one will notice. (Take a quick stroll through almost any office, and you're likely to spot a number of not-so-cleverly disguised passwords.) Wireless networks often "feel" private, but that deceptive illusion can cost you time and money.[8]

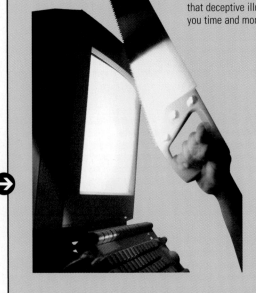

© NICK KOUDIS/PHOTODISC/GETTY IMAGES

When businesses do make mistakes, apologizing to consumers doesn't guarantee renewed sales. But a sincere apology can definitely restore a company's reputation, which can ultimately lead to greater profits. Two recent examples make this point clear:

- *Trapped!* Due to a huge snowstorm on Valentine's Day 2007, ten jetBlue planes were stranded on the tarmac at New York's JFK airport, trapping furious passengers—with no information, no power, and limited refreshments—for as long as eight hours. In the wake of the storm, jetBlue canceled more than 1,000 additional flights. JetBlue CEO David Neeleman responded with a profuse apology, reimbursing customers and establishing a customer bill of rights. The airline estimates that the total cost of the crisis was between $20 million and $30 million. But in 2008, jetBlue won its fourth consecutive customer service award from J.D. Power and Associates, clear evidence that the apology worked to regain customer trust.[10]

- *Apple Angst:* Apple introduced the iPhone on June 29, 2007, to rave reviews and stellar sales, despite the $599 price tag. But two months later, Apple dropped the price of the phone by $200, in order to expand the user base yet further. Not surprisingly, early adopters were livid—why, they demanded, did Apple repay their trust and support by ripping them off? CEO Steve Jobs quickly apologized and offered every $599 iPhone customer a $100 Apple store credit. The response seemed to work. In 2008, Apple's ranking in the American Customer Satisfaction Index climbed 8%, a full ten percentage points ahead of its nearest competitor in an industry where ratings in general are sinking.[11]

Responsibility to Investors: Fair Stewardship and Full Disclosure

The primary responsibility of business to investors is clearly to make money—to create an ongoing stream of profits. But companies achieve and maintain long-term earnings in the context of responsibility to *all* stakeholders, which may mean trading short-term profits for long-term success. Responsibility to investors starts by meeting legal requirements, and in the wake of recent corporate scandals, the bar is higher than ever. The 2002 **Sarbanes-Oxley Act** limits conflict of interest issues by restricting the consulting services that accounting firms can provide for the companies they audit. Sarbanes-

Oxley also requires that financial officers and CEOs personally certify the validity of their financial statements. (See Chapter 8 for more detail on the Sarbanes-Oxley Act.)

But beyond legal requirements, companies have a number of additional responsibilities to investors. Spending money wisely would be near the top of the list. For instance, are executive retreats to the South Pacific on the company tab legal? They probably are. Do they represent a responsible use of corporate dollars? Now that seems unlikely. Honesty is another key responsibility that relates directly to financial predictions. No one can anticipate exactly how a company will perform, and an overly optimistic or pessimistic assessment is perfectly legal. But is it socially responsible? It probably isn't, especially if it departs too far from the objective facts—which is, of course, a subjective call.

Responsibility to the Community: Business and the Greater Good

Beyond increasing everyone's standard of living, businesses can contribute to society in two main ways: philanthropy and responsibility. **Corporate philanthropy** includes all business donations to nonprofit groups, including both money and products. The Giving USA Foundation reported that total corporate donations in 2007 exceeded $15 billion, an increase of nearly 2% versus 2006, despite rising worries about the economy. But since corporate giving ties closely to corporate profits, philanthropy will likely decrease in 2008 and beyond. "As goes the economy, so goes corporate giving…only more so," says Patrick M. Rooney of the Center on Philanthropy at Indiana University.

Corporate philanthropy also includes donations of employee time; in other words, some companies pay their employees to spend time volunteering at nonprofits. Timberland, an outdoor clothing company, is a leader in corporate philanthropy, not only donating goods but also giving employees paid six-month sabbaticals to work for nonprofits.[12]

Some companies contribute to nonprofits through

Sarbanes-Oxley Act Federal legislation passed in 2002 that sets higher ethical standards for public corporations and accounting firms. Key provisions limit conflict-of-interest issues and require financial officers and CEOs to certify the validity of their financial statements.

corporate philanthropy All business donations to nonprofit groups, including money, products, and employee time.

cause-related marketing. This involves a partnership between a business and a nonprofit, designed to spike sales for the company and raise money for the nonprofit. Unlike outright gifts, these dollars are not tax deductible for the company, but they can certainly build the company's brands.

Corporate responsibility relates closely to philanthropy but focuses on the actions of the business itself rather than donations of money and time. The Home Depot, for instance, employs more Olympic hopefuls than any other U.S. company through its Olympic Job Opportunities Program. The firm offers athletes full-time pay and benefits for a flexible 20-hour workweek to accommodate demanding training and competition schedules. Taking a different approach to corporate responsibility, Cisco Systems has developed relationships with the different branches of the military to help make recruitment and hiring of disabled veterans a standard part of their hiring practices. Both of these policies ultimately benefit society as a whole.

Responsibility to the Environment Protecting the environment is perhaps the most crucial element of responsibility to the community. Business is a huge consumer of the world's limited resources, from oil, to timber, to fresh water, to minerals. In some cases, the production process decimates the environment and spews pollution into the air, land, and water, sometimes causing irreversible damage. And the products created by business can cause pollution as well, such as the smog generated by cars, and the sometimes-toxic waste caused by junked electronic parts.

The government sets minimum standards for environmental protection at the federal, state, and local levels. But a growing number of companies are going further, developing innovative strategies to build their business while protecting the environment. Many have embraced the idea of **sustainable development**: doing business to meet the needs of this generation without harming the ability of future generations to meet their needs. This means weaving environmentalism throughout the business decision-making process. Since sustainable

development can mean significant long-term cost savings, the economic crisis may even push forward environmentally friendly programs—especially as government stimulus spending kicks in to fuel investment.

The results of sustainability programs have been impressive across a range of industries. McDonald's, for instance, produces mountains of garbage each year, as do virtually all major fast food chains. But the Golden Arches stands above the others in its attempts to reduce the problem. An article from the Sustainability Institute reports some encouraging statistics:

- "The company used to ship orange juice to its restaurants in ready-to-serve containers. Now it ships frozen concentrate, which reduces orange juice packaging by 75%—4 million pounds less garbage a year."

- "Soft drinks were shipped as syrup in cardboard containers. The local restaurants added the water and the fizz. Now the syrup is delivered by trucks that pump it directly into receiving tanks at the restaurants. No packaging is needed at all. Savings: 68 million pounds of cardboard per year."[13]

Reducing the *amount* of trash is better than recycling, but recycling trash clearly beats dumping it in a landfill. McDonald's participates in this arena as well, through their extensive recycling programs, but more importantly as a big buyer of recycled products.

Taking an even broader perspective, some firms have started to measure their carbon footprint, with an eye toward reducing it. **Carbon footprint** refers to the amount of harmful greenhouse gases that a firm emits throughout its operations, both directly and indirectly. The ultimate goal is to become carbon neutral—either to emit zero harmful gasses, or to counteract the impact of emissions by removing a comparable amount from the atmosphere through projects such as planting trees. Dell Inc. became fully carbon neutral in mid-2008, fulfilling its quest to become "the greenest technology on the planet." More recently, PepsiCo calculated the carbon footprint for its Tropicana orange juice brand and was surprised to learn that about a third of its emissions came from applying fertilizer to the orange groves. According to the Conference Board, business leaders have begun to see their carbon footprint—both measurement and reduction—as a burgeoning opportunity.[14]

> **Currently, the average U.S. office worker uses a sheet of paper every 12 minutes—a ream per person every 2.5 working weeks—and disposes of 100–200 lbs. of paper every year.**
>
> Trees, Water, and People

A growing number of companies use **green marketing** to promote their business. This means marketing environmental products and practices to gain a competitive edge. Patagonia, for example, markets outdoor clothing using 100% organic cotton and natural fibers such as hemp. But green marketing represents a tough challenge: while most people support the idea of green products, the vast majority won't sacrifice price, performance, or convenience to actually buy those products. Sometimes, however, green marketing can be quite consistent with profitability. The Toyota Prius hybrid car offers an interesting example. The Prius costs several thousand dollars more than a standard car, but as gas prices skyrocketed through the summer of 2008, consumers flooded the dealerships, snapping up Prius hybrids faster than Toyota could ship them. Yet when the economy dropped in late 2008, Toyota sales plummeted along with the rest of the industry, suggesting that the environment may be a fair-weather priority for consumers.[15]

LO5 Ethics and Social Responsibility in the Global Arena: A House of Mirrors?

Globalization has made ethics and social responsibility even more complicated for workers at every level. Bribery and corruption are among the most challenging issues faced by companies and individuals that are involved in international business. Transparency International, a leading anticorruption organization, publishes a yearly index of "perceived corruption" across 146 countries. No country scores a completely clean 10 out of 10, and the United States scores a troubling 7.5. Not surprisingly, the world's poorest countries fall largely in the bottom half of the index, suggesting rampant corruption is part of their business culture.[16]

Corruption wouldn't be possible if companies didn't offer bribes, so Transparency International also researched the likelihood of firms from industrialized countries to pay bribes abroad. The 2008 results indicated that firms from export powers Russia, China, and Mexico rank among the worst, with India following close behind. U.S. corporations, forbidden to offer bribes since 1977 under the Foreign Corrupt Practices Act, show a disturbing inclination to flout the law. The United States scored 7.5 out of a possible 10, falling below many Western European countries.[17]

These statistics raise some thought-provoking questions:

Going Green – It's Not Just Governments

While governments and grassroots groups around the world have led the global push to "go green," make no mistake, multinational businesses have played a leadership role as well, making major contributions to the greening of the planet. Some examples:

- Bank of America reduced paper use by 32% from 2000 to 2005, despite a 24% growth in its customer base. Bank of America also runs an internal recycling program that recycles 30,000 tons of paper each year, good for saving roughly 200,000 trees for each year of the program's operation.
- DuPont, not historically known for earth-friendly practices, successfully reduced greenhouse gas emissions during the '90s by 63%—far ahead of the timetable set forth in the controversial Kyoto Protocol.
- Anheuser-Busch now saves 21 million pounds of metal per year by trimming an eighth of an inch off the diameter of its beer cans without reducing the volume of beer "one bit."
- By opting to use coffee-cup sleeves made of recycled paper, Starbucks has saved roughly 78,000 trees per year since 2006.
- Tesla Motors is developing environmentally friendly sports cars that offer blazing speed and formidable power with virtually no emissions.
- Hewlett-Packard owns gigantic e-waste recycling plants that reclaim not just steel and plastic but also toxic chemicals like mercury. HP takes back any brand of equipment, not just its own 100% recyclable machines. HP also audits its top suppliers for eco-friendliness.[18]

- When does a gift become a bribe? The law is unclear, and perceptions differ from country to country.

- How can corporations monitor corruption and enforce corporate policies in their foreign branches?

- What are other ways to gain a competitive edge in countries where bribes are both accepted and expected?

Other challenging issues revolve around business responsibility to workers abroad. At minimum, businesses should pay a living wage for reasonable hours in a safe working environment. But exactly what this means is less clear-cut. Does a living wage mean enough to support an individual or a family? Does "support" mean enough to subsist day to day, or enough to live in modest comfort? Should American businesses mandate no child labor in countries where families depend on their children's wages to survive? Companies must address these questions individually, bringing together their own values with the laws of both the United States and their host countries.

The most socially responsible companies establish codes of conduct for their vendors, setting clear policies for human rights, wages, safety, and environmental impact. In 1991, Levi Strauss became the first global company to establish a comprehensive code of conduct for its contractors. Over the years, creative thinking has helped it maintain its high standards, even in the face of cultural clashes. An example from Bangladesh, outlined in the *Harvard Business Review*, illustrates its preference for win-win solutions. In the early 1990s, Levi Strauss "discovered that two of its suppliers in Bangladesh were employing children under the age of 14—a practice that violated the company's principles but was tolerated in Bangladesh. Forcing the suppliers to fire the children would not have ensured that the children received an education,

and it would have caused serious hardship for the families depending on the children's wages. In a creative arrangement, the suppliers agreed to pay the children's regular wages while they attended school and to offer each child a job at age 14. Levi Strauss, in turn, agreed to pay the children's tuition

WITHOUT A MAP... CHARTING AN ETHICAL COURSE

Choosing Between a Loaf of Bread and a Packet of Shampoo

Three-quarters of the world's population—nearly 4 billion people—earn less than $2 per day. But C.K. Prahalad, a well-respected consultant and economist, claims that if the "aspirational poor" had a chance to consume, they could add about $13 trillion in annual sales to the global economy. Unilever, a global marketing company headquartered in Europe, has aggressively pursued this market with consumer products. Their customers might not have electricity, running water, or even enough for dinner, but many of them do have packets of Sunsilk shampoo and Omo detergent. Electronics companies have experienced marketing success as well. In Dharavi, for instance—one of the largest urban slums in India—more than 85% of households own a television set.

Critics suggest that the corporate push to reach impoverished consumers will enrich multinationals at the expense of their customers, representing exploitation of the world's poorest people. Ashvin Dayal, East Asia director for the antipoverty group Oxfam UK, expressed concern to *Time* magazine that corporate marketing might unseat locally produced products or encourage overspending by those who truly can't afford it. Citing heavily marketed candy and soda, he points out that "companies have the power to create needs rather than respond to needs."

But Prahalad counters that many people at the bottom of the economic pyramid accept that some of the basics—running water, for instance—are not likely to ever come their way. Instead, they opt to improve their quality of life through affordable "luxuries," such as single-use sachets of fragrant shampoo. He argues that "It's absolutely possible to do very well while doing good." Furthermore, he suggests that corporate marketing may kick-start the poorest economies, triggering entrepreneurial activity and economic growth. Since globalization shows no signs of slowing, let's hope that he's right.[19]

AP IMAGES/DENIS POROY; © ARKO DATTA/REUTERS/LANDOV

and provide books and uniforms." This creative solution allowed the suppliers to maintain their valuable contracts from Levi Strauss, while Levi Strauss upheld its values and improved the quality of life for its most vulnerable workers.[20]

Clearly, codes of conduct work best with monitoring, enforcement, and a commitment to finding solutions that work for all parties involved. Gap Inc. offers an encouraging example. In 1996, Gap published a rigorous Code of Vendor Conduct and required compliance from all of their vendors. Its 90 vendor-compliance officers strive to visit each of its 3,000 factories at least once a year. They have uncovered a troubling number of violations, proactively pulling contracts from serious violators and rejecting bids from suppliers who don't meet their standards.

Gap and Levi Strauss seem to be doing their part, but the world clearly needs universal standards and universal enforcement to ensure that the benefits of globalization don't come at the expense of the world's most vulnerable people.[21]

LO6 Monitoring Ethics and Social Responsibility: Who Is Minding the Store?

Actually, many firms are monitoring themselves. The process is called a **social audit**: a systematic evaluation of how well a firm is meeting its ethics and social responsibility objectives. Establishing goals is the starting point for a social audit, but the next step is determining how to measure the achievement of those goals, and measurement can be a bit tricky. As You Sow, an organization dedicated to promoting corporate social responsibility, recommends that companies measure their success by evaluating a "double bottom line," one that accounts for traditional financial indicators, such as earnings, and one that accounts for social responsibility indicators, such as community involvement.

Other groups are watching as well, which helps keep businesses on a positive track. Activist customers, investors, unions, environmentalists, and community groups all play a role. In addition, the threat of government legislation keeps some industries motivated to self-regulate. One example would be the entertainment industry, which uses a self-imposed rating system for both movies and TV, largely to fend off regulation. Many people argue the emergence of salads at fast food restaurants represents an effort to avoid regulation as well.

social audit A systematic evaluation of how well a firm is meeting its ethics and social responsibility goals.

The Big Picture

Clearly, the primary goal of any business is to earn long-term profits for its investors. But profits alone are not enough. As active participants in society, firms must also promote ethical actions and social responsibility throughout their organizations and their corresponding customer and supplier networks. Although every area matters, a few warrant special mention:

- In tough economic times, effective business leaders focus more than ever on integrity, transparency, and a humane approach to managing the workforce—especially during cutbacks.

- Building or maintaining a presence in foreign markets requires particularly careful attention to human rights and local issues.

- Sustainable development and other environmentally sound practices are not only fiscally prudent and customer-friendly, but also crucial for the health of our planet.

WHAT ELSE? *RIP & REVIEW* **CARDS IN THE BACK**

5

BUSINESS COMMUNICATION: CREATING AND DELIVERING MESSAGES THAT MATTER

LEARNING OBJECTIVES

After studying this chapter, you will be able to:

LO1 Explain the importance of excellent business communication

LO2 Describe the key elements of nonverbal communication

LO3 Compare, contrast, and choose effective communication channels

LO4 Choose the right words for effective communication

LO5 Write more effective business memos, letters, and emails

LO6 Create and deliver successful verbal presentations

> # Wise men talk because they have something to say; fools, because they have to say something.
>
> *Plato*

communication The transmission of information between a sender and a recipient.

noise Any interference that causes the message you send to be different from the message your audience understands.

communication barriers Obstacles to effective communication, typically defined in terms of physical, language, body language, cultural, perceptual, and organizational barriers.

intercultural communication Communication among people with differing cultural backgrounds.

LO1 Excellent Communication Skills: Your Invisible Advantage

Much of your success in business will depend on your ability to influence the people around you. Can you land the right job? Close the deal that makes the difference? Convince the boss to adopt your idea? Motivate people to buy your products? Excellent communicators are not only influential, but also well liked, efficient, and effective. Great communication skills can dramatically boost your chance for success, while poor communication skills can bury even the most talented people.

So what exactly are "excellent communication skills"? Many students believe that great business communication equates to a knack for speaking or a flair for writing. But if that's where you stop, you're likely to hit a brick wall again and again as you attempt to achieve your goals. Effective **communication** happens only when you transmit meaning—*relevant* meaning—to your audience.

Communication must be dynamic, fluid, and two-way, which includes listening. Seeking and understanding feedback from your audience—and responding appropriately—form the core of successful business communication. And it isn't as easy as you may think. American novelist Russell Hoban neatly summarized the issue: "When you come right down to it, how many people speak the same language even when they speak the same language?"

Communication Barriers: "That's Not What I Meant!"

Why is effective communication so challenging? The key issue is **noise**: any interference that causes the message you send to be different from the message your audience understands. Some experts define noise in terms of **communication barriers**, which arise in a number of different forms. As you read the definitions, keep in mind that with a bit of extra effort, most are surmountable, and we'll discuss strategies and tips as we move through the chapter.

- **Physical Barriers:** These can range from a document that looks like a wall of type, to a room that's freezing cold, to chairs in your office that force your visitors to sit at a lower level than you.

- **Language Barriers:** Clearly, if you don't speak the language you'll have trouble communicating. But even among people who do share the same language, slang, jargon, and regional accents can interfere with meaning.

- **Body Language Barriers:** Even if your words are inviting, the wrong body language can alienate and distract your audience so completely that they simply won't absorb the content of your message.

- **Perceptual Barriers:** How your audience perceives you and your agenda can create a significant obstacle to effective communication. If possible, explore their perceptions—both positive and negative—in advance!

- **Organizational Barriers:** Some companies have built-in barriers to effective communication, such as an unspoken rule that the people at the top of the organization don't talk to the people at the bottom. These barriers are important to understand but hard to change.

- **Cultural Barriers:** These can include everything from how you greet colleagues and establish eye contact to how you handle disagreement, eat business meals, and make small talk at meetings. As globalization gains speed, **intercultural communication** will become increasingly pivotal to long-term business success.

Identifying and understanding communication barriers is a vital first step toward dismantling them, in order to communicate more effectively with any audience.

LO2 Nonverbal Communication: Beyond the Words

Most of us focus on what we want to say, but *how* we say it matters even more. In fact, studies cited in the *Wall Street Journal's Career Journal* suggest that during face-to-face communication, only 7% of meaning comes from the verbal content of the message—38% comes from tone of voice and 55% comes from body language such as facial expressions, gestures, and posture.[1]

The goal of **nonverbal communication** should be to reinforce the meaning of your message. Random facial expressions and disconnected body language—arbitrary arm thrusts, for example—are at best distracting, and at worst clownish. But strong, deliberate nonverbal communication can dramatically magnify the impact of your messages. Here are a few examples of how this can work (but keep in mind that these examples do not necessarily translate from culture to culture):

- **Eye Contact:** Within American culture, sustained eye contact (different from a constant cold stare) indicates integrity, trust, and respectful attention, whether you're communicating with a subordinate, a superior, or a peer.

- **Tone of Voice:** Variation is the key to effectiveness, since paying attention to a monotone takes more concentration than most people are willing to muster. Also, even when you're angry or frustrated, try to keep your voice in a lower pitch to encourage listeners to stay with your message.

- **Facial Expressions:** People vary widely in terms of how much emotion they show on their faces, but virtually everyone communicates, whether or not they know it, through a wide range of expressions that include shy smiles, focused frowns, clenched jaws, squinted eyes, and furrowed brows.

- **Gestures and Posture:** How you handle your body speaks for you. For example, leaning forward can indicate interest, shrugging can suggest a lack of authority, and fidgeting can imply either impatience or nervousness. To increase the power of your message, both your gestures and your posture should be confident, open, and coherent.

As silly as it sounds, one of the easiest, most effective ways to improve your body language is to practice nonverbal communication in front of the mirror. Check out your gestures, notice your facial expressions, and focus on eye contact. If you have the time and ability, it's also helpful (though humbling!) to videotape

TechNotes

Social Media: A Basic Business Communication That's Here to Stay

According to social media expert Erick Qualman, social media is far more than a fad; instead, it represents a fundamental shift in how people communicate with each other, and a groundbreaking change in basic business communications. To succeed in tomorrow's workplace, students must be well versed in employer expectations regarding social media, not just for marketing, but also for more routine business communication. A comprehensive 2009 study of the Inc. 500 (the 500 fastest-growing private companies in the United States) showed that social media is here to stay, as an integral element of long-term business strategy. Key findings:

- 43% of Inc. 500 firms considered social media to be a central part of their strategic plans for the future of their business.

- With an eye on legal protection, 36% of the respondents' companies had a policy governing blogging by their employees.

- 68% monitored their brands or company name in the social media space.

- The majority of respondents used social media for business-to-business communication with other companies such as partners, vendors, or suppliers. Interestingly, 26% of this communication happened via Twitter, which may signal an important change in the popular conception of Twitter and how it is being used.

- Not surprisingly, 48% of the Inc. 500 used social networking sites such as Facebook, Linkedin, and Twitter to assist in recruiting and evaluating potential employees.

Illustrating the sheer scope of social media, the Social *Media Revolution 2* video released by the Social Media blog Socialnomics highlights the following statistics:

- Radio took 38 years to reach 50 million users , TV took 13 years, the World Wide Web took 4 years, and the iPod took 3 years.

- If Facebook were a country it would be the world's third largest, ahead of the United States and behind only China and India.

- 60 million status updates happen on Facebook daily.

- 50% of the mobile Internet traffic in the UK is for Facebook… people update anywhere, anytime…imagine what that means for bad customer experiences?

- Generations Y and Z consider email passé—some universities have stopped distributing email accounts.

- Wikipedia has over 15 million articles… studies show it's more accurate than *Encyclopedia Britannica*…78% of these articles are non-English.

- People care more about how their social graph ranks products and services than how Google ranks them.

Clearly, being ready for social media in the business world means more than just checking your Facebook every day. Explore *all* the social media tools. Use them proactively. Figure out how they could apply to the field that interests you. And use your new knowledge to market yourself to potential employers.[2]

PRNEWSFOTO/MARK

© THOMAS BARWICK/DIGITAL VISION/JUPITERIMAGES

those who listen better, so if you polish your listening skills, you're also likely to buff up the quality of what you know and when you know it. Exhibit 5.1 highlights some listening do's and don'ts (specific to American culture).[5]

yourself delivering both a formal and informal message, and ask a trusted friend to dissect the results with you.

Accurately discerning the body language of others is another powerful business communication tool. But keep in mind that you must evaluate others in the context of common sense. When your boss keeps yawning, she may be bored *or* she may just be tired. When your colleague crosses his arms, he may be indicating defensiveness *or* he might just normally stand that way.

Active Listening: The Great Divider

How we listen (or don't listen) also sends a high-impact, nonverbal message. In fact, an old Chinese proverb asserts that to listen well is as powerful a means of influence as to talk well. Those who do both are unstoppable.

Strong listening skills—**active listening**—play an obvious role in business success. The higher you go in an organization, the more you find that people are listening. Hourly employees may spend 30% of their time listening, while managers often spend 60%, and executives might spend 75% or more. Interestingly, top salespeople also tend to spend about 75% of their communication time listening.[3]

According to the International Listening Association website, 85% of our learning is derived from listening, yet listeners are distracted, forgetful, and preoccupied 75% of the time. If listening is so crucial, why do most of us have such a hard time engaging completely? One reason may be that people *listen* at about 125 to 250 words per minute, but *think* at about 1,000 to 3,000 words per minute—that's a significant gap. Common ways to fill the void include daydreaming, thinking about the past (e.g., last night), and planning for the future (e.g., later in the day).[4]

When you listen, try to use the extra thinking time to make yourself pay closer attention to the speaker. You'll find that people tend to tell more to

EXHIBIT 5.1 Tips for Better Listening

Listening Do's	Listening Don'ts
Use your extra mental capacity to summarize (to yourself!) what the speaker is saying. Ask yourself: Why does this matter? What's the key point?	Don't even glance at your emails or text messages. You won't fool anyone with those surreptitious peeks.
Take a few notes. It will not only help you concentrate but also communicate to the speaker that his or her thoughts really matter.	Don't begin speaking the moment the person stops talking. Take a brief pause to indicate that you're absorbing the message.
Listen with both your ears and your eyes. Notice any inconsistency between the speaker's words and body language.	Don't get overly comfortable. If your body is too relaxed, your mind may wander more easily.
Use nonverbal communication—nods, smiles, leaning forward—to indicate interest in the speaker.	Don't pick up your phone—or even look at your phone—when you're listening. And whenever it's practical, set your cell phone to vibrate when others are speaking.
Use verbal feedback and questions to indicate understanding and empathy: "So you're saying that…," or "Why do you think that?"	Don't interrupt or finish other people's sentences. There are few better ways to cut off future communication.

LO3 Choose the Right Channel: A Rich Array of Options

Figuring out the right way to send a message can be a daunting challenge, especially in light of the growing number of choices. The various options are called **communication channels**. Understanding the impact of each channel will help you make the best decision regarding which to use.

Communication channels differ from one another in terms of how much information—or richness—they communicate to the recipient. Exhibit 5.2 provides a brief overview of key channels.

What other channels can you identify? Possibilities include intranet postings, WebEx, and text messaging, among others. Where would these additional channels fall on the spectrum? Why?

EXHIBIT 5.2 Communication Channels

Communication Channel	Channel Richness	When Should You Use This Channel?
Memos/Reports	Very low: Your audience won't gain any information from your tone or your body language.	When your content is uncontroversial When you must reach a number of people with the same message When you must communicate lengthy or detailed information
Email	Very low: Here, too, your audience learns nothing beyond your words themselves.	When your content is uncontroversial When you must reach a number of people with the same message
Instant Message	Very low: Because so many of us IM with as few words as possible, your audience will pick up only the basics.	When your content is uncontroversial When you want a quick response regarding relatively simple issues When you know that your audience won't be annoyed by it
Voice Mail	Low: Your audience has the benefit of hearing your tone but not seeing your body language.	When your content is uncontroversial When you don't need a record of your message (but don't forget that the recipient can easily save or forward your voice mail)
Telephone Conversation	Moderate: Your audience benefits from hearing your tone and how it changes through the call.	When you need to either deliver your message or get a response quickly When your content is more personal or controversial When you need or want a spontaneous, dynamic dialogue with the recipient
Videoconferencing	High: Especially with state-of-the-art equipment, the channel conveys much of the richness of actually being there.	When you need to reach multiple people with complex or high-priority content When you need or want a spontaneous, dynamic dialogue with an audience that you cannot reach in person
In-Person Presentation	High: Your audience directly experiences every element of your communication, from verbal content, to tone, to body language.	When you need to reach a large audience with an important message When you need or want to experience the immediate response of your audience
Face-to-Face Meeting	Very high: Your audience experiences your full message even more directly.	When your message is personal, emotional, complex, or high-priority (but if the recipient might be volatile, you should consider using a less-immediate channel) When you need or want instant feedback from your audience

Consider the Audience: It's Not about You!

Clearly, the needs and expectations of your audience play a crucial role in your choice of communication channel. Even if the recipient's preferences seem absurd—for example, we probably all know someone who refuses to check email or voice mail—remember that your first priority is to communicate your message. If you send it through a channel that the audience doesn't expect or understand or like, you've crippled your chance for successful communication.

Analysis and consideration of your audience should also be a top priority after you choose your communication channel. Meeting the needs of your audience will give you a crucial edge in developing a message that works.

Companies that communicate effectively have a 47% higher return to shareholders.
BusinessWeek

LO4 Pick the Right Words: Is That Car Pre-Loved or Just Plain Used?!

Mark Twain once said, "The difference between the right word and almost the right word is the difference between lightning and the lightning bug." Perhaps that's a little extreme, but it may not be too far from the truth. In the business world, where your messages are competing

Preparing effective communication can be time-consuming, but it is always worthwhile.

- **Education:** The education level of the audience should drive the level of vocabulary and the complexity of the message.
- **Profession:** Some professions (e.g., website development) are rife with jargon and acronyms. How should this influence your message?

bias A preconception about members of a particular group. Common forms of bias include gender bias, age bias, and race, ethnicity, or nationality bias.

Be Concise

Jerry Seinfeld once said, "I will spend an hour editing an eight-word sentence into five." While Jerry might be going a bit too far, it pays to be clear and concise in virtually all business communication. But don't be concise at the expense of completeness; include all information that your audience may need (it'll save you time down the road).

Avoid Slang

Unless you're absolutely certain that your audience will understand and appreciate it, do not use slang in either written or verbal communication. The risk of unintentionally alienating yourself from your audience is simply too high.

Avoid Bias

Intentionally or unintentionally, words can communicate biases that can interfere with your message, alienate your audience, and call your own character into question. As a result, you will be less effective in achieving the immediate goals of your communication (and possibly any future communication as well). Three kinds of **bias** are common:

with so many others for the all-too-limited attention of the recipient, the right words can encourage your audience to stay with you long enough to absorb your message.

Analyze Your Audience

To find the right words, begin with the needs of your audience. Consider:

- **Expectations:** What kind of language do most people use in the organization? Is it formal or informal? Is it direct or roundabout? Should you differ from the norm? Why or why not?

> **I didn't have time to write a short letter, so I wrote a long one instead.**
> *Mark Twain*

Huh?!!

Between the Beijing Olympics in 2008 and the Shanghai World Expo in 2010, China has gained an increasingly high profile on the world stage, and so has Chinglish, a sometimes-bizarre blend of Chinese and mangled English language that seems to pop up on signs, menus, and labels throughout the tourist-heavy cities of China. For example:

- Plus-sized shoppers at the Scat clothing chain might find themselves needing to buy "fatso" or "lard-bucket" sizes.
- Before the Beijing Olympics, tourists could visit Racist Park, later rechristened Minorities Park to avoid sending a misleadingly negative message to visitors about Chinese culture.
- Port-a-potties have sometimes been located in the "urine district."
- Adventurous eaters can order fried enema at local eateries.
- In the past, the sick may have sought treatment at the Dongda Anus Hospital, now called the Dongda Proctology Hospital.

此段200米,当心落石,请靠岩壁行走,快速通过请勿逗留.
Within 200 meters, notice the rockslide, please is run about by cliff.

Although many of these language goofs are highly amusing, a number of Chinese find the snickers humiliating rather than funny. In fact, as the World Expo approached, the Chinese government established the Shanghai Commission for the Management of Language Use to eradicate by fiat the worst examples of mangled English. One of the chief translators, Jeffrey Yao, underscores that the purpose of signs is communication, not entertainment. "I want to see people nodding that they understand the message on these signs. I don't want to see them laughing."[5a]

Gender Bias Gender bias consists of words that suggest stereotypical attitudes toward a specific gender. Avoiding bias becomes tricky when you simply don't know the gender of your audience, which often happens when you apply for a job in writing. The best solution, of course, is to find out the recipient's name, but if you can't do that, do not address your message to "Dear Sir" or "Dear Madam"; rather, use the title of the position (e.g.,"Dear Hiring Manager").

Another common dilemma is establishing agreement in your sentences without creating gender bias. Consider the following example:

The guitarist who loses his instrument must buy a new one.

Technically, this sentence is correct, but it implies that all guitarists are men. A simple solution would be to convert to plural:

Guitarists who lose their instruments must buy new ones.

This approach almost always works to help you sidestep the gender bias issue. In the rare case that it doesn't, you can simply use the "his or her" option.

Age Bias Age bias refers to words that suggest stereotypical attitudes toward people of specific ages. In American culture, older people tend to experience negative age bias much more often than younger people. This happens despite specific federal legislation outlawing employment discrimination against people over 40 years old. The reason may be that American culture associates youth with highly valued qualities such as creativity, speed, independence, and individualism. This bias will become increasingly detrimental as the workforce ages. Here is an example of age bias:

We need someone young and dynamic in this position!
You could easily eliminate the negative bias by simply deleting the word "young," or by replacing it with the word "energetic." One clear benefit of eliminating bias in this case would be a broader applicant pool that might include an older person who is more dynamic than any of the younger applicants.

Race, Ethnicity, and Nationality Bias Words can also suggest stereotypical attitudes toward specific races, ethnicities, and nationalities. Leaving aside prejudice—which is clearly wrong—the problems in this area are usually unintentional and stem from unarticulated assumptions about a person's attitudes, opinions, and experiences. Your best plan for avoiding bias would be to forgo any references to race, ethnicity, or nationality unless they are directly relevant and clearly necessary. And of course, never simply assume that a single person embodies the attitudes, opinions, and experiences of a larger group. If you communicate with each person as an individual, you will not only avoid bias, but also develop deeper, more effective channels of communication.

Use Active Voice Whenever Possible

Active voice facilitates direct, powerful, concise communication. You have used **active voice** when the subject of your sentence *is* doing the action described by the verb. You have used **passive voice** when the subject of your sentence *is not* doing the action described by the verb.

Here's an example of a sentence that uses active voice:

Our team made a mistake in the sales forecast.
Our team, the subject of the sentence, did the action described by the verb (making a mistake). The same sentence in passive voice would read as follows:

A mistake was made in the sales forecast.

Language in Flux

As time goes by, language changes to reflect our changing experience. From the serious to the seriously silly, new words and expressions surface continually. For instance, "cyberspace," "wardrobe malfunction," and "soccer moms" entered common language only in the last couple of decades. But familiar words can also be used in new ways. Some clever examples currently circulating on the Internet:

- **Abdicate:** to give up all hope of ever having a flat stomach
- **Gargoyle:** olive-flavored mouthwash
- **Balderdash:** a rapidly receding hairline

Word lovers have also been known to redefine words by playing with the letters to create new meanings. A few witty examples from the Web:

- **"Sarchasm":** The gulf between the author of sarcastic wit and the person who doesn't get it.
- **"Dopeler effect":** The tendency of stupid ideas to seem smarter when they come at you rapidly.
- **"Giraffiti":** Vandalism spray-painted very, very high.

In this version, the subject of the sentence is the mistake, which clearly did not do the action. As you can see from these examples, another benefit of active voice is accountability, which can create deeper trust between you and your audience.

LO5 Write High-Impact Messages: Breaking through the Clutter

For many businesspeople, checking email—or even regular mail—is like approaching a fire hose for a sip of water. Goal number one is to crank down the pressure to get what you need without being knocked over by all the rest. To attain this goal, many people simply press the delete button.

Your challenge as a writer is to make your message a must-read, and the starting point should be the needs of your audience. Consider how the audience will respond to your message—think about how they will feel, not what they will do—and use that information to guide your writing. But keep in mind that it's hard to know for sure how the recipient will respond. For instance, each of the responses in Exhibit 5.3 could be reasonable for different people:

How do you know how your audience will respond? In most cases you must simply guess based on as much evidence as you can find. The value of making a thoughtful guess is that the chances of achieving your goal will soar if you happen to be correct.

The anticipated audience response should directly affect how you structure your writing.

- If the recipient will feel positive or neutral about your message, the memo or email should begin with your bottom line. What is your request or recommendation or conclusion? Why should the audience care? Once you've clarified those points, follow up with your rationale and explanations (keeping in mind that less is usually more for time-starved businesspeople).

EXHIBIT 5.3 Messages and Responses

Message	Possible Responses
Please note the new computer password procedures.	Positive: *Great! We've really needed this.* Neutral: *OK, no big deal.* Negative: *Not another change…*
The company plans to restructure your work team when the project is complete.	Positive: *I can hardly wait to work with new people!* Neutral: *It's all part of the job…* Negative: *Not another change!*

- If the recipient will feel negative about your message, start the memo or email with a couple of lines that present the rationale, before you give the bottom line. Follow up with alternatives if there are any, and be sure to end on a positive note (rather than an apology). This structure is less straightforward, but it's a more effective way to communicate your message.

See Exhibit 5.4 for sample emails based on different anticipated responses to messages in an Internet game development firm.

Strike the Right Tone

Good business writing sounds natural—it flows like spoken language and reads like a conversation on paper. To strike the right tone for any given message, remember that you can choose from a wide variety of conversational styles, from formal to chatty. Imagine yourself speaking to the recipient of your message, and you'll find that the right tone emerges naturally. A few guidelines will also help:

- Use common words in most situations (e.g., *use* versus *utilize*).
- Use active voice (e.g., *We made a mistake* versus *A mistake was made*).

EXHIBIT 5.4 Sample Emails: Same Message, Different Approach

If the recipient will feel neutral...

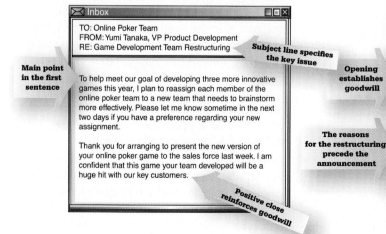

If the recipient will feel negative...

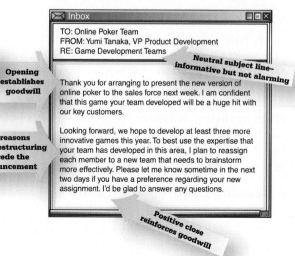

- Use personal pronouns (*I, you*) whenever appropriate.
- Use contractions (*I'll, don't, here's*) as often as you would when speaking.

Don't Make Grammar Goofs

Grammatical errors will distract your reader from your writing and undermine your credibility. Most business-people are aware of the more common grammatical errors, so they tend to jump off the page before the content of the message. But if you're uncertain about a particular point, look at how professionally edited publications handle similar issues. Finally, don't be afraid to do a commonsense check on any grammatical question.

Edward P. Bailey, noted professor and business communication author, points out that many writers make grammar mistakes based on phantom knowledge—"mythical" grammar rules that aren't even in grammar handbooks. His research firmly reassures us that:

- It is OK to end a sentence with a preposition when doing so sounds natural and does not involve excess words (e.g., *Where is this book from?* is much better than *From where is this book?*).

- It is OK to begin sentences with "And" or "But" (e.g., *Most teens enjoy videogames with a moderate level of violence. But a small, vocal minority strongly advocates a more clean-cut approach.*).

- It is OK to split infinitives (e.g., *Try to effectively film the next scene* is a perfectly acceptable sentence, even though "effectively" is inserted between "to" and "film.").

Once you accept these principles, your writing not only will sound more natural but also will flow more easily. Winston Churchill, renowned writer and speaker, was on-board with this common sense approach decades ago, as we can see from his joking comment that poked fun at tortured writing: "From now on, ending a sentence with a preposition is something up with which I will not put."[6]

Use Block Paragraphs

There are three elements to block paragraphs: (1) use single spacing, (2) double space between paragraphs, and (3) do not indent the first sentence of your paragraphs. This approach has become standard for business writing over the past decade, as writers have begun to include an increasing number of additional elements such as headings and illustrations. The block paragraphs create a more organized look for your page, guiding the reader's eye through the key elements of your structure.

Use Headings and Bulleted Lists Wherever Appropriate

Both headings and bulleted lists will guide your reader more easily through your writing. And the easier it is for

EXHIBIT 5.5 Ten Tips for Excellent Email

1. **Consider both your primary and secondary readers.** In other words, never forget that your reader may forward your email without considering the potential impact on you.

2. **Keep it short!** Many readers won't scroll down past whatever shows on their screen, so be sure to get your bottom line close to the top of your message.

3. **Don't forget to proofread.** This is especially important if you're asking someone to do something for you. And remember that your spell checker won't catch every mistake.

4. **Use standard writing.** Smiley faces, abbreviations, and five exclamation points are all fine if you're emailing your buddies, but in more formal messages they can make you look silly (or like you just don't care).

5. **Avoid attachments if possible.** They take time and space to open, and they don't always translate well to cell phones and PDAs. Instead, cut and paste relevant sections of the attachment into your email.

6. **Don't assume privacy.** Think of your emails as postcards that anyone (especially system administrators) can read along the way. In that light, try not to use email to communicate negative or critical messages.

7. **Respond promptly to emails.** If you don't have time to respond to the email itself, consider sending a message such as "Sorry, but I'm swamped right now—will get back to you early next week."

8. **Assume the best.** Since emails are often brief, they can cause unintentional offense. If you receive an off-key message, don't be afraid to inquire: "I'm not sure what you mean…could you please explain?"

9. **Create a compelling subject line.** Make your reader want to open your message. Briefly communicate the topic of your message and why your reader should care.

10. **Think before you write, and think again before you send!** Since it's so easy to send email, too many people send messages in an emotional moment that they later regret. Take time to think and think again.

your reader, the more likely that he or she will absorb your message, which is, of course, your ultimate goal.

- **Headings:** A heading is not a title; rather, it is a label for one of several parts. If you have only one part, skip the heading and use a title or a subject line. Consider using informative headings (e.g., Recruitment has stalled, rather than simply Recruitment), or question headings (e.g., Have we met our recruitment goals for this campaign?). And remember, headings are just as effective for letters and emails as they are for memos, and they are perfectly OK in one-page documents.

- **Bulleted Lists:** Bulleted lists are an invaluable tool that you can use to engage your reader's attention whenever you have more than one of anything in your writing (e.g., next steps, similar sections, questions). By formatting your lists with bullets, you are directing your reader's eye through your writing.

> ## Be sincere; be brief; be seated.
> *Franklin D. Roosevelt*

LO6 Create and Deliver Successful Verbal Presentations: Hook 'Em and Reel 'Em In!

What do people fear most? The *Book of Lists* asserts that public speaking ranks number one for the majority of people, high above the fear of death at number four. So when people say they would rather die than give a speech, they may really mean it! This section is designed to mitigate any fear you might have about public speaking by giving you guidance on how to create and deliver a high-impact verbal presentation.

As with most communication, the needs of the audience are the best place to begin. How does your audience feel about you and your topic? Are they interested? Hostile? Positive? What were they doing before your presentation? Dragging themselves out of bed after a late night at a sales meeting? Eating lunch? Use this information to guide how you develop your presentation. For instance, an eager, educated audience might not need as much background as a more lethargic, less-interested audience.

Opening

The opening of your presentation gives you a chance to grab the attention of the audience. If your opening hooks them, you've boosted the likelihood that you will hold their attention throughout the presentation. But developing that hook can be a challenge. The following are some suggestions for effective hooks:

- **An Interesting or Startling Statistic:** In a presentation regarding a risk management program, you could open by sharing that "Your odds of being killed in a plane crash are about 1 in 25 million, while your odds of being killed falling out of bed are about 1 in 2 million. What does this mean for us?"

- **Audience Involvement:** Pulling the audience into your opening can be very effective. For instance, in a presentation for a clothing company: "Imagine yourself with me at 11 P.M. on a Friday night, standing in line for admission to the hottest club in New York. As we inch forward, we suddenly realize that three other women in line are wearing the exact same dress as you...."

- **A Compelling Story or Anecdote:** This approach works best when it's completely genuine, using specific details that are directly relevant to the audience. For instance, in a presentation about employee benefits, you might want to share the story of a colleague who beat cancer using the company's innovative healthcare program.

- **A Relevant Simile or Metaphor:** Patricia Fripp, an award-winning keynote speaker, shares a simile that worked well to open a presentation for a colleague: "Being a scientist is like doing a jigsaw puzzle in a snowstorm at night...you don't have all the pieces... and you don't have the picture to work from."

- **Engaging Questions:** In a presentation about customer service, you could open by asking: "How many of you have spent far too long waiting on hold for customer service that was finally delivered by a surly agent who clearly knew nothing about your question?"

Google Presentations Software— The Next PowerPoint?

Although Microsoft PowerPoint remains the software option of choice for business presentations, Google Presentations software is swiftly gaining ground. Google Presentations is one of a growing number of applications based in "the cloud." This means that when you buy a new computer, you don't need to spend hundreds of dollars buying PowerPoint. You simply log into your Google account, use the Google Presentations software, and save your finished product on Google's servers. Since your work is stored on the Internet, you can access it from any device with a Web connection—you don't need to email it to yourself, or store it on a temperamental local drive, or worry about saving your changes as you move from work to home to school.

But Google Presentations is far from perfect. If you temporarily lose your Internet connection—on a plane or a bus, for instance—you cannot access your work. Security might be a worry, since Web-based data may be vulnerable to hackers. If Google disables your account for any reason, your work is lost. And Google Presentations does not yet include all the features available in PowerPoint, such as chart-making tools and advanced slide animations. The price, though, is pretty attractive: free! And that includes new versions and updates.

From a long-term perspective, another key benefit of Google Presentations—and all other cloud computing applications—is environmental. *Newsweek* writer Brian Braiker points out that "conducting affairs in the cloud is not only convenient, it's also greener: less capital and fewer printouts means less waste." All of which suggests that the forecast for Google Presentations is far from cloudy.[7]

Body

The most common presentation mistake is to include too many key ideas in the body of your presentation. Audiences simply cannot absorb more than two to four main points, and three are ideal. Specific examples and vivid comparisons will illustrate your points and bring them to life, while trusted sources, specific data, and expert quotations will increase your credibility and persuasiveness. Regardless of the length of your presentation, be sure to use clear transitions as you move from point to point.

Just before launching into the body of your presentation, you should tell the audience your key points, ideally with visual reinforcement. Then as you move to each new point, you can refer to the blueprint that you established upfront. A clear, explicit structure will help the audience track with you as you move through your material.

Close

Ideally, the close of your presentation will summarize your key points. Then circle back to your introduction, so that the beginning and the end serve as "bookends" for the body of your presentation. For instance, if you began by asking questions, end by answering them. If you began with an anecdote, end by referring to the same story. As an alternative (or maybe an addition), consider sharing a quotation or a bit of humor relevant to your content.

Also, keep in mind that you should verbally signal to your audience that you are about to conclude. Once you do so—by saying "in summary," for instance—be sure that you actually do conclude. Nothing alienates an audience more quickly than launching into another point after you've told them you're finished! Your body language will support your conclusion if you turn off your projector, and move toward the audience to answer questions. And even if you aren't so eager to field questions, try to paste a receptive look on your face—it'll increase your credibility and set a positive tone for the Q&A session.

Questions

At the start of your presentation, decide whether you want to handle questions throughout your talk or save them for the end. Tell your audience your preference upfront; most of the time they will respect it. But if you do receive unwanted questions in the middle of your presentation, don't ignore them. Simply remind the questioner that you'll leave plenty of time for questions at the end.

Not surprisingly, the best tip for handling questions is to be prepared. Since it's tough to anticipate questions for your own presentation, you may want to enlist the help of a trusted colleague to brainstorm the possibilities. And don't just come up with the questions—prepare the answers too!

Visual Aids

Studies suggest that three days after a presentation, people retain 10% of what they heard from an oral presentation, 35% from a visual presentation, and 65% from a combined visual and oral presentation. The numbers are compelling: visual aids matter. Depending on your audience, effective, high-impact visual aids could range from props to charts to mounted boards. But in business communication, PowerPoint slides are the most common option. If you use PowerPoint, consider these suggestions:

- **Showing Works Better Than Simply Telling:** Use pictures and other graphics whenever possible.
- **Less Is More:** Keep this helpful guideline in mind: no more than seven words per line, no more than seven lines per slide.
- **Don't Just Read Your Slides Aloud:** Instead, paraphrase, add examples, and offer analysis and interpretation.

Handling Hostility

We've all seen hostile questioners who seem determined to undermine presenters. It can be awful to watch, but it's surprisingly easy to handle. Here are a few tips:

- Stay calm and professional. Right or wrong, the hostile questioner has won the day if you get defensive or nervous.
- Don't be afraid to pause before you answer to gather your thoughts and allow the hostility to diffuse (a sip of water can provide good cover for a thought-gathering moment).
- Once you've answered the question, don't reestablish eye contact with the questioner. Doing so would suggest that you are seeking approval for your response, which only invites further hostile follow-up.
- If the questioner insists on follow-up, you may need to agree to disagree. If so, be decisive: "Sounds like we have two different points of view on this complex issue."
- Use body language to reinforce that you are done interacting with the questioner. Take a couple of steps away, and ask another part of the group if they have any questions.

Chapter 5   Business Communication: Creating and Delivering Messages that Matter

- **Go Easy on the Special Effects:** Too many sounds and too much animation can be painfully distracting.
- **Don't Let Your Slides Upstage You:** Look at your audience, not at the slides. And dim the screen when you're not specifically using it.[8]

Handling Nerves

Believe it or not, most experts agree that nervousness can be useful before a presentation. A little adrenalin can help you perform better, think faster, and focus more completely. But we all know that out-of-control nerves can interfere with effectiveness. Here are some ideas to mitigate speech anxiety:

- Send yourself positive messages; visualize success. Examples: "I will be dynamic and engaging." "They will completely support my new product idea."
- Take ten slow, deep breaths—use the yoga approach of breathing in through your nose and out through your mouth.
- Take a sip of water to loosen your throat muscles and mitigate a shaking voice (water also gives you a way to fill pauses).
- Pick a friendly face or two in the audience, and imagine yourself speaking only to those people (but don't stare at them!).
- Remind yourself that the audience wants you to succeed. Focus on their needs rather than your own nerves.

Incorporating Humor

Everyone likes to be funny, but incorporating humor in a business presentation can be risky. Only do it if you're very, very sure that it's funny. Even so, double-check that your jokes are appropriate and relevant. You should never, ever laugh at the expense of any member of your audience. Even laughing at yourself is chancy, since you risk diminishing your credibility. (But a joke at your own expense is always effective if you make a mistake; there's no better way to recover the goodwill of your audience.)

Delivery

Some people are naturals, but for the rest of us, **dynamic delivery** is a learned skill. It begins and ends with preparation, but keep in mind that practice doesn't always make perfect—in fact, practice more often just makes permanent. So be sure that you practice with an eye toward improvement. If possible, you should set up a practice situation that's close to the real thing. If you'll be standing to present, stand while you practice, since standing makes many people feel more vulnerable. Consider practicing in front of a mirror to work on eye contact and gestures. Also, try recording your voice to work on a lively tone. Finally, practice in front of a trusted friend or two who can give you valuable feedback. See Exhibit 5.6 for Ten Tips for Dynamic Delivery.

dynamic delivery Vibrant, compelling presentation delivery style that grabs and holds the attention of the audience.

EXHIBIT 5.6: Ten Tips for Dynamic Delivery

1. PRACTICE!
2. Know your material, but never memorize it word for word.
3. Look directly at members of your audience at least 50% of the time.
4. Vary your voice, your facial expressions, and your body language.
5. Use selective notes (but keep them inconspicuous).
6. Stick to your allotted time.
7. Slow down and listen to yourself.
8. Don't apologize (unless you really did something wrong!).
9. Remember to use natural gestures.
10. PRACTICE!

The Big Picture

Effective communication saves time and money—boosting performance and morale—across every area of business. But one vital principle holds true regardless of the more specific nature of your communication: the best way to achieve your goals is to focus on your audience, not on yourself. If you understand the goals, expectations, and needs of your audience, you can tailor your communication to boost your chances (sometimes dramatically) of accomplishing your objectives.

As globalization and technological change continue to accelerate, new communication challenges will likely develop across the spectrum of business. To ensure that your communication continues to be effective, keep an open mind. Pay attention to differences among cultures, to language usage in professional publications, and to new communication technology. And don't be afraid to consult an up-to-date communication website or handbook every so often. When other resources aren't available, rely on courtesy, consideration, and common sense—valuable tools to guide your communication in any situation.

WHAT ELSE? *RIP & REVIEW* **CARDS IN THE BACK**

6

BUSINESS FORMATION: CHOOSING THE FORM THAT FITS

LEARNING OBJECTIVES

After studying this chapter, you will be able to...

LO1 Describe the characteristics of the four basic forms of business ownership

LO2 Discuss the advantages and disadvantages of a sole proprietorship

LO3 Evaluate the pros and cons of the partnership as a form of ownership

LO4 Explain why corporations have become the dominant form of business ownership

LO5 Explain why limited liability companies are becoming an increasingly popular form of ownership

LO6 Evaluate the advantages and disadvantages of franchising

> **A corporation is an artificial being, invisible, intangible, and existing only in the contemplation of the law.**
>
> *John Marshall, fourth Chief Justice of the United States*

LO1 Business Ownership Options: The Big Four

One of the most important decisions entrepreneurs must make when they start a new business is the form of ownership they'll use. The form they choose will affect virtually every aspect of establishing and operating their firm, including the initial cost of setting up the business, the way the profits are distributed, the types of taxes (if any) the business itself must pay, and the types of regulations it must obey. Choice of ownership also determines the degree to which each owner has personal liability for the firm's debts and the sources of funds available to the firm to finance future expansion.

The vast majority of businesses in the United States are owned and organized under one of four forms:

1. A **sole proprietorship** is a business that is owned, and usually managed, by a single individual. As far as the law is concerned, a sole proprietorship is simply an extension of the owner. Any earnings of the company are treated as income of the owner; likewise, any debts the company incurs are considered to be the owner's personal debts.

2. A **partnership** is a voluntary agreement under which two or more people act as co-owners of a business for profit. As we'll see later in the chapter, there are several types of partnerships. In its most basic form, known as a **general partnership**, each partner has the right to participate in the company's management and share in profits—but also has unlimited liability for any debts the company incurs.

3. A **corporation** is a business entity created by filing a form (known in most states as the **articles of incorporation**) with the appropriate state agency, paying the state's incorporation fees, and meeting certain other requirements (the specifics vary among states). Unlike a sole proprietorship or a partnership, a corporation is considered to be a legal entity that is separate and distinct from its owners. In many ways, a corporation is like an artificial person. It can legally engage in virtually any business activity a natural person can pursue. For example, a corporation can enter into binding contracts, borrow money, own property, pay taxes, and initiate legal actions (such as lawsuits) in its own name. It can even be a partner in a partnership or an owner of another corporation. Because of a corporation's status as a separate legal entity, the owners of a corporation have **limited liability**—meaning they aren't personally responsible for the debts and obligations of their company.

4. A **limited liability company (LLC)** is a hybrid form of business ownership that is similar in some respects to a partnership while having other characteristics that are similar to a corporation. Like a corporation, a limited liability company is considered a legal entity separate from its owners. Also like a corporation—and as its name implies—an LLC offers its owners limited liability for the debts of their business. But it offers more flexibility than a corporation in terms of tax treatment; in fact, one of the most interesting characteristics of an LLC is that its owners can elect to have their business taxed either as a corporation *or* a partnership. Many states even allow individuals to form single-person LLCs that are taxed as if they were sole proprietorships.

sole proprietorship A form of business ownership with a single owner who usually actively manages the company.

partnership A voluntary agreement under which two or more people act as co-owners of a business for profit.

general partnership A partnership in which all partners can take an active role in managing the business and have unlimited liability for any claims against the firm.

corporation A form of business ownership in which the business is considered a legal entity that is separate and distinct from its owners.

articles of incorporation The document filed with a state government to establish the existence of a new corporation.

limited liability When owners are not personally liable for claims against their firm. Limited liability owners may lose their investment in the company, but their personal assets are protected.

limited liability company (LLC) A form of business ownership that offers both limited liability to its owners and flexible tax treatment.

Sole proprietorships, partnerships, and corporations have been around in some form since the beginning of our nation's history, but limited liability companies are a relatively new form of ownership in the United States. In 1977 Wyoming passed the first state statute allowing LLCs, and in 1982 Florida became the second state to do so. But it wasn't until a ruling by the Internal Revenue Service (IRS) in 1988 clarifying the tax treatment of LLCs that most other states followed suit. Today every state has enacted LLC legislation, and the LLC has become a very popular ownership option. In many states, filings to form LLCs now outnumber filings to form corporations.[1]

Exhibits 6.1 and 6.2 provide some interesting insights about the relative importance of each form of ownership. As shown in Exhibit 6.1, the sole proprietorship is by far the most common type of business organization in the United States. In 2006 almost 22 million individuals reported operating nonfarm sole proprietorships. This represented more than 71.5% of the total number of business enterprises. As a group, these sole proprietorships reported almost $1.28 trillion in revenue and almost $278 billion in net income (profit). But while these figures are impressive in aggregate, most individual sole proprietorships are quite small. According to the U.S. Census Bureau's *2010 Statistical Abstract*, more than two-thirds of all sole proprietorships reported annual revenue of less than $25,000, while only a tiny fraction of 1% reported receipts in excess of $1 million.[2]

As Exhibit 6.2 shows, when it comes to economic impact, the corporate form of ownership rules. Though only about 19% of all business firms are incorporated, in 2006 (and most other years) corporations reported about 68% of all business profits. Corporations like Walmart, Exxon-Mobil, General Electric, Apple, and Boeing have annual sales revenues measured in the billions (sometimes hundreds of billions) of dollars. But not all corporations are multibillion-dollar enterprises. In 2006, about 23% of all corporations reported total revenues of less than $25,000.[3]

As you can see from Exhibit 6.1, partnerships are less common than sole proprietorships or corporations. Still, in 2006 about 2.9 million businesses were classified as partnerships in the United States. And partnerships tend to be both larger and more profitable than sole proprietorships. As Exhibit 6.2 shows, in aggregate partnerships earned substantially higher total net income than sole proprietorships, despite the fact that sole proprietorships outnumbered partnerships by a ratio of almost eight to one![4]

You've probably noticed that Exhibits 6.1 and 6.2 don't include specific information about limited liability companies. That's because these exhibits are based on information taken from annual business tax returns submitted to the Internal Revenue Service (IRS). The IRS doesn't track LLC information separately. Instead, it classifies each LLC based on the tax treatment the company selects. LLCs that choose to be taxed as partnerships are classified as partnerships, while those choosing to be taxed as corporations are classified as corporations. (The vast majority of LLCs elect to be taxed as partnerships, so most LLC earnings are reported in the partnership category.)

We'll see that each form of ownership has distinct advantages and disadvantages. As a company grows and matures, the form of ownership that's best suited to its needs may change. Fortunately, the form of ownership for a business isn't set in stone. For example, it is possible—and in fact quite common—for business owners to convert from a sole proprietorship to a corporation, or from a corporation to a limited liability company.

EXHIBIT 6.1 Total Number of Businesses by Form of Ownership[5]

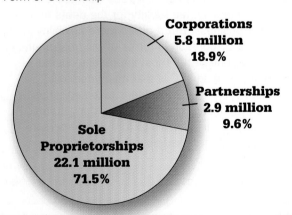

Corporations
5.8 million
18.9%

Partnerships
2.9 million
9.6%

Sole Proprietorships
22.1 million
71.5%

EXHIBIT 6.2 Total Net Income by Form of Ownership[6]

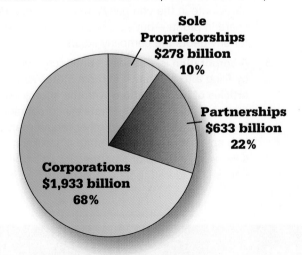

Sole Proprietorships
$278 billion
10%

Partnerships
$633 billion
22%

Corporations
$1,933 billion
68%

LO2 Advantages and Disadvantages of Sole Proprietorships

Our look at Exhibits 6.1 and 6.2 raises two questions about sole proprietorships. First, why is this form of ownership so popular? Second, why do sole proprietorships usually remain relatively small? A look at the advantages and disadvantages of sole proprietorships can help answer these questions.

Advantages

Sole proprietorships offer some very attractive advantages to people starting a business:

*   **Ease of Formation:** Compared to the other forms of ownership we'll discuss, the paperwork and costs involved in forming a sole proprietorship are minimal. No special forms must be filed, and no special fees must be paid. Entrepreneurs who are eager to get a business up and running quickly can find this a compelling advantage.

*   **Retention of Control:** As the only owner of a sole proprietorship, you're in control. You have the ability to manage your business the way you want. If you want to "be your own boss," a sole proprietorship might look very attractive.

*   **Pride of Ownership:** One of the main reasons many people prefer a sole proprietorship is the feeling of pride and the personal satisfaction they gain from owning and running their own business.

*   **Retention of Profits:** If your business is successful, *all* the profits go to you—minus your personal taxes, of course.

*   **Possible Tax Advantage:** No taxes are levied directly on the earnings of sole proprietorships as a business. Instead, the earnings are taxed only as income of the proprietor. As

we'll see when we discuss corporations, this avoids the undesirable possibility of double taxation of earnings.

Disadvantages

Entrepreneurs thinking about forming sole proprietorships should also be aware of some serious drawbacks:

*   **Limited Financial Resources:** Raising money to finance growth can be tough for sole proprietors. With only one owner responsible for a sole proprietorship's debts, banks and other financial institutions are often reluctant to lend it money. Likewise, suppliers may be unwilling to provide supplies on credit. This leaves sole proprietors dependent on their own wealth plus money that their firms generate.

*   **Unlimited Liability:** Because the law views a sole proprietorship as an extension of its owner, the debts of the firm become the personal debts of the owner. If someone sues your business and wins, the court could seize your personal possessions—even those that have nothing to do with your business—and sell them to pay the damages. This unlimited personal liability means operating as a sole proprietorship is a risky endeavor.

*   **Limited Ability to Attract and Maintain Talented Employees:** Most sole proprietors are unable to pay the high salaries and offer the perks that highly qualified, experienced employees get when they work for big, well-established companies.

*   **Heavy Workload and Responsibilities:** Being your own boss can be very rewarding, but it can also mean very long hours and a lot of stress. Sole proprietors—as the ultimate authority in their business—often must perform tasks or make decisions in areas where they lack expertise.

*   **Lack of Permanence:** Because a sole proprietorship is just an extension of the owner, it lacks permanence. If the owner dies, retires, or withdraws from the business for some other reason, the company legally ceases to exist. Even if the company continues to operate under new ownership, in the eyes of the law it becomes a different firm.

LO3 Partnerships: Two Heads (and Bankrolls) Can Be Better Than One

There are several types of partnerships, each with its own specific characteristics. We'll focus our discussion mainly on the most basic type, known as a general partnership. However, we'll also take a quick look at limited partnerships and limited liability partnerships.

Formation of General Partnerships

There is no specific upper limit on the number of partners that can participate in a general partnership, but most partnerships consist of only a few partners—often just two. The partnership is formed when the partners enter into a voluntary partnership agreement. It is legally possible to start a partnership on the basis of a verbal agreement, but doing so is often a recipe for disaster. It's much safer to get everything in writing and to seek expert legal assistance when drawing up the agreement. A typical partnership agreement spells out such details as the initial financial contributions each partner will make, the specific duties and responsibilities each will assume, how they will share profits (and losses), how they will settle disagreements, and how they will deal with the death or withdrawal of one of the partners. A well-written agreement can prevent a lot of misunderstandings.

Advantages of General Partnerships

Partnerships offer some key advantages relative to both sole proprietorships and corporations:

- **Ability to Pool Financial Resources:** With more people investing in the company, a partnership is likely to have a stronger financial base than a sole proprietorship.

- **Ability to Share Responsibilities and Capitalize on Complementary Skills:** Partners can share the burden of running the business, which can ease the workload. They can also benefit from complementary skills and interests, splitting up the tasks so they use their skills to best advantage.

- **Ease of Formation:** Compared to corporations, partnerships are relatively easy to set up. All that's needed is an agreement among two or more people to operate a business as co-owners.

- **Possible Tax Advantages:** Similar to a sole proprietorship, the earnings of a partnership

"pass through" the business—untouched by the Internal Revenue Service (IRS)—and are taxed only as the partners' personal income. Again, this avoids the potential for double taxation endemic to corporations.

Disadvantages of General Partnerships

General partnerships also have some serious disadvantages. As you read about them, keep in mind that a well-written partnership agreement can mitigate some of the drawbacks:

- **Unlimited Liability:** As a general partner you're not only liable for your own mistakes, but also for the mistakes of your partners. In fact, all general partners have unlimited liability for the debts and obligations of their business. So, if the assets they've invested in the business aren't sufficient to meet these claims, the personal assets of the partners are at risk. When someone sues a partnership, the lawsuit can target *any* individual partner or group of partners. In fact, lawsuits often go after the partners with the deepest pockets, even if they did not personally participate in the act that caused the legal action. In other words, if you have more personal wealth than the other partners, you could lose more than they do even if they were the ones at fault!

> It's very much like a marriage, though I get along better with my wife.
>
> *Zane Carter, general partner in Carter Cosgrove and Co. on his relationship with his partners*

- **Potential for Disagreements:** If general partners can't agree on how to run the business, the conflict can complicate and delay decision-making. A well-drafted partnership agreement usually specifies how disputes will be resolved, but disagreements among partners can create friction and hard feelings that harm morale and undermine the cooperation needed to keep the business on track.

- **Lack of Continuity:** If a current partner withdraws from the partnership, the relationship among the participants will clearly change, potentially

ending the partnership. This creates uncertainty about how long a partnership will remain in business.

- **Difficulty in Withdrawing from a Partnership:** A partner that withdraws from a partnership remains personally liable for any debts or obligations the firm had *at the time of withdrawal*—even if those obligations were created by the actions of other partners.

Limited Partnerships

A **limited partnership** is a partnership arrangement that includes at least one general partner *and* at least one limited partner. Both types of partners contribute financially to the company and share in its profits. But in other respects they play different roles:

- General partners may contribute money, property, and personal services to the partnership. They also have the right to fully participate in managing the partnership, and they have unlimited personal liability for any of its debts—just like the partners in a general partnership.

- Limited partners may contribute money and property to the company, but *cannot* actively participate in its management. Limited partners have limited liability; they are liable for the debts of the firm *only* to the extent of their actual investment. As long as they do not actively participate in management, their personal wealth is not at risk.

Limited Liability Partnerships

The **limited liability partnership (LLP)** is the newest form of partnership. It is similar to a limited partnership in some ways, but it has the advantage of allowing *all* partners to take an active role in management, while also offering *all* partners some form of limited liability. In other words, there's no need to distinguish between limited and general partners in an LLP.

The amount of liability protection offered by LLPs varies among states. In some states, LLPs offer "full-shield" protection, meaning that partners have limited liability for all claims against their company, except those resulting from *their own* negligence or malpractice. In other states, partners in LLPs have a lesser "partial-shield" protection. In these states, each partner has limited liability for the negligence or malpractice of other owners but still has unlimited liability for any other debts. Only certain types of professional businesses are allowed to organize as LLPs in most states. For example, California law allows only accountants, lawyers, and architects to form LLPs.

LO4 Corporations: The Advantages and Disadvantages of Being an Artificial Person

There are several types of corporations. The most common is called a **C corporation**; when people use the term "corporation" without specifying which type, they are generally referring to a C corporation. Because it's the most common, we'll devote most of our discussion to C corporations. However, we'll also describe three

---

limited partnership A partnership that includes at least one general partner who actively manages the company and accepts unlimited liability and one limited partner who gives up the right to actively manage the company in exchange for limited liability.

limited liability partnership (LLP) A form of partnership in which all partners have the right to participate in management and have limited liability for company debts.

C corporation The most common type of corporation, which is a legal business entity that offers limited liability to all of its owners, who are called stockholders.

Keeping It All in the Family

In recent years, limited partnerships have become increasingly popular in a surprising place: the family. Many families have set up family limited partnerships (called FLIPs) with the parents as the general partners and the children as the limited partners. Why do this? By using this structure, parents can transfer family assets to their children, thus greatly reducing gift and inheritance taxes. Since the parents are the general partners, they retain control over family assets even though they are now held by the children. Also, because (as limited partners) the children have limited liability, this structure can protect family assets from lawsuits or creditors.

Anyone thinking about setting up a FLIP should seek legal advice; this type of arrangement needs to be carefully structured to avoid problems. The IRS has expressed concern that many people are abusing this type of partnership and has vowed to be diligent in looking for such abuse. Thus, setting up a FLIP is likely to significantly increase your chances of an audit by the IRS![7]

corporate bylaws
The basic rules governing how a corporation is organized and how it conducts its business.

stockholder
An owner of a corporation.

institutional investor An organization that pools contributions from investors, clients, or depositors and uses these funds to buy stocks and other securities.

other types of corporations: S corporations, statutory close (or closed) corporations, and nonprofit corporations.

Forming a C Corporation

As we mentioned earlier, the formation of a corporation requires filing articles of incorporation and paying filing fees. It also requires the adoption of **corporate bylaws**, which are detailed rules that govern the way the corporation is managed and operates. Because of these requirements, forming a corporation tends to be more expensive and complex than forming a sole proprietorship or partnership. But the exact requirements vary among the states. Some states are known for their simple forms, inexpensive fees, low corporate tax rates, and "corporation-friendly" laws and court systems. In these states, forming a corporation is not much harder or more expensive than setting up a sole proprietorship. Not surprisingly, many large companies choose to incorporate in states with such favorable environments—even if they intend to do the majority of their business in other states. Delaware, in particular, has been very successful at attracting corporations. You may not think of Delaware as the home of corporate power, but about half of all publicly traded corporations—and 63% of the firms listed in the Fortune 500—are incorporated in Delaware.[8]

Ownership of C Corporations

Ownership of C corporations is represented by shares of stock, so owners are called "**stockholders**" (or "shareholders"). Common stock represents the basic ownership interest in a corporation, but some firms also issue preferred stock. One key difference between the two types of stock involves voting rights; common stockholders normally have the right to vote in stockholders' meetings, while preferred stockholders do not. Some large corporations issue billions of shares of stock and have hundreds of thousands—or even millions—of stockholders. For example, in February 2009 AT&T had 5.9 billion shares of common stock outstanding, held by 1,448,975 stockholders.[10]

Stock in large corporations is usually publicly traded, meaning anyone with the money and inclination to do so can buy and sell their shares. But many smaller corporations are owned by just a handful of stockholders who don't actively trade their stock. It's even possible for individuals to incorporate their business and be the sole shareholder in their corporation.[11]

Stockholders don't have to be individuals. Organizations such as mutual funds, insurance companies, pension funds, and endowment funds pool money from a large number of individual contributors and use these funds to buy stocks and other securities. These organizations, called **institutional investors**, own the majority of stock in many large corporations.

The Role of the Board of Directors

It's not practical for all of the stockholders of a large corporation to actively participate in the management of their company. Besides, most stockholders don't have the time, management skills, or desire to effectively manage such a complex business enterprise. Thus, in accordance with corporate bylaws, the stockholders

A New Form of Business Aims for Social Responsibility

In April of 2010, Maryland became the first state to pass a law allowing the formation of an entirely new business entity called a benefit corporation. Formation of a benefit corporation is similar to that of a C corporation, but with the additional requirement that the company's bylaws must include provisions identifying specific social or environmental goals, which the law then holds the board of directors accountable for achieving.

Despite their social orientation, benefit corporations aren't nonprofit organizations. They are allowed—indeed, expected—to earn a satisfactory financial return for their owners. But Maryland's law explicitly allows directors of benefit corporations to give equal or greater priority to other stakeholders such as employees, customers, or environmentalists. This gives a benefit corporation's board legal cover to pursue social and environmental goals without fear of stockholder lawsuits. As Maryland state senator Jamie Raskin, one of the sponsors of the Maryland law, put it, "We are giving companies a way to do good and do well at the same time. The benefit corporations will tie public and private purposes together."

It is too early to tell whether benefit corporations will become a popular type of business entity. But some early developments suggest that it has attracted considerable attention. Many privately held corporations have already expressed interest in converting to this new business entity. And benefit corporation legislation has already been introduced in several other states, with Vermont becoming the second state to legalize B corporations in May 2010.[9]

The board of directors is responsible for protecting the interests of a corporation's stockholders.

board of directors The individuals who are elected by stockholders of a corporation to represent their interests.

elect a **board of directors** and rely on this board to oversee the operation of their company and protect their interests.

The board of directors establishes the corporation's mission and sets its broad objectives. But board members seldom take an active role in the day-to-day management of their company. Instead, again in accordance with corporate bylaws, the board appoints a chief executive officer (CEO) and other corporate officers to manage the company on a daily basis. The board is responsible for monitoring the performance of these corporate officers to ensure that their decisions are consistent with stockholder interests. It also provides advice to these officers on broad policy issues, approves their major proposals, and ensures that the company adheres to major regulatory requirements.

Advantages of C Corporations

There are several reasons why corporations have become the dominant form of business ownership:

- **Limited Liability:** As we've already explained, stockholders are not personally liable for the debts of their company. If a corporation goes bankrupt, the stockholders might find that their stock is worthless, but their other personal assets are protected.

- **Permanence:** Unless the articles of incorporation specify a limited duration, corporations can continue operating as long as they remain financially viable and the majority of stockholders want the business to continue. Unlike a sole proprietorship or partnership, a general corporation is unaffected by the death or withdrawal of an owner.

- **Ease of Transfer of Ownership:** It's easy for stockholders of publicly traded C corporations to withdraw from ownership—they simply sell their shares of stock.

- **Ability to Raise Large Amounts of Financial Capital:** Corporations can raise large amounts of financial capital by issuing shares of stock or by selling long-term IOUs called corporate bonds. The ability to raise money by issuing these securities gives corporations a major financial advantage over most other forms of ownership.

- **Ability to Make Use of Specialized Management:** Large corporations often find it easier to hire highly qualified professional managers than proprietorships and partnerships. Major corporations can typically offer attractive salaries and benefits, and their permanence and potential for growth offer managers opportunities for career advancement.

Disadvantages of C Corporations

In addition to their significant benefits, C corporations also have a number of drawbacks:

- **Expense and Complexity of Formation and Operation:** As we've already seen, establishing a corporation is more complex and expensive than forming sole proprietorships and partnerships. Corporations are also subject to more formal operating requirements. For example, they are required to hold regular board meetings and keep accurate minutes.

> **CEOs of major corporations are usually *very* well paid. But there are exceptions. For the past decade, Apple CEO Steve Jobs has agreed to total compensation of $1. But don't feel sorry for Jobs; he owns 5.5 million shares of Apple stock worth several billion dollars!**
>
> *USA Today*

- **Complications When Operating in More Than One State:** When a business that's incorporated in one state does business in other states, it's called a "*domestic* corporation" in the state where it's incorporated and a "*foreign* corporation" in the other states. A corporation must register or qualify to do business as a foreign corporation in order to operate in any state other than the one in which it incorporated. This typically requires additional paperwork and fees.

- **Double Taxation of Earnings and Additional Taxes:** The IRS considers a C corporation to be a separate legal entity and taxes its earnings accordingly. Then any dividends (earnings the corporation distributes to stockholders) are taxed *again* as the personal income of the stockholders. This double taxation can take a big bite out of the company's earnings that are distributed to shareholders. (But note that corporations often reinvest some or all of their profits back into the business. Shareholders don't pay income taxes on these retained earnings.) In addition, most states also impose an annual franchise tax on both domestic and foreign corporations that operate within their borders.

- **More Paperwork and More Regulation:** Corporations are more closely regulated than other forms of business. Large, publicly traded corporations are required to send annual statements to all shareholders and to file detailed quarterly and annual reports with the Securities and Exchange Commission (SEC). Anyone can look at the forms filed with the SEC, making it difficult to keep financial information secret from competitors.

- **Possible Conflicts of Interest:** The corporate officers appointed by the board are supposed to further the interests of stockholders. But some top executives pursue policies that further their *own* interests (such as prestige, power, job security, high pay, and attractive perks) at the expense of the stockholders. The board of directors has an obligation to look out for the interests of stockholders, but—as our feature on the Troubled Asset Relief Program explains—in recent years the boards of several major corporations have come under criticism for failure to provide proper oversight.

Other Types of Corporations: Same but Different

Now that we've described C corporations, let's take a quick look at three other types of corporations:

WITHOUT A MAP... CHARTING AN ETHICAL COURSE

This TARP Has Executive Pay Covered

A C corporation's board of directors is supposed to protect the interests of the stockholders who elect them. But critics charge that board members at some corporations seem to be more interested in protecting the interests of their CEOs than those of the owners.

The issue of executive compensation has been a sore spot with stockholders for many years. But it came to a head in 2008 as the economy spiraled into a deep recession. Many boards continued to approve high salaries and lavish bonuses for their CEOs even as their companies posted huge losses—a practice that angered not only stockholders, but also the general public and Congress. Exorbitant CEO pay was particularly upsetting in the financial sector, which was in such bad shape in late 2008 that the Bush administration asked Congress to approve a $700 billion financial sector bailout called the Troubled Asset Relief Program (TARP). A special provision was later approved that allowed struggling U.S. automakers (which also had many executives earning attractive salaries and bonuses) to also have access to TARP funds.

When reports surfaced that many of the top executives at the companies pleading for TARP money were due to receive huge bonuses, the public outcry was deafening. Congress quickly responded by placing restrictions on CEO compensation as a condition for receiving TARP bailout money. For example, it limited the corporate tax deduction for CEO compensation to $500,000. It also required boards to remove incentives from compensation packages that encouraged CEOs to take excessive risks.

In June of 2009 the new Obama administration put even more teeth in the government's efforts to curb executive pay by appointing Kenneth Feinberg to the position of executive compensation czar. Feinberg's assignment: review pay plans for top executives at all corporations still receiving "exceptional assistance" under the TARP program, and restructure those compensation packages he deemed to be excessive.

Feinberg took his job seriously. In early 2010 he announced a plan that would reduce the number of executives who worked for companies still receiving TARP funds and earned more than $500,000 from 65 in 2009 to only 5 by the end of 2010.[12]

© GREG FIUME/GETTY IMAGES

S corporations, **statutory close corporations,** and **nonprofit corporations**. Like C corporations, each is created by filing the appropriate paperwork with a government agency. Also like general corporations, these corporations are considered legal entities that stand apart from their owners and can enter into contracts, own property, and take legal action in their own names. But in other key respects they are quite different from C corporations—and from each other. Exhibit 6.3 summarizes the basic features of these corporations.

Corporate Restructuring

Large corporations constantly look for ways to grow and achieve competitive advantages. Some corporations work to achieve these goals, at least in part, through mergers, acquisitions, and divestitures. We'll close our discussion of corporations by taking a quick look at these forms of corporate restructuring.

Mergers and Acquisitions In the news and casual conversation, the terms "merger" and "acquisition" are often used interchangeably. However, there's a difference between the two. An **acquisition** occurs when one firm buys another firm. The firm making the purchase is called the "acquiring firm," and the firm being purchased is called the "target firm." After the acquisition, the target firm ceases to exist as an independent entity while the purchasing firm continues in operation and its stock is still traded. But not all acquisitions are on friendly terms. When the acquiring firm buys the target firm despite the opposition of the target's board and top management, the result is called a "hostile takeover."

In a **merger**, instead of one firm buying the other, the two companies agree to a combination of equals, joining together to form a new company out of the two previously independent firms. Exhibit 6.4 describes the three most common types of corporate combinations.

Divestitures: When Less Is More Sometimes corporations restructure by subtraction rather than by addition. A **divestiture** occurs when a firm transfers total or partial ownership of some of its assets to investors or to

S corporation A form of corporation that avoids double taxation by having its income taxed as if it were a partnership.

statutory close (or closed) corporation A corporation with a limited number of owners that operates under simpler, less formal rules than a C corporation.

nonprofit corporation A corporation that does not seek to earn a profit and differs in several fundamental respects from C corporations.

acquisition A corporate restructuring in which one firm buys another.

merger A corporate restructuring that occurs when two formerly independent business entities combine to form a new organization.

divestiture The transfer of total or partial ownership of some of a firm's assets to investors or to another company.

EXHIBIT 6.3 Characteristics of S, Statutory Close, and Nonprofit Corporations

Type	Key Advantages	Limitations
S Corporation	• The IRS does not tax earnings of S corporations separately. Earnings pass through the company and are taxed only as income to stockholders, thus avoiding the problem of double taxation associated with C corporations. • Stockholders have limited liability.	• It can have no more than 100 stockholders. • With only rare exceptions, each stockholder must be a U.S. citizen or permanent resident of the United States. (No ownership by foreigners or other corporations.)
Statutory Close (or Closed) Corporation	• It can operate under simpler arrangements than conventional corporations. For example, it doesn't have to elect a board of directors or hold an annual stockholders' meeting. • All owners can actively participate in management while still having limited liability.	• The number of stockholders is limited. (The number varies among states but is usually no more than 50.) • Stockholders normally can't sell their shares to the public without first offering the shares to existing owners. • Not all states allow formation of this type of corporation.
Nonprofit (or Not-for-Profit) Corporation	• Earnings are exempt from federal and state income taxes. • Members and directors have limited liability. • Individuals who contribute money or property to the nonprofit can take a tax deduction, making it easier for these organizations to raise funds from donations.	• It has members (who may pay dues) but cannot have stockholders. • It cannot distribute dividends to members. • It cannot contribute funds to a political campaign. • It must keep accurate records and file paperwork to document tax-exempt status.

horizontal merger A combination of two firms that are in the same industry.

vertical merger A combination of firms at different stages in the production of a good or service.

conglomerate merger A combination of two firms that are in unrelated industries.

EXHIBIT 6.4 Types of Mergers and Acquisitions

Type of Merger	Definition	Common Objective	Example
Horizontal Merger	A combination of firms in the same industry.	Increase size and market power within the industry Improve efficiency by eliminating duplication of facilities and personnel.	The 2009 acquisition of Wachovia by Wells Fargo to create the most extensive financial services company in North America.
Vertical Merger	A combination of firms that are at different stages in the production of a good or service, creating a "buyer-seller" relationship.	It provides tighter integration of production and increased control over the supply of crucial inputs.	The 1996 merger of Time Warner (a major provider of cable television) with Turner Broadcasting (owner of several cable networks, such as CNN and TNT).
Conglomerate Merger	A combination of firms in unrelated industries.	It reduces risk by making the firm less vulnerable to adverse conditions in any single market.	The 2006 acquisition by Berkshire Hathaway (a highly diversified company that holds stock in a wide variety of companies) of Iscar, a privately held company that makes cutting tools.

another company. Firms often use divestitures to rid themselves of a part of their company that no longer fits well with their strategic plans. This allows them to streamline their operations and focus on their core businesses. In many (but not all) cases, divestitures involve the sale of assets to outsiders, which raises financial capital for the firm.

One common type of divestiture, called a "spin-off," occurs when a company issues stock in one of its own divisions or operating units and sets it up as a separate company—complete with its own board of directors and corporate officers. It then distributes the stock in the new company to its existing stockholders. After the spin-off, the stockholders end up owning two separate companies rather than one. They can then buy, sell, or hold either (or both) stocks as they see fit. While a spin-off

Veiled Threats?

One of the primary advantages of incorporating a business is that doing so provides the owners with the protection of limited liability. In legal terms, the creation of a corporation establishes a separation, called a "corporate veil," between the assets of the business and those of its stockholders. This separation means that the owners' personal wealth normally isn't at risk if the company's assets aren't sufficient to cover payments to creditors or claims that result from a lawsuit.

But there are limits to this protection. Under certain conditions a court may "pierce the corporate veil" during lawsuits or bankruptcy proceedings, ruling that stockholders are *personally* liable for *all* claims against their corporation. The court will reach such a verdict when it finds evidence that the corporation is not a legitimate business, but rather a sham or "front" set up to protect the personal assets of individuals engaged in financially risky or fraudulent behavior.

The courts look at many factors in order to determine whether to pierce the veil. One red flag arises when the courts find the assets of one or more major stockholders are commingled with those of the corporation—such as when the firm shares a bank account with a shareholder instead of having a separate account. The courts may also pierce the veil if the firm fails to hold required meetings, keep required financial records, or follow other corporate formalities, thus raising concerns that it isn't a legitimate business.[13]

Chapter 6   Business Formation: Choosing the Form that Fits

allows a corporation to eliminate a division that no longer fits in its plans, it doesn't actually generate any additional funds for the firm.

A "carve-out" is like a spin-off in that the firm converts a particular unit or division into a separate company and issues stock in the newly created corporation. However, instead of distributing the new stock to its current stockholders, it sells the stock to outside investors, thus raising additional financial capital. In many cases the firm sells only a minority of the total shares, so that it maintains majority ownership.

© TIM BOYLE/GETTY IMAGES

LO5 The Limited Liability Company: The New Kid on the Block

As the newest form of business ownership, state laws concerning the legal status and formation of LLCs are still evolving. Several states have recently revised their statutes to make forming LLCs simpler and to make transfer of ownership easier. Other states have kept more restrictive requirements intact. This diversity of state requirements, and the continuing evolution of LLC statutes, makes it difficult to provide meaningful generalizations about this form of ownership.[14]

Forming and Managing an LLC

In many respects, forming an LLC is similar to forming a corporation. As with corporations, LLCs are created by filing a document (which goes by a variety of names, such as *certificate of organization* or *articles of organization*) and paying filing fees in the state where the business is organized. Organizers of most LLCs also draft an operating agreement, which is similar to the bylaws of a corporation. Some states also require LLCs to publish a notice of intent to operate as a limited liability company.

Because LLCs are neither corporations nor partnerships, their owners are called *members* rather than stockholders or partners. Members of LLCs often manage their own company under an arrangement similar to the relationship among general partners in a partnership. However, some LLCs hire professional managers who have responsibilities much like those of the CEO and other top officers of corporations.

Advantages of LLCs

Why are LLCs becoming so popular? This form of ownership offers significant advantages:

- **Limited Liability:** Similar to a corporation, *all* owners of an LLC have limited liability.

- **Tax Pass-Through:** As we mentioned at the beginning of this chapter, for tax purposes the owners of LLCs may elect to have their companies treated as either a corporation or a partnership—or even as a sole proprietorship if it is owned by a single person. The default tax classification for LLCs with more than one owner—and the one most LLCs choose—is the partnership option. Under this arrangement, there is no separate tax on the earnings of the company. Instead, earnings "pass through" the company and are taxed only as income of the owners. This eliminates the double taxation of profits that is endemic to

> LLCs are new in the United States, but they have existed in other countries for over a century. Wyoming's 1977 LLC law was based on a German business entity first established in 1892 known as a Gesellschaft mit beschränkter Haftung (GmbH), which is German for "company with limited liability."
>
> *Investopedia*

franchise A licensing arrangement whereby a franchisor allows franchisees to use its name, trademark, products, business methods and other property in exchange for monetary payments and other considerations.

franchisor The business entity in a franchise relationship that allows others to operate their business using resources it supplies in exchange for money and other considerations.

franchisee The party in a franchise relationship that pays for the right to use resources supplied by the franchisor.

distributorship a type of franchising arrangement in which the franchisor makes a product and licenses the franchisee to sell it.

business format franchise A broad franchise agreement in which the franchisee pays for the right to use the name, trademark, and business and production methods of the franchisor.

general corporations. However, there are some cases where it makes sense for LLCs to elect to be taxed as a corporation. For example, the owner of a single-person LLC can avoid paying self-employment taxes by electing to have the LLC treated as a corporation rather than as a sole proprietorship.

- **Simplicity and Flexibility in Management and Operation:** Unlike corporations, LLCs aren't required to hold regular board meetings. Also, LLCs are subject to less paperwork and fewer reporting requirements than corporations.

- **Flexible Ownership:** Unlike S corporations, LLCs can have any number of owners. Also unlike S corporations, the owners of LLCs can include foreign investors and other corporations. However, some states do make it difficult to transfer ownership to outsiders.

Limitations and Disadvantages of LLCs

Despite their increasing popularity, LLCs have some limitations and drawbacks:

- **More Complex to Form Than Partnerships:** Because of the need to file articles of organization and pay filing fees, LLCs can take more time and effort to form than sole proprietorships and general partnerships.

- **Annual Franchise Tax:** Even though they may be exempt from corporate income taxes, many states require LLCs to pay an annual franchise tax.

- **Foreign Status in Other States:** Like corporations, LLCs must register or qualify to operate as "foreign" companies when they do business in states other than the state in which they were organized. This results in more paperwork, fees, and taxes.

- **Limits on Types of Firms That Can Form LLCs:** Most states do not permit banks, insurance companies, and nonprofit organizations to operate as LLCs.

- **Differences in State Laws:** As we've already mentioned, LLC laws are still evolving—and their specific requirements vary considerably among the states. In 2006 the National Conference of Commissioners

on Uniform State Laws created a Revised Uniform Limited Liability Company Act that could be used as a model by all states. To date, only a few states have adopted this law. Until there is more uniformity in state laws, operating LLCs in more than one state is likely to remain a complex endeavor.[15]

LO6 Franchising: Proven Methods for a Price

A **franchise** is a licensing arrangement under which one party (the **franchisor**) allows another party (the **franchisee**) to use its name, trademark, patents, copyrights, business methods, and other property in exchange for monetary payments and other considerations. Franchising has become a very popular way to operate a business. A 2008 study conducted by PricewaterhouseCoopers for the International Franchising Association (IFA) reported that more than 909,000 franchises operated in the United States, contributing more than $2.3 trillion in sales to the U.S. economy. According to this study, franchising now provides more jobs in the U.S. economy than either the durable manufacturing sector or the financial activities sector.[16]

The two most popular types of franchise arrangements are **distributorships** and **business format franchises**. In a distributorship, the franchisor makes a product and grants distributors a license to sell it. The most common example of this type of franchise is the arrangement between automakers and the dealerships that sell their cars. In a business format franchise, the franchisor grants the franchisee the right to both make *and* sell its good or service. Under this arrangement the franchisor usually provides a wide range of services to the franchisee, such as site selection, training, and help in obtaining financing, but also requires the franchisee to follow very specific guidelines while operating the business. You're no doubt very familiar with business format franchises; examples include Papa John's, Wendy's, Supercuts, Jiffy Lube, Jenny Craig, and Massage Envy.

Franchising in Today's Economy

Franchising is now a well-established method of operating a business—but that doesn't mean it's static. Let's look at some ways the world of franchising is changing.

One of the biggest trends in franchising for the past several years has been an expansion into foreign markets. Franchisors in a variety of industries have found that opportunities for franchise growth are greater in foreign countries because competition is less intense and markets are less saturated than in the United States. At the end of 2009, McDonald's had 12,510 franchise outlets in foreign countries (slightly more than it had in the United States), Subway had 6,484, and Curves had 2,714.[17] Of course, operating in foreign countries can pose special challenges. Differences in culture, language, laws, demographics, and economic development mean that franchisors, like other types of business owners, must adjust their business methods—and the specific products they offer—to meet the needs of foreign consumers.

Another notable trend has been the growth in the number of women franchisees. Reliable statistics on women in franchising are difficult to find, but the International Franchising Association (IFA) estimates that women now own about 30% of all franchises, and anecdotal evidence suggests that the trend toward more women-owned franchisees is continuing. A number of women, such as JoAnne Shaw (founder of the Coffee Beanery), Maxine Clark (founder of Build-A-Bear), and Linda Burzynski (owner and CEO of Liberty Fitness) also have become very successful franchisors. But, despite these highly visible success stories, the number of women franchisors hasn't grown nearly as fast as the number of women franchisees.[18]

Minority participation in franchises, both as franchisees and franchisors, has been relatively low. African Americans, Hispanics, Asian Americans, and Native Americans make up about a third of the population, and that share is expected to steadily grow over the next several decades. Yet according to C. Everett Wallace, a past chair of the IFA's Minorities in Franchising Committee, less than 10% of all franchisees are minorities. One of the main reasons for such low minority involvement in franchising is a lack of awareness of franchising opportunities within minority communities. But many franchisors are now making a strong effort to actively recruit minority franchisees.[19]

Two major initiatives have given the efforts to reach minority franchising a boost in recent years. The first, known as the National Minority Franchising Initiative (NMFI), was founded in 2000. The NMFI's website currently maintains a directory of over 500 franchisors who actively promote minority franchise ownership. The second initiative, called MinorityFran, was established in early 2006 by the IFA. This initiative has the cooperation of a variety of organizations interested in promoting minority business ownership, including the National Urban League, the Association of Small Business Development Centers, the U.S. Pan Asian American Chamber of Commerce, and the Minority Business Development Agency. Franchisors participating in the program receive information and marketing materials designed to help them reach potential minority franchisees more effectively. As of June 2009, MinorityFran had approximately 60 participating franchisors, including many of the largest in the United States. Many MinorityFran participants provide special incentives, such as reduced franchise fees or additional

training, to help minority franchisees get started.[20]

Advantages of Franchising

Both the franchisee and the franchisor must believe they'll benefit from the franchise arrangement; otherwise they wouldn't participate. The advantages of franchising for the franchisor are fairly obvious. It allows the franchisor to expand the business and bring in additional revenue (in the form of franchising fees and royalties) without investing its own capital. Also, franchisees—business owners who are motivated to earn a profit—may have a greater incentive than salaried managers to do whatever it takes to maximize the success of their outlets.

From the franchisee's perspective, franchising offers several advantages:

- **Less Risk:** Franchises offer access to a proven business system and product. The systems and methods offered by franchisors have an established track record. People who are interested in buying a franchise can do research to see how stores in the franchise have performed and can talk to existing franchisees before investing.

- **Training and Support:** The franchisor normally provides the franchisee with extensive training and support. For example, Subway offers two weeks of training at its headquarters and additional training at meetings. The franchisor also sends out newsletters, provides Internet support, maintains a toll-free number for phone support, and provides on-site evaluations.[21]

- **Brand Recognition:** Operating a franchise gives the franchisee instant brand-name recognition, which can be a big help in attracting customers.

- **Easier Access to Funding:** Bankers and other lenders may be more willing to loan you money if your business is part of an established franchise than a new, unproven business.

Disadvantages of Franchising

Franchising also has some drawbacks. From the franchisor's perspective, operating a business with perhaps thousands of semi-independent owner–operators can be complex and challenging. With such a large number of owners it can be difficult to keep all of the franchisees satisfied, and disappointed franchisees sometimes go public with their complaints, damaging the reputation of the franchisor. In fact, it isn't unusual for disgruntled franchisees to sue their franchisors.

Franchisees are also likely to find some disadvantages:

- **Costs:** The typical franchise agreement requires franchisees to pay an initial franchise fee when they enter into the franchise agreement and an ongoing royalty (usually a percentage of monthly sales revenues) to the franchisor. In addition, the franchisor may assess other fees to support national advertising campaigns or for other purposes. These costs vary considerably, but for high-profile franchises, they can be substantial. Exhibit 6.5 compares the franchise fees, royalties, and total investment for several well-established franchises. (Total investment reflects the fact that the cost of starting a franchise generally requires the franchisee to invest in property, equipment, and inventory in addition to paying the franchise fee.)

- **Lack of Control:** The franchise agreement usually requires the franchisee to follow the franchisor's procedures to the letter. People who want the freedom and flexibility to be their own boss can find these restrictions frustrating.

- **Negative Halo Effect:** The irresponsible or incompetent behavior of a few franchisees can create a negative perception that adversely affects not only the franchise as a whole but also the success of other franchisees.

EXHIBIT 6.5 Franchisee Costs for Selected Franchises[22]

Franchise	Type of Business	Franchise Fee	Royalty*	Estimated Minimum Total Investment
McDonald's	Fast food	$45,000	12.5%	$995,900
Jiffy Lube	Automobile maintenance	$35,000	4%	$229,000
Jenny Craig	Weight loss	$25,000	7%	$169,600
Papa John's	Pizza delivery	$25,000	5%	$113,823
Supercuts	Hair styling	$22,500	6%	$111,000
Merle Norman	Cosmetics and skin care	$0	0%	$33,300
Anytime Fitness	Health club	$10,999 to $17,999	$419/mo.	$33,074
Coffee News	Local newsletters	$8,000	$75/wk.	$8,925

*Royalty is expressed as a percentage of gross revenues unless otherwise specified.

- **Growth Challenges:** While growth and expansion are definitely possible in franchising (many franchisees own multiple outlets), strings are attached. Franchise agreements usually limit the franchisee's territory and require franchisor approval before expanding into other areas.

- **Restrictions on Sale:** Franchise agreements normally prevent franchisees from selling their franchises to other investors without prior approval from the franchisor.

- **Poor Execution:** Not all franchisors live up to their promises. Sometimes the training and support are of poor quality, and sometimes

© ANTHONY BLAKE PHOTO LIBRARY/PHOTOLIBRARY

Some Franchisees Are Quite Happy When They Don't Earn a Profit

While most franchisees are out to make a profit, a small but growing number of nonprofit organizations such as CenterForce (a provider of services to people with developmental disabilities), Common Ground (a provider of shelter for the homeless), and the Chicago Children's Choir have turned to franchising as a new way to raise funds. Everybody seems to win from this arrangement:

- Many customers like doing business with nonprofit franchisees; they get a well-known product while supporting a worthy cause.
- Franchisors view their arrangements with nonprofit franchisees as a good way to meet their social responsibilities and build goodwill within local communities.
- The nonprofits gain access to a business with proven products and methods. This can boost their fundraising efforts at a time when funds from more traditional sources are no longer growing fast enough to keep up with needs. In addition, some nonprofit youth organizations have found that operating a franchise allows them to offer employment opportunities to the teenagers they serve.

Several well-known franchisors, including Krispy Kreme, ServiceMaster, Maggie Moo's, AIM Mail Centers, and Popeye's have entered into arrangements with nonprofit franchisees in recent years. But Ben & Jerry's has taken the most proactive approach, establishing a special program called PartnerShops to help nonprofits get started in franchising. The company has even taken its efforts global, opening up a Ben & Jerry's PartnerShop with the Cresco Trust (an organization serving disadvantaged youth) in Northern Ireland.[23]

the company does a poor job of screening franchisees, leading to the negative halo effect we mentioned previously.

These considerations suggest that before buying a franchise, potential owners should carefully research the franchise opportunity.

> ## It's not hard to meet expenses. They're everywhere.
> *Anonymous franchisee*

Entering into a Franchise Agreement

To obtain a franchise, the franchisee must sign a **franchise agreement**. This agreement is a legally binding contract that specifies the relationship between the franchisor and the franchisee in great detail. There's no standard form for the contract, but some of the key items normally covered include:

- **Terms and Conditions:** The franchisee's rights to use the franchisor's trademarks, patents, and signage, and any restrictions on those rights. It also covers how long the agreement will last and under what terms (and at what cost) it can be renewed.

- **Fees and Other Payments:** The fees the franchisee must pay for the right to use the franchisor's products and methods, and when these payments are due.

- **Training and Support:** The types of training and support the franchisor will provide to the franchisee.

- **Specific Operational Requirements:** The methods and standards established by the franchisor that the franchisee is required to follow.

- **Conflict Resolution:** How the franchisor and franchisee will handle disputes.

- **Assigned Territory:** The geographic area in which the franchisee will operate and whether the franchisee has exclusive rights in that area.

It's vital for anyone thinking about entering into a franchise agreement to know all the facts before signing on the dotted line. Fortunately, the Federal Trade Commission (FTC) requires franchisors to provide potential franchisees with a document known as a **Franchise Disclosure Document (FDD)**. This long, complex document (covering 23 separate major topics and sometimes running well over 100 pages) can be an invaluable source of information about virtually every aspect of the franchise arrangement. For example, the FDD must provide contact information for at least 100 current franchisees. (If the franchisor has fewer than 100 current franchisees it must list all of them.) This gives a potential franchisee the ability to contact other franchisees and ask them about their experiences with the franchisor. As an added bonus, the FTC requires the FDD to be written in "plain English" rather than in the complex legal jargon that often characterizes such documents. This rule means you actually have a chance to understand what you're reading![24]

Under FTC rules, the franchisor must give the franchisee at least 14 calendar days to review the FDD before the franchise agreement can be signed. A careful study of the FDD can go a long way toward ensuring that the franchisee makes an informed decision. Even though the FDD is written in "plain English," it's a good idea to have a lawyer who is knowledgeable about franchise law review it. You'll have to pay for any legal advice, but entering into a bad franchise agreement can be a lot more expensive (and stressful) than a lawyer's fees.

The Big Picture

In this chapter we've discussed the forms of business ownership. Each form of ownership offers advantages and drawbacks. One of the most interesting developments in recent years has been the evolution of limited liability companies from a business novelty in the early 1990s to one of the most popular forms of ownership by the early part of the 21st century.

Many Americans view business ownership as a means of achieving both personal satisfaction and financial success. In fact, millions of Americans have chosen to pursue those goals by starting (or buying) and operating their own small business, most commonly in the form of a sole proprietorship.

But starting and running a small business require specific talents and an entrepreneurial spirit that not everyone possesses. Another way to participate in business ownership and pursue financial goals is to buy stock in a publicly traded corporation. Corporate stock has proven a popular investment for many people—and over the long term, stock ownership often provides attractive financial returns. But as recent events suggest, investing in the stock market isn't for the faint of heart.

WHAT ELSE? *RIP & REVIEW* **CARDS IN THE BACK**

franchise agreement The contractual arrangement between a franchisor and franchisee that spells out the duties and responsibilities of both parties.

Franchise Disclosure Document (FDD) A detailed description of all aspects of a franchise that the franchisor must provide to the franchisee at least 14 calendar days before the franchise agreement is signed.

SMALL BUSINESS AND ENTREPRENEURSHIP: ECONOMIC ROCKET FUEL

LEARNING OBJECTIVES

After studying this chapter, you will be able to...

LO1 Explain the key reasons to launch a small business

LO2 Describe the typical entrepreneurial mindset and characteristics

LO3 Discuss funding options for small business

LO4 Analyze the opportunities and threats that small businesses face

LO5 Discuss ways to become a new business owner and tools to facilitate success

LO6 Explain the size, scope, and economic contributions of small business

{ **Do what you love. This way, whether you make money at it or not, at least you're enjoying yourself.** }

Guy Kawasaki, venture capitalist

LO1 Launching a New Venture: What's in It for Me?

Over time, the entrepreneurship rate has played a powerful, positive role in the U.S. economy. Despite the raging recession, new business creation increased steadily from 2007 to 2009. Among teenagers, interest in someday launching their own business fell from 60% to 50% in 2009—a significant drop, likely due to the recession. In 2009, overall U.S. entrepreneurship rates reached their highest level in 14 years, driven in part by unemployed workers looking to stay afloat as they seek new jobs, representing a hopeful sign for the future of our economy, as job seekers become potential job creators.[1]

Make no mistake: starting a new business can be tough—very tough. Yet for the right person, the advantages of business ownership far outweigh the risk and hard work. Although people start their own ventures for a variety of reasons, most are seeking some combination of greater financial success, independence, flexibility, and challenge. Others are simply seeking survival.[2]

Greater Financial Success

Although you can make a pretty good living working for someone else, your chances of getting really rich may be higher if you start your own business. The *Forbes* magazine annual list of the 400 richest Americans is dominated by **entrepreneurs**, such as Bill Gates and Paul Allen (founders of Microsoft), Phil Knight (founder of Nike), Michael Dell (founder of Dell Inc.), and Sergey Brin and Larry Page (founders of Google). And many people feel that their chances of even moderate financial success are higher if they're working for themselves rather than someone else. The opportunity to make more money is a primary motivator for many entrepreneurs, although other factors clearly play a role as well.[3]

Independence

Being your own boss is a huge benefit of starting your own business. You answer to no one other than yourself and any investors that you invite to participate in your business. Bottom line: you are the only one who is ultimately responsible for your success or failure. This setup is especially compelling for people who have trouble being subordinates because of their personalities (and we probably all know someone who fits that description!). But while independence is nice, it's important to keep in mind that every business depends on meeting the needs of its customers, who can be even more demanding than the toughest boss.

{ **Business opportunities are like buses... there's always another one coming.** }

Richard Branson, founder, Virgin Enterprise

Flexibility

The ability to set your own hours and control your own schedule is a hugely appealing benefit for many business owners, especially parents seeking more time with their kids or retirees looking for extra income. Given current technological tools—from email to eBay—it's easy for small business owners to manage their firms on the go or after hours. Of course, there's often a correlation between hours worked and dollars earned (it's rare to work less and earn more). But when more money isn't the primary goal, the need for flexibility can be enough to motivate many entrepreneurs to launch their own enterprise.

Challenge

Running your own business provides a level of challenge unmatched by many other endeavors. Most business owners—especially new business owners—never find themselves bored! Starting a business also offers endless opportunities for learning that can provide more profound satisfaction for many people than grinding out the hours as an employee.

Survival

Although most entrepreneurs launch their business in response to an opportunity with hopes of improving their lives, some entrepreneurs—called "necessity entrepreneurs"—launch their business because they believe it is their *only* economic option. Necessity entrepreneurs range from middle-aged workers laid off from corporate jobs, to new immigrants with limited English and heavy accents, to those who experience discrimination in the standard workplace. For each of these types of people, small business ownership can be the right choice in the face of few other alternatives.

LO2 The Entrepreneur: A Distinctive Profile

Successful entrepreneurs tend to stand out from the crowd in terms of both their mindset and their personal characteristics. As you read this section, consider whether you fit the entrepreneurial profile.

The Entrepreneurial Mindset: A Matter of Attitude

Almost every entrepreneur starts as a small businessperson—either launching a firm or buying a firm—but not every small businessperson starts as an entrepreneur. The difference is a matter of attitude. From day one, a true entrepreneur—such as Sam Walton of Walmart, Steve Jobs of Apple, or Jeff Bezos of Amazon—aims to change the world through blockbuster goods or services. That isn't the case for all small-business owners. Most people who launch new firms expect to better themselves, but they don't expect huge, transformative growth; in fact, nearly 70% of small business owners say they don't want to grow any larger.[4]

However, classic entrepreneurs who deliver on the promise of their best ideas can dramatically change the economic and social landscape worldwide. Examples of business owners who thought and delivered big include Henry Ford, founder of the Ford Motor Company and originator of assembly line production; Walt Disney, founder of The Walt Disney Company and creator of Mickey Mouse; Bill Gates, founder of Microsoft; Mary Kay Ash, founder of a cosmetics powerhouse; Martha Stewart, lifestyle innovator for the masses; George Lucas, creator of the *Star Wars* empire; Pierre Omidyar, founder of eBay; and Oprah Winfrey, media mogul.

> **Oprah Winfrey is the most inspirational entrepreneur to American women, and Donald Trump is the most inspirational entrepreneur to American men.**
> *USA Today*

Entrepreneurial Characteristics

While experts sometimes disagree about the specific characteristics of successful entrepreneurs, virtually all include vision, self-reliance, energy, confidence, tolerance of uncertainty, and tolerance of failure. (See Exhibit 7.1.) Most successful entrepreneurs have all of these qualities and more, but they come in a huge variety of combinations that highlight the complexity of personality: there is no one successful entrepreneurial profile.

Vision Most entrepreneurs are wildly excited about their own new ideas, which many seem to draw from

EXHIBIT 7.1 Entrepreneurial Characteristics

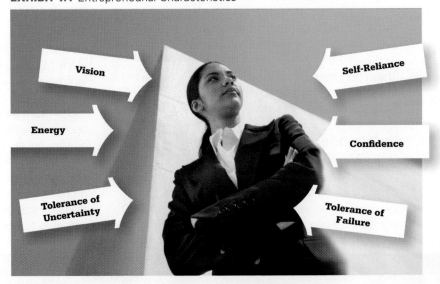

Vision · Self-Reliance · Energy · Confidence · Tolerance of Uncertainty · Tolerance of Failure

a bottomless well. Entrepreneurs find new solutions to old problems, and they develop new products that we didn't even know we needed until we had them. And entrepreneurs stay excited about their ideas, even when friends and relatives threaten to call the loony bin. For instance, Fred Smith, founder of the FedEx empire, traces the concept for his business to a term paper he wrote at Yale, which supposedly received a C from a skeptical professor. But that didn't stop him from creating a business logistics system that transformed the industry.

Self-Reliance As an entrepreneur, the buck stops with you. New business owners typically need to do everything themselves, from getting permits, to motivating employees, to keeping the books—all in addition to producing the product or service that made them start the business in the first place. Self-reliance seems to come with an **internal locus of control**, or a deep-seated sense that the individual is personally responsible for what happens in his or her life. When things go well, people with an internal locus of control feel that their efforts have been validated, and when things go poorly, those same people feel that they need to do better next time. This sense of

responsibility encourages positive action. In contrast, people with an **external locus of control** rely less on their own efforts, feeling buffeted by forces such as random luck and the actions of others, which they believe will ultimately control their fate.

Energy Entrepreneurs simply can't succeed without an enormous amount of energy. Six or seven 12-hour workdays are not atypical in the start-up phase of running a business. A survey by the Wells Fargo/Gallup Small Business Index found that today's small-business owner works an average of 52 hours per week, with 57% working at least six days a week, and more than 20% working all seven. Even a day off isn't *really* off—Discover Financial Services learned that only 36% of small business owners describe a day off as

internal locus of control A deep-seated sense that the individual is personally responsible for what happens in his or her life.

external locus of control A deep-seated sense that forces other than the individual are responsible for what happens in his or her life.

Your Entrepreneurial IQ

Entrepreneur.com, a leading website for growing businesses, developed a new way to gauge your entrepreneurial readiness. Take this quiz, and see where you land:

1. I am…
   a) …an only child
   b) …a younger sibling
   c) …an older sibling
   d) …part of the Brady Bunch

2. "I watch a lot of mindless TV"
   a) True
   b) False

3. If I start my own business, I should expect…
   a) …to work around the clock tirelessly, until the nice men in the white coats come to get me.
   b) …not work around the clock. All work and no play makes Jack and Jill a dull couple, you know?

4. Your chances of succeeding in business are better if…
   a) …you've taken business classes in college
   b) …you haven't

5. I'm usually convinced that…
   a) …the glass is half full

   b) …the glass is going to fall off the table, break, cut me and send me to the emergency room, where I'll have to deal with my HMO.

Scoring:
1. Whatever you circled, give yourself 10 points. As long as you don't wind up trashing your family on *The Jerry Springer Show*, it really doesn't matter whether you're an only child or one of a crowd.

2. The best entrepreneurs get their inspiration anytime, anywhere; their minds are always working. If you said "true," give yourself 10 points. If you said "false," subtract 37 points for either lying or being out of touch with the rest of America.

3. Anything worth anything is a struggle to achieve. If you picked "a," give yourself 10 more points. If you picked "b," give yourself 5.

4. Education never hurt anyone. If you

circled "a," give yourself 10 points. But since plenty of people succeed without an education, give yourself 9 if you circled "b."

5. If you're going to start your own business, you've got to have a positive attitude. If you circled "a," give yourself 10 points. If you marked "b," subtract 42.

Meaning:

High score of 50 points: Congratulations! You have what it takes to be a successful entrepreneur. Go start your business with our blessings.

Low score of negative 57 points: What, you're going to let a silly quiz tell you how to run your life? Start your business anyway. And have a blast! But don't forget to have a Plan B.[5]

completely work free, versus 58% of the rest of working Americans. But small business owners seem to find the grind worthwhile: 47% of small business owners said that if they won $10 million in the lottery, they would still work in their current job. Only 9% would stop working, and 8% would combine work, volunteering, and other areas of interest.[6]

Confidence Successful entrepreneurs typically have confidence in their own ability to achieve, and their confidence encourages them to act boldly. But too much confidence has a downside. Entrepreneurs must take care not to confuse likelihood with reality. In fact, many could benefit from the old adage "Hope for the best and plan for the worst." A study for the Small Business Administration Office of Advocacy confirmed that entrepreneurs are typically overconfident regarding their own abilities. As a result they're sometimes willing to plunge into a new business, but they don't always have the skills to succeed.[7]

Tolerance of Uncertainty More often than others, entrepreneurs see the world in shades of gray, rather than simply black and white. They tend to embrace uncertainty in the business environment, turning it to their advantage rather than shying away. Uncertainty also relates to risk, and successful entrepreneurs tend to more willingly accept risk—financial risk, for instance, such as mortgaging their home for the business, and professional risk, such as staking their reputation on the success of an unproven product.

Tolerance of Failure Even when they fail, entrepreneurs seldom label themselves losers. They tend to view failure as a chance to learn, rather than as a sign that they just can't do it (whatever "it" may be for them at any given moment). Interestingly, Isaac Fleischmann, director of the U.S. Patent Office for 36 years, pointed out that "During times of economic decline when unemployment increases, so does the number of patents. Dark days often force us to become more ingenious, to monitor and modify the ways we reached failure and reshape them into a new pattern of success." Failure can actually be an effective springboard for achievement.[9]

LO3 Finding the Money: Funding Options for Small Businesses

For many entrepreneurs, finding the money to fund their business is the top challenge of their start-up year. The vast majority of new firms are funded with the personal resources of their founder. In fact, 94% of companies on the "Inc. 500 List" of fastest-growing firms raised start-up funds from personal accounts, family, and friends. Other key funding sources include bank loans, angel investors, and venture capital firms.[10]

Personal Resources

While the idea of using just your own money to open a business sounds great, the financial requirements of most new firms typically force entrepreneurs to also tap personal resources such as family, friends, and credit cards. If you do borrow from family or friends, virtually every small business expert recommends that you keep the relationship as professional as possible. If the business fails, a professional agreement can preserve personal ties. And if the business succeeds, you'll need top-quality documentation of financing from family and friends to get larger-scale backing from outside sources.

Personal credit cards can be an especially handy—though highly risky—financing resource. In fact, a recent survey found that nearly half of all start-ups are funded with plastic. (It's no wonder, given that those

© DANNY MOLOSHOK/REUTERS/LANDOV

Roach Coaches Minus the Roaches

When most people think of lunch trucks, unappetizing images, such as limp French fries, greasy mystery meat, and scuttling cockroaches may jump to mind. But the roach coaches of yesterday may soon go the way of rotary phones and VHS tapes. Lunch trucks today have gone way upscale, a good number featuring high end ethnic fusion food, such as Korean/Mexican tacos, or gourmet desserts, such as crème brulee, or even green options, such as "sustainability harvested" fish tacos, and locally grown pizza toppings. Today's big city food truck owners tend to be tech-savvy entrepreneurs, building loyal customers via social media, and alerting followers about their whereabouts via Twitter. The famed Kogi BBQ truck in Los Angeles, for instance, has 28,000 active Twitter followers, and attributes 70% of its sales directly to social media. Building a successful lunch truck business is no easy task, but high-end food trucks are transforming the restaurant business, particularly in large cities.[8]

solicitations just keep on coming.) Credit cards do provide fast, flexible money, but watch out—if you don't pay back your card company fast, you'll find yourself socked with financing fees that can take years to pay off.[11]

Loans

Getting commercial loans for a new venture can be tough. Banks and other lenders are understandably hesitant to fund a business that doesn't have a track record. And when they do, they require a lot of paperwork and often a fairly long waiting period. Given these hurdles, only 20% of new business owners launch with commercial loans. And virtually no conventional lending source—private or government—will lend 100% of the start-up dollars for a new business. Most require that the entrepreneur provide a minimum of 25 to 30% of total start-up costs from personal resources.[12]

Another source for loans may be the U.S. Small Business Administration (SBA). The SBA doesn't give free money to start-up businesses—neither grants nor interest-free loans—but they do partially guarantee loans from local commercial lenders. This reduces risk for the lender, who is, in turn, more likely to lend money to a new business owner. The SBA also has a microloan program that lends small amounts of money—$13,000 on average—to start-up businesses through community nonprofit organizations.[13]

Angel Investors

Angel investors aren't as saintly—or as flighty—as they sound. Angels are wealthy individuals who invest in promising start-up companies for one basic reason: to make money for themselves. According to Jeffrey Sohl, director of the Center for Venture Research, angels look for companies that seem likely to grow at 30 to 40% per year and will then either be bought or go public. He estimates that 10 to 15% of private companies fit that description, but points out that finding those firms isn't easy. It doesn't help, he says, that "80% of entrepreneurs think they're in that 10 to 15%." The economic crisis has had a punishing impact on angel investing. Half of the investors surveyed in November 2008 by the Angel Capital Association, the industry's trade group, said they invested less than they had predicted in 2008. In 2009, angel investments decreased 8.3% versus 2008, while the average deal size declined 11.1%, suggesting a more cautious approach to angel investing in an uncertain economic climate.[14]

Venture Capital

Venture capital firms fund high-potential new companies in exchange for a share of ownership, which can sometimes be as high as 60%. These deals tend to be quite visible, but keep in mind that only a tiny fraction of new businesses receive any venture capital money. The economic crisis has drastically reduced venture

funding, and the advice and guidance that come with the dollars can be quite significant. David Barger, chief executive officer of jetBlue Airways, remembers that he and jetBlue's founder, David Neeleman, originally planned to call the airline Taxi and to fly bright yellow planes. But an influential venture capitalist changed their minds. He called them into his office and said, "If you call this airline Taxi, we're not going to invest." The name changed, and the venture capitalist stayed.[15]

The economic crisis has drastically reduced venture capital spending. In the fourth quarter of 2008, as the economy began to shudder, venture capital investments dropped 33% versus fourth quarter 2007, and annual venture investments dropped 8% in 2008 overall. But the environment was a bright spot: dollars invested in the clean technology sector grew more than 50% in 2008. In 2009, total venture spending decreased 37% versus 2008; venture spending on clean technology such as alternative energy and pollution reduction was $1.9 billion in 2009, well below the $4 billion investment in 2008.[16]

LO4 Opportunities and Threats for Small Business: A Two-Sided Coin

Most small businesses enjoy a number of advantages as they compete for customers. But they also must defuse a range of daunting potential threats in order to succeed over the long term.

Small Business Opportunities

Small businesses enjoy a real competitive edge across a range of different areas. Because of their size, many small firms can exploit narrow but profitable market niches, offer personal customer service, and maintain lower overhead costs. And due to advances in technology, small firms can compete more effectively than ever in both global and domestic markets.

Market Niches Many small firms are uniquely positioned to exploit small but profitable **market niches**. These sparsely occupied spaces in the market tend to have fewer competitors because they simply aren't big enough—or enough high-profile—for large firms. They nonetheless offer more than enough potential for small, specialized companies. For example, Kazoo & Company, a relatively small toy store, competes effectively with Walmart, Target, and Kmart by stocking different—and complementary—products, deliberately zigging when the big players zag.[17]

Personal Customer Service With a smaller customer base, small firms can develop much more personal relationships with individual customers. Shel Weinstein, for instance, former owner of a Los Angeles corner pharmacy, knew his customers so well that they would call him at home in the middle of the night for help with medical emergencies. The personal touch can be especially beneficial in some foreign markets, where clients prize the chance to deal directly with top management.

Lower Overhead Costs With entrepreneurs wearing so many hats, from CEO to customer service rep, many small firms have lower overhead costs. They can hire fewer managers and fewer specialized employees. Perhaps more importantly, smaller firms—due to a lack of resources—tend to work around costs with tactics such as establishing headquarters in the owner's garage or offering employees flexible schedules instead of costly healthcare benefits.

Technology The Internet has played a powerful role in opening new opportunities for small businesses. Using a wealth of online tools, from eBay to eMachineshop, companies-of-one can create, sell, publish, and even manufacture goods and services more easily than ever before. The Internet has also created international opportunities, transforming small businesses into global marketers. The London-based Anything Left-Handed retail store, for instance, evolved into an award-winning global wholesaler of left-handed items within a year of launching its website. Founder Keith Milsom comments "our website has allowed us to communicate with potential customers and market our business worldwide at very little cost, making international development possible."[18]

> **More than 50% of Americans trust small business owners to guide the economy compared with less than 15% who trust members of Congress.**
> *Washington Post*

Small Business Threats

While small businesses do enjoy some advantages, they also face intimidating obstacles, from a high risk of failure to too much regulation.

High Risk of Failure Starting a new business involves risk—a lot of risk—but the odds improve significantly if you make it past the crucial 4-year mark. Check out the 7-year survival rate in Exhibit 7.2. Notice that it declines much more slowly after Year 4.

© SPIDERSTOCK/ISTOCKPHOTO.COM

Taking Stock and Stepping Up

For several decades, women have been launching new businesses at twice the rate of men, and their growth rates have outpaced the economy, yet women-owned businesses are still small compared to businesses owned by men – as of 2008, the average sales of women-owned businesses were still only 27% of those of men. So what holds these women back? According to Sharon Hadary, who has studied this issue for decades, and writes about it for *The Wall Street Journal*, the problem seems to be twofold: 1) many woman business owners hold themselves back through self-limiting thinking, and 2) many woman business owners are held back by "the stereotypes, perceptions and expectations of business and government leaders." Research shows that the only statistically significant predictor of business growth is the entrepreneur's goals for growth. Men tend to start businesses to be their own boss and to grow the business as large as possible. Women tend to start businesses to be personally challenged and to integrate work and family, and they want to stay small enough to personally oversee all aspects of the business. Women also tend to enter industries such as retail and personal services, which have lower cost of entry and less growth potential. Compounding these issues, many women lack the resources for expansion, in part because they avoid debt as a "bad thing," neglect to build relationships with bankers, and don't believe that they would receive significant credit even if they did apply, so many don't even bother to apply. To close the success-rate gap between men and women business owners, Ms. Hadary recommends that women business owners think BIG from the earliest stages of the enterprise, and think even BIGGER as the enterprise begins to grow. Ms. Hadary also stresses the importance of women learning from women about the specifics of getting the job done. She also emphasizes the critical role of networking. Aspiring women entrepreneurs who follow these recommendations today may well become tomorrow's blockbuster success stories.[18a]

EXHIBIT 7.2 New Business Survival Rates[19]

Year in Business	Survival Rate	Change vs. Prior Year (percentage points)
Year 1	81%	–19
Year 2	66%	–15
Year 3	54%	–12
Year 4	44%	–10
Year 5	38%	–6
Year 6	34%	–4
Year 7	31%	–3

Even though these numbers may look daunting, it's important to remember that owners shut down their businesses for many reasons other than the failure of the firm itself. The possibilities include poor health, divorce, better opportunities elsewhere, and interestingly, an unwillingness to make the enormous time commitment of running a business. Small business expert David Birch jokingly calls this last reason—which is remarkably common—the "I had no idea!" syndrome. It highlights the importance of anticipating what you're in for *before* you open your doors.[20]

Lack of Knowledge and Experience People typically launch businesses because they either have expertise in a particular area—like designing websites or cooking Vietnamese food—or because they have a breakthrough idea—like a new way to develop computer chips or run an airline. But in-depth knowledge in a specific area doesn't necessarily mean expertise in running a business. Successful business owners must know everything from finance to human resources to marketing.

Too Little Money The media is filled with stories of business owners who made it on a shoestring, but lack of start-up money is a major issue for most new firms. Ongoing profits don't usually begin for a while, which means that entrepreneurs must plan on some lean months—or even years—as the business develops momentum. That means a real need to manage money wisely and to resist the temptation to invest in fixed assets, such as fancy offices and advanced electronics, before sufficient regular income warrants it. It also requires the nerve to stay the course despite initial losses.[22]

Bigger Regulatory Burden Complying with federal regulations can be challenging for any business, but it can be downright overwhelming for small firms. A study sponsored by the federal government shows that firms with fewer than 20 employees spend an average of $7,647 per employee abiding by federal regulations, compared with $5,282 spent by firms with more than 500 employees. The overall burden is 45% greater for small business than for its larger business counterparts. But relief may be on the way: in mid-2008, Congress began to examine ways to reduce the growing regulatory burden on small businesses—an urgent need in the face of the struggling economy.[23]

Higher Health Insurance Costs Administrative costs for small health plans are much higher than for large businesses, making it even tougher for small firms to offer coverage to their employees. Given skyrocketing healthcare costs in general, the best employees are likely to demand a great insurance plan, putting small business at a real disadvantage in terms of building a competitive workforce.[24] But this may change as healthcare reform goes into effect over the next decade.

LO5 Launch Options: Reviewing the Pros and Cons

When you imagine starting a new business, the first thought that comes to mind would probably be the process of developing your own big idea from an abstract concept to a thriving enterprise. But that's not the only

© JUSTIN SULLIVAN/GETTY IMAGES

Failing with Style

A surprising number of 20th-century entrepreneurial stars experienced significant failure in their careers, yet bounced back to create wildly successful ventures. Early in his career, for instance, Walt Disney was fired from an ad agency (in hindsight, a rather foolish ad agency) for a "singular lack of drawing ability." Ray Kroc, the man who made McDonald's into a fast food empire, couldn't make a go of real estate, so he sold milkshake machines for much of his life. He was 52 years old, and in failing health, when he discovered the McDonald brothers' hamburger stand and transformed it into a fast food empire. And Steve Jobs, founder of Apple computer, found himself unceremoniously dumped by his board of directors less than ten years after introducing the world's first personal computer. After another decade, he returned in triumph, restoring Apple's polish with blockbuster new products such as the iMac and the iPod. So next time you fail, keep your eyes open for opportunity—your failure may be the first step of the next big thing.[21]

option. In fact, it may make more sense to purchase an established business, or even buy a franchise such as a Pizza Hut or Subway restaurant. Each choice, of course, involves pros and cons. The trick is finding the best fit for you: the combination that offers you the least harmful downsides and the most meaningful upsides. Broadly speaking, it's less risky to buy an established business or franchise, but it can be more satisfying to start from scratch. Exhibit 7.3 offers a more detailed overview of the pros and cons.

Making It Happen: Tools for Business Success

Whatever way you choose to become a small business owner, several strategies can help you succeed over the long term: gain experience in your field, learn from others, educate yourself, access **Small Business Administration (SBA)** resources, and develop a business plan.

Gain Experience Getting roughly three years of experience working for someone else in the field that interests you is a good rule of thumb. That way, you can learn what does and doesn't fly in your industry with relatively low personal risk (and you'd be making any mistakes on someone else's dime). You can also start developing a vibrant, relevant network before you need to ask for favors. But if you stay much longer than three years, you may get too comfortable to take the plunge and launch your own venture.

Learn from Others You should actively seek opportunities to learn from people who've succeeded in your field. If you don't know anyone personally, use your network to get introductions. And don't forget industry associations, local events, and other opportunities to build relationships. Also, remember that people who failed in your field may be able to give you valuable insights (why make the same mistakes they did?). As a bonus, they may be more willing to share their ideas and their gaffes if they're no longer struggling to develop a business of their own.

Educate Yourself The opportunities for entrepreneurial learning have exploded in the past decade. Many colleges and universities now offer full-blown entrepreneurship programs that help students both develop their plans and secure their initial funding. But education shouldn't stop there. Seek out relevant press

articles, workshops, websites, and blogs so that your ongoing education will continue to boost your career.

Access SBA Resources The SBA offers a number of resources beyond money (which we'll discuss in the next section). The SBA website, www.sba.gov, provides a wealth of information from industry-specific statistics, to general trends, to updates on small business regulations. The SBA also works hand in hand with individual

EXHIBIT 7.3 Pros and Cons of Starting a Business from Scratch versus Buying an Established Business

Starting Your Business from Scratch

Key Pros	Key Cons
It's all *you*. Your concept, your decisions, your structure, and so on.	It's all *you*. That's a lot of pressure.
You don't have to deal with the prior owner's bad decisions.	It takes time, money, and sheer sweat equity to build a customer base.
	Without a track record, it's harder to get credit from both lenders and suppliers.
	From securing permits to hiring employees, the logistics of starting a business can be challenging.

Buying an Established Business

Key Pros	Key Cons
The concept, organizational structure, and operating practices are already in place.	Working with someone else's idea can be a lot less fun for some entrepreneurs.
Relationships with customers, suppliers, and other stakeholders are established.	You may inherit old mistakes that can range from poor employee relations to pending lawsuits.
Getting financing and credit is less challenging.	

Buying a Franchise

Key Pros	Key Cons
In most cases, you're buying your own piece of a well-known brand and proven way of doing business.	You have less opportunity for creativity since most agreements tie you to franchise requirements.
Typically, management expertise and consulting come with the franchise package.	If something goes wrong with the national brand (e.g., *E. coli* at a burger joint), your business will suffer, too.
Franchisers occasionally offer not just advice but also the financing that can make the purchase possible.	The initial purchase price can be steep, and that doesn't include the ongoing percent-of-sales royalty fee.[25]
These advantages add up to a very low 5% first-year failure rate.	

states to fund local **Small Business Development Centers (SBDCs)**. SBDCs provide a range of free services for small businesses from developing your concept, to consulting on your business plan, to helping with your loan applications. And the SBA supports **SCORE**, the Service Corps of Retired Executives at www.score .org. They provide free, comprehensive counseling for small businesses from qualified volunteers.

Develop a Business Plan Can a business succeed without a plan? Of course. Many do just fine by simply seizing opportunity as it arises and changing direction as needed. Some achieve significant growth without a plan. But a **business plan** does provide an invaluable way to keep you and your team focused on success. And it's absolutely crucial for obtaining outside funding, which is why many entrepreneurs write a business plan after they've used personal funding sources (such as savings, credit cards, and money from family and friends) to get themselves up and running. Even then, the plan may be continually in flux if the industry is rapidly changing.

An effective business plan, which is usually 25 to 50 pages long, takes about six months to write. While the specifics may change by industry, the basic elements of any business plan answer these core questions:

- What service or product does your business provide, and what needs does it fill?
- Who are the potential customers for your product or service, and why will they purchase it from you?
- How will you reach your potential customers?
- Where will you get the financial resources to start your business?
- When can you expect to achieve profitability?[26]

The final document should include all of the following information:

- Executive summary (two to three pages)
- Description of business (include both risks and opportunities)
- Marketing
- Competition (don't underestimate the challenge)
- Operating procedures
- Personnel
- Complete financial data and plan, including sources of start-up money (be realistic!)
- Appendix (be sure to include all your research on your industry)[27]

Check out the SBA business-planning site for more information on how to write your own business plan and for samples of actual business plans (http://www.sba.gov/smallbusinessplanner/index. html). Other excellent resources (among many) on the Internet include the sample business plan resource center (www.bplans.com/) and the business plan pages of AllBusiness .com (www.allbusiness.com/).

LO6 Small Business and the Economy: An Outsized Impact

The most successful entrepreneurs create goods and services that change the way people live. Many build blockbuster corporations that power the stock market and dominate pop culture through ubiquitous promotion. But small businesses—despite their lower profile—also play a vital role in the U.S. economy. Here are a few statistics from the U.S. Small Business Administration:

- In 2008, 99.9% of the 29,600,000 businesses in the United States had fewer than 500 employees.
- About three-quarters of those business owners—21,700,000 people, totaling about 7% of the population—ran their businesses without any employees.
- Yet these small businesses generate about half of the U.S. gross domestic product.
- Over the last 15 years, small businesses created 64% of the net new jobs in the United States.
- In total, small business provides jobs for about half of the nation's private workforce.[28]

> **Bill Gates, Steve Jobs, and Michael Dell built blockbuster firms without a college degree, but 57% of those who start a business in high income countries do have a college degree.**
> *Global Entrepreneurship Monitor*

Small Business Development Centers (SBDCs) Local offices—affiliated with the Small Business Administration—that provide comprehensive management assistance to current and prospective small business owners.

SCORE (Service Corps of Retired Executives) An organization—affiliated with the Small Business Administration—that provides free, comprehensive business counseling for small business owners from qualified volunteers.

business plan A formal document that describes a business concept, outlines core business objectives, and details strategies and timelines for achieving those objectives.

The statistics, of course, depend on the definition of small business. For research purposes, the SBA defines small business as companies with up to 500 employees, including the self-employed. But the SBA also points out that the meaning of small business differs across industries. To officially count as "small," the number of employees can range from less than 100 to 1,500, and the average revenue can range from $0.75 million to $28.5 million, depending on the type of business. But regardless of the specific definition, the fact is clear: small business is a big player in the U.S. economy.

Beyond the sheer value of the goods and services they generate, small businesses make a powerful contribution to the U.S. economy in terms of creating new jobs, fueling innovation, and vitalizing inner cities.

- Creating New Jobs: Small businesses with employees start up at a rate of more than 600,000 per year. Four years after they launch, 44% of those businesses—and many of the jobs they create—remain viable. In 2005 (the most recent year with data), small firms created 79% of the net new jobs in the economy, while large firms created only 21%. But while small businesses are quick to add new jobs, they're often the first to contract when times are tough; instability comes with the territory.[29]

- Fueling Innovation: Small businesses are much more likely to develop revolutionary new ideas. Small patenting firms produce about 13% more patents per employee than their large-firm counterparts, and those patents are twice as likely to be found among the top 1% of highest-impact patents. Small firms tend to be effective innovators for a number of reasons. Perhaps most importantly, their very reason for being often ties to a brand new idea. In the early years, they need innovation

in order to simply survive. And they often display a refreshing lack of bureaucracy that allows new thinking to take hold.[31]

- Vitalizing Inner Cities: New research shows that small businesses are the backbone of urban economies, finding opportunity in niches that may not be worthwhile for larger firms. Small business comprises more than 99% of inner-city business establishments. In addition to creating new jobs, these small businesses generate 80% of total employment in American inner cities, providing a springboard for economic development. [32]

Entrepreneurship Around the World

Research suggests that entrepreneurship has an economic impact in countries around the world. For the past decade, the Global Entrepreneurship Monitor (GEM) has measured the annual rate of new business start-ups across a range of countries across the globe, adding new nations each year. The 10th annual GEM study included 43 countries. The research for this study was conducted mostly in May and June of 2008—the global economic crisis loomed on the horizon, but had yet to hit with full force. Even so, respondents perceived an overall decline in opportunities to start a new business. Surprisingly, though, intentions to launch a business in the next three years did not decline as sharply as perceived opportunities. Possible reasons: 1) People who are afraid of losing their jobs might consider entrepreneurship more seriously. 2) Potential entrepreneurs may be highly optimistic about their own ability to cope. ("This crisis may be a problem for everyone else, but not for me.") 3) Potential

© ANDRESR/ISTOCKPHOTO.COM

Tempting Targets

Over the past decade, a growing number of big firms have turned their sights onto small business, eager to reap the potential profits. Google, a small firm itself not so long ago, was among the first to recognize that the customers of small commercial websites—because of their sheer numbers—add up to big business. Marissa Mayer, a vice president at Google, points out that small companies were the early purchasers of Google's innovative "sponsored link" advertising program. She credits small businesses—such as the one that bought a sponsored link tied to extreme ironing—with attracting their biggest clients to the program. Other major search sites, like Yahoo! and MSN, have followed Google's lead, transforming a critical mass of interactive advertising from in-your-face pop-ups to relevant text-only ads.

Countless other opportunities have stemmed from the rise of "minipreneurs," which Trendwatching.com defines as "an army" of individuals launching super-small-scale enterprises. Players include micro businesses, freelancers, side businesses, weekend entrepreneurs, Web-driven entrepreneurs, free agents, and more. Big business has rushed to serve these emerging customers with products and services that ease their way. JetBlue, for instance, helps small business owners meet face-to-face with partners, clients, and suppliers at a truly affordable price. FedEx makes it easy—and relatively cheap—for small business owners to send products around the world through their Kinko/FedEx centers. Even the 800-pound gorilla IBM actively targets small businesses with customized consulting services. As the sheer number of small businesses grows, big businesses will likely find brand-new ways to help them thrive.[30]

entrepreneurs may be planning to delay their launches until the end of the three-year period, assuming the economy will get back on a better track.

> In 15,000 single room factories, local entrepreneurs handle at least 80% of plastic recycling in Mumbai, India's largest city.
>
> *Time*

The current entrepreneurship rate varies dramatically from country to country, ranging from a high of 45.6% in Bolivia to a low of 4.4% in Russia. (See Exhibit 7.4 for the ten nations with the highest and lowest entrepreneurship rates.) The differences among countries seem to depend largely on three key factors: What is the national per-capita income? What will the entrepreneur need to give up (i.e., the opportunity costs)? How strongly do the national culture and political environment support business start-ups?

Per-Capita Income In low-income countries such as Bolivia and Angola, a high percentage of entrepreneurs start their own businesses because they simply have no other options. This contributes heavily to the startlingly high overall level of entrepreneurship. The rate of such "necessity entrepreneurship" declines in higher-income countries such as the United States and Japan, where entrepreneurs are more likely to strike out on their own in response to an opportunity that they spot in the marketplace.

Opportunity Costs Entrepreneurship rates are significantly lower in countries that provide a high level of employment protection (it's hard to get fired) and strong unemployment insurance (financial support if you do get fired). With these benefits in place, the sense of urgency regarding entrepreneurship tends to fall. The European Union provides a number of clear examples.

EXHIBIT 7.4 Entrepreneurship Rates[33]

Top Ten Entrepreneurship Rates		Bottom Ten Entrepreneurship Rates	
Country	Entrepreneurship rate	Country	Entrepreneurship rate
Bolivia	45.6%	Russia	4.4%
Colombia	36.7%	Belgium	5.3%
Peru	32.7%	Romania	5.9%
Argentina	29.6%	Germany	7.7%
Ecuador	28.1%	France	8.2%
Dominican Republic	27.9%	Denmark	8.4%
India	27.6%	Latvia	9.4%
Brazil	26.4%	South Africa	9.9%
Angola	26.0%	Israel	10.6%
Macedonia	24.8%	Turkey	10.7%

Cultural/Political Environment Extensive, complex regulations can hinder entrepreneurship by raising daunting barriers. And a lack of cultural support only compounds the problem. These factors certainly contribute to the relatively low entrepreneurship rates in much of the European Union and Japan. Entrepreneurs in more supportive nations such as the United States and New Zealand get a boost from limited regulation and strong governmental support. A thriving "cowboy culture" helps, too—standout individuals who break free of old ways attract attention and admiration in many of the countries with higher entrepreneurship rates.[34]

The Big Picture

Successful entrepreneurs need more than simply a great idea. Bringing that idea to market—and earning a profit in the process—requires deep knowledge of every area of business. Finding money, attracting customers, and absorbing risk are only some of the challenges. But for the right person, the payoff can be huge in terms of everything from financial success to scheduling flexibility. The key is finding something you love to do that offers value to others. While that doesn't guarantee success, building on a passion suggests that you'll at least enjoy the journey. Looking forward from the global economic crisis in 2009, entrepreneurship seems likely to become a way of life, either part-time or full-time, for a growing swath of the population. The ideal result would be a higher standard of living—and a higher quality of life—for business owners and their customers worldwide.

WHAT ELSE? *RIP & REVIEW* **CARDS IN THE BACK**

8

ACCOUNTING: DECISION MAKING BY THE NUMBERS

LEARNING OBJECTIVES

After studying this chapter, you will be able to...

LO1 Define accounting and explain how accounting information is used by a variety of stakeholders

LO2 Discuss the career opportunities open to accountants

LO3 Identify the goals of generally accepted accounting principles

LO4 Describe the key elements of the major financial statements

LO5 Describe the information provided in the independent auditor's report and endnotes to financial statements

LO6 Explain how managerial accounting can help managers with product costing, incremental analysis, and budgeting

Visit 4ltrpress at www.cengagebrain.com.

accounting A system for recognizing, organizing, analyzing, and reporting information about the financial transactions that affect an organization.

LO1 Accounting: Who Needs It?

Accounting is a system for recognizing, organizing, analyzing, and reporting information about the financial transactions that affect an organization. The goal of this system is to provide its users with relevant, timely information that allows them to make sound economic decisions.

Who uses the information that accounting provides? It's a long list; after all, everyone wants to make sound economic decisions. In fact, managers and other business stakeholders rely so heavily on accounting information that it's sometimes called the language of business. Key users of accounting information include:

- Managers: Marketing managers, for instance, need information about sales in various regions and for various product lines. Financial managers need up-to-date facts about debt, cash, inventory, and capital.

- Stockholders: As owners of the company, most stockholders have a keen interest in its financial performance, especially as indicated by the firm's financial statements. Has management generated a strong enough return on their investment?

- Employees: Strong financial performance would help employees make their case for nice pay raises and hefty bonuses. But if earnings drop—especially multiple times—layoffs might be in the offing, so many employees might decide to polish their résumés!

- Creditors: The late, great comedian Bob Hope once defined a bank as a place that would only lend you money if you could prove you didn't really need it. That's a bit of an exaggeration, but it is true that responsible bankers and other lenders will want to assess a firm's creditworthiness by looking at its accounting statements before granting a loan.

- Suppliers: Like bankers, companies that provide supplies want to know that the company can pay for the orders it places.

- Government agencies: Accurate accounting information is critical for meeting the reporting requirements of the Internal Revenue Service (IRS), the Securities and Exchange Commission, and other federal and state agencies.

A number of other groups—including the news media, competitors, and unions—might also have a real interest in a firm's accounting information—whether the firm wants them to have it or not! If you have any interest in managing, investing in, or working for a business, the ability to understand accounting information is extremely valuable.

LO2 The Accounting Profession: More Than Just Recording Transactions

Accounting is a popular major among business students. But many students who are just beginning their study of business don't really know much about the profession. What do accountants do, and what kind of education and training do they need to succeed? Let's take a look.[1]

> **Before becoming the most famous of ancient Chinese philosophers, Confucius worked as an accountant.**
> *ChinaCulture.org*

What Accountants Do

People unfamiliar with accounting sometimes think it's the same as bookkeeping. But even though the two are related, accounting involves more than bookkeeping. In general, bookkeeping covers the routine procedures involved in classifying and recording financial transactions. Accounting goes

© ANGEL HERRERO DE FRUTOS/ ISTOCKPHOTO.COM

beyond these functions to analyze and interpret the recorded information and to communicate findings to end users.

Today virtually all firms use computers and sophisticated accounting software to help perform the routine functions of accounting, such as those normally performed by bookkeepers. In fact, computers have given accountants the ability to store and retrieve data, manipulate it, and create meaningful reports much more quickly than they could with manual systems. So knowledge of how to work with computers is important to accountants. But the issues and problems accountants deal with still require a great deal of human insight and expertise. Computers haven't replaced accountants—they've just given them the ability to work more effectively.

Accounting is a broad field that encompasses many possible careers paths. Let's look at the duties and responsibilities of three types of accountants.

- **Management accountants**: Many accountants, known as management accountants (or private accountants), work within an organization, preparing reports and analyzing financial information specific to that organization. These accountants perform a wide variety of tasks, including the development of budgets, cost management, performance appraisal, and asset management. They often prepare reports for managers and financial statements for owners and other stakeholders. Most private accountants work within profit-seeking businesses; many, however, work for nonprofit organizations, such as charities, private schools, and churches. *Internal auditors* are private accountants who are responsible for verifying the accuracy of their organization's internal records and the validity of its accounting procedures. They can help a firm improve its performance by identifying areas where mismanagement, waste, and fraud may exist. The job market for internal auditors has been quite strong in recent years.

- **Public accountants**: Other accountants, called public accountants, provide a broad range of accounting and consulting services to clients on a fee basis. These clients may be individuals, corporations, nonprofit organizations, or government agencies. Typical services include income tax preparation, external auditing services, and consultation on a variety of accounting issues and problems. Public accountants often help new companies design their accounting systems and procedures and mature companies update and improve their accounting systems.

- **Government accountants**: As their name implies, government accountants work for a wide variety of government agencies at the local, state, and federal levels. Many of these accountants work to ensure that government agencies properly manage and account for the public funds they use. Others are employed by government regulatory agencies to audit the finances of private firms or individuals to ensure that government regulations are met and that all appropriate taxes are paid.

LO3 Financial Accounting: Intended for Those on the Outside Looking In

Financial accounting is the branch of accounting that addresses the needs of external stakeholders, including stockholders, creditors, and government regulators. These stakeholders are seldom interested in poring over detailed accounting information about the individual departments or divisions within a company. Instead, they're interested in the financial performance of the firm as a whole. They often want to know how a firm's financial performance has changed over a period of several years or to compare its results to those of other firms in the same industry. The major output of financial accounting is a set of financial statements designed to provide this broad type of information. We'll describe these statements in the next section.

Role of the Financial Standards Accounting Board

Imagine how confused and frustrated investors, creditors, and regulators would become if every firm could just make up its own financial accounting rules as it went along and change them whenever it wanted! To reduce

CPA or CSI? A Look at Accounting's Private Eyes

On March 12, 2009 Bernie Madoff was sentenced to 150 years in prison for perpetrating the biggest investment fraud in U.S. history. Madoff's scheme hit thousands of individual and institutional investors like a ton of bricks. Many charitable foundations and pension funds were devastated, as were the personal portfolios of many rich and famous (and supposedly sophisticated) individuals who trusted Madoff with their savings. How could $50 billion seemingly vanish? Where had it gone? Could any of it be recovered?

Law enforcement agencies, insurance companies, trial lawyers, and government regulatory agencies often turn to financial sleuths known as "forensic accountants" to follow the money trail in scandals such as the Madoff case. "I liken it to *CSI* or *Law and Order*," says Terry McCarthy, audit partner at Green & Seifter, in Syracuse, NY. "But instead of figuring out the trajectory of a bullet, you're trying to find out how a transaction occurred."

Like the forensic scientists on the television series *CSI*, forensic accountants often have impressive credentials. Many are Certified Public Accountants or Certified Fraud Examiners who also hold additional degrees in fields like law enforcement and criminal justice. They are mystery solvers who must use all of their skills to analyze financial transactions that often are intended to be misleading. "Forensic accountants untangle events and details that are tangled by design," says Barry Mukamal of Rachlin Cohen & Holtz, a forensic accounting practice in Miami.

Many forensic accountants work for private companies, but the federal government is also a major employer—the FBI alone has between 500 and 600 of these accounting specialists on its payroll. With billions of dollars lost to corporate fraud each year and with identity theft on the rise, it's not surprising that forensic accounting has been one of the fastest-growing occupations over the past few years. And there's no sign that employment prospects are going to slow down anytime soon. As Andrew Bernstein, a director of forensic services with Miami-based Berkowitz Dick Pollack & Brant puts it, "Fraud is a growth industry. There's never been a shortage of bad people doing bad things."[2]

AP IMAGES/KATHY WILLENS

confusion and provide external stakeholders with consistent and accurate financial statements, the accounting profession has adopted a set of **generally accepted accounting principles (GAAP)** that guide the practice of financial accounting. In the United States, the Securities and Exchange Commission (SEC) has the ultimate legal authority to set and enforce accounting standards. In practice, however, the SEC has delegated the responsibility for developing these rules to a private organization known as the **Financial Accounting Standards Board (FASB)**. This board consists of five members appointed by the Financial Accounting Foundation. Each member serves a five-year term and can be reappointed to serve one additional term. In order to preserve independence and impartiality, the members are required to sever all ties with any firms or institutions they served prior to joining the Board.

Through GAAP, the FASB aims to ensure that financial statements are:

- Relevant: They must contain information that helps the user understand the firm's financial performance and condition.

- Reliable: They must provide information that is objective, accurate, and verifiable.

- Consistent: They must provide financial statements based on the same core assumptions and procedures over time; if a firm introduces any significant changes in how it prepares its financial statements, GAAP requires it to clearly identify and describe these changes.

- Comparable: They must present accounting statements in a reasonably standardized way, allowing users to track the firm's financial performance over a period of years and compare its results with those for other firms.

The FASB faces a challenging task in setting these principles. Businesses of different sizes and in different industries vary considerably in the ways they operate. Accounting methods that work well for one firm are often inappropriate for another firm. Over the years, as the FASB has attempted to deal with a variety of special cases and complex situations, GAAP has evolved into what many observers view as a cumbersome and complex set of rules in serious need of an overhaul. In fact, in recent years the SEC itself has made a strong push to scrap the current GAAP framework and replace it with an entirely different system. Such a change would have far-reaching consequences for the practice of financial accounting in the United States.

generally accepted accounting principles (GAAP) A set of accounting standards that is used in the preparation of financial statements.

Financial Accounting Standards Board (FASB) The private board that establishes the generally accepted accounting principles used in the practice of financial accounting.

Ethics in Accounting

Even clear and well-established accounting principles won't result in accurate and reliable information if managers and accountants flaunt them. A series of accounting scandals rocked the American business world during the late 1990s and the first few years of the 21st century. Between October 2001 and July 2002, several large corporations—Enron, Tyco, WorldCom, and Adelphia, to name only a few—were implicated in major accounting scandals. In many cases these firms overstated earnings by billions of dollars or hid billions of dollars in debts. Once their accounting improprieties became known, most of these firms suffered severe financial difficulties. Some of the companies went bankrupt, leaving stockholders with worthless stock and employees without jobs or pension plans. Many of the CEOs and top financial officers for these companies ended up in jail.[3]

These scandals served as a wake-up call to the accounting profession that their ethical training and standards need major improvement. In the wake of the scandals, many state accounting boards passed new ethics-related requirements.

LO4 Financial Statements: Read All About Us

One of the major responsibilities of financial accounting is the preparation of three basic financial statements: the balance sheet, income statement, and statement of cash flows. Taken together, these financial statements provide external stakeholders with a broad picture of an organization's financial condition and its recent financial performance. Large corporations with publicly traded stock must send an annual report containing all three statements to all stockholders. They also must file quarterly and annual reports, including financial statements with the SEC. Let's take a look at the information each statement provides.

The Balance Sheet: What We Own and How We Got It

The **balance sheet** summarizes a firm's financial position at a specific point in time. Though the balance sheets of different firms vary in specifics, all of them are organized to reflect the most famous equation in all of accounting—so famous that it is usually referred to simply as the **accounting equation**:

$$\text{Assets} = \text{Liabilities} + \text{Owners' Equity}$$

Exhibit 8.1 shows a simplified balance sheet for Bigbux, a hypothetical company we'll use to illustrate the information provided by financial statements. As you look over this exhibit, keep in mind that real-world balance sheets may include additional accounts and that different firms sometimes use different names for the same type of account. Despite these differences, Exhibit 8.1 should help you understand the basic

Will Going Global Zap GAAP?

Are GAAP's days numbered? These venerable U.S. accounting standards now face some stiff competition from a set of rules known as the International Financial Reporting Standards (IFRS). Many nations in Europe and Asia have already adopted the IFRS, and the United States may soon follow suit. In February 2010 the SEC announced a timeline that could require U.S. firms to switch from GAAP to IFRS in 2015. But in making the announcement, the SEC admitted that a switch to IFRS would be challenging and complex, so it left open the possibility that it might delay the timeline—or perhaps scrap it altogether.

Despite its less than definitive endorsement, the SEC clearly views the potential adoption of IFRS as a major development. As SEC Chief Accountant Jim Kroeker put it, "The decision to incorporate IFRS into our financial reporting system would be, to say the least, highly significant."

If the switch does occur, American firms will have to make significant changes in their accounting practices. GAAP and IFRS have different criteria for recognizing certain types of revenue, for valuing inventory, and for reporting interest expense and pension costs. There are even some financial instruments that GAAP classifies as owners' equity but IFRS classifies as liabilities! Clearly, the values reported on the balance sheets and income statements of U.S. firms could look quite different if the move to IFRS actually takes place. The good news for American firms is that a recent study of the differences between GAAP and IFRS suggests that most U.S. corporations would end up reporting higher earnings under the international system![4]

structure common to all balance sheets. Notice that the three major sectors of this statement reflect the key terms in the accounting equation. Once we've defined each of these terms, we'll explain the logic behind the accounting equation and how the balance sheet illustrates this logic.

- **Assets** are things of value that the firm owns. Balance sheets usually classify assets into at least two major categories. The first category, called *current assets*, consists of cash and other assets that the firm expects to use up or convert into cash within a year. For example, in Bigbux's balance sheet the value for *accounts receivable* refers to money owed to Bigbux by customers who bought its goods on credit. These receivables are converted into cash when customers pay their bills. *Inventory* is the other current asset listed on Bigbux's balance sheet. For a wholesale or retail company, inventory consists of the stock of goods it has available for sale. For a manufacturing firm, inventory includes not only finished goods but also materials and parts used in the production process as well as any unfinished goods.

  Property, plant, and equipment is the other major category of assets shown on most balance sheets. This category lists the land, buildings, machinery, equipment, and other long-term assets that Bigbux owns. With the exception of land, all of these assets have a limited useful life, so accountants subtract *accumulated depreciation* from the original value of these assets to reflect the fact that these assets are being used up over time.

  Though Bigbux doesn't do so, some companies list a third category of assets, called *intangible assets*. These are assets that have no physical existence—you can't see or touch them—but they still have value. Examples include patents, copyrights, trademarks, and even the goodwill a company develops with its stakeholders.

- **Liabilities** indicate what the firm owes to non-owners—in other words, the claims non-owners have against the firm's assets. Balance sheets usually organize liabilities into two broad categories: current liabilities and long-term liabilities. *Current liabilities*

are debts that come due within a year of the date on the balance sheet. Accounts payable—what the firm owes suppliers when it buys supplies on credit—is a common example of a current liability. Wages payable, which indicate what the firm owes to workers for work they have already performed, is another example. *Long-term liabilities* are debts that don't come due until more than a year after the date on the balance sheet. The only long-term liability that Bigbux lists is a long-term loan, which is a formal written IOU with a due date more than a year after the date on the balance sheet.

- **Owners' (or Stockholders') equity** refers to the claims the owners have against their firm's assets. The specific accounts listed in the owners' equity section of a balance sheet depend on the form of business ownership. As Exhibit 8.1 shows, common stock is a key owners' equity account for corporations. So for corporations such as Bigbux, the owners' equity section is usually titled *stockholders' equity*. Also notice that retained earnings, which are the accumulated earnings reinvested in the company (rather

assets Resources owned by a firm.

liabilities Claims that outsiders have against a firm's assets.

owners' equity The claims a firm's owners have against their company's assets (often called stockholders' equity on balance sheets of corporations).

EXHIBIT 8.1 The Balance Sheet for Bigbux

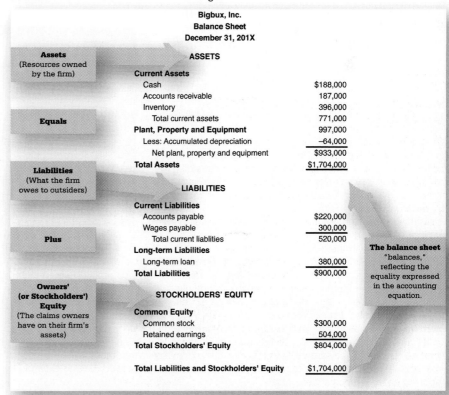

Bigbux, Inc. Balance Sheet December 31, 201X		
Assets (Resources owned by the firm)	**ASSETS**	
	Current Assets	
	Cash	$188,000
	Accounts receivable	187,000
	Inventory	396,000
	Total current assets	771,000
Equals	**Plant, Property and Equipment**	997,000
	Less: Accumulated depreciation	–64,000
	Net plant, property and equipment	$933,000
	Total Assets	$1,704,000
Liabilities (What the firm owes to outsiders)	**LIABILITIES**	
	Current Liabilities	
	Accounts payable	$220,000
	Wages payable	300,000
	Total current liablities	520,000
Plus	**Long-term Liabilities**	
	Long-term loan	380,000
	Total Liabilities	$900,000
Owners' (or Stockholders') **Equity** (The claims owners have on their firm's assets)	**STOCKHOLDERS' EQUITY**	
	Common Equity	
	Common stock	$300,000
	Retained earnings	504,000
	Total Stockholders' Equity	$804,000
	Total Liabilities and Stockholders' Equity	$1,704,000

The balance sheet "balances," reflecting the equality expressed in the accounting equation.

income statement
The financial statement that reports the revenues, expenses, and net income that resulted from a firm's operations over an accounting period.

revenue Increases in a firm's assets that result from the sale of goods, provision of services, or other activities intended to earn income.

accrual-basis accounting The method of accounting that recognizes revenue when it is earned and matches expenses to the revenues they helped produce.

than paid to owners), is another major component of the owners' equity section.

The logic behind the accounting equation is based on the fact that firms must finance the purchase of their assets, and owners and non-owners are the only two sources of funding. The accounting equation tells us that the value of a firm's assets must equal the amount of financing provided by owners (as measured by owners' equity) plus the amount provided by creditors (as indicated by the firm's liabilities) to purchase those assets. Because a balance sheet is based on this logic, it must *always* be in balance. In other words, the dollar value of the assets *must* equal the dollar value of the

> ## It sounds extraordinary, but it's a fact that balance sheets can make fascinating reading.
>
> *Baroness Mary Archer, Cambridge University Lecturer and Chairwoman of the National Energy Foundation*

liabilities plus owners' equity. This is true for *all* firms, from the smallest sole proprietorship to the largest multinational corporation. Notice in Exhibit 8.1 that the $1,704,000 in total assets listed on Bigbux's balance sheet matches the $1,704,000 in liabilities plus owners' equity.

The Income Statement: So, How Did We Do?

The **income statement** summarizes the financial results of a firm's operations over a given period of time. The figure that attracts the most attention on the income statement is net income, which measures the company's profit or loss. In fact, another name for the income statement is the *profit and loss statement* (or, informally, the P&L). Just as with the balance sheet, we can use a simple equation to illustrate the logic behind the organization of the income statement:

$$\text{Revenue} - \text{Expenses} = \text{Net Income}$$

In this equation:

- **Revenue** represents the increase in the amount of cash and other assets (such as accounts receivable) the firm earns in a given time period as the result of its business activities. A firm normally earns revenue by selling goods or by charging fees for providing services (or both). Accountants use **accrual-basis accounting** when recognizing revenues. Under the accrual approach, revenues are recorded when they are earned and payment is reasonably assured. It's important to realize that

© UPI/APPLE INC./LANDOV

Intangible Assets Take a Big Bite out of Apple's Balance Sheet

On September 26, 2009, Apple, Inc.'s balance sheet reported that the total value of its stockholders' equity was $31.64 billion. But the actual market value of Apple's outstanding common stock on that date was more than $166 billion— more than five times the balance sheet figure. What accounts for this huge discrepancy?

Many of Apple's most valuable resources, including the patents it holds on innovative products such as iPads and iPhones, along with the goodwill it has established with its fanatically loyal customers, are intangible assets that were created by Apple's own design teams, software programmers, and marketers. The fact that these intangibles were developed internally creates a big problem for Apple's accountants. When a company buys an intangible asset (such as rights to use a patent) from an external seller, the purchase price gives accountants an objective measure of value that they can record on the balance sheet. But when Apple's own employees create these assets, there is no purchase price for accountants to record. Lacking an objective measure of their value, Apple's accountants (in accordance with today's GAAP) write off the cost of creating these assets as an expense rather than recording their value on the balance sheet.

While Apple's balance sheet omits internally created intangible assets, investors are keenly aware of how incredibly valuable they are—and they are willing to pay for this extra value when they buy the company's stock. Thus, these unrecorded intangible assets are a major reason why the market value of Apple's stock far exceeds the value of stockholders' equity reported on its balance sheet.[5]

this is not always when the firm receives cash from its sales. For example, if a firm sells goods on credit, it reports revenue before it receives cash. (The revenue would show up initially as an increase in accounts receivable rather than as an increase in cash.)

- **Expenses** indicate the cash a firm spends, or other assets it uses up, to carry out the business activities necessary to generate its revenue. Under accrual-basis accounting, expenses aren't necessarily recorded when cash is paid. Instead, expenses are matched to the revenue they help generate. The specific titles given to the costs and expenses listed on an income statement vary among firms—as do the details provided. But the general approach remains the same: costs are deducted from revenue in several stages to show how net income is determined. The first step in this process is to deduct *costs of goods sold*, which are costs directly related to buying, manufacturing, or providing the goods and services the company sells. (Manufacturing companies often use the term *cost of goods manufactured* for these costs.) The difference between the firm's revenue and its cost of goods sold is its *gross profit*. The next step is to deduct *operating expenses* from gross profit. Operating expenses are costs the firm incurs in the regular operation of its business. Most income statements divide operating expenses into *selling expenses* (such as salaries and commissions to salespeople and advertising expenses) and *general* (or *administrative*) *expenses* (such as rent, insurance, utilities, and office supplies). The difference between gross profit and operating expenses is *net operating income*. Finally, interest expense and taxes are deducted from net operating income to determine the firm's net income.

- **Net income** is the profit or loss the firm earns in the time period covered by the income statement. If net income is positive, the firm has earned a profit. If it's negative, the firm has suffered a loss. Net income is called the "bottom line" of the income statement because it is such an important measure of the firm's operating success. But income statements usually include additional information below the net income, so it isn't literally the bottom line. For example, the income

statement for Bigbux indicates how much of the net income was retained and how much was distributed to stockholders in the form of dividends.

Take a look at Exhibit 8.2 to see how the income statement for Bigbux is organized. See if you can identify the accounts that represent the revenue, expense, and income concepts we've just described.

> { **Remind people that profit is the difference between revenue and expense. This makes you look smart.** }
>
> *Scott Adams, creator of Dilbert*

Statement of Cash Flows: Show Me the Money

The last major financial statement is the **statement of cash flows**. Cash is the lifeblood of any business organization. A firm must have enough cash to pay what it owes to workers, creditors, suppliers, and

EXHIBIT 8.2 Income Statement for Bigbux

	Bigbux, Inc. Income Statement For Year Ending December 31, 201X	
Revenue: (What the firm earns)	Sales Revenue	890,000.00
	Cost of goods sold	550,000.00
Minus	Gross Profit	340,000.00
	Operating Expenses	
	Selling expenses	79,000.00
	Administrative expenses	86,000.00
Costs and Expenses (Cash spent and other resources used up)	Total Operating Expenses	165,000.00
	Net Operating Income	175,000.00
	Interest expense	12,000.00
	Taxable Income	163,000.00
Equals	Taxes	62,000.00
	Net Income	101,000.00
Net Income (Profit if positive or loss if negative)	Dividends	55,000.00
	Transfer to Retained Earnings	46,000.00

taxing authorities—hopefully with enough left to pay its owners a return on their investment! So it's not surprising that a firm's stakeholders want to know not only *how much* the firm's cash balance changed over the accounting period, but also *why* it changed. The statement of cash flows shows how and why the firm's cash position changed by identifying the amount of cash that flowed into and out of the firm from three types of activities:

1. Cash flows from *operating activities* show the amount of cash that flowed into the company from the sale of goods or services, as well as cash from dividends and interest received from ownership of the financial securities of other firms. It also shows the amount of cash Bigbux used to cover expenses resulting from operations and any cash payments to purchase securities held for short-term trading purposes. Remember that under the accrual method not all revenues and expenses on the income statement represent cash flows, so operating cash flows may differ substantially from the revenues and expenses shown on the income statement.

2. Cash flows from *investing activities* show the amount of cash received from the sale of fixed assets (such as land and buildings) and financial assets bought as long-term investments. It also shows any cash used to buy fixed assets and long-term financial investments.

3. Cash flows from *financing activities* show the cash the firm received from issuing additional shares of its own stock or from taking out long-term loans. It also shows cash outflows from payment of dividends to shareholders and to repay principal on loans.

Exhibit 8.3 shows the Statement of Cash Flows for Bigbux. You can see that Bigbux experienced a substantial increase in its total cash balance. You can also see that this increase in cash was primarily due to two factors. First, a look at operating cash flows shows that the cash Bigbux collected from customer payments exceeded its cash payments for inventory and operating expenses by a significant margin. Second, the section on financing activities shows that Bigbux took out a large long-term loan. The net increases in cash from these sources more than offset the net cash outflow from investing due to the

purchase of new equipment. Note that the cash balance at the end of the period matches the amount of cash reported in the current balance sheet (see Exhibit 8.1 again)—as it always should.

Other Statements

In addition to the three major statements we've just described, firms usually prepare either a statement of retained earnings or a stockholders' equity statement. Let's take a quick look at each of these statements.

The *statement of retained earnings* is a simple statement that shows how retained earnings have changed from one accounting period to the next. The change in retained earnings is found by subtracting dividends paid to shareholders from net income.

Firms that have more complex changes in the owners' equity section sometimes report these changes in notes to the financial statements in the annual report. But they often disclose these changes by providing a *stockholders' equity statement*. Like the statement of retained earnings, this statement shows how net income and dividends affect retained earnings. But it also shows other changes in stockholders' equity, such as those that arise from the issuance of additional shares of stock.

LO5 Interpreting Financial Statements: Digging Beneath the Surface

The financial statements we've just described contain a lot of important information. But they don't necessarily tell the whole story. In fact, the numbers they report can be misleading if they aren't put into proper context.

EXHIBIT 8.3 Bigbux's Statement of Cash Flows

Bigbux Corporation Statement of Cash Flows For Year Ended December 31, 201X		
Operating Cash Flow		
Cash payments from customers	$804,000	
Purchase of inventory	(576,000)	
Cash operating expenses	(155,000)	
Net Cash Provided from Operations		$73,000
Investing Cash Flow		
Sale of land	$50,000	
Purchase of equipment	(85,000)	
Net Cash Used by Investing		(35,000)
Financing Cash Flow		
Increase in long-term bank loans	$63,000	
Payments of cash dividends	$(55,000)	
Net Cash Provided from Financing		$8,000
Total Cash Flow		$46,000
Cash at beginning of period		$142,000
Cash at End of Period		$188,000

Operating cash flows
(Cash flows related to producing and selling)

Plus

Investing cash flows
(Cash flows from the purchase and sale of long-term assets)

Plus

Financing cash flows
(Cash flows related to long-term financing activities)

Equals

Total Cash Flow

Thus, in addition to looking at the statements, it's also important to check out the independent auditor's report and read the management discussion and footnotes that accompany these statements. It's also a good idea to compare the figures reported in current statements to those from earlier statements to see how key account values have changed.

The Independent Auditor's Report: A Necessary Stamp of Approval

U.S. securities laws require publicly traded corporations in the United States to have an independent CPA firm (an accounting firm that specializes in providing public accounting services) perform an annual external audit of their financial statements. The purpose of the audit is to verify that the statements were properly prepared in accordance with generally accepted accounting principles, and that they fairly present the financial condition of the firm. The results of the audit are presented in an independent auditor's report, which is included in the annual report the firm sends to its stockholders.

If the auditor doesn't find any problems with the way a firm's financial statements were prepared and presented, the report will offer an *unqualified opinion* (also referred to as a *clean opinion*). If the auditor identifies limited problems with the firm's accounting methods or financial statements, but believes that in all other respects these statements are fair and accurate, the report will express a *qualified opinion*. But when auditors discover more serious and widespread problems with a firm's statements, they offer an *adverse opinion*. An adverse opinion indicates that the

© FUSE/JUPITERIMAGES

External auditors carefully examine a company's financial records before rendering their opinion.

© JUSTIN HORROCKS/ISTOCKPHOTO.COM

New Accounting Trend: Stretching a Single into a Triple

Accounting has always focused on measures of the *financial* performance of an organization. But many of today's leading accounting firms are heeding a call to develop a much broader set of performance measures called the triple bottom line (TBL). The TBL approach evaluates the company's performance in three key areas:

- Profits: how well the company satisfies the traditional goal of providing a fair financial return for stockholders
- People: how well the company meets the needs of other stakeholders such as employees, customers, and community
- Planet: the extent to which the company pursues environmentally sound and sustainable practices.

The TBL concept was first described by social responsibility guru John Elkington in 1994. But in the 1990s most accounting firms were reluctant to devote the time and effort needed to develop measures of TBL performance. So for several years TBL was more a catchphrase than a real-world approach to evaluating corporate performance. That began to change soon after the turn of the century, as a wave of corporate accounting scandals, growing concerns about global warming, and a devastating financial crash convinced many in the accounting and finance professions that a narrow focus on financial performance was distorting corporate incentives.

Gradually, a consensus emerged that broader measures of corporate performance were needed. As Rodger Hill, Head of Financial Management Advisory for accounting giant KPMG, observed, "The days of purely measuring business performance by financial result may well be numbered. In its place, I believe that discerning investors will look for something broader to measure an entity's real contribution and performance." And according to Hill, that broader approach should be the triple bottom line.

Today virtually most major accounting firms, including all of the "Big 4" accounting firms that perform the vast majority of external audits of public companies, have developed their own versions of triple bottom line accounting.[6]

auditor believes the information contained in the statements was not prepared according to generally accepted accounting principles and that the statements may be inaccurate and unreliable. Such an opinion should set off alarm bells, warning others to view the information in the firm's financial statements with real skepticism.

In order for CPA firms to perform audits with integrity, they must be independent of the firms they audit. During the 1990s, many of the major CPA firms entered into very lucrative consulting contracts with some of the businesses they were auditing. It became increasingly difficult for these CPA firms to risk losing these high-paying contracts by raising issues about accounting practices when they audited the books of their clients. In other words, the auditors ceased to be truly independent and objective. The lack of rigorous oversight by external auditors contributed to the accounting scandals we mentioned earlier in this chapter.

In the aftermath of the scandals, Congress passed the **Sarbanes-Oxley Act of 2002** (commonly referred to as "SOX" or "Sarbox"). This law banned business relationships that might create conflicts of interest between CPA firms and the companies they audit. It also established a private-sector nonprofit corporation known as the Public Company Accounting Oversight Board (PCAOB). The PCAOB defines its mission as "to protect the interests of investors and further the public interest in the preparation of informative, fair, and independent audit reports."[7]

Notes to Financial Statements: Reading the Fine Print

Some types of information can't be adequately conveyed by numbers alone. Annual reports include notes (often *many* pages of notes) that disclose additional information about the firm's operations, accounting practices, and special circumstances that clarify and supplement the numbers reported on the financial statements. These notes can be *very* revealing. For example, GAAP often allows firms to choose among several options when it comes to certain accounting procedures—and the choices the firm makes can affect the value of assets, liabilities, and owners' equity on the balance sheet and the revenues, costs, and net income on the income statement. The notes to financial statements explain the specific accounting methods used to recognize revenue, value inventory, and depreciate

> ### In 2004 a horse named "Read The Footnotes" ran in the Kentucky Derby.
> *Securities and Exchange Commission*

fixed assets. They might also provide details about the way the firm funds its pension plan or health insurance for its employees. They must also disclose *changes* in accounting methods that could affect the comparability of the current financial statements to those of previous years. Even more interesting, the notes might disclose important facts about the status of a lawsuit against the firm or other risks the firm faces. Stakeholders who ignore these notes are likely to miss out on important information.

Another important source of information is the section of the annual report usually titled "Management's Discussion and Analysis." As its name implies, this is where the top management team provides its take on the financial condition of the company. SEC guidelines require top management to disclose any trends, events, or risks likely to have a significant impact on the firm's financial condition in this section of the report.

Comparative Statements: Trendy Analysis

The SEC requires publicly traded corporations to provide comparative financial statements. This simply means that the statements list two or three years of figures side by side, making it possible to see how account values have changed over a period of time. Many firms that aren't publicly traded also present comparative statements, even though they are not required to do so by GAAP.

Comparative balance sheets allow users to trace what has happened to key assets and liabilities over the past two or three years, and whether its owners' equity had increased. Comparative income statements allow users to determine whether the firm's net income had increased or decreased and what has happened to revenues and expenses over recent years. Using comparative statements to identify changes in key account values over time is called **horizontal analysis**.

LO6 Managerial Accounting: Inside Intelligence

Now that we've looked at financial accounting, let's turn our attention to the other major branch of accounting, **managerial (or management) accounting**. As its name implies, this branch of accounting is designed to meet the needs of a company's managers, though in recent years many firms have empowered other employees and given them access to some of this information as well. Exhibit 8.4 identifies several ways that managerial accounting differs from financial accounting.

Managers throughout an organization rely on information created by managerial accountants to make important decisions. The accuracy and reliability of this information can make a huge difference in the performance of a firm. In fact, many firms view their management accounting systems as a source of competitive advantage and regard the specifics of these systems as highly valuable company secrets.[8]

We'll close this chapter by describing three types of management responsibilities that rely on information provided by managerial accounting: determining product costs, performing incremental analysis, and developing budgets. Keep in mind that the discussion that follows is only a "sampler" of the areas where managerial accounting plays an important role.

Product Costing: As Simple as ABC?

Managers must have an accurate measure of the costs incurred to produce their firm's goods and services. Without good information on costs, managers would be operating in the dark as they try to set prices, determine the most desirable mix of products, and locate areas where efficiency is lagging. A firm's management accounting system helps managers throughout an organization measure costs and assign them to the correct products and activities.

Some costs are easy to assign. The costs of labor and materials used directly in the production of a product are usually easy to identify and measure. These are called *direct labor* and *direct materials costs*. Unfortunately, many other costs aren't tied in such a simple and direct way to the production of a specific product. For example, a firm typically pays property taxes on its factory building and pays premiums on an insurance policy to cover losses due to fire or storm damage. It also incurs general maintenance costs for upkeep of the building. These costs are for the entire production facility and aren't directly tied to the production of any specific product. Such costs are called *overhead costs*.

In the past, managerial accountants often relied on very simple rules to determine how much of the overhead costs

managerial (or management) accounting The branch of accounting that provides reports and analysis to managers to help them make informed business decisions.

EXHIBIT 8.4 Comparison of Financial and Managerial Accounting

	Financial Accounting	Managerial Accounting
Purpose	Primarily intended to provide information to external stakeholders, such as stockholders, creditors, and government regulators. Information provided by financial accounting is available to the general public.	Primarily intended to provide information to internal stakeholders, such as the managers of specific divisions or departments. This information is proprietary—meaning that it isn't available to the general public.
Type of information presented	Focuses almost exclusively on financial information.	Provides both financial and nonfinancial information.
Nature of reports	Prepares a standard set of financial statements.	Prepares customized reports to deal with specific problems or issues.
Timing of reports	Presents financial statements on a predetermined schedule (usually quarterly and annually).	Creates reports upon request by management rather than according to a predetermined schedule.
Adherence to accounting standards?	Governed by a set of generally accepted accounting principles (GAAP).	Uses procedures developed internally that are not required to follow GAAP.
Time period focus	Summarizes past performance and its impact on the firm's present condition.	Provides reports dealing with past performance, but also involves making projections about the future when dealing with planning issues.

activity-based costing (ABC) A technique to assign product costs based on links between activities that drive costs and the production of specific products.

incremental analysis An evaluation of the financial impact different alternatives would have in a particular decision-making situation.

incremental costs Costs that change as the result of a decision.

to assign to different products. One common approach was to allocate overhead in proportion to the number of direct labor hours involved in the production of each product—products that required the most labor to produce were assigned the most overhead costs. But, while this approach was simple, it often provided misleading information. Many overhead costs aren't related to the amount of direct labor used to produce a product. For example, changes in the amount of labor used to produce a product may have no impact on the cost of an insurance premium or property taxes.

In recent years managerial accountants have developed more sophisticated ways to allocate costs. One promising new approach is called **activity-based costing (ABC)**. This approach is more complex and difficult to implement than the direct labor method. However, it's likely to provide more meaningful results because it is based on a systematic examination of what actually creates (or drives) overhead costs. It assigns these costs to specific products by linking the production of those products to the specific activities that create the costs.

Incremental Analysis: Focusing on Change

Incremental analysis evaluates the financial impact of different alternatives in a decision-making situation. Typical examples include analysis of whether a firm should:

- Make parts and components itself, or buy them from suppliers
- Repair its existing equipment or buy new equipment
- Eliminate or sell off an existing product line—or even an entire division or subsidiary

To make the best decision in each of these situations, managers must correctly identify how each alternative would affect the company's revenues and costs—not always an easy task, but one that's crucial to making sound decisions. Let's look at an example to see why.

Suppose an electronics firm produces high-definition LCD televisions at a rate of 10,000 per month. It currently makes its own digital tuners for the televisions, and the various types of costs it incurs to produce the tuners are listed in Exhibit 8.5. Dividing the total costs

EXHIBIT 8.5 Costs of Making Digital Tuners Per Month

Direct labor costs	$140,000
Direct materials costs	$85,000
Manufacturing overhead costs	$75,000
Total costs	$300,000
Costs per unit (at 10,000 units per month)	$30

by the number of TVs produced per month shows that the average cost of tuners per TV is $30.

Now suppose that a supplier offers to sell the firm tuners of similar quality at a cost of $25 per television. At first glance it might appear that the firm could lower its costs by accepting the offer; after all, $25 per tuner is less than $30.

But a more careful look, using incremental analysis, might suggest that this would be a bad move. In particular, incremental analysis would almost certainly find that many of the overhead costs assigned to the production of the tuners are unaffected by how many tuners the company produces. Insurance premiums, property taxes, and depreciation expenses on the production facility are examples. The firm would still incur most of these costs even if it bought the tuners from another firm!

To correctly analyze the impact of buying tuners rather than making them, incremental analysis identifies which costs would actually *change* if the company discontinued its production of the tuners. These are called the **incremental costs** of the decision. The direct labor and materials costs are incremental; if the firm doesn't produce the tuners, it won't incur these costs. But most of the manufacturing overhead costs aren't incremental, so they have no bearing on our decision.

Let's assume that all of the direct material and labor costs are incremental but that the firm would still incur $65,000 of its overhead costs. Exhibit 8.6 shows that the decision to buy tuners would completely eliminate direct labor and direct materials costs, but would reduce overhead costs by only $10,000. When these remaining overhead costs are added to the cost of buying the tuners, you can see that the firm's total costs would be $15,000 higher if it bought the tuners than if it continued to produce them itself.

© MATJAZ BONCINA/ISTOCKPHOTO

EXHIBIT 8.6 Incremental Analysis: Make or Buy Tuners?

Type of Cost	Make	Buy
Direct labor costs	$140,000	$0
Direct materials costs	$85,000	$0
Manufacturing overhead	$75,000	$65,000
Cost of purchasing speakers ($25 × 10,000 units)	$0	$250,000
Total monthly cost	$300,000	$315,000

Budgeting: Planning for Accountability

Management accountants also provide much of the information used in the development of budgets. **Budgeting** is a management tool that explicitly shows how a firm will acquire and use the resources it needs to achieve its goals over a specific time period. The budgetary process facilitates planning by requiring managers to translate goals into measurable quantities and identify the specific resources needed to achieve these goals. But budgeting offers other advantages as well. If done well, budgeting:

- Requires managers to clearly specify how they intend to achieve the goals they set during the planning process. This should lead to a better allocation of the organization's limited resources.

- Encourages communication and coordination among managers and employees in various departments within the organization. As we'll see in the next section, the budget process can give middle and first-line managers and employees an opportunity to provide top managers with important feedback about the challenges facing their specialized areas and the resources they need to meet those challenges.

- Serves as a motivational tool. Good budgets clearly identify goals *and* demonstrate a plan of action for acquiring the resources needed to achieve them. Employees tend to be more highly motivated when they understand the goals their managers expect them to accomplish and when they view these goals as ambitious but achievable.

- Provides an effective way to monitor progress and evaluate performance. Managers can compare actual performance to budgetary figures to determine whether various departments and functional areas are making adequate progress toward achieving their organization's goals. If actual performance falls short of budgetary goals, managers can look for reasons and, if necessary, take corrective action.

> **budgeting** A management tool that explicitly shows how a firm will acquire and use the resources needed to achieve its goals over a specific time period.

Preparing the Budget: Top-Down or Bottom-Up?

There are two different approaches to budget preparation. In some organizations top management prepares the budget with little or no input from middle and supervisory managers—a process known as *top-down budgeting*. Supporters of this approach point out that top management knows the long-term strategic needs of the company and is in a better position to see the big picture when making budget decisions.

The other approach to budget development is called *bottom-up* or *participatory budgeting*. Organizations that use a participatory process allow middle and supervisory managers to actively participate in

Abandon the Budget?

The budgeting process is widely entrenched in corporate America, with many managers viewing it as an invaluable tool for planning and control. But some financial managers believe that budgeting is a badly flawed practice. They argue that traditional budgeting creates fixed performance targets that managers expect subordinates to meet. These targets often prove unrealistic, resulting in frustrated employees who may feel pressured to "fudge the numbers." Another problem is that the annual nature of budgeting encourages managers to become so focused on meeting short-term budget targets that they lose track of important longer-term implications of their decisions.

Some companies have become so disenchanted with budgeting that they've sought ways to replace it with more flexible planning and control systems. In fact, several major corporations that have abandoned traditional budgeting have formed a consortium called the Beyond Budgeting Round Table (BBRT) to share ideas and publicize their approach. The BBRT's membership list is global in scope and includes major U.S. corporations such as Time Warner and American Express. Several other highly successful U.S. corporations, such as Google and Southwest Airlines, have adopted practices consistent with the BBRT philosophy.[9]

operating budgets Budgets that communicate an organization's sales and production goals and the resources needed to achieve these goals.

financial budgets Budgets that focus on the firm's financial goals and identify the resources needed to achieve these goals.

master budget A presentation of an organization's operational and financial budgets that represents the firm's overall plan of action for a specified time period.

the creation of the budget. Proponents of this approach maintain that it has two major advantages. First, lower-level managers are likely to know more about the issues and challenges facing their departments—and the resources it will take to address them—than top management. Second, middle and first-line managers are likely to be more highly motivated to achieve budgetary goals when they have a say in how those goals are developed. On the negative side, the bottom-up approach is more time consuming and resource intensive to carry out than the top-down approach. Also, some middle managers may be tempted to overstate their needs or set low budget goals in order to make their jobs easier—an outcome known as *budgetary slack*.[10]

Developing the Key Budget Components: One Step at a Time

Budgeting actually involves the preparation of several different budget documents. These documents are organized into two broad classes: operating budgets and financial budgets.

Operating budgets are budgets that identify projected sales and production goals and the various costs the firm will incur in order to meet these goals. These budgets are developed in a specific order, with the information from earlier budgets used in the preparation of later budgets.

The preparation of operating budgets begins with the development of a *sales budget* that provides quarterly estimates of the number of units of each product the firm expects to sell, the selling price, and the total dollar value of expected sales. The sales budget must be created first because the production and cost figures that go into other operating budgets depend directly or indirectly on the level of sales. Once the sales budget is complete, the next step is to develop the production budget and administrative and selling expenses budgets. And once the production budget is completed, the information it contains is used to prepare budgets for direct labor costs, direct materials costs, and manufacturing overhead. The final stage in the preparation of operating budgets is the creation of a *budgeted income statement*. This budget looks much like the income statement we described earlier, but instead of describing the actual results of the firm's past operations, it combines the revenue projections from the sales budget and the cost projections from

Budgeting encourages communication and coordination among managers and employees.

© DMITRIY SHIRONOSOV/ISTOCKPHOTO.COM

the other operating budgets to present a forecast of *expected* net income.

Financial budgets focus on the firm's financial goals and identify the resources needed to achieve these goals. The two main financial budget documents are the *cash budget* and the *capital expenditure budget*. The cash budget identifies short-term fluctuations in cash flows, helping managers identify times when the firm might face cash flow problems—or when it might have a temporary surplus of cash that it could invest. The capital expenditure budget identifies the firm's planned investments in major fixed assets and long-term projects. (We'll discuss the cash budget and capital expenditure budget in more detail in Chapter 9.) The information from these two financial budgets and the budgeted income statement are combined to construct the *budgeted balance sheet*. This is the last financial budget; it shows how the firm's operations, investing, and financing activities are expected to affect all of the asset, liability, and owners' equity accounts.

The firm's **master budget** brings together all of the documents in the operating and financial budgets into a unified whole, representing the firm's overall plan of action for a specified time period. In other words, the master budget shows how all of the pieces fit together to form a complete picture. Exhibit 8.7 shows all of the budget documents that are included in a typical master budget. The arrows indicate the order in which the

EXHIBIT 8.7 Development of the Master Budget

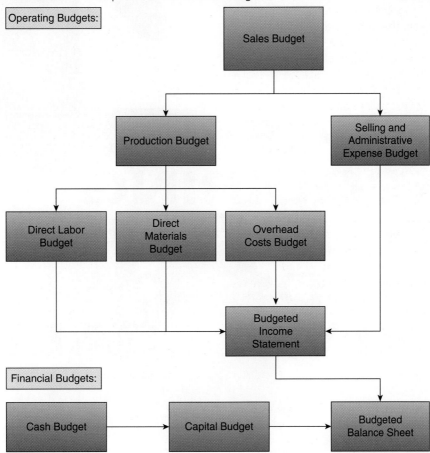

budgets are developed, starting with the sales budget and ending with the budgeted balance sheet.

The Big Picture

Accounting provides vital information to both the internal and external stakeholders of a firm. The balance sheet, income statement, and statement of cash flow that are the main output of financial accounting help external stakeholders, such as owners and creditors, evaluate the financial performance of a firm. And managerial accounting helps managers throughout an organization make better decisions by providing them with relevant and timely information about the costs and benefits of the choices they have to make. Clearly, a basic knowledge of accounting concepts will help you succeed in just about any career path you choose.

Looking ahead, it's likely that employment opportunities in accounting will grow rapidly over the next few years. In part this is because recent economic events have reinforced the importance of making good financial decisions—and good financial decisions depend on the information that accountants provide. But another reason for this growth is that the accounting profession faces a host of interesting new opportunities and challenges. For example, recent high-profile cases of accounting and investment fraud and other white-collar crimes have increased the demand for skilled accountants to trace the money trails that result from such illegal schemes. On a more positive note, the desire of businesses to meet their environmental responsibilities has led to the development of new accounting techniques to measure the costs and benefits of "green" business practices—and a demand for accountants who know how to use them. Finally, the possibility of a major overhaul of the generally accepted accounting principles governing financial accounting may open up opportunities for a new breed of accountants who are well-versed in the application of the new principles.

WHAT ELSE? *RIP & REVIEW* **CARDS IN THE BACK**

9

FINANCE: ACQUIRING AND USING FUNDS TO MAXIMIZE VALUE

LEARNING OBJECTIVES

After studying this chapter, you will be able to...

LO1 Explain how maximizing share-holder value relates to social responsibility

LO2 Describe how financial managers use key ratios to evaluate their firm

LO3 Discuss how financial managers use budgeted financial statements and cash budgets

LO4 Explain the significance of working capital management

LO5 Explain how financial managers evaluate capital budgeting proposals

LO6 Identify the key issues involved in determining a firm's capital structure

Visit CourseMate at **www.cengagebrain.com.**

> { **The waste of money cures itself, for soon there is no money to waste.** }
>
> *M. W. Harrison*

LO1 What Motivates Financial Decisions?

Our nation's recent economic history clearly shows how important good financial management can be to the success (and even survival) of a business organization. As the world economy plunged into an ever-deeper recession in 2008 and 2009, sound financial management became increasingly critical—and increasingly challenging. Firms found that raising funds to finance long-term investments in plant, machinery, and property became almost impossible as the primary markets for their securities dried up. Even well-run firms experienced short-term cash flow problems as sales declined and more customers paid their bills late (or not at all). And when these companies tried to borrow money to meet their payroll or finance their inventory, they found that their short-term credit had dried up because many lenders were in bigger trouble than they were! It's no exaggeration to say that the whole global financial system literally teetered on the brink of collapse.

Because of these financial problems, many companies—including some major financial corporations that had been considered icons of free-market capitalism—went belly-up during this period. In fact, firms with almost $1.2 trillion in assets filed for bankruptcy in 2008. To put that in perspective, the total asset value of all of the firms that went bankrupt in the post 9/11 recession of 2001–2002 (a downturn that included the bankruptcies of Enron, WorldCom and several other huge corporations) was less than $500 billion. And it could have been worse; without massive assistance by the federal government, many other major corporations might have suffered the same fate.[1]

Shareholder Value and Social Responsibility: Does Good Behavior Pay Off?

Firms use funds for a variety of purposes. Some cash is needed to meet short-term obligations, such as paying wages and salaries to employees, bills from suppliers, dividends to owners, and taxes to the government. Other funds are used to finance major long-term projects, such as investments in plant and equipment or the launch of a new product line. Companies also have a variety of ways to raise the funds they need: cash generated through business operations, loans from bankers and other creditors, and (for corporations) money obtained by issuing stocks and bonds. In a nutshell, financial management is responsible for finding, among all these alternatives, the best sources of funds and the best ways to use them.

The decisions of a firm's financial management team can have a critical impact on the firm's overall success.

But how do financial managers determine the "best" sources and uses of funds? In other words, what criteria do financial managers use to make their decisions? Historically, the goal of financial management has been to *maximize the value of the firm to its owners*. For corporations with publicly traded stock, this goal translates into finding the sources and uses of cash that will maximize the market price of the company's common stock.

One reason financial managers emphasize the goal of maximizing the market price of stock is that they believe that the board (and the top management team it assembles) has a legal and ethical obligation to make decisions consistent with the financial interests of their firm's owners. Stockholders elect the board of directors to represent and protect their interests. This puts board members in a position of trust; they must act in the best interests of the stockholders.

Another reason for emphasizing shareholder wealth is more practical. Stockholders have invested their money and assumed the risks associated with business ownership. Most shareholders accept these risks only when they believe that

financial ratio analysis Computing ratios that compare values of key accounts listed on a firm's financial statements.

liquid asset An asset that can quickly be converted into cash with little risk of loss.

liquidity ratios Financial ratios that measure the ability of a firm to obtain the cash it needs to pay its short-term debt obligations as they come due.

asset management ratios Financial ratios that measure how effectively a firm is using its assets to generate revenues or cash.

doing so offers an opportunity to benefit financially. Thus, in order to continue attracting financial resources needed to grow and prosper, a firm must provide value to its stockholders.

The emphasis that financial management places on maximizing shareholder value may seem to conflict with social responsibility—the business obligation to consider the needs of all stakeholders, not just owners, but also employees, customers, creditors, suppliers, and even society as a whole. Fortunately, this broader view of social responsibility *can* be (and often is) consistent with the goal of shareholder wealth maximization—especially if the managers take a long-term perspective. Treating customers, employees, suppliers, creditors, and other stakeholders with fairness, honesty, and respect can build goodwill. This often results in satisfied customers (who may recommend the company to their friends and colleagues), more productive and loyal workers (and less employee turnover), better cooperation from suppliers, and a more favorable business climate—all of which can contribute to a more profitable company and an increase in shareholder value.[2]

But it isn't always that simple. Diverse stakeholder groups can have very different goals, and finding the right balance among the competing interests of these groups of stakeholders can be difficult. When conflicts arise between the long-term interests of owners and those of other stakeholders, financial managers generally adopt the policies they believe are most consistent with the interests of ownership.

Given the goal of shareholder wealth maximization, the major duties and responsibilities of financial managers usually involve the following tasks:

- Evaluating the firm's current financial condition to determine current strengths and weaknesses.

- Planning for the effective use of financial resources to take advantage of these strengths and to correct for any weaknesses.

- Managing the firm's working capital to achieve the right mix of current assets and current liabilities.

- Evaluating long-run investment opportunities to identify investments in property, plant, equipment, and other assets and activities that are likely to increase shareholder value.

- Determining the appropriate mix of debt and equity to meet the long-term financial needs of the company.

In the remainder of this chapter we'll take a look at how financial managers perform each of these functions.

LO2 Evaluating Current Conditions: Where Do We Stand?

Before financial managers can determine the best financial strategies for their firms, they must identify their existing strengths and weaknesses. One way they do this is by computing ratios that compare values of key accounts listed on their firm's financial statements—a technique called **financial ratio analysis.** Over the years, financial managers have developed an impressive array of specific ratios. But all of these ratios fall into four basic categories:

1. **Liquidity ratios**: In finance a **liquid asset** is one that can be quickly converted into cash with little risk of loss. **Liquidity ratios** measure the ability of an organization to convert assets into the cash it needs to pay off liabilities that come due in the next year.

   One of the simplest and most commonly used liquidity ratios is the *current ratio*, which is computed by dividing a firm's current assets by its current liabilities. Current assets include cash and other assets expected to be converted into cash in the next year, while current liabilities are the debts that must be repaid in the next year. The larger the current ratio, the easier it should be for a firm to obtain the cash needed to pay its short-term debts. Many firms strive for a current ratio of 2 or greater, meaning that current assets are at least twice as great as current liabilities. The idea is to give the firm a "cushion" in case some of its current assets turn out to be harder to convert into cash than expected. But this is a guideline rather than a hard and fast rule; firms with strong cash flows from operations may experience no liquidity problems even if their current ratio is less than 1. Clearly, however, a sharp decline in the current ratio can signal a situation where the firm may struggle to come up with cash when debts come due. Liquidity concerns became a major issue for many companies in 2008 when declining sales cut into operating cash flows and credit markets dried up with the onset of the recession.

2. **Asset management ratios**: **Asset management ratios** (also sometimes called activity ratios) provide measures of how effectively an organization is using its assets to generate net income. For example, the *inventory turnover ratio*—computed by dividing the firm's cost of goods sold by average inventory—measures how many times a firm's inventory is sold and replaced each year. Up

to a point, a high turnover ratio is good because it indicates that the firm's products are moving quickly. On the other hand, a low inventory turnover indicates that goods may be sitting on the firm's shelves or stored in its warehouses for long periods of time—usually not a positive sign. However, it is possible for an inventory turnover ratio to be *too* high. For instance, a high ratio could mean that the company isn't keeping enough goods in stock, causing frequent stockouts. This can frustrate customers and result in lost sales if they take their business elsewhere.

For firms that sell a lot of goods on credit, the *average collection period* is another important asset management ratio. This ratio is computed by dividing accounts receivable by average daily credit sales. A value of 45 for this ratio means that customers take 45 days (on average) to pay for their credit purchases. In general, the smaller the ratio the better, since a lower value indicates that the firm's customers are paying for their purchases more quickly. But we'll see in our discussion of working capital management that low collection periods can also have drawbacks.

3. **Leverage ratios:** **Financial leverage** is the use of debt to meet a firm's financing needs; a *highly leveraged* firm is one that relies heavily on debt. While the use of leverage can benefit a firm when times are good, a high degree of leverage is very risky. The extensive use of financial leverage played a major role in the financial meltdown that began during the latter part of the last decade. **Leverage ratios** measure the extent to which a firm is employing financial leverage. Two common leverage ratios are the *debt ratio*, computed by dividing a firm's total liabilities by its total assets, and the *debt-to-equity ratio*, which is found by dividing total liabilities by total owners' equity. If a firm financed half its assets with debt and half with owners' equity, its debt ratio would be .5 (or 50%). The same firm's debt-to-equity ratio would be 1.0 (or 100%).

4. **Profitability ratios:** Firms are in business to earn a profit, and **profitability ratios** provide measures of how successful they are at achieving this goal. There are many different profitability ratios, but we'll look at just a couple of examples. *Return-on-equity* (ROE), calculated by dividing net income (profit) by owners' equity, measures the income earned per dollar invested by the stockholders. If a firm issues both common and preferred stock, the computation of this ratio typically measures only the return to the common stockholders, since they are considered to

financial leverage
The use of debt in a firm's capital structure.

leverage ratios
Ratios that measure the extent to which a firm relies on debt financing in its capital structure.

profitability ratios
Ratios that measure the rate of return a firm is earning on various measures of investment.

© STEPHEN MORRIS/ISTOCKPHOTO.COM

Choose Your Poison: Toxic Assets as Executive Bonuses

Like most financial institutions in 2008, Swiss multinational financial services giant Credit Suisse faced two big problems: a lot of highly risky mortgage-backed assets on its balance sheet and a public backlash against the big bonuses traditionally paid to top managers in the face of the company's poor financial performance. But unlike other financial institutions, Credit Suisse came up with a novel strategy to tackle its problems. First, it used $5 billion of its riskiest securities—what media pundits often referred to as "toxic" assets—to create a new fund it called the Partner Asset Facility. Next, it paid "bonuses" to its top managers by giving them shares in any earnings generated by this fund. Finally, it made the bonuses from the fund payable over a period of many years, so the amount managers received depended on the *long-term* performance of the fund's toxic assets.

The Credit Suisse strategy appeased many critics of executive bonuses because managers were no longer guaranteed a fat check—they would only receive whatever the toxic assets in the Partner Asset Facility earned. Most observers considered this fair, since the company's managers were the ones who approved the strategy of investing heavily in these risky securities.

The strategy also had another benefit: placing the toxic assets in the Partner Asset Facility effectively removed them from Credit Suisse's balance sheet. This meant that the company no longer had to take huge write-downs if these assets continued to decline in value. As Dirk Hoffman-Becking of Sanford C. Berstein Ltd. put it, "It's monstrously clever."

Actually, the strategy turned out to be not only clever, but also quite lucrative for the executives who received shares in the fund—at least in the first year. As the world economy improved during 2009 many of the fund's assets increased dramatically in value. At the end of the first year the fund's value was up an impressive 72%, resulting in some very attractive executive bonuses.[3]

be the true owners of the company. Thus, dividends paid to preferred stockholders are subtracted from net income in the numerator when computing ROE because these dividends aren't available to common stockholders. Similarly, the denominator of this ratio includes only equity provided by common stockholders and retained earnings.

Another profitability ratio, called *earnings per share* (EPS), indicates how much net income a firm earned per share of common stock outstanding. It is calculated by dividing net income minus preferred dividends by the average number of shares of common stock outstanding.

Exhibit 9.1 summarizes the ratios we've mentioned and describes a few other ratios as well. Interpreting ratios correctly isn't always easy. For one thing, there's no single "best" value for a specific ratio; whether a particular ratio value is good or bad depends, in part, on the industry. For example, grocery stores normally have high inventory turnover ratios, meaning goods move through them quickly—a good thing, since few people want to buy bananas, bread, milk, or tomatoes that have been sitting in the store for several months! But it's not unusual for a furniture store or art gallery to have some expensive and distinctive pieces in stock for months before they are sold. So it's not surprising that the average inventory turnover of food stores is 18.33, while the average for furniture stores, for example, is 6.76.[4]

A comparison of a firm's ratios with the average ratios for other firms in the *same* industry (or with the ratios for a firm recognized as an industry leader) can help determine whether they're in the right ballpark. But even these comparisons can be misleading if they

EXHIBIT 9.1 Key Financial Ratios

Ratio	Type	What It Measures	How It Is Computed
Current	Liquidity: measures ability to pay short-term liabilities as they come due.	Compares current assets (assets that will provide cash in the next year) to current liabilities (debts that will come due in the next year).	$\dfrac{Current\ Assets}{Current\ Liabilities}$
Inventory turnover	Asset management: measures how effectively a firm is using its assets to generate revenue.	How quickly a firm sells its inventory to generate revenue.	$\dfrac{Cost\ of\ Goods\ Sold}{Average\ Inventory}$
Average collection period	Asset management: measures how effectively a firm is using its assets to generate revenue.	How long it takes for a firm to collect from customers who buy on credit.	$\dfrac{Accounts\ Receivable}{\left(\dfrac{Annual\ Credit\ Sales}{365}\right)}$
Debt-to-equity	Leverage: measures the extent to which a firm relies on debt to meet its financing needs.	Compares the total amount of debt financing to the amount of equity (owner-provided) financing. A high ratio indicates that the firm is "highly leveraged."	$\dfrac{Total\ Debt}{Total\ Owners'\ Equity}$
Debt-to-assets	Leverage: measures the extent to which a firm relies on debt to meet its financing needs.	Similar to debt-to-equity, but compares debt to assets rather than equity. This is another way of measuring the degree of financial leverage, or debt, the firm is using.	$\dfrac{Total\ Debt}{Total\ Assets}$
Return on equity	Profitability: compares the amount of profit to some measure of resources invested.	Indicates earnings per dollar invested by the owners of the company. Since common stockholders are the true owners, preferred stockholders' dividends are deducted from net income before computing this ratio.	$\dfrac{Net\ Income - Preferred\ Dividends}{Average\ Common\ Stockholders\ Equity}$
Return on assets	Profitability: compares the amount of profit to some measure of resources invested.	Indicates the amount of profit earned on each dollar the firm has invested in assets.	$\dfrac{Net\ Income}{Average\ Total\ Assets}$
Earnings per share	Profitability: compares the amount of profit to some measure of resources invested.	Measures the net income per share of common stock outstanding.	$\dfrac{Net\ Income - Preferred\ Dividends}{Average\ Number\ of\ Common\ Share\ Outstanding}$

aren't carefully interpreted. The accounting profession allows firms some flexibility in such matters as how they measure inventory and cost of goods sold and how they depreciate their assets. Because of this flexibility, two firms in the *same* industry with very similar real-world performance could report very different values for profitability or asset management ratios simply because they used different—but equally acceptable—accounting methods to develop their statements.

LO3 Financial Planning: Providing a Road Map for the Future

Financial planning is an important part of the firm's overall planning process. Assuming that the overall planning process has established appropriate goals and objectives for the firm, financial planning must answer the following questions:

- What specific assets must the firm obtain in order to achieve its goals?

- How much additional financing will the firm need to acquire these assets?

- How much financing will the firm be able to generate internally (through additional earnings), and how much must it obtain from external sources?

- When will the firm need to acquire external financing?

The planning process involves input from a variety of areas. In addition to seeking input from managers in various functional areas of their business, financial managers usually work closely with the firm's accountants during the planning process.

Basic Planning Tools: Budgeted Financial Statements and the Cash Budget

The budgeting process provides financial managers with much of the information they need for financial planning. In fact, the **budgeted income statement** and **budgeted balance sheet** are two key financial planning tools. Also called *pro forma financial statements*, they provide a framework for analyzing the impact of the firm's plans on the financing needs of the company.

- The budgeted income statement uses information from the sales budget and various cost budgets (as well as other assumptions) to develop a forecast of net income for the planning period.

- The budgeted balance sheet forecasts the types and amounts of assets a firm will need to implement its future plans. It also helps financial managers to determine the amount of additional financing (liabilities and owners' equity) the firm must arrange in order to acquire those assets.

The **cash budget** is another important financial planning tool. Financial managers use cash budgets to get a better understanding of the *timing* of cash flows within the planning period. Cash budgets normally cover a one-year period and show projected cash inflows and outflows for each month. This helps financial managers determine when the firm is likely to need additional funds to meet short-term cash shortages, and when surpluses of cash will be available to pay off loans or to invest in other assets.

Even firms with growing sales can experience cash flow problems, especially if many of their customers buy on credit. To meet increasing sales levels, growing firms must hire more labor and buy more supplies. The firm may have to pay for these additional inputs *before* its credit customers pay their bills, leading to a temporary cash crunch. Exhibit 9.2 illustrates this type of situation by presenting a partial cash budget for a hypothetical firm called Oze-Moore.

Notice that Oze-Moore's sales increase significantly in both March and April, but that most of its customers buy on credit. Thus, much of the cash Oze-Moore receives in March actually is from payments by credit customers for purchases they made in *February*. Because February sales are much lower than sales in March, the cash available in March falls short of the amount Oze-Moore needs to pay its bills. In fact, since the cash budget assumes that Oze-Moore wants to maintain at least $10,000 in its cash account at all times, it will have to arrange for a short-term loan of $11,750 to cover the shortfall and maintain its desired cash balance.

A look at the other months in Exhibit 9.2 shows that Oze-Moore also will need to arrange additional loans in April. This is valuable information to the firm's financial managers. Knowing in advance that they will need additional funds in March and April gives them time to seek the best sources for the needed funds.

The cash budget also shows that Oze-Moore is likely to generate a large cash surplus in May, enabling it to repay the short-term loans it obtained in March and April. In fact, the cash budget projects that May's surplus is likely to be so large that even after repaying the loans, Oze-Moore will have more cash than it needs. Knowing about this ahead of time may give managers a chance to find some short-term interest-earning investments where they can temporarily "park their cash."

budgeted income statement A projection showing how a firm's budgeted sales and costs will affect expected net income. (Also called a *pro forma* income statement.)

budgeted balance sheet A projected financial statement that forecasts the types and amounts of assets a firm will need to implement its future plans and how the firm will finance those assets. (Also called a *pro forma* balance sheet.)

cash budget A detailed forecast of future cash flows that helps financial managers identify when their firm is likely to experience temporary shortages or surpluses of cash.

LO4 Managing Working Capital: Current Events

A firm's **net working capital** is the difference between its current assets and current liabilities. In part, working capital management involves maintaining the appropriate level of current assets such as cash, inventories, and accounts receivable. But another concern is deciding the amount and type of current liabilities needed to finance the firm's short-term need for funds.

Managing Current Assets

Holding current assets involves trade-offs; either too much or too little of these assets can spell trouble. Effective management of working capital involves making the right investment decisions with respect to the type and amount of each current asset.

Managing Cash A company must have cash to pay its workers, suppliers, creditors and taxes. Many firms also need cash to pay dividends. And most firms also want to

hold enough cash to meet unexpected contingencies. But cash has one serious shortcoming compared to other assets: it earns little or no return. If a firm holds a lot more cash than necessary to meet its required payments, stockholders are likely to ask why the excess cash isn't being invested in more profitable assets. And if the firm can't find a profitable way to invest the money, the stockholders are likely to ask management why it doesn't use the excess cash to pay them a higher dividend—most shareholders can think of plenty of ways *they'd* like to use the cash!

In the narrowest sense, a firm's cash refers to its holdings of currency (paper money and coins issued by the government) plus demand deposits (the balance in the company's checking account). However, when most firms report their cash holdings on their balance sheet, they take a broader view, including **cash equivalents** along with their actual cash. Cash equivalents are very safe and highly liquid assets that can be converted into cash so easily that firms view them as part of their cash holdings. Commercial paper, U.S. Treasury Bills (T-bills), and money market mutual funds are among the most popular cash equivalents. The advantage of these cash equivalents is that they offer a better financial return (in the form of interest) than currency or demand deposits.

© JAMES BLINN/ISTOCKPHOTO.COM

EXHIBIT 9.2 Cash Budget for Oze-Moore

Cash Budget for Oze-Moore

	February	March	April	May
Sales	$75,000	$110,000	$125,000	$90,000
Cash balance at beginning of month		$10,000	$10,000	$10,000
Receipts of Cash				
Cash sales		$16,500	$18,750	$13,500
Collection of accounts receivable from last month's sales		$63,750	$93,500	$106,250
Total Cash Available		$90,250	$122,250	$129,750
Disbursements of Cash				
Payment of accounts payable		$60,500	$68,750	$49,500
Wages and salaries		$27,500	$31,250	$22,500
Fixed costs (rent, interest on debt, etc.)		$8,000	$8,000	$8,000
Purchase of new computers			$6,500	
Total Cash Payments		$96,000	$114,500	$80,000
Excess or Deficit of Cash for Month		-$5,750	$7,750	$49,750
Loans needed to maintain cash balance of $10,000		$15,750	$2,250	$0
Amount of cash available to repay short-term loans		$0	$0	$39,750
Cash balance at end of month		$10,000	$10,000	$31,750
Cumulative loans		$15,750	$18,000	$0

Sales increase in both March and April. But since most of Oze-Moore's customers buy on credit, its receipt of cash lags behind these sales increases.

While receipts of cash lag behind sales, Oze-Moore's payments of wages and accounts payable are due in the same month as sales.

Despite big increases in sales in March and April, Oze-Moore suffers a shortfall of cash because of the difference in *timing* between cash receipts and cash payments.

Financial managers want to have at least $10,000 in the cash balance at the beginning of each month. When cash falls below this amount they take out a short-term loans.

In May, Oze-Moore has a surplus in cash. This gives it enough cash to pay off the loans from earlier months.

Commercial paper consists of short-term promissory notes (IOUs) issued by major corporations with excellent credit ratings. Historically, commercial paper has been unsecured—meaning it isn't backed by a pledge of collateral. It is usually offered only by firms with excellent credit ratings because firms with less-than-stellar financial reputations that tried to issue unsecured commercial paper would be unlikely to find many buyers. In recent years a new class of commercial paper has emerged, called *asset-backed commercial paper*. This type of paper is backed by financial securities.

Even though commercial paper can be issued for up to 270 days, firms typically issue it for much shorter periods—sometimes for as little as two days. Corporations sell commercial paper at a *discount*, meaning that it is initially sold at a lower price than the amount the company will pay the holder when the paper comes due. The difference between the initial price and the price paid to the holder when the paper comes due represents the interest earned on the note.

U.S. Treasury bills, or "T-bills," are short-term IOUs issued by the U.S. government. Most T-bills mature (come due) in 4, 13, or 26 weeks. Like commercial paper, the bills are sold at a discount, and the holder receives the full par value of the bill at maturity. There is a very active secondary market for T-bills, meaning that their owners can sell them to other investors before they mature. Thus, T-bills are highly liquid. And since the U.S. government backs them, they're essentially risk-free. The safety and liquidity of T-bills make them very attractive cash equivalents.

Money market mutual funds raise money by selling shares to large numbers of investors. They then pool these funds to purchase a portfolio of short-term, liquid securities. (In fact, money market mutual funds often include large holdings of commercial paper and T-bills.) Money market mutual funds are an affordable way for small investors to get into the market for securities, which would otherwise be beyond their means. This affordability also makes these funds a particularly

> **commercial paper** Short-term (and usually unsecured) promissory notes issued by large corporations.

> **U.S. Treasury bills (T-bills)** Short-term marketable IOUs issued by the U.S. federal government.

> **money market mutual funds** A mutual fund that pools funds from many investors and uses these funds to purchase very safe, highly liquid securities.

> Households and businesses aren't the only customers who pay late. Faced with plummeting tax revenues in 2009, many state governments began delaying payments to suppliers.
>
> *Smallbiz.com*

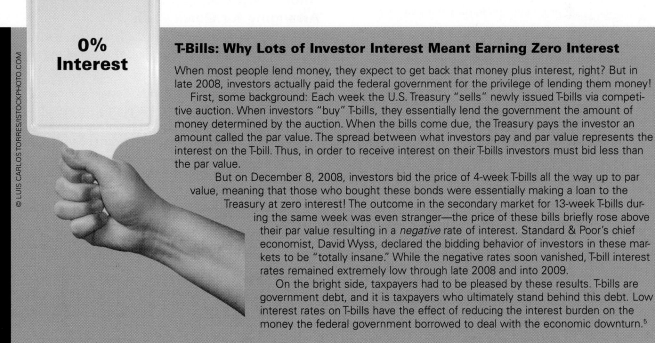

0% Interest

T-Bills: Why Lots of Investor Interest Meant Earning Zero Interest

When most people lend money, they expect to get back that money plus interest, right? But in late 2008, investors actually paid the federal government for the privilege of lending them money!

First, some background: Each week the U.S. Treasury "sells" newly issued T-bills via competitive auction. When investors "buy" T-bills, they essentially lend the government the amount of money determined by the auction. When the bills come due, the Treasury pays the investor an amount called the par value. The spread between what investors pay and par value represents the interest on the T-bill. Thus, in order to receive interest on their T-bills investors must bid less than the par value.

But on December 8, 2008, investors bid the price of 4-week T-bills all the way up to par value, meaning that those who bought these bonds were essentially making a loan to the Treasury at zero interest! The outcome in the secondary market for 13-week T-bills during the same week was even stranger—the price of these bills briefly rose above their par value resulting in a *negative* rate of interest. Standard & Poor's chief economist, David Wyss, declared the bidding behavior of investors in these markets to be "totally insane." While the negative rates soon vanished, T-bill interest rates remained extremely low through late 2008 and into 2009.

On the bright side, taxpayers had to be pleased by these results. T-bills are government debt, and it is taxpayers who ultimately stand behind this debt. Low interest rates on T-bills have the effect of reducing the interest burden on the money the federal government borrowed to deal with the economic downturn.[5]

attractive cash equivalent for smaller firms.

Managing Accounts Receivable Accounts receivable represents what credit customers owe the firm. Allowing customers to buy on credit can significantly increase sales. But, as our discussion of the cash budget showed, credit sales can create cash flow problems because they delay the receipt of cash the firm needs to meet its financial obligations. Credit customers who pay late or don't pay at all only exacerbate the problem. So it's important for firms to have a well-thought-out policy that balances the advantages of offering credit with the costs. The key elements of this policy should include:

- Setting credit terms: For how long should the firm extend credit? What type of cash discount should the firm offer to encourage early payments?

- Establishing credit standards: How should the firm decide which customers qualify for credit? What type of credit information should it require? How strict should its standards be?

- Deciding on an appropriate collection policy: How aggressive should the firm be at collecting past-due accounts? At what point does it make sense to take (or at least threaten to take) legal action against late-paying customers, or to turn over the accounts to collection agencies? When does it make sense to work out compromises?

In each area, firms face trade-offs. For example, a firm that extends credit for only 30 days will receive its payments faster than a firm that allows customers 60 or 90 days. But setting short credit periods may also result in lost sales, especially if competitors give customers more time to pay. Similarly, setting high credit standards reduces the likelihood a firm will have problems with customers who pay late (or not at all). Yet these strict standards may prevent many good customers from getting credit, resulting in lower sales. Finally, an aggressive collection policy may help the firm collect payments that it would otherwise lose. But an aggressive policy might alienate customers who make hon-

est mistakes, causing them to take future business to competitors.

In recent troubled times, some firms have found that being flexible and creative about the form of payment can help them get at least some of what they are owed. Sometimes barter arrangements work better than demanding cash. For example, a health spa took payments from one of its customers in the form of hundreds of granola bars. Similarly, the owner of a bookkeeping firm agreed to accept payment from a veterinarian in the form of emergency surgery on her pet cat![6]

Managing Inventories Inventories are the stocks of finished goods, work-in-process, and parts and materials that firms hold as a part of doing business. Clearly, businesses must hold inventories to operate. For example, you'd probably be disappointed if you visited a Best Buy store and were confronted with empty shelves rather than with a wide array of electronic gadgets to compare and try out. Similarly, a manufacturing firm must hold an inventory of parts and materials to produce its products.

But for many firms, the funds tied up in inventories represent a major investment, and the cost of storing and insuring inventory items is a significant expense. While inventory management is an important part of overall working capital management, inventory policies are usually designed and implemented within the broader context of a firm's overall operations management strategy. In recent years many firms have become very aggressive about controlling inventories in order to reduce costs and improve efficiency.

Short-Term Financing: Arranging for Quick Cash

Firms often have several options when it comes to raising short-term financing. Let's look at some of the more important sources.

Spontaneous Sources of Funds Certain sources of funding arise naturally, during the normal course of business operations. This type of financing is called **spontaneous financing** because the firm doesn't have to make special arrangements to acquire it. **Trade credit**, which arises when suppliers ship materials, parts, or goods to a firm without requiring payment at the time of delivery, is the major source of spontaneous

> { **Sometimes your best investments are the ones you don't make.**
> *Donald Trump* }

financing for many firms. In most cases, the terms of trade credit are presented on the invoice for the shipment. For example, an invoice might list the terms as 2/10 net 30. The "net 30" indicates that the supplier allows the buyer 30 days before payment is due. But the "2/10" tells the buyer that the supplier is offering a 2% discount off the invoice price if it pays within 10 days.

At first glance, the 2% discount may not seem like a big deal. But failing to take the discount can be very costly. Consider the terms we mentioned above: 2/10, net 30. If the firm fails to pay within 10 days it loses the discount and must pay the full amount 20 days later. Paying 2% more for the use of funds for only 20 days is equivalent to an *annual* finance charge of over 37%![7]

Suppliers will grant trade credit only after they've evaluated the creditworthiness of the firm. But once they've granted this credit to a company once, they generally continue offering it as long as the firm satisfies the terms of the credit arrangements. Although firms of all sizes use this type of financing, trade credit is a particularly important source of financing for small businesses. The Federal Reserve Board's *Survey of Small Business Finances* indicates that about 60% of all small businesses relied on this form of financing—the highest percentage of any source of short-run financial capital.[8]

Short-Term Bank Loans Banks are another common source of short-term business financing. Short-term bank loans are usually due in 30 to 90 days, though they can be up to a year in length. When a firm negotiates a loan with a bank, it signs a *promissory note*, which specifies the length of the loan, the rate of interest the firm must pay, and other terms and conditions of the loan. Banks sometimes require firms to pledge collateral, such as inventories or accounts receivable, to back the loan. That way, if the borrower fails to make the required payments, the bank has a claim on specific assets that can be used to pay off the amount due.

Rather than going through the hassle of negotiating a separate loan each time they need more funds, many firms work out arrangements with their bankers to obtain preapproval so that they can draw on funds as needed. One way firms do this is by establishing a **line of credit**. Under this type of arrangement, a bank agrees to provide the firm with funds up to some specified limit, as long as the borrower's credit situation doesn't deteriorate.

A **revolving credit agreement** is similar to a line of credit, except that the bank makes a formal, legally binding commitment to provide the agreed-upon funds. A revolving credit agreement is like a *guaranteed* line of credit. In exchange for the binding commitment to provide the funds, the bank requires the borrowing firm to pay a commitment fee based on the *unused* amount of funds. Thus, under the terms of a revolving credit agreement, the firm will pay interest on any funds it borrows, and a commitment fee on any funds it does not borrow. The commitment fee is much lower than the interest on the borrowed funds, but it can amount to a fairly hefty charge if the firm has a large unused balance.

Factoring Firms can also obtain short-term financing by using the services of a factor. A **factor** is a company that buys the accounts receivables of other firms. The factor makes a profit by purchasing the receivables at a discount from the firm and collecting the full amount from the credit customer.

Although firms that use factors don't receive the full amount for their accounts receivables, the use of factors offers some definite advantages. Instead of having to wait for credit customers to pay, the firm gets its money almost immediately. Also, using a factor allows the firm to outsource its collection efforts, so it doesn't have to maintain its own collection department. Factoring now provides more than a trillion dollars in short-term financing to firms—an amount that's more than tripled since the early 1990s.[9]

Commercial Paper We defined commercial paper in our discussion of cash equivalents. Well-established corporations with strong credit reputations often issue commercial paper to meet their short-term financing needs. A key reason commercial paper is popular with such companies is that this form of financing typically carries a lower interest rate than commercial banks

line of credit A financial arrangement between a firm and a bank in which the bank pre-approves credit up to a specified limit, provided that the firm maintains an acceptable credit rating.

revolving credit agreement A guaranteed line of credit in which a bank makes a binding commitment to provide a business with funds up to a specified credit limit at any time during the term of the agreement.

factor A company that provides short-term financing to firms by purchasing their accounts receivables at a discount.

charge on short-term loans. By far the biggest issuers of commercial paper are financial institutions, but other large corporations also use this form of financing.

The market for commercial paper normally is huge—often close to $2 trillion—but it can fluctuate dramatically as economic conditions change. Investors tend to view commercial paper as significantly riskier than T-bills, so the demand for these corporate IOUs often drops sharply during economic downturns. In fact, the market for commercial paper essentially dried up in late 2008 as the economy sank into a deep recession. This put a tremendous strain on many of the struggling financial institutions that relied on commercial paper to meet their short-term cash needs. The situation became so grim that in October of 2008 the Fed established the Commercial Paper Funding Facility, a limited liability company funded by the Federal Reserve Bank of New York. This facility, which the Fed operated until February 1, 2010, ultimately purchased several hundred billion dollars of commercial paper, providing a crucial infusion of cash into this stressed market.[10]

LO5 Capital Budgeting: In It for the Long Haul

So far we've looked at how a firm manages its current assets and liabilities and how it arranges to meet short-term financing needs. We'll conclude the chapter with a look at how firms make decisions about investing in fixed assets and how they arrange for long-term financing.

Capital budgeting refers to the procedure a firm uses to plan for its investment in assets or projects that it expects will yield benefits for more than a year. The capital budgeting process evaluates proposals such as:

- replacing existing machinery and equipment with more advanced models;

- buying additional new machinery and equipment to expand production capacity;

- building a new factory, warehouse, or office building;

- introducing a new product line or service into the firm's product mix.

A firm that makes a poor capital budgeting choice may need to live with the consequences of its decision for a long time, or sell expensive assets at a substantial loss. For example, a multibillion-dollar plant Intel builds

to fabricate computer chips may be so specialized in its design and layout that firms in other industries couldn't use it without expensive modifications. If Intel found that it really didn't need the extra capacity, it might have a hard time finding a firm interested in buying the plant.

Evaluating Capital Budgeting Proposals

Financial managers measure the benefits and costs of a long-term investment proposal in terms of the cash flows it will generate. But accurately forecasting these cash flows can be quite a challenge, since financial managers must analyze only *relevant* cash flows—those that are expected to *change* as the result of a capital budgeting decision. Identifying and estimating the size of these cash flows can be tough.

To illustrate one challenge in measuring cash flows, suppose a beverage company is evaluating a proposal to market a new type of soft drink that its research shows would be very popular with young adults. Let's assume that the firm believes that sales of the new drink will result in cash revenue of $12 million per month, while the cost of producing and distributing the drink will require cash payments of $7 million per month. At first glance it might appear that this would result in a net cash inflow of $5 million per month (the $12 million inflow minus the $7 million outflow). But suppose some of the new drink's sales occur because customers switch from the firm's existing product line—an outcome known as *cannibalization*. If so, much of the supposed increase in cash may be offset by decreases in sales of other beverages. Financial managers would have to estimate these cannibalization effects in order to measure the true incremental cash flows generated by the new drink.

Another problem is that the cash flows from a long-term investment are spread over several years. Cash flows are likely to be negative at the start of a project because money must be spent to get the project up and running. But a project must eventually generate enough positive cash flows to more than offset these expenditures if it is to benefit the company.

When financial managers compare cash flows that occur at different times, they must take the time

Time is money.

Ben Franklin

value of money into account. The **time value of money** reflects the fact that a dollar received today is worth *more* than a dollar received in the future because the sooner you receive a sum of money, the sooner you can put that money to work to earn even *more* money.

Let's illustrate the time value of money with a simple example. Suppose your favorite aunt is extremely proud of your decision to enroll in a business course—as well she should be! In fact, she's so pleased that she decides to send you $1,000 to reward your good judgment. Let's also suppose that you decide to invest your aunt's gift in a certificate of deposit (CD) at your local bank that pays 5% interest. (We realize that you might have other ways to use the $1,000, but humor us for now.) How much money will you have a year from the day you buy the CD? The answer is $1,050—your original $1,000 *plus* the $50 interest you earned on the CD.

Now let's change our assumptions. Suppose your aunt still gives you $1,000 but doesn't send you the money until next year. Because you receive the money later, you lose the opportunity to earn a year's worth of interest. Receiving your aunt's gift today means that *you are $50 better off next year than you would be if you'd received the $1,000 a year from today.* Clearly, the earlier you receive a given sum of money, the better off you are from a financial standpoint.

Because money has a time value, the value of an investment doesn't just depend on the *amount* of cash an investment generates but also on *when* it generates that cash.

When financial managers compare different investments, each with complex cash flows over a period of many years, they take the time value of these cash flows into account by converting them into their present values.

The **present value** of a cash flow received in a future time period is the amount of money which, if invested *today* at an assumed rate of interest, would grow to become that future amount of money. For example, take a look at Exhibit 9.3. It shows that $1,000 invested today at 6% grows to a future value of $1,262.48 in four years. Thus, $1,000 is the present value of $1,262.48 received in 4 years.

> **time value of money** The principle that a dollar received today is worth more than a dollar received in the future.
>
> **present value** The amount of money that, if invested today at a given rate of interest, would grow to become some future amount in a specified number of time periods.

EXHIBIT 9.3 How a Present Value of $1,000 Grows to a Future Value of $1,262.48 in Four Years

Now
- Deposit $1000.00 (Present value)
- Earn 6% per year

After 1 year you'll have
- $1000.00 + $60 interest earned over first year (6% of $1000) =
- $1060.00

After 2 years you'll have
- $1060.00 + $63.60 interest earned over second year (6% of $1060) =
- $1123.60

After 3 years you'll have
- $1123.60 + $67.42 interest earned over third year (6% of $1123.60) =
- $1191.02

After 4 years you'll have
- $1191.02 + $71.46 interest earned over fourth year (6% of $1191.02) =
- $1262.48 (Future Value)

For a Socially Responsible Firm in Need of Funds, There's No Need to Fear...

Venture capital (VC) firms have long been an important source of financing for hot new companies offering the potential for rapid growth. VCs are limited partnerships or limited liability companies that pool funds from wealthy individuals and institutional investors (such as pension funds and college endowments) and invest those funds in firms with high profit potential. Many of today's best-known corporations, including Staples, Google, Apple, and Starbucks, got their first major funding from venture capitalists.

Traditional venture capital firms focus almost exclusively on the bottom line. They are willing to invest in "green" companies (and often do), but only if the firms offer potentially high (and quick) returns. But over the past decade a new breed of "green" VC firm has emerged. These new firms still seek a solid financial return, but that isn't their *only* goal. They exist to fund firms that pursue worthy social and environmental goals—and do so even if the expected financial return is a bit lower and they have to wait longer to receive it.

Consider Underdog Ventures, a VC firm whose managing partner, David Berge, was listed in *Inc. Magazine* in 2009 as one of 30 entrepreneurs who were "saving the world." Underdog invests *only* in firms that exhibit socially responsible business practices. And it is more patient with its investments, putting less pressure on the firms to create a quick return. Another difference between Underdog and traditional VC firms is that it allows investors to specify the type of firm they want to fund and to target certain demographic or geographic opportunities, such as businesses owned and operated by women or minorities, or those located in depressed areas. Finally, it has set up its own philanthropic organization, called the Underdog Foundation, to support socially responsible projects that cannot be satisfied by profit-seeking investments. Even more impressive: *every* investor in Underdog Ventures and *every* firm that has received funds from Underdog has contributed to the foundation.[11]

net present value (NPV) The sum of the present values of expected future cash flows from an investment minus the cost of that investment.

capital structure The mix of equity and debt financing a firm uses to meet its permanent financing needs.

covenants Conditions lenders place on firms that seek long-term debt financing.

Today, financial calculators and spreadsheet software make computing present values easy. All a manager needs to do is enter the amount and timing of the estimated cash flow into the calculator (or spreadsheet) along with the discount rate. The calculator or software will handle all of the number crunching.

Using Net Present Value to Evaluate Capital Budgeting Proposals

The most commonly used method to evaluate capital budgeting proposals is to compute their **net present value (NPV)**. The NPV of an investment proposal is found by adding the present values of *all* of its estimated future cash flows and subtracting the initial cost of the investment from the sum. A positive NPV means the present value of the expected cash flows from the project is greater than the cost of the project. In other words, the benefits from the project exceed its cost even after accounting for the time value of money. Financial managers are likely to approve projects with positive NPVs. A negative NPV means that the present value of the expected future cash flows from the project is less than the cost of the investment. This would indicate that the cost of the project outweighs its cash flow benefits. Financial managers would reject proposals with negative NPVs. (See Exhibit 9.4.)

EXHIBIT 9.4 Decision Rule for Capital Budgeting

Result of NPV Calculation	Decision
NPV ≥ 0	Accept proposal ✔
NPV < 0	Reject proposal ✘

LO6 Choosing the Sources of Long-Term Capital: Loaners vs. Owners

Our last major financial management topic deals with how firms meet their long-term financing needs. Most firms use a combination of equity and debt to acquire needed assets and to finance their operations. Owners provide equity financing, while creditors (lenders) provide debt financing. The extent to which a firm relies on various forms of debt and equity to satisfy its financing needs is called that firm's capital structure. To simplify our discussion, we'll focus mainly on the **capital structure** of corpo-rations, but keep in mind that many of the basic issues and principles apply to any form of ownership.

Pros and Cons of Debt Financing

When a firm borrows funds, it enters into a contractual agreement with the lenders. This arrangement creates a *legally binding* agreement to repay the money borrowed (called the principal) *plus interest*. These payments take precedence over any payments to owners. In fact, lenders often require the firm to pledge collateral, such as real estate, financial securities, or equipment, to back the loan. Should the firm be unable to make the required payments, the lenders can use this collateral to recover what it is owed.

Debt financing offers some advantages to firms. For instance, the interest payments a firm makes on debt are a tax-deductible expense. So Uncle Sam (in the form of the IRS) subsidizes the interest payments. For example, if the corporation's tax rate is 30%, then each dollar of interest expense reduces the firm's taxes by $.30—meaning the true cost to the firm of each dollar of interest is only $.70.

Another advantage of debt is that it enables the firm to acquire additional funds without requiring existing stockholders to invest more of their own money or the sale of stock to new investors (which would dilute the ownership of existing owners). Moreover, if the firm invests the borrowed funds profitably, the use of debt can substantially improve the return on equity to the shareholders. We'll illustrate this result in our discussion of financial leverage.

An obvious disadvantage of debt is the requirement to make fixed payments. This can create real problems when the firm finds itself in an unexpectedly tight financial situation. In bad times, these fixed payments can eat up most (or all) of the earnings, leaving little or no return to the firm's owners. And if the firm is unable to meet these fixed payments it can be forced into bankruptcy.

Another disadvantage of debt financing is that creditors often impose restrictions, called **covenants**, on the borrower. Covenants sometimes place restrictions on the amount of dividends a firm can pay or a limit on the amount of additional debt financing the firm can obtain. They sometimes even limit the level of salaries and bonuses the firm can pay its employees. The purpose of covenants is to protect creditors by preventing the borrower from pursuing policies that might put the lenders' funds at greater risk. Covenants are desirable from the perspective of the lender, but they limit the flexibility of management.

Pros and Cons of Equity Financing

For corporations, equity financing comes from two major sources: money directly invested by stockholders who purchase newly issued stock, and **retained earnings**, which are earnings a company reinvests.

Equity financing provides a company with more flexibility and less risk than debt financing. Unlike debt, equity imposes no required payments. A firm can skip dividend payments to stockholders without having to worry that it will be pushed into bankruptcy. And a firm doesn't have to agree to burdensome covenants to acquire equity funds.

On the other hand, equity financing doesn't yield the same tax benefits as debt financing. In addition, existing owners may not want a firm to issue more stock, since doing so might dilute their share of ownership. Finally, a company that relies mainly on equity financing forgoes the opportunity to use financial leverage. But as we've already noted, leverage can be a two-edged sword. We'll illustrate the risks and rewards of leverage in our next section.

Financial Leverage: Using Debt to Magnify Gains (And Losses)

As we mentioned in our discussion of ratios, firms that rely on a lot of debt in their capital structure are said to be *highly leveraged*. The main advantage of financial leverage is that it increases the expected return on the stockholders' investment. Its main disadvantage is that it also increases the firm's financial risk.

Let's illustrate both the advantages and disadvantages of financial leverage with a simple example. Exhibit 9.5 shows the revenues, expenses, and earnings that two firms—Eck-Witty Corporation and Oze-Moore International—would experience for two different levels of sales, one representing a strong year and the other a weak year. To keep our example simple, let's assume that Eck-Witty and Oze-Moore are *identical* in all respects *except* their capital structure. Thus, any differences in the financial performance of these firms results from differences in their use of debt and equity financing. We'll use return on equity (ROE) to measure the financial performance of each firm from the perspective of its stockholders. (See Exhibit 9.1 if you need a reminder about how this ratio is computed.)

Note that *both* firms have invested in a total of $1 million of assets, but they've met their financing needs in different ways. Eck-Witty used only common stock and retained earnings in its capital structure, so it has $1 million in equity and no debt. Oze-Moore's capital structure consists of $400,000 in owners' equity and $600,000 in debt, so it is highly leveraged. The interest rate on its debt is 10%, so Oze-Moore has to make required interest payments of $60,000 per year to its lenders. Both companies must pay taxes equal

retained earnings
That part of net income that a firm reinvests.

Is Too Big to Fail a Thing of the Past?

A key factor leading to the economic crisis beginning in 2008 was the extremely risky (some would say reckless) behavior of many of our nation's largest banks and financial institutions. The extensive use of leverage at many of these firms left them highly vulnerable to a downturn in the economy. A few of these huge firms went under in late 2008—Lehman Brothers and Washington Mutual among the best known—and their failures contributed to the panic and financial turmoil. Government officials quickly concluded that they couldn't allow other financial giants such as Citigroup, Goldman Sachs, and Bank of America to go under. They reasoned that these firms were so huge and so interdependent that the collapse of one of them could bring down the entire U.S. financial system and devastate the economy. In other words, they were deemed "too big to fail." This line of reasoning led the government to hastily create a huge bailout program for the financial sector.

While most experts agreed that the government's bailout was necessary, they also agreed that it sent the wrong message for the future. As long as financial institutions are too big to fail, they are likely to continue making excessively risky decisions, since they believe the government will protect them from any negative consequences of these risks. In other words, "heads we win, tails the taxpayers lose."

But the days of "too big to fail" may be over. In 2010 Congress passed a far-reaching (and controversial) financial reform bill. One goal of this legislation was to eliminate the problem of "too big to fail." Among the law's key provisions:

- **Tighter restrictions on financial leverage:** the reform bill requires big banks to hold larger amounts of capital against their debts, effectively limiting their use of risky financial leverage.
- **Requirement for funeral plans:** large financial institutions are required to develop plans for their rapid and orderly shutdown should they go under.
- **Prohibition of government bailouts for individual banks:** while the Fed can still engage in broad-based emergency lending during a future crisis, bailouts that target specific companies are now prohibited.[12]

to 30% of their earnings, but Oze-Moore's total tax bill will be lower than Eck-Witty's because its interest payments are tax deductible.

Exhibit 9.5 shows the results for the two firms under both sales scenarios. Note that, although the revenue and operating expenses for the firms are identical under both scenarios, Oze-Moore's net income is lower than Eck-Witty's because it also must pay interest on its debt. But also remember that the owners of Eck-Witty contributed much more of their _own_ money than the owners of Oze-Moore.

As you can see in Exhibit 9.5, when sales are good Oze-Moore's leverage really pays off: under the strong sales scenario its return on equity is 24.5%, while Eck-Witty's ROE is only 14%. This occurs because interest payments on debt financing are _fixed_. Oze-Moore pays its creditors $60,000—no more, no less—whether times are good or bad. When it earns a return that is higher than the interest rate on debt, _any additional earnings_

on investments Oze-Moore financed using debt go to the _owners_, even though creditors provided the funds. When earnings are strong, this really boosts the returns to the stockholders!

But in the weak sales scenario, the $60,000 of _required_ interest payments wipes out all of Oze-Moore's earnings (and then some), leaving the company with a negative net income and an ROE of -1.75%. Even worse, if Oze-Moore fails to make the required interest payments, creditors could force it into bankruptcy. This illustrates the risk associated with financial leverage. In comparison, notice that Eck-Witty still earns a small profit in the weak sales scenario; granted its return on equity of 3.5% isn't spectacular, but it sure beats the negative return experienced by Oze-Moore.

Our example contains important lessons for the real world—lessons that recent financial history clearly illustrates. During the economic boom between 2003 and early 2007, many companies found that the use

EXHIBIT 9.5 How Financial Leverage Affects the Return on Equity

How Leverage Affects Returns

Interest Rate	10%	
Tax Rate	30%	

Eck-Witty (Capital structure uses only equity)			Oze-Moore (Capital structure is 40% equity and 60% debt)		
Equity (Funds supplied by owners)	$1,000,000		Equity (Funds supplied by owners)	$400,000	
Debt (Funds obtained by borrowing)	$0		Debt (Funds obtained by borrowing)	$600,000	

Market Conditions:	Strong Sales	Weak Sales	Market Conditions:	Strong Sales	Weak Sales
Revenue	$800,000	$480,000	Revenue	$800,000	$480,000
Cost of goods sold	350,000	250,000	Cost of goods sold	350,000	250,000
Operating expenses	250,000	180,000	Operating expenses	250,000	180,000
Income before interest and taxes	200,000	50,000	Income before interest and taxes	200,000	50,000
Interest	0	0	Interest	60,000	60,000
Taxable earnings	200,000	50,000	Taxable earnings	140,000	-10,000
Income taxes	60,000	15,000	Income taxes	42,000	-3,000
After Tax Income	140,000	35,000	**After Tax Income**	98,000	-7,000
Return on Equity	14.00%	3.50%	**Return on Equity**	24.50%	-1.75%

Compared to Oze-Moore's risky use of leverage, Eck-Witty's use of only equity financing results in a lower ROE when sales are strong, but a better ROE when sales are weak.

Oze-Moore's use of leverage magnifies returns on equity when sales are strong, but the need to make fixed interest payments leads to negative returns when sales are weak.

Oops! what were they THINKING?!

© PHOTODISC/GETTY IMAGES

Will Leverage in the Movie Business Lead to "Marvel-ous" Returns?

Moviegoers around the globe got caught in a web of excitement in May of 2007 when *Spider-Man 3* played to huge audiences. The third installment in the Marvel Comics franchise earned over $750 million at the box office. Executives at Sony Pictures, the film studio that produced the *Spider-Man* series under a licensing agreement with Marvel, were thrilled. But executives at Marvel Entertainment weren't nearly as excited—and for good reason. Financial analysts who looked into the cash flows concluded that very little of the money generated by *Spider-Man 3* found its way into Marvel's coffers. Sony clearly got the better end of the licensing deal.

Apparently this wasn't an isolated incident. Until recently, Marvel superheroes seemed to have special powers for making *other* companies rich while leaving Marvel's earnings nearly invisible by comparison. Fox's 2005 movie *The Fantastic Four* grossed hundreds of millions of dollars but delivered only $13 million to Marvel. Likewise the *X-Men* action-film series earned a combined $2 billion, but only $26 million found its way into Marvel's bank account.

Feeling shortchanged by its licensing strategy, Marvel decided to produce its own films. The first of Marvel Studios' independently developed movies was *Iron Man*, which debuted in May of 2008. The movie was a huge success; its box office receipts for 2008 ranked second only to the Batman blockbuster *The Dark Knight*. Marvel's second major production, *The Incredible Hulk*, hit the screens only a few months after *Iron Man*. While not quite the smash hit of *Iron Man*, it still earned a respectable profit. And the company's success continued when *Iron Man 2* proved to be yet another box office triumph when it was released in May of 2010. Flush with these successes, the company plans to release an ambitious slate of movies over the next few years.

Marvel's move is a bold attempt to reap the profits generated by its superheroes. But moviemaking is risky, and Marvel made it riskier when it entered into a $525 million debt financing deal, using the film rights to its superhero characters as collateral. If the gamble works—and the successes of *Iron Man* and *The Incredible Hulk* and *Iron Man 2* were certainly encouraging—the company's use of financial leverage could provide a truly "Marvel-ous" return on its investment. But if future movies bomb and Marvel can't generate enough cash to pay its debts, lenders will own the film rights to Captain America and other Marvel creations. [13]

---

of leverage magnified their ROEs. In fact, in their quest to generate ever-higher returns, firms began underestimating the risks of leverage and continued to take on additional debt. When the housing bubble burst and the economy slowed, the required interest and principal payments on their debt became a heavy burden on heavily leveraged firms. The highfliers of 2006 and 2007 experienced huge losses as their fixed payments ate up all of their earnings. As we mentioned at the beginning of this chapter, many of these firms ended up in bankruptcy.

By late 2008 many of the highly leveraged firms that survived the initial carnage were frantically looking for ways to reduce the amount of debt in their capital structure—a strategy known as *deleveraging*. This required them to either raise more equity or to liquidate (sell off) assets in order to pay off debt. Unfortunately, many firms found deleveraging to be a slow and painful process. The poor performance of these firms meant their earnings were low, so they couldn't use retained earnings to build their financial capital. And their poor economic condition also made it difficult to convince investors to buy their stock. So raising equity was extremely difficult. But it was just as difficult to raise money needed to deleverage by selling off assets; with so many firms liquidating financial assets at the same time, the value of these assets plunged. The moral

of the story: if the financial returns of leverage seem too good to be true, over the long run they probably are. Sound financial management requires keeping a level head and considering the riskiness of financial decisions as well as their return. [14]

The Big Picture

In this chapter we discussed the tasks financial managers perform as they attempt to find the best sources and uses of financial resources. Recent history amply illustrates how important sound financial management is to the success of a firm—and how devastating poor financial decisions can be. Indeed, the recent decline and fall of some of the biggest and best-known U.S. corporations can be traced in large measure to poor financial decisions—especially decisions that failed to adequately take risk into account, resulting in the use of too much leverage.

These lessons from the recent past will probably result in a different approach to financial management over the next several years. As firms recover from the trauma of a severe recession, they are likely to be more conservative in their view of what constitutes the best sources and uses of funds. Firms are likely to shy away from excessive debt and put more emphasis on equity financing. They also are less likely to use their funds to invest in highly risky or speculative assets.

WHAT ELSE? *RIP & REVIEW* **CARDS IN THE BACK**

10

SECURITIES MARKETS: TRADING FINANCIAL RESOURCES

LEARNING OBJECTIVES

After studying this chapter, you will be able to...

LO1 Describe the three basic types of securities issued by corporations

LO2 Explain how securities are issued in the primary market and traded on secondary markets

LO3 Discuss how the government and private organizations regulate securities markets

LO4 Compare several strategies that investors use to invest in securities

LO5 Explain the investor appeal of mutual funds and exchange traded funds

LO6 Describe how investors can track the performance of their investments

Visit CourseMate at www.cengagebrain.com.

← 22-51
WALL

> **Anyone who thinks there is safety in numbers hasn't looked at the stock market pages.**
>
> *Irene Peter, American writer*

LO1 Basic Types of Financial Securities

Securities markets transfer funds from investors who want to earn a return on their money to firms that need financial resources to achieve their long-term goals. Without these markets companies would find it difficult to obtain the financial resources they need to expand, create jobs, introduce new products, and compete effectively in global markets. But securities markets don't just benefit the businesses that issue the securities. Investors who buy securities obtain financial assets they expect to enhance their wealth.

You can, and most likely will, participate in these markets. In fact, doing so may be the key to achieving your personal financial goals. Making wise investment decisions can help you buy your dream home, put your kids through college, and live comfortably when you retire. But as recent history has shown, investing in securities can result in losses as well as gains. This chapter will help you understand both the rewards *and* the risks of investing in corporate securities. Let's begin by describing the three major types of securities that are traded in securities markets.

Common Stock: Basic Ownership

Common stock is the basic form of ownership in a corporation. Exhibit 10.1 shows stock certificates representing ownership in several different corporations. As owners, common stockholders have certain key rights:

- **Voting Rights:** Owners of common stock have the right to vote on important issues in the annual stockholders' meeting. One of the key issues stockholders vote on is the selection of members to the corporation's board of directors. They also may vote on other major issues, such as the approval of a merger with another firm or a change in the corporation's bylaws. Under the most common arrangement, stockholders can cast one vote for each share of stock they own.

- **Right to Dividends:** Dividends are a distribution of profits to the corporation's owners. All common stockholders have the right to receive a dividend, *if* the board of directors declares one. Of course, if a firm has a bad year, there may not be any profits to distribute. And even if the company is profitable, the board may choose to reinvest the earnings in the company rather than distribute them as dividends. Thus, *there is no guarantee stockholders will receive a dividend.*

- **Capital Gains:** Stockholders also *may* receive another type of return on their

EXHIBIT 10.1 Common Stock Certificate: A Share of Corporate Ownership

Common stock is the basic form of ownership in a corporation.

AP IMAGES/KEVIN P. CASEY

© ISTOCKPHOTO.COM

capital gain The return on an asset that results when its market price rises above the price the investor paid for it.

preferred stock A type of stock that gives its holder preference over common stockholders in terms of dividends and claims on assets.

investment, called a **capital gain**, when the price of the stock rises above the amount they paid for it. Capital gains can create very attractive financial returns for stockholders. To take an extreme example, the market price of Google stock on September 3, 2004, closed at $100.01 per share. A little over three years later, on November 7, 2007, the closing price of a share of Google's stock was $741.79. Investors who bought stock in 2004 were no doubt very happy with this result.

Of course, stock prices can also fall, so investors sometimes realize *capital losses* instead of gains—as many investors found during the recent stock market crash. The price of Google's stock dropped from $741.79 per share on November 7, 2007, to $257.44 on

> ## Some companies have a long history of paying dividends. For example, on May 13, 2010, the Dow Chemical Company announced its 395th consecutive quarterly dividend, a string going all the way back to 1912.
>
> *Yahoo! Finance website*

November 24, 2008—a decline of more than $484 in a little over a year. Investors who bought Google stock when it was near its peak in 2007 were no doubt a bit disappointed with this result.[1]

- **Preemptive Right:** If a corporation issues new stock, existing stockholders may have a preemptive right to purchase new shares in proportion to their existing holdings before the stock is offered to the general public. For example, if you own 5% of the existing shares of stock, then the preemptive right gives you the right to purchase 5% of the new shares. This could be important for large stockholders who want to maintain control over a significant share of votes.
- **Right to a Residual Claim on Assets:** The final stockholder right is a residual claim on assets. If the

corporation goes out of business and liquidates its assets, stockholders have a right to share in the proceeds in proportion to their ownership. But note that this is a *residual* claim—it comes *after all other claims* have been satisfied. In other words, the firm must pay any back taxes, legal expenses, wages owed to workers, and debts owed to creditors before the owners get anything. By the time all of these other claims have been paid, little or nothing may be left for the owners.

Preferred Stock: Getting Preferential Treatment

Common stock is the basic form of corporate ownership, but some companies also issue **preferred stock**, so named because—compared to common stock—it offers its holders preferential treatment in two respects:

- **Claim on Assets:** Holders of preferred stock have a claim on assets that comes before common stockholders if the company goes out of business. This gives preferred stockholders a better chance than common stockholders of recovering their investment if the company goes bankrupt.
- **Payment of Dividends:** Unlike dividends on common stock, dividends on preferred stock are usually a stated amount. And a company that issues preferred stock can't pay *any* dividend to its common stockholders unless it pays the full stated dividend on preferred stock. Still, it is important to note that a corporation has no *legal* obligation to pay a dividend to *any* stockholders, not even those who hold preferred stock.

Preferred stock often includes a *cumulative feature*. This means that when the firm skips a preferred dividend in one quarter, the amount it must pay the next quarter is equal to the dividend for that quarter *plus* the amount of the dividend it skipped in the previous quarter. Any additional skipped dividends continue to accumulate, and the firm can't pay any dividends to common stockholders until *all* accumulated dividends are paid to preferred stockholders. A cumulative provision gives the board of directors a strong incentive to make regular dividend payments to preferred stockholders.

Preferred stock isn't necessarily "preferred" to common stock in all respects. For instance, preferred stockholders normally don't have voting rights, so they can't vote on issues that come up during stockholders meetings. And even though preferred stockholders are more likely to receive a dividend, there is no guarantee that the fixed dividend paid to preferred stockholders will always be greater than the dividend the board declares for common stockholders. Finally, when a company experiences strong earnings, the market price of its common stock can—and often does—appreciate more in value than the price of its preferred stock. Once capital gains are taken into account, the overall return that common stockholders earn can be much greater than the total return earned by preferred stockholders.

Bonds: Earning Your Interest

A **bond** is a formal long-term IOU issued by a corporation or government entity. Bonds come in many different varieties. Our discussion will focus on the basic characteristics and features of bonds issued by corporations.

The date a bond comes due is called its **maturity date,** and the amount the issuer owes the bondholder at maturity is called the bond's **par value** (or face value). Bonds issued by corporations usually mature ten to 40 years after issuance, but even longer maturities are possible. During the 1990s, several major corporations, including Disney, Coca-Cola, and IBM, issued *century bonds* that matured 100 years after they were issued. The par value of bonds is usually $1,000 or some multiple of that amount.[2]

Like stocks, bonds are marketable securities, meaning that bondholders can sell their bonds to other investors before they mature. Bond prices fluctuate with conditions in the bond market. When a bond's market price is above its par value, it is selling at a *premium*; when its price is below par value, it is selling at a *discount*.

The firm issuing bonds typically pays interest to bondholders each year until the bond matures.

The **coupon rate** on the bond expresses the annual interest payment as a percentage of the bond's par value. For example, investors who own a bond with a par value of $1,000 and a coupon rate of 7.5% receive $75 in interest (7.5% of $1,000) each year until the bond reaches maturity—or until they sell their bonds to someone else. But since bonds can sell at a premium or a discount, the coupon rate doesn't necessarily represent the rate of return investors earn on the amount they actually *paid* for the bond. The **current yield** expresses a bond's interest payment as a percentage of the bond's current market price rather than its par value. If the market price of the bond in our example was $833.33, then the current yield would be 9% (found by dividing the $75 interest payment by $833.33).

Unlike dividends on stock, a firm has a *legal obligation* to pay interest on bonds—and to pay the bondholder par value of the bond when it matures. Thus, bondholders are more likely to receive a financial return than stockholders. But that doesn't mean that bonds are without risk. Corporations that get into serious financial

bond A long-term debt instrument issued by a corporation or government entity.

maturity date The date when a bond will come due.

par value (of a bond) The value of a bond at its maturity; what the issuer promises to pay the bondholder when the bond matures.

coupon rate The interest paid on a bond expressed as a percentage of the bond's par value.

current yield The amount of interest earned on a bond expressed as a percentage of the bond's current market price.

© BURKE/TRIOLO PRODUCTIONS/BOTANICA/GETTY IMAGES

Could Your Best Investment Be a Piece of Junk?

Bonds are generally considered to be safer investments than common stocks. However, there are definitely some exceptions to this rule. Junk bonds are bonds issued by companies with poor credit ratings. Investors who hold such bonds face the real possibility that the issuer will be unable to make the required payments of interest and principal. And the risk increases when the economy weakens. In 2007 only 22 companies in the world defaulted on their bonds. But with the deepening recession, that number soared to 126 companies in 2008.

Given this risk, why would anyone invest in junk bonds? The answer is that with high risk comes the possibility of attractive returns. Firms with poor credit ratings must offer higher returns to entice investors to buy their riskier bonds. Thus, junk bonds pay higher rates of interest—sometimes much higher rates—than safer "investment grade" bonds. And these bonds generally sell at a deep discount, making their current yields even higher than their coupon rates. Toward the end of 2008, yields on many junk bonds exceeded 20%—more than double the yield earned on safer "investment grade" bonds.

By late 2008 many investors concluded that the high yield on these bonds made the risks of investing in junk bonds worth taking—especially given the poor performance of stocks during the same period. Investing in junk became a hot strategy. But most investors who bought junk bonds did so in moderation, limiting their holdings of junk bonds to only a small part of a broadly diversified portfolio of securities.[3]

difficulties sometimes *default* on their bonds, meaning that they are unable to make required payments. When that happens, bankruptcy proceedings usually allow bondholders to recover some (but not all) of what they are owed; historically the average amount recovered has been about 72 cents on the dollar. While that is better than what stockholders can expect when a company goes through bankruptcy, it is far short of being risk free![4]

Exhibit 10.2 illustrates a bond certificate. See if you can locate the par value, coupon rate, and maturity date for the bond in this exhibit. Ownership of most bonds is now electronically recorded, so actual paper certificates like the one in this exhibit are becoming quite rare. Bonds that register ownership electronically are called *book entry bonds.*

Securing bonds Most companies issue **secured bonds**, meaning that they back (secure) these IOUs by pledg-

ing specific assets, such as property or equipment, as collateral. Should the issuer fail to make the required payments of interest and principal, the bondholders can require it to use these assets to satisfy their claims.

Some bonds, called *debentures*, aren't secured by the pledge of specific assets. Instead, they are backed only by the earning capacity and general creditworthiness of the issuing firm. Most investors are willing to buy debentures from businesses with excellent financial reputations—such as General Electric and AT&T. Even so, debentures typically carry a higher coupon rate than similar secured bonds.

Methods of Retiring Bonds Corporations that issue bonds usually make specific provisions to ensure an orderly repayment of principal. Firms that fail to do so might find themselves faced with the need to make large repayments at a time when they were strapped for cash. One approach is to offer **serial bonds**, which are issued at the same time but mature in different years. This enables the issuer to spread the repayment over time. Another common method is to establish a **sinking fund**. When a firm uses a sinking fund, it periodically deposits money into a fund that is used to buy back some of the bonds each year. Like a serial bond issue, a sinking fund allows the firm to repay the principal gradually instead of making all of the payments in the same year.

Special Characteristics of Bonds Bonds often include special features that can make them more attractive to both the investor and the issuing firm. Let's take a look at two common examples.

Callable bonds include a provision that allows the firm to call in (or "redeem") *all* of the bonds at a specified price prior to their maturity date. This allows firms to take advantage of drops in interest rates after they issue their bonds. For example, a firm that issued $100 million in callable bonds that paid 10% interest would have to make $10 million in interest payments each year (10% of $100 million). If interest rates fell to 7%, the firm could issue new

EXHIBIT 10.2 Bond Certificate: A Long-Term Corporate IOU

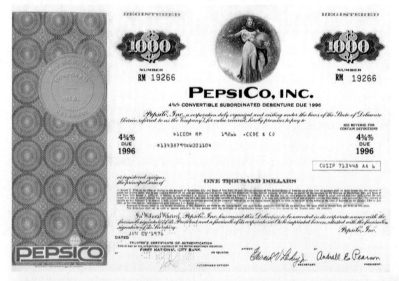

© TERRI L. MILLER/E-VISUAL COMMUNICATIONS, INC.

bonds at the lower rate and use the proceeds to call in the 10% bonds. This would reduce the firm's annual interest expense from $10 million to $7 million, saving the company millions of dollars in interest payments over the life of the bonds.

Of course, bondholders who own bonds paying high interest rates are likely to be unhappy when they are called. In order to attract investors, callable bonds typically include a few "sweeteners." For instance, callable bonds usually carry a slightly higher coupon rate than similar bonds that aren't callable. Also, in most cases the company promises to pay the bondholder more than the par value when it calls a bond. The additional amount is known as the *call premium*. The size of the premium usually declines as the bond approaches its maturity date.

Convertible bonds allow bondholders to exchange their bonds for a stated number of shares of the corporation's common stock. The *conversion ratio* states the number of shares of stock exchanged for each convertible bond. For example, if the conversion ratio is 20, then each bond can be exchanged for 20 shares of common stock.

Owning a convertible bond allows investors to take advantage of a rise in stock prices, while limiting their risk if stock prices fall. The firm also can benefit from issuing convertible bonds. Since bondholders like the convertible feature, the firm can offer a lower coupon rate on convertible bonds, reducing its interest expense. Also, if the investor exchanges the bonds for stock, the firm no longer has to make interest payments or repay the principal on the bonds. But there is one important group that may be unhappy with this arrangement; the corporation's existing stockholders may be displeased by the fact that the new stock issued to former bondholders dilutes their share of ownership—and their share of any profits.

LO2 Trading Securities: The Primary and Secondary Markets

There are two distinct types of securities markets: the primary securities market and the secondary securities market. The **primary securities market** is where corporations raise additional financial capital by selling *newly issued* securities. The **secondary securities market** is where *previously issued* securities are traded. Let's take a look at how each of these markets works.

The Primary Securities Market: Where Securities Are Issued

There are two methods of issuing securities in the primary market:

- In a **public offering** securities are sold to anyone in the investing public who is willing (and financially able) to buy them.

- In a **private placement** securities are sold to one or more large investors under terms negotiated between the issuing firm and the private investors.

Public Offerings Many corporations are initially owned by a small number of people who don't actively trade the stock to outsiders. But rapidly growing corporations often need to obtain more financial capital than such a small group can provide. Such firms may *go public* by issuing additional stock and offering it to the general public. The first time a corporation sells its stock in a public offering, the sale is called an **initial public offering (IPO)**. After its IPO a firm can raise more financial capital by issuing additional new shares. The sale of this additional stock is known as a *seasoned equity offering*.

Most firms that go public seek the help of a financial intermediary known as an **investment bank**. The investment bank assists the firm at every step of the IPO, from the planning and market assessment until the day of the actual offering. One of the key responsibilities of the investment bank is to arrange for the actual sale of the securities. The investment bank typically uses either a *best efforts* or a *firm commitment* approach. Under the best efforts approach the bank provides advice about pricing and marketing and assists in finding potential buyers. But it doesn't guarantee that the firm will sell all of its securities at a high enough price to meet its financial goals. The investment bank earns a commission on all of the shares sold under a best efforts approach. Under a *firm-commitment* arrangement, the investment bank **underwrites** the issue. This means that the investment bank itself purchases *all* of the shares, which guarantees that the firm issuing the stock will receive a known amount of new funds directly from the investment bank and seeks to make a profit by reselling the stock to investors at a higher price.

Before going public, a firm must file a registration statement with the Securities and Exchange

convertible bond A bond that gives its holder the right to exchange it for a stated number of shares of common stock in some specified time period.

primary securities market The market where newly issued securities are traded. The primary market is where the firms that issue securities raise additional financial capital.

secondary securities market The market where previously issued securities are traded.

public offering A primary market issue in which new securities are offered to any investors who are willing and able to purchase them.

private placement A primary market issue that is negotiated between the issuing corporation and a small group of accredited investors.

initial public offering (IPO) The first time a company issues stock that may be bought by the general public.

investment bank A financial intermediary that specializes in helping firms raise financial capital in primary markets.

underwriting An arrangement under which an investment banker agrees to purchase all shares of a public offering at an agreed-upon price.

Commission (SEC)—a government watchdog we will describe later in this chapter. The registration statement provides a detailed description of both the firm and the securities, including the firm's key financial statements plus additional financial information. It consists of two parts. The first, called the prospectus, contains specific information the firm must provide to potential investors. Part II contains more detailed information required by the SEC but which the company does not have to report to investors.

Private Placements Private placements are usually quicker, simpler, and less expensive than public offerings. In a private placement, the issuing firm negotiates the terms of the offer directly with a small number of **accredited investors**. These are individuals, businesses, or other organizations that meet specific requirements set by the SEC. An investment banker often helps the firm identify and contact accredited investors and assists the firm as it negotiates the terms of the private placement.

The main reason private placements are simpler and less expensive than public offerings is that privately placed securities are exempt from the requirement to register with the SEC. (The SEC's rationale is that accredited investors are more sophisticated than other investors, so they don't need protection provided by the registration process.) The ability to obtain financing without having to prepare complex registration documents can be a real attraction. But because the pool of potential investors is limited to accredited investors, private placements normally don't have the potential to raise as much money as public offerings. Another drawback is that securities that haven't been registered with the SEC can't be sold to anyone except other accredited investors.

Secondary Securities Markets: Trading Between Investors

The firms issuing the stocks and bonds don't receive any additional funds when their securities are traded in the secondary markets. But secondary markets still matter to the corporations that issue these securities. The price of a firm's stock in the secondary market directly reflects investor opinion about how well the firm is being managed. Also, few investors would want to buy securities issued in the primary markets without the possibility of earning capital gains by selling these securities in the secondary markets.

Securities Exchanges A securities exchange (or stock exchange) is an organization that provides a venue for stockbrokers or securities dealers to trade listed stocks and other securities for clients. Each exchange establishes requirements for the stocks it lists. Specific listing requirements vary among the exchanges, but they're typically based on the earnings of the company, the number of shares of stock outstanding, and the number of shareholders. In addition to meeting listing requirements, exchanges also require firms to pay an initial fee at the time their securities are first listed and an annual listing fee to remain listed on the exchange.

The **New York Stock Exchange (NYSE)** and **NASDAQ** are the two largest exchanges in the United States. Most of the nation's largest and best-known corporations, such as ExxonMobil, Walmart, Coca-Cola, and General Electric, are listed on the NYSE. Many prominent

AP IMAGES/DAVID KARP

high-tech firms, such as Apple, Google, Intel, and Microsoft are listed on the NASDAQ exchange. These two exchanges are now the dominant secondary markets for securities of large, nationally traded corporations.

Prior to 2008 the American Stock Exchange (Amex) was also recognized as a national exchange, though it was much smaller than either the NYSE or NASDAQ. In recent years its major significance was as an important market for exchange traded funds (ETFs)—a relatively new type of investment that we'll describe later in this chapter. However, the NYSE acquired Amex in 2008 and changed its name to NYSE Alternext.[5]

Stock exchanges aren't unique to the United States. Exhibit 10.3 identifies the world's largest exchanges ranked by market capitalization, a measure of the total market value of all of the securities traded on the exchange. Both the NYSE and NASDAQ have broadened their global reach by pursuing mergers with foreign exchanges. In early 2007, the NYSE merged with a large European stock exchange known as Euronext. (After the merger the parent company of the exchange officially became NYSE Euronext, but in the United States

EXHIBIT 10.3 Major Global Stock Exchanges

Exchange	Country	2009 Market Capitalization (in $Trillions)
NYSE Group	USA	11.84
Tokyo Stock Exchange	Japan	3.31
NASDAQ Stock Market	USA	3.24
London Stock Exchange	United Kingdom	2.80
Shanghai Stock Exchange	China	2.70
Hong Kong Exchanges	Hong Kong (China)	2.31
TSX Group	Canada	1.68
BME Spanish	Spain	1.43

Source: Spreadsheet EQUITY109 linked through the World Federation of Exchanges website: http://www.world-exchanges.org/statistics/annual/2009/equity-markets/total-value-share-trading (accessed June 4, 2010).

the exchange itself is still called NYSE.) That same year NASDAQ merged with OMX, an exchange based in Sweden, to form the NASDAQ OMX Group.[6]

The NYSE and NASDAQ have always operated in fundamentally different ways. Until very recently, the vast majority of trades on the NYSE took place at a physical location—a group of trading floors in the heart of New York's financial district—where brokers representing buyers and sellers of listed securities met to conduct business. Each stock listed on the NYSE traded at a particular spot on a floor where a *specialist* for that stock was located. The specialist organized bidding on the stock, essentially acting as an auctioneer. Because of this arrangement, the NYSE was called an *auction market*.

The newer NASDAQ exchange has never had a physical trading location. Instead, dealers who participate in NASDAQ are linked by telephone and computer networks. Thus, NASDAQ is often called an *electronic exchange*.

The key players in NASDAQ's market are dealers known as **market makers**. These are investment companies that specialize in buying and selling specific NASDAQ-listed stocks. Each NASDAQ stock has several market makers who compete against each other by posting two prices for each stock: the *bid price* indicates how much the market maker will pay to buy a share of the stock while the *ask price* indicates the price at which it will sell the same stock. The ask price is always just slightly higher than the bid price; the difference is called the bid/ask spread (or just the spread) and is the source of the market maker's profit.

market makers Investment companies that specialize in buying and selling specific stocks traded on the NASDAQ exchange or OTC market.

NASDAQ has no trading floors. All trades on this exchange are carried out through a network of securities dealers linked by phone and computer networks.

The bid and ask prices of all market makers for a specific stock are quoted on computer screens. Competition among the market makers usually keeps the spread from being more than a few pennies per share. But market makers trade such large numbers of shares each day that those pennies can really add up.

Big Changes at the NYSE In 2006 and 2007 the NYSE implemented a new system for trading securities, known as the **NYSE Hybrid Market**. The new system still allows investors to trade securities via the traditional auction market. But it also gives them the option of carrying out a broad range of trades using a newer system called NYSE Direct+, which is a computerized system that automatically matches buyers and sellers.[7] Implementation of the NYSE Hybrid Market led to a dramatic decline in auction market activity on NYSE trading floors as many investors opted to use the automated system.

The evolution of the NYSE Hybrid Market continued in 2008 when the NYSE replaced its specialists with dealers called *designated market makers* (DMMs). These new players perform most of the duties of the old market specialists; in particular, they maintain orderly markets by organizing auctions for specific stocks. But DMMs also actively participate in the market for those specific stocks, much like the market makers on the NASDAQ exchange.[8]

The Over-the-Counter Market Many corporations don't meet the requirements for listing on an organized exchange; some are too small, and others haven't experienced satisfactory business performance. Other corporations meet requirements to list on the NYSE or NASDAQ but choose not to do so because they don't want to pay the listing fees the exchanges charge. The **over-the-counter market (OTC)** is where the stocks of such companies are traded. OTC stocks are traded through a system of market makers much like stocks are traded on the NASDAQ exchange. However, the market for most OTC stocks is much less active than for stocks listed on the major exchanges.

Electronic Communications Networks **Electronic communications networks** are a relatively new type of

The United States Takes Stock of GM (and We Mean That Literally)

In market-based economies like the United States, corporate stock normally is owned by private individuals and institutional investors. But in 2009, the old General Motors Corporation—which as recently as 2007 was the largest automaker in the world—was transformed by bankruptcy proceedings into a "new GM" complete with a new majority owner: the U.S. federal government. Uncle Sam received 61% of the stock in the new GM when the Obama administration agreed to supply the new company with $50 billion in federal financial support under a special provision of the Troubled Asset Relief Program (TARP). The United Automobile Workers union and the Canadian government received most of the remaining stock. Meanwhile, private stockholders who owned the old prebankruptcy GM were left holding virtually worthless stock in a company known as the Motors Liquidation Company.

The Obama administration claimed to be a reluctant investor in GM, with little interest in using its majority ownership to influence corporate policy. In the words of President Obama, "We are a shareholder but we are not an active shareholder. We have specifically said that we are not in the business of running a car company." Indeed, federal officials repeatedly stated that the government would hold its majority stake only until the company's financial situation improved enough to attract private investors.

In early 2010, GM's financial situation began to improve—aided not only by an upturn in auto sales, but also by the leaner cost structure it achieved through its bankruptcy proceedings. By April of that year Ed Whitacre, CEO of the new GM, felt confident enough in the company's turnaround to announce a plan to hold an initial public offering of the company's stock by the end of the year. One goal of the IPO was to allow the government to eventually sell its shares, thus returning the company to private ownership and recouping much of the taxpayer money that had been invested in the company.[9]

© BILL PUGLIANO/GETTY IMAGES

computer-based securities market. ECNs are entirely automated. When an investor places an order for a certain security on an ECN, the system automatically checks to see if there is a matching order to sell. If so, it immediately executes the transaction. The use of ECNs can speed up transactions and lower trading costs. ECNs have also made it possible for more investors to trade securities "after hours" when the large U.S. exchanges are closed.[10] By early 2005, both the NYSE and NASDAQ saw ECNs as a threat to their market positions *and* as an opportunity for growth—and both reacted in much the same way. On April 20, 2005, the NYSE announced plans to buy Archipelago, one of the largest and best-known ECNs. Two days later, NASDAQ announced its intention to buy Instinet, another major ECN. Both exchanges quickly completed their acquisitions and have now integrated ECN technology into their operations.

LO3 Regulation of Securities Markets: Establishing Confidence in the Market

Securities markets work well only if participants have confidence in the integrity and fairness of the system. To ensure that this confidence is justified, a mix of state, federal, and private efforts regulates the markets. Let's look at some of the major players.

State Regulations

In the early 20th century, unscrupulous securities dealers took advantage of the lack of government oversight to sell stocks in highly risky (and sometimes completely fictitious) businesses to naïve customers. The result was financial ruin for many of these investors—and a public outcry calling for government action.

State governments responded to these unethical practices more quickly than the federal government. In 1911, Kansas passed the first state law dealing with securities fraud. Over the next few years, virtually every state passed similar laws, which soon came to be called *blue sky laws*. (There's some debate about who first coined the "blue sky" name, but many historians trace its origins to early supporters of such laws who argued that, left unregulated, unscrupulous securities dealers would try to sell unsophisticated citizens shares of stock in thin air or the blue sky.)[11]

Though they vary in their specifics, the state laws typically require all securities sold in the state to be registered with a state regulatory agency. They also required all securities dealers and brokerage firms to register with the state and gave investors the right to sue when injured by securities fraud.

Federal Legislation

The federal government got involved in regulating the securities industry during the Depression years, following the great stock market crash that began in October 1929. The first two federal laws dealing with securities markets were the Securities Act of 1933 and the Securities Exchange Act of 1934. These two laws still provide the foundation for the federal approach to the regulation of securities markets.

A key objective of the **Securities Act of 1933** was to restore public faith and trust in the securities markets that had been battered by the crash in 1929. This act deals mainly with securities issued in the primary market. It prohibits misrepresentation, deceit, or other forms of fraud in the sale of new securities. It also requires firms issuing new stock to file a registration statement with the SEC, as we mentioned in our discussion of initial public offerings.

The **Securities Exchange Act of 1934** dealt mainly with the regulation of secondary security markets. This law created the **Securities and Exchange Commission** and gave it broad powers to oversee and regulate the securities industry. The law required that all publicly traded firms with at least 500 shareholders and $10 million in assets file quarterly and annual financial reports with the SEC, and that brokers and dealers register with the SEC.

The Securities Exchange Act also gave the SEC the power to prosecute individuals and companies that engaged in fraudulent securities market activities. For example, the SEC has the authority to go after individuals who engage in illegal *insider trading*, which is the practice of using inside information (important information about a company that isn't available to the general investing public) to profit from trading in a company's securities. In a recent case, the SEC accused Raj Rajaratnam, billionaire manager of the Galleon Group hedge fund, and several associates of earning over $20 million in illegal profits by trading inside information about Google, IBM, and other high-tech firms. Although the outcome of Rajaratnam's trial was unknown at the time this book went to press, several associates involved in the case pleaded guilty and were cooperating with prosecutors.[12]

The Role of Self-Regulatory Organizations

Although the SEC retains ultimate regulatory authority over securities markets, it relies on **self-regulatory organizations (SROs)** to oversee the operations of these markets. SROs are nongovernmental organizations that develop and enforce the rules governing the behavior of

Securities Act of 1933 The first major federal law regulating the securities industry.

Securities Exchange Act of 1934 A federal law dealing with securities regulation that established the Securities and Exchange Commission to oversee the securities industry.

Securities and Exchange Commission The federal agency with primary responsibility for regulating the securities industry.

self-regulatory organizations (SROs) Private organizations that develop and enforce standards governing the behavior of their members.

diversification A strategy of investing in a wide variety of securities in order to reduce risk.

their members. The SEC reviews and approves (or disapproves) any new rules or regulations the SROs propose.

Until recently, NASDAQ and the NYSE maintained separate SROs. However, in July 2007, these two SROs merged to form the Financial Industry Regulatory Authority (FINRA). The new SRO oversees approximately 5,000 brokerage firms and 656,000 brokers and dealers—making it by far the largest nongovernmental regulator of U.S. securities markets.[13]

LO4 Personal Investing

Would investing in stocks, bonds, and other securities make sense for you? If so, how could you get started? What are the potential risks and rewards of various investment strategies? Since this chapter is about securities markets, we'll focus on personal investing in stocks and bonds, but keep in mind that other types of investments could also help you achieve your financial goals.

Investing in securities requires you to think carefully about your specific situation and your personal goals and attitudes:

- What are your short-term and long-term goals?
- Given your budget, how much are you able to invest?
- How long can you leave your money invested?
- How concerned are you about the tax implications of your investments?
- How much tolerance do you have for risk?

The best types of securities for you, and the best investment strategies for you to use, will depend in large part on your answers to questions such as these.

Notice that the last question deals with your attitudes toward risk. Most people are not comfortable with high levels of risk. But no investment strategy completely avoids risk. And in general, the riskier the approach, the greater the *potential* rewards. To achieve your goals, you'll need to find the balance between risk and return that works for you.

Diversification—investing in many different types of securities in many different sectors—is one way to reduce risk. If you put all of your investment dollars into a small number of securities, a setback in one or two could have a devastating financial impact, but if you hold many different securities in different sectors of the economy, then losses on some securities may be offset by gains on others. But diversification can only *reduce* risk; it can't entirely eliminate it. Recent history is a good illustration: in 2008, even investors who held many different securities in many different companies located in many different countries saw the value of their investment portfolios decline dramatically as the global economy faltered.

Symbolic Logic: Do You LUV this HOG's DNA?

Every publicly traded corporation is identified by a unique combination of letters known as its stock symbol. The use of symbols began in the mid-1800s when people began sending information about stock prices via telegraph. The symbols allowed telegraph operators to tap out a few letters rather than having to spell out a company's entire name.

Although we no longer rely on the telegraph for stock quotes, the symbols are still used today. For example, symbols are used to quote stock prices on those scrolling tickers at the bottom of many financial news channels on cable TV. And many financial websites require you to enter a company's symbol in order to get the latest quotes and statistics for its stock.

The combination of letters used in a symbol is usually tied to the company's business, but the connection can be a bit subtle. For example, the stock symbol for Anheuser-Busch InBev on the NYSE is BUD, reflecting the fact that the giant brewery's most famous product—at least in the United States—is its Budweiser beer. (On the Euronext exchange in Europe the same company's symbol is ABI.) See if you can identify the well-known corporation that uses each of the symbols listed in the table above. (Answers are given below.)[14]

GOOG	HOG
MMM	DNA
JAVA	LUV

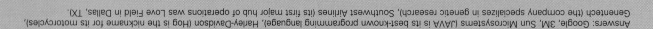

© RUBBERBALL/JUPITERIMAGES

Answers: Google, 3M, Sun Microsystems (JAVA is its best-known programming language), Harley-Davidson (Hog is the nickname for its motorcycles), Genentech (the company specializes in genetic research), Southwest Airlines (its first major hub of operations was Love Field in Dallas, TX).

Choosing a Broker: Gaining Access to the Markets

Members of the general public cannot directly trade stocks and other securities on the exchanges we described earlier in the chapter. Thus, most investors enlist the services of a brokerage firm with access to these exchanges. Choosing the right broker is the first step in implementing your investment plans.

A *full service broker* provides a wide range of services—such as market research, investment advice, and tax planning—in addition to carrying out your trades. *Discount brokers* provide the basic services needed to buy and sell securities, but offer fewer additional services. As you might expect, discount brokers tend to charge significantly lower commissions than full service brokers. In fact, many discount brokers charge flat fees of only a few dollars per trade for basic transactions.

In recent years, competition among brokerage firms has blurred the distinction between full service and discount brokers. To stop clients from defecting to discount brokers, many full-service firms have lowered their commissions. At the same time, many discount brokers have begun offering a broader range of services to attract more clients.

Buying Securities: Let's Make a Deal

Once you've chosen your broker you can place orders to buy or sell securities. To do so, you'd contact your broker and indicate the stock you want to buy and how many shares you want to purchase. You can also specify the type of order you want to place. The most common types of orders are market orders and limit orders:

- **Market orders** instruct the broker to buy or sell a security at the current market price. Placing a market order virtually guarantees that your order will be executed. The downside is that you may end up buying at a higher price than you expected to pay (or selling your stock for less than you expected to receive).

- **Limit orders** place limits on the prices at which orders are executed. A buy limit order tells a broker to buy a stock *only* if its price is at or below a specified value. You'd use this approach if you wanted to make sure you didn't pay more for the stock than you thought it was worth. A sell limit order tells your broker to sell the shares only if the price is at or above a specified value. This prevents your broker from selling your stock at a price you believe is too low.

Strategies for Investing in Securities

How do you choose specific securities to buy? Should you buy and sell on a regular basis? Or should you hold on to securities and ignore short-term fluctuations? Your answers to these questions will reflect the investing strategy you choose. We'll provide an overview of the more common approaches, but as you'll see, none of these approaches is foolproof—alas, there is no single strategy that is guaranteed to earn you millions.

Investing for Income Some investors focus on buying bonds and preferred stocks in order to generate a steady, predictable flow of income. Recall that bonds pay a stated amount of interest each year and that preferred stock usually pays a fixed dividend on a regular basis. These investors may also buy common stock in large, well-established firms with a reputation for paying

market order An order telling a broker to buy or sell a specific security at the best currently available price.

limit order An order to a broker to buy a specific stock only if its price is below a certain level, or to sell a specific stock only if its price is above a certain level.

Stockbrokers place orders to buy and sell stocks and other securities for their clients.

© TETRA IMAGES/JUPITERIMAGES

Oops! what were they THINKING?!

Did a Tech Wreck Cause a Flash Crash?

The stock market has always been volatile, but its gyrations on May 6, 2010 were of an entirely different order of magnitude. The Dow Jones Industrial Average, the most widely followed index of stock prices, dropped by over 1,000 points in the course of a few minutes—by far the biggest single-day drop in market history. The market partially recovered, but still ended the day down by 348 points. The most disconcerting aspect of this "flash crash" was that there was no obvious reason for the wild swings. Even after 12 days of intense investigation, the SEC was forced to conclude that it couldn't provide a clear explanation.

Many financial analysts suspect that the crash was caused in part by high-frequency trading (HFT), a completely automated technique used by high-tech traders. HFT employs a set of rules, called algorithms, which allow computers to very quickly take advantage of miniscule price differences for securities traded on different exchanges. These price differences are often only a penny or two per share, but the computers trade so many shares so quickly that those pennies add up.

HFT became increasingly popular after 2005, and as it grew it attracted more controversy. Defenders of the technique argued that intense competition among HFT investors narrowed the spread between bid and ask prices. This, they claimed, allowed even traditional (i.e., human) investors to benefit from the ability to sell at higher prices and buy at lower prices. But other experts remained leery. As market guru Paul Wilmott put it in early 2010, "High frequency trading is the next big bandwagon, and everyone is jumping onboard. Wall Street always jumps on the next thing, and it always blows up."

Some observers believe that Wilmott's words were prophetic. They suggest that a variety of unusual conditions caused HFT algorithms to break down on May 6, 2010. The result was that too many computers tried to sell at the same time, putting intense downward pressure on prices. Because these transactions were generated by computers, the downward spiral occurred much too fast for human intervention to halt the slide. As *Bloomberg Businessweek* magazine put it, "Panic combined with automation leads to much faster panic."[15]

---

regular dividends. This approach is popular with retirees who want to supplement their retirement income. The drawback is that the return on such low-risk securities is relatively low, and their market value seldom increases much over time. Thus, it probably isn't the best strategy for younger investors who are trying to grow their wealth.

Market Timing Investors who rely on market timing use a variety of analytical techniques to try to predict when prices of specific stocks are likely to rise and fall. Market timers try to make quick gains by buying low and selling high over a relatively short time horizon.

The problem with market timing is that so many factors can influence stock prices—some of them random in nature—that it's tough to consistently identify the timing and direction of short-run stock price changes. Market timing also requires investors to make frequent trades. Given the commissions and fees the investor pays on every trade, this approach may do a better job of enriching the broker than enriching the investor!

Value Investing Investors who favor value investing try to find stocks that are undervalued in the market. They believe other investors will eventually recognize the true value of these stocks. When this happens, the demand for the stocks will increase, and the market value will rise, generating an attractive return. This approach requires a lot of research to identify discrepancies between a company's true (or intrinsic) value and its current market price.

The drawback with value investing is that you are in competition with thousands of other investors trying to do the same thing, so the competition to locate good buys is intense. Unless you're among the first to discover an undervalued stock, the investors who beat you to it will rush to buy up the stock, increasing demand and driving up the stock's price so that it is no longer undervalued.

Investing for Growth Investors who focus on growth look for companies that have the potential to grow much faster than average for a sustained period of time, which they believe will lead to stock price growth. Investors using this strategy often invest in stocks of relatively small new companies with innovative products in a hot sector of the economy.

Investing for growth entails a lot of risk. By their very nature, small new companies don't have an established track record. Rapidly expanding industries also tend to attract a lot of start-up companies, so competition can be intense. It's hard to predict which firms will be winners; even experts often make the wrong choice.

Buying and Holding If you're a patient person with steady nerves, a buy-and-hold approach might appeal to you. This strategy involves purchasing a diversified set of securities and holding them for a long period of time. Investors who use the buy-and-hold approach don't usually worry about detailed analysis of individual stocks. Instead, they invest in a broad range of securities and put their faith in the ability of the *overall market* to continue the long-run upward trend it has exhibited throughout its history. The buy-and-hold strategy seldom enables someone to "get rich quick," but it usually results in a solid financial return over the long haul.

> ## Unless you can watch your stock holding decline by 50% without becoming panic stricken, you should not be in the stock market.
>
> *Warren Buffet, billionaire, investment guru and CEO of conglomerate Berkshire Hathaway*

Obviously, the buy-and-hold strategy will work only if you can afford to leave your money invested for a long time. When the stock market takes a dive, it can sometimes take years for stocks to recover and start to show solid returns. Some people who think they're comfortable with a buy-and-hold strategy end up getting "happy feet" after a few days of significant declines in stock prices. They panic and sell off their stocks at exactly the wrong time, locking in big losses. For the buy-and-hold strategy to work, you've got to have the patience—and mental toughness—to ride out short-term downturns in the market.

LO5 Other Investment Options: Mutual Funds and Exchange Traded Funds

So far we've discussed a wide variety of strategies and techniques that involve investing directly in specific securities. But, for reasons we'll describe in this section, many investors find it more attractive to invest in securities indirectly. Two ways to do this are by investing in mutual funds and exchange traded funds. Let's see why these investment options have become so popular.

Mutual Funds: Strength in Numbers

Mutual funds are investment companies that pool money from large numbers of individual investors and invest these funds in a variety of stocks, bonds, government securities, and other assets. Each individual investor then shares in the earnings from these investments in proportion to the amount invested.

Several features make mutual funds a popular choice for investors:

- **Diversification at Relatively Low Cost:** Since you're pooling your funds with thousands of other investors, investing in mutual funds lets you invest in a broader portfolio of securities than you could afford as an individual.

- **Professional Management:** Many individual investors don't have the time, inclination, or expertise to make complex investment decisions. Most mutual funds have full-time professional managers to make these decisions.

- **Variety:** Whatever your investment goals and philosophy, you can probably find a fund that's a good match. There are many different types of funds; some invest only in certain types of securities (such as municipal bond funds or stocks of large corporations), others invest in specific sectors of the economy (such as energy or health care) and yet others seek more balanced and broad-based portfolios.

- **Liquidity:** It's usually easy to withdraw funds from a mutual fund. However, it's worth noting that regardless of when you initiate your withdrawal, redemptions are not carried out until the end of the day, when the major stock exchanges close.

Like all investments, mutual funds have some drawbacks. Perhaps the most serious is that the professional management touted by many funds doesn't come cheap. Investors in mutual funds pay for the fund manager and for other costs associated with their funds through a variety of fees that typically range from 1% to 3% of the amount invested. And funds assess these fees even when they perform poorly.

It is also important to realize that highly specialized mutual funds, such as those that invest in only one sector of the economy, don't really offer the benefits of diversification. (Just ask anyone who bought mutual funds that invested heavily in dot-com firms in the first two years of the 21st century. To say that most of these funds tanked in 2001–2002 is putting it kindly.) But even funds that are highly diversified can post negative earnings when the stock market as a whole goes through a downturn. And unlike bank deposits, investments in mutual funds are not insured or guaranteed by the government.

Exchange Traded Funds: Trading Market Baskets of Securities

An **exchange traded fund (ETF)** is a hybrid investment that looks something like a stock and something like a mutual fund. When you buy a share in an ETF, you're purchasing ownership in a "market basket" of many different stocks, similar to a mutual fund. Just as there are many types of mutual funds, there are many types of ETFs. Most ETFs are based on a highly diversified market basket of stocks. In fact, the stocks in

mutual fund An investment vehicle that pools the contributions of many investors and buys a wide array of stocks or other securities.

exchange traded fund (ETF) Shares traded on securities markets that represent the legal right of ownership over part of a basket of individual stock certificates or other securities.

many ETFs are chosen to reflect the composition of a broad-based stock index, such as the S&P 500. (We'll discuss stock indices later in this chapter.) But in recent years more specialized ETFs have appeared on the market.

From an investor's perspective, the major difference between ETFs and mutual funds is that shares of ETFs are sold exactly like stocks. Unlike mutual funds, which allow investors to buy and sell only after the major stock exchanges close, you can buy and sell ETFs any time of the day. Also compared to mutual funds, ETFs usually have lower costs and fees. However, one drawback of ETFs compared to mutual funds is that you have to pay brokerage commissions every time you buy or sell shares. Thus, while you *could* buy only a few ETF shares at a time, the commissions could take a big bite out of any gains. In recent years ETFs have become a hot investment option.

LO6 Keeping Tabs on the Market

Once you've begun to invest in securities, you'll want to keep track of how your investments are doing. Using the Internet, you can easily access information about both general market trends and the performance of specific securities.

Stock Indices: Tracking the Trends

One of the most common ways to track general market conditions and trends is to follow what's happening to various stock indices. A **stock index** provides a means of tracking the prices of a large group of stocks that meet certain defined criteria. Many investors like to compare how the stocks in their own portfolio compare to the performance of these broad indices. Let's look at some of the best-known and most widely followed indices:

- The **Dow Jones Industrial Average:** Often called the "DJIA" or just "the Dow," it is the most widely followed stock index. The Dow is based on the adjusted average price of 30 stocks picked by the

> **There are approximately 8,000 mutual funds now in the United States—far more than the total number of individual stocks listed on the NYSE and NASDAQ combined.**
>
> *Investment Company Institute*

Does Green Investing Earn Green Returns?

Is it possible to meet your personal financial goals while also satisfying your desire to invest in companies that pursue environment-friendly policies? Several so-called "green" mutual funds claim to help you do just that. The New Alternatives Fund, established in 1982, was the first fund that selected stocks based primarily on environmental considerations. In recent years the fund's portfolio has emphasized firms that develop alternative energy sources, recycle waste, and produce pollution abatement equipment.

The number of green funds has grown in recent years, reflecting our society's increased concern about environmental issues. But green funds vary in terms of the criteria they use for selecting their stocks. For instance, the Winslow Green Growth Fund invests aggressively in small-growth firms that meet their environmental responsibilities. The more conservative Portfolio 21 selects large, well-established companies that emphasize environmental sustainability. In 2010 its portfolio of over 100 stocks included such well-known corporations as Nike, Staples, Google, and Johnson & Johnson.

An obvious question is whether these *environmentally* green funds provide investors with the *other* type of "green" investors seek—namely, an attractive *financial* return. Over the long haul, the answer appears to be yes. The Winslow Green Growth Fund had an average annual return of 12.1% from its inception in 1994 through April 2010. That significantly outperformed the average return on stock indices such as the S&P 500 over the same time period. Likewise, the New Alternatives Fund and the Portfolio 21 Fund both performed better than the S&P 500 over the five-year period ending on March 31, 2010. But, as is the case for most specialized mutual funds, these average returns concealed big fluctuations over shorter time periods. For instance, the Winslow fund earned an eye-popping total return of 92% in 2003, but saw returns plunge to a disastrous -60% in 2008—and then rise again by 43.7% in 2009. The returns reported by New Alternatives and Portfolio 21's returns fluctuated by similar amounts over the same time period.[16]

editors of *The Wall Street Journal*. All of the Dow firms are huge, well-established corporations, such as American Express, General Electric, Coca-Cola, Hewlett-Packard, and Disney.

- The **Standard & Poor's 500 (S&P 500):** With 500 stocks instead of just 30, the S&P 500 is a much broader index than the DJIA. Still, like the Dow, all of the companies included in the S&P 500 are large, well-established American corporations.

- The **NASDAQ Composite Index:** This includes all the domestic and foreign common stocks traded on the NASDAQ exchange.

Exhibit 10.4 identifies several other well-known indices, including some that track prices of stocks in foreign securities markets.

EXHIBIT 10.4 Major Stock Price Indices

Index	What It Tracks
Wilshire 5000	Stock prices of all U.S. corporations with actively traded stock. Despite the 5000 in its name, this index actually includes well over 6000 stocks (the exact number changes frequently).
Russell 2000	Stock prices of 2000 relatively small but actively traded U.S. corporations.
FTSE 100	Stock prices of 100 of the largest and most actively traded companies listed on the London Stock Exchange.
Nikkei 225	Stock prices of 225 of the largest and most actively traded companies listed on the Tokyo Stock Exchange.
SSE Composite	Stock prices of all stocks listed on the Shanghai Stock Exchange.
Hang Seng	Stock prices of 43 large companies listed on the Hong Kong Stock Exchange.

Tracking the Performance of Specific Securities

Many newspapers offer daily stock market reports, but you can find more current and detailed information by visiting one of the many websites that specialize in financial news. To check out a specific stock, you simply type its *stock symbol*—a short combination of letters that uniquely identifies a corporate security—into a "Get Quote" box. (Don't worry if you don't know the symbol; most sites have a lookup feature that finds the symbol if you type in the company's name.)

Exhibit 10.5 illustrates the information a popular financial website, Yahoo! Finance (http://finance.yahoo.com/), provides about Harley-Davidson's common stock. Some of the key figures reported for Harley-Davidson include:

- *Last trade*: The price of Harley-Davidson's common stock for the last trade of the day while the NYSE was open was $27.35.

- *Change*: The closing price of Harley-Davidson's stock on this day was $1.88 lower than the closing price on the previous day.

- *Bid and Ask*: The highest price a buyer is offering for Harley-Davidson stock is $27.38, while the lowest price a seller is willing to accept for its stock is $27.68.

- *Day's range*: The highest price for the stock during the day was $28.35, and the lowest price was $27.16.

- *52-Week range*: The highest price for Harley-Davidson stock over the previous 52 weeks was $36.13, while its lowest price was $14.99.

- *Volume*: 5,825,985 shares of the stock were traded during the day.

- *Market Cap*: The total market value of all shares of Harley-Davidson common stock outstanding was $6.44 billion. This is found by multiplying the price per share times the number of shares of common stock outstanding.

- *P/E*: The price earnings is found by dividing the price per share by the stock's earnings per share. However, the P/E ratio for companies with negative earnings per share (such as Harley-Davidson in this case) is usually reported as N/A. In general, a higher P/E ratio means investors expect a greater growth in earnings over time.

Standard & Poor's 500 A stock index based on prices of 500 major U.S. corporations in a variety of industries and market sectors.

NASDAQ Composite A stock index based on all domestic and foreign stocks listed on the NASDAQ exchange.

EXHIBIT 10.5 Yahoo! Finance Quote for a Stock

Harley-Davidson, Inc. Common St (NYSE: HOG)
After Hours: 27.35 0.00 (0.00%) 6:11pm EDT

Last Trade:	27.35	Day's Range:	27.16 - 28.35
Trade Time:	4:01pm EDT	52wk Range:	14.99 - 36.13
Change:	↓1.88 (6.43%)	Volume:	5,825,985
Prev Close:	29.23	Avg Vol (3m):	4,452,440
Open:	28.33	Market Cap:	6.44B
Bid:	27.38 x 900	P/E (ttm):	N/A
Ask:	27.68 x 100	EPS (ttm):	-0.60
1y Target Est:	36.45	Div & Yield:	0.40 (1.40%)

Source: Yahoo! Finance stock quote accessed June 4, 2010. Reproduced with permission of Yahoo! Inc. YAHOO! and the YAHOO! logo are registered trademarks of Yahoo! Inc.

- *EPS (earnings per share)*: Harley-Davidson earned –$0.60 per share of common stock outstanding. EPS is computed by dividing the net income available to common stockholders by the number of shares of common stock outstanding.

- *Div & Yield*: The sum of dividends paid by Harley-Davidson over the past 12 months was $0.40 per share. Yield is found by dividing the dividend per share by the previous day's price per share. It tells us that at that price the dividend paid by Harley-Davidson represented a 1.4% return to the investor. (But keep in mind that the dividend isn't the only return investors might earn. In fact, when stocks are rising in value the capital gain may offer a much greater return than the dividend.)

Financial websites also provide information about other types of securities such as mutual funds, ETFs, and bonds. Exhibit 10.6 shows the information the Yahoo! Finance site reports for a well-established mutual fund, the Janus Balanced Fund.

EXHIBIT 10.6 Yahoo! Finance Quote for a Mutual Fund

JANUS BALANCED FUND T SHARES

Net Asset Value:	**23.71**
Trade Time:	**Jun 4**
Change:	↓0.39 (1.62%)
Prev Close:	24.10
YTD Return*:	3.46%
Net Assets*:	5.85B
Yield*:	1.59%

* As of 30-Apr-10

Source: Yahoo! Finance stock quote accessed June 4, 2010. Reproduced with permission of Yahoo! Inc. YAHOO! and the YAHOO! logo are registered trademarks of Yahoo! Inc.

You can see that quotes for mutual funds aren't as detailed as the quotes for common stocks. But they still provide some very useful information:

- **Net Asset Value:** The Janus Balanced Fund's $23.71 **Net Asset Value (NAV)** represents the price at which the fund may be bought or redeemed; it is essentially the

market value of a mutual fund on a per share basis. A fund's NAV is computed at the end of each trading day by dividing the sum of the closing market values of all of the fund's cash and securities (less any liabilities) by the number of shares outstanding.

- **Change:** The fund's NAV decreased by $0.39 from its value at the close of the previous trading day.

- **YTD Return (year-to-date return):** The percentage increase or decrease in the NAV since the beginning of the year. The YTD return for this fund was positive, meaning that it had increased in value since the beginning of the year—which was true of the vast majority of funds during the first half of 2010, the time period when this quote was taken.

- **Yield:** The yield of 1.59% indicates the dividends or earnings of the fund distributed to investors as a percentage of its NAV. But keep in mind that, as with stocks, these dividends aren't the only return shareholders of mutual funds can earn; they may also earn a capital gain.

The Big Picture

Securities markets play a vital role in the global economy. The funds corporations raise when they issue stocks and bonds in these markets are critical to every functional area of their operations. Without these funds the marketing department would lack the resources needed to develop new products, information technology professionals would be unable to update hardware and software, and operations managers would be unable to acquire the machinery and equipment needed to produce the goods and services the company sells to earn its profits.

On the other side of these markets, investors who buy corporate securities do so to acquire assets that they hope will help them achieve their own financial goals. But investing in securities also involves risk. Over any short-run time period there is simply no guarantee that stocks and bonds will provide investors with the returns they expect. The good news—at least if you plan to invest—is that history shows that over the long run the return on these securities is positive. In other words, given enough time (and patience), investing in stocks and other securities is likely to result in a substantial increase in wealth.

WHAT ELSE? *RIP & REVIEW* CARDS IN THE BACK

LEARN YOUR WAY!

SHE DID

We know that no two students are alike. You come from different walks of life and with many different preferences. You need to study just about anytime and anywhere. **BUSN4** was developed to help you learn Introduction to Business in a way that works for you.

Not only is the format fresh and contemporary, it's also concise and focused. And, **BUSN4** is loaded with a variety of study tools, like in-text review cards, printable flashcards, and more.

Go to CourseMate for BUSN4 to find plenty of resources to help you study—no matter what learning style you like best! Access at www.cengagebrain.com.

11

MARKETING: BUILDING PROFITABLE CUSTOMER CONNECTIONS

LEARNING OBJECTIVES

After studying this chapter, you will be able to...

LO1 Discuss the objectives, the process, and the scope of marketing

LO2 Identify the role of the customer in marketing

LO3 Explain each element of marketing strategy

LO4 Describe the consumer and business decision-making process

LO5 Discuss the key elements of marketing research

LO6 Explain the roles of social responsibility and technology in marketing

> ## You need to give customers what they want—not what you *think* they want.
>
> *John Ilhan, Australian entrepreneur*

LO1 Marketing: Getting Value by Giving Value

What comes to mind when you hear the term **marketing**? Most people think of the radio ad they heard this morning, or the billboard they saw while driving to school. But advertising is only a small part of marketing; the whole story is much bigger. The American Marketing Association defines marketing as *the activity, set of institutions, and processes for creating, communicating, delivering, and exchanging offerings that have value for customers, clients, partners, and society at large.*

The ultimate benefit that most businesses seek from marketing is long-term profitability. But attaining this benefit is impossible without first delivering value to customers and other stakeholders. A successful marketer delivers value by filling customer needs in ways that exceed their expectations. As a result, you get sales today and sales tomorrow and sales the next day, which—across the days and months and years—can translate into long-term profitability. Alice Foote MacDougall, a successful entrepreneur in the 1920s, understood this thinking early on: "In business you get what you want by giving other people what they want." **Utility** is the ability of goods and services to satisfy these wants. And since there is a wide range of wants, products can provide utility in a number of different ways:

- *Form utility* satisfies wants by converting inputs into a finished form. Clearly, the vast majority of products provide some kind of form utility. For example, Jamba Juice pulverizes fruit, juices, and yogurt into yummy smoothies, and Burger King slices, dices, and sizzles potatoes into french fries.

- *Time utility* satisfies wants by providing goods and services at a convenient time for customers. For example, FedEx delivers some parcels on Sunday, LensCrafters makes eyeglasses within about an hour, 7-Eleven opens early and closes late, and e-commerce, of course, provides the ultimate 24-7 convenience.

- *Place utility* satisfies wants by providing goods and services at a convenient place for customers. For example, ATMs offer banking services in many large supermarkets, Motel 6 lodges tired travelers at the bottom of highway off-ramps, and vending machines refuel tired students at virtually every college campus.

- *Ownership utility* satisfies wants by smoothly transferring ownership of goods and services from seller to buyer. Virtually every product provides some degree of ownership utility, but some offer more than others. Apple, for example, has created a hassle-free purchase process that customers can follow by phone, by computer, and in-person.

Satisfying customer wants—in a way that exceeds expectations—is a job that never ends. Jay Levinson, a recognized expert in breakthrough marketing, comments, "Marketing is … a process. You improve it, perfect it, change it, even pause it. But you never stop it completely."

The Scope of Marketing: It's Everywhere!

For many years, businesspeople have actively applied the principles of marketing to goods and services that range from cars, to fast food, to liquor, to computers, to movies. But within the last decade or two, other organizations have successfully adopted marketing strategies and tactics to further their goals.

Nonprofit organizations—in both the private and public sectors—play a significant role in our economy, employing more people than the federal government and all 50 state governments combined (not to mention an army of volunteers!). These organizations use marketing, sometimes quite assertively, to achieve their objectives. The U.S. Army's advertising budget, for example, is nearly $300 million per year, which ranks on the list of top U.S. advertisers. Your own college probably markets itself to both prospective students and potential alumni donors. Private-sector nonprofit organizations also use marketing strategies for everything from marshalling AYSO soccer coaches for kids, to boosting attendance at the local zoo, to planning cultural events.[1]

Nonprofit organizations play a pivotal role in the expansion of marketing across our economy to include people, places, events, and ideas. But for-profit enterprises have also begun to apply marketing strategies and tactics beyond simply goods and services.

- **People Marketing:** Sports, politics, and art dominate this category, but even some businesspeople merit mentioning. Top banking executives, for instance, took a beating from a marketing standpoint during the financial meltdown at the end of 2008. Also in 2008, President Barack Obama was named Ad Age Marketer of the Year, edging out powerhouse consumer brands that were also on the short list, such as Apple, Nike, and Coors. He became a living symbol of change in the minds of the electorate. Countless entertainers and athletes have used people marketing to their advantage as well. Consider, for example, Paris Hilton, who appeared to build her career on promotion alone. In fact, as you pursue your personal goals—whether you seek a new job or a Friday night date—people marketing principles can help you achieve your objective. Start by figuring out what your "customer" needs,

and then ensure that your "product" (you!) delivers above and beyond expectations.[2]

- **Place Marketing:** This category involves drawing people to a particular place. Cities and states use place marketing to attract businesses. Delaware, for instance, the second-smallest state in the Union, is home to more than half of the Fortune 500 firms because Delaware deliberately developed a range of advantages for corporations. But more visibly, cities, states, and nations use place marketing to attract tourists. Thanks to powerful place marketing, most people have probably heard that "What happens in Vegas stays in Vegas." But in late 2008, Las Vegas shelved the high-rolling campaign in favor of a more recession-proof strategy: the "Take a Break USA" campaign. While the campaign features traditional television and newspaper advertising, it also includes a YouTube component meant to involve consumers at a more personal level.[3]

- **Event Marketing:** This category includes marketing—or sponsoring—athletic, cultural, or charitable events. Partnerships between the public and private sectors are increasingly common. Examples include the Olympics, the Super Bowl, and the Music For Relief concert to benefit victims of the 2004 Indian Ocean tsunami.

- **Idea Marketing:** A whole range of public and private organizations market ideas that are meant to change how people think or act. Recycle, don't pollute, buckle your seatbelt, support our political party, donate blood, don't smoke; all are examples of popular causes. Often, idea marketing and event marketing are combined, as we see in the annual Avon Walk for Breast Cancer. The planners actively market the idea of annual mammograms, as they solicit contributions for breast cancer research and participation in the event itself.

The Evolution of Marketing: From the Product to the Customer

The current approach to marketing evolved through a number of overlapping stages, as you'll see in Exhibit 11.1. But as you read about these eras, keep in mind that some businesses have remained lodged—with varying degrees of success—in the thinking of a past era.

Production Era Marketing didn't always begin with the customer. In fact, in the early 1900s, the customer was practically a joke. Henry Ford summed up the prevailing mindset when he reportedly said "You can have your Model T in any color you want as long as it's black." This attitude made sense from a historical perspective, since consumers didn't have the overwhelming number of choices that are currently available; most products were purchased as soon as they were produced and distributed to consumers. In this context, the top business priority was to produce large quantities of goods as efficiently as possible.

Selling Era By the 1920s, production capacity had increased dramatically. For the first time, supply in many categories exceeded demand, which caused the emergence of the hard sell. The selling focus gained momentum in the 1930s and 1940s, when the Depression and World War II made consumers even more reluctant to part with their limited money.

Marketing Era The landscape changed dramatically in the 1950s. Many factories that had churned out military supplies converted to consumer production, flooding the market with choices in virtually every product category. An era of relative peace and prosperity emerged, and—as soldiers returned from World War II—marriage and birthrates soared. To compete for the consumer's dollar, marketers attempted to provide goods and services that met customer needs better than anything else on the market. As a result, the marketing concept materialized in the 1950s. The **marketing concept** is a philosophy that makes customer satisfaction—now and in the future—the central focus of the entire organization. Companies that embrace this philosophy strive to delight customers, integrating this goal into all business

> **marketing concept**
> A business philosophy that makes customer satisfaction—now and in the future—the central focus of the entire organization.

EXHIBIT 11.1 The Evolution of Marketing

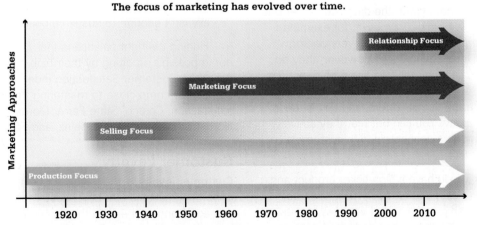

The focus of marketing has evolved over time.

While individual firms differ in their approach to marketing, the prevailing view at leading edge firms has changed over time as shown here.

activities. The marketing concept holds that delivering unmatched value to customers is the only effective way to achieve long-term profitability.

Relationship Era The marketing concept has gathered momentum across the economy, leading to the current era, unfolding over the last decade, which zeros in on long-term customer relationships. Acquiring a new customer can cost five times more than keeping an existing customer. Retaining your current customers—and getting them to spend additional dollars—is clearly cost effective. Moreover, satisfied customers can develop into advocates for your business, becoming powerful generators of positive "word of mouth."

LO2 The Customer: Front and Center

Customer relationship management (CRM) is the centerpiece of successful, 21st century marketing. Broadly defined, CRM is the ongoing process of acquiring, maintaining, and growing profitable customer relationships by delivering unmatched value. CRM works best when marketers combine marketing communication with one-on-one personalization. Amazon is a champion player at CRM, greeting customers by name, recommending specific products, and providing streamlined checkout. Clearly, information is an integral part of this process—you simply can't do CRM without collecting, managing, and applying the right data at the right time for the right person (and every repeat customer is the "right person"!).

Limited Relationships Clearly the scope of your relationships will depend not just on the data you gather but also on your industry. Colgate-Palmolive, for example, can't forge a close personal bond with every person who buys a bar of Irish Spring soap. However, they do invite customers to call their toll-free line with questions or comments, and they maintain a vibrant website with music, an e-newsletter, special offers, and an invitation to contact the company. You can bet that they actively gather data and pursue a connection with customers who do initiate contact.

Full Partnerships If you have a high-ticket product and a smaller customer base, you're much more likely to pursue a full partnership with each of your key clients. Colgate-Palmolive, for instance, has dedicated customer service teams working with key accounts such as

Walmart and Costco. With a full partnership, the marketer gathers and leverages extensive information about each customer, and often includes the customer in key aspects of the product development process.

Value

You know you've delivered **value** when your customers believe that your product has a better relationship between the cost and the benefits than any competitor. By this definition low cost does not always mean high value. In fact, a recent survey suggests that loyal customers are often willing to pay *more* for their products rather than switch to lower-cost competitors. Apple provides a clear example. We probably all know at least a handful of Apple fanatics who gladly pay far more for their PowerBooks (or iPhones, or iPads) than they would pay for a competing product.

Perceived Value Versus Actual Value The operative idea here is *perceived*. Simply creating value isn't enough; you also must help customers believe that your product is uniquely qualified to meet their needs. This becomes a particular challenge when you're a new business competing against a market leader with disproportionately strong perceived value.

Customer Satisfaction

You know you've satisfied your customers when you deliver perceived value above and beyond their expectations. But achieving **customer satisfaction** can be tricky. Less savvy marketers frequently fall into one of two traps:

- The first trap is overpromising. Even if you deliver more value than anyone else, your customers will be disappointed if your product falls short of overly high expectations. The messages that you send regarding your product influence expectations—keep them real!

- The second trap is underpromising. If you don't set expectations high enough, too few customers will be willing to try your product. The result will be a tiny base of highly satisfied customers, which usually isn't enough to sustain a business.

Finding the right balance is tricky, but clearly not impossible. Judging by their high scores on the American Customer Satisfaction Index, the following companies come close to mastering the art of customer satisfaction: Costco, State Farm, Clorox Company, Nordstrom, Amazon, H.J. Heinz, and FedEx.[4]

Customer Loyalty

Customer loyalty is the payoff for delivering value and generating satisfaction. Loyal customers purchase from you again and again—and they sometimes even pay more for your product. They forgive your mistakes. They provide valuable feedback. They may require less service. They refer their friends (and sometimes even strangers). Moreover, studying your loyal customers can give you a competitive edge for acquiring new ones, since people with a similar profile would likely be a great fit for your products.[5]

LO3 Marketing Strategy: Where Are You Going and How Will You Get There?

In marketing terms, the question becomes: who is your target audience, and how will you reach them? Many successful firms answer this question by developing a formal **marketing plan**, updated on a yearly basis; other firms handle their planning on a more informal basis. But regardless of the specific approach, the first step in planning your marketing strategy should be to determine where to target your efforts. Who are those people who are most likely to buy your products? The first step is **market segmentation**—dividing your marketing into groups of people, or segments, that are similar to one another and different from everyone else. One or more of these segments will be your target market. Once you've identified your target market, your next step is to determine how you can best use marketing tools to reach them. And finally, you need to anticipate and respond to changes in the external environment. This section will define target market, explain market segmentation, introduce the marketing mix, and review the key factors in the marketing environment. Taken together, these elements will shape an effective marketing strategy, as shown in Exhibit 11.2.

EXHIBIT 11.2 Marketing Strategy
The marketer creates the marketing mix but responds to the marketing environment with a single-minded focus on the target market.

Target Market

Your **target market** is the group of people who are most likely to buy your product. This is where you should concentrate your marketing efforts. But why not target your efforts toward everyone? After all, even if most middle-aged moms wouldn't buy purple polka-dotted miniskirts, an adventurous few just might do it. Well, you can always hope for the adventurous few, but virtually every business has limited resources, and marketing toward the people who are most likely to buy your flamboyant minis—say, teenage girls—will maximize the impact of each dollar you spend. A well-chosen target market embodies the following characteristics:

- Size: There must be enough people in your target group to support a business.

- Profitability: The people must be willing and able to spend more than the cost of producing and marketing your product.

- Accessibility: Your target must be reachable through channels that your business can afford.

- Limited competition: Look for markets with limited competition; a crowded market is much tougher to crack.

Consumer Markets Versus Business Markets

Consumer marketers (B2C) direct their efforts to people who are buying products for personal consumption (e.g., candy bars, shampoo, and clothing), whereas **business marketers (B2B)** direct their efforts to customers who are buying products to use either directly or indirectly to produce other products (e.g., tractors, steel, and cash registers). But keep in mind that the distinction between the market categories is not in the products themselves; rather, it lies in how the buyer will use the product. For instance, shampoo that you buy for yourself is clearly a consumer product, but shampoo that a hair stylist buys for a salon is a business product. Similarly, a computer that you buy for yourself is a consumer product, but a computer that your school buys for the computer lab is a business product. Both B2C and B2B marketers need to choose the best target, but they tend to follow slightly different approaches.

marketing plan A formal document that defines marketing objectives and the specific strategies for achieving those objectives.

market segmentation Dividing potential customers into groups of similar people, or segments.

target market The group of people who are most likely to buy a particular product.

consumer marketers (also known as business-to-consumer or B2C) Marketers who direct their efforts toward people who are buying products for personal consumption.

business marketers (also known as business-to-business or B2B) Marketers who direct their efforts toward people who are buying products to use either directly or indirectly to produce other products.

demographic segmentation Dividing the market into smaller groups based on measurable characteristics about people such as age, income, ethnicity, and gender.

geographic segmentation Dividing the market into smaller groups based on where consumers live. This process can incorporate countries, cities, or population density as key factors.

psychographic segmentation Dividing the market into smaller groups based on consumer attitudes, interests, values, and lifestyles.

behavioral segmentation Dividing the market based on how people behave toward various products. This category includes both the benefits that consumers seek from products and how consumers use the product.

Geographic segmentation can mean zeroing in on the right target neighborhood.

© ETHEL DAVIES/PHOTOLIBRARY

Consumer Market Segmentation

Choosing the best target market (or markets) for your product begins with dividing your market into segments, or groups of people who have similar characteristics. But people can be similar in a number of different ways, so not surprisingly, marketers have several options for segmenting potential consumers.

Demographic B2C **demographic segmentation** refers to dividing the market based on measurable characteristics about people such as age, income, ethnicity, and gender. Demographics are a vital starting point for most marketers. Mattel, for example, targets kids, while Howard Stern targets young men, and BMW targets the wealthy. Sometimes the demographic makeup of a given market is tough to discern; African American artists, for instance, create the bulk of rap music, yet Caucasian suburban males form the bulk of the rap music market.

Geographic B2C **geographic segmentation** refers to dividing the market based on where consumers live. This process can incorporate countries, or cities, or population density as key factors. For instance, Toyota Sequoia does not concentrate on European markets, where tiny, winding streets and nonexistent parking are common in many cities. Cosmetic surgeons tend to market their services more heavily

in urban rather than rural areas. And finding a great surfboard is easy in California, but more challenging in South Dakota.

Psychographic B2C **psychographic segmentation** refers to dividing the market based on consumer attitudes, interests, values, and lifestyles. Porsche Cayenne, for instance, targets consumers who seek the thrill of driving. A number of companies have found a highly profitable niche providing upscale wilderness experiences for people who seek all the pleasure with none of the pain (you enjoy the great outdoors, while someone else lugs your gear, pours your wine, slices your goat cheese, and inflates your extra-comfy air mattress). And magazine racks are filled with products geared toward psychographic segments, from *People* magazine, to *Sports Illustrated,* to *InfoWorld,* to *Cosmopolitan.* NOTE: Marketers typically use psychographics to complement other segmentation approaches, rather than to provide the core definition.

Behavioral B2C **behavioral segmentation** refers to dividing the market based on how people behave toward various products. This category includes both the benefits that consumers seek from products and how consumers use the product. The Neutrogena Corporation, for example, built a multimillion-dollar hair care business by targeting consumers who wanted an occasional break from their favorite shampoo. Countless products such as Miller Lite actively target the low-carbohydrate consumer. But perhaps the most common type of behavioral segmentation is based on usage patterns. Fast food restaurants, for instance, actively target heavy users (who, ironically, tend to be slender): young men in their 20s and 30s. This group consumes about 17% of their total calories from fast food, compared to 12% for adults in general. Understanding the usage patterns of your customer base gives you the option of either focusing on your core users, or trying to pull light users into your core market.

Business Market Segmentation

B2B marketers typically follow a similar process in segmenting their markets, but they use slightly different categories:

Geographic B2B geographic segmentation refers to dividing the market based on the concentration of customers. Many industries tend to be highly clustered in certain areas, such as technology in California, and auto suppliers in the "auto corridor" that stretches south from Michigan to Tennessee. Geographic segmentation, of course, is especially common on an international basis, where variables such as language, culture, income, and regulatory differences can play a crucial role.

Customer-based B2B customer-based segmentation refers to dividing the market based on the characteristics of customers. This approach includes a range of possibilities. Some B2B marketers segment based on customer size. Others segment based on customer type. Johnson & Johnson, for example, has a group of salespeople dedicated exclusively to retail accounts such as Target and Publix, while other salespeople focus solely on motivating doctors to recommend their products. Other potential B2B markets include institutions—schools and hospitals, for instance, are key segments for Heinz Ketchup—and the government.

Product-use–based B2B product-use–based segmentation refers to dividing the market based on how customers will use the product. Small and midsized companies find this strategy especially helpful in narrowing their target markets. Possibilities include the ability to support certain software packages or production systems or the desire to serve certain customer groups, such as long-distance truckers or restaurants that deliver food.

The Marketing Mix

Once you've clearly defined your target market, your next challenge is to develop compelling strategies for product, price, distribution, and promotion. The blending of these

© GINES VALERA MARIN/ISTOCKPHOTO.COM

Color Me . . . Hungry?!

Have you ever noticed that fast food restaurants typically feature vivid shades of red, yellow, and orange in both their logos and their décor? Think McDonald's, KFC, Burger King, and Pizza Hut. The color choice is no coincidence.

Marketing researchers have learned that consumers in the United States associate red with energy, passion, and speed. Yellow suggests happiness and warmth, while orange suggests playfulness, affordability, and fun. A simulated cocktail party study found that partygoers in red rooms reported feeling hungrier and thirstier than others, and guests in yellow rooms ate twice as much as others. The implication? Surrounding customers with red, yellow, and orange encourages them to eat a lot quickly and leave, which aligns nicely with the goals of most fast food chains.

Color psychology is a powerful—though often overlooked—marketing tool. Colors evoke emotions and trigger specific behaviors, which can dramatically influence how people buy your product. Here is a list of common colors and some of their associations in U.S. mainstream culture.

- Red: Love, passion, warmth, food, excitement, action, danger, need to stop
- Blue: Power, trustworthiness, calm, success, seriousness, boredom
- Green: Money, nature, health, healing, decay, illness
- Orange: Playfulness, affordability, youth, fun, low quality, cheap
- Purple: Royalty, luxury, dignity, spirituality, nightmares, craziness
- White: Purity, innocence, simplicity, mildness
- Black: Sophistication, elegance, seriousness, sexuality, mystery, evil

Keep in mind that while some color associations are universal, others can differ significantly among cultures. White, for instance, signifies death and mourning in Chinese culture, while purple represents death in Brazil.

As a marketer, your goal should be to align your color choice with the perceptions of your target market and the features of your product. The result should be more green for your bottom line![6]

marketing mix The blend of marketing strategies for product, price, distribution, and promotion.

elements becomes your **marketing mix,** as shown below in Exhibit 11.3.

- **Product Strategy:** Your product involves far more than simply a tangible good or a specific service. Product strategy decisions range from brand name, to product image, to package design, to customer service, to guarantees, to new product development, and more. Designing the best product clearly begins with understanding the needs of your target market.

- **Pricing Strategy:** Pricing is a challenging area of the marketing mix. To deliver customer value, your prices must be fair, relative to the benefits of your product. Other factors include competition, regulation, and public opinion. Your product category plays a critical role, as well. A low-cost desk, for instance, might be appealing, but who would want discount-priced knee surgery?

- **Distribution Strategy:** The goal is to deliver your product to the right people, in the right quantities, at the right time, in the right place. The key decisions include shipping, warehousing, and selling outlets (e.g., the Web versus network marketing versus brick-and-mortar stores). The implications of these decisions for product image and customer satisfaction can be significant.

- **Promotion Strategy:** Promotion includes all of the ways that marketers communicate about their products. The list of possibilities is long and growing, especially as the Internet continues to evolve

EXHIBIT 11.3 Marketing Mix

Product Strategy

Pricing Strategy

Promotion Strategy

Distribution Strategy

WITHOUT A MAP... CHARTING AN ETHICAL COURSE

When Less Is More...

It's not your imagination—the food you buy at the market really does disappear faster, even though you may not have realized that the package was smaller. In 2008, about 30% of all packaged goods got smaller, most of them unnoticed by consumers. Skippy peanut butter jars, for instance, got about 10% smaller, but the jar looks just the same—it's the dimple in the bottom that's more indented. PepsiCo reduced the size of its orange juice jugs by 7 ounces, but touted the container's "new ergonomic design" and "easy-pour lid." The agenda, some say, was to distract consumers from the *de facto* price increase. And cereal makers have reduced the depth of their packages—much less noticeable than reducing the height or width.

Food manufacturers assert that these size reductions—and the associated cost cuts—are crucial in the face of skyrocketing food and fuel costs. Some analysts also point out that the reductions are ultimately good for the environment, because less packaging eliminates waste. But others see deception. "It's become a game," said Susan Broniarczyk, a professor of marketing at the University of Texas at Austin. "How far can you go in reducing the size of a package while flying under the consumers' radar screen?" Consumer advocate Ben Popken takes an even harder line: "This is the packaging equivalent of three-card monte. By changing several factors at the same time, food companies disguise the fact that you're getting less for the same price."

What do you think? Are food firms playing fair? Or are they going too far in an attempt to deliberately mislead customers? Whatever your conclusions, it clearly makes sense to shop carefully, looking at both the price tag *and* the cost per unit.[7]

AP IMAGES/STEVEN SENNE

at breakneck speed. Key elements today include advertising, personal selling, sales promotion, public relations, word of mouth, and product placement. Successful promotional strategies typically evolve in response to both customer needs and competition. A number of innovative companies

Advertising is the 'wonder' in Wonder Bread.

Jef I. Richards, advertising professor and author

are even inviting their customers to participate in creating their advertising through venues such as YouTube. Check out Exhibit 11.4 to see how easily you can analyze promotional strategies.

The Global Marketing Mix

As you decide to enter foreign markets, you'll need to reevaluate your marketing mix for each new country. Should it change? If so, how should it change? Many business goods simply don't require much change in the marketing mix, since their success isn't dependent on culture. Examples include heavy machinery, cement, and farming equipment. Consumer products, however, often require completely new marketing mixes to effectively reach their consumers.

Nike's approach to marketing in China offers an interesting example of how one firm managed the complex process of building a successful business in a foreign market. When Nike first entered China in the

1990s, the company seemed to face an insurmountable challenge: not only did a pair of Nike sneakers cost twice the Chinese average monthly salary, but most Chinese just didn't play sports, according to Terry Rhoads, then director of Nike sports marketing. So he boldly set out to change that. Rhoads created a Nike high school basketball league, which has since spread to 17 cities. To loosen up fans, he blasted canned cheering during games and arranged for national TV coverage of the finals. He even leveraged connections with the NBA to bring Michael Jordan for visits.

The gamble quickly paid off, as the Chinese middle class emerged—along with more individualistic values, which are a strong fit with the Nike ethos. By 2001, Nike had dubbed its marketing approach "hip hoop," which they described as an effort to "connect Nike with a creative lifestyle." Sales in 2008 exceeded $1 billion, about a year ahead of when Nike had anticipated. And a recent survey suggests that Chinese youth rank Nike as their favorite sports brand. Winning over young buyers is especially important, according to researcher Mary Bergstrom, because young people are China's "most influential" consumers, often affecting what the whole household buys.[8]

The Marketing Environment

While marketers actively influence the elements of the marketing mix, they must anticipate and respond to the elements of the external environment, which

EXHIBIT 11.4 Analyzing Promotional Strategies
Who is the target audience for each of these ads? How does each ad position the product relative to the competition? Which strategy is most effective? Why?

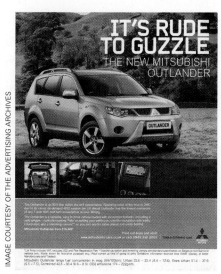

they typically cannot control. **Environmental scanning** is a key tool; the goal is simply to continually collect information from sources that range from informal networks, to industry newsletters, to the general press, to customers, to suppliers, to the competition, among others. The key elements of the external environment include the following components:

Competitive The dynamic competitive environment probably affects marketers on a day-to-day basis more than any other element. Understanding the competitive environment often begins with analysis of **market share,** or the percentage of the marketplace that each firm controls. To avoid ambushes—and to uncover new opportunities—you must continually monitor how both dominant and emerging competitors handle each element of their marketing mix. And don't forget indirect competitors, who meet the same consumer needs as you but with a completely different product (e.g., cable TV and Internet games).

Economic The only certainty in the economic environment is change, but the timing of expansions and contractions is virtually impossible to predict. Your goal as a marketer is to identify and respond to changes as soon as possible, keeping in mind that a sharp eye sees opportunity even in economic downturns. For instance, affordable luxuries and do-it-yourself enterprises can thrive during recessions.

Social/Cultural The social/cultural element covers a vast array of factors, including lifestyle, customs, language, attitudes, interests, and population shifts. Trends can change rapidly, with a dramatic impact on marketing decisions. Anticipating and responding to trends can be especially important in industries such as entertainment, fashion, and technology. Motorola, for instance, had a runaway hit with its RAZR phone, introduced in 2004, but when consumer tastes turned elsewhere, it just wasn't ready. By 2008, Motorola's share of the mobile phone handset market had plummeted by about half.[9]

Technological Changes in technology can be very visible to consumers (e.g., the introduction of the iPhone). However, technology often affects marketers in ways that are less directly visible. For example, technology allows mass customization of Levi's blue jeans at a reasonable price and facilitates just-in-time inventory management for countless companies that see the results in their bottom lines.

Political/Legal The political/legal area includes laws, regulations, and political climate. Most U.S. laws and regulations are clear (e.g., dry counties in certain states), but others are complex and evolving (e.g., qualifications for certain tax breaks). Political climate includes changing levels of governmental support for various business categories. Clearly, the political/legal issues affect heavily regulated sectors (e.g., telecommunications and pharmaceuticals) more than others.

The Global Marketing Environment

As the Internet has grown, the world market has become accessible to virtually every business. This boosts the importance of understanding each element of the marketing environment—competitive, economic, social/cultural, technological, and political/legal—in each of your key markets. Among the biggest global challenges are researching opportunities in other countries and delivering your product to customers in other countries.

LO4 Customer Behavior: Decisions, Decisions, Decisions!

If successful marketing begins with the customer, then understanding the customer is critical. Why do people buy one product but not another? How do they use the products they buy? When do they get rid of them? Knowing the answers to these questions will clearly help you better meet customer needs.

Consumer Behavior

Consumer behavior refers specifically to how people act when they are buying products for their own personal consumption. The decisions they make often seem spontaneous (after all, how much thought do you give to buying a pack of gum?), but they often result from a complex set of influences, as shown in Exhibit 11.5.

Marketers, of course, add their own influence through the marketing mix. For instance, after smelling

EXHIBIT 11.5 Elements That Influence the Consumer Decision-Making Process

Influence	Description
Cultural	*Culture*: The values, attitudes, and customs shared by members of a society
	Subculture: A smaller division of the broader culture
	Social Class: Societal position driven largely by income and occupation
Social	*Family*: A powerful force in consumption choices
	Friends: Another powerful force, especially for high-profile purchases
	Reference Groups: Groups that give consumers a point of comparison
Personal	*Demographics*: Measurable characteristics such as age, gender, or income
	Personality: The mix of traits that determine who you are
Psychological	*Motivation*: Pressing needs that tend to generate action
	Attitudes: Lasting evaluations of (or feelings about) objects or ideas
	Perceptions: How people select, organize, and interpret information
	Learning: Changes in behavior based on experience

purchase choices. One example might be postpurchase mailings that highlight the accolades received by an expensive product.

But does every consumer go through every step of the process all the time? That's clearly not the case! People make low-involvement decisions (such as buying that pack of gum) according to habit … or even just on a whim. But when the stakes are high—either financially or socially—most people move through the five steps of the classic decision-making process. For example, most of us wouldn't think of buying a car, a computer, or the "right" pair of blue jeans without stepping through the decision-making process.

Business Buyer Behavior

Business buyer behavior refers to how people act when they're buying products to use either directly or indirectly to produce other products (e.g., chemicals, copy paper, computer servers). Business buyers typically have purchasing training and apply rational criteria to their decision-making process. They usually buy according to purchase specifications and objective standards, with a minimum of personal judgment or whim. Often, business buyers are integrating input from a number of internal sources, based on a relatively formal process. And finally, business buyers tend to seek (and often secure) highly customized goods, services, and prices.

cognitive dissonance Consumer discomfort with a purchase decision, typically for a higher-priced item.

business buyer behavior Describes how people act when they are buying products to use either directly or indirectly to produce other products.

pretzels in the mall and tasting pretzel morsels from the sample tray, many of us would at least be tempted to cough up the cash for a hot, buttery pretzel of our own … regardless of any other factors! Similarly, changes in the external environment—for example, a series of hurricanes in Florida—dramatically affect consumer decisions about items such as flashlights, batteries, and plywood.

All these forces shape consumer behavior in each step of the process regarding purchase decisions. Exhibit 11.6 shows how the consumer decision process works.

Clearly, marketing can influence the purchase decision every step of the way, from helping consumers identify needs (or problems), to resolving that awful feeling of **cognitive dissonance** (or kicking oneself) after a major purchase. Some marketers attempt to avoid cognitive dissonance altogether by developing specific programs to help customers validate their

EXHIBIT 11.6 Consumer Decision Process

Need Recognition
Your best friend suddenly notices that she is the only person she knows who still wears high-rise blue jeans to class...problem alert!

Information Search
Horrified, your friend not only checks out your style, but also notices what the cool girls on campus are wearing. AND she snitches your copy of *Cosmo* to leaf through the ads.

Evaluation of Alternatives
Your friend compares the prices and styles of the various brands of blue jeans that she identifies.

Purchase Decision
After a number of conversations, your friend finally decides to buy True Religion jeans for $215.

Postpurchase Behavior
Three days later, she begins to kick herself for spending so much money on jeans, because she can no longer afford her daily Starbucks habit.

marketing research
The process of gathering, interpreting, and applying information to uncover marketing opportunities and challenges, and to make better marketing decisions. •

secondary data
Existing data that marketers gather or purchase for a research project.

primary data New data that marketers compile for a specific research project.

observation research Marketing research that *does not* require the researcher to interact with the research subject.

survey research Marketing research that requires the researcher to interact with the research subject.

LO5 Marketing Research: So What Do They REALLY Think?

If marketing begins with the customer, marketing research is the foundation of success. **Marketing research** involves gathering, interpreting, and applying information to uncover opportunities and challenges. The goal, of course, is better marketing decisions: more value for consumers and more profits for businesses that deliver. Companies use marketing research to:

- Identify external opportunities and threats (from social trends to competition).
- Monitor and predict customer behavior.
- Evaluate and improve each area of the marketing mix.

Types of Data

There are two main categories of marketing research data—**secondary data** and **primary data**—each with its own set of benefits and drawbacks, as shown in Exhibit 11.7.

Clearly, it makes sense to gather secondary data before you invest in primary research. Look at your company's internal information. What does previous research say? What does the press say? What can you find on the Web? Once you've looked at the secondary research, you may find that primary research is unnecessary. But if not, your secondary research will guide your primary research and make it more focused and relevant, which ends up saving time and money.

Primary Research Tools

There are two basic categories of primary research: observation and survey. **Observation research** happens when the researcher *does not* directly interact with the research subject. The key advantage of watching versus asking is that what people actually *do* often differs from what they *say*—sometimes quite innocently. For instance, if an amusement park employee stands

EXHIBIT 11.7 Research Data Comparison

Secondary Data:	Primary Data:
Existing data that marketers gather or purchase	New data that marketers compile for the first time
Tends to be lower cost	Tends to be more expensive
May not meet your specific needs	Customized to meet your needs
Frequently outdated	Fresh, new data
Available to your competitors	Proprietary—no one else has it
Examples: U.S. Census, *The Wall Street Journal*, *Time* magazine, your product sales history	Examples: Your own surveys, focus groups, customer comments, mall interviews

outside an attraction and records which way people turn when they exit, he may be conducting observation research to determine where to place a new lemonade stand. Watching would be better than asking because many people could not honestly say which way they'd likely turn. Examples of observation research include:

- Scanner data from retail sales.
- Traffic counters to determine where to place billboards.
- Garbage analysis to measure recycling compliance.

Observation research can be both cheap and amazingly effective. A car dealership, for instance, can survey the preset radio stations on every car that comes in for service. That information helps them choose which stations to use for advertising. But the biggest downside of observation research is that it doesn't yield any information on consumer motivation—the reasons behind consumer decisions. The preset radio stations wouldn't matter, for example, if the bulk of drivers listen only to CDs in the car. **Survey research** happens when the researcher *does*

© MIKE SEGAL/PHOTOLIBRARY

Chapter 11   Marketing: Building Profitable Customer Connections

Oops! what were they THINKING?!

"If you can't be a good example, then you'll just have to serve as a horrible warning."

Even the heavy-hitters make marketing gaffes. Their biggest mistakes are often entertaining, but they also serve as a powerful warning to consult with the customer *before* taking action. A few amusing examples:

• In mid-2009, Microsoft showed a photo on its U.S. website of three office workers—white, Asian American, and African American—and then changed the photo on the Polish version of the website to replace the head of the African American man with the head of a white man, while leaving the original hand of the African American man clearly visible. Although Microsoft quickly apologized and pulled the photo from its Polish site, they didn't clearly explain why they thought it made sense to mask the diversity of the photo in the first place.

• In 2007, Hershey's introduced Ice Breakers Pacs, nickel-sized dissolvable pouches with a powdered sweetener inside. But they discontinued production in early 2008, in response to concerns from police narcotics officers and other community leaders that the mints too closely resembled tiny heat-sealed bags used to sell powdered street drugs. Announcing that the candy would be discontinued, Hershey's CEO commented that the company was "sensitive to these concerns." Apparently they weren't sensitive enough.

• In 2009, Tropicana introduced a new package for its premium orange juice. The redesign supplanted the longtime Tropicana brand symbol—an orange from which a straw protrudes—with a picture of a glass of orange juice. Consumers were outraged. They described the package as "ugly," "stupid," and "generic." One even asked, "Do any of these package design people actually shop for orange juice?" Deluged with negative feedback, the company scrapped the new packaging less than two months after they introduced it.

These fiascos only highlight the importance of *marketing research*. But sometimes, of course, even research isn't enough to identify marketing issues before they hit. At that point the priority should shift to dealing with the mistake openly, honestly, and quickly, which can help a company win the game, despite the gaffe.[10]

---

interact with research subjects. The key advantage is that you can secure information about what people are thinking and feeling, beyond what you can observe. For example, a carmaker might observe that the majority of its purchasers are men. They could use this information to tailor their advertising to men, or they could do survey research and possibly learn that even though men do the actual purchasing, women often make the purchase decision ... a very different scenario! But the key downside of survey research is that many people aren't honest or accurate about their experiences, opinions, and motivations, which can make

"It Ain't Easy Being Green"

Globally, despite financial concerns, consumers plan to spend more on green products, particularly in emerging powerhouse countries, such as China, India, and Brazil. To establish themselves as green in the minds of consumers, brands must take genuine environmental action in every area from energy efficiency, to packaging, to green innovation. Consumers expect a comprehensive approach. According to the 2009 ImagePower Green Brands survey, U.S. consumers rank the following brands "greenest":

1. Clorox Green Works	6. P&G
2. Burt's Bees	7. Walmart
3. Tom's of Maine	8. IKEA
4. SC Johnson	9. Disney
5. Toyota	10. Dove

It's not surprising that each of these brands touts green credentials *and* performance in a simple, compelling message. Successful green marketers know that if a product doesn't perform, you won't buy it twice. They also know that hardcore green activists won't let them rest if their green claims are bogus. Delivering on both fronts—without a wallet-busting price—is a tough challenge that more and more marketers are racing to meet. Worldwide, intellectuals and activists are the most credible spokespeople about green products, and to achieve success, marketers must reach them in a way that creates a groundswell of positive "buzz."[11]

survey research quite misleading. Examples of survey research include:

- Telephone and online questionnaires
- Door-to-door interviews
- Mall-intercept interviews
- Focus groups
- Mail-in questionnaires

An International Perspective

Doing marketing research across multiple countries can be an overwhelming challenge. In parts of Latin America, for instance, many homes don't have telephone connections, so the results from telephone surveys could be very misleading. Door-to-door tends to be a better approach. But in parts of the Middle East, researchers could be arrested for knocking on a stranger's door, especially if they aren't dressed according to local standards. Because of these kinds of issues, many companies hire research firms with a strong local presence (often based in-country) to handle their international marketing research projects.

LO6 Social Responsibility and Technology: A Major Marketing Shift

Two key factors have had a dramatic impact on marketing in the last couple of decades: a surge in the social responsibility movement and the dramatic emergence of the Internet and digital technology. This section will cover how each factor has influenced marketing.

Marketing and Society: It's Not Just About You!

Over the past couple of decades the social responsibility movement has accelerated in the United States, demanding that marketers actively contribute to the needs of the broader community. Leading-edge marketers have responded by setting a higher standard in key areas such as environmentalism, abolishment of sweatshops, and involvement in the local community. Starbucks, Target, and General Electric, for instance,

© MEDIABLITZIMAGES (UK) LIMITED/ALAMY

Innovation Unleashed!

In today's hyper-competitive marketplace, businesses must differentiate their products from an astonishing array of alternatives. While life-changing innovation is rare, many successful products simply provide a new twist on an existing product. Examples include Go-Gurt's portable yogurt in a tube, Arrowhead's Sport Top water bottles, and Colgate's pump toothpaste dispenser.

To help you make those kinds of jumps, the game in this box uses rebus puzzles to stretch your creativity. Rebus puzzles present common words and phrases in novel orientation to each other. The goal is to determine the meaning. The puzzles are below, and the answers are at the bottom of the box.

ARREST YOU'RE	HISTORY HISTORY HISTORY	Chimadena	RIGHT RIGHT	BAN ANA
abcdefghjmo pqrstuvwxyz	TimeTime	YYYGuy	MEREPEAT	BPULSEIANSEUSRSE

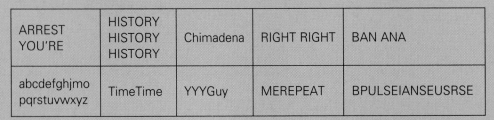

Answers: You're under arrest, missing link, history repeats itself, time after time (or double time), made in China, wise guy, equal rights, repeat after me, banana split, mixing business with pleasure.

green marketing The development and promotion of products with ecological benefits.

mass customization The creation of products tailored for individual consumers on a mass basis.

all publish corporate responsibility reports that evaluate the social impact of how the companies run their businesses, and all highlight their programs on their corporate websites.

Green Marketing Companies employ **green marketing** when they actively promote the ecological benefits of their products. Toyota has been especially successful promoting the green benefits of its Prius (although like all carmakers, Toyota has struggled during the global financial crisis). Its strategy highlights fuel economy *and* performance, implying that consumers can "go green" without making any real sacrifices. Environmentally friendly fashion offers another emerging example of green marketing. Over the past few years, a number of designers have rolled out their versions of upscale ecofashion. In addition to clothing made of organic cotton, recent entries include vegan stilettos with four-inch heels, bamboo dresses, biodegradable umbrellas, and solar-powered jackets (these jackets feature solar cells, integrated into the collar, that collect solar energy and route it to charge devices). Green marketing items are aimed at a growing number of consumers who make purchase decisions based (at least in part) on their convictions. But reaching these consumers may be an increasing challenge in tough economic times, when low prices trump all other considerations for a growing swath of the population.[12]

Technology and Marketing: Power to the People!

The emergence of the digital age has revolutionized every element of marketing. Perhaps the most dramatic change has been a shift in power from producers to customers. The Internet gives customers 24/7 access to information and product choices from all over the world. In response, competition has intensified as marketers strive to meet an increasingly high standard of value.

But technology has also created opportunities for marketers. The Internet has opened the door for **mass customization:** creating products tailored for individual consumers on a mass basis. Using sophisticated data collection and management systems, marketers can now collect detailed information about each customer, which allows them to develop one-on-one relationships and to identify high-potential new customers. Through the Web, marketers can tap into (or even create) communities of users that yield valuable information about their goods and services. Technology also helps marketers lower costs, so they can deliver greater value to their customers.

The digital boom has also created an abundance of promotional opportunities as marketers reach out to consumers via new tools, such as interactive advertising, virtual reality displays, text messaging, and video kiosks. We'll discuss these tools in more detail in Chapter 12.

The Big Picture

Since the ultimate goal of most marketing is long-term profitability, a core marketing principle must infuse every facet of a successful organization: the need to deliver products that exceed customer expectations. The customer must come first for *every* department—including finance, accounting, engineering, manufacturing, and human resources—although the specifics of how that plays out will clearly differ for each organizational function. Competition in the future will only intensify. Customer choices will continue to multiply as globalization and technology march forward. While these forces will weed out the weaker players, firms with a deeply engrained marketing orientation and a strong customer focus will continue to flourish—delivering value to their stakeholders and dollars to their bottom line.

WHAT ELSE? *RIP & REVIEW* **CARDS IN THE BACK**

PRODUCT AND PROMOTION: CREATING AND COMMUNICATING VALUE

Customers buy for their reasons, not yours.

Orvel Ray Wilson, consultant

Product and promotional strategy are the two most visible elements of the promotional mix: what benefits are you offering consumers, and how are you communicating those benefits? This chapter covers product and promotional strategies separately, but as you read, keep in mind that effective marketers carefully interweave all the elements of the marketing mix—including distribution and pricing strategies—to create a coherent whole that's even stronger than the sum of the parts.

LO1 Product: It's Probably More Than You Thought

When most people hear the term "product," they immediately think of the material things that we buy and use and consume every day: a can of Coke, a Nokia cell phone, a pair of 7 jeans. But from a marketing standpoint, product means much more. A **product** can be anything that a company offers to satisfy consumer needs and wants; the possibilities include not only physical goods, but also services and ideas. A car wash, laser eye surgery, and a cooking lesson all qualify as products.

When you buy a product, you also "buy" all of the attributes associated with the product. These encompass a broad range of qualities, such as the brand name, the image, the packaging, the reputation, and the guarantee. Keep in mind that—from a consumer standpoint—these attributes (or the lack of these attributes) are part of the product purchase, even if they don't add to its value. As a marketer, it's worth your while to carefully consider each element of your product to ensure that you're maximizing value without sacrificing profitability. For example, with the introduction of the translucent, multicolored iMac computers in 1998, Apple established its reputation for creating value through product design—an attribute that other PC manufacturers completely overlooked as they churned out their inventories of boring, beige boxes. Over the years, Apple has continued to polish its reputation by introducing sleek, elegantly designed products such as its iPad tablet computers and its iPhones.

Services: A Product by Any Other Name...

If a "product" includes anything that satisfies consumer needs, services clearly fit the bill. But services have some obvious differences from tangible goods. You often cannot see, hear, smell, taste, or touch a service, and you can virtually never "own" it. After a haircut, for example, you might possess great-looking hair, but you don't own the haircutting experience (at least not literally). Most services embody these qualities:

- **Intangibility:** As we discussed, you typically cannot see, smell, taste, or touch a service before you buy it. Clearly, this creates a lot of uncertainty. Will the purchase really be worthwhile? Smart marketers mitigate the uncertainty by giving clues that suggest value. For example, the Formosa Café, a funky, old-time Hollywood bar and restaurant, plasters the walls with signed pictures of movie stars, providing "evidence" of its movie biz credentials.

- **Inseparability:** Try as you might, you simply can't separate the buyer of a service from the person who renders it. Delivery requires interaction between the buyer and the provider, and the customer directly contributes to the quality of the service. Consider a trip to the doctor. If you accurately describe your symptoms, you're likely to get a correct diagnosis. But if you simply say, "I just don't feel normal," the outcome will likely be different.

- **Variability:** This one ties closely to inseparability. A talented masseuse would probably help you relax, whereas a mediocre one might actually create tension. And even the talented masseuse might give better service at the end of the day than at the beginning, or worse service on the day she breaks up with her boyfriend. Variability also applies to the difference among providers. A massage at a top-notch spa, for example, is likely to be better than a massage at your local gym.

- **Perishability:** Marketers cannot store services for delivery at peak periods. A restaurant, for instance, only has so many seats; they can't (reasonably) tell their 8 P.M. dinner customers to come back the next day at 5 P.M. Similarly, major tourist destinations, such as Las Vegas, can't store an inventory of room service deliveries or performances of Cirque du Soleil. This creates obvious cost issues; is it worthwhile to prepare for a peak crowd but lose money when it's slow? The answer depends on the economics of your business.

Goods Versus Services: A Mixed Bag

Identifying whether a product is a good or a service can pose a considerable challenge, since many products contain elements of both. A meal at your local Italian restaurant, for instance, obviously includes tangible goods: You definitely own that calzone. But someone else took your order, brought it to the table, and (perhaps most importantly) did the dishes! Service was clearly a crucial part of the package.

A goods and services spectrum can provide a valuable tool for analyzing the relationship between the two. (See Exhibit 12.1.) At one extreme, **pure goods** don't include any services. Examples include a bottle of shampoo or a package of pasta. At the other extreme, **pure services** don't include any goods. Examples include financial consulting or math tutoring. Other products— such as a meal at Pizza Hut—fall somewhere between the poles.

Product Layers: Peeling the Onion

When customers buy products, they actually purchase more than just the good or service itself. They buy a complete product package that includes a core benefit, the actual product, and product augmentations. (See Exhibit 12.2.) Understanding these layers is valuable, since the most successful products delight consumers at each one of them.

Core Benefit At the most fundamental level, consumers buy a *core benefit* that satisfies their needs. When you go to a concert, for instance, the core benefit is entertainment. When you buy a motorcycle, the core benefit is transportation. And when you go to the gym, the core benefit is fitness. Most products also provide secondary benefits that help distinguish them from other goods and services that meet the same customer needs. A secondary benefit of a motorcycle, for example, might include the ease of parking.

Actual Product

This *actual product* layer, of course, is the product itself: the physical good or the delivered service that provides the core benefit. A U2 concert is the actual "service" that provides a live music experience. A Kawasaki Ninja is the actual product that provides a thrilling ride. Sports Club LA is the actual gym that provides fitness. Identifying the actual product is sometimes tough when the product is a service. For example, the core benefit of personal training might be weight loss, but the actual product may be some very fit person haranguing you to do ten more sit-ups. Keep in mind that the actual product includes all of the attributes that make it unique, such as the brand name, the features, and the packaging.

Augmented Product Most marketers wrap their actual products in additional

© PROFIMEDIA INTERNATIONAL S.R.O. / ALAMY

EXHIBIT 12.1 Goods and Services Spectrum

Pure Goods

Bottle of Shampoo
Can of Cola

Financial Consulting
Math Tutoring

Pure Services

EXHIBIT 12.2 The Three Product Layers: Camera Phone

Core Benefit
- Communication
- Entertainment
- Image

Augmented Product
- Warranty
- Owner's Manual
- Insurance
- Customer Service

GREAT!!

Actual Product
- Lightness
- Thinness
- Look and Feel
- Ease of Use
- Ring Tone
- Game Options

goods and services, called the *augmented product*, that sharpen their competitive edge. Augmentations come in a range of different forms, such as warranties, free service, instruction manuals, installation, and customer help lines. A U2 concert might give fans a chance to win backstage passes. The Kawasaki Ninja usually comes with a two-year warranty and free dealer prep. And Sports Club LA offers valet parking, overnight laundry service, and delicious smoothies.

> ## In the factory, we make cosmetics; in the store, we sell hope.
> *Charles Revson, founder, Revlon Cosmetics*

Product Classification: It's a Bird, It's a Plane...

Products fall into two broad categories—consumer products and business products—depending on the reason for the purchase. **Consumer products** are purchased for personal use or consumption, while **business products** are purchased to use either directly or indirectly in the production of another product. The bag of chips that you buy to eat, for instance, is a consumer product, while the bag of chips that a Subway owner buys to sell is a business product.

Consumer Product Categories Marketers further divide consumer products into several different subcategories, as shown below. Understanding the characteristics of the subcategories can help marketers develop better strategies.

- *Convenience products* are the inexpensive goods and services that consumers buy frequently with limited consideration and analysis. Distribution tends to be widespread, with promotion by the producers. Examples include staples such as milk and toothpaste, impulse items such as candy bars and magazines, and emergency products such as headache tablets and plumbing services.

- *Shopping products* are the more expensive products that consumers buy less frequently. Typically, as consumers shop, they search for the best value and learn more about features and benefits through the shopping process. Distribution is widespread, but more selective than for convenience products. Both producers and retailers tend to promote shopping products. Examples include computers, appliances, and maid services.

- *Specialty products* are those much more expensive products that consumers seldom purchase. Most people perceive specialty products as being so important that they are unwilling to accept substitutes. Because of this, distribution tends to be highly selective (consumers are willing to go far out of their way for the "right" brand). Both producers and retailers are apt to promote specialty products, but to a highly targeted audience. Some specialty product examples are Lamborghini sports cars, Tiffany jewelry, and Rolex watches.

- *Unsought products* are the goods and services that hold little interest (or even negative interest) for consumers. Price and distribution vary wildly, but promotion tends to be aggressive to drum up consumer interest. Home warranties, prepaid legal services, and blood donations are some examples.

Business Product Categories Marketers also divide business products into subcategories. Here, too, understanding the subcategories can lead to better marketing strategies.

- *Installations* are large capital purchases designed for a long productive life. The marketing of installations emphasizes personal selling and customization. Examples include industrial robots, new buildings, and railroad cars.

consumer products
Products purchased for personal use or consumption.

business products
Products purchased to use either directly or indirectly in the production of other products.

- *Accessory equipment* includes smaller, movable capital purchases, designed for a shorter productive life than installations. Marketing focuses on personal selling, but includes less customization than installations. Examples include personal computers, copy machines, and furniture.

- The *maintenance, repair, and operating products* category consists of small-ticket items that businesses consume on an ongoing basis, but don't become part of the final product. Marketing tactics emphasize efficiency. Examples include brooms, nails, pens, and lubricants.

- *Raw materials* include the farm and natural products used in producing other products. Marketing emphasizes price and service rather than product differentiation. Examples include milk, cotton, turkeys, oil, and iron.

- *Component parts and processed materials* include finished (or partially finished) products used in producing other products. Marketing emphasizes product quality as well as price and service. Examples include batteries for cars and aluminum ingots for soda cans.

- *Business services* are those services that businesses purchase to facilitate operations. Marketing focuses on quality and relationships; the role of price can vary. Examples include payroll services, marketing research, and legal services.

LO2 Product Differentiation and Planning: A Meaningful Difference

While some products have succeeded with little or no forethought, you'll dramatically boost your chance of a hit with careful planning. **Product differentiation** should be a key consideration. Winning products must embody a real or perceived difference versus the glut of goods and services that compete in virtually every corner of the market. As we'll discuss in the next section, areas to consider include product quality, features and benefits, branding, and packaging. But different alone isn't enough; different from and better than the competition is the shortest path to success. A quick look at some high-profile product failures illustrates the point.

- **Nehru suits:** In the 1960s, fashion experts predicted that Nehru suits—with their oddly tailored collars—would be a major hit. Few were disappointed when that trend fizzled.

- **Clear Beer:** In the 1990s, several companies introduced clear beers, reflecting an ill-fated obsession with clear products, including shampoo, soap, and the short-lived, clear Crystal Pepsi.

- **Funky French Fries:** In 2002, Ore-Ida introduced Funky Fries. The flavors included cinnamon-sugar, chocolate, and "radical blue." Not surprisingly, they were off the market in less than a year.

Product Quality

Product quality relates directly to product value, which comes from understanding your customer.

Agricultural products such as milk and beef are classified as raw materials.

© LIQUIDLIBRARY/JUPITERIMAGES

Peter Drucker, a noted business thinker, writer, and educator, declared:

Quality in a product or service is not what the supplier puts in. It's what the customer gets out and is willing to pay for. A product is not quality because it is hard to make and costs a lot of money . . . this is incompetence. Customers pay only for what is of use to them and gives them value. Nothing else constitutes quality.

In other words, a high-quality product does a great job meeting customer needs. Seimans, a huge electronics conglomerate, embodies this thinking in its approach to quality: "Quality is when our customers come back and our products don't."

But the specific definition of quality—and the attributes that indicate quality—changes across product categories. Here are a few examples:

EXHIBIT 12.3 Product Quality Indicators

Product Category	Some Quality Indicators
Internet search engines	Fast, relevant, and far-reaching results
Stylish blue jeans	High-profile designer, high price, and celebrity customers
TV editing equipment	Reliability, flexibility, and customer service
Roller coasters	Thrill factor, design, and setting
Chain saws	Effectiveness, safety, and reliability

Regardless of product category, the two key aspects of quality are level and consistency. **Quality level** refers to how well a product performs its core functions. You might think that smart companies deliver the highest possible level of performance, but this is seldom profitable, or even desirable. For instance, only a tiny group of consumers would pay for a jet ski to go 200 mph, when 80 mph offers a comparable thrill (at least for most of us!). The right level of product performance is the level that meets the needs of your consumers, and those needs include price. Decisions about quality level must also consider the competition. The goal is to outperform the other players in your category, while maintaining profitability.

{ **Quality is remembered long after the price is forgotten.** }

Gucci family slogan

The second dimension of quality is **product consistency**. How consistently does your product actually deliver the promised level of quality? With a positive relationship between price and performance, consistent delivery can offer a competitive edge at almost any quality level.

Honda offers an excellent example. When most people consider the Accord, the Civic, and the CRV, all Honda-owned models, quality quickly comes to mind. And all three dominate their markets. But clearly, the quality *level* (and price) is different for each. The Accord serves the upper, more conservative end of the market; the Civic tends to appeal to younger, hipper, more budget-minded consumers; the CRV tends to appeal to middle-of-the-road shoppers seeking a reliable, small SUV. In short, Honda succeeds at delivering product consistency at several markedly different quality levels.

Perhaps the exact opposite of automotive quality was the Yugo, imported from the former Yugoslavia in the mid-1980s. See the *Oops!* box on the next page to learn more.

Features and Benefits

Product features are the characteristics of the product you offer. If a product is well designed, each feature corresponds to a meaningful **customer benefit**. The marketer's challenge is to design a package of features that offers the highest level of value for an acceptable price. And the equation must also account for profitability goals.

One winning formula may be to offer at least some low-cost features that correspond to high-value benefits. Creating an "open kitchen" restaurant, for instance, has limited impact on costs, but gives patrons an exciting, up-close view of the drama and hustle of professional food preparation. Exhibit 12.4 lists some other examples of product features and their corresponding customer benefits.

EXHIBIT 12.4 Product Features and Customer Benefits

Product	Product Feature	Customer Benefit
Subway sandwiches	Lower fat	Looser pants
Contact lenses	Different colors	A new-looking you
High-definition TV	46-inch screen	The party's at your house
Hybrid car	Better gas mileage	More cash for other needs
Triple latte	Caffeine, caffeine, caffeine	More time to, uh, study

quality level How well a product performs its core functions.

product consistency How reliably a product delivers its promised level of quality.

product features The specific characteristics of a product.

customer benefit The advantage that a customer gains from specific product features.

Glossary (margin)

product line A group of products that are closely related to each other, either in terms of how they work, or the customers they serve.

product mix The total number of product lines and individual items sold by a single firm.

cannibalization When a producer offers a new product that takes sales away from its existing products.

brand A product's identity—including product name, symbol, design, reputation, and image—that sets it apart from other players in the same category.

brand equity The overall value of a brand to an organization.

Product Lines and the Product Mix

Some companies focus all of their efforts on one product, but most offer a number of different products to enhance their revenue and profits. A **product line** is a group of products that are closely related to each other, either in terms of how they work or the customers they serve. Amazon's first product line, for instance, was books. To meet the needs of as many book lovers as possible, Amazon carries well over a million different books in its product line. A **product mix** is the total number of product lines and individual items sold by a single firm. Amazon's product mix includes a wide range of product lines, from books, to electronics, to toys (to name just a few!). Please see Exhibit 12.5 for an illustration of Amazon's product line and product mix.

Decisions regarding how many items to include in each product line and in the overall product mix can have a huge impact on a firm's profits. With too few items in each line, the company may be leaving money on the table. With too many items, the company may be spending unnecessarily to support its weakest links.

One reason that firms add new product lines is to reach completely new customers. Gap, for instance, added Old Navy to reach younger, lower-income customers, and Banana Republic to reach older, higher-income customers. Each line includes a range of different products designed to meet the needs of their specific customers. But the risk of adding new

lines—especially lower-priced lines—is **cannibalization**, which happens when a new entry "eats" the sales of an existing line. This is especially dangerous when the new products are lower priced than the current ones. You could see the problem, for instance, if a $20 blue jean purchase from Old Navy replaces a $50 blue jean purchase from Gap; the company has lost more than half its revenue on the sale. Like other companies with multiple lines, Gap carefully monitors the cannibalization issue and works to differentiate its lines as fully as possible.

Branding

At the most basic level, a **brand** is a product's identity that sets it apart from other players in the same category. Typically, brands represent the combination of elements such as product name, symbol, design, reputation, and image. But today's most powerful emerging brands go far beyond the sum of their attributes. They project a compelling group identity that creates brand fanatics: loyal customers who advocate for the brand better than any advertising a marketer could buy. The overall value of a brand to an organization—the extra money that consumers will spend to buy that brand—is called **brand equity**.

Since 2001, *BusinessWeek* and Interbrand, a leading brand consultancy, have teamed up to publish a ranking of the 100 Best Global Brands by dollar value.

EXHIBIT 12.5 Amazon's Product Line and Product Mix

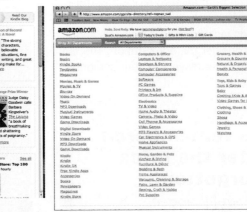

Oops! what were they THINKING?!

Oops! If You Drive a Yugo, Maybe You Will Go and Maybe You Won't Go...

The tiny Yugo hatchback hit the U.S. market with great fanfare in the summer of 1985. Billed as the cheapest new car in the United States, the Yugoslavian import captured the imagination of the consumer market. Eager buyers stormed the dealerships before the first cars were off the boat. The price was an unimaginably low $3,990.

But low price wasn't enough. As buyers began to actually drive their cars, they uncovered flaw after flaw, including major issues such as premature engine failure and poor dealer service. Reviewers described the Yugo as more of a toy than a car. Not surprisingly, sales plummeted, leading to bankruptcy in 1989.

The short life of the Yugo was long enough to establish its place as a cultural icon of cheap. Countless disillusioned owners competed to coin the best description of their Yugo. Sample comments from the CarTalk website (which featured the Yugo as the worst car of the millennium):

"The Yugo's first stop after the showroom was the service department; `Fill 'er up and replace the engine!'"

"At least it had heated rear windows—so your hands would stay warm while you pushed."

But despite its problems (or perhaps because of them!) the Yugo also spawned a remarkable artistic effort. A professor at the NYC School of Visual Arts challenged his students several years ago to turn discarded Yugos into something useful. The results, displayed for a time in New York City's Union Station, included a toaster, a Port-o-Potty, a confessional, a diner, and a submarine.[1]

© PHOTODISC/GETTY IMAGES
© JAMAL A. WILSON/AFP/GETTY IMAGES

The top ten brands are listed in Exhibit 12.6, but you can find the complete list at Interbrand's website.

Brand Name A catchy, memorable name is among the most powerful elements of your brand. While the right name will never save a bad business, it can launch a good business to new heights. But finding the right name can be tough. According to the respected Brighter Naming consulting group, the following characteristics can help:

1. Short, sweet, and easy to pronounce and spell: Examples include Dell, Gap, Dove, Tide, Kool-Aid.
2. Unique within the industry: Think Apple, Monster, jetBlue, and Victoria's Secret.
3. Good alliteration, especially for long names: The words should roll off your tongue. Some examples are Coca-Cola, BlackBerry, and Minute Maid.[3]

Brand names typically fall into four categories, as described in Exhibit 12.7.

EXHIBIT 12.6 *BusinessWeek*/Interbrand Top Ten Global Brands[2]

Brand	Country of Ownership
Coca-Cola	United States
IBM	United States
Microsoft	United States
GE	United States
Nokia	Finland
McDonald's	United States
Google	United States
Toyota	Japan
Intel	United States
Disney	United States

EXHIBIT 12.7 Brand Name Categories

Category	Description	Examples
Location-based	Refers to either the area served or the place of origin	Southwest Airlines, Bank of America, Best Western Hotels
Founder's name	Can include first name, last name, or both	McDonald's, Suzy's Sub Sandwiches, Ford, Disney, Hewlett-Packard
Descriptive or functional	Describes what the product is or how it works	eBay, U.S. News and World Report, Weight Watchers, Krispy Kreme
Evocative	Communicates an engaging image that resonates with consumers	Yahoo!, Craftsman, Virgin, Intel, Lunchables, Cosmopolitan, Starbucks

Line Extensions versus Brand Extensions As companies grow, marketers look for opportunities to grow their businesses. **Line extensions** are similar products offered under the same brand name. Possibilities include new flavors, sizes, colors, ingredients, and forms. One example is Coca-Cola, which offers versions with lemon, lime, vanilla, with caffeine, without caffeine, with sugar, and without sugar. The marketing challenge is to ensure that line extensions steal market share from competitors, rather than from the core brand.

Brand extensions, on the other hand, involve launching a product in a new category under an existing brand name. The Bic brand, for instance, is quite elastic, stretching nicely to include diverse products such as pens, glue, cigarette lighters, and disposable razors. The Virgin brand demonstrates similar elasticity, covering more than 350 companies that range from airlines, to cell phones, to soft drinks, to cars. But the concept of brand extension becomes most clear (and most entertaining) through examining brand extension failures. Examples include Bic perfume, Budweiser Dry, and Harley-Davidson Cologne.[4]

Licensing Some companies opt to license their brands from other businesses. **Licensing** means purchasing—often for a substantial fee—the right to use another company's brand name or symbol. The benefits, of course, are instant name recognition, an established reputation, and a proven track record. On a worldwide basis, the best-known licensing arrangements are probably character names, which range from Mickey Mouse to Bart Simpson and appear on everything from cereal, to toys, to underwear. Many movie producers also do high-profile licensing, turning out

truckloads of merchandise that features movie properties such as Harry Potter and *Twilight*.

Another fast-growing area is the licensing of corporate names. Coca-Cola, for instance, claims to have more than 300 licensees who sell over a billion dollars of licensed merchandise each year. The potential benefits for Coca-Cola are clear: more promotion, increased exposure, and enhanced image. But the risk is significant. If licensed products are of poor quality or overpriced, the consumer backlash hits the core brand rather than the producer of the licensed product.

Cobranding **Cobranding** is when established brands from different companies join forces to market the same product. This cooperative approach has a long history, but is currently enjoying a new popularity. Examples include:

- Dreyer's markets various Girl Scout Cookie-flavored ice creams.
- Kohl's markets Vera Wang's fashions under the name Simply Vera.
- Kmart markets Martha Stewart housewares.

Cobranding can offer huge advantages to both partners, by leveraging their strengths to enter new markets and gain more exposure. Through the Kohl's–Wang agreement, Vera Wang gained exposure to a mass audience (and their shopping dollars), while Kohl's bolstered its image by gaining exclusive rights to trendy fashions. But cobranding can be risky. If one partner makes a major goof (think Martha Stewart), the fallout can damage the reputation of the other partner as well.

National Brands Versus Store Brands **National brands,** also called manufacturers' brands, are brands that the producer owns and markets. Many are well-known and widely available such as Pantene shampoo, Tide detergent, and 7-Up. Although most retailers carry lots of national brands, an increasing number have opted to also carry their own versions of the same products, called **store brands**, or private label. Deep discounters such as Walmart and Costco have had particular success with their private-label brands (e.g., Sam's Choice and Kirkland).

Many national brand names are recognizable around the world.

© RYAN BORN/WIREIMAGE/GETTY IMAGES

Private labels play a growing role in grocery stores, as well. In the United States, about one out of four grocery purchases is private label, and the numbers are even higher in Europe. As the global recession deepened in 2008 and 2009, private-label sales increased by more than 7%. The growing influence of low-end private-label brands increases the pressure on national brands to continually innovate while holding down prices.[5]

At the upper end of the market—especially in the clothing business—key retailers specialize in private brands to create and protect a consistent, upscale image. Examples include Neiman Marcus, Coldwater Creek, and Saks Fifth Avenue. Private-label clothing accounts for about 40% of all U.S. apparel sales.[6]

Packaging

Great packaging does more than just hold the product. It can protect the product, provide information, facilitate storage, suggest product uses, promote the product brand, and attract buyer attention. Great packaging is especially important in the crowded world of grocery stores and mass merchandisers. In the average supermarket, for instance, the typical shopper passes about 300 items per minute and makes anywhere from 20% to 70% of purchases on sheer impulse. In this environment, your package must call out to your target customers and differentiate your product from all the others lined up beside it. Yet, in attracting consumer attention, a good package cannot sacrifice the basics such as protecting the product.[7]

Bottom line, great packaging stems from consumer needs, but it usually includes at least a smidge of creative brilliance. Examples include yogurt in a pouch that doesn't need a spoon, soup to-go that can be microwaved in the can, and single-serving baby carrot packets that moms can toss into kids' lunches.

LO3 Innovation and the Product Life Cycle: Nuts, Bolts, and a Spark of Brilliance

For a business to thrive long term, effective new product development is vital. And the process works only if it happens quickly. As technological advances hit the market at breakneck speed, current products are becoming obsolete faster than ever before. The need for speed compounds as hungry competitors crowd every niche of the market. But the rush is risky, since new product development costs can be in the millions, and the success rate is less than a third. Marketers who succeed in this challenging arena devote painstaking effort to understanding their customers, but they also nurture the creativity they need to generate new ideas. An example of how this can work: The 3M Corporation—makers of Post-It notes and Scotch Tape—introduces about 500 new products per year by pushing its employees to "relentlessly ask 'What if?'." 3M also encourages workers to spend 15% of their work time (paid work time!) on projects of personal interest.[8]

> { **If you're not failing every now and again, it's a sign you're not doing anything very innovative.** }
>
> *Woody Allen, film director*

Types of Innovation

Clearly the first personal computer represented a higher degree of newness than the first personal computer with a color screen. And the computer with a color

Wacky Labels

As product lawsuits take on a life of their own, manufacturers are responding with warning labels that seem increasingly wacky. To call attention to this trend, a Michigan anti-lawsuit group called M-LAW sponsors the annual Wacky Warning Label Contest. Top finishers over the past few years included the following gems:

- A toilet brush tag that says "Do not use for personal hygiene."
- A bag of livestock castration rings warns, "For animal use only."
- A label on a baby-stroller storage pouch that warns "Do not put child in bag."
- A small, 1" x 4" LCD panel that cautions, "Do not eat the LCD panel."
- A disappearing ink marker that cautions "The Vanishing Fabric Marker should not be used as a writing instrument for signing checks or any legal documents."[9]

screen represented a higher degree of newness than the first low-cost knockoff. Levels of innovation fall along a spectrum, as shown in Exhibit 12.8.

Discontinuous Innovation *Discontinuous innovations* are brand-new ideas that radically change how people live. Examples include the first car, the first plane, the first television, and the first computer. These dramatic innovations require extensive customer learning, which should guide the marketing process.

Dynamically Continuous Innovation *Dynamically continuous innovations* are characterized by marked changes to existing products. Examples include cell phones, MP3 players, and digital cameras. These types of innovations require a moderate level of consumer learning in exchange for significant benefits.

Continuous Innovation A slight modification of an existing product is called a *continuous innovation*. Examples include new sizes, flavors, shapes, packaging, and design. The goal of continuous innovation is to distinguish a product from the competition. The goal of a knockoff, on the other hand, is simply to copy a competitor and offer a lower price.

The New Product Development Process

An efficient, focused development process will boost your chances of new product success. The standard model includes six stages:

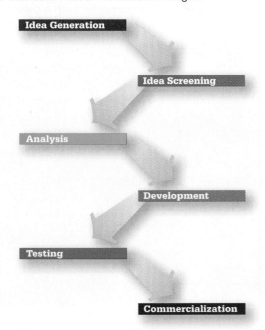

Discontinuous Innovation

Dynamically Continuous Innovation

Continuous Innovation

EXHIBIT 12.8
Levels of Innovation

Each stage requires management to "green light" ideas before moving forward to ensure that the company doesn't waste resources on marginal concepts.

- **Idea Generation:** Some experts estimate that it takes 50 ideas for each new product that makes it to market, so you should definitely cast a wide net. Ideas can come from almost anywhere, including customer research, customer complaints, salespeople, engineers, suppliers, and competitors.

- **Idea Screening:** The purpose of this stage is to weed out ideas that don't fit with the company's objectives and ideas that would clearly be too expensive to develop. The Walt Disney Company, for instance, would certainly eliminate the idea of a XXX cable channel because it just doesn't fit their mission.

- **Analysis:** The purpose of the analysis stage is to estimate costs and forecast sales for each idea to get a sense of the potential profit and of how the product might fit within the company's resources. Each idea must meet rigorous standards to remain a contender.

- **Development:** The development process leads to detailed descriptions of each concept with specific product features. New product teams sometimes also make prototypes, or samples, that consumers can actually test. The results help fully refine the concept.

- **Testing:** This stage involves the formal process of soliciting feedback from consumers by testing the product concept. Do they like the features? Are the benefits meaningful? What price makes sense? Some companies also test-market their products, or sell them in a limited area to evaluate the consumer response.

- **Commercialization:** This stage entails introducing the product to the general market. Two key success factors are gaining distribution and launching promotion. But a product that tested well doesn't always mean instant success. The VW Beetle, for example, sold only 330 cars during its first year in the United States, but it later became a hit.

New Product Adoption and Diffusion

In order to become a commercial success, new products must spread throughout a market after they are introduced. That process is called *diffusion*. But clearly diffusion happens at different speeds, depending on the individual consumer and on the product itself.

Product Adoption Categories Some consumers like to try new things; others seem terrified of change. These attitudes clearly affect the rate at which individual people are willing to adopt (or begin buying and using) new products. The first adopters, about 2.5% of the total, are adventurous risk takers. The laggards, about 16% of the total, sometimes adopt products so late that earlier adopters have already moved to the next new thing. The rest of the population falls somewhere in between. Keep in mind that individuals tend to adopt new products at different rates. For instance, we probably all know someone who is an innovator in technology, but a laggard in fashion, or vice-versa.

Product Diffusion Rates Some new products diffuse into the population much more quickly than others. For example, Apple iPods and Segway Human Transporters appeared on the market around the same time; iPods have become a pop culture icon, while Segways remain on the fringe. What accounts

for the difference? Researchers have identified five product characteristics that affect the rate of adoption and diffusion. The more characteristics a product has, the faster it will diffuse into the population.

- **Observability:** How visible is the product to other potential consumers? Some product categories are easier to observe than others. If you adopt a new kind of car, for instance, the whole neighborhood will know, plus anyone else who sees you on the streets and highways.

- **Trialability:** How easily can potential consumers sample the new product? Trial can be a powerful way to create new consumers, which is why many markets fill their aisles with sample tables during popular shopping hours. Other examples of trial-boosting strategies include test driving cars, sampling music, and testing new fragrances.

- **Complexity:** Can potential consumers easily understand what your product is and how it works? If your product confuses people—or if they find it hard to explain to others—adoption rates will slow. For example, many people who test-ride Segway Human Transporters love the experience, but they have trouble explaining to others how it works or why it beats other transportation options.

Which Shade of Green Works for You?

Even in the midst of the Great Recession, about 50% of consumers still purchased just as many green products as before the downturn—many of which cost more—while 19% purchased even more green products. But green is a broad term—possibly too broad to be useful. Capitalizing on this trend means zeroing in on the right angle for your specific product.

Trendwatching, an international trend-spotting firm, has made this analysis easier by pinpointing several hot subcategories within the broader green marketplace. The following are some highlights from the report:

- *Eco-Iconic*: These are green products that make a bold, audacious statement about the owner's green credentials to everyone who sees him or her using the product. The example is to use these products to flaunt a green lifestyle. Examples include GoinGreen's G-Wiz electric cars, a current hit in London, and Corland Solar Powered Bags, which allow for recharging a cell phone or an iPod.
- *Eco-Embedded*: These are green products that rely on government regulation to essentially "force" consumers out of environmental complacency. Five large German cities, for example, have applied a complete ban on cars that do not have a catalytic converter or diesel particulate filter.
- *Eco-Boosters:* These worthy products don't just offset their own negative environmental impacts; they actually offset additional negative impacts as well. Fiji Water, for instance, as part of its sustainable growth initiative, will offset its total carbon footprint by 120%. Also, London-based Ecoigo, a "green" car service, aims to be carbon positive, offsetting double the emissions from every trip as well as from energy used by its office.

Can you think of other products or service ideas that fit each category? What are other niches in the sustainable marketplace? Clearly, finding the right shade of green for your product can mean a bright shade of green for your bottom line.[10]

- **Compatibility:** How consistent is your product with the existing way of doing things? Cordless phones, for example, caught on almost instantly, since they were completely consistent with people's prior experiences—only better!

- **Relative Advantage:** How much better are the benefits of your new product compared to existing products? When gas prices climb, for example, the benefits of a hybrid car take on a much higher value relative to standard cars. As a result, demand skyrockets.

The Product Life Cycle: Maximizing Results over Time

When marketers introduce a new product, they hope it will last forever, generating sales and profits for years to come. But they also realize that all products go through a **product life cycle**: a pattern of sales and profits that typically changes over time. The life cycle can be dramatically different across individual products and product categories, and predicting the exact shape and length of the life cycle is virtually impossible. But most product categories do move through the four distinct stages shown in Exhibit 12.9.

- **Introduction:** This is a time of low sales and nonexistent profits as companies invest in raising awareness about the product and the product category.

Some categories, such as the microwave, languish in this phase for years, while other categories, such as computer memory sticks, zoom through this phase. And some categories, of course, never get beyond introduction (think clear beers).

- **Growth:** During the growth period, sales continue to rise, although profits usually peak. Typically, competitors begin to notice emerging categories in the growth phase. They enter the market—often with new variations of existing products—which further fuels the growth. Portable MP3 players, for example, are currently in the growth phase, and a number of competitors are challenging Apple's hold on the market.

- **Maturity:** During maturity, sales usually peak. Profits continue to decline as competition intensifies. Once a market is mature, the only way to gain more users is to steal them from competitors, rather than to bring new users into the category. Weaker players begin to drop out of the category. Gasoline-powered cars and network TV are in maturity in the United States.

- **Decline:** During this period, sales and profits begin to decline, sometimes quite rapidly. The reasons usually relate to either technological change or change in consumer needs. For instance, the introduction of word processing pushed typewriters into decline, and a change in consumer taste and habits pushed hot cereal into decline. Competitors continue to drop out of the category.

EXHIBIT 12.9 Product Life Cycle for a Typical Product Category

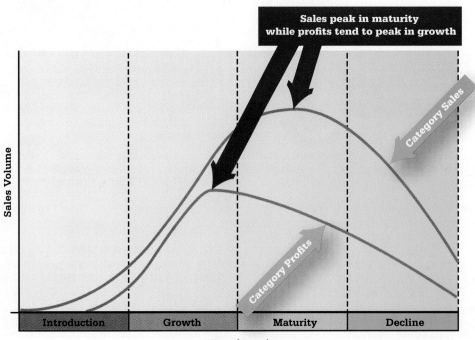

Chapter 12   Product and Promotion: Creating and Communicating Value

Familiarity with the product life cycle helps marketers plan effective strategies for existing products and identify profitable categories for new products. Exhibit 12.10 summarizes typical marketing strategies and offers examples for each phase.

Individual products also have life cycles that usually follow the category growth pattern but sometimes vary dramatically. Clearly, it's in the marketer's best interest to extend the profitable run of an individual brand as long as possible. There are several ways to make this happen: finding new uses for the product, changing the product, and changing the marketing mix. M&Ms, for example, created a splash in the market by adding new colors based on customer voting.

LO4 Promotion: Influencing Consumer Decisions

Promotion is the power to influence consumers—to remind them, to inform them, to persuade them. The best promotion goes one step further, building powerful consumer bonds that draw your customers back to your product again and again. But don't forget that great promotion only works with a great product. Bill Bernbach, an ad industry legend, captures this concept by noting that "A great ad campaign will make a bad product fail faster. It will get more people to know it's bad."

Marketers can directly control most promotional tools. From TV advertising to telephone sales, the marketer creates the message and communicates it directly to the target audience. But, ironically, marketers *cannot* directly control the most powerful promotional tools: publicity, such as a comment on *Oprah*, or a review in *Consumer Reports*, and word-of-mouth such as a recommendation from a close friend or even a casual acquaintance. Marketers can only influence these areas through creative promotional strategies.

Promotion in Chaos: Danger or Opportunity?

Not coincidentally, the Chinese symbol for crisis resembles the symbols for danger and opportunity—a perfect description of promotion in today's market. The pace of change is staggering. Technology has empowered consumers to choose how and when they interact with media, and they are grabbing control with dizzying speed. Cable-based on-demand video continues to soar, and digital movie downloads are poised for explosive growth. In 2007, Internet users spent an average of nearly 33 hours per week surfing the Web, almost twice as much time as watching TV. Meanwhile, more passive forms of entertainment, such as network television, are slowly losing their audience. And those people who do still watch TV are gleefully changing the schedules and zapping the ads with TiVo or similar devices. As media splinters across an array of entertainment options, usage patterns have changed as well: tech-savvy viewers are more prone to consume media in on-the-fly snacks rather than sit-down meals. Rising consumer power and the breakneck pace of technology have created a growing need—and a stunning opportunity—for marketers to zero in on the right customers, at the right time, with the right message.[11]

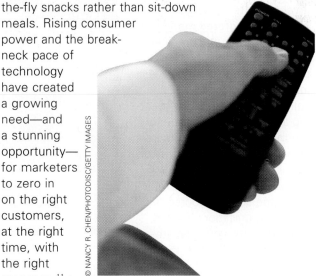

© NANCY R. CHEN/PHOTODISC/GETTY IMAGES

promotion
Marketing communication designed to influence consumer purchase decisions through information, persuasion, and reminders.

EXHIBIT 12.10 The Product Life Cycle and Marketing Strategies

Phase	Examples	Sales/Profits	Key Marketing Strategies
Introduction	Virtual reality games, fuel cell technology	Low sales, low profits	Build awareness, trial, and distribution
Growth	Hybrid cars, flat-screen TVs, video cell phones, Internet gambling	Rapidly increasing sales and profits	Reinforce brand positioning, often through heavy advertising
Maturity	Airlines, DVD players, food processors, personal computers, online stock trading	Flat sales and declining profits	Target competitors, while defending franchise with new product features, competitive advertising, promotion, and price cuts
Decline	Pagers, videocassettes	Declining sales and profits	Reduce spending and consider terminating the product

Integrated Marketing Communication: Consistency and Focus

How many marketing messages have you gotten in the past 24 hours? Did you flip on the TV or radio? Surf the Web? Notice a billboard? Glance at the logo on a T-shirt or cap? Grab a flyer for a party? Chat with a friend about some product he likes? Marketing exposure quickly snowballs: the typical consumer receives about 3,000 advertising messages each day. Some of those messages are hard to avoid as marketers find new, increasingly creative ways to promote their products to a captive audience. The venues include elevators, taxicabs, golf carts, and other surprising settings.[12]

Given the confounding level of clutter, smart companies use **integrated marketing communication** to coordinate their messages through every promotional vehicle—including their advertising, website, salespeople, and so on—creating a coherent impression in the minds of their customers. Why bother coordinating all of these elements? The answer is clear. Consumers don't think about the specific source of the communication; instead, they combine—or integrate— the messages from *all* the sources to form a unified impression about your product. If the messages are out of sync or confusing, busy consumers won't bother to crack the code. They'll simply move on to the next best option.

Can you really control every message that every consumer sees or hears about your product? It's not likely. But if you accurately identify the key points of contact between your product and your target market, you can focus on those areas with remarkable effectiveness. For instance, the most common points of contact for McDonald's are probably advertising and the in-store experience. From upbeat commercials, to smiling employees, to brightly striped uniforms, McDonald's spends millions of dollars to support its core message of fast, tasty food in a clean,

Dell promotes its brand heavily and effectively through its website.

© GEORGE FREY/LANDOV

friendly environment—heavily concentrated in the areas that are key to its brand.

Other companies are likely to encounter the bulk of their customers through different channels. You'd probably learn about Dell computers, for example, through either its website or word-of-mouth. Dell has invested heavily in both areas. The company maintains an innovative, user-friendly website that allows even novice users to create customized systems. And Dell delivers award-winning customer service and technical support, which gets its customers to recommend its products to family and friends.

Coordinating the Communication

Even after you've identified the key points of contact, coordinating the messages remains a challenge. In many companies, completely different teams develop the different promotional areas. Salespeople and brand managers often have separate agendas, even when the same executive manages both departments. And frequently, disconnected outside agencies handle advertising, Web development, and sales promotion programs. Coordinating the messages will happen only with solid teamwork, which must begin at the top of the organization.

Information also plays a crucial role. To coordinate marketing messages, everyone who creates and manages them must have free access to knowledge about the customer, the product, the competition, the market, and the strategy of the organization. Some of this information, such as strategic goals, will come from the top down, but a fair amount, such as information about the customer, should come from the bottom up. Information must also flow laterally, across departments and agencies. The marketing research department, for instance, might have critical information about product performance, which might help the Web management agency create a feature page that might respond to competitive threats identified by the sales force. When all parties have access to the same data, they are much more likely to remain on the same page.

LO5 A Meaningful Message: Finding the Big Idea

Your promotional message begins with understanding how your product is different from and better than the competition. But your **positioning statement**—a brief statement that articulates how you want your target market to envision your product relative to the competition—seldom translates directly into the promotional message. Instead, it marks the beginning of the creative development process, often spearheaded by ad agency creative professionals. When it works, the creative development process yields a *big idea*—a meaningful, believable, and distinctive concept that cuts through the clutter. Big ideas are typically based on either a rational or an emotional premise. Here are a few examples from the last decade:

Rational:	Science:	Clinique: "Allergy tested. 100% fragrance free."
	Price:	Walmart: "Always low prices. Always."
	Engineering:	BMW: "The ultimate driving machine."
Emotional:	Sex:	Axe: "Bom Chicka Wah Wah"
	Security:	Allstate: "You're in good hands."
	Humor:	Mountain Dew: "Do the Dew"

Not surprisingly, funny ads are a consumer favorite, although humor can be risky. For a record ten years in a row, from 1998 through 2008, Budweiser—known for using humor effectively—nabbed the top spot in *USA Today*'s annual Ad Meter consumer ranking of Super Bowl ads. But in 2009, a very funny "Free Doritos" ad—created by talented amateurs in an online contest sponsored by Frito-Lay—knocked Budweiser off its pedestal.[13]

The best big ideas have entrenched themselves in popular culture, spawning both imitators and parodies. A small sampling includes:

- L'Oréal: "Because you're worth it"
- The Energizer Bunny
- "Got Milk?"
- Budweiser: "Whassssuuup?!"
- Motel 6: "We'll leave the light on for you."

An International Perspective

Some big ideas translate well across cultures. The Marlboro Man, for instance, now promotes rugged in-dividualism across the globe. But other big ideas don't travel as smoothly. DeBeers, for example, tried running ads in Japan using their proven strategy in the West: fabulously dressed women smiling and kissing their husbands who have just given them glittering diamonds. The ads failed in Japan because a Japanese woman would be more likely to shed a few tears and feign anger that her husband would spend so much money. The revised DeBeers campaign featured a hardworking husband and wife in their tiny apartment. Receiving a diamond, the wife chides her extravagant husband: "Oh, you stupid!" The campaign was a wild success. Taking a big idea to a foreign market can mean big money and a powerful brand, but careful research should still be your first step.[14]

LO6 The Promotional Mix: Communicating the BIG IDEA

Once you've nailed your message, you need to communicate the big idea to your target market. The traditional communication tools—or **promotional channels**—include advertising, sales promotion, direct marketing, and personal selling. But more recently, a number of new tools have emerged, ranging from advergaming to Internet minimovies. The combination of communication

positioning statement A brief statement that articulates how the marketer would like the target market to envision a product relative to the competition.

promotional channels Specific marketing communication vehicles, including traditional tools, such as advertising, sales promotion, direct marketing, and personal selling, and newer tools such as product placement, advergaming, and Internet minimovies.

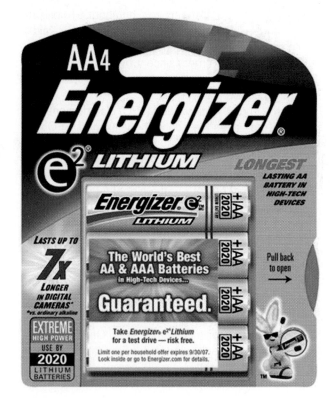

product placement
The paid integration of branded products into movies, television, and other media.

tools that you choose to promote your product is called your "promotional mix." We'll explore each area of the mix, beginning with the newest developments.

Emerging Promotional Tools: The Leading Edge

In the last decade, the promotional landscape has changed dramatically. Consumer expectations and empowerment have skyrocketed. Consumer tolerance for impersonal corporate communication has fallen. And digital technology has surged forward at breakneck speed. As a result, new promotional tools have emerged, and previously minor tools have burst into the mainstream. This section covers several leading-edge promotional tactics, but keep in mind that other tools—such as mobile phone promotion, social media marketing (e.g., Facebook) and widget-based marketing—are growing explosively, too.

Internet Advertising Internet advertising has been highly visible for more than a decade. But the industry has moved far beyond simple banner ads and annoying pop-up ads. The highest growth areas include paid search advertising, search engine optimization, and online video advertising.

Paid search advertising includes both sponsored links on Google that relate to the topic you've searched and targeted Google text ads on a number of different websites—both of which are at the heart of Google's outsized financial success. Industry expert *eMarketer* estimates that paid search advertising, including both Google and other similar services, hit about $10 billion in 2008 and may hit close to $20 billion by 2013. Paid search seems to be an especially attractive tactic during tough economic times, since it offers high accountability—marketers can tell exactly how well their limited advertising dollars are working.[15]

Search engine optimization (SEO) also demonstrated strong growth as the economy weakened. SEO involves taking specific steps to ensure that your website appears high on the list when customers look for your product or service via an Internet search engine such as Google or Yahoo!. Typically, the higher a firm appears, the more traffic that site will receive from potential customers. Predictions from *eMarketer* suggest that U.S. spending on search-engine marketing will nearly double from $12.2 billion in 2008 to $23.4 billion by 2013.[16]

Online video advertising represents another high-growth area. This includes the increasingly popular "pre-roll" ads, the 15- to 30-second spots that viewers often sit through before watching an online video on YouTube, Hulu, or many other sites. Online video advertising more than tripled in the first half of 2008 (although the base was miniscule compared to search advertising). According to *eMarketer* estimates, the growth will increase—even in the face of the global recession—from $505 million in 2008 to $5.8 billion in 2013, representing an extraordinary increase.[17]

Product Placement Product placement—the paid integration of branded products into movies and TV—exploded into big-screen prominence in 1982, when Reese's Pieces played a highly visible role in Steven Spielberg's blockbuster film *E.T.* Reese's Pieces sales shot up 65% (a major embarrassment for the marketers of M&Ms, who had passed on the opportunity). Over the years, product placement in movies has moved rapidly into the limelight. A few notable examples are:

- *Risky Business* (1983): This movie launched Tom Cruise and fueled a run on Ray-Ban sunglasses. The shades got another boost in 1997 with *Men in Black*.
- *You've Got Mail* (1998): AOL scored big in this Tom Hanks–Meg Ryan romance that etched the AOL signature mail call onto the national consciousness.
- James Bond: This longstanding movie icon hawked so many products in recent movies (e.g., Omega watches, Heineken beer, and British Airways), that it triggered a backlash from annoyed moviegoers and critics.[18]

Product placement on TV has catapulted into the mainstream in response to the growing prominence of digital video recorders (DVRs) such as TiVo. By 2009, more than 30% of U.S. households had at least one DVR, up from fewer than 10% in 2005. DVRs allow consumers not only to watch on their own schedule, but also to zap ads. Worried marketers see product placement as a chance to "TiVo-proof" their messages by integrating them into the programming. In 2007 they poured $2.9 billion into television product placement, and spending will likely continue to soar.[19]

Product placement works best for marketers if the product seamlessly integrates into the show as a player rather than simply a prop. For instance, it's hard to miss Coke in *American Idol*. The judges are seldom without their Coca-Cola—emblazoned cups, and the contestants sit on a Coca-Cola couch in a Coca-Cola room as they wait to hear their fate. The price tag for this exposure—including commercial time and online content—is about $35 million. Media buyers often negotiate product placement deals as part of a package that includes regular ads, which reinforce the product that appeared in the program (unless, of course, the ads are zapped).[20]

Whether in TV or movies, product placement offers marketers huge sales potential in a credible environment, which may be why experts predict that global paid product placement will hit $7.6 billion by the end of 2010. But product placement is risky—if your show is a dud, your placement is worthless. And the cost is high and growing, which only increases the financial risk. The benefits of product placement are tough to measure as well, especially for existing brands. But in the end, the

Chapter 12 Product and Promotion: Creating and Communicating Value only measure that really counts is consumer acceptance, which may disappear if product placement intrudes too much on the entertainment value of movies and TV.

Advergaming Interactive games have exploded into pop culture, with about 72% of U.S. consumers playing some kind of videogame. Not surprisingly, marketers have followed closely behind, developing a new promotional channel: **advergaming**. Market analysts expect that spending in the advergame industry will increase from $295 million in 2007 to $650 million in 2012.[21]

According to Massive, an advertising network that specializes in video games, advergaming works for marketers. Gamers exposed to embedded ads show a 64% increase in brand familiarity, a 37% increase in brand rating, and a 41% increase in purchase consideration. But Massive isn't the only game in town. In early 2007, Google purchased AdScape, a nimble video game advertising company, and independent agency Double Fusion also provides fierce competition. Given the effectiveness of advergaming and the explosive growth, gamers may soon see a cyberworld filled with as much promotion as the real world.[22]

Buzz Marketing A recent study defined "buzz" as the transfer of information from someone who is in the know to someone who isn't. Buzz is essentially word-of-mouth, which now influences two-thirds of all consumer product purchases. And it makes sense. In a world that's increasingly complex, people turn to people they know and trust to help sort the garbage from the good stuff. Other popular terms for **buzz marketing** are "guerrilla marketing" and "viral marketing."

Not surprisingly, marketers have actively pursued buzz for their brands, especially with the rising cost and diminishing effectiveness of more traditional media channels. Innovative buzz campaigns are typically custom-designed to meet their objectives, and they often cost significantly less than more traditional

approaches. Here are some notable examples:

- **The Subservient Chicken:** In line with its "Have it your way" slogan, Burger King launched the Subservient Chicken website to introduce its new TenderCrisp Chicken sandwich. The site shows an actor in a chicken suit who invites the viewer to "Get chicken the way you want it. Type in your command here." With a few obvious exceptions, the chicken will do just about anything you ask, from laying an egg to throwing pillows. After the link was seeded in some popular chat rooms, it exploded across the Web. The site has garnered more than 14 million unique visitors, becoming a pop culture favorite. And even though Burger King didn't release specific sales results, it did report "significantly increased" chicken sandwich sales.[23]

- **Tremor:** Procter & Gamble, known for its traditional marketing, has mobilized buzz marketing on an unprecedented scale. Its Tremor marketing group, launched in 2001, recruited about 200,000 sociable kids, ages 13 to 19, to talk up products to their peers. These teens talk for free—or if not for free, for the chance to influence companies and get the early inside scoop on new products. In addition to P&G brands, Tremorites have worked on heavy-hitters such as Sony Electronics, DreamWorks SKG, and Coca-Cola. The results have been impressive. A dairy foods firm, for instance, introduced a new chocolate malt milk in Phoenix and Tucson with the same marketing mix and the same spending level. One exception: they used Tremor teens in Phoenix. After six months, sales in Phoenix were 18% higher than in Tucson. That kind of success tells its own story.[24]

Sponsorships Sponsorships certainly aren't new, but they are among the fastest-growing categories of promotional spending, hitting nearly $17 billion in 2009, although the growth rate slowed significantly as the global recession took hold. The reasons are clear. Sponsorships provide a deep association between a marketer and a partner (usually a cultural or sporting event). Even though sponsors can't usually provide more than simply their logo or slogan, consumers tend to view them in a positive light, since they are clearly connected to events that matter to the target audience. The best sponsorship investments,

advergaming A relatively new promotional channel that involves integrating branded products and advertising into interactive games.

buzz marketing The active stimulation of word-of-mouth via unconventional, and often relatively low-cost, tactics. Other terms for buzz marketing are "guerrilla marketing" and "viral marketing."

sponsorship A deep association between a marketer and a partner (usually a cultural or sporting event), which involves promotion of the sponsor in exchange for either payment or the provision of goods.

PRNEWSFOTO/JUST BORN, INC.

of course, occur when the target audience for the marketer completely overlaps the target audience for the event. The high level of integration between the sponsors and events can provide millions of dollars in valuable media coverage, justifying the hefty price.[25]

Traditional Promotional Tools: A Marketing Mainstay

Although new tools are gaining prominence, traditional promotional tools—advertising, sales promotion, public relations, and personal selling—remain powerful. In fact, many marketers use the new tools in conjunction with the traditional to create a balanced, far-reaching promotional mix.

Advertising The formal definition of **advertising** is paid, nonpersonal communication, designed to influence a target audience with regard to a product, service,

> # Doing business without advertising is like winking at a girl in the dark. You know what you are doing, but nobody else does.
>
> *Steuart Henderson Britt, psychologist and marketing expert*

organization, or idea. Most major brands use advertising not only to drive sales, but also to build their reputation, especially with a broad target market. Television (network broadcasts and cable combined) remains the number-one advertising media, with magazines and newspapers following. As mass media prices increase and audiences fragment, fringe media is roaring toward the mainstream. But measurement is tough, since alternative media tactics are buried in other categories, including magazines, outdoor, and Internet. The overall media spending patterns for 2009 are shown in Exhibit 12.11. As you review the table, note that Internet

EXHIBIT 12.11 2009 Measured Media Spending (billions)[26]

Measured Media	2009 Spending	Percentage of Total
Broadcast TV	$23,600	18.9%
Cable TV	$19,300	15.4%
Spot TV	$13,200	10.5%
Syndicated TV	$4,200	3.4%
Newspapers	$20,600	16.5%
Radio	$7,600	6.0%
Magazines	$23,500	18.8%
Outdoor	$3,400	2.7%
Internet*	$9,800	7.8%
TOTAL	$125,300	100%

BP: A Massive Environmental Disaster, and an Epic New Media Fail!

After a deadly explosion on one of its deep-sea oil-drilling rigs in spring 2010, BP began spewing thousands of barrels of oil each day into the Gulf of Mexico. As BP struggled to contain the spill and limit the damage, the company lost control of its public relations when a talented satirist opened a fake Twitter account called @BPGlobalPR with this message: "We regretfully admit that something has happened off of the Gulf Coast. More to come," followed by a stream of additional tweets, passed off as "real" PR statements from BP itself. A sampling:

© SAUL LOEB/AFP/GETTY IMAGES

- "The good news: Mermaids are real. The bad news: They are now extinct."
- "We've created something that will affect your children's children. Can YOU say the same about YOUR life?"
- "If we had a dollar for every complaint about this oil spill, it wouldn't compare to our current fortune. Oil is a lucrative industry!"
- "Negative people view the ocean as half empty of oil. We are dedicated to making it half full. Stay positive America!"
- "Doing our best to turn oil into oilinade. So far the stuff tastes TERRIBLE."
- "Just saw new satellite images of the spill. Actually, it kinda looks like the Earth has a beauty mark! Ooolala!"

In less than three weeks, the fake Twitter account garnered more than 25,000 followers, compared to fewer than 5,000 followers for the real BP account, which issued such tepid fare as "BP is committed to openness and transparency in our response to the oil spill in the Gulf of Mexico." Had BP used social media to create an open, authentic dialogue with the public, it might have emerged from the oil spill mess with at least a bit of its image intact. [27]

spending does not include search advertising or online video advertising, which are typically tracked separately. Please also note that overall media spending has dropped significantly in response to the recession.

Each type of media offers advantages and drawbacks, as summarized in Exhibit 12.12. Your goal as a marketer should be to determine which media options reach your target market efficiently and effectively, within the limits of your budget.

Sales Promotion Sales promotion stimulates immediate sales activity through specific short-term programs aimed at either consumers or distributors. Traditionally, sales promotion has been subordinate to other promotional tools, but spending has accelerated in

sales promotion Marketing activities designed to stimulate immediate sales activity through specific short-term programs aimed at either consumers or distributors.

EXHIBIT 12.12 Major Media Categories

Major Media	Advantages	Disadvantages
Broadcast TV	*Mass audience*: Season finales for top-rated shows garnered up to 20 million viewers in 2008. *High impact*: TV lends itself to vivid, complex messages that use sight, sound, and motion.	*Disappearing viewers*: The 20 million viewers for top-rated shows in 2008 are dwarfed by the 1983 record of 105 million viewers for the finale of *M*A*S*H*. *Jaded viewers*: Consumers who aren't zapping ads with TiVo are prone to simply tuning them out. *High cost*: A 30-second ad during Super Bowl 2009 cost a record $3 million, and a typical primetime ad cost $200,000 to $400,000, depending on the show.
Cable TV	*Targeted programming*: Cable helps advertisers target highly specialized markets (Zhong Tian Channel, anyone?). *Efficient*: The cost per contact is relatively low, especially for local buys. *High impact*: Cable offers the same sight, sound, and motion benefits as broadcast.	*DVRs*: As with broadcast TV, many viewers simply aren't watching ads. *Uneven quality*: Many cable ads are worse than mediocre, providing a seedy setting for quality products.
Newspapers	*Localized*: Advertisers can tailor their messages to meet local needs. *Flexible*: Turnaround time for placing and pulling ads is very short. *Consumer acceptance*: Readers expect, and even seek, newspaper ads.	*Short life span*: Readers quickly discard their papers. *Clutter*: It takes two or three hours to read the average metro paper from cover to cover. Almost no one does it. *Quality*: Even top-notch color newsprint leaves a lot to be desired.
Direct mail	*Highly targeted*: Direct mail can reach very specific markets. *International opportunity*: Less jaded foreign customers respond well to direct mail. *Email option*: Opt-in email can lower direct mail costs.	*Wastes resources*: Direct mail uses a staggering amount of paper. And most recipients don't even read it before they toss it. *High cost*: Cost per contact can be high, although advertisers can limit the size of the campaign. *Spam*: Unsolicited email ads have undermined consumer tolerance for all email ads.
Radio	*Highly targeted*: In L.A., for example, the dial ranges from Vietnamese talk radio, to urban dance music, each station with dramatically different listeners. *Low cost*: Advertisers can control the cost by limiting the size of the buy. *Very flexible*: Changing the message is quick and easy.	*Low impact*: Radio relies only on listening. *Jaded listeners*: Many of us flip stations when the ads begin.
Magazines	*Highly targeted*: From *Cosmo* to *Computerworld*, magazines reach very specialized markets. *Quality*: Glossy print sends a high-quality message. *Long life*: Magazines tend to stick around homes and offices.	*High cost*: A full-page, four-color ad in *People* can cost more than $300,000. *Inflexible*: Advertisers must submit artwork months before publication.
Outdoor	*High visibility*: Billboards and building sides are hard to miss. *Repeat exposure*: Popular locations garner daily viewers. *Breakthrough ideas*: Innovative approaches include cars and buses "wrapped" in ads, video billboards, and blimps.	*Simplistic messages*: More than an image and a few words will get lost. *Visual pollution*: Many consumers object to outdoor ads. Limited targeting: It's hard to ensure that the right people see your ad.
Internet	*24/7 global coverage*: Offers a remarkable level of exposure. *Highly targeted*: Search engines are especially strong at delivering the right ad to the right person at the right time. *Interactive*: Internet ads can empower consumers.	*Intrusive*: The annoyance factor from tough-to-close pop-ups alienates consumers, infuriating many. *Limited readership*: Web surfers simply ignore the vast majority of ads.

the past decade. Sales promotion falls into two categories: consumer and trade.

Consumer promotion is designed to generate immediate sales. Consumer promotion tools include premiums, promotional products, samples, coupons, rebates, and displays.

- **Premiums** are items that consumers receive free of charge—or for a lower than normal cost—in return for making a purchase. Upscale cosmetics companies use the gift-with-purchase approach on a regular basis. And fast food companies use premiums pretty much every time the major studios release a family movie. Successful premiums create a sense of urgency—"Buy me now!"—while building the value of the brand.

- **Promotional** products are also essentially gifts to consumers of merchandise that advertise a brand name. Nightclub promoters, for instance, often distribute free T-shirts plastered with their slogan. Or pizza delivery places give away refrigerator magnets with their logo and phone number. Promotional products work best when the merchandise relates to the brand, and it's so useful or fun that consumers will opt to keep it around.

- **Samples** reduce the risk of purchasing something new by allowing consumers to try a product before committing their cash. Dunkin' Donuts, for instance, gives away millions of cups of coffee during its annual Iced Coffee Day. Sampling also drives immediate purchases. At one time or another, most of us have probably bought food we didn't need after tasting a delicious morsel in the supermarket aisle. Costco and Trader Joe's do especially well with this angle on sampling.

- **Coupons** offer immediate price reductions to consumers. Instant coupons require even less effort, since they are attached to the package right there in the store. The goal is to entice consumers to try new products. But the downside is huge. Marketers who depend on coupons encourage consumers to focus on price rather than value, which makes it harder to differentiate brands and build loyalty. In categories with frequent coupons (such as soap and cereal), too many consumers wait for the coupon in order to buy. They end up getting great deals, but marketers pay the price in reduced profits.

- **Rebates,** common in the car industry and the electronics business, entice consumers with cash-back offers. This is a powerful tactic for higher-priced items, since rebates offer an appealing purchase

TechNotes

Tech Notes: Social Media Return on Investment

Clearly, social media is not a fad, but rather, a paradigm shift in how successful businesses market themselves. According to advertising heavyweight Alex Bogusky, "You can't buy attention anymore. Having a huge budget doesn't mean anything in social media... The old media paradigm was PAY to play. Now you get back what you authentically put in." And the evidence is building that social media offers a truly impressive return on investment, especially compared to traditional media. A few examples compiled by social media expert Erik Qualman underscore the potential return on investment:

- Wetpaint/Altimeter Study found companies that are both deeply and widely engaged in social media significantly surpass their peers in both revenues and profits. The study also found the company sales with the highest levels of social media activity grew on average by +18%, while those companies with the least amount of social activity saw their sales decline –6%.

- BlendTec increased its sales 5x by running the often humorous "Will It Blend" videos on YouTube, blending everything from an iPhone to a sneaker.
- Dell sold $3,000,000 worth of computers on Twitter.
- Ford Motor Company gave away 100 Fiestas to influential bloggers, resulting in 37% of Generation Y learning of the Ford Fiesta before it was launched in the United States.
- Software company Genius.com reports that 24% of its social media leads convert to sales opportunities.
- Web host provider Moonfruit more than recouped its $15,000 social media investment as its website traffic soared +300% while sales increased +20%.

Looking ahead, smart marketers of both large and small businesses are investing their limited resources in social marketing, and reaping an unprecedented return, forging the future of marketing promotion. [28]

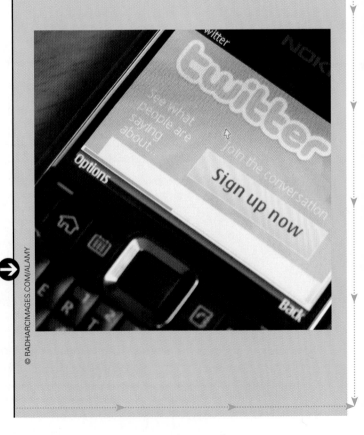

motivator. And rebates provide an incentive for marketers as well: breakage. Most people who buy a product because of the rebate don't actually follow through and do the paperwork to get the money (some estimates suggest that breakage rates are as high as 90 to 95%). This means that marketers can offer hefty discounts without actually coughing up the cash, so it isn't surprising that rebates are a popular promotional tool!

- **Displays** generate purchases in-store. Most experts agree that consumers make a hefty chunk of their purchase decisions as they shop, which means that displays can play a crucial role in sales success. Marketers of consumer products often give prefabricated display materials to grocery stores and mass merchandisers to encourage promotion.

Trade Promotion is designed to stimulate wholesalers and retailers to push specific products more aggressively. Special deals and allowances are the most common form of trade promotion, especially for consumer products. The idea is that if you give your distributors a temporary price cut, they will pass the savings on to consumers via a short-term "special."

Trade shows are another popular form of trade promotion. Usually organized by industry trade associations, trade shows give exhibitors a chance to display and promote their products to their distributors. They typically attract hundreds of exhibitors and thousands of attendees. Trade shows are especially common in rapidly changing industries such as toys and consumer electronics. Every year, for instance, the Consumer Electronics Association hosts "The world's largest annual trade show for consumer electronics!" in Las Vegas.

Other forms of trade promotion include contests, sweepstakes, and special events for distributors. A soda company, for instance, might sponsor a contest to see which grocery store can build the most creative summer display for its soda brands. Or a cable TV programmer might take a group of system managers to Key West to "learn more about their programming" (really an excuse for a great party that makes the system managers more open to the programmer's pitch).

Public Relations In the broadest sense, **public relations (or PR)** involves the ongoing effort to create positive relationships with all of a firm's different "publics," including customers, employees, suppliers, the community, the general public, and the government. But in a more focused sense, PR aims to generate positive **publicity**, or unpaid stories in the media that create a favorable impression about a company or its products. The endgame, of course, is to boost demand.

For the most part, the media covers companies or products that they perceive as newsworthy. To get coverage, smart firms continually scan their own companies for potential news—a hot product, for example,

or a major corporate achievement—and present that news to the media. But finding news on a regular basis can be tough. To fill the gaps, innovative PR people sometimes simply create "news." PR guru Bill Stoller offers some interesting ideas for how to invent stories that will grab media attention:

- **Launch a Hall of Fame:** Induct some luminaries from your industry, create a simple website, and send your press release to the media. Repeat each year, building your reputation along the way.

- **Make a List:** The best, the worst, the top ten, the bottom ten—the media loves lists, and the possible topics are endless! Just make sure that your list is relevant to your business.

- **Create a Petition:** The Web makes this tactic easy. Harness a growing trend or identify a need in your industry, and launch your petition. The more signatures you get, the better your chances for publicity.[29]

The biggest advantage of publicity is that it is usually credible. Think about it: Are you more likely to buy a product featured on the news or a product featured in a 30-second ad? Are you more likely to read a book reviewed by *The New York Times* or featured on a billboard? Publicity is credible because most people believe that information presented by the media is based on legitimate opinions and facts rather than on the drive to make money. And it also helps that publicity is close to free (excluding any fees for a PR firm).

But publicity has a major downside: the marketer has no control over how the media presents the company or its products. For example, in an effort to protect customers from a growing tide of solicitors in front of its stores, Target banned Salvation Army bell ringers in front of all its stores in 2004. The press cried foul, focusing not on the service to consumers, but rather on the disrespect to a venerable charity. Target's archrival Walmart, spotting an opportunity for itself at Target's expense, announced that it would match customer donations to the Salvation Army at all of its locations.

Personal Selling **Personal selling**—the world's oldest form of promotion—is person-to-person presentation of products to potential buyers. But successful selling typically begins long before the actual presentation and ends long afterward. In today's competitive

trade promotion
Marketing activities designed to stimulate wholesalers and retailers to push specific products more aggressively over the short term.

public relations (PR)
The ongoing effort to create positive relationships with all of a firm's different "publics," including customers, employees, suppliers, the community, the general public, and the government.

publicity Unpaid stories in the media that influence perceptions about a company or its products.

personal selling The person-to-person presentation of products to potential buyers.

environment, selling means building relationships on a long-term basis.

Creating and maintaining a quality sales force are expensive. Experts estimate that each business-to-business sales call costs nearly $400. So why are more than 10% of Americans employed in sales? Because nothing works better than personal selling for high-ticket items, complex products, and high-volume customers. In some companies, the sales team works directly with customers; in other firms, the sales force works with distributors who buy large volumes of products for resale.

Salespeople fall along a spectrum that ranges from order takers who simply process sales to order seekers who use creative selling to persuade customers. Most department stores, for instance, hire order takers who stand behind the counter and ring up sales. But Nordstrom hires creative order seekers who actively garner sales by offering extra services such as tasteful accessory recommendations for a clothing shopper.

A separate category of salespeople focuses on *missionary selling*, which means promoting goodwill for a company by providing information and assistance to customers. The pharmaceutical industry, for instance, hires a small army of missionary salespeople who call on doctors to explain and promote its products, even though the actual sales move through pharmacies.

The sales process typically follows six key stages. But as we explore each one, keep in mind that well before the process begins, effective salespeople seek a complete understanding of their products, their industry, and their competition. A high level of knowledge permeates the entire selling process.

© TETRA IMAGES/JUPITERIMAGES

1. **Prospect and Qualify**: Prospecting means identifying potential customers. Qualifying means choosing those who are most likely to buy your product. Choosing the right prospects makes salespeople more efficient, since it helps them focus their limited time in areas that will yield results. Companies find prospects in a number of different ways, from trade shows, to direct mail, to cold calling. In a retail environment, everyone who walks in the door is a prospect, so salespeople either ask questions or look for visual cues to qualify customers.

2. **Prepare:** Before making a sales call, research is critical, especially in a business-to-business environment. What are your prospect's wants and needs? What are his or her current product lines? Who are the key competitors? What are the biggest internal and external challenges? How much time is your prospect willing to give you? The answers to these questions will help you customize your presentation for maximum effectiveness.

3. **Present:** You've probably heard that you don't get a second chance to make a good first impression, and that's especially true in sales. With so many options and so little time, buyers often look for reasons to eliminate choices; a weak first impression provides an easy reason to eliminate you. Your presentation itself should match the features of your product to the benefits that your customer seeks (a chance to use all that preparation). Testimonials, letters of

praise from satisfied current customers, can push forward the sale by reducing risk for your prospect. And in many categories, a demonstration can be the clincher. For some products, a demonstration is a no-brainer—test-driving cars, for example. But in other categories, technology can help demonstrate products that are too big to move.

4. **Handle Objections:** The key to success here is to view objections as opportunities rather than criticism. Objections give you a chance to learn more about the needs of your prospects and to elaborate on the benefits of your product. You should definitely anticipate as many objections as possible and prepare responses. One response may be connecting prospects with others in your company who can better handle their concerns. This approach offers the additional benefit of deepening ties between your prospect and your company.

5. **Close Sale:** Closing the sale—or asking the prospect to buy—is at the heart of the selling process. The close should flow naturally from the prior steps, but often it doesn't—sealing the deal can be surprisingly tough. One approach may be a trial close: "Would you like the 15-inch screen or the 17-inch screen?" If your prospect is still reluctant to buy, you may want to offer another alternative, or a special financial incentive. Even if the prospect doesn't actually make the purchase, remember that he or she may be willing in the future, so keep the door open.

6. **Follow-up:** The sales process doesn't end when the customer pays. The quality of service and support plays a crucial role in future sales from the same customer, and getting those sales is much easier than finding brand new prospects. Great relationships with current customers also lead to testimonials and referrals that build momentum for long-term sales success.

Two personal selling trends are gathering momentum in a number of organizations: consultative selling and team selling. *Consultative selling* involves shifting the focus from the products to the customers. On a day-to-day basis, the practice involves a deep understanding of customer needs. Through lots and lots of active listening, consultative salespeople offer practical solutions to customer problems—solutions that use their products. While consultative selling generates powerful customer loyalty, it involves a significant—and expensive—time investment from the sales force.

Team selling tends to be especially effective for large, complex accounts. The approach includes a group of specialists from key functional areas of the company—not just sales, but also engineering, finance, customer service, and others. The goal is to uncover opportunities and respond to needs that would be beyond the capacity of a single salesperson. In these situations, a key part of the salesperson's role is to connect and coordinate the right network of contacts.

Choosing the Right Promotional Mix: Not Just a Science

There are no fail-safe rules for choosing the right combination of promotional tools. The mix varies dramatically among various industries, but also within specific industry segments. The best approach may simply be to consider the following questions in developing the mix that works best for your products.

Too Much of a Good Thing

Months after Kentucky Fried Chicken changed its name to KFC, consumers remembered that the "F" stands for "Fried." So KFC grilled chicken was a bit of a "disconnect" for many consumers. But undaunted, KFC pushed ahead with an Oprah Winfrey promotion, offering two free pieces of grilled chicken, two sides, and a biscuit to anyone who downloaded a coupon within a two-day period. But the offer went awry when KFC failed to execute effectively. KFC claimed that it prepared for a huge response, but it failed to account for consumers photocopying the coupon, and the response—magnified by Twitter—utterly swamped its stores. As a result of the overwhelming response, KFC canceled the promotion, forcing disappointed consumers to go back to KFC, fill out a form, and wait for another coupon to arrive in the mail to award them with a free Pepsi in lieu of their free chicken meal. Although the promotional concept certainly generated a lot of consumer buzz, it ultimately did more harm than good, since the fast-fooder was ultimately unable to deliver.[30]

- **Product Characteristics:** How can you best communicate the features of your product? Is it simple or complex? Is it high-priced or inexpensive? A specialized, high-priced item, for example, might require an investment in personal selling, whereas a simple, low-cost product might lend itself to billboard advertising.

- **Product Life Cycle:** Where does your product stand in its life cycle? Are you developing awareness? Are you generating desire? What about driving purchases? And building loyalty? The answers will clearly affect your promotional focus. For instance, if you're developing awareness, you might focus more on advertising, but if you're aiming to drive immediate sales, you'll probably emphasize sales promotion.

- **Target Audience:** How big is your target audience? Where do they live and work? A small target audience—especially if it's geographically dispersed—would lend itself to personal selling or direct mail. A sizable target audience might suggest advertising as an effective way to reach large numbers. Audience expectations should also play a role in your promotional mix decisions.

- **Push Versus Pull:** Does your industry emphasize push or pull strategies? A **push strategy** involves motivating distributors to "push" your product to the final consumers, usually through heavy trade promotion and personal selling. A **pull strategy** involves creating demand from your final consumers so that they "pull" your products through the distribution channels. Many successful brands use a combination of push and pull strategies to achieve their goals. P&G, for example, recently launched a consumer marketing campaign for Crest toothpaste featuring an "Irresistibility IQ" quiz for club-goers, but it also promotes heavily to dentists, hoping that those dentists will recommend Crest to their patients.

- **Competitive Environment:** How are your key competitors handling their promotional strategies? Would it make more sense for you to follow their lead or to forge your own promotional path? If all your competitors offer coupons, for instance, your customers may expect you to offer them as well. Or if the environment is cluttered, you might want to focus on emerging promotional approaches such as advergaming.

- **Budget:** What are your promotional goals? How much money will it take to achieve them? (Answering this question is tough, but it's clearly important.) How much are your competitors spending in each area of the mix? And how much money do you have for promotion? Even though available budget shouldn't drive the promotional mix, it plays a crucial role, especially for smaller businesses.

The Big Picture

The possibilities in both product development and promotional strategy have rapidly multiplied in the last few years alone. But companies can't deliver on the potential without well-oiled teamwork throughout the organization. For instance, the operations group must focus on quality, the accounting group must focus on cost, and the finance group must focus on funding—but from a big picture standpoint, all groups must work toward the same overarching goal: maximizing customer value. Promotion also requires coordination within the organization and among the outside suppliers who provide promotional services. Finally, the best ideas for both product and promotion can come from any department. Marketers who stay ahead of the curve will only sharpen their competitive edge in the decade to come.

WHAT ELSE? *RIP & REVIEW* **CARDS IN THE BACK**

© ANDERSEN ROSS/BLEND IMAGES/GETTY IMAGES

REVIEW!

HE DID

BUSN4 puts a multitude of study aids at your fingertips. After reading the chapters, check out these resources for further help:

• **Review Cards,** found in the back of your book, include all learning outcomes, key terms and definitions, and visual summaries for each chapter.

• **Online Printable Flashcards** give you additional ways to check your comprehension of key Introduction to Business concepts.

• Other great tools to help you review include **Interactive Business Decision Making Scenarios, Interactive Exhibits, Quizzes, Games, and More!**

Go to CourseMate for BUSN4 to find plenty of resources to help you *Review!* Access at www.cengagebrain.com.

13

DISTRIBUTION AND PRICING: RIGHT PRODUCT, RIGHT PERSON, RIGHT PLACE, RIGHT PRICE

LEARNING OBJECTIVES

After studying this chapter, you will be able to...

LO1 Define distribution and differentiate between channels of distribution and physical distribution

LO2 Describe the various types of wholesale distributors

LO3 Discuss strategies and trends in store and nonstore retailing

LO4 Explain the key factors in physical distribution

LO5 Outline core pricing objectives and strategies

LO6 Discuss pricing in practice, including the role of consumer perceptions

Visit CourseMate at **www.cengagebrain.com**.

Distribution and pricing are not the most glamorous elements of the marketing mix, but managed effectively, they can provide a powerful competitive advantage. While this chapter will cover distribution and pricing strategies separately, keep in mind that the two are linked both with each other, and with the product and promotional strategies of any successful brand.

LO1 Distribution: Getting Your Product to Your Customer

Next time you go to the grocery store, look around—the average U.S. supermarket carries more than 47,000 different products.[1] Is your favorite brand of soda part of the mix? Why? How did it get from the factory to your neighborhood store? Where else could you find that soda? How far would you be willing to go to get it? These are marketing distribution questions that contribute directly to the **distribution strategy**: getting the right product to the right person at the right place, at the right time.

The distribution strategy has two elements: channels of distribution and physical distribution. A **channel of distribution** is the path that a product takes from the producer to the consumer, while **physical distribution** is the actual movement of products along that path. Some producers choose to sell their products directly to their customers through a **direct channel**. No one stands between the producer and the customer. Examples range from Dell computers, to local farmers markets, to factory outlet stores. But most producers use **channel intermediaries** to help their products move more efficiently and effectively from their factories to their consumers. Coppertone, for example, sells sunblock to Costco—a channel intermediary—which may in turn sell it to you.

The Role of Distributors: Adding Value

You might be asking yourself why we need distributors. Wouldn't it be a lot less expensive to buy directly from the producers? The answer, surprisingly, is no. Distributors add value—additional benefits—to products. They charge for adding that value, but typically they charge less than it would cost for consumers or producers to add that value on their own. When distributors add to the cost of a product without providing comparable benefits, the middlemen don't stay in business. Fifteen years ago, for instance, most people bought plane tickets from travel agents. But when the Internet reduced the cost and inconvenience of buying tickets directly from airlines, thousands of travel agencies lost their customers.

One core role of distributors is to reduce the number of transactions—and the associated costs—for goods to flow from producers to consumers. As you'll see in Exhibit 13.1, even one marketing intermediary in the distribution channel can funnel goods from producers to consumers with far fewer costly transactions.

Distributors add value, or **utility**, in a number of different ways: form, time, place, ownership, information, and service. Sometimes the distributors deliver the value (rather than adding it themselves), but often they add new utility that wouldn't otherwise be present. As you read through the various types of utility, keep in mind that they are often interrelated, building on each other to maximize value.

Form Utility Form utility provides customer satisfaction by converting inputs into finished products. Clearly, form utility is primarily a part of manufacturing. Kellogg's, for instance, provides form utility by transforming wheat into cereal. But retailers can add form utility as well. Jamba Juice, for example, converts wheatgrass into juice and fruit into smoothies.

---

distribution strategy A plan for delivering the right product to the right person at the right place at the right time.

channel of distribution The network of organizations and processes that links producers to consumers.

physical distribution The actual, physical movement of products along the distribution pathway.

direct channel A distribution process that links the producer and the customer with no intermediaries.

channel intermediaries Distribution organizations—informally called "middlemen"—that facilitate the movement of products from the producer to the consumer.

utility The value, or usefulness, that a good or service offers a customer.

© PIXLAND/JUPITERIMAGES

Time Utility Time utility adds value by making products available at a convenient time for consumers. In our 24/7 society, consumers feel entitled to instant gratification, a benefit that distributors can provide more easily than most producers. Consider one-hour dry cleaning, or even vending machines. These distributors provide options for filling your needs at a time that works for you.

Place Utility Place utility satisfies customer needs by providing the right products in the right place. Gas stations and fast food, for instance, often cluster conveniently at the bottom of freeway ramps. ATMs—essentially electronic distributors—are readily available in locations that range from grocery stores to college cafeterias.

Ownership Utility Ownership utility adds value by making it easier for customers to actually possess the goods and services that they purchase. Providing credit, cashing checks, and delivering products are all examples of how distributors make it easier for customers to own their products.

Information Utility Information utility boosts customer satisfaction by providing helpful information. EB Games, for instance, hires gaming experts to guide its customers to the latest games and systems. Similarly, most skateboard stores hire skater salespeople who gladly help customers find the best board for them.

EXHIBIT 13.1 Reducing transactions through marketing intermediaries

Service Utility Service utility adds value by providing fast, friendly, personalized service. Examples would include placing a special order for that part you need to customize your car, or giving you a makeover in your favorite department store. Distributors that provide service utility typically create a loyal base of customers.

The Members of the Channel: Retailers Versus Wholesalers Many producers sell their goods through multiple channels of distribution. Some channels have many members, while others have only a few. The main distinction among channel members is whether they are retailers or wholesalers. **Retailers** are the distributors that most of us know and use on a daily basis. They sell products directly to final consumers. Examples include 7-Eleven markets, Starbucks, and Urban Outfitters. **Wholesalers**, on the other hand, buy products from the producer and sell them to businesses (or other nonfinal users such as hospitals, nonprofits, and the government). The businesses that buy from wholesalers can be retailers, other wholesalers, or business users. To complicate this fairly simple concept, some distributors act as both wholesalers and retailers. Sam's Club, for example, sells directly to businesses *and* to consumers.

LO2 Wholesalers: Sorting Out the Options

Some wholesalers are owned by producers and others are owned by retailers, but the vast majority—accounting for about two-thirds of

ATMs provide time and place utility, offering their customers 24/7 access to cash in a variety of convenient locations.

all the wholesale trade—are **independent wholesaling businesses**. These companies represent a number of different producers, distributing their goods to a range of customers. Independent wholesalers fall into two categories: (1) **merchant wholesalers**, who take legal possession, or title, of the goods they distribute, and (2) **agents/brokers**, who don't take title of the goods.

Merchant Wholesalers

Merchant wholesalers comprise about 80% of all wholesalers. By taking legal title to the goods they distribute, merchant wholesalers reduce the risk of producers' products being damaged or stolen—or even that they just won't sell. Taking title also allows merchant wholesalers to develop their own marketing strategies, including price.

- Full-service merchant wholesalers provide a complete array of services to the retailers or business users who typically purchase their goods. This includes warehousing, shipping, promotional assistance, product repairs, and credit.

- Limited-service merchant wholesalers provide fewer services to their customers. For example, some might warehouse products, but not deliver them. Others might warehouse and deliver, but not provide credit or marketing assistance. The specific categories of limited-service merchant wholesalers include the following:

  - *Drop Shippers:* Drop shippers take legal title of the merchandise, but they never physically process it. They simply organize and facilitate product shipments directly from the producer to their customers. Drop shippers are common in industries with bulky products, such as coal or timber. Amazon, however, successfully pioneered the use of drop shipping in e-commerce, where it has become a standard shipping method for a number of major websites.

  - *Cash and Carry Wholesalers:* These distributors service customers who are too small to merit in-person sales calls from wholesaler reps. Customers must make the trip to the wholesaler themselves and cart their own products back to their stores. Costco

and Staples are both examples.

  - *Truck Jobbers:* Typically working with perishable goods such as bread, truck jobbers drive their products to their customers, who are usually smaller grocery stores. Their responsibilities often include checking the stock, suggesting reorder quantities, and removing out-of-date goods.

Agents and Brokers

Agents and brokers connect buyers and sellers and facilitate transactions in exchange for commissions. But they do not take legal ownership of the goods they distribute. Many insurance companies, for instance, distribute via agents, while brokers often handle real estate and seasonal products such as fruits and vegetables.

LO3 Retailers: the Consumer Connection

Retailers represent the last stop on the distribution path, since they sell goods and services directly to final consumers. Given their tight consumer connection, retailers must keep in especially close touch with rapidly changing consumer needs and wants.

Smart retailers gain a competitive edge by providing more utility, or added value, than their counterparts. Low prices are only part of the equation. Other elements clearly include customer service, product selection, advertising, and location. The look and feel of the retailer—whether online or on-ground—is another critical element.

Retailing falls into two main categories: store and nonstore. But as we discuss each type, keep in mind that the lines between them are not always

independent wholesaling businesses Independent distributors that buy products from a range of different businesses and sell those products to a range of different customers.

merchant wholesalers Independent distributors who take legal possession, or title, of the goods they distribute.

agents/brokers Independent distributors who do not take title of the goods they distribute (even though they may take physical possession on a temporary basis before distribution).

©TIM BOYLE/GETTY IMAGES

clear. In fact, **multichannel retailing**—or encouraging consumers to buy through different venues—is an emerging phenomenon. Some marketers have sold their products through multiple channels for many years. For example, on any given day, you could purchase a Coke from a grocery store, a restaurant, or a vending machine. But the emergence of the Internet has provided a host of new opportunities for firms that hadn't previously considered a multichannel approach. An active relationship between on-ground and online outlets has become pivotal for many retailers.

Store Retailers

While other retail channels are growing, traditional stores remain the 800-pound gorilla of the retail industry, accounting for well over 90% of total retail. Stores range in size from tiny mom-and-pop groceries to multiacre superstores dwarfed only by their parking lots. Exhibit 13.2 highlights examples of different store types.

Both retailers and the producers who distribute through them must carefully consider their distribution strategy. The three key strategic options are intensive, selective, and exclusive.

Intensive Distribution Intensive distribution involves placing your products in as many stores as possible (or placing your stores themselves in as many locations as possible). This strategy makes the most sense for low-cost convenience goods that consumers won't travel too far to find. Marketers have chosen this strategy for Starbucks, Charmin, and *People* magazine, among thousands of other examples.

Selective Distribution Selective distribution means placing your products only with preferred retailers (or establishing your stores only in limited locations). This approach tends to work best for medium- and higher-priced products or stores that consumers don't expect to find on every street corner. Marketers have chosen this strategy for Nordstrom, Grand Lux Cafe, and most brands of paintball equipment.

Exclusive Distribution Exclusive distribution means establishing only one retail outlet in a given area. Typically that one retailer has exclusive distribution rights and provides exceptional service and selection. This strategy tends to work for luxury-good providers with a customer base that actively seeks their products. Examples include top-end cars such as Bentley and jewelers such as Tiffany.

The **wheel of retailing** offers another key strategic consideration. The wheel is a classic theory that suggests that retail firms—sometimes even entire retail categories—become more upscale as they go through their life cycles. For instance, it's easiest to enter a

EXHIBIT 13.2 Retail Store Categories

Store Type	Store Description	Examples
Category killer	Dominates its category by offering a huge variety of one type of product.	Home Depot, Best Buy, Staples
Convenience store	Sells a small range of everyday and impulse products, at easy-to-access locations with long hours and quick checkout.	7-Eleven, AM/PM markets, and a wide range of local stores
Department store	Offers a wide variety of merchandise (e.g., clothes, furniture, cosmetics), plus (usually) a high level of service.	Nordstrom, Neiman Marcus, JCPenney
Discount store	Offers a wide array of merchandise at significantly lower prices and with less service than most department stores.	Target, Walmart, Kmart
Outlet store	Producer-owned store sells directly to the public at a huge discount. May include discontinued, flawed, or overrun items.	Nike, Gap, Gucci, Versace, Quicksilver
Specialty store	Sells a wide selection of merchandise within a narrow category, such as auto parts.	Barnes & Noble, Victoria's Secret, Hot Topic, AutoZone
Supermarket	Offers a wide range of food products, plus limited nonfood items (e.g., toilet paper).	Kroger, Safeway, Albertson's, Whole Foods
Supercenter	Sells a complete selection of food and general merchandise at a steep discount in a single enormous location.	Walmart Supercenters, Super Target
Warehouse club	Sells discounted food and general merchandise to club members in a large warehouse format.	Costco, Sam's Club

business on a shoestring, gaining customers by offering low prices. But eventually businesses trade up their selection, service, and facilities to maintain and build their customer base. Higher prices then follow, creating vulnerability to new, lower-priced competitors. And thus the wheel keeps rolling.

> **Reed Hastings created Netflix—which revolutionized video distribution—partly out of anger that Blockbuster charged him $40 in late fees on his overdue rental of *Apollo 13*.**
>
> *Newsweek*

Although the wheel of retailing theory does describe many basic retail patterns, it doesn't account for stores that launch at the high end of the market (e.g., Whole Foods) and those that retain their niche as deep discounters (e.g., Big Lots! or Taco Bell). But the wheel theory does underscore the core principle that retailers must meet changing consumer needs in a relentlessly competitive environment.

Nonstore Retailers

While most retail dollars flow through brick-and-mortar stores, a growing number of sales go through other channels, or nonstore retailers. The key players represent online retailing, direct response retailing, direct selling, and vending.

Online retailing Also known as "e-tailing," online retailing grew at the astonishing rate of nearly 25% per year for most of the 2000s. But the torrid pace began to slow in 2008 with the onset of the recession. Looking forward, experts predict that annual growth will slow even further, but stay in positive territory. Much of the growth will likely come at the expense of on-ground retail, as consumers continue to shift to online channels. The bigger name brands—including online-only brands, such as Amazon, and on-ground brands with a strong Web presence, such as Best Buy—seem poised to benefit most, since cautious consumers are most familiar with them.[1a]

Online retailers, like their on-ground counterparts, have learned that great customer service can be a powerful differentiator. Simply "getting eyeballs" isn't enough, since—depending on the industry—less than 5% of the people visiting a typical website convert

WITHOUT A MAP... CHARTING AN ETHICAL COURSE

Your Shaving Cream May Be Spying on You!

Picture yourself ducking into your local drugstore to pick up a new can of shaving cream. As you walk to your car carrying your bags, a high-tech billboard in the parking lot identifies your purchases and flashes you an ad for a new razor. Have you just entered a sci-fi movie? No—but you have seen the intrusive potential of the latest retail tracking technology, radio frequency identification (RFID) tags.

RFID tags are essentially microchips embedded in products. The chips emit radio-frequency waves that allow users to monitor the location of any product at any given time. Until recently, marketers used RFID tags mostly to track the movement of pallets of goods through the supply chain (especially through warehouses). The cost per tag was simply too high to use on individual consumer products.

But then a number of major retailers—led by Walmart, Target, Albertson's, and Best Buy—mandated that their top suppliers adopt RFID. In a retail setting, the tags track the movement of products from stockrooms, to shelves, to the checkout counter. The potential benefits are huge: smoother inventory management, continually stocked shelves, less shoplifting, and more information about consumers—all of which adds up to huge cost reductions.

Yet privacy advocates are horrified. As RFID tags flood the retail sector, the possibilities for abuse multiply. Unwanted advertising is only part of the picture. What happens when anyone, including thieves, can check out the contents of your packages (or your purse, or your pockets, or your car)? Should marketers be allowed to track your shopping habits outside the store by tracking the products you carry with you? What about law enforcement or private investigators?

RFID industry advocates respond that these concerns are overblown. They point out that the tags emit signals only to readers within close range (less than five feet), which reduces the potential for abuse. And as standards develop, privacy policies will develop as well. But in the meantime, keep a close eye on your shaving cream![2]

into paying customers. Overstock.com, for instance, has been a pioneer in online customer service, hiring and training 60 specialists who engage customers in live chats, available 24/7. When a customer has a live chat with one of its specialists, the average purchase amount doubles. In fact, according to the National Retail Federation (NRF), shoppers have increasingly identified Internet-only retailers among those who offered the best customer service. In 2009, the annual NRF/American Express Customers' Choice survey included three online retailers—Overstock.com, Zappos.com, and Amazon.com—in its top five positions for retailers that offer the best customer service in any retail format.[3]

Online retailers have also learned to use technology to create a personal, in-the-moment shopping experience. Adidas and Land's End, for instance, encourage customers to custom-create branded merchandise, providing exclusivity at a reasonable price. But perhaps most importantly, technology allows online retailers to reach potential customers—anywhere, anytime—so long as they have a computer and Internet access.

Despite the advantages, online retailers face two major hurdles. The first is that products must be delivered, and even the fastest deliery services typically take at least a couple of days. But the truly daunting hurdle is the lack of security on the Web. As online retailers and software developers create increasingly secure systems, hackers develop more sophisticated tools to crack their new codes.

Direct Response Retailing This category includes catalogs, telemarketing, and advertising (such as infomercials) meant to elicit direct consumer sales. While many traditional catalog retailers have also established successful websites, the catalog side of the business continues to thrive. Victoria's Secret, for instance, sends a mind-boggling 395 million catalogs each year—that's four catalogs for every single American woman between the ages

of 15 and 64. Telemarketing, both inbound and outbound, also remains a potent distribution channel, despite the popular National Do Not Call list established in 2003.

Direct Selling This channel includes all methods of selling directly to customers in their homes or workplaces. Door-to-door sales has enjoyed a resurgence in the wake of the National Do Not Call list, but the real strength of direct selling lies in multilevel marketing, or MLM. Multilevel marketing involves hiring independent contractors to sell products to their personal network of friends and colleagues and to recruit new salespeople in return for a percentage of their commissions. Mary Kay Cosmetics and The Pampered Chef have both enjoyed enormous success in this arena, along with pioneering companies such as Tupperware.

{ **We own the relationship with the customer and we subcontract to others.**
Kevin Rollins, Dell CEO }

Vending Until about a decade ago, vending machines in the United States sold mostly soft drinks and snacks. But more recently, the selection has expanded (and the machines have gone more upscale) as marketers recognize the value of providing their products as conveniently as possible to their target consumers. Banana Boat, for example, has placed sunscreen vending units in high-traffic spots across sunny southern Florida. But other countries are far ahead of the United States in the vending arena. In Japan, for instance, people buy everything from blue jeans to beef from vending machines. As technology continues to roll forward, U.S. consumers are likely to see a growing number of vending machines for products as diverse as fresh-cooked french fries, digital cameras, and specialty coffee drinks.

AP IMAGES/LARRY CROWE

LO4 Physical Distribution: Planes, Trains, and Much, Much More

Determining the best distribution channels for your product is only the first half of your distribution strategy. The second half is physical distribution strategy: determining how your product will flow through the channel from the producer to the consumer.

The **supply chain** for a product includes not only its distribution channels, but also the string of suppliers who deliver products to the producers (see Exhibit 13.3). Planning and coordinating the movement of products along the supply chain—from the raw materials to the final consumers—is called **supply chain management** or **SCM**. **Logistics** is a subset of SCM that focuses more on tactics (the actual movement of products) than on strategy.

At one time, relationships among the members of the supply chain were contentious. But these days, companies that foster collaboration rather than competition have typically experienced more success. Vendor-managed inventory is an emerging strategy—pioneered by Walmart—that allows suppliers to determine buyer needs and automatically ship product. This strategy saves time and money, but also requires an extraordinary level of trust and information sharing among members of the supply chain.

In our turbocharged 24/7 society, supply chain management has become increasingly complex. Gap, for instance, contracts with more than 3,000 factories in more than 50 different countries, and distributes its products to about 3,000 stores in five different countries. The coordination requirements are mind-boggling. Key management decisions include the following considerations:

- **Warehousing:** How many warehouses do we need? Where should we locate our warehouses?

- **Materials Handling:** How should we move products within our facilities? How can we best balance efficiency with effectiveness?

- **Inventory Control:** How much inventory should we keep on hand? How should we store and distribute it? What about costs such as taxes and insurance?

- **Order Processing:** How should we manage incoming and outgoing orders? What would be most efficient for our customers and suppliers?

- **Customer Service:** How can we serve our customers most effectively? How can we reduce waiting times and facilitate interactions?

- **Transportation:** How can we move products most efficiently through the supply chain? What are the key tradeoffs?

- **Security:** How can we keep products safe from vandals, theft, and accidents every step of the way?

And fragile or perishable products, of course, require even more considerations.

Transportation Decisions

Moving products through the supply chain is so important that it deserves its own section. The various options—trains, planes, and railroads, for instance—are called **modes of transportation**. To make

supply chain All organizations, processes, and activities involved in the flow of goods from the raw materials to the final consumer.

supply chain management (SCM) Planning and coordinating the movement of products along the supply chain, from the raw materials to the final consumers.

logistics A subset of supply chain management that focuses largely on the tactics involved in moving products along the supply chain.

modes of transportation The various transportation options—such as planes, trains, and railroads—for moving products through the supply chain.

EXHIBIT 13.3 Elements of the Supply Chain
The Supply Chain highlights the links among the various organizations in the production and distribution process.

Raw Materials

Logistics (transportation, coordination, etc.)

Warehouse/Storage

Production

Warehouse/Storage

Logistics (transportation, coordination, etc.)

Distributors—Marketing and Sales

smart decisions, marketers must consider what each mode offers in terms of cost, speed, dependability, flexibility, availability, and frequency of shipments. The right choice, of course, depends on the needs of the business and on the product itself. See Exhibit 13.4 for a description of the transportation options.

Depending on factors such as warehousing, docking facilities, and accessibility, some distributors use several different modes of transportation. If you owned a clothing boutique in Las Vegas, for example, chances are that much of your merchandise would travel by boat from China to Long Beach, California, and then by truck from Long Beach to Las Vegas.

Proactive Supply Chain Management

A growing number of marketers have turned to supply chain management to build a competitive edge through greater efficiency. But given the complexity of the field, many firms choose to outsource this challenge to experts, rather than handling it internally. Companies that specialize in helping other companies manage the supply chain—such as UPS—have done particularly well in today's market.

LO5 Pricing Objectives and Strategies: A High-Stakes Game

Pricing strategy clearly has a significant impact on the success of any organization. Price plays a key role in determining demand for your products, which directly influences a company's profitability. Most people, after all, have a limited amount of money and a practically infinite number of ways they could spend it. Price affects their spending choices at a more fundamental level than most other variables.

But ironically, price is perhaps the toughest variable for marketers to control. Both legal constraints and marketing intermediaries (distributors) play a role in determining the final price of most products. Marketers must

also consider costs, competitors, investors, taxes, and product strategies.

In today's frenetic environment, stable pricing is no longer the norm. Smart marketers continually evaluate and refine their pricing strategies to ensure that they meet their goals. Even the goals themselves may shift in response to the changing market. Common objectives and strategies include building profitability, boosting volume, matching the competition, and creating prestige.

Building Profitability

Since long-term profitability is a fundamental goal of most businesses, profitability targets are often the starting point for pricing strategies. Many firms express these goals in terms of either return on investment (ROI) or return on sales (ROS). Keep in mind that profitability is the positive difference between revenue (or total sales) and costs. Firms can boost profits by increasing prices or decreasing costs, since either strategy will lead to a greater spread between the two. Doing both, of course, is tricky, but companies that succeed—such as Toyota—typically dominate their markets.

Boosting Volume

Companies usually express volume goals in terms of market share—the percent of a market controlled by a company or a product. Amazon.com, for example, launched with volume objectives. Its goal was to capture as many "eyeballs" as possible, in hopes of later achieving profitability through programs that depend on volume, such as advertising on its site. A volume objective usually leads to one of the following strategies:

Penetration Pricing Penetration pricing, a strategy for pricing new products, aims to capture as much of the market as possible through rock-bottom prices. Each individual sale typically yields a tiny profit; the real money comes from the sheer volume of sales. A key benefit of this strategy is that it tends to discourage competitors, who may be scared off by the slim margins. But penetration pricing makes sense only in categories that don't have a significant group of consumers who would be

EXHIBIT 13.4 Modes of Transportation[4]

Mode	Percentage of U.S. Volume Based on 2007 Ton-Miles	Cost	Speed	On-Time Dependability	Flexibility in Handling	Frequency of Shipments	Availability
Rail	39.5%	Medium	Slow	Medium	Medium	Low	Extensive
Truck	28.6%	High	Fast	High	Medium	High	Most extensive
Ship	12.0%	Lowest	Slowest	Lowest	Highest	Lowest	Limited
Plane	0.3%	Highest	Fastest	Medium	Low	Medium	Medium
Pipeline	19.6%	Low	Slow	Highest	Lowest	Highest	Most limited

> ## If automobiles had followed the same development cycle as the computer, a Rolls-Royce would today cost $100, get a million miles per gallon, and explode once a year, killing everyone inside.
>
> *Robert Cringely,*
> *technology journalist*

willing to pay a premium price (otherwise, the marketer would be leaving money on the table). For obvious reasons, companies that use penetration pricing are usually focused on controlling costs. jetBlue is a key example. Its prices are often unbeatable, but it strictly controls costs by using a single kind of jet, optimizing turnaround times at the gate, and using many non-major airports.

Everyday-low-pricing Also known as "sustained discount pricing," **everyday-low-pricing (EDLP)** aims to achieve long-term profitability through volume. Walmart is clearly the king of EDLP with "Always low prices. *Always!*" But Costco uses the same strategy to attract a much more upscale audience. Costco cus-

tomers boast an average salary of more than $95,000: these people are seeking everyday discounts because they want to, not because they need to. The product mix—eclectic and upscale—reflects the customer base. (Costco sells $600 million of discounted fine wine a year, and 55,000 low-priced rotisserie chickens a day.) While Costco posted years of healthy, sustained growth, the firm ran into trouble at the end of 2008. As the recession tightened its grip, sales began to soften, especially in non-food categories, suggesting that EDLP may be most effective for less upscale products.[5]

High/Low Pricing The **high/low pricing** strategy tries to increase traffic in retail stores by special sales on a limited number of products, and higher everyday prices on others. Often used—and overused—in grocery stores, drug stores, and department stores, this strategy can alienate customers who feel cheated when a product they bought for full price goes on sale soon after. High/low pricing can also train consumers to buy only when products are on sale.

Loss Leader Pricing Closely related to high/low pricing, **loss leader pricing** means pricing a handful of items—or

Right Is Always Right, But Sometimes Left Is Wrong

Confused? This twisted bit of wisdom comes from UPS, whose drivers worldwide log about 2 billion miles a year. In a determined effort to go green and reduce costs, UPS company leaders determined that eliminating left-hand turns from delivery routes—and the sitting in traffic that accompanies them—could dramatically improve gas mileage, so they implemented computer-generated delivery routes that eliminate as many left turns as possible. According to UPS, the new system "shaved nearly 30 million miles off UPS's delivery routes, saved 3 million gallons of gas, and reduced emissions by 32,000 metric tons of CO2—the equivalent of removing 5,300 passenger cars off the road for an entire year." The resulting publicity has drawn attention to relatively minor driving changes that even small businesses and individuals can make to waste less gas and create less pollution. Other high-impact driving "tweaks" include driving under 60 mph, maintaining recommended air pressure in tires, and replacing clogged air filters. UPS vividly demonstrated that small, positive changes can pay huge dividends for business and the environment alike.[6]

© STEPHEN CHERNIN/GETTY IMAGES

skimming pricing A new product pricing strategy that aims to maximize profitability by offering new products at a premium price.

loss leaders—temporarily below cost to drive traffic. The retailer loses money on the loss leaders, but aims to make up the difference (and then some) on other purchases. To encourage other purchases, retailers typically place loss leaders at the back of the store, forcing customers to navigate past a tempting array of more profitable items. The loss leader strategy has been used effectively by producers, as well. Gillette, for instance, gives away some shavers practically for free, but reaps handsome profits as consumers buy replacement blades. Similarly, Microsoft has sold its Xbox systems at a loss in order to increase potential profits from high-margin video games. But the loss leader strategy can't be used everywhere, since a number of states have made loss leaders illegal for anticompetitive reasons.[7]

Matching the Competition

The key goal is to set prices based on what everyone else is doing. Usually, the idea is to wipe out price as a point of comparison, forcing customers to choose their product based on other factors. Examples include Coke and Pepsi, Honda and Toyota, Chevron and Mobil, Delta and United. But sometimes one or two competitors emerge that drive pricing for entire industries. Marlboro, for instance, leads the pack in terms of cigarette pricing, with other brands falling into place behind.

Creating Prestige

The core goal is to use price to send consumers a message about the high quality and exclusivity of a product—the higher the price, the better the product. Of course, this strategy works only if the product actually delivers top quality; otherwise, nobody would buy more than once (and those who do so would clearly spread the word). Rolex watches, Mont Blanc pens, and Bentley cars all use prestige pricing to reinforce their image.

Skimming Pricing This new product pricing strategy is a subset of prestige pricing. **Skimming pricing** involves offering new products at a premium price. The idea is to entice price-insensitive consumers—music fanatics, for example—to buy high when a product first enters the market. Once these customers have made their purchases, marketers will often introduce lower-priced versions of the same product to capture the bottom of the market. Apple used this strategy with its iPod, introducing its premium version for a hefty price tag. Once it had secured the big spenders, Apple introduced the lower-priced iPod Nanos and Shuffles with a powerful market response. But keep in mind that skimming works only when a product is tough to copy in terms of design, brand image, technology, or some other attribute. Otherwise, the fat margins will attract a host of competitors.

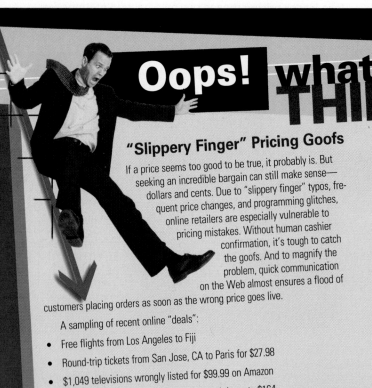

Oops! what were they THINKING?!

"Slippery Finger" Pricing Goofs

If a price seems too good to be true, it probably is. But seeking an incredible bargain can still make sense—dollars and cents. Due to "slippery finger" typos, frequent price changes, and programming glitches, online retailers are especially vulnerable to pricing mistakes. Without human cashier confirmation, it's tough to catch the goofs. And to magnify the problem, quick communication on the Web almost ensures a flood of customers placing orders as soon as the wrong price goes live.

A sampling of recent online "deals":

- Free flights from Los Angeles to Fiji
- Round-trip tickets from San Jose, CA to Paris for $27.98
- $1,049 televisions wrongly listed for $99.99 on Amazon
- $588 Hitachi monitors mistakenly marked down to $164

- $379 Axim X3i PDAs wrongly priced at $79 on Dell's site
- Five watches, worth $11,332, briefly sale priced at $0.0 (with free shipping) on Ashford.com

After the first few high-profile pricing disasters, online retailers have taken steps to protect themselves through specific disclaimers in their terms of use. And the courts have generally ruled that a company need not honor an offer if a reasonable person would recognize that it was a mistake.

But disclaimers and legal protections won't protect a retailer from customers who feel cheated. So companies that post pricing mistakes must choose between losing money by honoring offers or losing customer goodwill by canceling them—there simply isn't a winning option. But Travelocity—home of those unintended free tickets from Los Angeles to Fiji—has at least found a way to handle snafus with grace. Its Travelocity Guarantee program notes "If, say, we inadvertently advertise a fare that's just 'too good to be true,' like a free trip to Fiji, we'll work with you and our travel partners to make it up to you and find a solution that puts a smile on your face." So—happy shopping!

© PHOTODISC/GETTY IMAGES

LO6 Pricing in Practice: A Real-World Approach

At this point, you may be wondering about economic theory. How do concepts such as supply and demand and price elasticity affect pricing decisions?

Even though most marketers are familiar with economics, they often don't have the information they need to apply the theories to their specific pricing strategies. Collecting data for supply and demand curves is expensive and time consuming, which may be unrealistic for rapidly changing markets. From a real-world standpoint, most marketers consider market-based factors—especially customer expectations and competitive prices—but they rely on cost-based pricing. The key question is: what price levels will allow me to cover my costs and achieve my objectives?

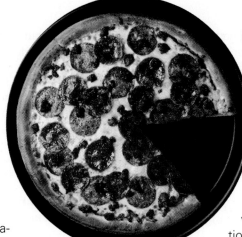

© C SQUARED STUDIOS/PHOTODISC/GETTY IMAGES

Breakeven Analysis

Breakeven analysis is a relatively simple process that determines the number of units a firm must sell to cover all costs. Sales above the breakeven point will generate a profit; sales below the breakeven point will lead to a loss. The actual equation looks like this:

$$\text{Breakeven Point (BP)} = \frac{\text{Total fixed costs (FC)}}{\text{Price/Unit (P)} - \text{Variable cost/unit (VC)}}$$

If you were selling pizza, for example, your fixed costs might be $300,000 per year. Fixed costs stay the same regardless of how many pizzas you sell. Specific fixed costs might include the mortgage, equipment payments, advertising, insurance, and taxes. Suppose your variable cost per pizza—the cost of the ingredients and the cost of wages for the baker—was $4 per pizza. If your customers would pay $10 per pizza, you could

breakeven analysis
The process of determining the number of units a firm must sell to cover all costs.

Hitting the Right Note with Music Pricing

Not so long ago, you just couldn't buy that hot new song without shelling out nearly twenty bucks for the whole CD—never mind whether or not you wanted all the other songs. The model worked great for the big record labels, which thrived through the 1990s. But all that changed in 2000, when Napster exploded onto the scene with free file-sharing.

In 2003, Steve Jobs found a new money-making model with the introduction of iTunes. But downloads of single tracks didn't come close to making up for plummeting album sales. And despite the success of iTunes, illegal file sharing continued to thrive.

In late 2007 British rock group Radiohead tried a different approach. The band released its new album online—on its own record label—and invited fans to pay whatever they thought the music was worth.

Worldwide, 62% of downloaders paid nothing for the album. But 38% of downloaders *did* pay, shelling out an average of $6.00 worldwide, and $8.05 in the United States. The band and fans alike celebrated this bold move as a success, but the "pay what you want" model hasn't taken hold in the industry overall. One reason may be that most artists might find it tough to convince 40% of their listeners to pay for their music.

In 2009, Apple introduced a new digital music pricing model that may favor record labels. They launched three pricing tiers: 69 cents for most songs, 99 cents for some songs, and $1.29 for the most popular songs.

The record labels are happy because this strategy breaks the $1 price barrier, which opens the door for bundling songs, videos, and other digital goodies together, at a price that might seem like a relative discount. In fact, record labels were so pleased that they granted Apple licensing for over-the-air downloads to the iPhone.

Looking forward, one thing seems sure: as more and more music consumers go digital, the music industry—labels and artists alike—will need to shift with them in order to survive.[8]

© LEIGH SCHINDLER/iSTOCKPHOTO.COM

profit margin The gap between the cost and the price of an item on a per product basis.

use the breakeven equation to determine how many pizzas you'd need to sell in a year so that your total sales were equal to your total expenses. Remember: a company that is breaking even is not making a profit.

Here's how the breakeven analysis would work for our pizza business:

$$BP = \frac{FC}{P - VC} = \frac{\$300,000}{\$10 - \$4} = \frac{\$300,000}{\$6} = 50,000 \text{ pizzas}$$

Over a one-year horizon, 50,000 pizzas would translate to about 303 pizzas per day. Is that reasonable? Could you do better? If so, fire up those ovens! If not, you have several choices, each with its own set of considerations:

- **Raise Prices:** How much do other pizzas in your neighborhood cost? Are your pizzas better in some way? Would potential customers be willing to pay more?

- **Decrease Variable Costs:** Could you use less expensive ingredients? Is it possible to hire less expensive help? How would these changes affect quality and sales?

- **Decrease Fixed Costs:** Should you choose a different location? Can you lease cheaper equipment? Would it make sense to advertise less often? How would these changes affect your business?

Clearly, there isn't one best strategy, but a breakeven analysis helps marketers get a sense of where they stand and the hurdles they need to clear before actually introducing a product.

Fixed Margin Pricing

Many firms determine upfront how much money they need to make for each item they sell. The **profit margin**—which is the gap between the cost and the price on a per product basis—can be expressed as a dollar amount, but more often is expressed as a percent. There are two key ways to determine margins.

1. **Cost-Based Pricing:** The most popular method of establishing a fixed margin starts with determining the actual cost of each product. The process is more complex than it may initially seem, since fixed costs must be allocated on a per product basis, and some variable costs fluctuate dramatically on a daily or weekly basis. But once the per product cost is set, the next step is to layer the margin on the cost to determine the price. Costco, for instance, has a strict policy that no branded item can be marked up by more than 14%, and no private-label item by more than 15%. Supermarkets, on the other hand, often mark up merchandise by 25%, and department stores by 50% or more. Margins in other industries can be much thinner.[9]

2. **Demand-Based Pricing:** This approach begins by determining what price consumers would be willing to pay. With that as a starting point, marketers subtract their desired margin, which yields their target costs. This method is more market focused than

AP IMAGES/CAROLYN KASTER

Go Figure!!

Classic economics—plus common sense—says that as prices dip, we'll buy more, and as prices rise we'll buy less. But in the real world, consumers aren't that rational. Our emotions trump our minds when marketers press pricing hot buttons—especially FREE and 99 CENTS.

Nearly 50 years ago, Dan Gold owned a liquor store that sold various wines for 79¢, 89¢, 99¢, and $1.49. But Gold recounted, "We always noticed that the 99¢ sold much better." So they changed all the prices of wine to 99¢. The results were fascinating: "The 79¢ sold better at 99¢, the 89¢ sold better at 99¢, and of course the $1.49 sold better at 99¢." In 1982, Gold used this insight to launch the successful 99 Cent Only chain. Economist Dan Ariely highlighted the power of FREE to subvert reason in his best-selling book, *Predictably Irrational.* Ariely and some colleagues experimented with chocolate—expensive, delicious Lindt truffles, and cheap, ordinary Hershey's Kisses. When they offered people a 15¢ Lindt truffle, or a 1¢ Hershey's Kiss, 73% bought the truffle. But when they dropped the price of both by a penny—so the truffle was 14¢ and the Hershey's Kiss was FREE—only 31% bought the truffle. Does this make sense? Clearly not! The chocolates were the same, but the word FREE lured people to take the chocolate they didn't *really* want. Go figure!

The good news, according to Ariely, is that consumers are irrational in predictable ways—with real-world lessons. In 2010, William Poundstone, in his book *Priceless: The Myth of Fair Value,* reviews the idea of "anchoring"—introducing products with such high prices that everything else looks affordable by comparison. Key takeaway: "be first to name a price in a negotiation, and don't worry about being overly reasonable."[10]

cost-based pricing, but it's also more risky, since profits depend on achieving those target costs. A number of Japanese companies, such as Sony, have been very successful with this approach, achieving extraordinarily efficient production.

Consumer Pricing Perceptions: The Strategic Wild Card

You just don't know if you've found the right price until you figure out how consumers perceive it. And those perceptions can sometimes defy the straightforward logic of dollars and cents. Two key considerations are price–quality relationships and odd pricing.

The link between price and perceived quality can be powerful. Picture yourself walking into a local sporting goods store, looking for a new snowboard. They have several models of your favorite brand, most priced at around $450. But then you notice another option—same brand, same style—marked down to $79. Would you buy it? If you were like most consumers, you'd probably assume that something was wrong with a board that cheap. Would you be right? It's hard to know. Sometimes the relationship between price and quality is clear and direct, but that is not always the case. Regardless, consumers will use price as an indicator of quality unless they have additional information to guide their decision. Savvy marketers factor this tendency into their pricing strategies.

Marketers also must weigh the pros and cons of **odd pricing**, or ending prices in numbers below even dollars and cents. A micro stereo system at Target, for instance, costs $99.99. Gasoline, of course, uses odd pricing to 99/100ths of a cent. But wouldn't round numbers be easier? Does that extra penny really make a difference? While the research is inconclusive, many marketers believe that jumping up to the

"next" round number sends a message that prices have hit a whole new level. In other words, they believe that the *perceived* gap between $99.99 and $100.00 is much greater than the *actual* gap of 1%. And it certainly makes sense from an intuitive standpoint.

Odd prices have also come to signal a bargain, which is often—but not always—a benefit for the marketer. For instance, a big-screen TV for $999.99 might seem like a great deal, while knee surgery for $4,999.99 sounds kind of scary—you'd probably rather that your doctor charge $5,000. Likewise, a fast food joint might charge $3.99 for its value meal, while fine restaurants almost always end their prices in zeros. Marketers can determine whether odd pricing would work for them by evaluating the strategy in light of the messages it sends to the target market.

odd pricing The practice of ending prices in numbers below even dollars and cents in order to create a perception of greater value.

The Big Picture

Distribution and pricing are two fundamental elements of the marketing mix. In today's frenzied global economy, marketers are seeking a competitive edge through distribution management. Creating a profitable presence in multiple retail venues requires constant focus throughout the organization. And managing the supply chain—how products move along the path from raw materials to the final consumer—plays a crucial role in controlling costs and providing great customer service. Integrating effective technology during the entire process can separate the winners from the losers.

Pricing objectives and strategies are also pivotal since they directly impact both profitability and product image. As the market changes, successful companies continually reevaluate and modify their approach, working hand in hand with their accountants.

Looking ahead, a growing number of companies will probably move toward collaboration rather than competition as they manage their supply chains. And pricing will likely become even more dynamic in response to the changing market.

WHAT ELSE? *RIP & REVIEW* CARDS IN THE BACK

© KARL WEATHERLY/PHOTODISC/GETTY IMAGES

14

MANAGEMENT, MOTIVATION, AND LEADERSHIP: BRINGING BUSINESS TO LIFE

LEARNING OBJECTIVES

After studying this chapter, you will be able to...

LO1 Discuss the role of management and its importance to organizational success

LO2 Explain key theories and current practices of motivation

LO3 Outline the categories of busi-

> ## A typical day at the office for me begins by asking: What is impossible that I'm going to do today?
>
> *Daniel Lamarre, president and COO, Cirque du Soleil*

LO1 Bringing Resources to Life

To grow and thrive every business needs resources—money, technology, materials—and an economic system that helps enterprise flourish. But those resources, or factors of production, are nothing without **management** to bring them to life. Managers provide vision and direction for their organizations, they decide how to use resources to achieve goals, and they inspire others—both inside and outside their companies—to follow their lead. By formal definition, managers achieve the goals of an organization through planning, organizing, leading, and controlling organizational resources including people, money, and time.

In simple terms, **planning** means figuring out where to go and how to get there. **Organizing** means determining a structure for both individual jobs and the overall organization. **Leading** means directing and motivating people to achieve organizational goals. And **controlling** means checking performance and making adjustments as needed. In today's chaotic, hyper-competitive business environment, managers face daunting challenges. But for the right people, management positions can provide an exhilarating—though sometimes exhausting—career.

As the business pace accelerates and the environment continues to morph—especially in the wake of economic turmoil—the role of management has radically transformed. The successful manager has changed from boss to coach, from disciplinarian to motivator, from dictator to team builder. But the bottom-line goal has remained the same: to create value for the organization.

Management Hierarchy: Levels of Responsibility

Most medium and large companies have three basic levels of management: **top management**, **middle management**, and **first-line (or supervisory) management**. The levels typically fall into a pyramid of sorts, with a small number of top managers and a larger number of supervisory managers. Responsibilities shift as managers move up the hierarchy, and the skills that they use must shift accordingly. Here are the differences between three key levels:

- **Top management** sets the overall direction of the firm. Top managers must articulate a vision, establish priorities, and allocate time, money, and other resources. Typical titles include chief executive officer (CEO), president, and vice president.

- **Middle management** manages the managers. (Say that three times!) Middle managers must communicate up and down the pyramid, and their primary contribution often involves coordinating teams and special projects with their peers from other departments. Typical titles include director, division head, and branch manager.

- **First-line management** manages the people who do the work. First-line managers must train, motivate, and evaluate nonmanagement employees, so they are heavily involved in day-to-day production issues. Typical titles include supervisor, foreman, and section leader.

Smaller companies usually don't have a hierarchy of management. Often the owner must act as the top, middle, and first-line manager, all rolled into one. This clearly requires enormous flexibility and well-developed management skills.

Management Skills: Having What It Takes to Get the Job Done

Given the turbulence of today's business world, managers must draw on a staggering range of skills to do their jobs efficiently and effectively.

management Achieving the goals of an organization through planning, organizing, leading, and controlling organizational resources including people, money, and time.

planning Determining organizational goals and action plans for how to achieve those goals.

organizing Determining a structure for both individual jobs and the overall organization.

leading Directing and motivating people to achieve organizational goals.

controlling Checking performance and making adjustments as needed.

top management Managers who set the overall direction of the firm, articulating a vision, establishing priorities, and allocating time, money, and other resources.

middle management Managers who supervise lower-level managers and report to a higher-level manager.

first-line management Managers who directly supervise nonmanagement employees.

technical skills Expertise in a specific functional area or department.

human skills The ability to work effectively with and through other people in a range of different relationships.

conceptual skills The ability to grasp a big-picture view of the overall organization, the relationship between its various parts, and its fit in the broader competitive environment.

Maslow's hierarchy of needs theory A motivation theory that suggests that human needs fall into a hierarchy and that as each need is met, people become motivated to meet the next highest need in the pyramid.

Most of these abilities cluster into three broad categories: technical skills, human skills, and conceptual skills.

- **Technical Skills: Technical skills** refer to expertise in a specific functional area or department. Keep in mind that technical skills don't necessarily relate to technology. People can have technical skills—or specific expertise—in virtually any field, from sales, to copywriting, to accounting, to airplane repair, to computer programming.

- **Human Skills: Human skills** refer to the ability to work with and through other people in a range of different relationships. Human skills include communication, leadership, coaching, empathy, and team building. A manager with strong human skills can typically mobilize support for initiatives and find win–win solutions for conflicts.

- **Conceptual Skills: Conceptual skills** refer to the ability to grasp a big-picture view of the overall organization and the relationship between its various parts. Conceptual skills also help managers understand how their company fits into the broader competitive environment. Managers with strong conceptual skills typically excel at strategic planning.

All three categories of skill are essential for management success. But their importance varies according to the level of the manager. Front-line managers must have a high degree of technical skills, which help them hire, train, and evaluate employees; avoid mistakes; and ensure high-quality production. Middle-level managers need an especially high level of human skills. They typically act as the bridge between departments, coordinating people and projects that sometimes have mismatched priorities. Top-level managers must demonstrate excellent conceptual skills in order to formulate a vision, interpret marketplace trends, and plan for the future. To move up in an organization, managers must constantly learn and grow, nurturing skills that reflect their new tasks.

Across all three skill sets, critical thinking and decision-making abilities have become increasingly important. Critical thinking helps managers find value even in an overload of information, while decision-making skills help them respond wisely and rapidly, with an unwavering focus on customer satisfaction.

Managers who expect to grow in the company hierarchy must expect to foster new skills. Too often, workers get promotions because of great technical skills—e.g., the top salesperson lands the sales manager slot—but they struggle to move further because they don't fully develop their human and conceptual skills.

LO2 Motivation: Lighting the Fire

Standout managers motivate others to reach for their best selves—to accomplish more than they ever thought possible. Motivated workers tend to feel great about their jobs, and workers who feel great tend to produce more. But the thinking about *how* to motivate workers has changed dramatically over time. In the

The Big Mouth Boss

Anyone who has watched Steve Carell as the self-proclaimed "World's Best Boss" in *The Office*, has likely wondered how many blowhard bosses are raking in the big bucks by just faking it. The answer is: more than you may think. A recent study in the *Journal of Personality and Social Psychology* revealed that we rate those who speak up more often to be better leaders AND to be more competent—even when the proof of performance shows otherwise. In the study, volunteers—who offered their SAT math scores in advance to researchers—competed on teams to solve computational problems. Rating each other after the exercise, participants gave the highest marks for leadership to those who offered the most answers—even though the most vocal participants did *not* give the most correct answers and did *not* have the highest math SAT scores. So, in the workplace, don't hesitate to put in your two cents, and you might end up raking in the big bucks yourself.[1]

WORLD'S BEST BOSS

© STOCKBYTE/GETTY IMAGES

Oops! what were they THINKING?!

© PHOTODISC/GETTY IMAGES

Bad Decisions, Big Impacts

Every day, managers around the globe make high-stakes decisions, from expanding overseas, to introducing new products, to closing factories. The great decisions have become the stuff of legends, shaping the business world as we know it today. Bad choices also abound, although we tend to hear a lot less about them. Consider these five business decisions that made history for their silliness:

- Faced with the opportunity to buy rights to the telephone in 1876, Western Union, the telegraph behemoth, rejected the newfangled device: "This 'telephone' has too many shortcomings to be seriously considered as a means of communication. The device is inherently of no value to us."

- In 1899 two young attorneys approached Asa Chandler—owner of the briskly selling new fountain drink Coca-Cola—with an innovative proposal to bottle the beverage. Chandler sold them exclusive rights to bottle Coke across most of the United States for the grand sum of $1. Oops.

- Reviewing technology at the dawn of the television age, *The New York Times*—a bellwether for key trends in business and otherwise—decided that TV just wasn't happening: "The problem with television is that people must keep their eyes glued to a screen; the average American family hasn't time for it." Imagine their surprise a few short years later…

- Gordon Moore of Intel sheepishly admits to a major gaffe: "In the mid-1970s, someone came to me with an idea for what was basically the PC. I personally didn't see anything useful in it, so we never gave it another thought."

- Mike Smith, one of the executives in charge of evaluating new talent for the London office of Decca Records, rejected the Beatles in 1962 with the now infamous line: "Groups are out; four-piece groups with guitars particularly are finished." Not so much…

With the help of hindsight, momentous decisions may seem almost inevitable. But these bloopers clearly show that in the fog of the moment, the right choice can be anything but clear.

---

early 1900s, key management thinkers focused on efficiency and productivity, dictating precisely how workers should do each element of their jobs. But more recent research suggests that people's thoughts and feelings play a vital role in motivation, which leads to a range of new theories.

Theories of Motivation

Maslow's Hierarchy of Needs Theory Noted psychologist Abraham Maslow theorized that people are motivated to satisfy only unmet needs. He proposed a hierarchy of human needs—from basic to abstract—suggesting that as each need is met, people become motivated to meet the next highest need in the pyramid. Maslow's five specific needs are shown in Exhibit 14.1. While he didn't develop his theory based on the workplace, Maslow's ideas can illuminate the needs behind motivation at work.

From a workplace perspective, the idea that people are motivated only by unmet needs clearly holds true for the first two levels of the hierarchy. Finding a job that pays the bills, for instance, is the primary motivator for most people who don't have any job at all. People who have a job, but no healthcare, would find health insurance much more motivating than, say, a company picnic geared toward meeting social needs.

EXHIBIT 14.1 Maslow's Hierarchy of Needs and the Workplace

Maslow's Need	Description	Workplace Examples
Physiological	Need for basic survival—food, water, clothing, and shelter	A job with enough pay to buy the basics
Safety	Need to feel secure—free of harm and free of fear	Safety equipment, healthcare plans, retirement plans, job security
Social (Belonging)	Need to feel connected to others—accepted by family and friends	Teamwork, positive corporate culture, company lunchroom
Esteem	Need for self-respect and respect from others—recognition and status	Acknowledgment, promotions, perks
Self-Actualization	Need for fulfillment, the need to realize one's fullest potential	Challenging, creative jobs; work that ties to a greater good

But once physiological and safety needs are met, the other needs are motivating to different degrees in different people. An employee with strong social connections outside work, for instance, might be more motivated by a promotion that meets esteem needs than by a company outing that meets social needs. A number of firms actually use self-actualization needs as a starting point for motivating employees, by creating a mission statement that communicates the importance of the work. Google, for instance, inspires employees through its lofty purpose: to organize the world's information and make it universally accessible and useful.

Theory X and Theory Y

Psychologist Douglas McGregor, one of Maslow's students, studied workplace motivation from a different angle. He proposed that management attitudes toward workers would directly affect worker motivation. His research suggested that management attitudes fall into two opposing categories, which he called **Theory X and Theory Y**, described in Exhibit 14.2.

McGregor proposed that managers should employ Theory Y assumptions in order to capitalize on the imagination and intelligence of every worker. In American business today, some organizations use a Theory X approach, but a growing number have begun to at least experiment with Theory Y, tapping into a rich pool of employee input.

Job Enrichment A number of researchers have focused on creating jobs with more meaningful content, under the assumption that challenging, creative work will motivate employees to give their best effort. **Job enrichment** typically includes the following factors:

1. **Skill Variety**: Workers can use a range of different skills.

2. **Task Identity**: Workers do complete tasks with clear beginnings and endings.

3. **Task Significance**: Workers understand the impact of the task on others.

4. **Autonomy**: Workers have freedom and authority regarding their jobs.

5. **Feedback**: Workers receive clear, frequent information about their performance.

> # Leadership is the art of getting someone else to do something you want done because he wants to do it.
> *Dwight D. Eisenhower*

Richard Branson, maverick founder of the Virgin Group, relies on job enrichment—especially autonomy and feedback—to keep people motivated at his 350-company empire (which includes a startling range of firms, such as Virgin Atlantic Airlines, Virgin Music, Virgin mobile phones, and Virgin Galactic space travel). Branson gives his managers a stake in their companies and then tells them "to run it as if it's their own." He says, "I intervene as little as possible. Give them that, and they will give everything back." Due in large part to Branson's motivational approach, the Virgin workforce is fully engaged with the company, contributing to its remarkable long-term success.[2]

Expectancy Theory Usually attributed to researcher Victor Vroom, **expectancy theory** deals with the relationship among individual effort, individual performance, and

EXHIBIT 14.2 Theory X and Theory Y

Theory X Assumptions about Workers	Theory Y Assumptions about Workers
• Workers dislike work and will do everything they can to avoid it.	• Work is as natural as play or rest—workers do not inherently dislike it.
• Fear is motivating—coercion and threats are vital to get people to work toward company goals.	• Different rewards can be motivating—people can exercise self-direction and self-control to meet company goals.
	• People can accept and even seek responsibility.
• People prefer to be directed, avoiding responsibility and seeking security.	• The capacity for imagination, creativity, and ingenuity is widely distributed in the population.
	• The intellectual capacity of the average worker is underutilized in the workplace.

individual reward. The key concept is that a worker will be motivated if he or she believes that effort will lead to performance, and performance will lead to a meaningful reward.

Effort ➠ Performance ➠ Reward

The theory suggests that if any link in the chain is broken, the employee will not be motivated.

Retailer Hot Topic has done a great job implementing every step of the equation, especially the link between effort and performance. A Hot Topic employee describes the connection, saying, "I've worked for HT for five years, and the best thing I've learned is that if you work hard enough and dedicate enough of yourself to something, you can achieve your goals!" Perhaps it's no coincidence that Hot Topic was one of the few retail chains that continued to perform well, even as the recession tightened its grip in late 2008 and early 2009.[3]

Motivated employees have played a central role in Hot Topic's strong performance.

© RICHARD LEVINE/ALAMY

Equity Theory Pioneered by J. Stacy Adams, **equity theory** proposes that perceptions of fairness directly affect worker motivation. The key idea is that people won't be motivated if they believe that the relationship between what they contribute and what they earn is different from the relationship between what others contribute and what others earn. For example, if you worked ten-hour days, and earned less than the guy in the next cube who works seven-hour days, you'd probably think it was pretty unfair. To restore a sense of balance, you might:

- Demand a raise
- Start working seven-hour days
- Convince yourself that the other guy is about to be fired

- Look for another job

The response to perceived inequity almost always involves trying to change the system, changing your own work habits, distorting your perceptions, or leaving the company.

But keep in mind that equity theory is based on perceptions, which are not always on the mark. People are all too prone to overestimate their own contributions, which throws perceived equity out of balance. The best way to combat equity issues is through clear, open communication from management.[4]

Motivation Today

Companies today use a range of approaches to motivation, although several key themes have emerged. Most firms no longer seek to make their employees happy; instead, they want their workers to be productive and engaged. Yet for employees, work is about more than just productivity. University of Michigan business school professor David Ulrich points out that even in today's hyper-competitive environment, "people still want to find meaning in their work and in the institutions that employ them."[5]

A growing emphasis on corporate culture has captured the best of both worlds for companies that do it right. A distinctive, positive culture tends to create productive employees who are deeply attached to their work and their companies. Software giant SAS, for instance, *Fortune* magazine's "Best Company to Work for in 2010," earned its number-one slot due to "trust between our employees and the company," which becomes clear via unlimited sick days, a medical center staffed by four physicians and ten nurse practitioners (at no cost to employees), a free 66,000-square-foot fitness center and natatorium, a lending library, and a summer camp for children. Not surprisingly, turnover at SAS is the industry's lowest at 2%, and the firm is highly profitable.

Building contractor DPR Construction pays employees up to $20,000 for successfully recommending people for jobs with the company. Atlantic Health gives new hires 18, 23, or 28 vacation days depending on their positions. SC Johnson & Son offers onsite concierge service that will mail your packages, send flowers to loved ones, pick up and deliver groceries, find the best deals on car insurance, change the oil in your car, and even stand in line to wait for your concert tickets. And computer chipmaker Intel offers all full-time employees in the United States and Canada an eight-week paid sabbatical every seven years.[6]

Finally, a growing number of businesses have expanded their range of employee incentives beyond just cash. While money certainly matters, *Fortune*

equity theory A motivation theory that proposes that perceptions of fairness directly affect worker motivation.

strategic planning
High-level, long-term planning that establishes a vision for the company, defines long-term objectives and priorities, determines broad action steps, and allocates resources.

tactical planning
More specific, shorter-term planning that applies strategic plans to specific functional areas.

operational planning Very specific, short-term planning that applies tactical plans to daily, weekly, and monthly operations.

magazine points out that "telling employees they're doing a great job costs nothing but counts big." Employee training is a noncash motivational tactic gaining momentum across the economy in response to the growing array of complex skills needed by the workforce. The emphasis on training and education is especially motivating given that more and more employees identify themselves based on their field of expertise rather than their organization.[7]

Successful businesses ensure that their workforce has up-to-date training in an array of skills.

© TOMMLI/ISTOCKPHOTO.COM

LO3 Planning: Figuring Out Where to Go and How to Get There

The planning function—figuring out where to go and how to get there—is the core of effective management. A survey in *The Wall Street Journal* found that 80% of executives identify planning as their most valuable management tool. But even though planning is critical, it's also highly risky in light of cutthroat competition, rapid change, and economic uncertainty. The best plans keep the organization on track, without sacrificing flexibility and responsiveness; they incorporate ways to respond to change both inside and outside the organization.[8]

Although all managers engage in planning, the scope of the process changes according to the manager's position as shown in the table below. Top-level managers focus on **strategic planning**. They establish a vision for the company, define long-term objectives and priorities, determine broad action steps, and allocate resources. Middle managers focus on **tactical planning**, or applying the strategic plan to their specific areas of responsibility. And first-line managers focus on **operational planning**, or applying the tactical plans to daily, weekly, and monthly operations. Successful firms often encourage a flow of feedback up and down the organization to ensure that all key plans are sound and that all key players "buy in." Some typical planning decisions and timeframes are shown in Exhibit 14.3.

EXHIBIT 14.3 Managerial Planning

Type of Planning	Management Level	Scope of Planning	Examples of Planning Questions and Concerns
Strategic Planning	Senior management	Typically five-year timeframe	Should we acquire a new company?
			Should we begin manufacturing in China?
			Should we take our company public?
Tactical Planning	Middle management	Typically one-year timeframe	Should we invest in new production equipment?
			Should we spend more time servicing each customer?
			Should we spend fewer ad dollars on TV and more on the Web?
Operational Planning	First-line management	Daily, weekly, and monthly timeframe	How should we schedule employees this week?
			When should we schedule delivery for each batch of product?
			How should customer service people answer the phones?

A fourth category of planning has gained new prominence in the last decade: **contingency planning**, or planning for unexpected events. Senior management usually spearheads contingency planning, but with input from the other levels of management. Contingency plans consider what might go wrong—both inside the business and with the outside environment—and develop responses. Potential issues include:

- How should we respond if our competitors start a price war?
- What should we do if the government regulates our industry?
- How can we restart our business if a natural disaster destroys our plant?
- How will we evacuate employees if terrorists strike our headquarters?

Clearly, anticipating every potential problem is impossible (and impractical!). Instead, effective contingency plans tend to focus only on the issues that are most probable, most potentially harmful, or both (see Exhibit 14.4).

EXHIBIT 14.4 Contingency planning paradigm
Businesses tend to focus their contingency plans on issues that are most probable *and* most potentially harmful.

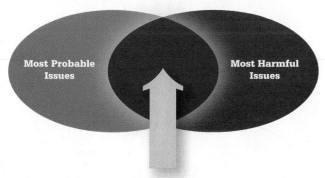

Most Probable Issues

Most Harmful Issues

Focus Area for Contingency Plans

For example, a southern California amusement park might concentrate its contingency plans on earthquake response, while a national airline might focus its plans on responding to a pilots' strike.

Strategic Planning: Setting the Agenda

Strategic planning is the most fundamental part of the planning process, since all other plans—and most major management decisions—stem from the strategic plan. The strategic planning process typically includes these steps:

1. Define the mission of the organization.
2. Evaluate the organization's competitive position.
3. Set goals for the organization.
4. Create strategies for competitive differentiation.
5. Implement strategies.
6. Evaluate results and incorporate lessons learned.

Defining Your Mission The mission of an organization articulates its essential reason for being. The **mission** defines the organization's purpose, values, and core goals, providing the framework for all other plans (see Exhibit 14.5). Most large companies present their mission as a simple, vivid, compelling statement that everyone involved with the company—from the janitor to the CEO, from customers to investors—can easily understand. Mission statements tend to vary in their length, their language, and even their names, but they share a common goal: to provide a clear, long-term focus for the organization.

Evaluating Your Competitive Position Strategy means nothing in a vacuum—every firm must plan in

contingency planning Planning for unexpected events, usually involving a range of scenarios and assumptions that differ from the assumptions behind the core plans.

mission The definition of an organization's purpose, values, and core goals, which provides the framework for all other plans.

EXHIBIT 14.5 Examples of Mission Statements

Company	Mission Statement
House of Blues	To create a profitable, principled, global entertainment company
	To celebrate the diversity and brotherhood of world culture
	To promote racial and spiritual harmony through love, peace, truth, righteousness, and non-violence
Cold Stone Creamery	We will make people happy around the world by selling the highest quality, most creative ice cream experience with passion, excellence, and innovation.
Google	Google's mission is to organize the world's information and make it universally accessible and useful.

SWOT analysis A strategic planning tool that helps management evaluate an organization in terms of internal strengths and weakness, and external opportunities and threats.

the context of the marketplace. Many companies use a **SWOT analysis** (strengths, weaknesses, opportunities, and threats) to evaluate where they stand relative to the competition. Strengths and weaknesses are internal to the organization, and they include factors that would either build up or drag down the firm's performance. Opportunities and threats are external, and they include factors that would affect the company's performance, but are typically out of the company's control. Exhibit 14.6 offers some examples.

Initial information about internal strengths and weaknesses usually comes from careful analysis of internal reports on topics such as budget and profitability. But to better understand strengths and weaknesses, executives should actively seek firsthand information—on a personal basis—from key people throughout the company, from front-line workers to the board of directors.

Gathering information about external opportunities and threats can be more complex, since these areas include

both current and potential issues (which can be tough to predict). Information about external factors can come from many different sources, including the news, government reports, customers, and competitors.

EXHIBIT 14.6 SWOT Analysis

Potential internal strengths:	Potential external opportunities:
• Premium brand name • Proven management team • Lower costs/higher margins	• Higher consumer demand • Complacent competitors • Growth in foreign markets
Potential internal weaknesses:	Potential external threats:
• Low employee satisfaction • Inadequate financial resources • Poor location	• A powerful new competitor • A deep recession • New government regulations

Attitude and Expectations

Generation Y—which includes the 76 million kids born between 1978 and 1998—is changing the face of the workforce. These self-confident, outspoken young people have posed a new set of challenges for managers across the economy. A quick profile of Generation Y—also known as millennials, echo-boomers, and Gen F (for Facebook)—highlights their key characteristics. As you read, keep in mind that no general overview can clearly describe each member of Generation Y. Yet chances are strong that you recognize at least parts of yourself in this profile. Companies that understand you and your peers—and figure out how to harness your talents—will find themselves with a sharp competitive edge in the years to come.

© IMAGE SOURCE BLACK/JUPITERIMAGES

- **Goal Driven**: Gen Yers expect to perform for their rewards. But they tend to find smaller, short-term goals much more motivating than long-term goals. The reason: a week in their fast-paced world is more like a year was for their parents.
- **NOW Focused**: Gen Yers often look for instant gratification. They typically expect to make an impact in their companies right away, and they are less willing to "pay dues" or "suck up" to people they don't respect in order to make it happen.
- **Change Oriented**: Gen Yers actively embrace change and excitement. Many anticipate—even hope—to change jobs frequently. They don't share the expectation of long-term employment that disillusioned so many of their parents.
- **Tech Savvy**: Gen Yers are masters of the Internet and the iPod. They often expect top technology in the workplace, and they use virtually all of it (often at the same time!) to boost their performance.
- **Diverse**: Gen Y is among the most diverse demographic groups—one in three is a minority—and most don't believe that their ethnicity defines their character. Many were born in other countries and speak multiple languages fluently.
- **Idealistic**: Gen Yers grew up in a scary world, marked by violence in their own backyards. Yet they remain convinced that they can make a positive difference, seeking solutions through a refreshing commitment to volunteerism.
- **Fulfillment Focused**: Gen Yers tend to deeply value their families and their personal lives. They fully expect to achieve their lofty career goals without sacrificing time for themselves and the people they care about.[9]

Setting Your Goals **Strategic goals** represent concrete benchmarks that managers can use to measure performance in each key area of the organization. They must fit the firm's mission and tie directly to its competitive position. The three most effective goals are:

1. **Specific and Measurable**: Whenever possible, managers should define goals in clear numerical terms that everyone understands.

2. **Tied to a Timeframe**: To create meaning and urgency, goals should be linked to a specific deadline.

3. **Realistic but Challenging**: Goals that make people stretch can motivate exceptional performance.

Exhibit 14.7 offers examples of how weak goals can transform into powerful goals.

EXHIBIT 14.7 Goal Setting: Getting It Right

Weak Goal	Powerful Goal
Improve customer satisfaction.	Increase average customer satisfaction ratings to 4.5 by the end of the fiscal year.
Reduce employee turnover.	Retain 90% of new employees for two or more years.
Increase market share.	Become the #1 or #2 brand in each market where we compete by the end of 2012.

Creating Your Strategies **Strategies** are action plans that help the organization achieve its goals by forging the best fit between the firm and the environment. The underlying aim, of course, is to create a significant advantage versus the competition. Sources of competitive advantage vary, ranging from better product quality, to better technology, to more motivated employees. The most successful companies build their advantage across several fronts. Southwest Airlines, for example, has a more motivated workforce and a lower cost structure. Nordstrom has better customer service and higher product quality. And Procter & Gamble has more innovative new products and strong core brands.

The specifics of strategy differ by industry and by company, but all strategies represent a roadmap. The SWOT analysis determines the starting point, and the objectives signify the immediate destination. Since speed matters, you must begin mapping the next leg of the journey even before you arrive.

For added complexity, you never know—given the turbulent environment—when you might hit roadblocks. This means that strategies must be dynamic and flexible. Top managers have responded to this challenge by encouraging front-line managers to participate in the process more than ever before.

Implementing Your Strategies Implementation should happen largely through tactical planning. Middle managers in each key area of the company must develop plans to carry out core strategies in their area. If the strategic plan, for example, calls for more new products, marketing would need to generate ideas, finance would need to find funding, and sales would need to prepare key accounts. And all of these steps would require tactical planning.

Evaluating Your Results and Incorporating Lessons Learned Evaluation of results should be a continual process, handled by managers at every level as part of their controlling function, covered further in this chapter. But for evaluation to be meaningful, the lessons learned must be analyzed objectively and factored back into the next planning cycle.

LO4 Organizing: Fitting Together the Puzzle Pieces

The organizing function of management means creating a logical structure for people, their jobs, and their patterns of interaction. And clearly, the pieces can fit together in a number of different ways. In choosing the right structure for a specific company, management typically considers many factors, including the goals and strategies of the firm, its products, its use of technology, its size, and the structure of its competitors. Given the potential for rapid change in each of these factors, smart companies continually reexamine their structure and make changes whenever necessary. Microsoft, for instance, restructures its organization every couple of years as new challenges emerge.

To be effective, reorganizations—and their purpose—must be clear to employees throughout the company. In order to help employees understand how they and their jobs fit within the broader organization, most firms issue an **organization chart**, or a visual

strategic goals Concrete benchmarks that managers can use to measure performance in each key area of the organization.

strategies Action plans that help the organization achieve its goals by forging the best fit between the firm and the environment.

organization chart A visual representation of the company's formal structure.

degree of centralization The extent to which decision-making power is held by a small number of people at the top of the organization.

representation of the company's formal structure, as shown in Exhibit 14.8. Looking at the company represented by Exhibit 14.8, you would probably assume that the vice president of production has more power than a regular employee in the marketing department. And in terms of formal power, you'd be absolutely right. But if the marketing employee babysits on the weekend for the president's granddaughter, the balance of power may actually be a bit different than it seems. Make no mistake: the formal structure matters. But knowing how power flows on an informal basis could dramatically increase your effectiveness as well, by helping you target your ideas to the right managers and marshal the support of the most influential employees.

Key Organizing Considerations

In developing the organizational structure, management must make decisions about the degree of centralization, the span of management control, and the type of departmentalization that makes the most sense at any given time.

Centralization The **degree of centralization** relates directly to the source of power and control. In central-

EXHIBIT 14.8 Sample Organization Chart

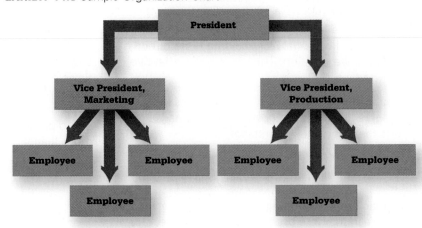

ized companies, a small number of people at the top of the organization have the power to make decisions. This approach is simple and efficient, and the result tends to be a strong corporate image and a uniform customer approach across the front lines. But the downside is that centralized companies typically respond more slowly to customer needs and have lower employee morale. The trade-off may be worthwhile in steady, stable markets, but those are rare.

Faced with today's turbulent environment, most firms are moving toward greater decentralization, pushing power to the lower levels of the organization. Employees with the power to make decisions can respond to customer needs more quickly and effectively.

Green to the Core

When most people think of green business, they envision the flood of environmentally friendly products that have poured into the market in the last five years. But outdoor clothing company Patagonia has been leading the movement since its inception nearly 40 years ago. Yvon Chouinard, the quirky 70+-year-old founder, manages every facet of his firm according to its mission: *Make the best product, cause no unnecessary harm, and use business to inspire and implement solutions to the environmental crisis.*

Chouinard and his team hire people who appreciate the outdoors and give them ample opportunity to enjoy it, providing flextime, for instance, when the surf is up. And Chouinard's production methods tread lightly on the environment. Examples: switching to organic cotton and using recycled plastic soft-drink bottles as raw materials for pricey jackets.

So far, it works—both for the world and for the bottom line. Chouinard claims that every time Patagonia has elected to do the right thing for the environment—even when it costs twice as much—it's turned out to be more profitable. This alone may inspire other firms to follow his example. Chouinard is particularly tickled that Walmart has taken notice: "I'm blown away by Walmart. If Walmart does one-tenth of what they say they're going to do, it will be incredible."

As the green business movement continues to gain momentum, Chouinard gets closer and closer to fulfilling the core of Patagonia's mission.[10]

© JEAN-MARC GIBOUX/LIAISON AGENCY/GETTY IMAGES

They can also capitalize on opportunities that would likely vaporize in the time it would take to get permission to act. But for decentralization to work, every employee must fully understand the firm's mission, goals, and strategy; otherwise, the company could develop a fragmented image, which would undermine its long-term strength. Also, active communication across departments is essential so that all employees can benefit from innovations in other parts of the organization.

Span of Control The **span of control**, or span of management, refers to the number of people that a manager supervises. There is no ideal number for every manager. The "right" span of control varies based on the abilities of both the manager and the subordinates, the nature of the work being done, the location of the employees, and the need for planning and coordination. Across industries the general trend has moved toward wider spans of control as a growing number of companies have pruned layers of middle management to the bare minimum.

Departmentalization Departmentalization means breaking workers into logical groups. A number of different options make sense, depending on the organization.

- **Functional:** Dividing employees into groups based on area of expertise, such as marketing, finance, and engineering, tends to be efficient and easy to coordinate. For those reasons it works especially well for small to medium-sized firms.

- **Product:** Dividing employees into groups based on the products that a company offers helps workers develop expertise about products that often results in especially strong customer relations.

- **Customer:** Dividing employees into groups based on the customers that a company serves helps companies focus on the needs of specific customer groups. Many companies have separate departments for meeting the needs of business and consumer users. This approach is related to product departmentalization.

- **Geographical:** Dividing employees into groups based on where

customers are located can help different departments better serve specific regions within one country. Similarly, many international firms create a separate department for each different country they serve.

- **Process:** Dividing into groups based on what type of work employees do is common in manufacturing, where management may divide departments by processes such as cutting, dyeing, and sewing.

As companies get larger, they usually adopt several different types of departmentalization at different levels of the organization. This approach, shown in Exhibit 14.9 on the following page, is called "hybrid departmentalization."

Organization Models

Company structures tend to follow one of three different patterns: line organizations, line-and-staff organizations, and matrix organizations. But these organizational models are not mutually exclusive. In fact, many management teams build their structure using elements of each model at different levels of the organization.

Line Organizations A **line organization** typically has a clear, simple chain of command from top to bottom. Each person is directly accountable to the person immediately above, which means quick decision making and no fuzziness about who is responsible for what. The downside is a lack of specialists to provide advice or support for line managers. This approach tends to work well for small businesses, but for medium-sized and large companies the result can be inflexibility, too much paperwork, and even incompetence since experts aren't available to give their input into key decisions.

Line-and-Staff Organizations A **line-and-staff organization** incorporates the benefits of a line organization

span of control Span of management; refers to the number of people that a manager supervises.

departmentalization The division of workers into logical groups.

line organizations Organizations with a clear, simple chain of command from top to bottom.

line-and-staff organizations Organizations with line managers forming the primary chain of authority in the company, and staff departments working alongside line departments.

line managers Managers who supervise the functions that contribute directly to profitability: production and marketing.

staff managers Managers who supervise the functions that provide advice and assistance to the line departments.

matrix organizations Organizations with a flexible structure that brings together specialists from different areas of the company to work on individual projects on a temporary basis.

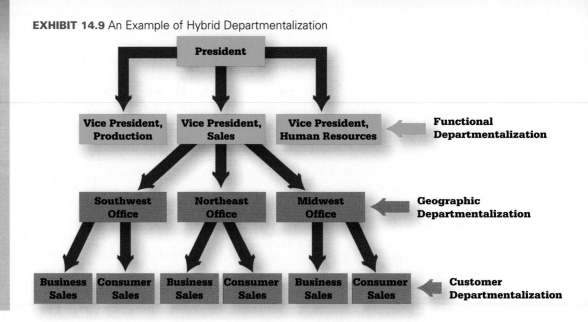

EXHIBIT 14.9 An Example of Hybrid Departmentalization

President

Vice President, Production — Vice President, Sales — Vice President, Human Resources ← **Functional Departmentalization**

Southwest Office — Northeast Office — Midwest Office ← **Geographic Departmentalization**

Business Sales | Consumer Sales | Business Sales | Consumer Sales | Business Sales | Consumer Sales ← **Customer Departmentalization**

without all the drawbacks. **Line managers** supervise the functions that contribute directly to profitability: production and marketing. **Staff managers**, on the other hand, supervise the functions that provide advice and assistance to the line departments. Examples include legal, accounting, and human resources. In a line-and-staff organization, the line managers form the primary chain of authority in the company. Staff departments work alongside line departments, but there is no direct reporting relationship (except at the top of the company). Since staff people don't report to line people, their authority comes from their know-how. This approach, which overlays fast decision making with additional expertise, tends to work well for medium-sized and large companies. But in some firms, the staff departments gain so much power that they become dictatorial, imposing unreasonable limitations on the rest of the company.

Matrix Organizations **Matrix organizations** build on the line-and-staff approach by adding a lot more flexibility. A matrix structure brings together specialists from different areas of the company to work on individual projects on a temporary basis. A new product development team, for instance, might include representatives from sales, engineering, finance, purchasing, and advertising. For the course of the project, each specialist reports to the project manager and to the head of his or her own department (e.g., the vice president of marketing). The matrix approach has been particularly popular in the high-tech and aerospace industries.

The matrix structure offers several key advantages. It encourages teamwork and communication across the organization. It offers flexibility in deploying key people. It lends itself to innovative solutions. And not surprisingly—when managed well—the matrix structure creates a higher level of motivation and satisfaction for employees. But these advantages have a clear flip side. The need for constant communication can bog down a company in too many meetings. The steady state of flux can be overwhelming for both managers and employees. And having two bosses can cause conflict and stress for everyone.

LO5 Leadership: Directing and Inspiring

While most people easily recognize a great leader, defining the qualities of leaders can be more complex, since successful leaders have a staggering range of personalities, characteristics, and backgrounds. Most researchers agree that true leaders are trustworthy, visionary, and inspiring. After all, we don't follow people who don't know where they're going, and we definitely don't follow people we don't trust. Other key leadership traits include empathy, courage, creativity, intelligence, and fairness.

{ **Management is doing things right; leadership is doing the right things.**

Peter Drucker, management researcher, writer, and speaker }

Leadership Style

How a leader uses power defines his or her leadership style. While the range of specific styles is huge, most seem to cluster into three broad categories: autocratic, democratic, and free-rein. The categories fall along a continuum of power, with the manager at one end and the employees at the other, as shown in Exhibit 14.10.

EXHIBIT 14.10 The Continuum of Leadership and Power

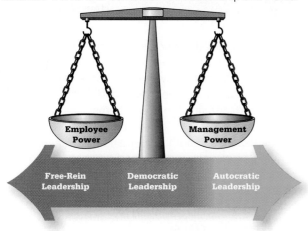

Employee Power — Management Power

Free-Rein Leadership — Democratic Leadership — Autocratic Leadership

Autocratic leaders hoard decision-making power for themselves, and they typically issue orders without consulting their followers. **Democratic leaders** share power with their followers. Even though they still make final decisions, they typically solicit and incorporate input from their followers. **Free-rein leaders** set objectives for their followers but give them freedom to choose how they accomplish those goals.

Interestingly, the most effective leaders don't use just one approach. They tend to shift their leadership style, depending on the followers and the situation. When a quick decision is paramount, autocratic leadership may make the most sense. An army officer, for example, probably shouldn't take a vote on whether to storm a hill in the middle of a firefight. But when creativity is the top priority—during new product brainstorming, for instance—free-rein management would probably work best. Likewise, a brand-new worker might benefit from autocratic (but friendly) management, while a talented, experienced employee would probably work best under free-rein leadership.

Another vital consideration is the customer. When the customer seeks consistency in the delivery of the product—in fast food, for instance—the autocratic leadership style may be appropriate. But when the customer needs flexibility and problem-solving assistance—a consulting client, for example—the free-rein leadership

autocratic leaders Leaders who hoard decision-making power for themselves and typically issue orders without consulting their followers.

democratic leaders Leaders who share power with their followers. While they still make final decisions, they typically solicit and incorporate input from their followers.

free-rein leaders Leaders who set objectives for their followers but give them freedom to choose how they accomplish those goals.

© JOSE LUIS PELAEZ INC./BLEND IMAGES/JUPITERIMAGES

Power Play

Leadership traits and practices go hand in hand with power and influence. Power in business—the ability to push forward ideas, generate change, and influence others—can come from a number of sources:

- **Position**: The power of position gives a leader formal authority to either reward or punish employees with tools such as pay and job schedules. The chief financial officer, for example, has position power over the accountants.
- **Expertise**: The power of expertise comes from a person's abilities and experience. The best computer programmer, for instance, tends to have power in technology-dependent organizations.
- **Personality**: The power of personality comes from a person's character. Some people—often those with great communication skills and well-developed empathy—influence others simply through who they are.

While any one of these types of power could be effective alone, leaders have the best chance of success if they cultivate all three sources.

When you build your own base of power, don't forget that powerful leaders are seldom bullies. Research suggests that the nice guys do get ahead: A recent study showed that companies with farsighted, tolerant, humane, and practical CEOs yielded a 758% return over the course of a decade, versus a 128% return for the S&P 500 overall, during the same time period.[11]

style may be most effective. The democratic leadership style typically provides customers with a balance of consistency and flexibility, which works across a wide range of industries.

LO6 Controlling: Making Sure It All Works

Controlling may be the least glamorous of the management functions, but don't be fooled: it's critically important. Controlling means monitoring performance of the firm—or individuals within the firm—and making improvements when necessary. As the environment changes, plans change. And as plans change, the control process must change as well, to ensure that the company achieves its goals. The control process includes three key steps:

1. Establish clear performance standards.
2. Measure actual performance against standards.
3. Take corrective action if necessary.

Establishing clear standards—or performance goals—begins with planning. At every level of planning, objectives should emerge that are consistent with the company's mission and strategic plan. The objectives must be (1) specific and measurable, (2) realistic but challenging, and (3) tied to a timeframe. Individual managers may need to break these goals into smaller parts for specific employees, but the subgoals should retain the same three qualities as the original objective.

Measuring performance against standards should happen well before the end of the timeframe attached to the goal. A strong information tracking system is probably management's best tool in this phase of the control process.

If the company or individual is not on track to meet the goals, management's first response should be communication. Employees with full information are far more likely to improve their perfor-

90% of managers believe that they're in the top 10% of performers.

BusinessWeek

mance than employees who never learn that they're falling behind. But sometimes workers need more than information—they may need additional resources or coaching in order to meet their goals. If they still don't succeed, perhaps the goals themselves need reexamination as part of a dynamic planning process. Given the expense in both human and financial terms, disciplining employees for poor performance should come only after exploring the reasons for not meeting goals and making changes if necessary.

The Big Picture

In the past decade, management has become more complex and demanding than ever before. Managers in every area of the business must carry out their roles—planning, organizing, leading, and controlling—in a relentlessly fast-paced world, seething with constant change. While management isn't for everyone, it's often a fit for people with vision, courage, integrity, energy, and a passionate commitment to their companies.

Looking forward, the role of management will continue to evolve in response to the environment. Regardless of how the changes unfold, several key factors will be absolutely vital for successful managers in the 21st century: a constant focus on the customer, a commitment to globalization, excellent judgment, and the right mix of talented, motivated employees.

WHAT ELSE? *RIP & REVIEW* **CARDS IN THE BACK**

SPEAK UP!

THEY DID

BUSN4 was built on a simple principle: to create a new teaching and learning solution that reflects the way today's faculty and students teach and learn. Through conversations, focus groups, surveys, and interviews, we collected data that drove the creation of the version of BUSN4 that you are using today.

But it doesn't stop there – in order to make BUSN4 an even better learning experience, we'd like you to SPEAK UP and tell us how BUSN4 works for you. What do you like about it? What would you change? Do you have additional ideas that would help us build a better product for next year's Introduction to Business students?

Speak Up! Go to CourseMate for BUSN4. Access at **www.cengagebrain.com.**

HUMAN RESOURCE MANAGEMENT: BUILDING A TOP-QUALITY WORKFORCE

LEARNING OBJECTIVES

After studying this chapter, you will be able to...

LO1 Explain the importance of human resources to business success

LO2 Discuss key human resource issues in today's economy

LO3 Outline challenges and opportunities that the human resources function faces

LO4 Discuss human resource planning and core human resources responsibilities

LO5 Explain the key federal legislation that affects human resources

Visit CourseMate at **www.cengagebrain.com.**

> # If you hire good people, give them good jobs, and pay them good wages, something good is going to happen.
>
> *Jim Sinegal, founder of Costco*

LO1 Human Resource Management: Bringing Business to Life

As competition accelerates across the globe, leading firms in every business category have recognized that a quality workforce can vault them over the competition. Southwest Airlines was early to recognize the untapped potential of its people. Executive Chairman Herb Kelleher declared, "We value our employees first. They're the most important, and if you treat them right, then they treat the customers right, and if you treat the customers right, then they keep coming back and shareholders are happy." His attitude has more than paid off. Southwest Airlines has posted profits for 37 consecutive years, even as other airlines have spiraled into decline.

As the Great Recession constricted the economy in 2009, managing human resources remained a top priority for Southwest CEO Gary Kelly. "We've never had a layoff. We've never had a pay cut. And we're going to strive mightily, especially this year, to avoid them once again..." Instead, he says, "We're being more creative about encouraging employees to move about the company. We are not threatening people with their jobs." He points out that "Southwest Airlines has to be a great place to work to get great people to come and stay. We're known for being the greatest company to work for and at the top of the customer service rankings."[1]

Companies that get the most from their people often consider their human resources their biggest investment. They view the core goal of **human resource (HR) management** in a similar light: to nurture their human investment so that it yields the highest possible return. HR can achieve that goal by recruiting world-class talent, promoting career development, and boosting organizational effectiveness. But clearly this can happen only in partnership with key managers throughout the company, especially senior executives. (In smaller companies, of course, the owners usually do HR management in addition to their other responsibilities.)

LO2 Human Resource Management Challenges: Major Hurdles

Building a top-quality workforce can be tougher than it may initially seem. Human resource managers—and their counterparts throughout the company—face huge challenges. The best strategies still aren't clear, but forward-thinking firms tend to experiment with new approaches.

Layoffs and Outsourcing

As high-tech, high-end jobs follow low-tech, low-end jobs out of the country—or even just to local contractors—human resources find themselves in turmoil. Many jobs have disappeared altogether as companies have contracted in response to the Great Recession. How can businesses boost the morale and the motivation level of the employees who are left behind? Does less job security translate to less worker loyalty? How can human resources continue to add value as the ground shifts beneath them—and as they wonder how long their own jobs will last?[2]

Wage Gap

Comparing CEO pay to worker pay demonstrates a startling wage gap, bigger in the United States than in any other developed country. In 2007, the average CEO earned 275 times the average worker. As a point of comparison, 30 years ago, chief executives averaged only 30 to 40 times the average American worker's paycheck. In 2009, median CEO salaries at 200 large, publicly held U.S. firms fell –0.9%, while net income decreased by 5%. Most observers don't object to the pay gap when top CEO pay ties to top performance. But as the value of formerly high-flying corporations began to evaporate in 2008 and 2009, public rage over senior management salaries and bonuses hit new highs. This clearly represents a strategic challenge for HR management.[3]

Older Workers

As the oversized Baby Boomer generation begins turning 60, their employers—which include virtually every major American company—face a potential crisis: the loss of key talent and experience through massive retirements. Enlightened companies have responded with programs to retain their best employees through flexible schedules, training opportunities, and creative pay schedules. But as companies aggressively trimmed their payrolls in 2008 and 2009, the priority of these kinds of programs plummeted, which may leave some firms with a critical dearth of highly experienced workers when the economy revs back up.

Younger Workers

As twentysomethings enter the workforce, they often bring optimism, open minds, technological know-how, a team orientation, and a multicultural perspective. But a number of them also bring an unprecedented sense of entitlement. This can translate into startlingly high expectations for their pay, their responsibilities, and their job flexibility, but little willingness to "pay dues." Many have no expectation that their employers will be loyal to them, and they don't feel that they owe their companies strong loyalty. Managing this group can sometimes be a challenge, but companies that do it well stand to deliver results for years to come.[4]

Women Workers

Over the last few decades, women have made enormous strides in terms of workplace equality. But several large-scale studies confirm that women continue to face daunting discrimination in terms of both pay and promotions. While unfair treatment has been an issue for many years, recent legal changes have made it easier for women to sue, costing companies millions of dollars in the last decade alone. And the flood of lawsuits shows no signs of slowing. Many women have responded to the unfriendly business environment by leaving the workforce to raise children, start their own companies, or pursue other interests. As a result, we are experiencing a harmful, ongoing brain drain.[5]

Work-Life Balance

Over the last decade, workers across all ages and both genders have actively pursued more flexibility and work–life balance in their jobs. But as the recession deepened in 2009, companies began to cut back on these initiatives, describing them as "nice to have" programs in a time when "need to have" goals—such as meeting payroll each month—are tough to attain. Middle-level managers are also apt to demonstrate bias against worker flexibility, even when top management actively supports work–life balance programs. In spite of these issues, insightful HR managers try hard to offer enough flexibility to keep their best workers without jeopardizing their company's business goals.[6]

Lawsuits

The United States has become a wildly litigious society, with employees, customers, and shareholders levying lawsuit after lawsuit against firms of all sizes. Even though many of the lawsuits are legitimate—some profoundly important—a good number are just plain silly. But even if a lawsuit is frivolous, even if it's thrown out of court, it can still cost a company millions of dollars. Even more importantly, a frivolous lawsuit can cost a business its reputation. Avoiding employee lawsuits by knowing the law and encouraging legal practices is a growing human resources challenge.

LO3 Human Resources Managers: Corporate Black Sheep?

The Problem

The human resource management function is clearly critical, but human resources departments—and the people who work in them—face major challenges. Leading-edge firms expect every department to offer "big picture," strategic contributions that boost company value. But a report in *Fast Company* suggests that most HR professionals lack sufficient strategic skills. Among other data, the report quotes a respected executive at a top U.S. company: "Business acumen is the single biggest factor that HR professionals in the U.S. lack today."[7]

But even highly qualified, strategically focused HR managers face daunting perception problems. A management professor at a leading school comments that "The best and the brightest just don't go into HR." Once in the workforce, many employees see the human resources department as irrelevant—or even worse, as the enemy. This perception clearly undermines their effectiveness.

The Solution

To gain respect from both senior management and their peers, human resources executives must earn a seat at the table. The first step is to know the company.

> ## HR matters enormously in good times. It defines you in the bad.
>
> *Jack and Suzy Welch*

What are the strategic goals? Who is the core customer? Who is the competition? Respected HR departments typically figure out ways to quantify their impact on the company in dollars and cents. They determine how to raise the value of the firm's human capital, which in turn increases the value of the firm itself. Effective HR people also remain open to exceptions even as they enforce broad company policies.

But clearly, these solutions will work only if senior management recognizes the potential value of effective human resource management. One simple test of senior management commitment is the reporting relationship. If the HR department reports to the CFO, it may be on the fast track to outsourcing. But if the HR department reports to the CEO, the strategic possibilities are unlimited.

LO4 Human Resource Planning: Drawing the Map

Great human resource management begins with great planning: Where should you go? And how should you get there? Your objectives, of course, should flow from the company's master plan, and your strategies must reflect company priorities.

What is your "job description" and what are your "job specifications" as a student?

© DOUG MENUEZ/PHOTODISC/GETTY IMAGES

One of the first steps in the HR planning process should be to figure out where the company stands in terms of human resources. What skills does the workforce already have? What skills do they need? A company-wide **job analysis** often goes hand in hand with evaluating the current workforce. Job analysis examines what exactly needs to be done in each position to maximize the effectiveness of the organization—independent of who might be holding each job at any specific time. Smaller companies often handle job analysis on an informal basis, but larger companies typically specify a formal **job description** and **job specifications** (or specs).

A job description defines the jobholder's responsibilities, and job specs define the qualifications for doing the job. Consider your professor's position. The job description might include the number of classes to be taught as well as other required campus activities. The job specs might include the type of education and teaching experience required. Taken together, the two might look something like Exhibit 15.1.

The next step is to forecast future human resource requirements. The forecasting function requires a deep understanding of the company goals and strategies. HR managers must also assess the future supply of workers. Assessing supply can be a real challenge, since the size and quality of the workforce shift continually. But key considerations should include retirement rates, graduation rates in relevant fields, and the pros and cons of the international labor market.

A complete HR plan—which falls under the company's strategic planning umbrella—must cover

job analysis The examination of specific tasks that are assigned to each position, independent of who might be holding the job at any specific time.

job description An explanation of the responsibilities for a specific position.

job specifications The specific qualifications necessary to hold a particular position.

EXHIBIT 15.1 Job Description and Job Specifications: Professor

Job Description	Job Specifications
Teach five business classes each semester either face to face or online.	A master's degree in business from an accredited graduate school
Consult with students for five hours each week on an individual basis.	A minimum of three years business teaching experience
Participate actively in college governance.	Excellent interpersonal and communication skills

each core area of human resource management (see Exhibit 15.2):

- Recruitment
- Selection
- Training
- Evaluation
- Compensation
- Benefits
- Separation

Recruitment: Finding the Right People

Finding people to hire is easy—especially as the unemployment rate hit new highs in 2009—but finding *qualified* employees can still be a daunting challenge. The U.S. Census Bureau points out that a college degree typically doubles earning power, and the U.S. Bureau of Labor Statistics attests that most of the fastest-growing fields in the next five years will require college graduates. But only 28% of adults over the age of 25 have a college degree. And as highly trained, highly educated Baby Boomers hit retirement, HR recruiters may face a hiring crunch. In addition to finding qualified hires, recruiters also must find new employees who fit with the company culture in terms of both personality and style.[8]

New employees come from two basic sources: internal and external. **Internal recruitment** involves transfer-

Job fairs and professional conferences provide opportunities for external recruitment.

© KEVORK DJANSEZIAN/GETTY IMAGES

ring or promoting employees from other positions within the company. This approach offers several advantages:

- Boosts employee morale by reinforcing the value of experience within the firm
- Reduces risk for the firm since current employees have a proven track record
- Lowers costs of both recruitment and training

But companies often find that they don't have the right person within their organization. The firm may be too small, or perhaps no one has the right set of skills to fill the immediate needs. Or maybe the firm needs the fresh thinking and energy that can come only from outside. When this is the case, companies turn to **external recruitment**.

External recruitment, or looking for employees outside the firm, usually means tapping into a range of different resources. The possibilities include employment websites, newspaper ads, trade associations, college and university employment centers, and employment agencies. But the most promising source of new hires may be referrals from current employees. A growing number of organizations offer their current employees a cash bonus—typically $1,000 to $2,000—for each person they refer to the company who makes it past a probationary period. As an added benefit, employees who come through referrals have an excellent chance at success, since the person who recommended them has a stake in their progress. Employee referral programs also represent a real bargain for employers, compared to the average cost per new hire of more than $4,000. Not surprisingly, a higher level of employee referrals correlates to a higher level of shareholder returns, although lack of diversity may become a long-term problem with relying on employee referrals. [9]

Selection: Making the Right Choice

Once you have a pool of qualified candidates, your next step is to choose the best person for the job. This, too, is easier said than done, yet making the right selection is crucial. The costs of a bad hire—both the direct costs such

EXHIBIT 15.2 Human Resource Management

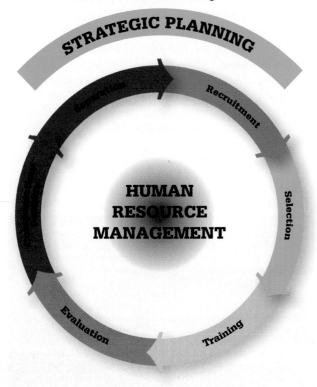

STRATEGIC PLANNING

HUMAN RESOURCE MANAGEMENT

Separation
Recruitment
Selection
Training
Evaluation

as placing ads and the intangibles such as lost productivity and morale—can drain company resources. A typical selection process includes accepting applications, interviewing, testing, checking references and background, and making the job offer. Keep in mind, though, that small businesses often follow a more streamlined process.

> { **A company is known by the people it keeps.** }
> *Meehan & Meehan*

Applications Many companies use written applications simply as an initial screening mechanism. Questions about education and experience will determine whether a candidate gets any further consideration. In other words, the application is primarily a tool to reject unqualified candidates, rather than to actually choose qualified candidates.

Interviews Virtually every company uses interviews as a central part of the selection process. In larger companies, the HR department does initial interviews and then sends qualified candidates to the hiring manager for the actual selection. The hiring manager usually recruits coworkers to participate in the process.

Although employers frequently give interviews heavy weight in hiring decisions, interviews often say surprisingly little about whether a candidate will perform on the job. Too many managers use the interview as a get-to-know-you session, rather than focusing on the needs of the position. To help ensure that interviews better predict performance, experts recommend a **structured interview** process: developing a list of questions beforehand and asking the same questions to each candidate. The most effective questions are typically behavioral: they ask the candidate to describe a situation that he or she faced at a previous job—or a hypothetical situation at the new job—and to explain the resolution. Interviewers should gear the specific questions toward behaviors and experiences that are key for the new position. Consider the following examples of how these questions could be worded:

- Describe a time when you had to think "outside the box" to find a solution to a pressing problem.
- If you realized that a co-worker was cheating on his expense report, how would you handle the situation?
- What would you do if your boss asked you to complete a key project within an unreasonable timeframe?

Cultural differences also affect interview performance. As the U.S. labor pool becomes more diverse, even domestic companies must be aware of cultural

structured interviews An interviewing approach that involves developing a list of questions beforehand and asking the same questions in the same order to each candidate.

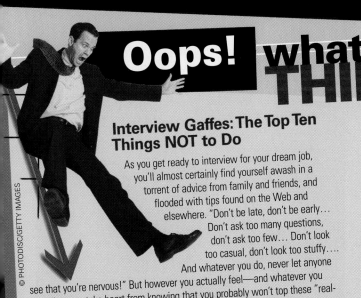

© PHOTODISC/GETTY IMAGES

Oops! what were they THINKING?!

Interview Gaffes: The Top Ten Things NOT to Do

As you get ready to interview for your dream job, you'll almost certainly find yourself awash in a torrent of advice from family and friends, and flooded with tips found on the Web and elsewhere. "Don't be late, don't be early... Don't ask too many questions, don't ask too few... Don't look too casual, don't look too stuffy.... And whatever you do, never let anyone see that you're nervous!" But however you actually feel—and whatever you actually say—take heart from knowing that you probably won't top these "real-life" interview question blunders:

1. Question: "What five or six adjectives best describe you?"
   Answer: "Really, really, really, really, really cool!"

2. Question: "Were you late because you got lost?"
   Answer: "No. It was such a nice day that I didn't mind driving slowly."

3. Question: "Why should I hire you?"
   Answer: "Because they say you should always hire people better than yourself."

4. Question: "What do you find interesting about this job?
   Answer: "The money. I don't really care what your company does."

5. Question: "Is it important to you to get benefits right away?"
   Answer: "I don't believe in healthcare. If I broke my leg, I'd just live with it."

6. Question: "What is your greatest strength?"
   Answer: "I'm a quick learner if I'm in the mood to pay attention."

7. Question: "What can you tell me about your creative ability?"
   Answer: "My answers to most of your questions are pretty good indicators."

8. Question: "Would you be willing to take a drug test?"
   Answer: "Sure. What kind of drugs do I get to test?"

9. Question: "What would your boss say about you?"
   Answer: "That I'm insubordinate."

10. Question: "How would you define a 'problem person'?"
    Answer: "Anyone who disagrees with me."[10]

differences. And it isn't simply a matter of legality or ethics. Firms that hire the best people regardless of cultural background will gain a critical edge in our increasingly competitive world.

Testing Either before or after the interview process (and sometimes at both points), a growing number of companies have instituted employment testing of various sorts. The main categories include skills testing, personality testing, drug testing, and physical exams. Skills testing and personality testing carry a fair amount of legal risk, since these tests must measure skills and aptitudes that relate directly to the job itself. Virtually 100% of Fortune 500 companies do pre-employment drug testing, as do most other companies. Physical exams are also standard but are highly regulated by state and federal law to ensure that firms don't use them just to screen out certain individuals.

References and Background Checks Even if you feel absolutely certain that a candidate is right for the job, don't skip the reference check before you make an offer. Research from the Society for Human Resource Managers suggests that more than 50% of job candidates lie on their résumé in some way. Although it may be tough to verify contributions and accomplishments at former jobs, it's pretty easy to uncover lies about education, job titles, and compensation. And it's quite worthwhile, given that the costs of bringing an unethical employee on board can be staggering. Furthermore, if you happen to hire a truly dangerous employee, you can open the door to negligent hiring lawsuits for not taking "reasonable care." But surprisingly—despite the high risk—employment expert John Challenger estimates that only about 15% of candidates are thoroughly vetted by the companies that consider them.[11]

Job Offers After a company finds the right person, the next hurdle is designing the right job offer and getting your candidate to accept it. To hook an especially hot contender, you may need to get creative. A phone call from top management, the royal treatment, and special perks go a long way, but most superb candidates also want to know in very specific terms how their contributions would affect the business. And no matter how excited you are about your candidate, be certain to establish a **probationary period** upfront. This means a specific timeframe (typically three to six months) during which a new hire can prove his or her worth on the job. If everything works out, the employee will move from conditional to permanent status; if not, the company can fire the employee fairly easily.

Contingent Workers Companies that experience a fluctuating need for workers sometimes opt to hire **contingent workers**—or employees who don't expect regular, full-time jobs—rather than permanent, full-time workers. Specifically, contingent employees include temporary full-time workers, independent contractors, on-call workers, and temporary agency or contract agency workers. As a group, these contingent workers account for about 11% of U.S. employment.[12]

Employers appreciate contingent workers because they offer flexibility, which can lead to much lower costs. But the hidden downside can be workers who are less committed and less experienced. Too much reliance on contingent workers could unwittingly sabotage company productivity and the customer experience.

Training and Development: Honing the Competitive Edge

For successful companies in virtually every field, training and development have become an ongoing process rather than a one-time activity. Even in a recession, training and development must gather speed for companies and individuals to maintain their competitive edge. Experts offer five key reasons that relate directly to a healthy bottom line:

1. Increased innovation in strategies and products

2. Increased ability to adopt new technologies

On-the-job training often works best for relatively simple jobs.

3. Increased efficiency and productivity

4. Increased employee motivation and lower employee turnover

5. Decreased liability (e.g., sexual harassment lawsuits)

Training programs take a number of different forms, from orientation to skills training, to management development, depending on the specific employee and the needs of the organization.

Orientation Once you hire new employees, **orientation** should be the first step in the training and development process. Effective orientation programs typically focus on introducing employees to the company culture (but without sacrificing need-to-know administrative information). Research consistently shows that strong orientation programs significantly reduce employee turnover, which lowers costs.[13]

The Boeing aerospace company has mastered the art of employee orientation. Boeing Military Aircraft and Missile Systems revamped its orientation process to include mentoring, meetings with senior executives, and an after-work social program. A highlight of the orientation—meant to crystallize the "wow" factor of working at Boeing—is the chance to take the controls of an F/A-18 fighter plane flight simulator. Management rightfully sees the program as a chance to develop "future leaders...the ones who will make sure that Boeing continues to be a great place to work."[14]

On-the-Job Training **On-the-job training** is popular because it's very low-cost. Employees simply begin their jobs—sometimes under the guidance of more experienced employees—and learn as they go. For simple jobs this can make sense, but simple jobs are disappearing from the U.S. market due to the combined impact of offshoring and technology. On-the-job training can also compromise the customer experience. Have you ever waited for much too long in a short line at the grocery store because the clerk couldn't figure out how to use the cash register? Multiplied across hundreds of customers, this kind of experience undermines the value of a company's brand.

Formal apprenticeship programs tend to be a more effective way of handling on-the-job training. **Apprenticeship** programs mandate that each beginner serve as an assistant to a fully trained worker for a specified period of time before gaining full credentials to work in the field. In the United States, apprenticeships are fairly common in trades such as plumbing and bricklaying. But in Europe, apprenticeships are much more common across a wide range of professions, from bankers to opticians.

Off-the-Job Training Classroom training happens away from the job setting, but typically during work hours. Employers use classroom training—either on- or off-site—to teach a wide variety of topics from new computer programming languages, to negotiation skills, to stress management, and more. Going one step further than classroom training, some employers train workers off-site on "real" equipment (e.g., robots) similar to what they would actually use on the job. This approach is called "vestibule training." Police academies, for instance, often use vestibule training for firearms. Job simulation goes even further than vestibule training, by attempting to duplicate the exact conditions that the trainee will face on the job. This approach makes sense for complex, high-risk positions such as astronaut or airline pilot.

Computer-Based Training Computer-based training—mostly delivered via the Web—now plays a crucial role in off-the-job training. Broadband technology has turbocharged audio and visual capabilities, which support engaging and interactive online training programs. Online training also standardizes the presentation of the material, since it doesn't depend on the quality of the individual instructor. And the Web helps employers train employees wherever they

orientation The first step in the training and development process, designed to introduce employees to the company culture, and provide key administrative information.

on-the-job training A training approach that requires employees to simply begin their jobs—sometimes guided by more experienced employees—and to learn as they go.

apprenticeships Structured training programs that mandate that each beginner serve as an assistant to a fully trained worker before gaining full credentials to work in the field.

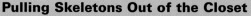

Pulling Skeletons Out of the Closet

With criminal convictions for CEOs splashed across the headlines, companies are spending a lot more time and money on background checks for key executives. According to *Forbes* magazine, top investigative firms find that 10 to 20% of their executive searches expose issues that range from fake degrees to criminal filings. Peter Turecek, a managing partner of a business intelligence and investigations practice, comments, "We came across...an executive at an acquisition target company who turned out to have been a bagman in a murder. We also discovered a CFO that stole his neighbor's sod because he couldn't wait to finish his lawn. What's he doing if he can't meet his quarterly numbers?" That's a scary thought...[15]

© STOCKBYTE/GETTY IMAGES

management development Programs to help current and potential executives develop the skills they need to move into leadership positions.

performance appraisal A formal feedback process that requires managers to give their subordinates feedback on a one-to-one basis, typically by comparing actual results to expected results.

compensation The combination of pay and benefits that employees receive in exchange for their work.

may be in the world, at their own pace and convenience. But there is a key drawback: it takes a lot of discipline to complete an online program, and some people simply learn better through direct human interaction.

Management Development As the bulk of top-level U.S. executives move toward retirement (or lose their jobs in the recession), developing new leaders has become a priority in many organizations. **Management development** programs help current and potential executives develop the skills they need to move into leadership positions. These programs typically cover specific issues that the business faces, but also less-tangible—yet equally important—topics, such as communication, planning, business-analysis, change-management, coaching, and team-building skills.

Evaluation: Assessing Employee Performance

Straightforward, frequent feedback is a powerful tool to improve employee performance. The best managers provide informal feedback on a constant basis so that employees always know where they stand. But most companies also require that managers give formal feedback through periodic **performance appraisals**, usually every six months or once a year. Typically, managers conduct the appraisals by sitting down with each employee on a one-to-one basis, and comparing actual results to expected results. The performance appraisal affects decisions regarding compensation, promotions, training, transfers, and terminations.

The HR role in performance appraisals begins with the strategic process of creating evaluation tools that tie directly into the company's big picture objectives. Then, on a day-to-day basis, HR coordinates the actual appraisal process, which typically involves volumes of paperwork. HR must also ensure that managers are trained in how to provide relevant, honest, objective feedback, and that workers at every level know how to respond if they believe their appraisal is not fair.

Both giving and receiving evaluations tend to be awkward for everyone

involved, and unfortunately, uncomfortable people tend to make mistakes. As you read the following list, you'll probably find that you've been at the receiving end of at least a couple of the most common appraisal goofs.

1. **Gotcha!** Too many managers use the performance appraisal as a chance to catch employees doing something wrong, rather than doing something right.

2. **The Once-a-Year Wonder** Many companies mandate annual reviews, but some managers use that as an excuse to give feedback only once a year.

3. **Straight from the Gut** Although "gut feel" can have real value, it's no substitute for honest, relevant documentation of both expectations and accomplishments.

4. **What Have You Done for Me Lately?** Many managers give far too much weight to recent accomplishments, discounting the early part of the review period.

5. **The "Me Filter"** While appraisals are a bit subjective by their very nature, some managers filter every comment through their personal biases. Here are some examples:

   • **Positive Leniency:** "I'm a nice guy so I give everyone great scores."

   • **Negative Leniency:** "I have high expectations so I give everyone low scores."

   • **Halo Effect:** "I like this employee so I'll give her top scores across the board."

For a performance appraisal to be effective, the manager must focus on fairness, relevance, objectivity, and balance. Equally important, the manager should give feedback on a continual basis to eliminate surprises and maximize performance.

Compensation: Show Me the Money

The term **compensation** covers both pay and benefits, but when most people think about compensation, they think about cash. Yet your paycheck is only part of the picture. Many companies also offer noncash benefits such as healthcare, which can be worth up to 30% of each employee's pay. Researching, designing, and managing effective compensation systems are core HR functions.

From a company perspective, compensation—both cash and noncash—represents a big chunk of product costs, especially in labor-intensive businesses such as banks, restaurants, and airlines. Although many firms opt to cut labor costs as far as possible, others boost compensation above the norm to find and keep the best workers. In fact, research suggests that companies that offer higher-than-average compensation generally outperform their competitors in terms of total return to shareholders—both stock price and dividend payouts.[16]

Regarding specific individuals and positions, companies typically base compensation on a balance of the following factors:

- **Competition:** How much do competing firms offer for similar positions?
- **Contribution:** How much does a specific person contribute to the bottom line?
- **Ability to Pay:** How much can the company afford?
- **Cost of Living:** What would be reasonable in light of the broader local economy?
- **Legislation:** What does the government mandate?

The most common compensation systems in the United States are wages and salaries. **Wages** refer to pay in exchange for the number of hours or days that an employee works. Variations can be huge, starting at the federal minimum wage of $7.25 per hour (as of mid-2009) and ranging up to more than $50 per hour. Jobs that require less education—such as flipping burgers—typically pay hourly wages. Federal law requires companies to pay wage earners overtime, 50% more than their standard wage, for every hour worked over 40 hours per week.

Salaries on the other hand, cover a fixed period, most often weekly or monthly. Most professional, administrative, and managerial jobs pay salaries. While salaries are usually higher than wages, salaried workers do not qualify for overtime, which means that sometimes a low-level manager's overall pay may be less than the pay of wage-based employees who work for that manager.

Pay for Performance In addition to wages and salaries, many organizations link some amount of worker pay directly to performance. The idea, of course, is to motivate employees to excel. Exhibit 15.3 lists some common approaches.

As you look over the various variable pay options, which would you find most motivating? Why? What type of business might use each form of variable pay? Why?

Benefits: From Birthday Cakes to Death Benefits

Benefits represent a significant chunk of money for employers, but for many years workers took benefits for granted. No longer. As the unemployment rate skyrocketed in 2009, employees began to appreciate their benefits more than ever, recognizing that health care, dental care, paid sick days, retirement plans, and other perks add enormous value to their paychecks—and can be yanked at the discretion of their employer.[17]

In fact, a number of budget-minded employers already stick to the legally mandated basics: Social Security and Medicare contributions, payments to state unemployment and workers' compensation programs, and job protection per the Federal Family and Medical Leave Act. However, socially responsible employers—and companies that seek a competitive advantage through a top-notch workforce—tend to offer far more. Optional benefits usually include some or all of the following:

- Paid vacation days and holidays
- Paid sick days
- Health insurance
- Retirement programs
- Product discounts

A smaller number of companies also offer less traditional benefits such as backup childcare options, free massage, subsidized concierge services, tuition reimbursement, and paid time off for volunteering. During the recession of 2009, companies that offered "extras" focused extra attention on perks that would boost morale without an outrageous price tag.[18]

In the past decade, a growing number of companies have begun to offer **cafeteria-style benefits**. This approach involves giving their employees a set dollar

---

wages The pay that employees receive in exchange for the number of hours or days that they work.

salaries The pay that employees receive over a fixed period, most often weekly or monthly.

benefits Noncash compensation, including programs such as health insurance, vacation, and childcare.

cafeteria-style benefits An approach to employee benefits that gives all employees a set dollar amount that they must spend on company benefits, allocated however they wish within broad limitations.

EXHIBIT 15.3 Performance Pay Options

Variable Pay System	Description
Commission	Commission involves payment as a percentage of sales. Usually, larger commissions go with smaller base pay.
Bonuses	Bonuses are lump-sum payments, typically to reward strong performance from individual employees.
Profit sharing	Profit-sharing plans reward employees with a share of company profits above and beyond predetermined goals.
Stock options	Stock options are the right to buy shares of company stock at some future date for the price of the shares on the day that the company awarded the options.
Pay for knowledge	This approach involves awarding bonuses and pay increases in exchange for increases in knowledge such as earning an MBA.

flextime A scheduling option that allows workers to choose when they start and finish their workdays, as long as they complete the required number of hours.

compressed workweek A version of flextime scheduling that allows employees to work a full-time number of hours in less than the standard workweek.

telecommuting Working remotely—most often from home—and connecting to the office via phone lines, fax machines, and broadband networks.

amount per person that they must spend on company benefits. The key to these plans is choice, which allows employees to tailor their benefits to their individual needs.

Over the past couple of decades, employees across the U.S. economy have demanded more flexibility from their employers, and companies have responded. Flexible scheduling options include flextime, telecommuting, and job-sharing plans, discussed in detail below. But unfortunately, as massive, widespread layoffs swept across the economy in 2009, workers began to give up flexible schedules—or to stop even asking about them in the first place—out of fear that they would appear less committed to their jobs.[19]

Flextime A **flextime** plan gives workers some degree of freedom in terms of when they start and finish their workday, as long as they complete the required number of hours. Typically, companies with flextime scheduling oblige their employees to start work between mandated hours in the morning—say, anytime between 7 A.M. and 10 A.M.—to take lunch between certain hours in the middle of the day, and to complete work at the end of eight hours. This approach ensures that everyone is present during core hours for communication and coordination, but provides choice outside those parameters. Flextime tends to increase employee morale and retention. But it makes less sense in jobs that entail extensive teamwork and customer interaction. It also requires careful management to avoid abuse.

The **compressed workweek**, another version of flextime scheduling, allows employees to work a full-time number of hours in less than the standard workweek. The most popular option is to work four ten-hour days rather than five eight-hour days. Major companies such as Intel have developed successful compressed workweek programs at a number of their facilities.

Telecommuting Working remotely—most often from home—is a growing phenomenon on a global scale. Booming technological advances allow employees to "commute" to the office via phone lines, fax machines, and broadband networks. About 40% of companies allow **telecommuting**, and about a third of Americans telecommute at least occasionally. The bottom-line benefits for companies that embrace the approach can be significant. Telecommuting employees are 10 to 45% more productive than their office-bound colleagues. And direct savings from decreased costs add up fast, as well. By establishing telecommuting programs, employers

WITHOUT A MAP... CHARTING AN ETHICAL COURSE

The Brouhaha Over Bonuses

When AIG—which accepted a multibillion-dollar bailout from the U.S. Treasury—paid millions of dollars in bonuses to some of the same people who engineered the global financial crisis, a firestorm of outrage swept across the country. Never mind that nine of the top ten earners returned the money in full—the damage had already been done.

Furious, President Obama instructed his Treasury Secretary to "pursue every single legal avenue to block these bonuses and make the American taxpayers whole." Both politicians and regular people demanded that the government step in to cancel bonus contracts. And Congress seriously considered a 90% tax against all bonus recipients.

But as the outrage over AIG reached a fevered pitch, it eclipsed some more positive news. Bollinger Insurance CEO Jack Windolf, for instance, opted to share his $500,000 bonus with his workforce. Windolf gave a $1,000 check to each of his 434 employees, in what he dubbed the "Bollinger Mini Stimulus package." Other firms cut executive bonuses completely to avoid layoffs.

The 2009 executive bonus drama raised some crucial long-term questions about compensation. How much bonus is too much? How closely should bonuses be tied to performance? Do executives have an ethical obligation to turn down unearned money? If they don't step up, does the government have a right to step in? How much regulation is too much? The answers to these questions may ultimately affect the money in your pocket as an executive, a taxpayer, or both.[20]

can realize annual cost savings of $5,000 per employee, which adds up to hundreds of millions of dollars each year for big players, such as IBM and AT&T.[21]

While telecommuting sounds great at first glance, it offers benefits and drawbacks for organizations and employees alike, as you'll see in Exhibit 15.4.

Job Sharing Job sharing allows two or more employees to share a single full-time job. Typically job share

EXHIBIT 15.4: An Analysis of Telecommuting

	Benefits	Drawbacks
Organization	• Lower costs for office space, equipment, and upkeep • Higher employee productivity due to better morale, fewer sick days, and more focused performance • Access to a broader talent pool (not everyone needs to be local)	• Greater challenges maintaining a cohesive company culture • Greater challenges fostering teamwork • Greater challenges monitoring and managing far-flung employees
Employee	• Much more flexibility • Zero commute time (less gas money) • Better work–family balance • Every day is casual Friday (or even pajama day!) • Fewer office politics and other distractions	• Less fast-track career potential • Less influence within the organization • Weaker connection to the company culture • Isolation from the social structure at work[22]

participants split salary equally, but they often need to allocate full benefits to just one of the partners. On a nationwide basis, fewer than 20% of employers (e.g., American Express and Quaker Oats) offer job-sharing programs and reap the benefits such as higher morale and better retention.[23]

Separation: Breaking Up Is Hard to Do

Employees leave jobs for a number of different reasons. Experiencing success, they may be promoted or lured to another firm. Experiencing failure, they may be fired. Or in response to changing business needs, their employer might transfer them or lay them off. And of course, employees also leave jobs for completely personal reasons such as family needs, retirement, or a change in career aspirations.

When companies terminate employees, they must proceed very carefully to avoid wrongful termination lawsuits. The best protection is honesty and documentation. Employers should always document sound business reasons for termination and share those reasons with the employee.

But employees can still lose their jobs for reasons that have little to do with their individual performance. In response to the recession, employers eliminated 5.1 million jobs between December 2007 and March 2009. Many experts anticipate that massive layoffs will continue. As companies have become leaner, the remaining workers have experienced enormous stress. Managers can mitigate the trauma most effectively by showing empathy and concern for employees who remain, and by treating the laid-off employees with visible compassion.[24]

© LAJOSREPASI/ISTOCKPHOTO.COM

Commuting at Zero Gallons per Mile

Countless studies confirm that telecommuting can offer real benefits for both employers and employees. But it can also make a world of difference for our planet.

More telecommuters mean fewer vehicles spewing pollution on the roads. In fact, the 3.9 million workers who telecommuted in 2007 reduced CO_2 emissions at a level roughly equal to removing 2 million vehicles from the road for the entire year. According to the National Technology Readiness Survey, we could save about 1.35 billion gallons of fuel per year, if everyone who was able to telecommute did so just 1.6 days per week.

Telecommuting can also go a long way toward reducing the overall carbon footprint of many businesses. Sun Microsystems, which boasts a robust telecommuting program, found that its 24,000 telecommuting U.S. employees *avoided* producing 32,000 metric tons of CO_2 by driving to and from work less often.

But the environmental benefits don't stop there. Sun also found that employees used less energy at home than they did at the office. "Office equipment energy consumption rate at a Sun office was two times that of home office equipment energy consumption, from approximately 64 watts per hour at home to 130 watts per hour at a Sun office." A key reason: laptops—used by most telecommuting employees—require less power than traditional desktop PC/monitor combos.

Factoring in the environmental benefits, we might conclude that the overall cost of telecommuting is even less than zero.[25]

Civil Rights Act of 1964 Federal legislation that prohibits discrimination in hiring, firing, compensation, apprenticeships, training, terms, conditions, or privileges of employment based on race, color, religion, sex, or national origin.

Title VII A portion of the Civil Rights Act of 1964 that prohibits discrimination in hiring, firing, compensation, apprenticeships, training, terms, conditions, or privileges of employment based on race, color, religion, sex, or national origin for employers with 15 or more workers.

Equal Employment Opportunity Commission (EEOC) A federal agency designed to regulate and enforce the provisions of Title VII.

> # Even a small layoff shocks and demoralizes survivors so much that voluntary quit rates rise an average of 31% above previous levels.
>
> *The Wall Street Journal*

LO5 Legal Issues: HR and the Long Arm of the Law

Even when the company is right—even when the company wins—employment lawsuits can cost millions of dollars and deeply damage the reputation of your organization, as we briefly discussed earlier in this chapter. To avoid employment lawsuits, most firms rely on HR to digest the complex, evolving web of employment legislation and court decisions, and to ensure that management understands the key issues.

The bottom-line goal of most employment legislation is to protect employees from unfair treatment by employers. Some would argue that the legislation goes so far that it hinders the ability of companies to grow. But regardless of your personal perspective, the obligation of an ethical employer is to understand and abide by the law as it stands—even if you're working within the system to change it.

The most influential piece of employment law may be the **Civil Rights Act of 1964**. **Title VII** of this act—which applies only to employers with 15 or more workers—outlaws discrimination in hiring, firing, compensation, apprenticeships, training, terms, conditions, or privileges of employment based on race, color, religion, sex, or national origin. Over time, Congress has supplemented Title VII with legislation that prohibits discrimination based on pregnancy, age (40+), and disability.

Title VII also created the **Equal Employment Opportunity Commission (EEOC)** to enforce its provisions. And in 1972, Congress beefed up the EEOC with additional powers to regulate and to enforce its mandates, making the EEOC a powerful force in the human resources realm.

Here are some additional key pieces of employment legislation:

- **Fair Labor Standards Act of 1938:** Established a minimum wage and overtime pay for employees working more than 40 hours a week.

- **Equal Pay Act of 1963:** Mandated that men and women doing equal jobs must receive equal pay.

- **Occupational Safety and Health Act of 1970:** Required safety equipment for employees and established maximum exposure limits for hazardous substances.

Some Weighty Issues

Can your boss put you on a diet? Can he force you to stop smoking after work? Can he make you run laps? Not quite—but your boss can definitely make it worth your while to be healthy.

A growing number of big U.S. businesses are offering wellness programs that include financial rewards for healthy behaviors—and some include financial penalties for a lack of results. Big businesses certainly have an incentive: effective wellness programs can reduce medical and absenteeism costs by up to 30% in less than four years. In fact, year-round comprehensive corporate wellness programs have shown savings-to-cost ratios of over $3 saved for each $1 invested.

But these programs aren't without controversy. According to a recent survey, more than 60% of business owners plan to implement a wellness incentive program, but—not surprisingly—only 12% of employees want their bosses involved in their health.

No one argues against voluntary health assessments, weight-loss programs, and stop-smoking programs. But what happens when "voluntary" doesn't really mean optional? At Lincoln Industries, for instance, the CEO hesitates to call his company's wellness plan mandatory, but he does point proudly to 100% participation.

Some companies go even further. Scotts Miracle-Gro, for instance, forces employees who don't participate in their "voluntary" health-risk appraisal to pay a $40-per-month health insurance surcharge. Employees who do participate, but don't choose to change unhealthy behaviors, must pay a $67-per-month surcharge.

The legal limits of wellness programs are still unclear. But with skyrocketing healthcare costs, a growing number of firms are willing to push those limits as far as they can.[26]

- **Immigration Reform and Control Act of 1986:** Required employers to verify employment eligibility for all new hires.

- **Americans with Disabilities Act of 1990:** Prohibited discrimination in hiring, promotion, and compensation against people with disabilities and required employers to make "reasonable" accommodations for them.

- **Family and Medical Leave Act of 1996:** Required firms with 50 or more employees to provide up to 12 weeks of job-secure, unpaid leave on the birth or adoption of a child or the serious illness of a spouse, child, or parent.

Human resource managers are responsible for not only knowing this legislation in detail, but also for ensuring that management throughout their firm implements the legislation effectively, wherever it's applicable.

Affirmative Action: The Active Pursuit of Equal Opportunity

The term **affirmative action** refers to policies meant to increase employment and educational opportunities for minority groups—especially groups defined by race, ethnicity, or gender. Emerging during the American civil rights movement in the 1960s, affirmative action seeks to make up for the systematic discrimination of the past, by creating more opportunities in the present.

Over the past couple of decades, affirmative action has become increasingly controversial. Opponents have raised concerns that giving preferential treatment to some groups amounts to "reverse discrimination" against groups who do not get the same benefits. They claim that affirmative action violates the principle that all individuals are equal under the law. But supporters counter that everyone who benefits from affirmative action must—by law—have relevant and valid qualifications. They argue that proactive measures are the only workable way to right past wrongs and to ensure truly equal opportunity.

Recent Supreme Court decisions have supported affirmative action, pointing out that government has a "compelling interest" in assuring racial diversity. But the Supreme Court has rejected "mechanistic" affirmative action programs that amount to quota systems based on race, ethnicity, or gender.

The long-term fate of affirmative action remains unclear, but achieving the underlying goal—a diverse workplace with equal opportunity for all—stands to benefit both business and society as a whole.[27]

Sexual Harassment: Eliminating Hostility

Sexual harassment—which violates Title VII of the Civil Rights Act of 1964—involves discrimination against a person based on his or her gender. According to the EEOC, sexual harassment can range from requests for sexual favors to the presence of a hostile work environment. The EEOC also points out that a sexual harasser may be either a woman or a man, and the harasser doesn't need to be the victim's supervisor. The victim could be anyone affected—either directly or indirectly—by the offensive conduct. And clearly, to qualify as sexual harassment, the conduct must be unwelcome. The total number of sexual harassment charges filed with the EEOC in the last decade dropped 11% from 1998 to 2008, but the number of charges filed by men rose from 12.9% to 15.9%.[28]

Not just the perpetrator is liable for sexual harassment; employers may share accountability if they did not take "reasonable care" to prevent and correct sexually harassing behavior, or if they did not provide a workable system for employee complaints. Simply adopting a written policy against sexual harassment is not enough. Taking "reasonable care" also means taking proactive steps—such as comprehensive training—to ensure that everyone in the organization understands 1) that the firm does not tolerate sexual harassment, 2) that the firm has a system in place for complaints and will not tolerate retaliation against those who complain.[29]

The Big Picture

Effective human resource management can create an unbeatable competitive edge—a fair, productive, empowering workplace pays off in bottom-line results. In good times, a core HRM goal is to find, hire, and develop the best talent. While that function remains crucial in tough economic times, the focus changes to managing HR costs while maintaining morale. Looking forward, a growing number of firms will most likely outsource traditional HR tasks such as payroll and benefits administration to companies that specialize in these areas. HR departments could then focus on their core mission: working with senior management to achieve business goals by cultivating the firm's investment in human resources.

affirmative action Policies meant to increase employment and educational opportunities for minority groups—especially groups defined by race, ethnicity, or gender.

sexual harassment Workplace discrimination against a person based on his or her gender.

WHAT ELSE? *RIP & REVIEW* **CARDS IN THE BACK**

16

MANAGING INFORMATION AND TECHNOLOGY: FINDING NEW WAYS TO LEARN AND LINK

LEARNING OBJECTIVES

After studying this chapter, you will be able to...

LO1 Explain the basic elements of computer technology—including hardware, software, and networks—and analyze key trends in each area

LO2 Discuss the reasons for the increasing popularity of cloud computing

LO3 Describe how data becomes information and how decision support systems can provide high-quality information that helps managers make better decisions

LO4 Explain how Internet-based technologies have changed business-to-consumer and business-to-business commerce

LO5 Describe the problems posed by the rapid changes in Internet-based technologies, and explain ways to deal with these problems

Visit CourseMate at **www.cengagebrain.com.**

> ## { Any sufficiently advanced technology is indistinguishable from magic. }
> *Arthur C. Clarke, science fiction author*

LO1 Information Technology: Explosive Change

Over the past few decades, computer and communications hardware and software have changed dramatically. The capabilities of hardware have increased by orders of magnitude. In the late 1950s, for example, you would have needed 50 24-inch disks—costing tens of thousands of dollars—to store five megabytes of data. Today you can buy a flash memory device about the same size as a postage stamp that stores 16 gigabytes of data—over 3,000 times more data than that whole 1950s disk array—for under $30. Today's smartphones—or even basic calculators—have more processing power than early "mega computers" that took up a whole room and weighed several tons. Software has taken advantage of these dramatic improvements in hardware to become more versatile and powerful, and much easier to use.

But perhaps an even more important development than the increased power of hardware and sophistication of software is the degree to which today's technology is linked by networks. These networks allow businesses to coordinate their internal functions, serve their customers, and collaborate with their suppliers and partners in ways that could not have been envisioned even a quarter of a century ago. Such innovations have improved the efficiency and effectiveness of existing businesses while also opening up entirely new business opportunities. Of course, these new linkages pose challenges and threats as well as benefits and opportunities; a quarter of a century ago people hadn't heard of computer viruses, spyware, phishing, or spam (except for the Hormel meat product variety). Over the course of this chapter we'll take a look at both sides of this rapidly changing story.

Hardware and Software

Hardware refers to the physical components used to collect, input, store, organize, and process data and to distribute information. This hardware includes the various components of a computer system, as well as communications and network equipment. Examples include hard drives, keyboards, printers, modems, routers, and smart phones.

Software refers to the programs that provide instructions to a computer so that it can perform a desired task. There are two broad categories of software: system software and application software.

System software performs the critical functions necessary to operate a computer at the most basic level. The fundamental form of system software is the operating system, which controls the overall operation of the computer. It implements vital tasks, such as managing the file system, reading programs and data into main memory, and allocating system memory among various tasks to avoid conflicts. Operating system software also provides the interface that enables users to interact with the computer.

Utility programs, another type of system software, supplement operating system software in ways that increase the security or abilities of the computer system. High-profile examples include firewalls, antivirus software, and antispyware programs. Over the years, operating systems have incorporated basic versions of many of these utility programs.

Applications software is the software that helps users perform a desired task. *Horizontal applications software*, such as word processing, spreadsheet, and personal information management software, is used by many different businesses and occupations. *Vertical applications software* is designed for a specific industry or profession. For example, brokerage firms have special software that allows them to transact business on the stock exchanges, and hospitals and doctors' offices have software to help them track patient records.

hardware The physical tools and equipment used to collect, input, store, organize, and process data and to distribute information.

software Programs that provide instructions to a computer so that it can perform a desired task.

system software Software that performs the critical functions necessary to operate the computer at the most basic level.

applications software Software that helps a user perform a desired task.

Internet The world's largest computer network; essentially a network of computer networks all operating under a common set of rules that allow them to communicate with each other.

Internet2 (I2) A new high-tech Internet restricted to dues-paying members of a consortium. I2 utilizes technologies that give it a speed and capacity far exceeding the current Internet.

Networks

Today, most firms (and many households) use networks to enable users to communicate with each other and share both files and hardware resources. A network links computer resources using either a wired or wireless connection. Firms usually want to prevent outsiders from obtaining access to their networks for privacy and security reasons, but they sometimes allow customers or suppliers partial access to their private networks to strengthen their relationships with these important stakeholders.

Wireless networks and smartphones allow individuals to connect to the Internet from almost anywhere.

© DAVID KILPATRICK /ALAMY

The Internet and the World Wide Web The development and growth of the Internet is one of the great networking stories of the last two decades. The **Internet** is essentially the world's largest computer network. It's actually a network of networks, consisting of hundreds of thousands of smaller networks, operating under a common set of rules so that they can communicate with each other.

You probably experience the Internet through the World Wide Web. In fact, many people think that the Internet and the Web are the same thing, but they aren't. The Internet supports the Web and provides access to it, but it also includes many sites that aren't on the Web. Still, the Web is big enough in its own right; it consists of billions of documents—the number grows significantly every day—written and linked together using Hypertext Markup Language (HTML).

The increased availability of broadband Internet connections has fueled the popularity of the Web in the United States and other developed countries. Broadband refers to an Internet connection that has the capacity to transmit large amounts of data very quickly, allowing users to quickly download Web pages with graphic or audio content and to download huge files such as music, games, and movies. A survey by the

Pew Internet and American Life Project in late 2009 found that 60% of all U.S. adults had access to a broadband connection, up from 47% in 2007. From a business perspective, the growth in broadband penetration allows companies to offer richer, more interactive experiences to customers who visit their websites.[1]

But even today's broadband connections are too slow and inefficient for many advanced business and scientific applications. Such projects often require high-definition video and audio files to be shared among multiple sites at the same time. Beginning in 1996, several leading research universities, corporations, and other organizations formed a coalition to create a new generation of Internet technology based on fiber-optic cable, which they dubbed **Internet2**. Internet2 (or "I2") is up and running, but it isn't available to just anyone. Access is limited to dues-paying members of the Internet2 consortium, which today consists of over 200 major universities as well as 70 leading high-tech corporations, 45 government agencies, and about 50 international organizations.

Internet2 isn't just a faster way to surf the Web or send email. In fact, such routine uses of the current Internet aren't even allowed. Instead, it is a

> **At current speeds, Internet2 is capable of transmitting five feature-length DVD movies from one location to another in less than one second.**
>
> *Socaltech.com*

noncommercial network that uses high-speed connectivity to improve education, research, and collaboration. Member organizations see Internet2 as a way to bring together their researchers, scientists, and engineers at various locations in a way that allows real-time collaboration on complex and important topics. It also allows corporations to collaborate with other companies, universities, and organizations located thousands of miles apart. One of the missions of the Internet2 consortium is to "Develop and deploy advanced network applications and technologies, accelerating the creation of tomorrow's Internet." So, the benefits of Internet2 will eventually become commonplace on the Internet that the rest of us use.[2]

Intranets and extranets An **intranet** is a network that has the same look and feel as the Internet and uses the same browser software to display documents but is confined to a single firm's internal Web servers and available only to that firm's employees. When properly implemented, intranets enhance communication and collaboration among employees and provide an effective way to store and distribute information and applications useful to employees throughout the organization. Employees can usually log onto their company's intranet from remote locations using password-protected Internet access, allowing them to use company resources when working on the road or from home.

Firms sometimes also create **extranets** by opening up their intranets to give limited access to certain groups of stakeholders, such as key customers and suppliers. Extranets help firms provide extra services and information to their external stakeholders. For example, the firm might allow customers to check on the status of their order, or suppliers to check on the state of the firm's inventory to plan shipments of parts and materials.

intranet A network that has the look and feel of the Internet, and is navigated using a Web browser, but is confined to documents located on a single company's servers and is available only to the firm's employees.

extranet An intranet that allows limited access to a selected group of stakeholders, such as suppliers or customers.

The Role of the IT Department

Many business organizations have an information technology (IT) department to manage their information resources. But the role of this department varies significantly from one company to another. In some firms the IT department plays a strategic role, making and implementing key decisions about the technologies the firm will use. In other organizations the role of IT is largely operational; managers in functional departments make the key decisions about the computer and information resources their areas need, and the IT department simply maintains these resources and provides technical support to employees.

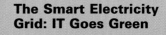

The Smart Electricity Grid: IT Goes Green

The Internet isn't the only complex network that is crucial to our nation's economy. Businesses also need a dependable power supply network. Providing this power is no small achievement; in fact, our nation's power grid has been called the world's most complex interconnected machine. At the beginning of the 21st century the National Academy of Engineering published a list of the 20 greatest engineering feats of the 20th century. The nation's electricity grid ranked first on the list. By way of comparison, the Internet ranked 13th.

As impressive as our current energy network is, new information technologies will soon make it even more reliable and efficient by creating a smart electricity grid. This new network will use high-tech sensors and meters to provide real-time information to both power companies and their customers.

Once in place, smart-grid technology will allow electric utilities to efficiently coordinate the generation and distribution of electricity from multiple sources—including environmentally friendly alternatives, such as wind, solar, and geothermal power. Even more importantly, it will help consumers and businesses monitor their use of electricity more accurately. Combined with pricing strategies that give users a cost break for using electricity during off-peak periods, the smart grid will result in a more efficient use of electricity. In fact, soon we will have "smart" appliances, such as air conditioners, dishwashers, and clothes driers that communicate with the grid to conserve energy and cut costs by adjusting the times when they operate.

A key benefit of smart grid technology is its ability to reduce environmental damage. The U.S. Department of Energy estimates that a 5% improvement in the efficiency of our nation's power grid—an easily attainable goal with the smart grid—would achieve the same reduction in greenhouse gases as permanently removing 53 million automobiles from our highways.[3]

© BSH STOCK/IMAGE SOURCE

cloud computing
The use of Internet-based storage capacity, processing power, and computer applications to supplement or replace internally owned information technology resources.

LO2 Cloud Computing: The Sky's the Limit!

In most companies, employees use applications and access data stored on their own computers or their companies' servers. But a new trend called "**cloud computing**" is challenging that approach. Cloud computing means going beyond a company's firewall to store data and run applications using Internet-based resources.

If you store and share photos on Flickr or Shutterfly you've already experienced a limited version of cloud computing and benefited from one of its key advantages—the ability to store large files without taking up valuable space on your computer's hard drive. You and others can access your photos from any computer with an Internet connection (or any Web-enabled mobile device)—another key advantage since it makes it very convenient to share your photos with friends and relatives.

Until recently most businesses were reluctant to embrace cloud computing, citing concerns about security and reliability as well as loss of internal control. Though security issues still remain, the number of firms using cloud-based services has grown significantly in recent years. This growth reflects the compelling advantages the cloud offers, including the ability to:

- access a vast array of computing resources without the need to invest heavily in expensive new hardware, software, and IT personnel;

- quickly adjust the amount of computer resources to meet their needs—and pay *only* for the resources that are *actually used*. This lowers costs and eliminates the problem of excess capacity. In fact, the cost reductions are often so great that even very small firms can afford to take advantage of sophisticated and powerful cloud computing resources;

- encourage collaboration among employees and business partners. Cloud resources aren't confined to a specific platform or operating system, so it is easy for people using different computer systems to share files and programs. In addition, many cloud-based applications include tools specifically designed to facilitate collaboration;

- take advantage of incredible gains in processing speed. Not only does cloud computing give users access to more resources, but also it enables them to use those resources more efficiently by taking advantage of a technique called *massively parallel computing*, which can combine the processing power of hundreds (or even thousands) of computers to work

on different elements of a problem *simultaneously*. The result is that data processing projects that used to take weeks to complete on a firm's internal computer resources can be completed in less than a day using cloud resources.[4]

Google and Amazon are two high-profile companies that already provide cloud computing services in a big way. Google offers a service known as Google App Engine that allows anyone (even small businesses) to use its vast and highly sophisticated computer infrastructure to develop and run their own applications on the Web. Google has also developed Google Apps, a set of web-based applications consisting of Gmail, Google Calendar, and Google Docs (which includes word processing, spreadsheet, and presentation applications) that are accessed via a web browser. While not quite as powerful or full-featured as office suites such as Microsoft Office, these programs have all the basic tools needed to handle everyday business tasks. In addition, all of the components of Google Docs include built-in tools that allow real-time collaboration among multiple users. The applications can be accessed from any computer with an Internet link and work with any operating system. Perhaps best of all from your perspective, Google provides an educational version of these applications to students and faculty at no charge, giving you a chance to experience some of the benefits of cloud computing at a personal level—although you may have to put up with some advertising.[5]

Amazon has moved into cloud computing just as aggressively as Google. It has developed a whole suite of cloud-based services known as "AWS" (which is short for Amazon Web Services). For instance, Amazon's Simple Storage Service (or S3) allows users to store virtually *any* amount of data on Amazon servers and retrieve it at any time. Another Amazon service, Elastic Compute Cloud (or EC2), gives clients the ability to harness the combined processing power of thousands of computers to handle complex and time-consuming computational tasks. Yet another Amazon service, SimpleDB, functions as an online database. All of these services are powerful and, compared to what it would cost a firm to purchase similar software and hardware, extremely cost effective.[6]

The New York Times used Amazon's cloud computing services to create an online archive allowing its subscribers to locate and view *any* article published over the paper's first seven decades in a format that had the same look and feel as the original article. The project to create this archive required the ability to scan and store over 11 *million* articles (amounting to over 4,000 gigabytes of data) and then convert these scanned documents into Internet-friendly PDF files. The project's managers estimated that this process would have tied up their newspaper's own computer resources for several weeks and would have been prohibitively expensive. But with storage provided by Amazon's S3 service and computational power provided by its EC2 service, the *Times* completed the whole project in two days and at a cost of less than $500. Amazingly, the project could have been completed even more quickly and at even lower cost but for a glitch in the PDF conversion process that required many of the files to be converted twice![7]

Cloud computing may revolutionize the role of IT departments.

data Raw, unprocessed facts and figures.

information Data that have been processed in a way that make them meaningful to their user.

database A file consisting of related data organized according to a logical system and stored on a hard drive or some other computer-accessible media.

Cloud computing is likely to bring about fundamental changes in the way firms acquire and use information technology resources. Some experts believe the very survival of IT departments—at least the ones that maintain and support only a firm's *internal* computer resources—is in doubt. Nicholas Carr, author of *The Big Switch: Rewiring the World from Edison to Google*, puts it this way: "In the long run, the IT department is unlikely to survive, at least not in its familiar form. It will have little left to do once the bulk of business computing shifts out of private data centers and into 'the cloud.'"[8]

LO3 Information Technology and Decision Making: A Crucial Aid

One of the vital functions of information technology—at least in relationship to business—is to transform data into useful information for decision makers. In order to make decisions, managers must have information about the current state of their business, their competitive environment, and the trends and market conditions that offer new opportunities. Where does this information come from? How can it be made more useful? How can managers process the information to make better decisions?

Data and Information

Let's start by distinguishing between data and information. **Data** are the facts and figures a firm collects. Data in their raw form have limited usefulness because they lack the context needed to give them meaning. Data become **information** when they are processed, organized, and presented in a way that makes them useful to a decision maker. Sometimes firms can obtain useful information from external sources, but sometimes they must create information by processing their own data. Given today's competitive environment, the speed with which managers obtain good-quality information can be a crucial competitive advantage.

Internally, every department of an organization generates facts and figures that the firm must store and track. Every time a financial transaction is completed, for example, the firm's accounting system must record the specific accounts affected. Similarly, a firm's human resource department must enter new data every time an employee is hired, fired, promoted, changes jobs, or retires. Firms must also keep track of the names, addresses, and credit information of each customer. This is hardly a complete list, but you get the picture; firms must store mountains of data and convert it into useful information.

Typically today's businesses store their data in **databases**, which are files of related data organized according to a logical system and stored on hard drives or some other computer-accessible storage media. It isn't unusual for a company to have many different databases, each maintained by a different department or functional area to meet its specific needs. For example, the human resources department might have a database of employee pay rates, and the marketing department may have another database of customer history.

Once all these data are stored, the firm must convert them into information. One common method is to *query* a database. A query is a request for the database management software to search the database for data that match criteria specified by the user. Suppose, for instance, that a marketing manager plans to introduce a product upgrade. She can enter a query that asks for the email addresses of all customers who have purchased the product in the past year. She can use this information to send a targeted email blast, promoting the upgrade to the customers who are most likely to buy it.

decision support system (DSS) A system that gives managers access to large amounts of data and the processing power to convert these data into high-quality information, thus improving the decision-making process.

business intelligence system A sophisticated form of decision support system that helps decision makers discover information that was previously hidden.

data warehouse A large, organization-wide database that stores data in a centralized location.

data mining The use of sophisticated statistical and mathematical techniques to analyze data and discover hidden patterns and relationships among data, thus creating valuable information.

expert system (ES) A decision-support system that helps managers make better decisions in an area where they lack expertise.

Characteristics of Good Information

We've seen that businesses have many sources of information. But not all information is of good quality. High-quality information is:

- **Accurate:** It should be free of errors and biases.
- **Relevant:** It should focus on issues that are important to making a decision.
- **Timely:** It should be available in time to make a difference.
- **Understandable:** It must help the user grasp its meaning.
- **Secure:** Confidential information must be secure from hackers and competitors.

Using Information Technology to Improve Decision Making

A company's information technology (IT) department frequently works closely with managers throughout the organization to support decision making. In fact, many companies develop **decision support systems (DSS)** that give managers access to large amounts of data and the processing power to convert the data into high-quality information quickly and efficiently.

Over the past two decades, a new class of decision support system has evolved to take advantage of the dramatic increase in data storage and processing capabilities. Called **business intelligence systems**, these systems help businesses discover subtle and complex relationships hidden in their data. Such systems can be a source of competitive advantage for the businesses that develop them.

One of the most common approaches to implementing a business intelligence system is to create a data warehouse and use data mining to discover unknown relationships. A **data warehouse** is a very large, organization-wide database that provides a centralized location for storing data from both the organization's own databases and external sources. **Data mining** uses powerful statistical and mathematical techniques to analyze the vast amounts of data in a data warehouse to identify useful information

> ### It used to be the big eat the small, but today the fast run over the slow.
> *Bob Helms, the former CEO of International Sematech*

that had been hidden. In recent years, data mining has had considerable success in areas as diverse as fraud and crime detection, quality control, scientific research, and even professional sports. For example, several NBA basketball teams have used data-mining techniques to discover the best combinations of players to put on the courts under various game situations.[9]

Expert Systems

Managers who use decision support systems usually already know quite a bit about the problem and how they want to solve it. They just need access to the right data and a system to "crunch the numbers" in a way that provides relevant, accurate, and timely information to help them make their decisions. But what happens when the problem is beyond the expertise of the manager? One way to deal with this problem is to set up an **expert system (ES)** to guide the manager through the decision-making process.

To develop expert systems, programmers ask experts in the relevant area to explain how they solve problems. They then devise a program to mimic the expert's approach, incorporating various rules or guidelines that the human expert uses. The finished program will ask a user a series of questions, basing each question on the response to the previous question. The program continues to ask questions until it has enough information to reach a decision and make a recommendation.

Expert systems routinely solve problems in areas as diverse as medical diagnoses, fraud detection, and consumer credit evaluation. The troubleshooting systems many companies have on the customer support pages of their websites are another type of expert system. If your product doesn't work, the troubleshooter will ask a series of questions designed to diagnose the problem and suggest solutions. Based on your responses to each question, the system selects the next question as it starts narrowing down the possible reasons for the problem until it identifies the cause and offers a solution. Often you can solve your problem without waiting on hold to talk to a human expert over the phone.[10]

Despite impressive results in many fields, expert systems have their limitations. Programming all of the decision rules into the system can be time consuming, complicated, and expensive. In fact, it's sometimes impossible because the experts themselves can't clearly explain how they make their decisions—they just "know" the answer based on their years of experience. If the experts can't clearly explain how they reach their conclusions, then programmers can't include the appropriate decision rules in the system. Finally, an expert system has little flexibility and no common sense. It probably won't be able to find a solution to a problem that deviates in any significant way from the specific type of problem it was programmed to solve.[11]

LO4 Information Technology and the World of e-Commerce

Over the past 20 years, advances in information technology have had a dramatic and widespread effect on how companies conduct their business. But in this chapter, we'll just concentrate on one key area: the growth and development of e-commerce.

E-commerce refers to using the Internet to facilitate the exchange of goods and services. You're probably most familiar with **business-to-consumer (B2C) e-commerce**. You participate in this form of e-commerce when you purchase some songs from iTunes, use Expedia to make travel arrangements, or buy stocks through an online broker such as Charles Schwab. However, **business-to-business (B2B) e-commerce**, which consists of markets where businesses sell supplies, components, machinery, equipment, or services to other businesses, actually accounts for a much larger volume of business.

While both B2C and B2B involve exchanging goods over the Internet, they differ in some important ways, as shown in Exhibit 16.1. Given these structural differences, it isn't surprising that the two markets operate so differently.

Using Information Technology in the B2C Market

Firms in the B2C market use information technology in a variety of ways. In this section we'll describe how firms use technology in general (and the Internet in particular) to attract new customers and strengthen the loyalty of existing customers.

Web 2.0 A major goal for most firms today is to develop stronger relationships with their customers. The Internet has proven to be an excellent tool for fostering such relationships—though it took a while for businesses to discover the best way to do so. In the early days of e-commerce, most companies tried to maintain tight control over all of the content presented on their websites. These websites presented information about products and allowed customers to place orders for goods and services, but offered little opportunity for user participation or involvement. However, by the early years of the 21st century, innovative businesses were developing ways to make e-commerce more interactive and collaborative. In doing so, they not only forged stronger relationships with the customers who posted this content, they also created a richer, more interesting, and more useful experience for *others* who visited the site. This new approach became known as **Web 2.0**.

e-commerce The marketing, buying, selling, and servicing of products over a network (usually the Internet).

business-to-consumer (B2C) e-commerce E-commerce in which businesses and final consumers interact.

business-to-business (B2B) e-commerce E-commerce in markets where businesses buy from and sell to other businesses.

Web 2.0 An approach to e-commerce that emphasizes interactive and collaborative commercial websites in order to develop consumer loyalty and create more value.

EXHIBIT 16.1 Key Differences Between B2C and B2B e-Commerce

	B2C	B2B
Type of customers	Individual final consumers	Other businesses
Number of customers in target market	Very large	Often limited to a few major business customers
Size of typical individual transaction	Relatively small (usually a few dollars to a few hundred dollars)	Potentially very large (often several thousand dollars, sometimes several million dollars)
Customer behavior	May do some research, but many purchases may be based on impulse	Usually does careful multiple research and compares vendors. May take bids.
Complexity of negotiations	Purchase typically involves little or no negotiation. Customer usually buys a standard product and pays the listed price.	Often involves extensive negotiation over specifications, delivery, installation, support, and other issues
Nature of relationship with customers	Firm wants to develop customer loyalty and repeat business but seldom develops a close working relationship with individual customers.	Buyers and sellers often eventually develop close and long-lasting relationships that allow them to coordinate their activities.

Two common tools found on Web 2.0 sites are wikis and blogs. A *wiki* is software that helps people collaborate by allowing them to create and edit web content on any web browser. A *blog* (short for web log) is an online journal or diary that is usually maintained by a single individual. Most blogs allow their readers to post comments.

Many Web 2.0 sites rely on users (or members) to provide most of their content. For instance, the online encyclopedia Wikipedia uses wiki software to allow users to comment on and contribute to its articles. And social networking sites such as Facebook, MySpace, and Twitter wouldn't exist without user-created material. The more users who participate on these sites, the more useful (and entertaining) they become—and the easier it is for them to attract even more visitors and contributors.

Interestingly, many companies have found that techniques used to encourage collaboration among their customers can be used to accomplish the same result with their employees. Major corporations such as HP, Wells Fargo, and Procter & Gamble now use blogs, wikis, and other Web 2.0 techniques to help their own employees work more effectively together. The use of Web 2.0 technologies within organizations is called Enterprise 2.0.[12]

Advertising on the Internet Many B2C companies have large target markets, so advertising is an important part of their marketing strategy. Internet advertising revenue grew rapidly in the early 21st century, increasing almost fourfold from 2002 to 2008. It dropped slightly in early 2009 (its first decline since 2002), but began rising again later that year. By the end of 2009 revenue from Internet advertising was nearly $23 billion, putting it ahead of magazine advertising revenue for the first time. If current trends continue it will soon surpass newspaper advertising—perhaps doing so by the time you read this. Ads placed on pages containing search results (such as those you see on Google or Bing) accounted for 47% of all Internet advertising revenues.[13]

Firms in B2C markets also use opt-in email as an advertising medium. Opt-in emails are messages that the receiver has explicitly chosen to receive. Customers often opt in when they register their products online and click to indicate that they would like to receive product information from the company. Since the customer has agreed to receive the message, opt-in emails tend to reach interested consumers. And, because email requires no envelopes, paper, or postage, it's much less expensive than direct mail.

Viral Marketing The Internet has also proven to be an effective medium for **viral marketing**, which attempts to get customers to communicate a firm's message to friends, family, and colleagues. Despite its name, legitimate viral marketing doesn't use computer viruses. Effective viral marketing campaigns can generate a substantial increase in consumer awareness of a product. As a strategy, viral marketing isn't unique to the Internet; even before the World Wide Web, marketers were adept at buzz marketing, the use of unconventional (and usually low-cost) tactics to stimulate word-of-mouth product promotion. But the Internet has made it possible to implement such strategies in clever ways and reach large numbers of people very quickly.

How Two Fans Changed the Face of Coke

Many Web 2.0 companies participate in social networking sites such as Facebook to forge stronger relationships with their customers. But sometimes the enthusiastic fans of a popular product just can't wait for the company to establish an official page. In early 2009 Dusty Sorg and Michael Jedrzejewski created a Coca-Cola fan page on Facebook. The page quickly became a huge success. Within a few months it boasted over 3.4 million fans, making it the second most popular page on Facebook—trailing only the page for President Barack Obama.

According to Facebook's policies, the company that produces a product has the right to its page. So Coca-Cola *could* have asked Facebook to shut down the fans' site and replaced it with an official corporate-managed page. But the company's management was impressed by the creativity of Sorg and Jedrzejewski's efforts. They also worried that thwarting the efforts of the page's creators might alienate many Coca-Cola fans who visited the page. So the soft drink giant invited Sorg and Jedrzejewski to its Atlanta headquarters, treated them royally during their visit, and negotiated an unusual arrangement. Under the terms of the agreement the two fans were allowed to keep their fan page in exchange for an agreement to collaborate with Coke officials on the development of content.[14]

© STEFAN KLEIN/ISTOCKPHOTO.COM

Handling Payments Electronically B2C e-commerce normally requires customers to pay at the time the purchase is made. Clearly, the use of cash and paper checks isn't practical. In the United States, most payments in the B2C market are made by credit cards. To ensure that such transactions are secure, most sites transmit payment information using a secure socket layer (SSL) protocol. You can tell if a site on which you're doing business is using SSL in two fairly subtle ways. First, the URL will begin with https:// instead of simply http://. (Note the "s" after http in the address.) Also, a small closed lock icon will appear near the bottom of your web browser (the exact location depends on the specific browser you are using). 🔒

Another common approach to sending electronic payments is to use a **cybermediary**—an Internet-based company that specializes in the secure electronic transfer of funds. By far the best-known cybermediary is PayPal. According to figures on its website, PayPal (which is owned by eBay) had over 220 million accounts worldwide as of mid-2010.[15]

A final way of making electronic payments is **electronic bill presentment and payment**. This is a relatively new method in which bills are sent to customers via email. The bill includes a simple mechanism (such as clicking on a button-shaped icon) that allows the customer to make a payment once the amount of the bill has been verified. Many banks now offer this payment method, as do services such as Quicken and Fiserv.

Using Information Technology in the B2B Market

Businesses that participate in B2B e-commerce typically don't surf multiple sites on the Web to find customers or suppliers. Instead, many participate in **e-marketplaces**, which are specialized Internet sites where many buyers and sellers in a specific B2B market can exchange information and buy and sell goods and services.

E-marketplaces provide a number of advantages to their participants:

- Compared to older methods, they reduce time, effort, and cost of doing business for both buyers and sellers.

cybermediary An Internet-based firm that specializes in the secure electronic transfer of funds.

electronic bill presentment and payment A method of bill payment that makes it easy for the customer to make a payment, often by simply clicking on a payment option contained in an email.

e-marketplace A specialized Internet site where buyers and sellers engaged in business-to-business e-commerce can communicate and conduct business.

> { **What new technology does is create new opportunities to do a job that customers want done.** }
>
> *Tim O'Reilly, founder and CEO of O'Reilly Media*

© AMANDA ROHDE/ISTOCKPHOTO.COM

Viral Marketing: Finding the Perfect Blend

Blendtec is a small company that specializes in one thing: making powerful high-quality blenders. The company, which was founded in 1999, has always claimed that its products will blend almost anything. But until recently the company had little success in convincing customers to believe those claims. Thus, despite the quality of its blenders, Blendtec remained a niche player in its market. The company's fortunes began to change soon after it hired George Wright as its first marketing director in 2006. Wright quickly began looking for ways to build public awareness of Blendtec's products. He knew his small company lacked the financial resources to mount a big conventional advertising campaign, so he decided to use viral marketing to generate the maximum amount of buzz at the lowest possible cost.

Wright recruited Tom Dickson, the company's CEO, to star in a series of "Will It Blend?" videos that featured Blendtec blenders reducing a weird assortment of items, such as garden rakes, marbles, and glow sticks, into finely chopped particles (or glowing goo in the case of the glow sticks). The initial video segments cost only about $50 to produce with the largest expense being the purchase of a white lab coat for Dickson to wear.

Wright initially featured the videos on the company website (www.willitblend.com) but soon decided to upload them to YouTube. Within weeks they were among the most popular videos on the site. One video, featuring a "golf ball smoothie," received 1.7 million views. The company saw sales of its home blenders soar by 43% in the first year after the videos were introduced. But that wasn't the only good news. Because the videos were so popular, other companies began begging Blendtec to feature their products in the videos. Soon Blendtec was able to charge these companies $5,000 for the privilege of having their products turned into "smoothies."[16]

radio frequency identification (RFID) a technology that stores information on small microchips than can transmit the information anytime they are within range of a special reader.

- Because they are Internet-based, they don't require expensive dedicated connections between firms, so even smaller firms can afford to participate.

- They enable sellers and buyers to contact and negotiate with a large number of market participants on the other side of the market.

- They often provide additional services—beyond simple trade—that allow firms to exchange information and collaborate.

Walmart was one of the earliest proponents of RFID technology. In 2003 it announced that it would require all of its major suppliers to include RFID chips on all of their shipments by 2006. But despite its clout, Walmart faced significant resistance from many suppliers who saw the new technology as too costly. Because of this resistance, Walmart fell far short of achieving its timetable; in fact, some of its large suppliers (and a majority of its smaller ones) still do not make extensive use of RFID. But those suppliers that have adopted the technology have generally reported very positive results.

> **Some Las Vegas casinos now include RFID chips in their poker chips, allowing them to calculate the average bet and won/loss rate of individual players.**
>
> *Technovelgy.com*

Once buyers and sellers have reached agreement in an e-marketplace, they may eventually develop a long-term working relationship that requires close coordination and collaboration. The relationships forged in e-marketplaces help the firms improve their supply chains. A *supply chain* is the network of organizations and activities needed to obtain materials and other resources, produce final products, and get those products to their final users.

In recent years many supply chains have begun using another information technology known as **radio frequency identification (RFID)**. This technology stores information on a microchip and transmits it to a reader when it's within range—which is usually limited to a few feet. The chips can be extremely small—some are difficult to see with the naked eye—and can be embedded in most types of tangible products. The chips are usually powered by the energy in the radio signal sent by the reader so they don't even need their own power supply.

RFID chips can store and transmit all sorts of information, but most commonly they transmit a serial number that uniquely identifies a product, vehicle, or piece of equipment. This type of information can be used to help track goods and other resources as they move through a supply chain. Deliveries can be recorded automatically without the need for manual record keeping. The chips also can make taking inventory much quicker and simpler since the items in stock identify themselves to readers. And the chips can be used to reduce the chances of pilferage. The result of these advantages is lower costs and a more efficient supply chain.

LO5 Challenges and Concerns Arising from New Technologies

So far we've concentrated on the benefits of advances in information technology—and it's clear that these benefits are enormous. But rapid technological advances also pose challenges and create opportunities for abuse. These problems affect businesses, their customers, and their employees, as well as the general public. In this section, we'll look at annoyances, security concerns, and legal and ethical issues.

> **Technology is so much fun, but we can drown in our technology. The fog of information can drive out knowledge.**
>
> *Daniel Boorstin, historian and former Librarian of Congress*

Spyware and Computer Viruses

As you almost certainly know, the Internet—for all its advantages—creates the possibility that unwanted files and programs may land on your computer. In many cases, this happens without your knowledge, much less your permission. Some of these files and programs are relatively benign (even useful), but others can create major problems.

© JULIEN TROMEUR/ISTOCKPHOTO.COM

Spyware is software that installs itself on your computer without permission and then tracks your computer behavior in some way. It might track which Internet sites you visit to learn more about your interests and habits in order to send you targeted ads. Or, more alarmingly, it might log every keystroke (thus capturing passwords, account numbers, and user names to accounts as you enter them), allowing someone to steal your identity. Some spyware even goes beyond passive watching and takes control of your computer, perhaps sending you to websites you didn't want to visit.

Computer viruses are small programs that install themselves on computers without the users' knowledge or permission and spread from one computer to another—sometimes very rapidly. (This ability to spread automatically to other computers is the key difference between virus software and spyware.) Some viruses are little more than pranks, but others can cause great harm. They can erase or modify data on your hard drive, prevent your computer from booting up, or find and send personal information you've stored on your computer to people who want to use it for identity theft. Viruses are often hidden in emails, instant messages, or files downloaded from the Internet.

How can you protect yourself from spyware and viruses? Take these common sense steps:

- Perform regular backups. This can come in handy should a virus tamper with (or erase) the data on your hard drive. Store the backed-up data in a separate place.

- Install high-quality antivirus and antispyware software and keep it updated. (Today's Internet security software utilities have the ability to automatically check for, download, and install updates, but they may need to be configured to do so.)

- Update your operating system regularly so that any security holes it contains are patched as soon as possible.

- Don't open email messages or attachments if you don't know and trust the sender.

- Read the licensing agreement of any programs you install—especially those of freeware you download from the Internet. The wording of these agreements will often indicate if other programs (such as spyware) will be installed along with your free program.

Spam, Phishing, and Pharming

Spam refers to unsolicited commercial emails, usually sent to huge numbers of people with little regard for whether they are interested in the product or not. It's hard to get exact measures of the amount of spam that is sent each year, but experts agree that it now comprises the vast majority of all email in the United States. It clogs email inboxes and makes it tough for people to find legitimate messages among all the junk. Spam filters exist that help detect and eliminate spam, but spammers are very good at eventually finding ways to fool these filters.[17]

The U.S. Congress enacted the Controlling the Assault of Non-Solicited Pornography and Marketing Act (usually called the CAN-SPAM Act) in 2003. This act requires senders of unsolicited commercial email to label their messages as ads and to tell the recipient how to decline further messages. It also prohibits the use of false or deceptive subject lines in email messages. But the rapid increase in the amount of spam in recent years suggests this law hasn't been an effective deterrent.

Phishing is another common use of spam. Phishers send email messages that appear to come from a legitimate business, such as a bank, credit card company, or retailer. The email attempts to get recipients to disclose personal information, such as their social security or credit card numbers, by claiming that there is a problem with their account. The messages appear authentic; in addition to official sounding language, they include official-looking graphics, such as corporate logos. The email also usually provides a link to a website where the recipient is supposed to log in and enter the desired information. When the victims of the scam click on this link, they go to a website that can look amazingly like

spyware Software that is installed on a computer without the user's knowledge or permission for the purpose of tracking the user's behavior.

computer virus Computer software that can be spread from one computer to another without the knowledge or permission of the computer users.

spam Unsolicited email advertisements usually sent to very large numbers of recipients, many of whom may have no interest in the message.

phishing A scam in which official-looking emails are sent to individuals in an attempt to get them to divulge private information such as passwords, usernames, and account numbers.

pharming A scam that seeks to steal identities by routing Internet traffic to fake websites.

hacker A skilled computer user who uses his or her expertise to gain unauthorized access to the computer (or computer system) of others, sometimes with malicious intent.

the site for the real company—but it's not. It's a clever spoof of the site where the phishers collect personal information and use it to steal identities.

Current versions of major web browsers include filters to block phishing scams, but phishers (like spammers in general) are very clever at finding ways to get around filters, so you need to take extra precautions. In addition to using a browser with an antiphishing filter, remember that reputable businesses almost never ask you for private information via email. Also, never click on a link in an email message to go to a website where you have financial accounts.

Not content with phishing expeditions, some scam artists have now taken to **pharming**. Like phishing, pharming uses fake websites to trick people into divulging personal information. But pharming is more sophisticated and difficult to detect than phishing because it doesn't require the intended victim to click on a bogus email link. Instead, it uses techniques to redirect Internet traffic to the fake sites. Thus, even if you type in the *correct* URL for a website you want to visit, you still might find yourself on a very realistic-looking pharming site. One way to check the validity of the site is to look for the indications that the site is secure, such as the https:// in the URL and the small closed lock icon mentioned earlier.[18]

Computers aren't the only devices plagued by these threats and annoyances. Cell phone users are facing increasing problems with spam delivered via text messaging. And, unlike email spam, many cell phone users end up paying extra for these unwanted messages. Even more alarming, some scammers have found ways to take their phishing expeditions to cell phones—a practice known as "smishing." A typical smishing ploy is to use text messaging to entice cell phone users to visit the scammer's fake website.[19]

Hackers: Break-Ins in Cyberspace

Hackers are skilled computer users who have the expertise to gain unauthorized access to other people's computers. Not all hackers intend to do harm, but some—called "black hat hackers" (or "crackers")—definitely have malicious intent. They may attempt to break into a computer system to steal identities or to disrupt a business. *Cyberterrorists* are hackers motivated by political or ideological beliefs who try to cause harm to those who don't share their views. Some experts predict that cyberterrorists may attempt to launch attacks on key industries (such as energy, finance, or transportation) that could cripple a nation's economy.[20]

Protecting against hackers requires individuals and businesses to be security conscious. Some of the precautions used against hackers, such as making frequent backups, are similar to those used to protect against

© JOSE LUIS PELAEZ INC./BLEND IMAGES/JUPITERIMAGES

Information Overload: Too Much of a Good Thing?

From email to cell phones (and text messaging) to Twitter updates to blogs on the Web, many of today's workers (and students) are connected to what seems to be an endless flow of information. But while the diversity and volume of the information generated by the communications technologies of the 21st century can be gratifying, it's also often distracting—and sometimes even intimidating.

Do you sometimes find yourself receiving so much information in such a short time period that you feel overwhelmed and unable to process it all? If so, you aren't alone. The problem is so common that there is even an organization—the Information Overload Research Group—dedicated to exploring its causes and cures.

How serious is information overload? One study, conducted by University of London psychiatrist Glenn Wilson, suggested that when workers were constantly bombarded with new information, their ability to remain focused and complete tasks was disrupted. In fact, he found information overload could actually temporarily reduce the worker's decision-making IQ by up to ten points!

Dealing with information overload requires discipline. If you find yourself swamped by too much information, try to set aside a few times a day when you will check and respond to emails and voicemails, read blogs, and surf the Web and leave other times free to concentrate on getting work done without these interruptions. Prioritize your work and don't let yourself get distracted by irrelevant (though often interesting) topics. Finally, resist the urge to subscribe to information sources such as newsletters and RSS feeds just because they are available and might be interesting—they won't help you if you never have time to read them.[21]

viruses. Another key to protecting against hackers is to make sure that all data transmitted over a network is encrypted, or sent in encoded form that can only be read by those who have access to a key. Security experts also suggest that organizations restrict access to computer resources by requiring users to have strong passwords. According to Microsoft, a strong password:

- is relatively long (eight or more characters);
- consists of a mix of lower- and uppercase letters, numbers, and special characters (such as #, @, &, ~);
- doesn't include the user's real name, username, a common word or simple sequences of letters or numbers;
- is not used for all accounts or for extended periods of time; use different passwords for different accounts and change them on a regular basis.

But strong passwords not only make it difficult for hackers to gain unauthorized access to a system, they also pose a challenge to legitimate users—it's tough to remember long random strings of letters, numbers, and characters—especially when you're supposed to use different passwords for different accounts and change them frequently. One security expert found that many people have such a hard time keeping up with their passwords that they simply write them down and hide them under their mouse pads—hardly a secure location![22]

Given these problems with passwords, many firms are now relying on *biometrics*—the use of personal characteristics to uniquely identify an individual to determine whether they should have access to computer resources. The most common current example of biometrics is the use of fingerprint readers, but other approaches, such as iris or retina scans, may become more common in the future.

Firewalls are another important tool to guard against hackers and other security threats. A firewall uses hardware or software (or sometimes both) to create a barrier that prevents unwanted messages or instructions from entering a computer system. As threats from spyware, hackers, and other sources have developed, the use of firewalls has become commonplace.

Ethical and Legal Issues

Information technology raises a number of legal and ethical challenges, such as the need to deal with privacy issues and to protect intellectual property rights. These issues are controversial and don't have simple solutions.

Personal Privacy We've already mentioned that firms now have the ability to track customer behavior in ways that were never before possible. So far, we've discussed the advantages to the firm and customer by emphasizing that such knowledge often allows firms to

offer better, more personalized service. But all this extra information comes at the expense of your privacy. Does the fact that firms know so much about your preferences and behavior make you a bit nervous?

Does it also bother you that your email messages lack confidentiality? When you send an email, it's likely to be stored on at least four computers: your personal computer, the server of your email provider, the server of your recipient's provider, and your recipient's own computer. If you send the email from your company's system, it's also likely to be stored when the company backs up its information. If you thought that deleting an email message from your own computer erased it permanently and completely, you need to think again.

Legal opinions about email are still evolving. In 2007 a panel of U.S. federal judges found that the Fourth Amendment protects emails from unreasonable search and seizure by the government. But judges of the Sixth Circuit Court of Appeals soon overturned this decision, leaving the question of whether email is protected from government search unresolved.[23]

The list of other ways you can lose your privacy is long and getting longer. For example, RFID chips are now embedded in U.S. passports and in many states' driver's licenses. Some privacy experts are concerned that such chips will make it easy for government organizations to track individuals. One reason government officials gave for embedding RFID chips in passports and driver's licenses was to make it harder for criminals and terrorists to forge IDs. But in 2009 a hacker publicly demonstrated the ability to read the information in these chips from a distance of several yards, leading to fears that identity thieves could use similar techniques to obtain personal information and perhaps even create convincing copies of these important identification documents. The U.S. government responded to these concerns by issuing assurances that passports and driver's licenses include additional security features that minimize such risks, but skeptics remain unconvinced.[24]

The bottom line is that there's no simple way to solve privacy concerns. Privacy is an elusive concept, and there is no strong consensus about how much privacy is enough.

Protecting Intellectual Property Rights **Intellectual property** refers to products that result from creative and intellectual efforts. There are many types of intellectual property, but we'll focus on forms of intellectual property that are protected by copyright law, such as books, musical works, computer programs, and movies.

firewall Software and/or hardware designed to prevent unwanted access to a computer or computer system.

intellectual property Property that is the result of creative or intellectual effort, such as books, musical works, inventions, and computer software.

Nintendo is just one of many companies concerned about piracy of their intellectual property.

© JOCHEN TACK/IMAGEBROKER.NET/PHOTOLIBRARY

Copyright law gives the creators of this property the exclusive right to produce, record, perform, and sell their work for a specified time period.

The rationale for copyright protection is that creators of intellectual property will receive little or no compensation for their efforts if their work can be copied, distributed, and used by others without permission and without payment. Without the chance to get paid for their work, many talented people might decide it's not worth the effort to create anything new.

The rapid rise and fall of the Napster file-sharing service in the early 2000s highlighted both how easy it was for literally millions of people to use the Internet to share musical works without permission and how aggressively the music industry would try to prevent such practices. The subsequent development of other music file-sharing networks and the lawsuits the music industry has filed against individual file swappers in recent years suggests that the struggle over this issue is far from over.[25]

Unauthorized music sharing isn't the only form of piracy. The Business Software Alliance estimates that globally 43% of all business software installed on personal computers in 2009 was illegally obtained, resulting in the loss of over $51 billion in revenue to software companies. Among larger nations, the piracy rate in China exceeded 80%. And it wasn't much better in India, where an estimated 65% of all business software was illegally obtained. The good news is that the piracy rate was much lower in the United States at 20%. But given the huge size of the U.S. software market, even this relatively low rate of piracy still resulted in losses of over $8.4 billion in revenue for software companies. Faced with such a widespread problem, many software publishers have become very aggressive at prosecuting firms and individuals engaged in software piracy.[26]

Video game and motion picture producers also face significant problems with piracy. Nintendo estimated that it lost almost $1 billion in revenues in 2007 due to the sale of pirated versions of games for its popular DS and Wii game systems. In late 2007 a raid on a factory in Hong Kong seized 10,000 machines used to illegally copy the company's games.[27]

Given how lucrative piracy can be, it's unlikely that this problem will go away anytime soon. You can expect the companies hurt by these practices to continue aggressively prosecuting pirates and to work on new technologies that make pirating digital media more difficult.

Hackers Take Stock of Profit Opportunities

© REMUS ESER/ISTOCKPHOTO.COM

In recent years hackers in search of quick profits have found the U.S. stock market a tempting target. In 2007, for example, a hacker gained illegal access to Thomson Financial's computer system and learned that a company named IMS Health, Inc. would soon report a substantial loss on its third quarter earnings. The hacker quickly bought hundreds of put options for the company's stock before the losses were made public. (A put option gives its holder the right to sell stock at a set price by a certain date.) When IMS Health's stock dropped dramatically he was able to sell the puts for a profit of over $287,000.

In both 2008 and 2009 the SEC uncovered even more blatant attempts by hackers to profit in the U.S. stock market. In both cases, the hackers engaged in "hack, pump, and dump" strategies. First, they bought stock in thinly traded companies. Then they hacked into brokerage firms and placed unauthorized orders to buy the same stocks at highly inflated prices. Having pumped up the prices, they sold (dumped) their own shares at huge profits.

The good news is that the SEC caught all of these hackers—we wouldn't be writing about them if their schemes had gone undetected! Other hackers may have found ways to profit without getting caught, but the SEC clearly is on task when it comes to cyber security.[28]

The Big Picture

Information technology plays a vital role in virtually every aspect of business operations. For instance, marketing managers use information technology to learn more about customers, reach them in novel ways, and forge stronger relationships with them—as we showed in our discussion of Web 2.0. Operations managers use RFID technologies to coordinate the movement of goods within supply chains and to keep more accurate inventory records. And financial managers use IT to track financial conditions and identify investment opportunities. Managers in all areas of a business can use decision support systems to improve their decision-making. They also can apply techniques such as data mining to obtain interesting new insights hidden in the vast streams of data that flow into their companies.

Cloud computing represents the newest and one of the most exciting new approaches to how companies acquire and utilize IT resources. The use of cloud-based resources not only has the potential to lower costs and increase flexibility, but it also offers the ability to magnify computation power to levels previously impossible to envision. If the popularity of cloud computing continues to grow as many experts predict, the role of IT departments will undergo a significant evolution.

The rapid changes in IT in recent years—especially those related to the rise of Internet as a business venue—have opened up exciting new commercial opportunities. But these changes have also created a host of legal and ethical challenges and security concerns as businesses and their stakeholders struggle to adapt to these new technologies. One thing is certain: business organizations that find ways to leverage the advantages of new IT developments while minimizing the accompanying risks are most likely to enjoy competitive success.

WHAT ELSE? *RIP & REVIEW* **CARDS IN THE BACK**

17

OPERATIONS MANAGEMENT: PUTTING IT ALL TOGETHER

LEARNING OBJECTIVES

After studying this chapter, you will be able to...

LO1 Describe the role of operations management in business

LO2 Discuss the key responsibilities of operations managers

LO3 Explain how technology has influenced operations management

LO4 Describe how operations managers integrate operations using supply chain management and enterprise resource planning

LO5 Discuss the ways operations managers can foster continuous quality improvement within their organizations

LO6 Explain the movement toward lean production

LO1 Operations Management: Doing It Right

Operations management is concerned with planning, organizing, leading, and controlling all of the activities involved in creating value by producing goods and services and distributing them to customers. When operations managers do their job well, their firms use the most effective and efficient methods to produce the *right* goods and services in the *right* quantities—and to distribute them to the *right* customers at the *right* time. Obviously, the decisions of operations managers can have a major impact on a firm's revenues and its costs, and thus on its overall profitability.

Over the past few decades, operations management has seen dramatic changes. Emerging technologies and global competition have fueled a range of new strategies. But before examining them in detail, let's look at some operations management basics.

Effectiveness versus Efficiency

The goals of operations management center on two key concepts: effectiveness and efficiency. **Effectiveness** means completing tasks and producing products that *create value* by satisfying wants. **Efficiency** refers to completing a task or producing a product at the *lowest cost*. Both efficiency and effectiveness are important; a firm must provide goods and services that satisfy consumers' wants—otherwise customers won't buy them. But in today's competitive markets it also must keep costs under control in order to earn an attractive profit.

The relationship between efficiency and effectiveness is subtle and complex. In the short run, improving effectiveness may increase costs, which would seem to reduce efficiency. But over the long haul, efficiency and effectiveness often go hand in hand; creating value can sometimes actually reduce costs.

Goods versus Services

Goods are tangible products that you can see and touch. *Durable goods* are expected to last three years or longer; examples include furniture and appliances. *Nondurable goods*, such as soft drinks and paper towels, are consumed more quickly. **Services** are intangible products, such as legal advice, entertainment, and medical care.

Historically, the U.S. economy has been a manufacturing powerhouse, with much of its labor and other resources focused on

producing goods. In fact, millions of Americans still work in the goods-producing sector. But over the last several decades, the American economy has experienced a fundamental shift away from manufacturing and toward the provision of services. From an operations management perspective, this shift has important implications. Exhibit 17.1 identifies some of the key differences between

operations management Planning, organizing, leading, and controlling the activities involved in producing goods and services and distributing them to customers.

effectiveness Using resources to create the greatest value.

efficiency Producing output or achieving a goal at the lowest cost.

goods Tangible products.

services Intangible products.

EXHIBIT 17.1 Differences between Goods and Services

Goods	Services
Are tangible: They have a physical form and can be seen, touched, handled, etc.	Are intangible: They can be "experienced," but they don't have a physical form.
Can be stored in an inventory.	Must be consumed *when* they are produced.
Can be shipped.	Must be consumed *where* they are provided.
Are produced independently of the consumer.	Often require the customer to be actively involved in their production.
Can have at least *some* aspects of their quality determined objectively by measuring defects or deviations from desired values.	Intangible nature means quality is based mainly on customer perceptions.

© JOHN LUND/STONE/GETTY IMAGES

value chain The net-work of relationships that channels the flow of inputs, information, and financial resources through all of the processes involved in producing and distributing goods and services.

goods and services from an operations perspective. As we move through the chapter, we'll see that the differences between goods and services directly affect many operations management decisions.

of relationships that channels the flow of inputs, information, and financial resources through all of the processes directly or indirectly involved in producing goods and services and distributing them to customers. The desired result of the value chain is to produce a combination of goods and services that create value for the target market at a cost that's low enough to allow the

> **The Bureau of Labor Statistics forecasts the U.S. service sector will generate 14.5 million new jobs between 2008 and 2018, while employment in the goods producing sector will remain unchanged over the same period.**
>
> *Bureau of Labor Statistics*

LO2 What Do Operations Managers Do?

Understanding the marketing definition of "product" plays a pivotal role in understanding what operations managers do. A product is more than a physical good—it includes a whole set of tangible and intangible features that create value for consumers by satisfying their needs and wants.

Marketing research typically determines which features a product should include to appeal to its target customers. Although operations managers don't normally have the primary responsibility for designing these goods and services, they provide essential information to those that do, especially regarding the challenges and constraints involved in creating actual products on time and within budget.

Once the actual goods and services are designed, operations managers must select and implement the processes needed to produce the goods and services and get them to the customer. A process is a set of related activities that transform inputs into outputs, thus adding value. The most obvious processes are those directly involved in the production of the final goods and services. But there are many other processes that play necessary "supporting roles." For example, purchasing and inventory management processes make sure that the firm has an adequate supply of high-quality materials, parts, and components. This creates value by ensuring that goods and services can be produced without delays or disruptions due to shortages of (or defects in) these inputs.

All of the processes a firm uses to create value must be integrated to ensure that they work seamlessly together. A **value chain** refers to the network

firm to make a profit while offering the goods and services at a competitive price.

Operations management is an ongoing process. Given the intense competition and rapid technological change that characterize today's business environment, firms must pursue continuous improvement in their operations. In particular, they must find ways to continuously improve quality while decreasing costs. We'll look at some ways firms try to accomplish these goals later in the chapter when we discuss several important quality initiatives and describe a relatively new trend called "lean manufacturing." But first, let's take a look at some of the key functions operations managers must perform to move goods and services from the drawing board to the final user.

Facility Location

There is an old saying in real estate that the three most important factors determining the value of a property are location, location, and location. While that may be a bit of an exaggeration for operations management, there is no doubt the location of a production facility is an important consideration.

For some types of facilities, the location decision is a no-brainer. A coal mine, for instance, must be located where there's coal. But for many other types of facilities, the decision is more complex. Exhibit 17.2 identifies some key factors that operations managers look at when they decide where to locate a facility. The importance of each factor in Exhibit 17.2 varies depending on the specific type of industry. Because of their need for direct interaction with customers, many service firms place primary interest on locating close to their markets. But manufacturing firms may be more concerned about the cost and availability of land and labor.

EXHIBIT 17.2 Factors That Affect Location Decisions

General Location Factors	Examples of Specific Considerations
Adequacy of utilities	Is the supply of electricity reliable?
	Is clean water available?
Land	Is adequate land available for a facility?
	How much does the land cost?
Labor market conditions	Are workers with the right skills available?
	How expensive is labor?
Transportation factors	Is the location near customers and suppliers?
	Is appropriate transportation nearby?
Quality of life factors	What is the climate like?
	Are adequate healthcare facilities available?
Legal and political environment	Does the local government support new businesses?
	What are the local taxes, fees, and regulations?

countries—has become an increasingly popular strategy in recent years. Low-wage labor is a major reason firms offshore their operations, but other factors also play a role. Land and other resources may be much less expensive in developing nations than in the United States. And some foreign governments, eager to attract U.S. investments, may offer financial incentives or other inducements. In addition, many foreign markets are growing much more rapidly than the relatively mature U.S. market. Firms often find it advantageous to locate production facilities close to these rapidly growing markets.

But offshoring can have drawbacks as well as benefits. Locating production facilities in foreign countries may require a firm to deal with unfamiliar laws, languages, and customs. Social unrest and unstable governments beset some developing nations. Roads, bridges, airports, and seaports in developing nations may have limited capacity or be in poor shape, making it difficult to ship goods and services. And electricity and other utilities may be unreliable, causing disruptions in production. It's also important to realize that low hourly *wages* in some foreign nations do not *always* translate into low costs of production. Workers in some developing nations have less education, less experience, and poorer health than American workers. For these reasons, they may be much less productive than their American counterparts. If the hourly wage of foreign workers is a third of what American workers earn, but the foreign workers produce only a fourth as much output per hour, their low wage isn't really a bargain.

> **offshoring** Moving production or support processes to foreign countries.

One of the most controversial issues concerning location decisions in recent years involves whether to move key processes overseas. **Offshoring**—the practice of moving production or support processes to foreign

© GUENTER SCHIFFMANN/BLOOMBERG VIA GETTY IMAGES

Seniors Have Their Moments at BMW

Soon after the turn of the 21st century, managers at BMW realized they faced a looming challenge. Germany's population was rapidly aging—and so was the upscale automaker's labor force. Evidence showed that as workers age, their health problems (and absenteeism) increased while their productivity decreased—not a good combination in the highly competitive auto market.

BMW's operations managers knew they needed to redesign their production processes to compensate for the limitations of their older workers. But they weren't sure what types of adjustments would be most effective. So in 2007 they set up an experimental "2017 production line" and staffed it with workers whose characteristics matched the profile of the older labor force BMW projected for 2017. This allowed them to try out a variety of changes and identify the ones that were most effective. A key element of the 2017 line was that managers actively sought the advice of the workers in the experiment. This turned out to be a great idea, because the workers came up with several inexpensive yet effective suggestions, such as:

- Replacing concrete floors with wooden floors to reduce strain on feet and knees.
- Installing height-adjustable work stations to reduce back strain.
- Changing the viewing angles of monitors to reduce neck strain.
- Encouraging workers to do stretching exercises during work breaks.

As simple as these changes were, they made a big difference in productivity and quality. Despite their older average age, the workers on the 2017 line quickly became just as productive as younger workers on other lines. They also achieved (and sustained) a zero defect rate. And absenteeism fell from 7% at the beginning of the project to 2% by the end of the first year—a rate that actually was lower than the average for workers on other production lines.[1]

Many labor leaders and politicians claim that offshoring results in widespread job losses for American workers. But some economists and business leaders contend that offshoring could actually increase domestic employment. They reason that offshoring reduces costs, enabling firms to become more competitive and increase their market share. This growth in market share may create more domestic jobs than were lost due to offshoring—although the types of jobs will be different. While this line of reasoning may be valid in some cases, it's been a tough sell to the American workforce. One problem is that the workers who lose jobs to offshoring may not have the skills to qualify for the new jobs that are created by the growth.[2]

Process Selection and Facility Layout

Once a firm has determined the design of its product, it must figure out the best way to produce it. This involves determining the most efficient processes, deciding the best way to sequence those processes, and designing the appropriate layout of the production facility so that materials, work in **process**, and finished goods move smoothly and efficiently through the production process.

Well-designed processes enable a firm to produce high-quality products effectively and efficiently, giving it a competitive advantage. Poorly designed processes can result in production delays, problems with quality, high costs, and other problems. But what considerations do operations managers use when they design these processes? And how should these processes be organized to achieve the goal of efficient production? Many factors influence the type of process that works best and how these processes should be organized. Two key considerations are the volume of production and the degree of standardization of the product.

Firms use *flow shop processes* when they produce goods that are relatively standardized and produced in large volumes. These processes use specialized machinery and equipment designed to produce a large quantity of a specific good or service very efficiently. The machinery and equipment used to perform these processes are often arranged in a product layout. This involves organizing the machinery, equipment, and tasks in a specific sequence. An assembly line is a common type of product layout. On an assembly line, the product being produced moves from one station to another in a fixed sequence, with the machinery and workers at each station performing specialized tasks. Services that provide a high volume of relatively standardized products can also use product

layouts. For example, fast food restaurants often prepare burgers, pizzas, or tacos in a standard sequence of steps that is not unlike a simple assembly line.

Flow shop processes aren't suited for the production of goods that require customization or that are produced individually or in small batches. Firms producing goods or services with these characteristics often use *job shop processes*. A job shop uses general-purpose equipment, sacrificing the efficiency of specialization for a greater degree of flexibility. Also, job shops don't require production to occur in a specific sequence of steps. Instead, the sequence of steps can be altered so that the shop can produce a variety of different goods without expensive retooling. Because they use general-purpose tools and perform a wider variety of tasks, workers in job shops must be more versatile than workers in flow shops. Job shops often use a process layout, which groups together machinery and equipment used to perform a specific task. For example, in a machine shop all of the drills may be located in one area, all of the lathes in another area, and all of the grinders in yet another. Service organizations that offer highly personalized service (such as hospitals) also often use a process layout.

A *cellular layout* falls between the process layout and the product layout. This arrangement is often used by companies that focus on lean production—a strategy we'll describe toward the end of this chapter. The cellular layout groups different types of machinery and equipment into self-contained cells. Each cell is set up for the efficient production of parts (or entire products) that require similar production processes. A shop might have several cells, each designed to produce a different type of output. Like an assembly line, the product progresses from one station in the cell to the next in a specific sequence. However, unlike most assembly lines, cells are relatively small and usually are designed to be operated by a small number of workers who perform a wider array of tasks than the assembly line workers.

A *project* involves the coordination of many complex activities to

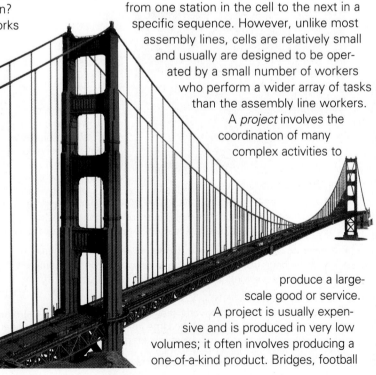

produce a large-scale good or service. A project is usually expensive and is produced in very low volumes; it often involves producing a one-of-a-kind product. Bridges, football

> # The "raw materials" of a service are time and motion, not plastic or steel.
>
> *G. Lynn Shostack,*
> *marketing consultant*

stadiums, and levees are examples. The creation of a Broadway play is an example of a project for a service. Projects often involve the production of goods that must be produced at a specific site (such as a building or a dam), or that are so large and bulky that it isn't feasible to move them from station to station (such as an ocean liner). Such products often use a *fixed position layout*. In this approach, the product stays fixed, and the employees, machinery, and equipment are brought to the fixed site when needed.

Special Characteristics of Service Processes Services are intangible and often require the customer to directly interact with the provider at the time the service is created. The inclusion of the customer in the process means that the creators of most services have less control over how the process is carried out, how long it takes to complete, and whether the result is satisfactory. For instance, the accuracy of a doctor's diagnosis often depends on how honestly and completely the patient answers the doctor's questions. And the amount of time the doctor spends with each patient will depend on the seriousness of the problem and the complexity of the diagnosis.

Because of the interaction between customers and service providers, the design of service facilities often must take the experiences of the participants into account. A **servicescape** is the environment in which the customer and service provider interact. A well-designed servicescape can have a positive influence on the attitudes and perceptions of both the customer and the employees who provide the service. A poor servicescape can have the opposite effect.[3]

The design of servicescapes centers on three types of factors: ambience; functionality; and signs, symbols, and artifacts. *Ambience* refers to factors such as decor, background music, lighting, noise levels, and even scents. For example, massage therapists often use low light, soothing background music, and pleasant scents to create a relaxing atmosphere for a massage. *Functionality* involves how easy is it for the customer to move through the facility and find what they are looking for. *Signs, symbols,* and *artifacts* convey information to customers and create impressions. Obviously signs like "Place Your Order Here" and "Pick Up Your Order Here" provide useful information that helps consumers maneuver through the service encounter. But other signs and symbols can be used to create favorable impressions. For instance, lawyers often prominently display their diplomas and awards in their offices to communicate their qualifications and professional accomplishments to their clients.

servicescape The environment in which a customer and service provider interact.

inventory Stocks of finished items, work in process, parts, materials, or other resources held by an organization.

Inventory Control: Don't Just Sit There

Inventories are stocks of goods or other items held by an organization. Manufacturing firms usually hold inventories of raw materials, components and parts, work in process, and finished goods. Retail firms are unlikely to hold work in process or raw materials, but they usually do hold inventories of finished goods and basic supplies that their business needs.

Deciding how much inventory to hold can be a real challenge for operations managers. Here are some of the reasons for holding large inventories:

- **Smooth Out Production Schedules:** A candy maker might produce more candy than it needs in August and September and hold the excess in inventory. That way it can meet the surge in demand in the weeks before Halloween without investing in more production capacity.

- **Meet Unexpected Increases in Demand:** Firms may lose sales to competitors if they run out of stock. They might hold additional inventory to meet unexpected increases in demand.

- **Reduce Costs Associated with Production Setup:** Rather than incurring frequent setup costs to produce items in small batches, firms may produce more than they need in the current time period, holding the rest in inventory for future periods.

- **Compensate for Forecast Errors:** Many firms base production schedules on sales forecasts. But sales forecasts aren't perfectly accurate. Any unsold goods will end up in inventory, at least for the short term.

But holding large inventories involves costs as well as benefits:

- **Tied-Up Funds:** Items in inventory don't generate revenue until they're sold, so holding large inventories can tie up funds that could be better used elsewhere within the organization.

- **Additional Costs:** Large inventories require the firm to rent, buy, or build more storage space—which can also mean extra costs for heating, cooling, taxes, insurance, and so on.

- **Increased Risk:** Holding large inventories exposes the firm to the risk of losses due to spoilage, depreciation, and obsolescence.

Operations managers determine the optimal amount of inventory by comparing the costs and benefits associated with different levels of inventory. In our discussion of lean manufacturing, we'll see that a recent trend has been toward finding ways to reduce inventory levels at every stage of the supply chain.

The demand for many types of services varies significantly depending on the season—or even on the time of day. Since services are consumed at the time they are created, service firms can't use inventories of work in process or finished goods to help them adapt to sudden changes in the level of demand. During peak lunch and dinner hours, popular restaurants tend to be very busy—often with crowds waiting to get a table. These same restaurants may be nearly empty during the midafternoon or late at night. Given this limitation, the selection of *capacity*—the number of customers the service facility can accommodate per time period—becomes a crucial consideration. If the capacity of a service facility is too small, customers may have to wait too long for service during peak periods and take their business elsewhere. But a large facility can be expensive to build, maintain, and insure, especially when it is used to full capacity only a few hours per day (or perhaps only a few days a year). Service firms often try to avoid this problem by finding ways to spread out demand so that big surges don't occur. One way to do this is to give customers an incentive to use the service at off-peak times. For instance, many bars and restaurants have "happy hours" or "early-bird specials."

Project Scheduling

Projects, such as the construction of a new office building or filming of a movie, are usually complex, important, and expensive. It's vital to plan and monitor them carefully to avoid major delays or cost overruns.

Gantt charts and **critical path method (CPM) networks** are two tools operations managers rely on to keep tabs on projects. A simple example can illustrate how both tools are used. We'll assume that the administration of a college wants to build a new sports arena and must complete several activities before it can hire a contractor and begin construction. Exhibit 17.3 lists the specific activities involved in the college's project.

Notice that Exhibit 17.3 identifies **immediate predecessors** for all of the activities except A. Immediate predecessors are activities that must

EXHIBIT 17.3 Activities Involved in College Arena Project

	Activity	Immediate Predecessor(s):	Time (Weeks)
A.	Survey of needs	None	2
B.	Determine site for arena	A	5
C.	Preliminary design developed	A	5
D.	Obtain major donation for funding	C	4
E.	Obtain board approval	B, D	4
F.	Select architect	E	3
G.	Establish budget	E	2
H.	Obtain remaining financing	F, G	10
I.	Finalize design	G	6
J.	Hire contractor	H, I	6

be completed before other activities can begin. For example, the administration believes that it must survey users of the arena to determine their needs and location preferences *before* they develop a preliminary design or select a site. Thus the survey of needs is an immediate predecessor for both the selection of the site and preliminary design.

Using a Gantt Chart to Get the Big Picture

Exhibit 17.4 on the following page illustrates a Gantt chart for this project. The Gantt chart lists all of the activities down its left margin and shows the elapsed time since the project began across the bottom of the chart. A bar is drawn for each activity, showing when it is expected to start and end. Notice that activities can't start until their immediate predecessors have been completed.

Once a project has begun, the bars for the activities on a Gantt chart can be filled in to indicate progress. In our example, the solid orange bars represent activities that are completed, the solid gray bars represent activities that haven't yet begun, and the bars that are part orange and part gray indicate activities that are currently under way. The chart shows us that as of week 22 the college is about a week behind schedule in finalizing its design since the orange part of the bar for this activity extends only to week 21. We can also see that the college is two weeks ahead of schedule in arranging final financing.

Using the Critical Path Method to Focus Efforts

Now look at Exhibit 17.5, which is a Critical Path Method diagram for the arena project. One benefit of a CPM network is that it clearly shows how all of the activities are related to each other. The direction of the arrows shows the immediate predecessors for each activity. For example, notice that arrows go from activities F *and* G to activity H. This indicates that *both* F

EXHIBIT 17.4 A Gantt Chart for the College Arena Project

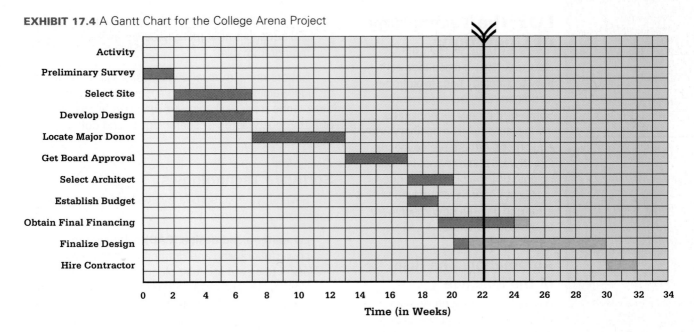

(selection of the architect) and G (establishing the budget) must be completed before activity H (obtaining final financing) can begin. But also notice that no arrow links activities H and I. This shows that these are independent activities, so the college could arrange financing and finalize the design for the arena at the same time.

We can use Exhibit 17.5 to illustrate some basic concepts used in CPM analysis. A *path* is a sequence of connected activities that *must be completed in the order specified by the arrows* for the overall project to be completed. You can trace several paths in our example by following a series of arrows from start to finish. For example, one path is A → B → E → G → I → J and another path is A → C → D → E → G → H → J.

All paths in a project are important, but some need more attention than others. The **critical path** consists of the sequence of activities that takes the longest to

complete. A *delay in any activity on a critical path is likely to delay the completion of the entire project*. Thus operations managers watch activities on the critical path very carefully and take actions to help ensure that they remain on schedule. We've shown the critical path for the arena project (A → C → D → E → F → H → J) with red arrows on our diagram.

Distinguishing between the critical path and other paths can help operations managers allocate resources more efficiently. Activities that aren't on the critical path can be delayed without causing a delay in the overall completion of the project—as long as the delay isn't too great. In CPM terminology, these activities have *slack*. When operations managers see delays in critical path activities, they may be able to keep the project on track by diverting manpower and other resources from activities with slack to activities on the critical path.

EXHIBIT 17.5 CPM Chart for the College Arena Project

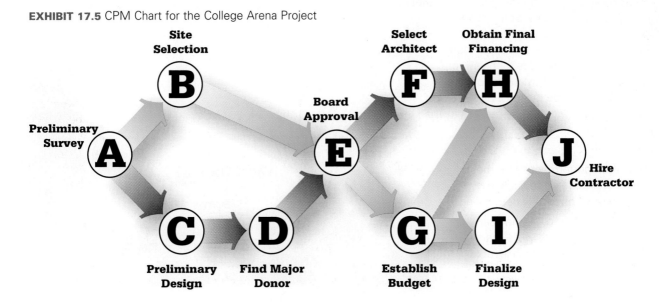

LO3 The Technology of Operations

Now let's take a close look at how technology has revolutionized operations management. Some of the new technologies involve automated machinery and equipment. Others are advances in software and information technology. But the biggest changes in recent years have involved efforts to link the new machinery to the new software.

Automation: The Rise of the Machine

For the past half century, one of the biggest trends in operations management has been increased **automation** of many processes. Automation means replacing human operation and control of machinery and equipment with some form of programmed control. Over the years, the use of automated systems has become increasingly common and increasingly sophisticated.

Automation began in the early 1950s with primitive programmed machines. But in recent decades, **robots** have taken automation to a whole new level. Robots are reprogrammable machines that can manipulate materials, tools, parts, and specialized devices in order to perform a variety of tasks. Some robots have special sensors that allow them to "see," "hear," or "feel" their environment. Many robots are mobile and can even be guided over rugged terrain.

Firms have found that robots offer many advantages:

- They often perform jobs that most human workers find tedious, dirty, dangerous, or physically demanding.

- They don't get tired, so they can work very long hours while maintaining a consistently high level of performance.

- They are flexible; unlike old dogs, robots *can* be taught new tricks because they are reprogrammable.

Robots perform a variety of tasks. Common uses include welding, painting, and assembling, but other uses range from packaging frozen pizza to disposing of hazardous wastes or searching for and defusing bombs.

Software Technologies

Several types of software have become common in operations management:

- **computer-aided design (CAD)** software provides powerful drawing and drafting tools that enable users to create and edit blueprints and design drawings quickly and easily. Current CAD programs allow users to create 3-D drawings.

- **computer-aided engineering (CAE)** software enables users to test, analyze, and optimize their designs through computer simulations. CAE software can help engineers find and correct design flaws *before* production.

- **computer-aided manufacturing (CAM)** software takes the electronic design for a product and creates the programmed instructions that robots must follow to produce that product as efficiently as possible.

Today, **computer-aided design and computer-aided manufacturing** software are often combined into a single system, called **CAD/CAM.** This enables CAD designs to flow directly to CAM programs, which then send instructions directly to the automated equipment on the factory floor to guide the production process.

When a CAD/CAM software system is integrated with robots and other high-tech equipment, the result

© PHOTOLINK/PHOTODISC/GETTY IMAGES

is **computer-integrated manufacturing (CIM)** in which the whole design and production process is highly automated. The speed of computers and the integration of all these functions make it possible to switch from the design and production of one good to another quickly and efficiently. CIM allows firms to produce custom-designed products for individual consumers quickly and at costs almost as low as those associated with mass production techniques—a strategy known as *mass customization*.

computer-integrated manufacturing (CIM) A combination of CAD/CAM software with flexible manufacturing systems to automate almost all steps involved in designing, testing, and producing a product.

LO4 Integrating Operations Management: Coordinating Efforts

The computer-integrated manufacturing we just discussed is one example of another important trend in operations management: the integration of formerly independent functions into highly coordinated systems. Two other major examples of this trend are supply chain management and enterprise resource planning (ERP).

How Operations Managers View Supply Chains

Operations managers view a *supply chain* as the part of a value chain that involves the physical movement of goods and materials through the production and distribution processes, along with the supporting flows of services and financial resources directly linked to this movement.[4]

Supply chains can be very complex, involving many firms, located in many countries, performing a wide range of production and distribution functions. Coordinating all of the flows among these organizations can be a real challenge. Today, operations managers rely heavily on specialized supply chain management software to help them plan and execute supply chain decisions. The market for this type of software has grown rapidly in recent years as firms have discovered the competitive advantages of efficient supply chain management.

The Internet has also provided new tools for managing supply chain relationships. For instance, e-marketplaces—websites that function as online meeting places for firms at different stages of a supply chain—now enable firms to negotiate, communicate, and collaborate more efficiently than ever before. Most e-marketplaces went through tough times during the dot-com bust a decade ago; in fact, many of them failed. But those that survived have staged a comeback and provide real benefits to their members. For example, Atlanta-based MFG.com supports buyers and sellers engaged in over 300 manufacturing processes. The site allows suppliers to precisely specify the types of jobs they are capable of performing. Buyers submit drawings and specifications for products or components they need

© STEVE COLE/ISTOCKPHOTO.COM

Doc Robot Is in the House

Robots are revolutionizing the practice of medicine. Doctors at many hospitals now use a robot developed by InTouch Health to check on their patients at times when they're unable to get to the hospital. The robot uses video cameras and a wireless Internet hookup to send information back to the doctor. The "head" of the robot is a video screen that allows the patient to see the physician, who can talk to the patient through the Internet hookup. Children, in particular, seem comfortable with this arrangement. When the robot rolls into the pediatric wing of a hospital decked out in a stethoscope and a superhero cape, the typical response is a roomful of giggles.

Now robots are even performing surgeries—although still under the guidance of experienced physicians. Intuitive Systems has developed a robotic system called the "da Vinci® Surgical System" that is capable of performing heart bypasses and other complex procedures. The da Vinci system was featured on the 2009 season finale of the popular ABC medical drama *Grey's Anatomy*. But the da Vinci system isn't just a star of fiction; by the end of 2009 almost 1,400 da Vinci systems had been installed and were in regular use in real-world hospitals throughout the world.

Doctors using da Vinci control the robot's movements from a console equipped with a 3-D monitor. The robot can perform surgeries with smaller incisions and steadier "hands" than unaided human surgeons. A study by the University of Maryland found that, compared to standard surgical procedures, the use of robots in heart bypass surgery resulted in shorter recovery times, fewer complications, and a better chance that the bypassed blood vessels would remain open.[5]

© 2008 INTUITIVE SURGICAL, INC.

vertical integration Performance of processes internally that were previously performed by other organizations in a supply chain.

outsourcing Arranging for other organizations to perform supply chain functions that were previously performed internally.

enterprise resource planning (ERP) Software-based approach to integrate an organization's systems in order to improve the flow of information among all departments and operating units.

produced, and MFG.com instantly directs the buyer's request to all sellers that possess the necessary expertise and the capacity to perform the job. Interested sellers can then bid on the job. The result is a very fast and efficient matching of buyers and sellers.[6]

One of the most important issues operations managers must consider when looking at how to improve supply chains is the trade-off between vertical integration and outsourcing. **Vertical integration** occurs when a firm attempts to gain more control over its supply chain by either developing the ability to perform processes previously performed by other organizations in the chain or by acquiring those organizations. **Outsourcing** is essentially the opposite of vertical integration; it involves arranging for other organizations in the supply chain to perform functions that were previously performed internally.

In recent years, the trend has been to rely more on outsourcing and less on vertical integration. Outsourcing allows a firm to shed functions it doesn't perform well in order to focus on its areas of strength. It also frees people and money that had been tied up in the outsourced activities, allowing these resources to be employed in more profitable ways.

It is important to realize that outsourcing is *not* the same thing as offshoring. Outsourcing doesn't require

a firm to go offshore; outsourced activities can be performed by other *domestic* firms. Similarly, offshoring doesn't necessarily involve outsourcing; a firm could accomplish processes overseas by directly investing in its *own* foreign facilities. Despite this distinction, many firms have combined outsourcing with offshoring, hiring foreign firms to carry out some of the processes that they previously performed at their own domestic facilities.

While foreign outsourcing can often reduce costs, it also can complicate supply chains and create coordination problems. And it can expose the firm to certain types of risks. When a firm outsources important functions, it may have to entrust others in its supply chain with confidential information and intellectual property, such as copyrighted material or patented products. These strategic assets have less legal protection in some countries than in the United States, so providing access to foreign firms may increase the risk that the firm's intellectual property will be pirated or counterfeited. This issue has been of greatest concern when firms have outsourced some of their supply chain functions to organizations in China.[7]

Enterprise Resource Planning: Creating One Big System

Enterprise resource planning (ERP) represents an even higher degree of operations integration than supply chain management. ERP is a computerized, organization-wide system that integrates the flow of information among *all* aspects of a business's operations—accounting, finance, sales and marketing, production, and human resources.

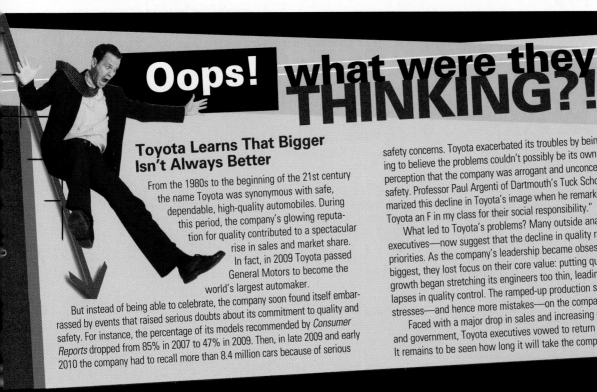

Oops! what were they THINKING?!

Toyota Learns That Bigger Isn't Always Better

From the 1980s to the beginning of the 21st century the name Toyota was synonymous with safe, dependable, high-quality automobiles. During this period, the company's glowing reputation for quality contributed to a spectacular rise in sales and market share. In fact, in 2009 Toyota passed General Motors to become the world's largest automaker.

But instead of being able to celebrate, the company soon found itself embarrassed by events that raised serious doubts about its commitment to quality and safety. For instance, the percentage of its models recommended by *Consumer Reports* dropped from 85% in 2007 to 47% in 2009. Then, in late 2009 and early 2010 the company had to recall more than 8.4 million cars because of serious

safety concerns. Toyota exacerbated its troubles by being slow to react, seeming to believe the problems couldn't possibly be its own fault. This created a perception that the company was arrogant and unconcerned about consumer safety. Professor Paul Argenti of Dartmouth's Tuck School of Business summarized this decline in Toyota's image when he remarked that "I would give Toyota an F in my class for their social responsibility."

What led to Toyota's problems? Many outside analysts—and key Toyota executives—now suggest that the decline in quality reflected a change in priorities. As the company's leadership became obsessed with becoming the biggest, they lost focus on their core value: putting quality first. The rapid growth began stretching its engineers too thin, leading to design errors and lapses in quality control. The ramped-up production schedules also created stresses—and hence more mistakes—on the company's production lines.

Faced with a major drop in sales and increasing criticism in the press and government, Toyota executives vowed to return to their focus on quality. It remains to be seen how long it will take the company to restore its image.[8]

© PHOTODISC/GETTY IMAGES

In fact, the newest versions of ERP software often include supply chain management as part of its system.

When one department enters data into the ERP system, it becomes immediately available to other departments, eliminating the need for each group to enter the data separately. In addition, the common information system makes it easier for departments throughout the enterprise to communicate and coordinate their activities. Once their ERP systems are fully in place, firms can see dramatic improvements in performance. But many companies have found that implementing ERP systems has been easier said than done. Several factors contribute to the cost and challenge of successfully implementing ERP systems:

- The scope and complexity of the software make it expensive, even without modifications. But most firms want to customize the software to meet their specific needs, adding to the complexity, cost, and timeframe.

- All the data from the old system must be transferred to the new system. This can be a time-consuming task since the data from different departments is often stored in different formats.

- ERP software requires employees throughout the organization to learn new ways of entering and accessing data. Productivity often falls until workers learn how to use the new system.[9]

Despite these challenges, ERP systems have become very popular. And they continue to evolve and take advantage of new technologies. One of the newest developments is the arrival of Web-based ERP systems that can be "rented" from online providers—a strategy that reduces the need for firms to invest in new hardware and software. The use of Web-based ERP services is an example of a relatively new trend in information technology known as cloud computing.[10]

LO5 Focus on Quality

Almost everyone agrees that quality is important. But the concept of quality is tough to define—even expert opinions differ. For our purposes, we'll adopt the view that quality is defined in terms of how well a good or service satisfies customer preferences.

Why is quality so important? Improvements in quality are a key to achieving competitive advantage because they enable a firm to improve both its effectiveness *and* its efficiency. The fact that high quality improves effectiveness (creates value) probably doesn't surprise you—consumers tend to place a high value on quality. But you might be surprised to learn that improved quality also can lower costs. After all, it's expensive to train workers in quality improvement, to install better equipment, set higher standards, and implement more rigorous procedures. But poor quality also comes with costs. When a firm detects defective products, it must scrap, rework,

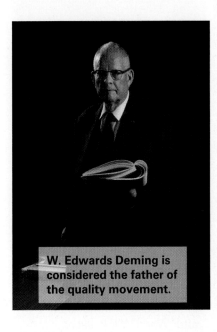

W. Edwards Deming is considered the father of the quality movement.

or repair them—all costly options. And the costs can be even higher when a firm *doesn't* catch defects before shipping products to consumers. These costs include handling customer complaints, warranty repair work, loss of goodwill, and the possibility of bad publicity or lawsuits. In the long run, firms often find that improving quality reduces these costs by more than enough to make up for their investment.

These ideas aren't especially new. W. Edwards Deming, viewed by many as the father of the quality movement, first proposed the relationship between quality and business success in the early 1950s. His ideas, which came to be known as the *Deming Chain Reaction*, are summarized in Exhibit 17.6. Unfortunately for American firms, Japanese companies were quicker to heed Deming's message than the Americans were.

EXHIBIT 17.6 The Deming Chain Reaction: Improved Quality Helps the Business's Bottom Line

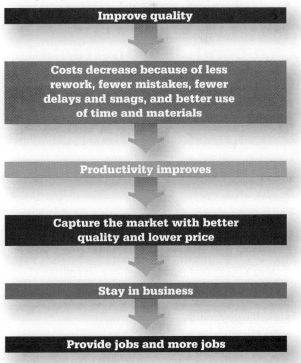

Improve quality

Costs decrease because of less rework, fewer mistakes, fewer delays and snags, and better use of time and materials

Productivity improves

Capture the market with better quality and lower price

Stay in business

Provide jobs and more jobs

Waking Up to the Need for Quality

The 1970s and early 1980s were a wake-up call for many American companies. During this period, Japanese firms in several key industries, including automobiles, electronics, and heavy machinery, rapidly gained global market share at the expense of American firms that had once faced little competition. One of the major reasons for the success of Japanese firms was that the quality of their goods was clearly superior. This was a remarkable turnaround because in the decades immediately after World War II, Japanese goods had a reputation for being downright shoddy.

How did the Japanese quality revolution occur? During the 1950s, many Japanese firms listened to quality experts such as W. Edwards Deming. They took the message to heart and began treating quality improvement as a *continuous* process—and as a goal that concerned every employee. It took a while, but the quality of Japanese goods slowly and steadily improved. By the early 1970s, many Japanese firms had achieved quality levels that exceeded those of companies in most other countries by a wide margin.

> **Quality is the result of a carefully constructed cultural environment. It has to be the fabric of the organization, not part of the fabric.**
>
> *Philip Crosby, 20th-century quality guru*

How American Firms Responded to the Quality Challenge

When key American firms realized how far they trailed the Japanese in quality, they made a real effort to change their ways. Like the Japanese a few decades earlier, American business leaders adopted a broader view of quality than they had previously held.

Total Quality Management The first result of this newfound emphasis on quality was the development of an approach called **total quality management**, better

known as TQM. There are several variations, but all versions of TQM share the following characteristics:

- **Customer Focus:** TQM recognizes that quality should be defined by the preferences and perceptions of customers.

- **Emphasis on Building Quality Throughout the Organization:** TQM views quality as the concern of every department and every employee.

- **Empowerment of Employees:** Most TQM programs give teams of workers the responsibility and authority to make and implement decisions to improve quality.

- **Focus on Prevention Rather Than Correction:** TQM pursues a strategy of preventing mistakes that create defects.

- **Long-Run Commitment to Continuous Improvement:** TQM requires firms to adopt a focus on making improvements in quality a way of life.

In many cases, American firms using TQM attempt to reduce defects by using **poka-yokes**—the Japanese term for "mistake proofing." Poka-yokes are simple procedures built into the production process that either prevent workers from making mistakes or help workers quickly catch and correct mistakes if they do occur. A simple example of a poka-yoke would be providing assembly workers with "kits" that contain exactly enough parts to complete one unit of work at a time. If the worker completes an assembly and sees a part left over, it's clear that a mistake has been made, and he or she can correct it on the spot.[11]

The Move to Six Sigma During the 1990s, another approach to total quality, known as **Six Sigma**, became increasingly popular. Six Sigma shares some characteristics with TQM, such as an organization-wide focus on quality, emphasis on finding and eliminating causes of errors or defects (prevention rather than correction), and a long-term focus on continuous quality improvement. Also like TQM, it relies on teams of workers to carry out specific projects to improve quality. At any given time, a firm may have several Six Sigma projects under way, and the goal of each is to achieve the Six Sigma level of quality.

But Six Sigma differs from TQM in other respects. Unlike TQM, it has a single unifying measure: to reduce defects of any operation or process to a level of no more than 3.4 per million opportunities. Attaining this level of quality represents a rigorous and challenging goal. Six Sigma also differs from TQM in its reliance on extensive (and expensive) employee training and reliance on expert guidance. The techniques used in the Six Sigma approach are quite advanced, and their application requires a high level of expertise.

Quality Standards and Quality Initiatives

Another way firms try to implement quality improvement is to launch programs designed to achieve certification or recognition from outside authorities. Two common approaches are to participate in the Baldrige National Quality Program and to seek certification under the International Organization for Standardization's ISO 9000 standards.

The Baldrige National Quality Program Congress passed the Malcolm Baldrige National Quality Improvement Act of 1987 in an effort to encourage American firms to become more competitive in the global economy by vigorously pursuing improvements in quality and productivity. Winners of the Baldrige Award must demonstrate excellence in seven criteria: leadership; strategic planning; customer and market focus; measurement, analysis, and knowledge management; human resource focus; process management; and business results.

Firms that participate in the **Baldrige National Quality Program** receive benefits even if they don't win the award. Every participating firm receives at least 300 hours of evaluation and review from highly qualified business and quality experts. At the end of the process, they receive a detailed report identifying areas of strength and areas where improvement is needed. Considering the normal fees that high-powered consulting firms charge for similar reports, the information and advice a firm gets for the fee charged to participate in the Baldrige program (which ranges from $1,000 to $6,000, depending on the type of organization) are a tremendous bargain![12]

ISO 9000 Certification Founded in 1947, ISO is a network of national standards institutes in more than 150 nations that work together to develop international standards for a wide array of industries. ISO standards ensure that goods produced in one country will meet the requirements of buyers in another country. This benefits consumers by giving them the ability to buy from foreign sellers with confidence, giving them a wider array of choices. It also benefits sellers by allowing them to compete more successfully in global markets.

Most of the standards established by the ISO are industry-specific. But in 1987 the ISO developed generic standards for quality management systems that could be applied to virtually any company in any industry in any country. Firms that satisfy these broad standards receive **ISO 9000** certification. Similar to many other quality initiatives, ISO 9000 standards define quality in terms of the ability to satisfy customer preferences and require the firm to implement procedures for continuous quality improvement. Since 1987, the ISO 9000 standards have been updated and modified several times. The latest update occurred in 2008.

In the late 1990s the International Organization for Standardization developed another set of standards called ISO 14000. This new set of standards focuses on environmental management. The goal is to ensure that qualifying firms minimize harm to the natural environment and achieve continuous improvement in environmental practices.

LO6 Lean Production: Cutting Waste to Improve Performance

Lean production refers to a set of strategies and practices to eliminate waste, which is defined as "any function or

---

Baldrige National Quality Program A national program to encourage American firms to focus on quality improvement.

ISO 9000 A set of generic standards for quality management systems established by the International Organization for Standardization.

lean production An approach to production that emphasizes the elimination of waste in all aspects of production processes.

Six Sigma Belts Quality Concerns

Six Sigma quality programs rely on sophisticated techniques that require highly trained and experienced leadership. Much like karate, Six Sigma identifies the proficiency of its practitioners with belt colors:

- **Yellow Belts** have some basic training in Six Sigma concepts, but they are not proficient enough to take responsibility for a project.
- **Green Belts** have a higher level of training than Yellow Belts and work on Six Sigma projects as part of their regular jobs. But they haven't acquired the depth of training needed to become Black Belts.
- **Black Belts** have a high enough level of training and experience to take charge of a Six Sigma team working on a specific project. They work full-time on Six Sigma projects.
- **Master Black Belts** have achieved the highest level of expertise in the statistical methods, quality improvement strategies, leadership, and other techniques needed to carry out Six Sigma projects. They are the teachers and mentors of Black Belts. Master Black Belts can achieve an almost superstar status within their organizations.[13]

activity that uses resources but doesn't create value." Eliminating waste can lead to dramatic improvements in efficiency. For example, Sanford, the maker of Paper Mate® pens and Sharpie® markers and highlighters, used lean thinking to dramatically cut its packaging costs. Before adopting lean thinking, Sanford developed different blister packs for every single product, resulting in literally hundreds of different packages. After applying lean thinking, the company was able to cut the number of package configurations down to 15, reducing setup time for packaging by 50%, cutting tooling costs by up to 80%, and reducing warehousing costs by up to 25%.[14]

Identifying Sources of Waste: Value Stream Mapping

Lean production begins by looking at all aspects of an organization's operations from the time that parts and raw materials first arrive until the production process is completed. The purpose of this process is to find and eliminate sources of waste. Value stream mapping is one of lean production's most important tools in this effort. A **value stream map** is a diagram that provides a detailed picture of the flows of all parts, materials, and information through

all of the activities involved in a manufacturing process or a service encounter. A value stream map also identifies the amount of labor and other resources used to carry out each process and indicates activity cycle time (the length of time needed to complete one full cycle of an activity).

Once the firm has identified areas of waste and developed solutions, operations managers draw a future state value map that incorporates the proposed changes. This allows them to visualize the new flow of activities, check for inconsistencies, and communicate their strategy to others in the organization.

Reducing Investment in Inventory: Just-in-Time to the Rescue

One of the hallmarks of lean systems is a tight control on inventories. In part, this reflects recognition of the inventory holding costs that we discussed earlier. But the lean approach also offers another reason for minimizing inventories. Large inventories serve as a buffer that enables the firm to continue operations when problems arise due to poor quality, faulty equipment, or unreliable suppliers. In the lean view, it's more efficient in the long run to improve quality, keep equipment in good working order, and develop reliable supply relationships than to continue compensating for these problems by holding large inventories.

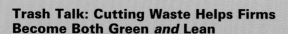

Trash Talk: Cutting Waste Helps Firms Become Both Green *and* Lean

Increasingly, firms across the United States are finding that one of the best ways to be lean is to also be "green." Firms that initiate projects to help the environment by cutting energy use and reducing waste often find that these projects quickly pay for themselves. For example:

- Fairmount Minerals dramatically cut fuel bills and shaved $400,000 per year from its operating costs by switching from trucks to a conveyor system to move sandstone. The company saved another $500,000 a year by repeatedly recycling the bags it used to ship its sand.
- AAMCO Transmissions' AAMCO Eco-Green program helps its franchisees dramatically reduce waste. Strategies include recycling cleaning solvents and using waste transmission fluid to heat stores. The average shop realizes a $40,000 to $50,000 annual return from savings on energy, waste removal, and cleaning product bills. As a side benefit, the popular green initiative also attracts more customers, thus bringing in more revenue as well as cutting costs.
- Subaru's Lafayette, Indiana, auto plant produces up to 180,000 cars each year, yet sends no waste to landfills. The Japanese automaker achieved its zero-landfill goal by finding innovative ways to recycle everything used in the plant from the wood in warehouse pallets to scrap steel left over after stamping fenders out of sheet metal. In the process it cut operating costs by several million dollars each year. One of the keys to Subaru's success has been its ability to convert employees into enthusiastic environmentalists who actively seek ways to cut waste. In fact, Denise Coogan, the plant's environmental affairs manager, likes to joke that Subaru's workers are now so proud of the project's accomplishments that they "can talk trash all day!"[15]

© JUSTIN HORROCKS/ISTOCKPHOTO.COM

© KRISTIAN STENSØNES/ISTOCKPHOTO.COM

> ## You seldom improve quality by cutting costs, but you can often cut costs by improving quality.
>
> *Karl Albrecht, author and futurist*

Lean manufacturing avoids overproduction and holding large inventories of finished goods by using **just-in-time (JIT) production** methods. The JIT approach produces only enough goods to satisfy current demand. This approach is called a *pull system* because actual orders "pull" the goods through the production process. The workers at the end of the production process produce just enough of the final product to satisfy actual orders and use just enough parts and materials from preceding stages of production to satisfy their needs. Workers at each earlier stage are expected to produce just enough output at their workstations to replace the amount used by the processes further along in the process—and in so doing they withdraw just the needed amount of parts and other supplies from even earlier processes.

JIT techniques obviously result in very small inventories of finished goods and work in process. But lean firms also hold only small inventories of materials and parts, counting on suppliers to provide them with these items as they need them to meet current demand. In a lean system, *all* organizations in the supply chain use the JIT approach, so that inventories are minimized at each stage. Clearly, this type of system requires incredible coordination among all parts of the supply chain; in fact, the movement toward JIT is a key reason supply chain management has become so crucial.

JIT does have some potential drawbacks. The most serious problem is that it can leave producers vulnerable to supply disruptions. If a key supplier is unable to make deliveries due to natural disasters or other problems, the manufacturer may quickly run out of supplies and have to shut down production. Toyota, the company many credit with the first major implementation of a JIT manufacturing system, experienced this drawback in 1997 when a fire at the main factory of one of its suppliers deprived it of a key brake component. Because of its limited inventory of the part, the giant automaker soon had to shut down 20 of its 30 Japanese assembly lines. Amazingly, however, Toyota was able to use its close connections with its network of suppliers to work out arrangements to obtain alternative supplies and was able to be back up and running in a matter of days.[16]

Lean Thinking in the Service Sector

Employing lean principles in the service sector can be quite a challenge because customers often participate in providing the service. This means a service firm usually has less control over how processes are conducted. But many service firms have benefited from creatively applying lean techniques. Southwest Airlines is well known for its efforts to reduce waste. It uses only one type of aircraft (the Boeing 737) to standardize maintenance and minimize training costs. It also has an extremely simple ticketing system (no assigned seating) and, when possible, flies into smaller or older airports where there is less congestion. This means less time and less fuel are spent circling airports waiting to land or sitting on runways waiting to take off. Despite a no-frills approach, Southwest almost always ranks near the top of the list in terms of airline customer satisfaction.[17]

The Big Picture

Operations management plays a crucial role in the success of a firm. Operations managers are responsible for "putting it all together" by developing and implementing the processes needed to produce goods and services and distribute them to the target market. Their decisions affect both revenues and costs, going a long way toward determining whether a firm makes a profit or suffers a loss.

The responsibilities of operations managers require them to work closely with other managers throughout their organizations. For example, they must work with marketers and designers to ensure that the desired goods and services move from the drawing board to the final customer on time and within budget. They must work closely with financial managers to ensure that the company invests in the capital goods needed to produce goods and services in the most efficient manner. And they must work effectively with human resource managers to attract and develop workers who possess the knowledge and skills needed to become world-class competitors. In fact, operations managers must even go beyond their own organization and work effectively with the suppliers and distributors who comprise the firm's value chain.

Operations managers must continuously adapt to changes in technology and in competitive conditions. Key challenges in recent years have centered on the need to continuously improve product quality while finding ways to reduce costs and protect the environment. You can expect the goals of becoming ever leaner—and ever greener—to remain a major focus of operations managers in years to come.

WHAT ELSE? *RIP & REVIEW* **CARDS IN THE BACK**

Chapter One

1 Global Entrepreneurship Monitor, 2008 Executive Report, by Niels Bosma, Zoltan J. Acs, Erkko Autio, and Alicia Coduras, Jonathan Levie, January 15, 2009, **http://www .gemconsortium.org/article.aspx?id=68,** accessed January 17, 2009; Taking Care of Business: Student Entrepreneurs by Tavia Evans, Roxana Hadad and Chris Diehl, FastWeb website, **http://www.fastweb.com/fastweb/resources/articles/ index/102542**, accessed January 17, 2009.

2 "The 400 Richest Americans," September 17, 2008, *Forbes* website, **http://www.forbes.com/lists/2008/54/400list08 _The-400-Richest-Americans_Rank.html**, accessed January 18, 2009.

3 "101 Dumbest Moments in Business" by editors of *Fortune*, updated January 16, 2008, CNNMoney (*Fortune*) website, **http://money.cnn.com/galleries/2007/fortune/0712/ gallery.101_dumbest.fortune/index.html**, accessed January 20, 2009; "101 Dumbest Moments in Business" by Adam Horowitz, David Jacobson, Tom McNichol, and Owen Thomas, CNNMoney (Business 2.0) website, **http://money.cnn.com/ galleries/2007/biz2/0701/gallery.101dumbest_2007/index .html**, accessed January 20, 2009.

4 Thaler, Richard H. and Sunstein, Cass R, *Nudge: Improving Decisions about Health, Wealth, and Happiness.* (New York: Penguin Group; 2009); "Easy Does It: How to make lazy people do the right thing," by Thaler and Sunstein, *The New Republic*, April 9, 2008, New Republic website; Stephen J. Dubner, "Who will climb the piano stairs?" Freakonomics: The Hidden Side of Everything. New York Times, October 13, 2009, **http://freakonomics.blogs.nytimes.com/2009/10/13/ who-will-climb-the-piano-stairs/?pagemode=print**, retrieved March 22, 2010. **http://articles.latimes.com/2008/apr/02/ opinion/oe-thalerandsunstein2 http://www.marcgunther .com/2009/11/16/whats-for-lunch-behaviorial-economics -meets-climate-change/**

5 7.2% of Americans work for nonprofit groups, study finds, by Suzanne Perry, December 19, 2006, The Chronicle of Philanthropy website, **http://philanthropy.com/free/ update/2006/12/2006121901.htm**, accessed January 19, 2009; Wages in the nonprofit sector: management, professional, and administrative support occupations by Amy Butler, October 28, 2008, Bureau of Labor Statistics website, **http://www.bls.gov/opub/cwc/cm20081022ar01p1.htm**, accessed January 19, 2008; Occupational Employment and Wages, 2007, May 9, 2008, Bureau of Labor Statistics website, **http://www.bls.gov/news.release/pdf/ocwage .pdf**, accessed January 19, 2009. Nonprofit sector needs to be better understood by Todd Cohen, February 22, 2010, Inside Philanthropy Blog, Philanthropy Journal website, **http:// philanthropyjournal.blogspot.com/2010/02/nonprofit -sector-needs-to-be-better.html,** retrieved March 23, 2010.

6 GNI Per Capita 2007 World Bank Data, revised October 17, 2008, **http://siteresources.worldbank.org/ DATASTATISTICS/ Resources/GNIPC.pdf**, accessed January 19, 2009; CIA World Factbook China, updated December 18, 2008, **https://www.cia.gov/library/publications/the-world -factbook/geos/ch.html**, accessed January 19, 2009; CIA World Factbook Russia, updated December 18, 2008, **https:// www.cia.gov/library/publications/the-world-factbook/ geos/rs.html**, accessed January 19, 2009; CIA World Factbook Hong Kong, updated December 18, 2008, **https://www.cia .gov/library/publications/the-world-factbook/geos/ hk.html**, accessed January 19, 2009.

7 The 6 myths of creativity by Bill Breen, December 19, 2007, Fast Company website, **http://www.fastcompany .com/magazine/89/creativity.html**, accessed January 20, 2009; The hidden secrets of the creative mind, Interview of R. Keith Sawyer by Francine Russo, January 8, 2006, *Time* website, **http://www.time.com/time/magazine/ article/0,9171,1147152,00.html**, accessed January 20, 2009; Ideas made here by Anne Fisher, June 11, 2007, **http://money.cnn.com/magazines/fortune/fortune _archive/2007/06/11/100061499/index.htm**, accessed January 20, 2009; You're bored, but your brain is tuned in by Benedict Carey, August 5, 2008, *New York Times* website, **http://www. nytimes.com/2008/08/05/health/ research/05mind.html**, accessed January 20, 2009.

8 American Customer Satisfaction Index, ASCI Scores, **http:// www.theacsi.org/index.php?option=com_content&task= view&id=150&Itemid=158&c=all&sort=Y2007**, accessed January 19, 2009.

9 Best Global Brands 2008, Interactive Table, September 18, 2008, *BusinessWeek* Online, **http://bwnt.businessweek .com/interactive_reports/global_brand_2008/?chan=magazi ne+channel_special+report**, accessed September 24, 2008.

10 Coping with the competition by Jack Trout, September 26, 2005, *Forbes*.com Entrepreneurs Newsletter, **http://www .forbes.com/ 2005/09/23/marketing-advertising-business -cx_jt_0926trout.html?partner=smallbusiness_newsletter**.

11 Why Webvan drove off a cliff by Joanna Glasner, Wired News, July 10, 2001, **http://www.wired.com/news/business/ 0,1367,45098,00.html.**

12 Honey, I shrunk the iPod. A lot. By Steven Levy, September 19, 2005, *Newsweek* magazine; Behind Apple's strategy: be second to market by John Boddie, August 29, 2005, Harvard Business School Working Knowledge, **http://hbswk .hbs.edu/item.jhtml?id=4970&t=technology**. "What's to become of Microsoft's answer to the iPod?" By John Letzing July 29, 2009, Marketwatch website, **http://www .marketwatch.com/story/microsofts-zune-continues-to -struggle-2009-07-29**, accessed April 1, 2010.

13 See note 12 above.

14 Giving employees what they want: the returns are huge, May 4, 2005, Knowledge@Wharton, Human Resources, **http:// knowledge.wharton.upenn.edu/article/1188.cfm**, accessed January 19, 2009; How Investing in Intangibles—Like Employee Satisfaction—Translates into Financial Returns, January 9, 2008, Knowledge@Wharton website, **http://knowledge**

.wharton.upenn.edu/article.cfm?articleid=1873, accessed January 19, 2009.

15 Editors name the greatest inventions of all time, *Encyclopedia Britannica* News Release, January 30, 2003, **http://corporate .britannica.com/press/releases/invention.html**; Encyclopedia Britannica's Great Inventions, accessed October 11, 2005, **http://corporate.britannica.com/press/inventions.html**.

16 Star search by Nanette Burns, October 10, 2005, *BusinessWeek* online, **http://www.businessweek.com/ magazine/content/ 05_41/b3954001.htm?campaign _id=nws_insdr_sep30&link_position=link1**.

17 Retail E-Commerce Update by Jeffrey Grau, December 2008, eMarketer website, **http://www.emarketer.com/Reports/ All/Emarketer_2000545.aspx**, accessed January 19, 2009.

18 An Older and More Diverse Nation by Midcentury, U.S. Census Bureau Press Release , August 14, 2008, Census Bureau website, **http://www.census.gov/Press-Release/www/ releases/archives/population/012496.html**, retrieved March 30, 2010; **http://www.census.gov/Press-Release/www/ releases/archives/population/012496.html**.

19 State and County Quick Facts, Mississippi, U.S. Census, Bureau website, **http://quickfacts.census.gov/qfd/ states/28000.html** Last Revised, February 23, 2010, retrieved March 30, 2010, Hawaii's Asian population at 55% is highest proportion in nation, May 1, 2009, Hawaii 24/7 website, **http:// www.hawaii247.org/2009/05/01/hawaiis-asian-population -at-55-is-highest-proportion-in-nation/**, retrieved March 30, 2010, State and County Quick Facts, New Mexico, U.S. Census Bureau website, **http://quickfacts.census.gov/qfd/ states/35000.html**, Last Revised, February, 23, 2010, retrieved March 30, 2010.

20 Translating Hispanic Marketing into Shareholder Value, Hispanic PR Wire/*Business Wire*, December 4, 2006, **http://www .hispanicprwire.com/print.php?l=in&id=7660**.

21 Diversity Awareness, Hershey Foods Corporation website, accessed October 4, 2005, **https://www.hersheysjobs.com/ Career/ControlPanel.aspx?ModuleCategoryID=1999999**.

22 Attitudes of young people toward diversity, CIRCLE fact sheet, February 2005, **http://www.civicyouth.org/PopUps/ FactSheets/Attitudes%202.25.pdf**.

23 CIA World FactBook, United States, updated December 18, 2008, **https://www.cia.gov/library/publications/the-world -factbook/geos/us.html**, accessed January 19, 2009; World Population Prospects, The 2006 Revision, Population Database, updated September 27, 2007, United Nations website, **http:// esa.un.org/unpp/p2k0data.asp**, accessed January 19, 2009.

24 Pending job flexibility act received mixed reviews by Sue Shellenbarger, WSJ Career Journal, **http://www .careerjournal.com/columnists/workfamily/20010426 -workfamily.html**, accessed October 4, 2005; Bad attitudes in the workplace by Les Christie, Sept 6, 2005, CNNMoney, **http://money.cnn.com/2005/08/24/pf/workplace _morale/?section=money_pf**; Inspiring worker loyalty one tough job by John Ellis, July 1, 2005, *East Bay Business Times* website, **http://www.bizjournals.com/eastbay/ stories/2005/07/04/focus1.html**.

25 The six sins of greenwashing, by TerraChoice Environmental Marketing Inc., November 2007, **http://www.terrachoice .com/files/6_sins.pdf**, accessed January 20, 2009; It's not easy being green by Matthew Knight, July 23, 2008, CNN website, **http://www.cnn.com/2008/TECH/science/07/16/ greenwash/**, accessed January 20, 2009; When Green Marketing Becomes Greenwashing by Carl Frankel, December 11, 2008, Matter Network website, **http:// featured.matternetwork.com/2008/12/short-history -green-marketing.cfm**, accessed January 20, 2009; Green or Greenwash? By Temma Ehrenfeld, July 7/July14, 2008, *Newsweek* magazine, p. 56.

26 Sustainability: Balancing Opportunity and Risk in the Consumer Products Industry, 2007 Report, Deloitte website, **http:// www.deloitte.com/dtt/cda/doc/content/us_cb**

_sustainability-study_june2007opt.pdf, accessed January 20, 2009; While Everything Else Stops, Green Still Means Go, by Sarah Fister Gale, January 19, 2009, GreenBiz website, **http:// greenbiz.com/feature/2009/01/19/green-still-means-go**, accessed January 20, 2009.

27 How Rising Wages Are Changing the Game in China by Dexter Roberts, March 27, 2006, *BusinessWeek* website, **http:// www.businessweek.com/magazine/content/06_13/ b3977049.htm**, accessed January 20, 2009; Good Luck Competing Against Chinese Labor Costs, Mfg. Job Growth in China Is Headed Up, Not Down; 109 Million Mfg. Workers in China Dwarfs Number in U.S., by Richard McCormack, May 2, 2006, *Manufacturing and Technology News* website, **http:// www.manufacturingnews.com/news/06/0502/art1.html**, accessed January 20, 2009; Cost of Chinese labor is on the rise by Scott Tong, July 6, 2007, Marketplace website, **http:// marketplace.publicradio.org/display/web/2007/07/06/ cost_of_chinese_labor_is_on_the_rise/**, accessed January 20, 2009; Manufacturing in China Today: Employment and Labor Compensation by Judith Banister, September 2007, The Conference Board website, **http://www.conference-board .org/economics/workingpapers.cfm**, accessed January 20, 2009.

28 Asian tsunami devastates Sri Lankan fishing industry by Jason Beaubien, January 10, 2005, NPR Morning Edition, **http:// www.npr.org/templates/story/story.php?storyId=4276161**; Phuket tourism industry crippled by mass cancellations by Sally Pook, January 8, 2005, Cyber Diver News Network, **http:// www.cdnn.info/news/travel/t050111.html**; Homeland security scuffle by Veronique de Rugy, October 15, 2004, *National Review* website, **http://www.nationalreview .com/comment/rugy200410150840.asp**; Bush brushes aside rebuilding cost concerns, September 19, 2005, Reuters News Service, MSNBC website, **http://www.msnbc.msn.com/ id/9374106/**.

29 Pomp and Circumspect by Daniel Pink, June 4, 2005, *New York Times* website, **http://select.nytimes.com/gst/abstract.html ?res=F60C1FFD3F5C0C778CDDAF0894DD404482**.

Pg. 14 Fact Box: The rise of a fierce yet agile superpower by Fareed Zakaria, *Newsweek*, January 7, 2008, page 38.

Chapter Two

1 TABLE B–1.—Gross domestic product, 1959–2008, Economic Report of the President: 2009 Spreadsheet Tables, updated January 14, 2009, Government Printing Office website, **http:// www.gpoaccess.gov/eop/tables09.html**, accessed January 20, 2009.

2 RealtyTrac's James J. Saccacio to Discuss Foreclosure Crisis Fallout at AFSA State Government Affairs Forum by RealtyTrac staff, RealityTrac website, October 1, 2008, **http://www .realtytrac.com/ContentManagement/pressrelease.aspx? ChannelID=9&ItemID=5284&accnt=64847**, accessed January 22, 2009. "REALTYTRAC® Year-end Rreport Shows Record 2.8 Million U.S. Properties With Foreclosure Filings in 2009," RealtyTrac Staff, January 14, 2010, RealtyTrac website, **http:// www.realtytrac.com/contentmanagement/pressrelease .aspx?itemid=8333**, accessed April 21, 2010.

3 Credit Crisis – The Essentials, Updated January 20, 2009, *New York Times* website, Automakers say if they go, millions of jobs will vanish by Sharon Silke Carty and Barbara Hagenbaugh, Updated November 21, 2008, *USA Today* website, Auto Industry Bailout Overview, Updated January 20, 2009, *New York Times* website, **http://topics.nytimes.com/topics/ reference/timestopics/subjects/c/credit_crisis/index.html**, accessed January 21, 2009; **http://www.usatoday.com/ money/autos/2008-11-17-automakers-bailout-impact_N .htm**, accessed January 21, 2009; **http://topics.nytimes.com/ top/reference/timestopics/subjects/c/credit_crisis/auto _industry/index.html**, accessed January 21, 2009.

4 One Trillion Dollars by Micheal Grunwald, January 26, 2009, *Time*, p. 27-31, **http://www.time.com/time/ politics/article/0,8599,1871769,00.html**. Economy adds jobs at fastest pace in three years by Jeannine Aversa and Christopher S. Rugaber, Apr 2, 2010, Associated Press, **http://www.google.com/hostednews/ap/article/ ALeqM5gNiyJ905Ho0Ur96V2TQhsBX19lGwD9ER6P402**, accessed April 20, 2010; Bernanke declares 'recession is very likely over' By Greg Robb, Sept. 15, 2009, MarketWatch website, **http://www.marketwatch.com/story/bernanke -declares-the-recession-over-2009-09-15**, accessed, April 20, 2010.

5 Brad Tuttle. "Movies for Cheap." *Time*. March 8, 2010. **<http://www.time.com/time/magazine/ article/0,9171,1968106,00.html>** (accessed April 8, 2010); Farhad Manjoo. "Little Known Redbox Proves the Power of In-Between Technology." *Fast Company*. July 1, 2009. **<http:// www.fastcompany.com/magazine/137/tech-edge-box -tops.html>** (accessed April 8, 2010); Chris Preimesberger. "How HP Envisions Making Printing Available Anywhere You Happen to Be." eWeek.com. April 23, 2010. **<http://www .eweek.com/c/a/Printers/How-HP-Envisions-Making -Printing-Available-Anywhere-You-Happen-to-Be-566907/>** (accessed April 27, 2010).

6 Money Stock Measures, Federal Reserve Statistical Release, February 5, 2009, Federal Reserve website, **http://www .federalreserve.gov/releases/h6/current/**, accessed February 11, 2009.

7 Federal receipts, outlays, surplus or deficit, and debt, fiscal years 2006-2011, Economic Report of the President, Spreadsheet Table B-81, Transmitted to the Congress February, 2010, GPO Access. **<http://www.gpoaccess.gov/eop/index .html>**, accessed April 27, 2010.

8 Historical Changes of the Target Federal Funds and Discount Rates, Federal Reserve Bank of New York website, **http:// www.newyorkfed.org/markets/statistics/dlyrates/fedrate .html**, accessed January 22, 2009.

9 Money Stock Measures, Federal Reserve Statistical Release, January 22, 2009, **http://www.federalreserve.gov/releases/ h6/current/**, accessed January 23, 2009.

10 Who is the FDIC?, FDIC website, October 27, 2008, **http:// www.fdic.gov/about/learn/symbol/index.html**, accessed January 22, 2009.

11 While everything else stops, green still means go by Sarah Fister Gale, January 19, 2009, GreenBiz website, **http://www .greenbiz.com/feature/2009/01/19/green-still-means -go**, accessed January 23, 2009; Walmart Completes Goal to Sell Only Concentrated Liquid Laundry Detergent, May 29, 2008, Walmart website, **http://walmartstores.com/ FactsNews/NewsRoom/8334.aspx**, accessed January 23, 2009; Technology industry going green to cut costs by Victor Godinez, February 22, 2008, *The Dallas Morning News* website, **http://www.dallasnews.com/sharedcontent/ dws/bus/stories/DN-edsenergy_22bus.ART.State. Edition1.399a338.html**, accessed January 23, 2009; Green really means business by Zachary Karabell, September 22, 2008, p. E6, *Newsweek* website, **http://www.newsweek .com/id/158586**, accessed January 23, 2009.

12 Federal Government, excluding Postal Services, U.S. Department of Labor Bureau of Labor Statistics website, March 12, 2008, **http://stats.bls.gov/oco/cg/cgs041.htm**, accessed August 16, 2008; Postal Service Workers, U.S. Department of Labor Bureau of Labor Statistics website, December 18, 2007, **http://stats.bls.gov/oco/ocos141.htm**, accessed August 16, 2008; Job Opportunities in the Armed Forces, U.S. Department of Labor Bureau of Labor Statistics website, December 18, 2007, **http://stats.bls.gov/oco/ocos249.htm**, accessed August 16, 2008.

13 Russia's flat tax miracle by Daniel J. Mitchell, PhD, The Heritage Foundation, March 24, 2003, **http://www.heritage .org/Press/Commentary/ed032403.cfm**; Russians do taxes

right by Deroy Murdock, *National Review* Online, March 1, 2002, **http://www.nationalreview.com/murdock/ murdock030102.shtml**; Russia: income taxes and tax laws, July 2005,Worldwide-Tax website, **http://www.worldwide -tax.com/russia/russia_tax.asp**; History of the U.S. taxsystem, U.S. Treasury website, **http://www.ustreas.gov/education/ fact-sheets/taxes/ustax.html**,accessed March 9, 2006.

14 Central Intelligence Agency. The World Factbook, North America; The United States: Economy: Overview Updated April 2009, **<https://www.cia.gov/library/publications/the -world-factbook/geos/us.html>**, accessed April 27, 2010.

15. Labor Force Statistics from the Current Population Survey: Unemployment Rate Table, U.S.Department of Labor Bureau of Labor Statistics website, **http://data.bls.gov/PDQ/servlet/ SurveyOutputServlet?data_tool=latest_numbers&series _id=LNS14000000**, accessed January 22, 2009.

16 Labor Force Statistics from the Current Population Survey: Unemployment Rate Table, U.S.Department of Labor Bureau of Labor Statistics website, **http://data.bls.gov/PDQ/servlet/ SurveyOutputServlet?data_tool=latest_numbers&series_id =LNS14000000**, accessed January 22, 2009.

Pg. 29 Fact Box: Expenditures on Children by Families, 2007, United States Department of Agriculture, March 2008, Center for Nutrition Policy and Promotion website, **http://www.cnpp .usda.gov/Publications/CRC/crc2007.pdf**, accessed January 26, 2009.

Chapter Three

1 Michael Mussa, "Global Economic Prospects for 2010 and 2011 Global Recovery Continues by April 8, 2010," Peterson Institute for International Economics, **http://www.iie.com/ publications/papers/mussa0410.pdf**, accessed May 11, 2010; CIA – The World Factbook, The World, Economy – Overview: updated, April 2010, **https://www.cia.gov/library/ publications/the-world-factbook/geos/xx.html**, accessed May 11, 2010; "World Economic Outlook Update: A Policy- Driven, Multispeed Recovery," International Monetary Fund, January 26, 2010, **http://www.imf.org/external/pubs/ft/ weo/2010/update/01/**, accessed May 11, 2010.

2 Rank Order Estimates, CIA—The World Factbook website: **https://www.cia.gov/library/publications/the-world -factbook/rankorder/2119rank.html**, accessed August 16, 2008, **https://www.cia.gov/library/publications/the-world -factbook/rankorder/2004rank.html**, accessed August 16, 2008, **https://www.cia.gov/library/publications/the-world -factbook/rankorder/2003rank.html**, accessed August 16, 2008.

3 Cell phones vital in developing world by Malcolm Foster, January 27, 2007, *Washington Post* website, **http://www .washingtonpost.com/wp-dyn/content/article/2007/01/27/ AR2007012700662.html**, accessed January 28, 2009; China's mobile users top 600 million: govt, July 24, 2008, Kioskea website, **http://en.kioskea.net/actualites/china-s-mobile -users-top-600-million-govt-10563-actualite.php3**, accessed January 28, 2009; Telecom sector regaining momentum by Anand Kumar, August 25, 2008, Dawn website, **http:// www.dawn.com/2008/08/25/ebr15.htm**, accessed January 28, 2009. Adam Hwang, "China market: Mobile phone users increase to nearly 766 million in February, says MIIT," *DigiTimes*, April 2, 2010, **http://www.digitimes.com/news/ a20100402vl200.html**, accessed May 4, 2010; Telecom Regulatory Authority of India, Press Release No. 20 /2010, New Delhi, April 26, 2010, Telecom Subscription Data as of March 31, 2010 **http://www.trai.gov.in/writereaddata/trai/ upload/pressreleases/732/pr26apr10no20.pdf**, accessed May 4, 2010

4 Dave Kiley and Burt Helm, "The Great Trust Offensive," *BusinessWeek*, September 17, 2009, **http://www .businessweek.com/magazine/content/09_39/ b4148038492933.htm**, accessed May 8, 2010.

5 Insperiences, Trendwatching newsletter, **http://www .trendwatching.com/trends/insperience.htm**, accessed January 12, 2006.

6 World Trade To Shrink In 2009: World Bank, December 9, 2008, NewsRoomAmerica website, **http://www .newsroomamerica.com/world/story.php?id=440169**, accessed January 29, 2009; WTO: developing, transition economies cushion trade slowdown, April 17, 2008, WTO Press Release, World Trade Organization website, **http:// www.wto.org/english/news_e/pres08_e/pr520_e.htm**, accessed January 29, 2009; Global Slump Hits Developing Countries as Credit Squeeze Impedes Growth and Trade; Tensions in Commodity Markets Ease, December 9, 2008, World Bank Press Release No:2009/160/DEC, World Bank website, **http://web.worldbank.org/WBSITE/EXTERNAL/ NEWS/0,,contentMDK:22003191~pagePK:64257043~piPK:4 37376~theSitePK:4607,00.html**, accessed January 29, 2009. CIA – The World Factbook, The World, Economy – Overview: updated, April 2010, **<https://www.cia.gov/library/ publications/the-world-factbook/geos/xx.html>**, accessed May 11, 2010.

7 Countertrade—an innovative approach to marketing by Dan West, Chairman American Countertrade Association, *BarterNews* issue #36, 1996, **http://barternews.com/ approach_marketing.htm**; Global Offset and Countertrade Association website, **http://www.globaloffset.org/index .htm**, accessed January 27, 2006.

8 As More Toys Are Recalled, Trail Ends in China by Eric S. Lipton and David Barboza, June 19, 2007, *New York Times* website, **http://www.nytimes.com/2007/06/19/business/ worldbusiness/19toys.html**, accessed January 29, 2009.

9 Normandy Madden, "Looking to grow in China? Ad Age has 10 surefire tips,". *Advertising Age*; May 4, 2009, 3-30; Geoff Dyer, "China's booming consumer demand," CNN.com, October 22, 2009, **<http://157.166.255.31/2009/BUSINESS/10/22/china .consumer.demand.ft/index.html>**, accessed May 7, 2010; Ray Kwong, "China's Barbie Doll Economics," *Forbes*, April 28, 2010, **<http://blogs.forbes.com/china/2010/04/28/chinas -barbie-doll-economics/>**, accessed May 7, 2010.

10 Thinking outside the border by Curtis, Minority Business Entrepreneur, September/October 2005, **http://www.export .gov/comm_svc/pdf/MBE_article.pdf.**

11 eBay to acquire Skype, Press Release, September 12, 2005, Skype website, **http://www.skype.com/company/ news/2005/skype_ebay.html**.

12 Intel to Build Advanced Chip-Making Plant in China by David Barboza, March 27, 2007, *New York Times* website, **http:// www.nytimes.com/2007/03/27/technology/27chip.html**, accessed January 30, 2009.

13 Rethink the value of joint ventures by Cynthia Churchwell, Harvard Business School Working Knowledge, May 10, 2004, **http://hbswk.hbs.edu/item.jhtml?id=4113&t=globalization**.

14 McDonald's country/market sites, **http://www.mcdonalds .com./countries.html**, accessed January 26, 2006. **<http:// www.dominos.com/Public-EN/Site+Content/Secondary/ Inside+Dominos/Pizza+Particulars/International+Speciality +Toppings/**; http://slice.seriouseats.com/archives/2008/02/ crazy-weird-asian-pizza-crusts-japanese-korean-hong -kong.html; http://recipes.howstuffworks.com/fresh-ideas/ dinner-food-facts/favorite-pizza-toppings-in-10-countries .htm; http://slice.seriouseats.com/archives/2008/02/crazy -weird-asian-pizza-crusts-japanese-korean-hong-kong.htm>**

15 Hyundai grows up by Michael Schuman, *Time* Global Business, July 2005, **http://www.time.com/time/globalbusiness/ article/0,9171,1074141,00.html**; At 5 feet 10 inches, I was too tall for Tokyo by Cathie Gandel, My Turn, *Newsweek*, December 12, 2005. Hyundai Bets Big On India and China by Moon Ihlwan, January 30, 2008, *BusinessWeek* website, **http://www.businessweek.com/globalbiz/content/ jan2008/gb20080130_061205.htm**, accessed January 30, 2009.

16 Selling to rural India, Springwise Newsletter, June 2003, **http://www.springwise.com/newbusinessideas/2003/06/ shakti.html**; Red herring: selling to the poor, April 11, 2004, The Next Practice website, **http://www.thenextpractice .com/news/red_herring_selling_to_the_poor.php**; Are you ready for globalisation 2.0? by Tim Weber, January 28, 2005, BBC News website, **http://news.bbc.co.uk/1/hi/ business/4214687.stm**.

17 John M. Broder, "Climate Goal Is Supported by China and India," *New York Times*, March 9, 2010, **<http://www .nytimes.com/2010/03/10/science/earth/10climate.html>**, accessed May 7, 2010; G-20 Clean Energy Economy FactBook Executive Summary, **<http://www.pewglobalwarming.org/ cleanenergyeconomy/pdf/PewG-20ExecSummary.pdf>**, accessed May 7, 2010.

18 World Internet Users and Population Stats, June 30, 2008, Internet World Stats website, **http://www .Internetworldstats.com/stats.htm**, accessed January 30, 2009; Credit card use in India lowest in world by Gaurie Mishra, May 31, 2007, *The Economic Times* website, **http:// economictimes.indiatimes.com/Personal_Finance/Credit _Cards/News/Credit_card_use_in_India_lowest_in_world/ rssarticleshow/2088097.cms**, accessed January 30, 2009.

19 Economy Rankings 2009, Doing Business – World Bank Group website, **http://www.doingbusiness.org/economyrankings/ ?direction=Asc&sort=10**, accessed January 30, 2009.

20 Many Countries Reducing Software Piracy, Study Says, But Problem Remains a Serious Drag on all Economies, BSA news release, May 12, 2009, **http://global.bsa.org/ globalpiracy2008/pr/pr_global.pdf**.

21 USTR releases 2002 inventory of trade barriers, Press Release, April 2, 2002, **http://www.useu.be/Categories/Trade/ Apr0202USTRReportForeignTradeBarriers.html**; U.S. targets non-tariff barriers to global trade, News Release, April 3, 2002, **http://www.usconsulate.org.hk/pas/pr/2002/040301.htm**.

22 The farm fight by Simon Robinson, Global Business, *Time*, December 2005, pages A13–A16; The WTO cotton case and U.S. domestic policy by Darren Hudson, C. Parr Rosson III, John Robinson, and Jaime Malaga, *Choices* magazine, 2nd Quarter, 2005, **http://www.choicesmagazine.org/2005-2/ wto/2005-2-10.htm**; "Cotton four" preparing new proposal on domestic support, WTO 2006 News Item, January 31, 2006, **http://www.wto.org/english/news_e/news06_e/ cotton_31jan06_e.htm**.

23 Debt Relief Under the Heavily Indebted Poor Countries (HIPC) Initiative, Factsheet – November 2008, International Monetary Fund website, **http://www.imf.org/external/np/exr/facts/ hipc.htm**, accessed January 30, 2009.

24 U.S. Total Trade Balance in Goods and Services (Exhibit 1) Seasonally Adjusted:January 1994 to November 2008, U.S. Census website, **http://www.census.gov/foreign-trade/ statistics/historical/gandsbal.pdf**, accessed January 30, 2009;Trade with NAFTA with Mexico (Consump): 2008, Jan– Nov, U.S. Census website, **http://www.census.gov/foreign -trade/balance/c0005.html#2008**, accessed January 30, 2009; Trade with NAFTA with Canada (Consump): 2008, Jan–Nov, U.S. Census website, **http://www.census.gov/foreign-trade/ balance/c0006.html**, accessed January 30, 2009.

25 Rank Order Estimates, CIA—The World Factbook website, **https://www.cia.gov/library/publications/the-world -factbook/rankorder/2119rank.html**, accessed August 16, 2008, **https://www.cia.gov/library/publications/the-world -factbook/geos/ee.html#Econ**, accessed August 16, 2008.

Pg. 34 Fact Box: Cell phones vital in developing world by Malcolm Foster, January 27, 2007, *Washington Post* website, **http://www.washingtonpost.com/wp-dyn/content/ article/2007/01/27/AR2007012700662_3.html**, accessed January 28, 2009.

Pg. 44 Fact Box: About the World Bank, FAQs, World Bank website, **http://web.worldbank.org/WBSITE/EXTERNAL/ EXTSITETOOLS/0,,contentMDK:20147466~menuPK:34418**

9~pagePK:98400~piPK:98424~theSitePK:95474,00.htm#14, accessed August 16, 2008.

Chapter Four

1 The Six Pillars of Character, Josephson Institute website, **http://josephsoninstitute.org/MED/MED-2sixpillars.html**, accessed February 2, 2009.

2 The Ethics of American Youth – 2008 summary, Josephson Institute Center for Youth Ethics website, **http://charactercounts.org/programs/reportcard/index.html**, accessed February 10, 2009. Josephson Institute, "Character Study Reveals Predictors of Lying and Cheating," October 29, 2009, <http://josephsoninstitute.org/surveys/index.html> (accessed May 13, 2010).

3 Big Three auto CEOs flew private jets to ask for taxpayer money by Josh Levs, November 19, 2008, CNN website, **http://www.cnn.com/2008/US/11/19/autos.ceo.jets/**, accessed February 2, 2009.

4 Divorce duel reveals Welch's perks, September 6, 2002, CNN Money website, **http://money.cnn.com/2002/09/06/news/companies/welch_ge/**, accessed February 2, 2009.

5 Why We'll Miss the Disney Trial by Barney Gimbel, *Fortune*, December 27, 2004, retrieved from CNNMoney website, **http://money.cnn.com/magazines/fortune/fortune_archive/2004/12/27/8217949/index.htm**; Disney's Basket Cases by Peter Bart, *Variety*, March 7, 2004, **http://www.variety.com/article/VR1117901299.html?categoryid=1&cs=1**.

6 National Business Ethics Survey: How Employees View Ethics in Their Organizations, 1994–2005, Ethics Resource Center, October 12, 2005, **http://www.ethics.org/research/2005-press-release.asp**. Ethics Resource Center, 2009 National Business Ethics Survey, <http://www.ethics.org/nbes/files/nbes-final.pdf> (accessed May 14, 2010).

7 'Seven Cows and a Dream' by Gary Hirshberg, February 25, 2008, *Newsweek* website, **http://www.newsweek.com/id/111716**, accessed February 10, 2009; Daily Star: Can Yunus create a poverty free world? by Gaziul Hasan Khan, May 10, 2008, Muhammad Yunus website, **http://muhammadyunus.org/content/view/139/128/lang,en/**, accessed February 10, 2009; Bill Gates Issues Call For Kinder Capitalism by Robert A. Guth, January 24, 2008, *Wall Street Journal* website, **http://online.wsj.com/article/SB120113473219511791.html?mod=fpa_whatsnews**, accessed February 10, 2009.

8 Wireless Quick FactsYear-End Figures, Dec 09, CTIA, The Wieless Association website, **http://www.ctia.org/advocacy/research/index.cfm/AID/10323**, accessed May 16, 2010. Micheline Maynard, "Toyota tried to hide defects from U.S., regulators say," *Press Democrat*, April 12, 2010, <http://www.pressdemocrat.com/article/20100412/business/4121070>, (accessed May 16, 2010); Angus MacKenzie, Scott Evans, "The Toyota Recall Crisis," *Motor Trend*, January 2010, <http://www.motortrend.com/features/auto_news/2010/112_1001_toyota_recall_crisis/index.html>, (accessed May 16, 2010.)

9 Complaining Customers Are Good for Business by Bob Leduc, Virtual Marketing Newsletter, May 11, 2004, **http://www.marketingsource.com/newsletter/05-11-2004.html**.

10 JetBlue paying millions to stranded flyers by John Springer, updated March 4, 2007, MSNBC website, **http://www.msnbc.msn.com/id/17237390/**, accessed February 3, 2009; JetBlue Airways Ranked 'Highest in Customer Satisfaction Among Low Cost Carriers...,' June 17, 2008, Press Release on Reuters website, **http://www.reuters.com/article/pressRelease/idUS120589+17-Jun-2008+PNW20080617**, accessed February 3, 2009.

11 Open letter to iPhone customers, Apple website, **http://www.apple.com/hotnews/openiphoneletter/**, accessed February 3, 2009; Apple's customer satisfaction up despite struggling industry by Jeff Smykil, August 19, 2008, Ars Technica website, **http://arstechnica.com/apple/news/2008/08/apples-customer-satisfaction-up-despite-struggling-industry.ars**, accessed February 3, 2009.

12 Charitable giving estimated to be $306.39 billion in 2007, June 23, 2008, Planned Giving Center website, **http://www.pgdc.com/pgdc/us-charitable-giving-estimated-be-30639-billion-2007**, accessed February 4, 2009; Corporate donors adjust to economic slump by Ret Boney, September 15, 2008, Philanthropy Journal website, **http://www.philanthropyjournal.org/resources/special-reports/corporate-giving/corporate-donors-adjust-economic-slump**, accessed February 4, 2009.

13 Bad and Good Environmental Marks for McDonald's by Donalla Meadows, Sustainability Institute website, **http://www.sustainer.org/dhm_archive/search.php?display_article=vn304mcdonaldsed**, accessed May 15, 2005.

14 'Carbon Footprint' Gaining Business Attention, October 18, 2006, Press Release, Conference Board website, **http://www.conference-board.org/UTILITIES/pressDetail.cfm?press_ID=2985**, accessed February 4, 2009; Green goal of 'carbon neutrality' hits limit by Jeffery Ball, December 30, 2008, *Wall Street Journal* website, **http://online.wsj.com/article/SB123059880241541259.html**, accessed February 4, 2009; How green is my orange? by Andrew Martin, January 22, 2009, *New York Times* website, **http://www.nytimes.com/2009/01/22/business/22pepsi.html?_r=1&scp=1&sq=How%20green%20is%20my%20orange&st=cse**, accessed February 4, 2009.

15 Marketing, Business and Sustainable Development: A Global Guide, Business and Sustainable Development website, **http://www.bsdglobal.com/markets/green_marketing.asp**, accessed February 4, 2009.

16 2008 Corruption Perceptions Index, Transparency International website, **http://www.transparency.org/news_room/in_focus/2008/cpi2008/cpi_2008_table**, accessed February 4, 2009.

17 Bribe Payers Index 2008, Transparency International website, **http://www.transparency.org/policy_research/surveys_indices/cpi/2009/cpi_2009_tabl**

18 Sources: BusinessPundit, "25 Big Companies That Are Going Green," July 29, 2008, <http://www.businesspundit.com/25-big-companies-that-are-going-green/>,(accessed May 17, 2010); CNNMoney, "Ten Green Giants," <http://money.cnn.com/galleries/2007/fortune/0703/gallery.green_giants.fortune/8.html> (accessed May 17, 2010).

19 Selling to the Poor by Kay Johnson, *Time* Bonus Section, May 2005; The Payoff for Investing in Poor Countries by C.K. Prahalad and Allen Hammond, Harvard Business School Working Knowledge website, **http://hbswk.hbs.edu/item.jhtml?id=3180&t=nonprofit&noseek=one**.

20 Values in Tension: Ethics Away from Home by Thomas Donaldson, *Harvard Business Review*, September/October 1996.

21 Gap, Inc. Social Reporting Award, December 20, 2004, Business Ethics website, **http://www.business-ethics.com/annual.htm#Gap%20Inc**.

Pg. 57 Fact Box: Survey Shows U.S. Teens Confident in Their Inventiveness; More Hands-On, Project-Based Learning May Be Needed, January 16, 2008, Press Release, Lemelson-MIT Program website, **http://web.mit.edu/invent/n-pressreleases/n-press-08index.html**, accessed February 6, 2009.

Chapter Five

1 Body Language Tactics That Sway Interviewers by Eugene Raudsepp, *Wall Street Journal* CareerJournal, December 5, 2002, **http://www.careerjournal.com/jobhunting/interviewing/20021205-raudsepp.html**.

2 Erik Qualman, "Social Media Revolution 2 (Refresh), Stats from Video," *Socialnomics*, May 5 2010, <http://socialnomics

.net/2010/05/05/social-media-revolution-2-refresh/>, accessed May 29, 2010; Nora Ganim Barnes and Eric Mattson, "Social Media in the 2009 Inc. 500: New Tools & New Trends," *Business Communication Blog*, **http://www .businesscommunicationblog.com/pdfs/socialmedia2009 .pdf**, accessed May 30, 2010.

3 The Listener Wins by Michael Purdy, Monster contributing writer, Monster.com, **http://featuredreports.monster.com/ listen/overview/**, accessed August 22, 2006; The Human Side of Business by Stephen D. Boyd, *Agency Sales* Magazine, February 2004, page 35, accessed via Infotrac College Edition.

4 We Learn More by Listening Than Talking by Harvey Mackay, *The Daily Herald*, January 16, 2005, page E6[SB14], **http://old .heraldextra.com/modules.php?op=modload&name=Ne ws&file=article&sid=45313**; Listening Factoids, International Listening Association, **http://www.listen.org/pages/factoids .html**, accessed August 22, 2006.

5 The Human Side of Business by Stephen D. Boyd, *Agency Sales* Magazine, February 2004, page 35, accessed via Infotrac College Edition; Learn to Listen: Closing the Mouth and Opening the Ears Facilitates Effective Communication by Marjorie Brody, *Incentive*, May 2004, page 57, accessed via Business and Company Resource Center.

5a Andrew Jacobs, "Shanghai Is Trying to Untangle the Mangled English of Chinglish," by Andrew Jacobs *New York Times*, May 2, 2010, **<New York Times website, http:// www.nytimes.com/2010/05/03/world/asia/03chinglish .html?pagewanted=1>**, accessed May 20, 2010.

6 Edward P. Bailey, *Writing and Speaking at Work*, (Prentice Hall, 2005), pages 82–89.

7 Bringing the cloud with you by Philip Tucker, March 31, 2008, Google Docs Blog, **http://googledocs.blogspot .com/2008/03/bringing-cloud-with-you.html**, accessed February 13, 2009; Living in the Clouds by Brian Braiker, June 10, 2008, *Newsweek* website, **http://www.newsweek.com/ id/140864**, accessed February 13, 2009; Comparing Google Docs with competing cloud computing applications by Michael Miller, February 9, 2009, InformIT website, **http://www .informit.com/articles/article.aspx?p=1323244&seqNum=3**, accessed February 13, 2009.

8 Presenting Effective Presentations with Visual Aids, U.S. Department of Labor, Occupational Safety and Health Administration, **http://www.osha.gov/doc/outreachtraining/ htmlfiles/traintec.html**, accessed August 22, 2006.

Chapter Six

1 Why States Should Adopt the Revised Uniform Limited Liability Company Act (2006), National Conference of Commissioners on Uniform State Laws website: **http://www.nccusl.org/ Update/uniformact_why/uniformacts-why-ullca.asp**, accessed January 29, 2009.

2 U.S. Census Bureau. The 2010 Statistical Abstract of the United States Table 728: **http://www.census.gov/ compendia/statab/2010/tables/10s0728.pdf**, accessed April 13, 2010.

3 U.S. Census Bureau. The 2010 Statistical Abstract of the United States Table 729: **http://www.census.gov/ compendia/statab/2010/tables/10s0729.pdf**, accessed April 13, 2010.

4 U.S. Census Bureau. The 2010 Statistical Abstract of the United States Table, 728: **http://www.census.gov/ compendia/statab/2010/tables/10s0728.pdf**, accessed April 13, 2010.

5 2010 Statistical Abstract of the United States Table 728: **http://www.census.gov/compendia/statab/2010/ tables/10s0728.pdf**, accessed April 13, 2010.

6 2010 Statistical Abstract of the United States Table 728: **http://www.census.gov/compendia/statab/2010/ tables/10s0728.pdf**, accessed April 13, 2010.

7 Is a Family Limited Partnership the Right Estate Tool for You?, Baby Boomer News website, **http://www.babyboomers .com/news/1008f.htm**; Protect Your Assets with a Family Partnership by Jeff Schnepper, MSN Money Central website, **http://articles.moneycentral.msn.com/Taxes/TaxShelters/ ProtectYourFamilyWithPartnership.aspx**, accessed August 1, 2009; Estate Planning With a Family Limited Partnership by Jason M. Woodward, NuWire Investor website, March 6, 2009: **http://www.nuwireinvestor.com/articles/estate-planning -with-a-family-limited-partnership-52666.aspx**.

8 Delaware Division of Corporations: **http://www.corp .delaware.gov/**, accessed July 31, 2009.

9 "The Ben & Jerry's Law: Principles Before Profit," by John Tozzi, *Bloomberg Business Week*, April 26, 2010, pp. 65-66; "Maryland Signs Benefit Corporation Law," by Tasha Petty, Little Green Submarine website, **http://www.littlegreensubmarine. com/maryland-signs-benefit-corporation-law/**; "Maryland First State in Union to Pass Benefit Corporation Legislation," CSR Newswire website, **http://www.csrwire.com/press/ press_release/29332-Maryland-First-State-in-Union-to-Pass- Benefit-Corporation-Legislation**.

10 AT&T Form 10-K for 2009, accessed through SEC Edgar Database: **http://www.sec.gov/Archives/edgar/ data/732717/000073271710000013/ex13.htm** and AT&T Annual Report (also accessed via Edgar Database), accessed April 16, 2010.

11 Setting Up a One Person Corporation by Karen Klein, November 7, 2007, *BusinessWeek* website: **http:// www.businessweek.com/smallbiz/content/nov2007/ sb2007117_803605.htm**.

12 "How TARP Is Totally Changing the Executive Pay Debate," by Joanna Ossinger, Fox News website: **http://www .foxbusiness.com/story/markets/economy/tarp-totally -changing-executive-pay-debate/**; "CEO Pay Takes a Hit in Bailout Plan," by Del Jones and Edward Iwata, October 2, 2008, *USA Today* website: **http://www.usatoday.com/ money/companies/management/2008-09-28-executive -pay-ceo_N.htm**; "Treasury Pay Czar Releases 2010 Salary Guidelines," *The Salt Lake Tribune* website: **http://www .sltrib.com/business/ci_14900040**; "Treasury Appoints Pay Czar to Oversee TARP Banks," by David Orol, Market Watch website: **http://www.marketwatch.com/story/treasury -appoints-pay-czar-to-oversee-tarp-banks**; "Pay Czar Imposes Salary Caps for Execs," by David Ellis and Ed Henry, CNN Money website: **http://money.cnn.com/2009/12/11/ news/companies/feinberg_compensation/index.htm**.

13 "Piercing the Corporate Veil," by Ken Laino, *Asset Protection Law Journal* website: **http://www. assetprotectionlawjournal.com/2009/06/articles/ohio-law/ piercing-the-corporate-veil/** (accessed June 2009); "Piercing the Corporate Veil," by Aaron Larson, *Expert Law* website: **http://www.expertlaw.com/library/business/corporate veil**.html (accessed March 6, 2010); "Piercing the Corporate Veil: How to Preserve Limited Liability," QuickMBA website: **http://www.quickmba.com/law/corporation/corporate- veil/** (accessed March 6, 2010); Cheeseman, Henry, *The Legal Environment of Business and Online Commerce, 5th edition* (Pearson Prentice Hall), pp. 348-349.

14 Why States Should Adopt the Revised Uniform Limited Liability Company Act (2006), National Conference of Commissioners on Uniform State Laws website: **http://www.nccusl.org/ Update/uniformact_why/uniformacts-why-ullca.asp**, accessed January 29, 2009.

15 Why States Should Adopt the Revised Uniform Limited Liability Company Act (2006), National Conference of Commissioners on Uniform State Laws website: **http://www.nccusl.org/ Update/uniformact_why/uniformacts-why-ullca.asp**, accessed January 29, 2009.

16 Franchising Outpaces Other Sectors of the Economy in Growth, Jobs, IFA website: **http://www.franchise.org/**

Franchise-News-Detail.aspx?id=38358, accessed February 1, 2009.

17 Entrepreneur.com website pages for individual franchisors: **http://www.entrepreneur.com/franchises/mcdonalds/282570-0.html; http://www.entrepreneur.com/franchises/subway/282839-0.html; http://www.entrepreneur.com/franchises/curves/282265-0.html**, accessed April 6, 2010.

18 Fit for Franchising, by Taylor Mallory, *Pink* Magazine June/July 2007, pinkmagazine.com website: **http://www.pinkmagazine.com/franchise/women/2007/burzynski.html**; Franchising Attracts More Women, Minorities by Julie Bennett, Startup Journal, accessed through Entrepreneur.com website: **http://www.entrepreneur.com/franchises/franchisezone/startupjournal/article61324.html**; Female Franchisors Few and Far Between by Julie M. Young, **e-magnify.com** website: **https://www.e-magnify.com/resources_articlearchiveresults.asp?categoryID=18**; Fit to Be a Franchisee: Many Businesswomen Choose Franchises that Connect With Personal Interests by Nancy Lacewell, June 7, 2006 Business First of Louisville website: **http://www.bizjournals.com/louisville/stories/2006/05/22/story2.html**.

19 Boosting Diversity in Franchising by Joan Szabo, December 5, 2006, *Franchise Update* website: **http://www.franchise-update.com/article/188/**.

20 Bridging the Gap Between the Minority Community and the Franchising Industry, Minority Franchising website: **http://www.minorityfranchising.com/**, accessed August 2, 2009; Minorities in Franchising, International Franchise Association website: **http://franchise.org/industrysecondary.aspx?id=40970**, accessed August 2, 2009.

21 Subway, Entrepreneur.com website, **http://www.entrepreneur.com/franchises/subway/282839-2.html**.

22 Individual franchise opportunity pages for each listed franchise on the Entrepreneur.com website, **http://www.entrepreneur.com/franchiseopportunities/index.html**, accessed April 6, 2010.

23 Ben & Jerry's website, **http://www.benjerry.com/scoop_shops/partnershops/**, accessed August 2, 2009; Nonprofit Owned Franchises: A Strategic Business Approach, prepared by Community Wealth Ventures and IFA Educational Foundation, March 2004, **http://www.franchise.org/uploadedFiles/Files/nonprofit_owned.pdf**; Franchise Chains: Nonprofits Team Up by Laura Sydell, Morning Edition, **javascript:launchPlayer('1644017', '1', '05-Feb-2004', '&topicName=Business&subtopicName= Business&prgCode=ME&hubId=1&thingId=1644016', 'RM,WM')**; February 5, 2004, **http://www.npr.org/templates/story/story.php?storyId=1644016**; Social Franchise Venture website: **http://www.socialfranchise.com/faq.asp?id=128304&page=1**, accessed August 2, 2009.

24 Franchise Rule Compliance Guide, Federal Trade Commission website: **http://www.ftc.gov/bcp/edu/pubs/business/franchise/bus70.pdf**, pages 20, 102-103, and 121.

Pg. 79 Fact Box: Executive Compensation 2007, *USA Today* website: **http://www.usatoday.com/money/graphics/ceo-comp/flash.htm**; Steve Jobs Salary in 2007: $1, MSNBC website: **http://www.msnbc.msn.com/id/22807978/**.

Pg. 83 Fact Box: LLC History, llc-reporter.com website: **http://www.llc-reporter.com/16.htm**, accessed August 2, 2009; Investopedia website: **http://www.investopedia.com/ask/answers/05/051305.asp**, accessed August 2, 2009.

Chapter Seven

1 Despite the recession U.S. entrepreneurial activity rate rises in 2009, May 20, 2010, Kauffman Foundation website **http://www.kauffman.org/newsroom/despite-recession-us-entrepreneurial-activity-rate-rises-in-2009.aspx**, accessed June 3, 2010.

2 Why Americans start their own business, October 27, 2007, Young Money Talks website, **http://www.youngmoneytalks.com/blog/index.php?p=257**, accessed February 15, 2008; Study: 72% of workers would rather work for themselves by Rhonda Abrams, October 11, 2008, *USA Today* website, **http://www.usatoday.com/money/smallbusiness/columnist/abrams/2007-10-11-workers-survey_N.htm**, accessed February 15, 2009.

3 The *Forbes* 400 edited by Matthew Miller and Duncan Greenberg, September 17, 2008, *Forbes* website, **http://www.forbes.com/2008/09/16/forbes-400-billionaires-lists-400list08_cx_mn_0917richamericans_land.html**, accessed February 15, 2009.

4 Discover Polls Reveal True Character of the American *Entrepreneur*, October 22, 2007, Press Release, Discover Financial Services website, **http://investorrelations.discoverfinancial.com/phoenix.zhtml?c=204177&p=irol-newsArticle&ID=1065373&highlight=**, accessed February 15, 2009.

5 Testing 1, 2 ... Your Business IQ by Geoff Williams, *Entrepreneur* magazine, November 1999, copyright Entrepreneur.com, Inc., 2004, **http://www.entrepreneur.com/Your_Business/YB_SegArticle/1,4621,231457,00.html**.

6 More than Half of Small Business Owners Work at Least Six-Day Weeks, Still Find Time for Personal Life, Wells Fargo News Release, August 9, 2005, **https://www.wellsfargo.com/press/20050809_GallupPersonalLife**. Discover Polls Reveal True Character of the American Entrepreneur, October 22, 2007, Press Release, Discover Financial Services website, **http://investorrelations.discoverfinancial.com/phoenix.zhtml?c=204177&p=irol-newsArticle&ID=1065373&highlight=**, accessed February 15, 2009.

7 Entrepreneurial Risk and Market Entry by Brian Wu and Anne Marie Knott, SBA Office of Advocacy, January 2005, **http://www.sba.gov/advo/research/wkpbw249.pdf**.

8 "Food Truck Nation," by Katy McLaughlin, June 5, 2009, *Wall Street Journal* website, **http://online.wsj.com/article/SB10001424052970204456604574201934018170554.html**, accessed June 3, 2010; "How to Open a (Successful) Food Truck," by Christine Lagorio, May 12, 2010, Inc. website, **http://preview.inc.com/guides/2010/05/opening-a-successful-food-truck.html**, accessed June 3, 2010.

9 Failure: Use It as a Springboard to Success, U.S. SBA Online Library, no attribution, **http://www.sba.gov/library/successXIII/19-Failure-Use-it.doc**, accessed December 28, 2005.

10 What Makes Them Tick by Keith McFarland, Inc 500, 2005, Inc website, **http://www.inc.com/resources/inc500/2005/articles/20051001/tick.html**.

11 Credit Cards Replace Small Business Loans by John Tozzi, August 20, 2008, *BusinessWeek* website, **http://www.businessweek.com/smallbiz/content/aug2008/sb20080820_288348.htm?chan=smallbiz_smallbiz+index+page_top+small+business+stories**, accessed February 15, 2009.

12 Start-up Information, updated April 28, 2008, Delaware Small Business Development Center website, **http://www.delawaresbdc.org/DocumentMaster.aspx?doc=1003#6**, accessed February 15, 2009.

13 Financial Assistance, Small Business Administration website, **http://www.sba.gov/services/financialassistance/index.html**, accessed February 15, 2009.

14 "The Angel Investor Market in 2009: Holding Steady but Changes in Seed and Startup Investments," by Jeffrey Sohl, Center for Venture Research, March 31, 2010. **http://www.unh.edu/news/docs/2009angelanalysis.pdf**, accessed June 4, 2010.

15 The Steady, Strategic Assent of jetBlue Airways, Strategic Management Knowledge at Wharton, December 14, 2005–January 10, 2006, **http://knowledge.wharton.upenn.edu/article/1342.cfm**; Charging Ahead by Bobbie Gossage,

January 2004, *Inc.* Magazine, **http://www.inc.com/ magazine/20040101/gettingstarted.html**.

16 "'Clean tech' deals among the largest in '09 venture capital spending," by Ben Geman, Jan 22, 2010, *The Hill* website, **http://thehill.com/blogs/e2-wire/677-e2-wire/77595 -clean-tech-deals-among-the-largest-in-09-venture-capital -spending**, accessed June 3, 2010.

17 Amplestuff website, **http://www.amplestuff.com/;** Kazoo v. Walmart, *Reveries* Magazine, November 29, 2005, **http:// www.reveries.com/?p=232.**

18 E-Commerce Award—June 2002, Anything Left-Handed website, **http://www.anythingleft-handed.co.uk/ pressreleases.html.**

18a "Why Are Women-Owned Firms Smaller Than Men-Owned Ones?," by Sharon Hadary, May 17, 2010, *Wall Street Journal* website **http://online.wsj.com/article/SB1000142405274870 4688604575125543191609632.html?mod=djem_jiewr_ES _domainid**, accessed June 3, 2010.

19 Business Employment Dynamics data: survival and longevity, II by Amy E. Knaup and Merissa C. Piazza, September 2007, Monthly Labor Review, Bureau of Labor Statistics website, **http://www.bls.gov/opub/mlr/2007/09/art1full.pdf**, accessed February 15, 2009.

20 Focus on Success, Not Failure by Rhonda Abrams, May 7, 2004, *USA Today* website money section, **http:// www.usatoday.com/money/smallbusiness/columnist/ abrams/2004-05-06-success_x.htm.**

21 Failure: Use It as a Springboard to Success, U.S. SBA Online Library, no attribution, **http://www.sba.gov/library/ successXIII/19-Failure-Use-it.doc**, accessed December 28, 2005.

22 Is Entrepreneurship for You? U.S. Small Business Administration, **http://www.sba.gov/starting_business/ startup/areyouready.html**, accessed December 15, 2005.

23 Committee Examines Ways to Ease Growing Regulatory Burden on Small Businesses, July 30, 2008, U.S. House of Representatives Press Release, House of Representatives website, **http://www.house.gov/smbiz/ PressReleases/2008/pr-7-30-08-regulatory.html**, accessed February 15, 2009.

24 Entrepreneurship in the 21st Century, Conference Proceedings, March 26, 2004, SBA Office of Advocacy and the Kauffman Foundation, **http://www.sba.gov/advo/stats/proceedings_a .pdf**. Health Care Costs Surface in Economic Stimulus Debate by Sharon McLoone, February 10, 2009, *Washington Post* website, **http://voices.washingtonpost.com/small -business/2009/02/health_care_costs_surface_in_e.html**, accessed February 15, 2009.

25 Five Reasons Why Franchises Flop by Steve Strauss, February 28, 2005, *USA Today* Money website, **http://www.usatoday .com/money/smallbusiness/columnist/strauss/2005-02-28 -franchise_x.htm**.

26 Business Plan Basics, U.S. SBA, **http://www.sba.gov/ starting_business/planning/basic.html**, accessed February 15, 2009.

27 Business Plan Basics, U.S. SBA, **http://www.sba.gov/ starting_business/planning/basic.html**, accessed February 15, 2009.

28 "Frequently Asked Questions," SBA Office of Advocacy, updated September 2009, SBA website **http://www.sba.gov/ advo/stats/sbfaq.pde**, accessed June 3, 2010.

29 Frequently Asked Questions, SBA Office of Advocacy, Updated September 2008, SBA website, **http://www.sba.gov/advo/ stats/sbfaq.pdf**, accessed February 17, 2009.

30 Minipreneurs, Trendwatching.com, **http://www .trendwatching.com/trends/MINIPRENEURS.htm**, accessed December 10, 2005; How Google tamed ads on the wild, wild Web by Randall Stross, November 20, 2005, *New York Times*, **http://select.nytimes.com/gst/abstract.html?res=FA0B11F D355A0C738EDDA80994DD404482**.

31 Frequently Asked Questions, SBA Office of Advocacy, Updated September 2008, SBA website, **http://www.sba.gov/advo/ stats/sbfaq.pdf**, accessed February 17, 2009.

32 Small Business Drives Inner City Growth and Jobs, NewsRelease, October 11, 2005, U.S. SBA Office of Advocacy, **http://www.sba.gov/advo/press/05-32.html**.

33 Global Entrepreneurship Monitor, 2008 Executive Report by Niels Bosma, Zoltan J. Acs, Erkko Autio, Alicia Coduras, and Jonathan Levie, Babson College and London School of Economics, **http://www.gemconsortium.org/article .aspx?id=76**, published January 15, 2009, accessed February 17, 2009.

34 Global Entrepreneurship Monitor, 2008 Executive Report by Niels Bosma, Zoltan J. Acs, Erkko Autio, Alicia Coduras, and Jonathan Levie, Babson College and London School of Economics, **http://www.gemconsortium.org/article .aspx?id=76**, published January 15, 2009, accessed February 17, 2009.

Pg. 90 Fact Box: Study: 72% of workers would rather work for themselves by Rhonda Abrams, October 11, 2008, *USA Today* website, **http://www.usatoday.com/money/smallbusiness/ columnist/abrams/2007-10-11-workers-survey_N.htm**, accessed February 17, 2009.

Pg. 94 Fact Box: How Do I...Get Some of That Venture Capital? By Sharon McLoone, October 6, 2008, *Washington Post* website, **http://voices.washingtonpost.com/small -business/2008/10/how_do_iget_some_of_that_ventu.html**, accessed February 17, 2009.

Pg. 97 Fact Box: Global Entrepreneurship Monitor, 2004 Executive Report, **http://www.gemconsortium.org/ download/1133331987906/GEM_2004_Exec_Report.pdf**, published May 27, 2005, accessed August 29,2008.

Pg. 99 Fact Box: Slumdog Entrepreneurs, *Time* magazine photo essay, by Daniel Berehulak, *Time* website, **http://www.time .com/time/photogallery/0,29307,1877000,00.html**, accessed February 17, 2009.

Chapter Eight

1 U.S. Bureau of Labor Statistics, *Occupational Outlook Handbook*: 2008-2009 website for accountants and auditors: **http://www.bls.gov/oco/ocos001.htm**, accessed February 11, 2009.

2 Accounting Sleuths on the Trail of Madoff Money by Rob Scherer, December 22, 2008, *Christian Science Monitor* website: **http://www.csmonitor.com/2008/1222/p01s01 -usec.html**; Post-Madoff, Forensic Accountants Seeing Increase in Business, Shareholders Foundation website: **http://shareholdersfoundation.com/news/post-madoff -forensic-accountants-seeing-increase-business**, accessed February 17, 2009; **http://www.webcpa.com/news/ Forensic-Accountants-Reconstruct-Madoff-Books-50484-1 .html; http://www.msnbc.msn.com/id/29612242/; http://online.wsj.com/article/SB124604151653862301 .html**; Forensic Teams Dig into Legal Disputes for Clients; Multidisciplinary Investigations Are Now a $6 Billion Business by Stan Luxenberg, *Crain's New York Business*, September 25, 2006; Forensic Accounting: Exponential Growth: The Work Varies Widely, the Credentials to Practice Are Sophisticated, Unique Marketing Is Needed, but the Engagements Are Very Lucrative by Jeff Stimpson, *The Practical Accountant*, February 2007; CFE: Certified Fraud Examiner? Forensic Accounting Is Catching On by Peter Vogt, MSN Encarta, August 2006, **http:// www.investigation.com/articles/library/2006articles/ articles6.htm**, accessed May 17, 2007.

3 Scandal Sheet, CBS Marketwatch website, **http://www .marketwatch.com/news/features/scandal_sheet.asp**; Corporate Scandal Sheet, Citizen Works website[SB36], **http://www.citizenworks.org/enron/corp-scandal.php**; The Corporate Scandal Sheet by Penelope Patsuris, *Forbes*,

August 26, 2002, **http://www.forbes.com/2002/07/25/accountingtracker.html**.

4 "SEC Delays Plan to Adopt IFRS," by Rachel Younglai, Reuters website: **http://www.reuters.com/article/idUSTRE61N6G220100224** (accessed May 7, 2010); "SEC Votes on Work Plan for Incorporating IFRS," by Michael Cohn, February 24, 2010, WebCPA website: **http://www.webcpa.com/news/SEC-Votes-Work-Plan-Incorporating-IFRS-53368-1.html**, accessed May 7, 2010; "No IFRS Requirement Until 2015 or Later Under New SEC Timeline," by Alexandra DeFelice and Matthew G. Lamoreaux, February 24, 2010, *Journal of Accountancy* website: **http://www.journalofaccountancy.com/Web/20102656.htm,** accessed May 7, 2010; "IFRS and US GAAP Similarities and Differences," PricewaterhouseCoopers IFRS Readiness Series, September 2008; "Closing the GAAP," August 28, 2008, Economist.com website: **http://www.economist.com/finance/displaystory.cfm?story_id=12010009**,accessed May 7, 2010.

5 When Balance Sheets Collide with the New Economy by Denise Caruso, The *New York Times*, Section 3, page 4, September 9, 2007; Albrecht, Stice, Stice and Swain, *Accounting Concepts and Applications, 9th ed.* (Cengage Learning), page 482; *The Hidden Value of Intangibles* by Ben McClure, Investopedia website, **http://www.investopedia.com/articles/03/010603.asp**, accessed August 29, 2008. The market capitalization of Apple stock was computed by the author using information for the number of shares of common stock outstanding reported on the Yahoo! Finance website: **http://finance.yahoo.com/q/ks?s=AAPL+Key+Statistics**. The price of Apple stock was found from a table of historical stock prices on the Yahoo! Finance website: **http://finance.yahoo.com/q/hp?s=AAPL,** accessed April 10, 2010.

6 "It's Time for Triple Bottom Line Reporting," by Daniel Tschopp, *The CPA Journal*, December 2003: **http://www.nysscpa.org/cpajournal/2003/1203/nv/nv3a.htm**; "Adapting Your Accounting Practices to Triple Bottom Line Reporting," by David Crawford, *CMA Management Magazine*, February 7, 2005, accessed on Greenbiz website: **http://www.greenbiz.com/business/research/report/2005/02/08/adapting-your-accounting-practices-triple-bottom-line-reporting**; "KPMG: The Triple Bottom Line of People, Planet and Profits," The Big Four Blog website, March 2, 2010: **http://bigfouralumni.blogspot.com/2010/03/kpmg-triple-bottom-line-of-people.html**; "What is Triple Bottom Line Reporting?," by Shane Thornton, eHow website: **http://www.ehow.com/about_5064070_triple-bottom-line-reporting.html** (accessed April 28, 2010); "Putting the Triple Bottom Line to Work," by Mark McElroy, November 11, 2009, Greenbiz website: **http://www.greenbiz.com/blog/2009/11/11/putting-triple-bottom-line-work**.

7 Mission statement on PCAOB website, **http://www.pcaobus.org/index.aspx**.

8 Albrecht, Stice, Stice, and Swain, *Accounting Concepts and Applications, 9th ed.* (Cengage Learning), page 758.

9 "The Origins of Beyond Budgeting and of the Beyond Budgeting Round Table (BBRT) – an Interview with Jeremy Hope," by Juergen Daum, Beyond Budgeting website: **http://www.beyondbudgeting.de/articles/Interview_Jeremy_Hope.pdf** (accessed May 10, 2010); "About Beyond Budgeting," Beyond Budgeting Round Table website: **http://www.bbrt.org/beyond-budgeting/beybud.html** (accessed April 5, 2010); "BBRT Current Member Organizations," Beyond Budgeting Round Table website, **http://www.bbrt.org/BBRT/bbrt-members.html** (accessed April 5, 2010); "Beyond Budgeting," by Juergen Daum, The Beyond Budgeting Info-Center website: **http://www.juergendaum.com/bb.htm** (accessed April 6, 2010).

10 *The Essentials of Finance and Budgeting*, Harvard Business School Press, Boston, MA, 2005, pp. 177–181.

Pg. 101 Fact Box: Confucius, ChinaCulture.org website: **http://www1.chinaculture.org/library/2008-02/08/content_23084.htm**, accessed February 18, 2009.

Pg. 110 Fact Box: A Beginner's Guide to Financial Statements, SEC website: **http://www.sec.gov/investor/pubs/begfinstmtguide.htm** ("Read The Footnotes" finished seventh in the 2004 Kentucky Derby.)

Chapter Nine

1 Numbers, *BusinessWeek*, February 9, 2009, p. 13.

2 See, for example, Moyer, McGuigan, and Rao, *Fundamentals of Contemporary Financial Management, 2nd ed.* (South-Western, Cengage Learning), page 3; Brigham and Houston, *Fundamentals of Financial Management, 11th ed.*, page 2.

3 Credit Suisse's Bonus Is Not Coal in the Stocking by Jim Cramer, TheStreet.com website: **http://www.thestreet.com/p/_search/rmoney/jimcramerblog/10454322.html**, December 19, 2008; Credit Suisse to Pay Bonuses in Toxic Debt by Stephen Foley, Independent.com website: **http://www.independent.co.uk/news/business/news/credit-suisse-to-pay-bonuses-in-toxic-debt-1203709.html** December 19 2008; How to Deleverage Balance Sheets by Barry Ritholtz, **http://www.ritholtz.com/blog/2008/12/how-to-deleverage-balance-sheets/** December 18, 2008; Investors, Pundits Welcome Credit Suisse Bonus Plan by Olesya Dmitracova and Raji Menon, Reuters Business and Finance website: **http://uk.reuters.com/article/marketsNewsUS/idUKLJ19930820081219?pageNumber=1** December 19, 2008. Credit Suisse to Use Illiquid Assets to Pay Bonuses by Christine Harper, Bloomberg website: **http://www.bloomberg.com/apps/news?pid=20601087&sid=auEEfFRNdqcs** December 18, 2008. "Bon Apétit: 'Toxic' Bonus Yields 72% at Credit Suisse," by Katharina Bart, *Wealth Bulletin* website: **http://www.wealth-bulletin.com/rich-life/rich-monitor/content/4058425398/26632/,** accessed April 16, 2010.

4 Inventory Turnover Ratios & Days Sales in Ending Inventories: U.S. National Averages, Bizstats.com website, **http://www.bizstats.com/inventory.htm**; Financial ratios for specific industries: Food and beverage stores, Bizstats.com website: **http://www.bizstats.com/reports/corp.asp?industry=Food+and+beverage+stores&profType=ratios&var=&coding=44.5.115**; Financial ratios for specific industries: Furniture and home furnishings, Bizstats website: **http://www.bizstats.com/reports/corp.asp?industry=Food+and+beverage+stores&profType=ratios&var=&coding=44.5.115**, accessed April 6, 2010.

5 The World's Biggest Mattress, NPR website: **http://www.npr.org/blogs/money/2008/12/worlds_biggest_mattress.html**; Treasury Bill Rates Go Negative; Loaning Money at a Guaranteed Loss by Mike Masnick, Techdirt website: **http://www.techdirt.com/articles/20081210/0329553074.shtml**, Zero Return on a T-Bill? Give US a Break by Dan Burrows, SmartMoney.com website: **http://www.smartmoney.com/investing/bonds/zero-return-on-a-t-bill-give-us-a-break/**; T-Bill rates Can Be Negative by Karl Smith: **http://modeledbehavior.blogspot.com/2008/03/t-bill-rates-can-be-negative.html**.

6 Getting Tough with Customers by Matthew Boyle and Olga Kharif, *BusinessWeek* March 9, 2009 p. 30.

7 The approximate "finance charge" of not taking the discount on credit can be computed using the following formula: where %discount is the discount the buyer receives for paying on or before the last day the discount is available, the Credit Discount Period is the number of days before payment of full invoice amount is due.

8 Financial Services Used by Small Businesses: Evidence from the 2003 Survey of Small Business Finances by Traci Mack and John D. Wolken, *Federal Reserve Bulletin*, October 2006, page A181.

9 Taking the Fear Out of Factoring by Martin Mayer, Inc.com website:**http://www.inc.com/magazine/20031201/factoring.html**.

10 New York Fed CPFF FAQs, New York Federal Reserve Bank website: **http://www.newyorkfed.org/markets/cpff_faq.html**, accessed March 13, 2009.

11 "Green and Social Venture Capital," Green VC website: **http://www.greenvc.org/green-and-social-venture-capital.html**; "30 Entrepreneurs Who Are Saving the World," by Kelly Fairchild, *Inc. Magazine*, November 1, 2009: **http://www.inc.com/magazine/20091101/30-entrepreneurs-who-are-saving-the-world.html**; "Do-Gooder Finance," by Natasha Tiku, *Inc. Magazine*, February 1, 2008: **http://www.inc.com/magazine/20080201/do-gooder-finance.html**; Underdog Ventures website: **http://www2.underdogventures.com/,** accessed April 19, 2010.

12 "Summary: Restoring American Financial Stability," Senate Committee on Banking, Housing and Urban Affairs: **http://banking.senate.gov/public/_files/FinancialReformSummaryAsFiled.pdf**; "Bernanke: Too Big to Fail a 'Pernicious' Problem," by Christina Cooke, Reuters website March 20, 2010: **http://www.reuters.com/article/idUSTRE62J0SM20100320**; "Details Still Scarce on WaMu's Failure," by Dan Fitzpatrick and John D. McKinnon, *The Wall Street Journal* website, April 13, 2010: **http://online.wsj.com/article/SB10001424052702304506904575180441067747062.html**; "Testimony of Chairman Ben S. Bernanke before the Committee on Financial Services of the U.S. House of Representatives," Federal Reserve website, April 20, 2010: **http://www.federalreserve.gov/newsevents/testimony/bernanke20100420a.htm**.

13 Calling All Superheroes: The Spider-Man Movies Have Made a Mint—But Not for Spidey's Publisher by Devin Leonard, *Fortune*, May 23, 2007, **http://money.cnn.com/magazines/fortune**; "Spider-Man 3" on Track to Beat Predecessors by Dean Goodman, Reuters, May 2, 2007, **http://www.reuters.com**; Form 10-K, **http://yahoo.brand.edgar-online.com/fetchFilingFrameset.aspx?dcn=0001116679-07-000580&Type=HTML**; Marvel Studios, Wikipedia: **http://en.wikipedia.org/wiki/Marvel_Studios**, accessed March 14, 2009; Top Ten Box Office Movies of 2008, Yahoo! Movies website: **http://movies.yahoo.com/photos/collections/gallery/1319/top-10-box-office-movies-of-2008#photo10**; Marvel Studios Confirms Upcoming Movies by Michael Hidkerson, Slice of SciFi website: **http://www.sliceofscifi.com/2008/11/05/marvel-studios-confirms-upcoming-movies/**, November 5, 2008. BoxOffice website: **http://www.boxoffice.com/**, accessed May 26, 2010.

14 Financial Sectors' New Buzzword Is Deleverage by Chris Arnold, NPR website: **http://www.npr.org/templates/story/story.php?storyId=94795760**, accessed August 9, 2009; Deleveraging, Now Only in Early Stages, Will Transform the Banking Industry by James Saft, *New York Times* website: **http://www.nytimes.com/2008/06/26/business/worldbusiness/26iht-col27.1.14006619.html?_r=1**, accessed August, 9, 2009; Deleveraging: A Fate Worse than Debt, *Economist* website: **http://www.economist.com/businessfinance/displaystory.cfm?story_id=12306060**, accessed August 9, 2009.

Pg. 123 Fact Box: Getting Tough with Customers by Matthew Boyle and Olga Kharif, *BusinessWeek* March 9, 2009 p. 30; Smallbiz.com: **http://www.smsmallbiz.com/profiles/When_States_Cant_Pay_Small_Employers_Face_Cash_Drought.html**.

Pg. 130 Fact Box: Citigroup Form 10-Q for September 30, 2008 accessed through SEC Edgar website: **http://www.sec.gov/Archives/edgar/data/831001/000104746908011506/a2188770z10-q.htm**.

Chapter Ten

1 Yahoo! Finance Historical Prices for Google Stock: **http://finance.yahoo.com/q/hp?s=GOOG&a=7&b=19&c=2004&d=2&e=19&f=2009&g=d&z=66&y=0**.

2 Century Bonds Lure the Rare Investor With a Truly Long-Term Outlook by Conrad D. Aenlle, *International Herald Tribune* website: **http://www.iht.com/articles/2001/03/31/mhund_ed2_.php**.

3 Defaults Stacking Up in the Junk Bond Market by Tom Petruno, *Los Angeles Times* website: **http://latimesblogs.latimes.com/money_co/2009/01/junk-bonds-the.html** January 26, 2009; There's Plenty of Juice in Junk Bonds by Mina Kimes, *Fortune* magazine, March 2, 2009, p. 40; Junk Bond Yields Are Crazy High, But Tread Carefully by John Waggoner, *USA Today*, December 5, 2008, Money Section, p. 3b.

4 The Coming Bond Default Wave by Richard Lehmann, *Forbes* Magazine website: **http://www.forbes.com/forbes/2008/1013/130.html**.

5 Amex Members Approve Acquisition of Amex by NYSE Euronext, Reuters website: **http://www.reuters.com/article/pressRelease/idUS137462+17-Jun-2008+BW20080617**.

6 About Us, NYSE Euronext website: **http://www.nyse.com/about/1088808971270.html**, accessed August 9, 2009; Nasdaq Milestones, Nasdaq website: **http://www.nasdaqomx.com/whoweare/milestones/milestonesnasdaq/**, accessed August 9, 2009.

7 NYSE Hybrid Market, NYSE website: **http://www.nyse.com/pdfs/hybrid_update.pdf**, accessed August 9, 2009.

8 2008 Review: NYSE Fights Back with Designated Market Makers by Peter Chapman, Tradersmagazine.com website, December 2008: **http://www.tradersmagazine.com/issues/20_289/102770-1.html**.

9 Investor Information, GM website: **http://www.gm.com/corporate/investor_information/**, accessed June 2, 2010; "Factbox: Ranking of World's Top 10 Auto Groups by Sales," Reuters website: **http://www.reuters.com/article/idUST8934920080901**, accessed June 2, 2010; "Obama Says 'Not Going to Meddle in GM's Decisions,'" by Caren Bohan, Jeff Mason, Kevin Krolici and John Crawley, Reuters website: **http://www.reuters.com/article/idUSTRE5AH3QC20091118**; "The Hottest IPO of 2010: GM?," MSN website: **http://articles.moneycentral.msn.com/Investing/Extra/the-hottest-ipo-of-2010-gm.aspx**; "GM IPO a Real Possibility in 2010: CEO," *The Economic Times* website: **http://economictimes.indiatimes.com/news/international-business/GM-IPO-a-real-possibility-in-2010-CEO/articleshow/5841584.cms**.

10 SEC website: **http://www.sec.gov/answers/ecn.htm and http://www.sec.gov/investor/pubs/afterhours.htm**, accessed August 9, 2009.

11 See for example, "How Kansas Drove Out a Set of Thieves" by Will Payne, *The Saturday Evening Post*, December 2, 1911, reproduced on the Office of Kansas Securities Commissioner's website: **http://www.securities.state.ks.us/edu/bluesky.html**.

12 "14 Charged in Galleon Insider Trading Case," by Pete Carey, *Mercury News* website: **http://www.mercurynews.com/galleon-insider-trading-case/ci_13720293?nclick_check=1** (accessed June 3, 2010); "Anil Kumar Pleads Guilty in Galleon Case," by Bess Levin, Dealbreaker.com website: **http://dealbreaker.com/2010/01/anil-kumar-pleads-guilty-in-galleon-case/** (accessed June 3, 2010); "State of Play in the Galleon Insider Trading Case," by Peter J. Henning, Dealbook.com website: **http://dealbook.blogs.nytimes.com/2010/03/30/state-of-play-in-the-galleon-insider-trading-case/** (accessed June 3, 2010).

13 About the Financial Industry Regulatory Authority, FINRA website, **http://www.finra.org/AboutFINRA/index.htm**, accessed August 29, 2008.

14 Investor FAQs, Anheuser Busch InBev website: **http://www.ab-inbev.com/go/investors/services/faqs.cfm#QA3**, accessed August 9, 2009; What Is a Stock Symbol and How Do I Find the Symbol for a Company?, BusinessKnowledgeSource.com website: **http://businessknowledgesource.com/investing/what_is_a_stock_symbol_and_how_do_i_find_the_symbol_for_a_company_021903.html**, accessed August 29, 2008; Stock Symbol Identifiers, StockMaven.com website, **http://www.stockmaven.com/symbols.htm**, accessed August 29, 2008; Stock Tickers and Ticker Symbols, Money-zine.com website, **http://www.money-zine.com/Investing/Stocks/Stock-Tickers-and-Ticker-Symbols/**, accessed August 9, 2009.

15 "Trading Shares in Milliseconds," by Bryant Urstadt, *Technology Review*, February 2010, pp. 44-49; "The Machines That Ate the Market," by Nina Mehta, Lynn Thomasson, and Paul Barrett. *Bloomberg Businessweek*, May 24, 2010, pp. 48-55; "The Flash Crash of May 6: What Happened?," Accountingweb website: **http://www.accountingweb.com/topic/technology/flash-crash-may-6-what-happened**; "US Markets Plunge, Then Stage a Rebound," by Graham Bowley, *New York Times* website, May 6. 2010: **http://www.nytimes.com/2010/05/07/business/07markets.html**.

16 Finding the Right Green Fund by Eugenia Levenson, Fortune magazine website November 6, 2008: **http://money.cnn.com/2008/11/05/magazines/fortune/levenson_greenfunds.fortune/index.htm**; Green Investments for Launderers by Will Ashworth, Investopedia website April 7, 2008: **http://community.investopedia.com/news/IA/2008/Green_Investments_For_Launderers.aspx?partner=YahooSA**; Winslow Green Growth Fund Performance, Winslow Management Company website: **http://www.winslowgreen.com/fund/performance.aspx**, accessed June 2, 2010; Portfolio 21 Performance, Portfolio 21 Investments website: **http://www.portfolio21.com/in_depth_perf.php**, accessed June 2, 2010; New Alternatives Fund Annual Report, December 31, 2009: **http://www.newalternativesfund.com/returns/NAF-AR-2009.pdf**, accessed June 2, 2010.

Pg. 134 Fact Box: Yahoo! Finance: **http://finance.yahoo.com/news/Dow-Declares-Quarterly-bw-665800093.html?x=0&.v=1**, accessed June 4, 2010.

Pg. 136 Fact Box: Perpetuity, Investopedia website: **http://www.investopedia.com/terms/p/perpetuity.asp**.

Pg. 146 Fact Box: Trends in Mutual Fund Investing January 2009, Investment Company Institute website: **http://www.ici.org/stats/mf/trends_01_09.html#TopOfPage,** accessed March 30, 2009.

Chapter Eleven

1 Army to Use Webcasts From Iraq for Recruiting by Stuart Elliott, November 10, 2008, *New York Times* website, **http://www.nytimes.com/2008/11/11/business/media/11adco.html**, accessed February 22, 2009.

2 What marketers can learn from Obama's campaign by Al Ries, November 5, 2008, *Advertising Age* website, **http://adage.com/moy2008/article?article_id=131810**, accessed February 22, 2009.

3 Vegas turns to reality show amid recession by Natalie Zmuda, January 2009, *Advertising Age* website, **http://adage.com/abstract.php?article_id=134193**, accessed February 22, 2009.

4 American Customer Satisfaction Index Quarterly Scores, Q1—Q4 2008, ASCI website, **http://www.theacsi.org/index.php?option=com_content&task=view&id=13&Itemid=31**, accessed February 24, 2009.

5 Eight reasons to keep your customers loyal by Rama Ramaswami, January 12, 2005, Mulitchannel Merchant website, **http://multichannelmerchant.com/opsandfulfillment/advisor/Brandi-custloyal**, accessed February 24, 2009.

6 The psychology of color in marketing by June Campbell, accessed March 19, 2005, UCSI website, **http://www.ucsi.cc/webdesign/color-marketing.html**; Color psychology in marketing by Al Martinovic, June 21, 2004, ImHosted website, **http://developers.evrsoft.com/article/web-design/graphics-multimedia-design/color-psychology-in-marketing.shtml**; Colors that sell by Suzanne Roman, November 29, 2004, ImHosted website, **http://developers.evrsoft.com/article/web-design/graphics-multimedia-design/colors-that-sell.shtml**; Reinvent Wheel? Blue Room. Defusing a Bomb? Red Room. By Pam Belluck, February 6, 2009, *New York Times* website, **http://www.nytimes.com/2009/02/06/science/06color.html**, accessed February 26, 2009.

7 It's true: Food packages shrunk last year by Chris Serres, December 31, 2008, *Chicago Sun-Times* website, **http://www.suntimes.com/news/nation/1356955,w-food-packages-shrinking-general-mills123108.article**, accessed February 26, 2008; That Shrinking Feeling, by Karen Springen, August 29, 2008, *Newsweek* website, **http://www.newsweek.com/id/156172**, accessed February 26, 2009; Shoppers beware: Products shrink but prices stay the same by Bruce Horovitz, June 13, 2008, **http://www.usatoday.com/money/industries/food/2008-06-11-shrinking-sizes_N.htm**, accessed February 26, 2009.

8 Shoe makers gunning for Olympian feat by Andria Cheng, May 9, 2008, Market Watch website, **http://www.marketwatch.com/news/story/story.aspx?guid={781CC2E2-2B3F-4FF5-A0C5-0FB962D7E204}**, accessed February 24, 2009.

9 TechSpin: Motorola's Lessons in Consumer Marketing by Joel Dreyfuss, March 26, 2008, *Red Herring* website, **http://www.redherring.com/Home/24017**, accessed February 24, 2009; Motorola's next move: it has to be a magic act by Phil Goldstein, February 3, 2009, Fierce Wireless website, **http://www.fiercewireless.com/story/motorolas-next-move-it-has-be-magic-act/2009-02-03**, accessed February 24, 2009.

10 Hershey stops making mints in coke-like packs, January 24, 2008, MSNBC website, **http://www.msnbc.msn.com/id/22827806/**, accessed February 26, 2009; Tropicana discovers some buyers are passionate about packaging by Stuart Elliott, February 23, 2009, *New York Times* website, accessed February 26, 2009; "Misrepresentation of our nation's ethnic diversity drives us all mad," by Ruth Mortimer, December 10, 2009, *MarketingWeek* website, **http://www.marketingweek.co.uk/misrepresentation-of-our-nations-ethnic-diversity-drives-us-all-mad/3007381.article** (accessed June 6, 2010).

11 "Green brands, global insight: Findings from the 2009 ImagePower Green Brands Survey," Landor Staff, September 2009, Landor website, **http://www.landor.com/index.cfm?do=thinking.article&storyid=749&bhcp=1** (accessed June 7, 2010).

12 Environment a fair-weather priority for consumers, June 3, 2008, Penn, Schoen & Bergland Press Release, Penn, Schoen & Bergland website, **http://www.psbresearch.com/press_release_Jun3-2008.htm**, accessed February 24, 2009; Green Fashion: Is It More Than Marketing Hype? By Gloria Sin, May 28, 2008, *Fast Company* website, **http://www.fastcompany.com/articles/2008/05/green-fashion-hype.html**, accessed February 24, 2009; "Green" Fashion, Formerly Hippie, Now Hip! February 21, 2008, CBS News website, **http://www.cbsnews.com/stories/2008/02/21/earlyshow/living/beauty/main3855868.shtml**, accessed February 24, 2009.

Pg. 164 Fact Box: Environment a fair-weather priority for consumers, June 3, 2008, Penn, Schoen & Bergland Press Release, Penn, Schoen & Bergland website, **http: //www.psbresearch.com/press_release_Jun3-2008.htm**, accessed February 24, 2009.

Chapter Twelve

1   The Years 1980, Histomobile website, **http://www
    .histomobile.com/histomob/internet/87/histo02.htm**,
    accessed April 16, 2005; Yugo Redux by Doug Donovan,
    April 23, 2002, *Forbes* website, **http://www.forbes
    .com/2002/04/23/0423yugo.html**; Worst Cars of the
    Millennium, CarTalk website, **http://www.cartalk.com/
    content/features/Worst-Cars/results5.html**; First Chinese
    Cars to Hit US Shores by Bill Vlasic, *The Detroit News*
    website, January 2, 2005, **http://www.detnews.com/2005/
    autoinsider/0501/02/A01-47455.htm**; Yugo Art photos from
    http://magliery.com/Graphics/YugoArt/diner.jpg.

2   *BusinessWeek* "100 Best Global Brands," **http://bwnt
    .businessweek.com/interactive_reports/best_global
    _brands_2009/**, accessed December 14, 2009.

3   Characteristics of a Great Name, The Brand Name Awards
    by Brighter Naming, **http://www.brandnameawards.com/
    top10factors.html**, accessed April 10, 2005.

4   Brand Extensions: Marketing in Inner Space by Adam Bass,
    Brand Channel website, **http://www.brandchannel.com/
    papers_review.asp?sp_id=296** accessed March 25, 2007;
    Brand Extensions We Could Do Without by Reena Jana,
    August 7, 2006, *BusinessWeek* website, **http://www
    .businessweek.com/magazine/content/06_32/b3996420
    .htm**.

5   "Private Label Growing Rapidly," by Alex Palmer, September
    22, 2009, *BrandWeek* website, **http://www.brandweek
    .com/bw/content_display/news-and-features/packaged
    -goods/e3i7c69fb437bbee15e35345c87bdf679fe** (accessed
    June 14, 2010).

6   "The USA Apparel Market Research Report," June 2010,
    Fashion. **http://www.infomat.com/fido/getpublication.fcn
    ?&type=research&SearchString=apparel&id=737870ST0000
    927&start=1&tr=17Infomat** (accessed June 14, 2010).

7   Not on the List? The Truth about Impulse Purchases, January
    7, 2009, Knowledge@Wharton website, **http://knowledge
    .wharton.upenn.edu/article.cfm?articleid=2132**, accessed
    February 28, 2009.

8   3M: Commitment to Sustainability, GreenBiz Leaders website,
    1999.

9   "Wacky Warning Labels 2009 Winners Announced," August
    16, 2009, Foundation for Fair Civil Justice website, **http://
    www.foundationforfairciviljustice.org/news/in_depth/
    wacky_warning_labels_2009_winners_announced/**
    (accessed June 14, 2010).

10 "Eco Iconic," June 2008, Trendwatching website, **http://
    trendwatching.com/trends/ecoiconic.htm**, accessed
    June 15, 2010. .

11 U.S. Consumer Online Behavior Survey Results 2007—
    Part One: Wireline Usage, International Data Corporation
    website, February 19, 2008, **http://www.idc.com/getdoc
    .jsp?containerId=prUS21096308**, accessed March 3, 2009;
    Why Video On Demand Is Still Cable's Game to Lose by Dan
    Frommer, September 5, 2008, The Business Insider website,
    **http://www.businessinsider.com/2008/9/why-video-on
    -demand-is-still-cable-s-game-to-lose**, accessed March
    3, 2009; Streaming vids boost Netflix profits by Glenn Abel,
    January 29, 2009, Download Movies 101 website, **http://
    downloadmovies101.com/wordpress-1/2009/01/29/
    streaming-vids-boost-netflix-profits/**, accessed March 3,
    2009; Casting the Big Movie Download Roles, September
    7, 2007, eMarketer website, **http://www.emarketer.com/
    Article.aspx?id=1005346**, accessed March 3, 2009.

12 Permission Marketing by William C. Taylor, December 18,
    2007, *Fast Company* website, **http://www.fastcompany
    .com/magazine/14/permission.html**, accessed March 3,
    2009.

13 'Two nobodies from nowhere' craft winning Super Bowl
    ad by Bruce Horovitz, February 4, 2009, *USA Today*
    website, **http://www.usatoday.com/money/advertising/
    admeter/2009admeter.htm**, accessed March 4, 2009.

14 Professor Paul Herbig, Tristate University, International
    Marketing Lecture Series, Session 6, International Advertising,
    http://www.tristate.edu/faculty/herbig/pahimadvstg.htm,
    accessed June 1, 2005; Taking Global Brands to Japan by
    Karl Moore and Mark Smith, The Conference Board website,
    **http://www.conference-board.org/worldwide/worldwide
    _article.cfm?id=243&pg=1**, accessed June 1, 2005.

15 Search Marketing Trends: Back to Basics,eMarketer website,
    February 2009, **http://www.emarketer.com/Report
    .aspx?code=emarketer_2000559**, accessed June 18, 2010.

16 eMarketer: Search Is Vital in a Recession by *Adweek* staff,
    February 25, 2009, *Brandweek* website, **http://www
    .brandweek.com/bw/content_display/news-and-features/
    digital/e3i195c363ab252f976a2dabde4d8ef2549**, accessed
    March 3, 2009.

17 U.S. Online Advertising Video Spending 2007 – 2013, August
    2008, eMarketer website, **http://www.marketingcharts
    .com/television/emarketer-revises-online-video-ad-spend
    -projections-downward-5679/emarketer-online-video-ad
    -spend-us-2007-2013jpg/**, accessed June 18, 2010.

18 Brandchannel's 2004 Product Placement Awards by Abram
    Sauer, February 21, 2005, **http://www.brandchannel.com/
    start1.asp?fa_id=251**; A Product Placement Hall of Fame by
    Dale Buss, *BusinessWeek* Online, June 22, 1998, **http://www
    .businessweek.com/1998/25/b3583062.htm**.

19 PQ Media Market Analysis Finds Global Product Placement
    Spending Grew 37% in 2006; Forecast to Grow 30% in 2007,
    Driven by Relaxed European Rules, Emerging Asian Markets;
    Double-Digit Growth in U.S. Decelerates, PQ Media website,
    March 14, 2007, **http://www.pqmedia.com/about-press
    -20070314-gppf.html**, accessed September 4, 2008. DVR
    Households Swelling Ranks by Jose Fermoso, December 16,
    2008, Portfolio website, **http://www.portfolio.com/views/
    blogs/the-tech-observer/2008/12/16/dvr-households
    -swelling-ranks**, accessed March 4, 2009; FCC opens inquiry
    into stealthy TV product placement, June 26, 2008, *USA Today*
    website, **http://www.usatoday.com/life/television/2008-06
    -26-fcc-advertising_N.htm**, accessed March 4, 2009; "DVRs
    now in 30.6% of U.S. Households," by Bill Gorman, April 30,
    2009, TV by the Numbers website, **http://tvbythenumbers
    .com/2009/04/30/dvrs-now-in-306-of-us-households/17779**
    (accessed June 16, 2010).

20 Ford, Coke & AT&T Pay More to Sponsor American Idol by
    Susan Gunelius, January 18, 2008, Bizzia website, **http://
    www.bizzia.com/brandcurve/ford-coke-att-pay-more
    -to-sponsor-american-idol/**, accessed March 4, 2009;
    "Global Paid Product Placement to Reach $7.6 billion
    By 2010: Report," by Amy Johannes, August 17, 2006,
    PromoMagazine website, **http://promomagazine.com/
    research/paidplacementreport/** (accessed June 16, 2010).

21 All Time High: 72% of U.S. Population Plays Video Games
    by Matt Peckham, April 3, 2008, *PC World* website, **http://
    blogs.pcworld.com/gameon/archives/006748.html**,
    accessed March 5, 2009; Video Game Advertising report,
    eMarketer website, **http://www.emarketer.com/Report
    .aspx?code=emarketer_2000485**, accessed March 5, 2009.

22 Massive Summary Research—Significant Findings, Massive
    website, **http://www.massiveincorporated.com/
    casestudiesa.html**, accessed March 4, 2009; Google to Buy
    Adscape by Nick Gonzalez, TechCrunch website, February 16,
    2007, **http://www.techcrunch.com/2007/02/16/google-to
    -buy-adscape-for-23-million/**, accessed March 5, 2009.

23 Dissecting "Subservient Chicken" by Mae Anderson, March
    7, 2005, *AdWeek* website, **http://www.adweek.com/aw/
    national/article_display.jsp?vnu_content_id=1000828049**.

24 Kid Nabbing by Melanie Wells, February 2, 2004,
    Forbes website, **http://www.forbes.com/free_forbes/2004/
    0202/084.html**. Tremor website, **http://tremor.com/index**

.html, accessed March 5, 2009; General Mills, Kraft Launch Word of Mouth Networks by Elaine Wong, October 5, 2008, *BrandWeek* website, **http://www.brandweek.com/bw/ content_display/news-and-features/packaged-goods/ e3i2db03fb29d573ec52722456845f5c274**, accessed March 5, 2009.

25 Sponsorship Spending To Rise 2.2 Percent in 2009, IEG Press Release, February 11, 2009, Sponsorship.Com website, **http://www.sponsorship.com/About-IEG/Press-Room/ Sponsorship-Spending-To-Rise-2.2-Percent-in-2009.aspx**, accessed March 5, 2009; "Sponsorship Spending To Rise 2.2 Percent in 2009," August 28, 2009, Sommerville Baddley Marketing website, **http://www.sbmktg.net/2009/08/ sponsorship-spending-to-rise-22-percent-in-2009/** (accessed June 16, 2010).

26 Top 100 Outlays Plunge 10% but Defying Spend Trend Can Pay Off by Bradley Johnson and Matthew Carmichael, *Advertising Age*, June 21, 2010, Vol. 81 Issue 25, p1-24, 10p, * Internet figures are based on display advertising. They do not include paid search or broadband video advertising.

27 "Fake BP Twitter Account: The most Ridiculous Tweets Yet," by Craig Kanalley, May 25, 2010, Huffington Post website, **http://www.huffingtonpost.com/2010/05/25/bp-fake -twitter-account-t_n_588675.html#s93278** (accessed June 11, 2010); "The Soul of Twit," by James Poniewozik, June 3, 2010, *Time* website, **http://www.time.com/time/magazine/ article/0,9171,1993863,00.html** (accessed June 11, 2010); "Fake BP Twitter account remains shrouded in mystery," by Caroline McCarthy, May 27, 2010, cNet News website, **http:// news.cnet.com/8301-13577_3-20006199-36.html** (accessed June 11, 2010).

28 "Social Media ROI Examples & Video," by Erik Qualman, posted November 12, 2009, Socialnomics, Social Media Blog, **http://socialnomics.net/2009/11/12/social-media-roi -examples-video/** (accessed June 28, 2010).

29 Publicity from Thin Air (Don't Just Wait for News to Happen) by Bill Stoller, Article Point website, **http://www.articlepoint .com/articles/public-relations/publicity-from-thin-air.php**, accessed June 15, 2005.

30 "Grilled Chicken a Kentucky Fried Fiasco," by Emily Bryson York, May 11, 2009, *Advertising Age* website, **http://adage .com/article?article_id=136551** (accessed June 28, 2010).

Chapter Thirteen

1 "Supermarket Facts, Industry Overview 2008," Food Marketing Institute website, **http://www.fmi.org/facts _figs/?fuseaction=superfact** (accessed June 30, 2010).

1a Report: Online retail could reach $156B in 2009 by Rachel Metz, January 29, 2009, The Industry Standard website, **http://www.thestandard.com/news/2009/01/29/report -online-retail-could-reach-156b-2009**, accessed March 13, 2009; eMarketer revises e-commerce forecast by Jeffrey Grau, March 5, 2009, eMarketer website, **http://www.emarketer .com/Article.aspx?id=1006948**, **http://www.emarketer .com/Article.aspx?id=1006948**.

2 Retailing the high-tech way by Pallavi Gogoi, July 6, 2005, *BusinessWeek* website, **http://www.businessweek.com/ technology/content/jul2005/tc2005076_5703.htm** accessed March 15, 2009; Walmart tagging fuels RFID market by Alorie Gilbert, December 22, 2004, ZD Net website, **http://news .zdnet.com/2100-9584_22-140442.html**, accessed March 15, 2009; RFID Chips: A Privacy And Security Pandora's Box? November 15, 2008, Science Daily website, **http://www .sciencedaily.com/releases/2008/11/081118141854.htm**, accessed March 15, 2009.

3 Fireclick Index, Top Line Growth, Fireclick website, **http://index.fireclick.com/fireindex.php?segment=0**, accessed March 13, 2009; L.L.Bean Once Again Number One in Customer Service, According to NRF Foundation/

American Express Survey, January 13, 2009, National Retail Federation website, **http://nrf.com/modules. php?name=News&op=viewlive&sp_id=653**, accessed March 13, 2009.

4 Table 1-46b: U.S. Ton-Miles of Freight (BTS Special Tabulation), 2007 data, Bureau of Transportation website, **http://www.bts .gov/publications/national_transportation_statistics/html/ table_01_46b.html (accessed June 30, 2010)**.

5 Sales soften at Costco, March 4, 2009, Retail Analysis IGD website, **http://www.igd.com/analysis/channel/news_hub .asp?channelid=1&channelitemid=9&nidp=&nid=5616**, accessed March 13, 2009.

6 "No left turns is actually right on," by Peter DeMarco, April 24, 2008, *The Boston Globe* website, **http://www.boston.com/ news/local/articles/2008/04/24/no_left_turns_is_actually _right_on/** (accessed June 30, 2010).

7 Loss Leader Strategy, Investopedia website (a *Forbes* Digital Company), **http://www.investopedia.com/terms/l/ lossleader.asp**, accessed March 14, 2009; Walmart not crying over spilt milk by Al Norman, August 22, 2008, The Huffington Post website, **http://www.huffingtonpost.com/al-norman/ wal-mart-not-crying-over_b_120684.html**, accessed March 14, 2009.

8 For Radiohead Fans, Does "Free" + "Download" = "Freeload"?, ComScore Press Release, November 5, 2007, ComScore website, **http://www.comscore.com/press/ release.asp?press=1883**, accessed March 15, 2009 Apple Changes Tune on Music Pricing by Ethan Smith and Yukari Iwatani Kane, January 9, 2009, *Wall Street Journal* website, **http://online.wsj.com/article/SB123126062001057765.html**, accessed March 15, 2009; Changes to iTunes prices raise music labels' hopes, January 14, 2009, *USA Today* website, **http://www.usatoday.com/tech/news/2009-01-14-online -music_N.htm**, accessed March 15, 2009; For Radiohead Fans, Does "Free" + "Download" = "Freeload"?, ComScore Press Release, November 5, 2007, ComScore website, **http://www .comscore.com/press/release.asp?press=1883**, accessed March 15, 2009.

9 How Costco Became the Anti Walmart by Steven Greenhouse, July 17, 2005, *New York Times* website, **http://www .nytimes.com/2005/07/17/business/yourmoney/17costco .html?adxnnl=1&pagewanted=1&adxnnlx=1122004143 -8Vfn2DFl1MJfernM1navLA**; Why Costco is so addictive by Matthew Boyle, October 25, 2006, CNNMoney website, **http://money.cnn.com/magazines/fortune/fortune _archive/2006/10/30/8391725/index.htm**, accessed March 14, 2009.

10 "Why the Price Is Rarely Right," by Peter Coy, January 10, 2010, *BusinessWeek* website, **http://www.businessweek .com/magazine/content/10_05/b4165077443953.htm** (accessed July 1, 2010).

Chapter Fourteen

1 Why bosses tend to be blowhards by Jeffrey Kluger, March 2, 2009, *Time*, page 48.

2 The Importance of Being Richard Branson, Leadership and Change, Knowledge@Wharton, January 12, 2005, **http:// knowledge.wharton.upenn.edu/article/1109.cfm**.

3 Hot Topic, Inc. Reports Fourth Quarter EPS Increases 19% to $0.32 Per Diluted Share; Provides Guidance for the 1st Quarter of 2009, March 11, 2009, News Blaze website, **http:// newsblaze.com/story/2009031112554500001.pz/topstory .html**, accessed March 25, 2009.

4 Motivate Your Staff by Larry Page, How to Succeed in 2005, Business 2.0 magazine, December 1, 2004, **http://money .cnn.com/magazines/business2/business2_archive/ 2004/12/01/8192529/index.htm**.

5 A New Game at the Office: Many Young Workers Accept Fewer Guarantees by Steve Lohr, *The New York Times*,

December 5, 2005, **http://select.nytimes.com/gst/abstract. html?res=F00F12FE38550C768CDDAB0994DD404482**.

6 "100 Best Companies to Work for 2010," *Fortune* website, **http://money.cnn.com/magazines/fortune/ bestcompanies/2010/index.html** (accessed July 2, 2010).

7 The 100 Best Companies to Work For 2006, *Fortune* magazine, January 23, 2006, pp. 71-74; Why the Economy Is a Lot Stronger Than You Think by Michael Mandel, *BusinessWeek* Online, February 13, 2006, **http://www.businessweek.com/ magazine/content/06_07/b3971001.htm**.

8 Don't Get Hammered by Management Fads by Darrell Rigby, *Wall Street Journal*, May 21, 2001.

9 Managing Generation Y—Part 1, Book Excerpt by Bruce Tulgan and Carolyn A. Martin, *BusinessWeek* Online, September 28, 2001, **http://www.businessweek.com/smallbiz/content/ sep2001/sb20010928_113.htm**; Managing Generation Y— Part 2, Book Excerpt by Bruce Tulgan and Carolyn A. Martin, *BusinessWeek* Online, October 4, 2001, **http://www .businessweek.com/smallbiz/content/oct2001/ sb2001105_229.htm**; Generation Y: They've Arrived at Work with a New Attitude by Stephanie Armour, *USA Today*, November 6, 2005, **http://www.usatoday.com/ money/workplace/2005-11-06-gen-y_x.htm**. The Facebook Generation vs. the Fortune 500 by Gary Hamel, March 24, 2009, The *Wall Street Journal* Blogs website, **http://blogs.wsj .com/management/2009/03/24/the-facebook-generation -vs-the-fortune-500/**, accessed March 30, 2009; What Gen Y Really Wants by Penelope Trunk, July 5, 2007, *Time* magazine website, **http://www.time.com/time/magazine/ article/0,9171,1640395,00.html**, accessed March 30, 2009; Managing Generation Y as they change the workforce by Molly Smith, January 8, 2008, Reuters website, **http://www .reuters.com/article/pressRelease/idUS129795+08-Jan -2008+BW20080108**, accessed March 30, 2009.

10 Founder of Patagonia became a businessman accidentally by Michelle Archer, October 30, 2005, *USA Today* Money, **http:// www.usatoday.com/money/books/reviews/2005-10-30 -patagonia_x.htm**; Patagonia: Blueprint for green business by Susan Casey, May 29, 2007, *Fortune* CNN Money website, **http://money.cnn.com/magazines/fortune/fortune _archive/2007/04/02/8403423/index.htm**, accessed March 30, 2009.

11 The CEO's new clothes by Yukio Shimizu, *Fast Company* website, September 2005, **http://www.fastcompany.com/ magazine/98/open_essay.html**, accessed September 4, 2008.

Pg. 220 Fact Box: Ten Years From Now… The Future of Work— The Poll, August 20, 2007, *BusinessWeek* website, **http:// www.businessweek.com/magazine/content/07_34/ b4047401.htm,** accessed March 30, 2009.

Chapter Fifteen

1 "Gary Kelly Southwest Airlines CEO on the Business of Building Trust," by Kate McCann, October 11, 2005, McCombs School of Business website, **http://www.mccombs.utexas .edu/news/pressreleases/lyceum05_kelly_wrap05.asp** (accessed July 2, 2010); "Southwest Airlines Reports Fourth Quarter Profit and 37th Consecutive Year of Profitability," January 21, 2010, PRNewsWire website, **http://www .prnewswire.com/news-releases/southwest-airlines -reports-fourth-quarter-profit-and-37th-consecutive-year -of-profitability-82241197.html** (accessed July 2, 2010).

2 A New Game at the Office: Many Young Workers Accept Fewer Guarantees by Steve Lohr, *New York Times*, December 5, 2005, **http://select.nytimes.com/gst/abstract.html?res=F 00F12FE38550C768CDDAB0994DD404482**.

3 "CEO pay vs. performance – Still a roll of the dice," (WSJ) by Dionysus on April 1, 2010, posted on Economatrix website, **http://www.economatix.com/ceo-pay-vs-performance -still-a-roll-of-the-dice-wsj** (accessed July 1, 2010); Figure 3AE

from MIshel, Lawrence, Jared Bernstein, and Heidi Shierholz, *The State of Working America 2009/2009. An Economic Policy Institute Book.* Ithaca, N.Y.: ILR Press, An Imprint of Cornell University Press, 2009 **http://www.stateofworkingamerica .org/tabfig/2008/03/SWA08_Chapter3_Wages_r2_Fig-3AE .jpg** (accessed July 1, 2010).

4 Facing Young Workers' High Job Expectations from Associated Press, *Los Angeles Times*, June 27, 2005; Tulgan, Bruce, *Not Everyone Gets a Trophy* (San Francisco: Jossey-Bass [Wiley Imprint], 2009).

5 How Corporate America Is Betraying Women by Betsy Morris, *Fortune*, January 10, 2005.

6 Featured Employee Rap Sheet, Hot Topic website, **http:// www.hottopic.com/community/rapsheets/emp_jodi .asp?LS=0&**, accessed April 11, 2006; A New Game at the Office: Many Young Workers Accept Fewer Guarantees by Steve Lohr, *New York Times*, December 5, 2005, **http://select .nytimes.com/gst/abstract.html?res=F00F12FE38550C768 CDDAB0994DD404482**; Work-life benefits fall victim to slow economy by Andrea Shim, April 4, 2009, *Los Angeles Times* website, **http://www.latimes.com/business/la-fi-flexible4 -2009apr04,0,4344887.story**, accessed April 4, 2009; Pending Job Flexibility Act Received Mixed Reviews by Sue Shellenbarger, *WSJ Career Journal*, **http://www. careerjournal.com/columnists/workfamily/20010426- workfamily.html**, accessed August 9, 2005. Work-life benefits fall victim to slow economy by Andrea Shim, April 4, 2009, *Los Angeles Times* website, **http://www.latimes.com/business/ la-fi-flexible4-2009apr04,0,4344887.story**, accessed April 4, 2009.

7 Work-life benefits fall victim to slow economy by Andrea Shim, April 4, 2009, *Los Angeles Times* website, **http://www .latimes.com/business/la-fi-flexible4-2009apr04,0,4344887 .story**, accessed April 4, 2009.

8 Why We Hate HR by Keith W. Hammonds, December 19, 2007, *Fast Company* website, **http://www.fastcompany .com/magazine/97/open_hr.html?page=0%2C1**, accessed April 4, 2009.

9 Table 1. The 30 fastest growing occupations covered in the 2008-2009 *Occupational Outlook Handbook*, Economic News Release, December 18, 2007, Bureau of Labor Statistics website, **http://www.bls.gov/news.release/ooh.t01.htm**, accessed April 7, 2009; Census Bureau Data Underscore Value of College Degree, U.S. Census Bureau News, October 26, 2006, Census Bureau website, **http://www.census.gov/ Press-Release/www/releases/archives/education/007660 .html**, accessed April 7, 2009.

10 SHRM Human Capital Benchmarking Study, 2008 Executive Summary, page 14, SHRM website, **http://www.shrm.org/ Research/Documents/2008%20Executive%20Summary _FINAL.pdf**, accessed April 7, 2009; Effective Recruiting Tied to Stronger Financial Performance, Watson Wyatt Worldwide news release, August 16, 2005, Watson Wyatt Worldwide website, **http://www.watsonwyatt.com/news/press .asp?ID=14959**, accessed April 7, 2009.

11 Top Five Resume Lies by Jeanne Sahadi, December 9, 2004, CNN Money website, **http://money.cnn.com/2004/11/22/pf/ resume_lies/**.

12 "You're Hired. At Least for Now," by Anne Kates Smith, March 2010, Kiplinger website, **http://www.kiplinger.com/ magazine/archives/employers-choose-temps-contract -workers.html** (accessed July 13, 2010).

13 Orientation: Not Just a Once-over-Lightly Anymore by Matt DeLuca HRO Today, April/May 2005, **http://www.hrotoday .com/Magazine.asp?artID=928**. New Emphasis on First Impressions by Leslie Gross Klaff, March 2008, Workforce Management website, **http://www.workforce.com/archive/ feature/25/41/58/index.php?ht=**, accessed April 7, 2009.

14 Show and Tell—Disney Institute's Four-Day Seminar on HR Management by Leon Rubis, *HR* magazine, April 1998; New Employee Experience Aims for Excitement Beyond the First

Day by Daryl Stephenson, Boeing Frontiers Online, May 2002, **http://www.boeing.com/news/frontiers/archive/2002/may/i_mams.html**.

15 Investigating the Executives by Penelope Patsuris, April 21, 2005, *Forbes* website, **http://www.forbes.com/smallbusiness/2005/04/21/cx_pp_0421ceosearch.html**.

16 Labor-Intensive by Sean McFadden, *Boston Business Journal*, November 19, 2004, **http://www.bizjournals.com/boston/stories/2004/11/22/smallb1.html**; The Costco Way; Higher Wages Mean Higher Profits. But Try Telling Wall Street by Stanley Holmes and Wendy Zelner, *BusinessWeek*, April 12, 2004; Study: Moderation in Hiring Practices Boosts Business Performance by Todd Raphael, Workforce Management, August 19, 2005, **http://www.workforce.com/section/00/article/24/14/03.html**.

17 Appreciating Benefits as Times Gets Tough by Carroll Lachnit, March 24, 2009, Blog: The Business of Management, Workforce Management website, **http://workforce.com/wpmu/bizmgmt/2009/03/24/benefits_in_tough_times/**, accessed April 9, 2009.

18 Perking Up: Some Companies Offer Surprising New Benefits by Sue Shellenbarger, March 18, 2009, *Wall Street Journal* website, **http://online.wsj.com/article/SB123733195850463165.html**, accessed April 9, 2009.

19 Questions and Answers about Flexible Work Schedules: A Sloan Work and Family Research Network Fact Sheet, updated September 2008, Sloan Work and Family Research Network website, **http://wfnetwork.bc.edu/pdfs/flexworksched.pdf**, accessed April 9, 2009; Work-life benefits fall victim to slow economy by Andrea Shim, April 4, 2009, *Los Angeles Times* website, **http://www.latimes.com/business/la-fi-flexible4-2009apr04,0,4344887.story**, accessed April 4, 2009.

20 Money for nothing by Dave Krasne, January 27, 2009, *New York Times* website, **http://www.nytimes.com/2009/01/27/opinion/27krasne.html?scp=3&sq=money%20for%20nothing&st=cse**, accessed April 11, 2009; Obama Orders Treasury Chief to Try to Block A.I.G. Bonuses by Helene Cooper, March 16, 2009, *New York Times* website, **http://www.nytimes.com/2009/03/17/us/politics/17obama.html**, accessed April 11, 2009; N.J. CEO Gives $1K "Stimulus Package" to Employees, April 2, 2009, NBC New York News website, **http://www.nbcnewyork.com/news/local/NJ-CEO-Gives-1K-Stimulus-Package--to-Employees.html**, accessed April 11, 2009.

21 Give telecommuting the green light by Ted Samson, June 7, 2007, InfoWorld website, **http://www.infoworld.com/d/green-it/give-telecommuting-green-light-628**, accessed April 10, 2009; Home Sweet Office: Telecommute Good for Business, Employees, and Planet by Brendan I. Koerner, September 22, 2008, *Wired* website, **http://www.wired.com/culture/culturereviews/magazine/16-10/st_essay**, accessed April 10, 2009.

22 Flexible Hours and Telecommuting—Not the Ticket to the Top of Corporate America, Five Questions for Susan DePhillips, Workforce Management, September 2005, **http://www.workforce.com/section/02/article/24/14/66.html**.

23 The New Job Sharers by Michelle V. Rafter, May 2008, Workforce Management website, **http://www.workforce.com/archive/feature/25/53/28/index.php**, accessed April 10, 2009; Study Attempts To Dispel Five Myths of Job Sharing by Stephen Miller, May 9, 2007, Society for Human Resource Management website, **http://moss07.shrm.org/Publications/HRNews/Pages/XMS_021497.aspx**, accessed April 10, 2009.

24 5.1 million jobs lost in this recession so far by Rex Nutting, April 3, 2009, MarketWatch website, **http://www.marketwatch.com/news/story/51-million-jobs-lost-recession/story.aspx?guid={CF54164C-6F7B-4501-B6FB-D7D1C8D710B9}&dist=msr_8**, accessed April 10, 2009; Boost Employee Morale After Layoffs, Workforce Management website, **http://www.workforce.com/archive/article/22/14/10.php**, accessed April 10, 2009.

25 Home Sweet Office: Telecommute Good for Business, Employees, and Planet by Brendan I. Koerner, September 22, 2008, *Wired* website, **http://www.wired.com/culture/culturereviews/magazine/16-10/st_essay**, accessed April 11, 2009; Give telecommuting the green light by Ted Samson, June 2, 2007, InfoWorld website, **http://www.infoworld.com/d/green-it/give-telecommuting-green-light-628**, accessed April 11, 2009; Sun, employees find big savings from Open Work telecommuting program by Ted Samson, June 19, 2008, InfoWorld website, **http://www.infoworld.com/d/green-it/sun-employees-find-big-savings-open-work-telecommuting-program-821**, accessed April 11, 2009. "National Study Finds Electronics Significantly Reduce Energy," Press Release, September 19, 2007, Telecommute Connecticut! website, **http://www.telecommutect.com/employers/pr_9_27_07.php** (accessed July 2, 2010).

26 Employee wellness programs prod workers to adopt healthy lifestyles, Larry Hand, Winter 2009, Harvard Public Health Review, Harvard School of Public Health website, **http://www.hsph.harvard.edu/news/hphr/winter-2009/winter09healthincentives.html**, accessed April 11, 2009; Lose weight or else! By Mina Kimes, July 3, 2008, CNNMoney website, **http://money.cnn.com/2008/06/30/smallbusiness/lose_weight.fsb/index.htm**, accessed April 11, 2009; Companies Win Savings As Workers Lose Pounds by Simona Covel, July 17, 2008, *Wall Street Journal* Small Business on the Smart Money Small Business website, **http://www.smsmallbiz.com/benefits/Companies_Win_Savings_As_Workers_Lose_Pounds.html**, accessed April 11, 2009; Drop that Weight or You're Fired! By Jennifer Barrett, April 14, 2008, *Newsweek* magazine, page 18. "Benefits of Corporate Wellness Programs," Infinite Health Coach website, **http://www.infinitehealthcoach.com/benefits-of-corporate-wellness-programs.html** (accessed July 2, 2010).

27 Flexible Hours and Telecommuting—Not the Ticket to the Top of Corporate America, Five Questions for Susan DePhillips, Workforce Management, September 2005, **http://www.workforce.com/section/02/article/24/14/66.html**.

28 Sexual Harassment Charges, EEOC & FEPAs Combined: FY 1997–FY 2008, EEOC website, updated March 11, 2009, **http://www.eeoc.gov/stats/harass.html**, accessed April 10, 2009.

29 Sexual Harassment, updated March 11, 2009, **http://www.eeoc.gov/types/sexual_harassment.html**, accessed April 10, 2009.

Pg. 234 Fact Box: Perking Up: Some Companies Offer Surprising New Benefits by Sue Shellenbarger, March 18, 2009, *Wall Street Journal* website, **http://online.wsj.com/article/SB123733195850463165.html**, accessed April 10, 2009.

Chapter Sixteen

1 Home Broadband Adoption 2009 by John B. Horrigan, Pew Internet and American Life Project: **http://www.pewinternet.org/Reports/2009/10-Home-Broadband-Adoption-2009.aspx**, accessed June 14, 2010.

2 About Internet2, Internet2 website: **http://www.Internet2.edu/resources/AboutInternet2.pdf**, accessed May 12, 2009.

3 Electronomics: Why We Need Smart Grid Technology and Infrastructure Today by Jesse Berst, Xconomy website February 12, 2009: **http://www.xconomy.com/seattle/2009/02/12/electronomics-why-we-need-smart-grid-technology-and-infrastructure-today/**; The Smart Grid: an Introduction, U.S. Department of Energy website: **http://www.oe.energy.gov/DocumentsandMedia/DOE_SG_Book_Single_Pages(1).pdf**, accessed May 7, 2009; Smart Grid Will Only Be as Good as the Security Behind It by William Jackson, Government Computer News website March 24, 2009: **http://**

www.gcn.com/Articles/2009/03/24/Smart-grid-security.aspx.

4 Special Report: Let it Rise, *Economist* website: http://www.economist.com/specialreports/displayStory.cfm?STORY_ID=12411882, October 23, 2008; Down to Business: Customers Fire a Few Shots at Cloud Computing by Rob Preston, Information Week website: http://www.informationweek.com/news/services/data/showArticle.jhtml?articleID=208403766; What Cloud Computing Really Means by Eric Knorr and Galen Gruman, InfoWorld.com: http://www.infoworld.com/d/cloud-computing/what-cloud-computing-really-means-031.

5 What Is Google App Engine? Google Code website: http://code.google.com/appengine/docs/whatisgoogleappengine.html accessed May 22, 2009; Google App Engine Lets Your Web App Grow Up by Brady Forrest, O'Reilly Radar website: http://radar.oreilly.com/2009/02/google-app-engine-lets-your-we.html; 7 Things You Should Know About Google Apps, Educause.edu website: http://net.educause.edu/ir/library/pdf/ELI7035.pdf, accessed May 22, 2009.

6 What Is AWS? Amazon Web Services website: http://aws.amazon.com/what-is-aws/ accessed, May 14, 2009; Cloud Computing. Available at Amazon.com Today by Spencer Reiss, *Wired* Magazine website April 21, 2008: http://www.wired.com/techbiz/it/magazine/16-05/mf_amazon.

7 Self-service, Prorated Super Computing Fun by Derek Gottfrid, The *New York Times*, November 1, 2007: http://open.blogs.nytimes.com/2007/11/01/self-service-prorated-super-computing-fun/; NY Times AWS Cloud Computing Mistake Costs $240, Green Data Center Blog, Noevember 5, 2008: http://www.greenm3.com/2008/11/nytimes-cloud-c.html; Early Experiments in Cloud Computing by Galen Gruman, InfoWorld website April 7, 2008: http://www.infoworld.com/d/virtualization/early-experiments-in-cloud-computing-020.

8 Carr, Nicholas, *The Big Switch: Rewiring the World from Edison to Google* (W. W. Norton & Company, 2008) Kindle edition, location 1124.

9 Data Mining Ready for a Comeback by Curt Monash, *ComputerWorld*, September 11, 2006, http://www.computerworld.com/action/article.do?command=viewArticleBasic&articleId=112733&pageNumber=2; A New Market Research Approach in Sport-Data Mining by Chen-Yueh Chen & Yi-Hsiu Lin, *The Sport Journal* website: http://www.thesportjournal.org/article/new-market-research-approach-sport-data-mining, Volume 12, Number 2, 2009; National Basketball Association, The Data Warehouse Institute website: http://www.tdwi.org/research/display.aspx?ID=5419 accessed May 24, 2009.

10 Effy Oz, *Management Information Systems*, 5th ed. (*Course Technology*, Cengage Learning, 2006), pages 332–338; "Expert Systems," AlanTuring.Net, http://www.cs.usfca.edu/www.AlanTuring.net/turing_archive/pages/Reference%20Articles/what_is_AI/What%20is%20AI07.html.

11 David M. Kroenke, *Experiencing MIS* (Pearson Prentice Hall, 2008), pages 340—341; What Are Expert Systems? Thinkquest.org website: http://library.thinkquest.org/11534/expert.htm accessed May 24, 2009.

12 Web 2.0 Definition Updated and Enterprise 2.0 Emerges, by Dion Hinchcliffe, ZDnet website: http://blogs.zdnet.com/Hinchcliffe/?p=71; The Ethics of Web 2.0: YouTube vs. Flickr, Revver, Eyespot, Bliptv, and Even Google, Lessig.org website: http://www.lessig.org/blog/2006/10/the_ethics_of_web_20_youtube_v.html, accessed May 24, 2009, Twitter, Blogs and Other Web 2.0 Tools Revolutionize Government Business by Doug Beizer, *Federal Computer Week* website March 6, 2009: http://www.fcw.com/Articles/2009/03/09/Web-2.0-in-action.aspx.

13 "IAB Internet Advertising Revenue Report: 2009 Full Year Results," by PricewaterhouseCoopers, IAB website: http://www.iab.net/media/file/IAB-Ad-Revenue-Full-Year-2009

.pdf; "A Milestone for Internet Ad Revenue," by Teddy Wayne, *New York Times* website, April 25, 2010: http://www.nytimes.com/2010/04/26/business/media/26drill.html.

14 Facebook Page Leaderboard, AllFacebook website: http://www.allfacebook.com/statistics/pages/leaderboard/, accessed April 25, 2009; How Do You Treat a Fan Who Owns Your Facebook Page? By Justin Smith http://www.insidefacebook.com/2009/03/18/how-do-you-treat-a-fan-who-owns-your-facebook-page/; Coke Fans' Facebook Page Draws Millions of Users by Joe Guy Collier, *Atlanta Journal-Constitution* March 30, 2009: http://www.ajc.com/business/content/business/coke/stories/2009/03/30/coke_facebook_page.html.

15 Paypal website: https://www.paypal-media.com/aboutus.cfm, accessed June 12, 2010.

16 Will it Blend website: http://www.willitblend.com/, accessed May 10, 2009; Viral Videos: How Sawdust and $50 Created Marketing Success for Blendtec.com by Scott Goodyear, Market Position website July 19, 2007: http://www.marketposition.com/blog/archives/2007/07/viral_videos_ho.html, accessed May 10, 2009; Marketing Videos Become a Hit in Their Own Right by Laura Lorber, *The Wall Street Journal* website, July 2, 2007: http://online.wsj.com/public/article/SB118330775119654449.html.html?mod=sblink_feature_articles; Blendtec: The Power of Viral Marketing, Bhatnatually website, June 6, 2008: http://www.lbhat.com/brands/blendtec-the-power-of-viral-marketing/.

17 Spammers Target Email Newsletters by David Utter, January 19, 2007, WebProWorld Security Forum, http://www.securitypronews.com/insiderreports/insider/spn-49-20070119SpammersTargetEmailNewsletters.html; Spammers Turn to Images to Fool Filters by Anick Jesdanun, *USA Today*, June 28, 2006, http://www.usatoday.com/tech/news/computersecurity/wormsviruses/2006-06-28-spam-images_x.htm.

18 Pharming: Is Your Trusted website a Clever Fake? Microsoft website January 3, 2007: http://www.microsoft.com/protect/yourself/phishing/pharming.mspx; Online Fraud: Pharming, Symantic website: http://www.symantec.com/norton/cybercrime/pharming.jsp, accessed May 24, 2009, Advisory: Watch Out for Drive-By-Pharming Attacks, Pharming.org website: http://www.pharming.org/index.jsp, accessed May 24, 2009.

19 Advertising Sent to Cell Phones Opens New Front in War on Spam by Kim Hart, Washingtonpost.com website, March 10, 2008, http://www.washingtonpost.com/wp-dyn/content/article/2008/03/09/AR2008030902213.html; The Ten Biggest Security Threats You Don't Know About by Andrew Brandt, *PC World* website, June 22, 2006, http://www.pcworld.com/article/id,126083-page,8/article.html, accessed September 11, 2008; "Smishing" Emerges as New Threat to Cell Phone Users by Mark Huffman, Consumer Affairs.com website: http://www.consumeraffairs.com/news04/2006/11/smishing.html accessed May 22, 2009; "SMiShing" Fishes for Personal Data Over Cell Phone by Eleanor Mills, CNet News website, February 24, 2009: http://news.cnet.com/8301-1009_3-10171241-83.html.

20 The Different Shades of Hackers, WindowSecurity.com, http://www.windowsecurity.com/articles/Different-Shades-Hackers.html; Preparing for Cyberterrorists, *Christian Science Monitor*, February 3, 2004, http://www.csmonitor.com/2004/0203/p08s01-comv.html; Cyberterrorism: How Real Is the Threat? by Gabriel Weimann, The United States Institute of Peace, December 2004, http://www.usip.org/pubs/specialreports/sr119.html; White Hat, Gray Hat, Black Hat by Michael Arnone, October 3, 2005, FCW.com, http://www.fcw.com/article90994-10-03-05-Print.

21 Email Addles the Mind by Benjamin Pimentel, May 4, 2005, SFGate.com, http://sfgate.com/cgi-bin/article.cgi?file=/c/a/2005/05/04/BUGOSCJGA41.DTL&type=printable; The Modern Brain, Besieged by Robert MacMillan, April 25, 2005,

washingtonpost.com, **http://www.washingtonpost.com/ wp-dyn/content/article/2005/04/25/AR2005042500342_pf.html.**; About the Information Overload Research Group, Information Research Overload Group website: **http://iorgforum.org/ AboutIORG.htm** accessed May 24, 2009.

22 Strong Passwords: How to Create and Use Them, Microsoft website: **http://www.microsoft.com/protect/yourself/ password/create.mspx**, accessed May 24, 2009; The Strong Password Dilemma by Richard E. Smith, PhD.: **http://www .cryptosmith.com/sanity/pwdilemma.html**, accessed May 24, 2009.

23 Email Privacy Gets a Win in Court by Reynolds Holding, June 21, 2007, *Time Magazine* website, **http://www.time.com/ time/nation/article/0,8599,1636024,00.html**; Federal Court: Stored Emails Are Protected by Martin Kaste, June 19, 2007, NPR.org, **http://www.npr.org/templates/story/story .php?storyId=11181164.** "Warshak: 6th Circuit Blinks," by Susan Brenner, CYB3RCRIM3 website: **http://cyb3rcrim3 .blogspot.com/2008/07/warshak-6th-circuit-blinks.html.**

24 Passport RFIDs Cloned Wholesale by $250 eBay Shopping Spree by Dan Goodin, *The Register* website February 2, 2009: **http://www.theregister.co.uk/2009/02/02/low_cost_rfid _cloner/**; Life With Big Brother: Radio Chips Coming Soon to Your Driver's License? By Bob Unruh, World Net Daily website February 28, 2009: **http://www.worldnetdaily.com/index .php?fa=PAGE.view&pageId=90008**; RFID Driver's Licenses Debated by Mark Baard, *Wired* website October 6, 2004: **http://www.wired.com/politics/security/ news/2004/10/65243.**

25 Anti-Napster Ruling Draws Mixed Reaction by Sam Costello, PCWorld.com. **http://www.pcworld.com/article/id,41327 -page,1/article.html**; 23 New Schools to Receive Latest Round of RIAA Pre-Lawsuit Letters, RIAA Pressroom, July 18, 2007, **http://www.riaa.com/newsitem.php?news _year_filter=&resultpage=&id=780E8751-0E03-4258-D651 -F991B66E1708.**

26 2008 Piracy Study, Business Software Alliance website: **http:// global.bsa.org/globalpiracy2008/studies/globalpiracy2008 .pdf.**

27 Nintendo Wants Action on Piracy by Emma Boyes, GameSpot website, February 15, 2008, **http://www.gamespot.com/ news/6186098.html**, accessed September 11, 2008; Nintendo Raid Hong Kong Pirates by Anthony Dickens, Nintendo Life website, October 24, 2007, **http://www.nintendolife.com/ articles/2007/10/24/nintendo_raid_hong_kong_pirates**, accessed September 11, 2008.

28 "Feds Crack Hackers' Stock Manipulation Cybercrime," by Larry Barrett, eSecurity Planet website: **http://www .esecurityplanet.com/news/article.php/3871176/Feds -Crack-Hackers-Stock-Manipulation-Cybercrime.htm**; "Hack, Pump and Dump," by Abhay Rao, *The Financial Express* website: **http://www.financialexpress.com/news/hack -pump-and-dump/369556/**; "SEC: Hacker Manipulated Stock Prices," by David Kravets, *Wired* website: **http://www .wired.com/threatlevel/2010/03/manipulated-stock-prices/**; "Ukranian Hacker Liable in SEC Insider Trading Case," by Dan Margolies, Reuters website: **http://www.reuters.com/ article/idUSTRE62S5DH20100329.**

Pg. 238 Fact Box: Internet2 Speed Record Team Launches Startup, Socaltech.com website: **http://www.socaltech.com/ Internet2_speed_record_team_launches_startup/s-0004916 .html**, accessed April 25, 2009.

Pg. 246 Fact Box: Shuffle Master Bets on RFID Poker Chips, Technovelgy.com website: **http://www.technovelgy.com/ct/ Science-Fiction-News.asp?NewsNum=304**, accessed May 21, 2009.

Chapter Seventeen

1 "Supply Chain News: BMW Uses Creative Thinking – and Employee Input – to Reduce Productivity Impact of Aging Workforce in Manufacturing," *Supply Chain Digest* website: **http://www.scdigest.com/ASSETS/ ON_TARGET/10-03-17-3.php?cid=3294**; "How BMW Is Planning for an Aging Workforce," by David Champion, *Harvard Business Review* website: **http://blogs.hbr.org/ hbr/hbreditors/2009/03/bmw_and_the_older_worker .html**; "How Could an Ageing Workforce Affect Supply Chain Management?" by Andrew Parker, EzineArticles.com website: **http://ezinearticles.com/?How-Could-an-Ageing- Workforce-Affect-Supply-Chain-Management?&id=4271775.**

2 Top Economists Square Off in Debate Over Outsourcing, CareerJournal.com website, **http://www.careerjournal. com/hrcenter/articles/20040520-aeppel.html**; Outsourcing Creates Jobs, Study Says, March 30, 2004, CNNMoney. com website, **http://money.cnn.com/2004/03/30/news/ economy/outsourcing/.**

3 Servicescapes: The Impact of Physical Surroundings on Customers and Employees by M. J. Bitner, *Journal of Marketing*, April 1992, pp. 57–71.

4 David A Collier and James R. Evans, *Operations Management, 2nd ed.* (Mason, OH: South-Western, Cengage Learning, 2007), p. 47.

5 Robot Reinvents Bypass Surgery by Steve Sternberg, *USA Today* website, April 29, 2008, **http://www.usatoday.com/ news/health/2008-04-29-robot-surgery_N.htm**, accessed September 11, 2008; Meet Mr. Rounder by Arlene Weintraub, *BusinessWeek* website, March 25,2005,**http://www .businessweek.com/magazine/content/05_13/b3926011 _mz001.htm**, accessed September 11, 2008; Report: For Heart Surgery Robot Beats Doctor by Sharon Gaudin, *Computer World* website, April 28, 2008, **http://www.computerworld .com/action/article.do?command=viewArticleBasic&tax onomyName=development&articleId=9081302&taxonom yId=11&intsrc=kc_top**, accessed September 11, 2008; Dr. Robot. Paging Dr. Robot by Anna Marie Kukek, *Daily Herald* website, April 10, 2008, **http://www.dailyherald.com/ story/?id=169962**, accessed September 11, 2008; Will Intuitive Surgical's Appearance on Grey's Anatomy Boost Sales? by Mike Huckman, SeekingAlpha website, May 17, 2009: **http:// seekingalpha.com/article/138034-will-intuitive-surgical-s -appearance-on-grey-s-anatomy-boost-sales**; About Intuitive, Intuitive Systems website: **http://www.intuitivesurgical .com/corporate/companyprofile/index.aspx**, accessed June 9, 2010. Intuitive Surgical website: **http://www .intuitivesurgical.com/products/faq/index.aspx#19**, accessed June 9, 2010.

6 Online Marketplaces Are Back in Play by Nick Zubko, *Industry Week*, April, 2008, pp. 34-36; e-Marketplaces 2.0 by Andrew K. Reese, *Supply & Demand Chain Executive Magazine* website: **http://www.sdcexec.com/publication/article .jsp?pubId=1&id=8885&pageNum=1**; Corporate Profile, MFG .com website: **http://www.mfg.com/en/about-mfg/mfg -corporate-profile.jsp**, accessed June 12, 2009.

7 Outsourcing: Ripoff Nation, BW Smallbiz Front Line, Winter 2006, *BusinessWeek* website: **http://www.businessweek .com/magazine/content/06_52/b4015435.htm?chan=rss _topStories_ssi_5**; Outsourcing in China: Five Basic Rules for Reducing Risk by Steve Dickinson, ezinearticles.com website, **http://ezinearticles.com/?Outsourcing-in-China:-Five -Basics-for-Reducing-Risk&id=17214.**

8 "Toyota Woes Follow Years of Slipping Quality," by Dan Carney, MSNBC website: **http://www.msnbc.msn.com/ id/35311172/ns/business-autos/**; "Can Toyota Recover Its Reputation for Quality?" by Wendy Kaufman, NPR website: **http://www.npr.org/templates/story/story .php?storyId=123519027**; "No Big Quality Problems at Toyota?" by Robert E. Cole, *Harvard Business Review* website: **http://blogs.hbr.org/cs/2010/03/no_big_quality_problems _at_toy.html.**

9 Cost of ERP—What Does ERP Really Cost? Systopia website, **http://www.sysoptima.com/erp/cost_of_erp.php**; Causes of

ERP Failures, BusinessKnowledgeSource.com website: **http://
businessknowledgesource.com/technology/causes_of_erp
_failures_006086.html**.

10 ERP and Cloud Computing: Delivering a Virtual Feast by David
Stodder, Intelligent Enterprise website: **http://intelligent
-enterprise.informationweek.com/channels/enterprise
_applications/showArticle.jhtml;jsessionid=OXN1PKNF
FTBJZQE1GHOSKH4ATMY32JVN?articleID=224701329**,
accessed June 9, 2010

11 Poka Yoke Mistake Proofing by Kerri Simon, iSixSigma website,
http://www.isixsigma.com/library/content/c020128a.asp;
Make No Mistake by Mark Hendricks, *Entrepreneur* Magazine,
October 1996, **http://www.entrepreneur.com/magazine/
entrepreneur/1996/october/13430.html**, accessed July
30,2007.

12 Why Apply? Baldrige National Quality Program website,
http://www.quality.nist.gov/Why_Apply.htm; Answers to
Frequently Asked Questions for the Baldrige National Quality
Program, National Institute of Standards and Technology,
**http://www.nist.gov/public_affairs/factsheet/baldfaqs
.htm**, accessed June 19, 2009.

13 Six Sigma Training by Charles Waxer, iSixSigma website,
http://www.isixsigma.com/library/content/c010225a

.asp**, accessed September 11, 2008; What is Six Sigma?,
GE website, **http://www.ge.com/sixsigma/SixSigma
.pdf**, accessed September 11, 2008; Six Sigma Black
Belt Certification, ASQ website, **http://www.asq.org/
certification/index.html**, accessed September 11, 2008.

14 Sanford "Pens" an Improved Blister-Pack Tale by Lauren R.
Hartman, *Packaging Digest*, January 2007, page 43.

15 Industry Warms to Sustainability by David Prizinsky *Crain's
Cleveland Business*, May 26, 2008, p16; It's Waste Not, Want
Not at Super Green Subaru Plant by Chris Woodyard, *USA
Today*, February 19, 2008, Section B, page 1; The Many Shades
of Green by Alan S. Brown, *Mechanical Engineering*, January
2009, pp. 22-29.].

16 The Toyota Group and the Aisin Fire by Toshihiro Nishiguchi
and Alexandre Beaudet, *Sloan Management Review*, Fall 1998,
pp. 49-59.

17 David A Collier and James R. Evans, *Operations Management*,
2nd ed. (Mason, OH: South-Western, Cengage Learning, 2007),
pages 751–753.

Pg. 254 Fact Box: *Occupational Outlook Handbook*, 2010-2011
Edition, BLS website: **http://www.bls.gov/oco/oco2003
.htm#industry**.

401(k), 403(b), and 457 plans
Employee contribution retirement plans that offer tax benefits. The plans are named for the section of the IRS tax code where they are described.

absolute advantage
The benefit a country has in a given industry when it can produce more of a product than other nations using the same amount of resources.

accounting
A system for recognizing, organizing, analyzing, and reporting information about the financial transactions that affect an organization.

accounting equation
Assets = Liabilities + Owners' Equity

accredited investors
An organization or individual investor who meets certain criteria established by the SEC and so qualifies to invest in unregistered securities.

accrual-basis accounting
The method of accounting that recognizes revenue when it is earned and matches expenses to the revenues they helped produce.

acquisition
A corporate restructuring in which one firm buys another.

active listening
Attentive listening that occurs when the listener focuses his or her complete attention on the speaker.

active voice
Sentence construction in which the subject performs the action expressed by the verb (e.g., *My sister wrote the paper*). Active voice works better for the vast majority of business communication.

activity-based costing (ABC)
A technique to assign product costs based on links between activities that drive costs and the production of specific products.

administrative law
Laws that arise from regulations established by government agencies.

advergaming
A relatively new promotional channel that involves integrating branded products and advertising into interactive games.

advertising
Paid, nonpersonal communication, designed to influence a target audience with regard to a product, service, organization, or idea.

affirmative action
Policies meant to increase employment and educational opportunities for minority groups—especially groups defined by race, ethnicity, or gender.

agent
A party who agrees to represent another party, called the principal.

agents/brokers
Independent distributors who do not take title of the goods they distribute (even though they may take physical possession on a temporary basis before distribution).

angel investors
Individuals who invest in start-up companies with high growth potential in exchange for a share of ownership.

annual percentage rate (APR)
The interest expense charged on a credit card expressed as an annual percentage.

applications software
Software that helps a user perform a desired task.

apprenticeships
Structured training programs that mandate that each beginner serve as an assistant to a fully trained worker before gaining full credentials to work in the field.

arbitration
A process in which a neutral third party has the authority to resolve a dispute by rendering a binding decision.

articles of incorporation
The document filed with a state government to establish the existence of a new corporation.

asset management ratios
Financial ratios that measure how effectively a firm is using its assets to generate revenues or cash.

assets
Resources owned by a firm.

autocratic leaders
Leaders who hoard decision-making power for themselves and typically issue orders without consulting their followers.

automation
Replacing human operation and control of machinery and equipment with some form of programmed control.

balance of payments
A measure of the total flow of money into or out of a country.

balance of payments deficit
Shortfall that occurs when more money flows out of a nation than into that nation.

balance of payments surplus
Overage that occurs when more money flows into a nation than out of that nation.

balance of trade
A basic measure of the difference in value between a nation's exports and imports, including both goods and services.

balance sheet
A financial statement that reports the financial position of a firm by identifying and reporting the value of the firm's assets, liabilities, and owners' equity.

Baldrige National Quality Program
A national program to encourage American firms to focus on quality improvement.

behavioral segmentation
Dividing the market based on how people behave toward various products. This category includes both the benefits that consumers seek from products and how consumers use the product.

benefits
Noncash compensation, including programs, such as health insurance, vacation, and childcare.

bias
A preconception about members of a particular group. Common forms of bias include gender bias, age bias, and race, ethnicity, or nationality bias.

board of directors
The individuals who are elected by stock-holders of a corporation to represent their interests.

bond
A long-term debt instrument issued by a corporation or government entity.

boycott
A tactic in which a union and its supporters and sympathizers refuse to do business with an employer with which they have a labor dispute.

brand
A product's identity—including product name, symbol, design, reputation, and image—that sets it apart from other players in the same category.

brand equity
The overall value of a brand to an organization.

brand extension
A new product, in a new category, introduced under an existing brand name.

breach of contract
The failure of one party to a contract to perform his or her contractual obligations.

breakeven analysis
The process of determining the number of units a firm must sell to cover all costs.

budget (personal)
A detailed schedule that documents your expected financial inflows (revenues earned and received) and outflows (expenses incurred and paid) in order to determine your net inflow or outflow for a given period of time.

budget deficit
Shortfall that occurs when expenses are higher than revenue over a given period of time.

budget surplus
Overage that occurs when revenue is higher than expenses over a given period of time.

budgeted balance sheet
A projected financial statement that fore-casts the types and amounts of assets a firm will need to implement its future plans and how the firm will finance those assets. (Also called a *pro forma* balance sheet.)

budgeted income statement
A projection showing how a firm's budgeted sales and costs will affect expected net income. (Also called a *pro forma* income statement.)

budgeting
A management tool that explicitly shows how firms will acquire and use the resources needed to achieve its goals over a specific time period.

business
Any activity that provides goods and services in an effort to earn a profit.

business buyer behavior
Describes how people act when they are buying products to use either directly or indirectly to produce other products.

business cycle
The periodic contraction and expansion that occur over time in virtually every economy.

business environment
The setting in which business operates. The five key components are: economic environment, competitive environment, technological environment, social environment, and global environment.

business ethics
The application of right and wrong, good and bad in a business setting.

business format franchise
A broad franchise agreement in which the franchisee pays for the right to use the name, trademark, and business and production methods of the franchisor.

business intelligence system
A sophisticated form of decision support system that helps decision makers discover information that was previously hidden.

business marketers (also known as business-to-business or B2B)
Marketers who direct their efforts toward people who are buying products to use either directly or indirectly to produce other products.

business plan
A formal document that describes a business concept, outlines core business objectives, and details strategies and timelines for achieving those objectives.

business products
Products purchased to use either directly or indirectly in the production of other products.

business technology
Any tools—especially computers, telecommunications, and other digital products—that businesses can use to become more efficient and effective.

business-to-business (B2B) e-commerce
E-commerce in markets where businesses buy from and sell to other businesses.

business-to-consumer (B2C) e-commerce
E-commerce in which businesses and final consumers interact.

buzz marketing
The active stimulation of word of mouth via unconventional, and often relatively low-cost, tactics. Other terms for buzz marketing are "guerrilla marketing" and "viral marketing."

C corporation
The most common type of business corporation, where ownership offers limited liability to all of its owners, also called stockholders.

cafeteria-style benefits
An approach to employee benefits that gives all employees a set dollar amount that they must spend on company benefits, allocated however they wish within broad limitations.

callable bond
A bond that the issuer can redeem at a given price prior to its maturity.

cannibalization
When a producer offers a new product that takes sales away from its existing products.

capital budgeting
The process a firm uses to evaluate long-term investment proposals.

capital gain
The return on an asset that results when its market price rises above the price the investor paid for it.

capital structure
The mix of equity and debt financing a firm uses to meet its permanent financing needs.

capitalism
An economic system—also known as the private enterprise or free market system—based on private ownership, economic freedom, and fair competition.

carbon footprint
Refers to the amount of harmful greenhouse gases that a firm emits throughout its operations, both directly and indirectly.

case law (also called common law)
Laws that result from rulings, called precedents, made by judges who initially hear a particular type of case.

cash budget
A detailed forecast of future cash flows that helps financial managers identify when their firm is likely to experience temporary shortages or surpluses of cash.

cash equivalents
Safe and highly liquid assets that many firms list with their cash holdings on their balance sheet.

cause-related marketing
Marketing partnerships between businesses and nonprofit organizations, designed to spike sales for the company and raise money for the nonprofit.

channel intermediaries
Distribution organizations—informally called "middlemen"—that facilitate the movement of products from the producer to the consumer.

channel of distribution
The network of organizations and processes that links producers to consumers.

Chapter 7 bankruptcy
A form of bankruptcy that discharges a debtor's debts by liquidating assets and using the proceeds to pay off creditors.

Chapter 11 bankruptcy
A form of bankruptcy used by corporations and individuals that allows the debtor to reorganize operations under a court-approved plan.

Chapter 13 bankruptcy
A form of bankruptcy that allows individual debtors to set up a repayment plan to adjust their debts.

Civil Rights Act of 1964
Federal legislation that prohibits discrimination in hiring, firing, compensation, apprenticeships, training, terms, conditions, or privileges of employment based on race, color, religion, sex, or national origin.

closed shop
An employment arrangement in which the employer agrees to hire only workers who already belong to the union.

cloud computing
The use of Internet-based storage capacity, processing power, and computer applications to supplement or replace internally owned information technology resources.

cobranding
When established brands from different companies join forces to market the same product.

code of ethics
A formal, written document that defines the ethical standards of an organization and gives employees the information they need to make ethical decisions across a range of situations.

cognitive dissonance
Consumer discomfort with a purchase decision, typically for a higher-priced item.

collective bargaining
The process by which representatives of union members and employers attempt to negotiate a mutually acceptable labor agreement.

commercial paper
Short-term (and usually unsecured) promissory notes issued by large corporations.

common market
A group of countries that has eliminated tariffs and harmonized trading rules to facilitate the free flow of goods among the member nations.

common stock
The basic form of ownership in a corporation.

communication
The transmission of information between a sender and a recipient.

communication barriers
Obstacles to effective communication, typically defined in terms of physical, language, body language, cultural, perceptual, and organizational barriers.

communication channels
The various ways in which a message can be sent, ranging from one-on-one, in-person meetings to Internet message boards.

communism
An economic and political system that calls for public ownership of virtually all enterprises, under the direction of a strong central government.

company matching
An amount contributed by the employer to an employee's retirement account that matches the employee's retirement contributions either dollar for dollar or based on a percentage of each dollar contributed by the employee.

comparative advantage
The benefit a country has in a given industry if it can make products at a lower opportunity cost than other countries.

compensation
The combination of pay and benefits that employees receive in exchange for their work.

compensatory damages
Monetary payments that a party who breaches a contract is ordered to pay in order to compensate the injured party for the actual harm suffered by the breach of contract.

compressed workweek
A version of flextime scheduling that allows employees to work a full-time number of hours in less than the standard workweek.

computer-aided design (CAD)
Drawing and drafting software that enables users to create and edit blueprints and design drawings quickly and easily.

computer-aided design/computer-aided manufacturing (CAD/CAM)
A combination of software that can be used to design output and send instructions to automated equipment to perform the steps needed to produce this output.

computer-aided engineering (CAE)
Software that enables users to test, analyze, and optimize their designs.

computer-aided manufacturing (CAM)
Software that takes the electronic design for a product and creates the programmed instructions that robots must follow to produce that product as efficiently as possible.

computer-integrated manufacturing (CIM)
A combination of CAD/CAM software with flexible manufacturing systems to automate almost all steps involved in designing, testing, and producing a product.

computer virus
Computer software that can be spread from one computer to another without the knowledge or permission of the computer users.

conceptual skills
The ability to grasp a big-picture view of the overall organization, the relationship between its various parts, and its fit in the broader competitive environment.

conglomerate merger
A combination of two firms that are in unrelated industries.

consideration
Something of value that one party gives another as part of a contractual agreement.

constitution
A code that establishes the fundamental rules and principles that govern a particular organization or entity.

consumer behavior
Description of how people act when they are buying, using, and discarding goods and services for their own personal consumption. Consumer behavior also explores the reasons behind people's actions.

consumer marketers (also known as business-to-consumer or B2C)
Marketers who direct their efforts toward people who are buying products for personal consumption.

consumer price index (CPI)
A measure of inflation that evaluates the change in the weighted-average price of goods and services that the average consumer buys each month.

consumer products
Products purchased for personal use or consumption.

consumer promotion
Marketing activities designed to generate immediate consumer sales, using tools such as premiums, promotional products, samples, coupons, rebates, and displays.

consumerism
A social movement that focuses on four key consumer rights: (1) the right to be safe, (2) the right to be informed, (3) the right to choose, and (4) the right to be heard.

contingency planning
Planning for unexpected events, usually involving a range of scenarios and assumptions that differ from the assumptions behind the core plans.

contingent workers
Employees who do not expect regular, full-time jobs, including temporary full-time workers, independent contractors, and temporary agency or contract agency workers.

contract
An agreement that is legally enforceable.

contraction
A period of economic downturn, marked by rising unemployment and falling business production.

controlling
Checking performance and making adjustments as needed.

convertible bond
A bond that gives its holder the right to exchange it for a stated number of shares of common stock in some specified time period.

copyright
The exclusive legal right of an author, artist, or other creative individual to own, use, copy, and sell their own creations and to license others to do so.

corporate bylaws
The basic rules governing how a corporation is organized and how it conducts its business.

corporate philanthropy
All business donations to nonprofit groups, including money, products, and employee time.

corporate responsibility
Business contributions to the community through the actions of the business itself rather than donations of money and time.

corporation
A form of business ownership in which the business is considered a legal entity that is separate and distinct from its owners.

countertrade
International trade that involves the barter of products for products rather than for currency.

coupon rate
The interest paid on a bond expressed as a percentage of the bond's par value.

covenants
Conditions lenders place on firms that seek long-term debt financing.

craft union
A union comprised of workers who share the same skill or work in the same profession.

credit
Allows a borrower to acquire an asset or to obtain a loan and repay the balance at a later time.

credit card
A card issued by a bank or other finance company that allows the cardholder to make a purchase now and to pay the credit card company later.

credit history
A summary of a borrower's open and closed credit accounts and the manner in which those accounts have been paid.

crime
A wrongful act against society defined by law and prosecuted by the state.

critical path
The sequence of activities in a project that is expected to take the longest to complete.

critical path method (CPM)
A project management tool that illustrates the relationships among all the activities involved in completing a project and identifies the sequence of activities likely to take the longest to complete.

current yield
The amount of interest earned on a bond expressed as a percentage of the bond's current market price.

customer benefit
The advantage that a customer gains from specific product features.

customer loyalty
When customers buy a product from the same supplier again and again—sometimes paying even more for it than they would for a competitive product.

customer-relationship management (CRM)
The ongoing process of acquiring, maintaining, and growing profitable customer relationships by delivering unmatched value.

customer satisfaction
When customers perceive that a good or service delivers value above and beyond their expectations.

cybermediary
An Internet-based firm that specializes in the secure electronic transfer of funds.

data
Raw, unprocessed facts and figures.

data mining
The use of sophisticated statistical and mathematical techniques to analyze data and discover hidden patterns and relationships among data, thus creating valuable information.

data warehouse
A large, organization-wide database that stores data in a centralized location.

database
A file consisting of related data organized according to a logical system and stored on a hard drive or some other computer-accessible media.

debit card
A card issued by the bank that allows the customer to make purchases as if the transaction involved cash. In a debit card purchase, the customer's bank account is immediately reduced at the time the purchase is made.

decision support system (DSS)
A system that gives managers access to large amounts of data and the processing power to convert these data into high-quality information, thus improving the decision-making process.

deflation
A period of falling average prices across the economy.

degree of centralization
The extent to which decision-making power is held by a small number of people at the top of the organization.

demand
The quantity of products that consumers are willing to buy at different market prices.

demand curve
The graphed relationship between price and quantity from a customer demand standpoint.

democratic leaders
Leaders who share power with their followers. While they still make final decisions, they typically solicit and incorporate input from their followers.

demographic segmentation
Dividing the market into smaller groups based on measurable characteristics about people such as age, income, ethnicity, and gender.

demographics
The measurable characteristics of a population. Demographic factors include population size and density and specific traits such as age, gender, and race.

departmentalization
The division of workers into logical groups.

depression
An especially deep and long-lasting recession.

direct channel
A distribution process that links the producer and the customer with no intermediaries.

direct investment
(or foreign direct investment) When firms either acquire foreign firms or develop new facilities from the ground up in foreign countries.

discount rate
The rate of interest that the Federal Reserve charges when it loans funds to banks.

discretionary costs
Expenditures for which the spender has significant control in terms of the amount and timing.

disinflation
A period of slowing average price increases across the economy.

distribution strategy
A plan for delivering the right product to the right person at the right place at the right time.

distributive bargaining
The traditional adversarial approach to collective bargaining.

distributorship
A type of franchising arrangement in which the franchisor makes a product and licenses the franchisee to sell it.

diversification
A strategy of investing in a wide variety of securities in order to reduce risk.

divestiture
The transfer of total or partial ownership of some of a firm's assets to investors or to another company.

Dow Jones Industrial Average
An index that tracks stock prices of 30 large, well-known U.S. corporations.

dynamic delivery
Vibrant, compelling presentation delivery style that grabs and holds the attention of the audience.

e-commerce
The marketing, buying, selling, and servicing of products over a network (usually the Internet).

economic system
A structure for allocating limited resources.

economics
The study of the choices that people, companies, and governments make in allocating society's resources.

economy
A financial and social system of how resources flow through society, from production, to distribution, to consumption.

effectiveness
Using resources to create the greatest value.

efficiency
Producing output or achieving a goal at the lowest cost.

electronic bill presentment and payment
A method of bill payment that makes it easy for the customer to make a payment, often by simply clicking on a payment option contained in an email.

electronic communications network (ECN)
An automated, computerized securities trading system that automatically matches buyers and sellers, executing trades quickly and allowing trading when securities exchanges are closed.

e-marketplace
A specialized Internet site where buyers and sellers engaged in business-to-business e-commerce can communicate and conduct business.

embargo
A complete ban on international trade of a certain item, or a total halt in trade with a particular nation.

employment at will
A legal doctrine that views employment as an entirely voluntary relationship that both the employee and employer are free to terminate at any time and for any reason.

enterprise resource planning (ERP)
Software-based approach to integrate an organization's systems in order to improve the flow of information among all departments and operating units.

entrepreneurs
People who risk their time, money, and other resources to start and manage a business.

environmental scanning
The process of continually collecting information from the external marketing environment.

Equal Employment Opportunity Commission (EEOC)
A federal agency designed to regulate and enforce the provisions of Title VII.

equilibrium price
The price associated with the point at which the quantity demanded of a product equals the quantity supplied.

equity theory
A motivation theory that proposes that perceptions of fairness directly affect worker motivation.

ethical dilemma
A decision that involves a conflict of values; every potential course of action has some significant negative consequences.

ethics
A set of beliefs about right and wrong, good and bad.

European Union (EU)
The world's largest common market, composed of 27 European nations.

everyday-low-pricing (EDLP)
Long-term discount pricing, designed to achieve profitability through high sales volume.

exchange rates
A measurement of the value of one nation's currency relative to the currency of other nations.

exchange traded fund (ETF)
Shares traded on securities markets that represent the legal right of ownership over part of a basket of individual stock certificates or other securities.

expansion
A period of robust economic growth and high employment.

expectancy theory
A motivation theory that deals with the relationship among individual effort, individual performance, and individual reward.

expenses
Resources that are used up as the result of business operations.

expert system (ES)
A decision-support system that helps managers make better decisions in an area where they lack expertise.

exporting
Selling products in foreign nations that have been produced or grown domestically.

external locus of control
A deep-seated sense that forces other than the individual are responsible for what happens in his or her life.

external recruitment
The process of seeking new employees from outside the firm.

extranet
An intranet that allows limited access to a selected group of stakeholders, such as suppliers or customers.

factor
A company that provides short-term financing to firms by purchasing their accounts receivables at a discount.

factors of production
Four fundamental elements—natural resources, capital, human resources, and entrepreneurship—that businesses need to achieve their objectives.

federal debt
The sum of all the money that the Federal Government has borrowed over the years and not yet repaid.

Federal Deposit Insurance Corporation (FDIC)
An independent agency created by Congress to maintain stability and public confidence in the nation's financial system, primarily by insuring bank deposits.

financial accounting
The branch of accounting that prepares financial statements for use by owners, creditors, suppliers, and other external stakeholders.

Financial Accounting Standards Board (FASB)
The private board that establishes the generally accepted accounting principles used in the practice of financial accounting.

financial budgets
Budgets that focus on the firm's financial goals and identify the resources needed to achieve these goals.

financial leverage
The use of debt in a firm's capital structure.

financial ratio analysis
Computing ratios that compare values of key accounts listed on a firm's financial statements.

firewall
Software and/or hardware designed to prevent unwanted access to a computer or computer system.

first-line management
Managers who directly supervise nonmanagement employees.

fiscal policy
Government efforts to influence the economy through taxation and spending.

flextime
A scheduling option that allows workers to choose when they start and finish their workdays, as long as they complete the required number of hours.

foreign franchising
A specialized type of foreign licensing in which a firm expands by offering businesses in other countries the right to produce and market its products according to specific operating requirements.

foreign licensing
Authority granted by a domestic firm to a foreign firm for the rights to produce and market its product or to use its trademark/patent rights in a defined geographical area.

foreign outsourcing
(also contract manufacturing) Contracting with foreign suppliers to produce products, usually at a fraction of the cost of domestic production.

franchise
A licensing arrangement whereby a franchisor allows franchisees to use its name, trademark, products, business methods, and other property in exchange for monetary payments and other considerations.

franchise agreement
The contractual arrangement between a franchisor and a franchisee that spells out the duties and responsibilities of both parties.

Franchise Disclosure Document (FDD)
A detailed description of all aspects of a franchise that the franchisor must provide to the franchisee at least 14 calendar days before the franchise agreement is signed.

franchisee
The party in a franchise relationship that pays for the right to use resources supplied by the franchisor.

franchisor
The business entity in a franchise relationship that allows others to operate their business using resources it supplies in exchange for money and other considerations.

free-rein leaders
Leaders who set objectives for their followers but give them freedom to choose how they accomplish those goals.

free trade
The unrestricted movement of goods and services across international borders.

Gantt chart
A chart used to track the progress of activities involved in completing a project.

General Agreement on Tariffs and Trade (GATT)
An international trade treaty designed to encourage worldwide trade among its members.

general partnership
A partnership in which all partners can take an active role in managing the business and have unlimited liability for any claims against the firm.

generally accepted accounting principles (GAAP)
A set of accounting standards that is used in the preparation of financial statements.

geographic segmentation
Dividing the market into smaller groups based on where consumers live. This process can incorporate countries, cities, or population density as key factors.

goods
Tangible products.

government accountants
Accountants who work for a wide variety of government agencies at the local, state, and federal levels.

grace period
The period of time that the credit-card holder has to pay outstanding balances before interest or fees are assessed.

green marketing
The development and promotion of products with ecological benefits.

grievance
A complaint by a worker that the employer has violated the terms of the collective bargaining agreement.

gross domestic product (GDP)
The total value of all final goods and services produced within a nation's physical boundaries over a given period of time.

hacker
A skilled computer user who uses his or her expertise to gain unauthorized access to the computer (or computer system) of others, sometimes with malicious intent.

hardware
The physical tools and equipment used to collect, input, store, organize, and process data and to distribute information.

high/low pricing
A pricing strategy designed to drive traffic to retail stores by special sales on a limited number of products, and higher everyday prices on others.

horizontal analysis
Analysis of financial statements that compares account values reported on these statements over two or more years to identify changes and trends.

horizontal merger
A combination of two firms that are in the same industry.

human resource management
The management function focused on maximizing the effectiveness of the workforce by recruiting world-class talent, promoting career development, and determining workforce strategies to boost organizational effectiveness.

human skills
The ability to work effectively with and through other people in a range of different relationships.

hyperinflation
An average monthly inflation rate of more than 50%.

immediate predecessors
Activities in a project that must be completed before some other specified activity can begin.

importing
Buying products domestically that have been produced or grown in foreign nations.

income statement
The financial statement that reports the revenues, expenses, and net income that resulted from a firm's operations over an accounting period.

incremental analysis
An evaluation of the financial impact different alternatives would have in a particular decision-making situation.

incremental costs
Costs that change as the result of a decision.

independent wholesaling businesses
Independent distributors that buy products from a range of different businesses and sell those products to a range of different customers.

industrial union
A union comprised of workers employed in the same industry.

inflation
A period of rising average prices across the economy.

information
Data that have been processed in a way that makes them meaningful to their user.

infrastructure
A country's physical facilities that support economic activity.

initial public offering (IPO)
The first time a company issues stock that may be bought by the general public.

institutional investor
An organization that pools contributions from investors, clients, or depositors and uses these funds to buy stocks and other securities.

integrated marketing communication
The coordination of marketing messages through every promotional vehicle to communicate a unified impression about a product.

intellectual property
Property that is the result of creative or intellectual effort, such as books, musical works, inventions, and computer software.

intercultural communication
Communication among people with differing cultural backgrounds.

interest-based bargaining
A form of collective bargaining that emphasizes cooperation and problem solving in an attempt to find a "win–win" outcome that benefits both sides.

internal locus of control
A deep-seated sense that the individual is personally responsible for what happens in his or her life.

internal recruitment
The process of seeking employees who are currently within the firm to fill open positions.

International Monetary Fund (IMF)
An international organization of 186 member nations that promotes international economic cooperation and stable growth.

Internet
The world's largest computer network; essentially a network of computer networks all operating under a common set of rules that allow them to communicate with each other.

Internet2 (I2)
A new high-tech Internet restricted to dues-paying members of a consortium. I2 utilizes technologies that give it a speed and capacity far exceeding the current Internet.

intranet
A network that has the look and feel of the Internet, and is navigated using a Web browser, but is confined to documents and data located on a single company's servers and is available only to the firm's employees.

inventory
Stocks of finished items, work in process, parts, materials, or other resources held by an organization.

investment bank
A financial intermediary that specializes in helping firms raise financial capital in primary markets.

investments
Reducing consumption in the current time period in order to build future wealth.

IRA
An individual retirement account that provides tax benefits to individuals who are investing for their retirement.

ISO 9000
A set of generic standards for quality management systems established by the International Organization for Standardization.

job analysis
The examination of specific tasks that are assigned to each position, independent of who might be holding the job at any specific time.

job description
An explanation of the responsibilities for a specific position.

job enrichment
The creation of jobs with more meaningful content, under the assumption that challenging, creative work will motivate employees.

job specifications
The specific qualifications necessary to hold a particular position.

joint ventures
When two or more companies join forces—sharing resources, risks, and profits, but not actually merging companies—to pursue specific opportunities.

just-in-time (JIT) production
A production system that emphasizes the production of goods to meet actual current demand, thus minimizing the need to hold inventories of finished goods and work in process at each stage of the supply chain.

Labor–Management Relations Act (Taft–Hartley Act)
Act passed in 1947 that placed limits on union activities, outlawed the closed shop, and allowed states to pass right-to-work laws that made union shops illegal.

labor union
A group of workers who have organized to work together to achieve common job-related goals, such as higher wages, better working conditions, and greater job security.

laws
Rules that are enforced by the government that govern the conduct and actions of people within a society.

leading
Directing and motivating people to achieve organizational goals.

lean production
An approach to production that emphasizes the elimination of waste in all aspects of production processes.

leverage ratios
Ratios that measure the extent to which a firm relies on debt financing in its capital structure.

liabilities
Claims that outsiders have against a firm's assets.

licensing
Purchasing the right to use another company's brand name or symbol.

limit order
An order to a broker to buy a specific stock only if its price is below a certain level, or to sell a specific stock only if its price is above a certain level.

limited liability
When owners are not personally liable for claims against their firm. Limited liability owners may lose their investment in the company, but their personal assets are protected.

limited liability company (LLC)
A form of business ownership that offers both limited liability to its owners and flexible tax treatment.

limited liability partnership (LLP)
A form of partnership in which all partners have the right to participate in management and have limited liability for company debts.

limited partnership
A partnership that includes at least one general partner who actively manages the company and accepts unlimited liability and one limited partner who gives up the right to actively manage the company in exchange for limited liability.

line-and-staff organizations
Organizations with line managers forming the primary chain of authority in the company, and staff departments working alongside line departments.

line extensions
Similar products offered under the same brand name.

line managers
Managers who supervise the functions that contribute directly to profitability: production and marketing.

line of credit
A financial arrangement between a firm and a bank in which the bank pre-approves credit up to a specified limit, provided that the firm maintains an acceptable credit rating.

line organizations
Organizations with a clear, simple chain of command from top to bottom.

liquid asset
An asset that can quickly be converted into cash with little risk of loss.

liquidity ratios
Financial ratios that measure the ability of a firm to obtain the cash it needs to pay its short-term debt obligations as they come due.

lockout
An employer-initiated work stoppage.

logistics
A subset of supply chain management that focuses largely on the tactics involved in moving products along the supply chain.

loss
When a business incurs expenses that are greater than its revenue.

loss leader pricing
Closely related to high/low pricing, loss leader pricing means pricing a handful of items—or loss leaders—temporarily below cost to drive traffic.

M1 money supply
Includes all currency plus checking accounts and traveler's checks.

M2 money supply
Includes all of M1 money supply plus most savings accounts, money market accounts, and certificates of deposit.

macroeconomics
The study of a country's overall economic issues, such as the employment rate, the gross domestic product, and taxation policies.

management
Achieving the goals of an organization through planning, organizing, leading, and controlling organizational resources including people, money, and time.

management accountants
Accountants who work within a business or nonprofit organization, preparing reports and analyzing financial information.

management development
Programs to help current and potential executives develop the skills they need to move into leadership positions.

managerial (or management) accounting
The branch of accounting that provides reports and analysis to managers to help them make informed business decisions.

market makers
Investment companies that specialize in buying and selling specific stocks traded on the NASDAQ exchange or OTC market.

market niche
A small segment of a market with fewer competitors than the market as a whole. Market niches tend to be quite attractive to small firms.

market order
An order telling a broker to buy or sell a specific security at the best currently available price.

market segmentation
Dividing potential customers into groups of similar people, or segments.

market share
The percentage of a market controlled by a given marketer.

marketing
An organizational function and a set of processes for creating, communicating, and delivering value to customers and for managing customer relationships in ways that benefit the organization and its stakeholders.

marketing concept
A business philosophy that makes customer satisfaction—now and in the future—the central focus of the entire organization.

marketing mix
The blend of marketing strategies for product, price, distribution, and promotion.

marketing plan
A formal document that defines marketing objectives and the specific strategies for achieving those objectives.

marketing research
The process of gathering, interpreting, and applying information to uncover marketing opportunities and challenges, and to make better marketing decisions.

Maslow's hierarchy of needs theory
A motivation theory that suggests that human needs fall into a hierarchy and that as each need is met, people become motivated to meet the next highest need in the pyramid.

mass customization
The creation of products tailored for individual consumers on a mass basis.

master budget
A presentation of an organization's operational and financial budgets that represents the firm's overall plan of action for a specified time period.

matrix organizations
Organizations with a flexible structure that brings together specialists from different areas of the company to work on individual projects on a temporary basis.

maturity date
The date when a bond will come due.

mediation
A method of dealing with an impasse between labor and management by bringing in a neutral third party to help the two sides reach agreement by reducing tensions and making suggestions for possible compromises.

merchant wholesalers
Independent distributors who take legal possession, or title, of the goods they distribute.

merger
A corporate restructuring that occurs when two formerly independent business entities combine to form a new organization.

microeconomics
The study of smaller economic units such as individual consumers, families, and individual businesses.

middle management
Managers who supervise lower-level managers and report to a higher-level manager.

mission
The definition of an organization's purpose, values, and core goals, which provides the framework for all other plans.

mixed economies
Economies that embody elements of both planned and market-based economic systems.

modes of transportation
The various transportation options—such as planes, trains, and railroads—for moving products through the supply chain.

monetary policy
Federal Reserve decisions that shape the economy by influencing interest rates and the supply of money.

money market mutual funds
A mutual fund that pools funds from many investors and uses these funds to purchase very safe, highly liquid securities.

money supply
The total amount of money within the overall economy.

monopolistic competition
A market structure with many competitors selling differentiated products. Barriers to entry are low.

monopoly
A market structure with one producer completely dominating the industry, leaving no room for any significant competitors. Barriers to entry tend to be virtually insurmountable.

multichannel retailing
Providing multiple distribution channels for consumers to buy a product.

mutual fund
An investment vehicle that pools the contributions of many investors and buys a wide array of stocks or other securities.

NASDAQ
A major stock exchange that handles trades through a computerized network.

NASDAQ Composite
A stock index based on all domestic and foreign stocks listed on the NASDAQ exchange.

national brands
Brands that the producer owns and markets.

National Labor Relations Act (Wagner Act)
Landmark pro-labor law enacted in 1935. This law made it illegal for firms to discriminate against union members and required employers to recognize certified unions and bargain with these unions in good faith.

natural monopoly
A market structure with one company as the supplier of a product because the nature of that product makes a single supplier more efficient than multiple competing ones. Most natural monopolies are government sanctioned and regulated.

negligence
An unintentional tort that arises due to carelessness or irresponsible behavior.

Net Asset Value (NAV)
The value of a mutual fund's securities and cash holdings minus any liabilities; usually expressed on a per share basis.

net income
The difference between the revenue a firm earns and the expenses it incurs in a given time period.

net present value (NPV)
The sum of the present values of expected future cash flows from an investment minus the cost of that investment.

net working capital
The difference between a firm's current assets and its current liabilities.

New York Stock Exchange (NYSE)
The largest securities exchange in the United States and the world. After its 2007 merger with a large European exchange, it is formally known as NYSE Euronext.

noise
Any interference that causes the message you send to be different from the message your audience understands.

nondiscretionary costs
Costs that the spender must incur but has little or no control over.

nonprofit corporation
A corporation that does not seek to earn a profit and differs in several fundamental respects from C corporations.

nonprofits
Business-*like* establishments that employ people and produce goods and services with the fundamental goal of contributing to the community rather than generating financial gain.

nonverbal communication
Communication that does not use words. Common forms of nonverbal communication include gestures, posture, facial expressions, tone of voice, and eye contact.

North American Free Trade Agreement (NAFTA)
The treaty among the United States, Mexico, and Canada that eliminated trade barriers and investment restrictions over a 15-year period starting in 1994.

NYSE Hybrid Market
A trading system established by the NYSE in 2006 that allows investors to execute trades through the traditional floor trading or through a newer automated trading system.

observation research
Marketing research that *does not* require the researcher to interact with the research subject.

odd pricing
The practice of ending prices in numbers below even dollars and cents in order to create a perception of greater value.

offshoring
Moving production or support processes to foreign countries.

oligopoly
A market structure with only a handful of competitors selling products that are either similar or different. Barriers to entry are typically high.

on-the-job training
A training approach that requires employees to simply begin their jobs—sometimes guided by more experienced employees—and to learn as they go.

open market operations
The Federal Reserve function of buying and selling government securities, which include treasury bonds, notes, and bills.

open shop
An employment arrangement in which workers who are represented by a union are not required to join the union or pay union dues.

operating budgets
Budgets that communicate an organization's sales and production goals and the resources needed to achieve these goals.

operational planning
Very specific, short-term planning that applies tactical plans to daily, weekly, and monthly operations.

operations management
Planning, organizing, leading, and controlling the activities involved in producing goods and services and distributing them to customers.

opportunity cost
The opportunity of giving up the second-best choice when making a decision.

organization chart
A visual representation of the company's formal structure.

organizing
Determining a structure for both individual jobs and the overall organization.

orientation
The first step in the training and development process, designed to introduce employees to the company culture, and provide key administrative information.

outsourcing
Arranging for other organizations to perform supply chain functions that were previously performed internally.

over-the-counter (OTC) market
The market where securities that are not listed on exchanges are traded.

owners' equity
The claims a firm's owners have against their company's assets (often called stockholders' equity on balance sheets of corporations).

par value (of a bond)
The value of a bond at its maturity; what the issuer promises to pay the bondholder when the bond matures.

partnership
A voluntary agreement under which two or more people act as co-owners of a business for profit.

passive voice
Sentence construction in which the subject does not do the action expressed by the verb; rather the subject is acted upon (e.g., *The paper was written by my sister*). Passive voice tends to be less effective for business communication.

patent
A legal monopoly that gives an inventor the exclusive right over the invention for a limited time period.

penetration pricing
A new product pricing strategy that aims to capture as much of the market as possible through rock-bottom prices.

performance appraisal
A formal feedback process that requires managers to give their subordinates feedback on a one-to-one basis, typically by comparing actual results to expected results.

personal selling
The person-to-person presentation of products to potential buyers.

pharming
A scam that seeks to steal identities by routing Internet traffic to fake websites.

phishing
A scam in which official-looking emails are sent to individuals in an attempt to get them to divulge private information such as passwords, user names, and account numbers.

physical distribution
The actual, physical movement of products along the distribution pathway.

picketing
A union tactic during labor disputes in which union members walk near the entrance of the employer's place of business, carrying signs to publicize their position and concerns.

planned obsolescence
The strategy of deliberately designing products to fail in order to shorten the time between purchases.

planning
Determining organizational goals and action plans for how to achieve those goals.

poka-yokes
Simple methods incorporated into a production process designed to eliminate or greatly reduce errors.

positioning statement
A brief statement that articulates how the marketer would like the target market to envision a product relative to the competition.

preferred stock
A type of stock that gives its holder preference over common stockholders in terms of dividends and claims on assets.

present value
The amount of money that, if invested today at a given rate of interest, would grow to become some future amount in a specified number of time periods.

primary data
New data that marketers compile for a specific research project.

primary securities market
The market where newly issued securities are traded. The primary market is where the firms that issue securities raise additional financial capital.

principal
A party who agrees to have someone else (called an agent) act on his or her behalf.

principal–agent relationship
A relationship in which one party, called the principal, gives another party, called the agent, the authority to act in place of, and bind the principal when dealing with, third parties.

private placement
A primary market issue that is negotiated between the issuing corporation and a small group of accredited investors.

privatization
The process of converting government-owned businesses to private ownership.

probationary period
A specific timeframe (typically three to six months) during which a new hire can prove his or her worth on the job before the hire becomes permanent.

process
A set of activities or steps that combine inputs in order to create a desired output.

producer price index (PPI)
A measure of inflation that evaluates the change over time in the weighted-average wholesale prices.

product
Anything that an organization offers to satisfy consumer needs and wants, including both goods and services.

product consistency
How reliably a product delivers its promised level of quality.

product differentiation
The attributes that make a good or service different from other products that compete to meet the same or similar customer needs.

product features
The specific characteristics of a product.

product life cycle
A pattern of sales and profits that typically changes over time.

product line
A group of products that are closely related to each other, either in terms of how they work, or the customers they serve.

product mix
The total number of product lines and individual items sold by a single firm.

product placement
The paid integration of branded products into movies, television, and other media.

productivity
The basic relationship between the production of goods and services (output) and the resources needed to produce them (input), calculated via the following equation: output / input = productivity.

profit
The money that a business earns in sales (or revenue), minus expenses, such as the cost of goods, and the cost of salaries.
Revenue – Expenses = Profit (or Loss)

profit margin
The gap between the cost and the price of an item on a per product basis.

profitability ratios
Ratios that measure the rate of return a firm is earning on various measures of investment.

promotion
Marketing communication designed to influence consumer purchase decisions through information, persuasion, and reminders.

promotional channels
Specific marketing communication vehicles, including traditional tools, such as advertising, sales promotion, direct marketing, and personal selling, and newer tools such as product placement, advergaming, and Internet minimovies.

property
The legal right of an owner to exclude non-owners from having access to a particular resource.

protectionism
National policies designed to restrict international trade, usually with the goal of protecting domestic businesses.

psychographic segmentation
Dividing the market into smaller groups based on consumer attitudes, interests, values, and lifestyles.

public accountants
Accountants who provide a variety of accounting services for clients on a fee basis.

public offering
A primary market issue in which new securities are offered to any investors who are willing and able to purchase them.

public relations (PR)
The ongoing effort to create positive relationships with all of a firm's different "publics," including customers, employees, suppliers, the community, the general public, and government.

publicity
Unpaid stories in the media that influence perceptions about a company or its products.

pull strategy
A marketing approach that involves creating demand from the ultimate consumers so that they "pull" your products through the distribution channels by actively seeking them.

pure competition
A market structure with many competitors selling virtually identical products. Barriers to entry are quite low.

pure goods
Products that do not include any services.

pure services
Products that do not include any goods.

push strategy
A marketing approach that involves motivating distributors to heavily promote—or "push"—a product to the final consumers, usually through heavy trade promotion and personal selling.

quality level
How well a product performs its core functions.

quality of life
The overall sense of well being experienced by either an individual or a group.

quotas
Limitations on the amount of specific products that may be imported from certain countries during a given time period.

radio frequency identification (RFID)
A technology that stores information on small microchips than can transmit the information anytime they are within range of a special reader.

recession
An economic downturn marked by a decrease in the GDP for two consecutive quarters.

recovery
A period of rising economic growth and employment.

reserve requirement
A rule set by the Fed, which specifies the minimum amount of reserves (or funds) a bank must hold, expressed as a percentage of the bank's deposits.

retailers
Distributors that sell products directly to the ultimate users, typically in small quantities, that are stored and merchandised on the premises.

retained earnings
That part of net income that a firm reinvests.

revenue
Increases in a firm's assets that result from the sale of goods, provision of services, or other activities intended to earn income.

revolving credit agreement
A guaranteed line of credit in which a bank makes a binding commitment to provide a business with funds up to a specified credit limit at any time during the term of the agreement.

right-to-work law
A state law that makes union shops illegal within that state's borders.

robot
A reprogrammable machine that is capable of manipulating materials, tools, parts, and specialized devices in order to perform a variety of tasks.

S corporation
A form of corporation that avoids double taxation by having its income taxed as if it were a partnership.

salaries
The pay that employees receive over a fixed period, most often weekly or monthly.

sale
A transaction in which the title (legal ownership) to a good passes from one party to another in exchange for a price.

sales promotion
Marketing activities designed to stimulate immediate sales activity through specific short-term programs aimed at either consumers or distributors.

Sarbanes-Oxley Act of 2002
Federal legislation passed in 2002 that sets higher ethical standards for public corporations and accounting firms. Key provisions limit conflict-of-interest issues and require financial officers and CEOs to certify the validity of their financial statements.

savings account
An interest-bearing account holding funds not needed to meet regular expenditures.

scope of authority (for an agent)
The extent to which an agent has the authority to act for and represent the principal.

SCORE (Service Corps of Retired Executives)
An organization—affiliated with the Small Business Administration—that provides free, comprehensive business counseling for small business owners from qualified volunteers.

secondary data
Existing data that marketers gather or purchase for a research project.

secondary securities market
The market where previously issued securities are traded.

secured bond
A bond backed by the pledge of specific assets.

Securities Act of 1933
The first major federal law regulating the securities industry.

Securities and Exchange Commission
The federal agency with primary responsibility for regulating the securities industry.

Securities Exchange Act of 1934
A federal law dealing with securities regulation that established the Securities and Exchange Commission to oversee the securities industry.

self-regulatory organizations (SROs)
Private organizations that develop and enforce standards governing the behavior of their members.

serial bonds
A series of bonds issued at the same time but having different maturity dates to spread out the repayment of principal.

services
Intangible products.

servicescape
The environment in which a customer and service provider interact.

sexual harassment
Workplace discrimination against a person based on his or her gender.

sinking fund
Funds a firm sets aside and uses to call in bonds or purchase bonds in order to assure an orderly repayment of principal.

Six Sigma
An approach to quality improvement characterized by very ambitious quality goals, extensive training of employees, and a long-term commitment to working on quality-related issues.

skimming pricing
A new product pricing strategy that aims to maximize profitability by offering new products at a premium price.

Small Business Administration (SBA)
An agency of the federal government designed to maintain and strengthen the nation's economy by aiding, counseling, assisting, and protecting the interests of small businesses.

Small Business Development Centers (SBDCs)
Local offices—affiliated with the Small Business Administration—that provide comprehensive management assistance to current and prospective small business owners.

social audit
A systematic evaluation of how well a firm is meeting its ethics and social responsibility goals.

social responsibility
The obligation of a business to contribute to society.

socialism
An economic system based on the principle that the government should own and operate key enterprises that directly affect public welfare.

sociocultural differences
Differences among cultures in language, attitudes, and values.

software
Programs that provide instructions to a computer so that it can perform a desired task.

sole proprietorship
A form of business ownership with a single owner who usually actively manages the company.

spam
Unsolicited email advertisements usually sent to very large numbers of recipients, many of whom may have no interest in the message.

span of control
Span of management; refers to the number of people that a manager supervises.

specific performance
A remedy for breach of contract in which the court orders the party committing the breach to do exactly what the contract specifies.

speed-to-market
The rate at which a new product moves from conception to commercialization.

sponsorship
A deep association between a marketer and a partner (usually a cultural or sporting event), which involves promotion of the sponsor in exchange for either payment or the provision of goods.

spontaneous financing
Funds that arise as a natural result of a firm's business operations without the need for special arrangements.

spyware
Software that is installed on a computer without the user's knowledge or permission for the purpose of tracking the user's behavior.

staff managers
Managers who supervise the functions that provide advice and assistance to the line departments.

stakeholders
Any groups that have a stake—or a personal interest—in the performance and actions of an organization.

Standard & Poor's 500
A stock index based on prices of 500 major U.S. corporations in a variety of industries and market sectors.

standard of living
The quality and quantity of goods and services available to a population.

statement of cash flows
The financial statement that identifies a firm's sources and uses of cash in a given accounting period.

statute of frauds
A requirement that certain types of contracts must be in writing in order to be enforceable.

statute of limitations
The time period within which a legal action must be initiated.

statutory close (or closed) corporation
A corporation with a limited number of owners that operates under simpler, less formal rules than a C corporation.

statutory law
Laws that are the result of legislative action.

stock index
A statistic that tracks how the prices of a specific set of stocks have changed.

stockholder
An owner of a corporation.

store brands
Brands that the retailer both produces and distributes (also called private-label brands).

strategic alliance
An agreement between two or more firms to jointly pursue a specific opportunity without actually merging their businesses. Strategic alliances typically involve less formal, less encompassing agreements than partnerships.

strategic goals
Concrete benchmarks that managers can use to measure performance in each key area of the organization.

strategic planning
High-level, long-term planning that establishes a vision for the company, defines long-term objectives and priorities, determines broad action steps, and allocates resources.

strategies
Action plans that help the organization achieve its goals by forging the best fit between the firm and the environment.

strike
A work stoppage initiated by a union.

structured interviews
An interviewing approach that involves developing a list of questions beforehand and asking the same questions in the same order to each candidate.

supply
The quantity of products that producers are willing to offer for sale at different market prices.

supply chain
All organizations, processes, and activities involved in the flow of goods from their raw materials to the final consumer.

supply chain management (SCM)
Planning and coordinating the movement of products along the supply chain, from the raw materials to the final consumers.

supply curve
The graphed relationship between price and quantity from a supplier standpoint.

survey research
Marketing research that requires the researcher to interact with the research subject.

sustainable development
Doing business to meet the needs of the current generation, without harming the ability of future generations to meet their needs.

SWOT analysis
A strategic planning tool that helps management evaluate an organization in terms of internal strengths and weakness, and external opportunities and threats.

system software
Software that performs the critical functions necessary to operate the computer at the most basic level.

tactical planning
More specific, shorter-term planning that applies strategic plans to specific functional areas.

target market
The group of people who are most likely to buy a particular product.

tariffs
Taxes levied against imports.

tax deferred revenue
A portion of earnings that is not taxed now but is taxed when the employee receives the cash distribution upon retirement.

technical skills
Expertise in a specific functional area or department.

telecommuting
Working remotely—most often from home—and connecting to the office via phone lines, fax machines, and broadband networks.

Theory X and Theory Y
A motivation theory that suggests that management attitudes toward workers fall into two opposing categories based on management assumptions about worker capabilities and values.

time value of money
The principle that a dollar received today is worth more than a dollar received in the future.

title
Legal evidence of ownership.

Title VII
A portion of the Civil Rights Act of 1964 that prohibits discrimination in hiring, firing, compensation, apprenticeships, training, terms, conditions, or privileges of employment based on race, color, religion, sex, or national origin for employers with 15 or more workers.

top management
Managers who set the overall direction of the firm, articulating a vision, establishing priorities, and allocating time, money, and other resources.

tort
A private wrong that results in physical or mental harm to an individual, or damage to that person's property.

total quality management (TQM)
An approach to quality improvement that calls for everyone within an organization to take responsibility for improving quality and emphasizes the need for a long-term commitment to continuous improvement.

trade credit
Spontaneous financing granted by sellers when they deliver goods and services to customers without requiring immediate payment.

trade deficit
Shortfall that occurs when the total value of a nation's imports is higher than the total value of its exports.

trade promotion
Marketing activities designed to stimulate wholesalers and retailers to push specific products more aggressively over the short term.

trade surplus
Overage that occurs when the total value of a nation's exports is higher than the total value of its imports.

trademark
A mark, symbol, word, phrase, or motto used to identify a company's goods.

trading bloc
A group of countries that has reduced or even eliminated tariffs, allowing for the free flow of goods among the member nations.

underwriting
An arrangement under which an investment banker agrees to purchase all shares of a public offering at an agreed upon price.

unemployment rate
The percentage of people in the labor force over age 16 who do not have jobs and are actively seeking employment.

Uniform Commercial Code (UCC)
A uniform act governing the sale of goods, leases, warranties, transfer of funds, and a variety of other business-related activities.

union shop
An employment arrangement in which a firm can hire nonunion workers, but these workers must join the union within a specified time period to keep their jobs.

universal ethical standards
Ethical norms that apply to all people across a broad spectrum of situations.

U.S. Treasury bills (T-bills)
Short-term marketable IOUs issued by the U.S. federal government.

utility (Chapter 11)
The ability of goods and services to satisfy consumer "wants."

utility (Chapter 13)
The value, or usefulness, that a good or service offers a customer.

value
A customer perception that a product has a better relationship than its competitors between the cost and the benefits.

value chain
The network of relationships that channels the flow of inputs, information, and financial resources through all of the processes involved in producing and distributing goods and services.

value stream map
A tool used in lean production to show the flows of materials and information from the beginning to the end of a production process; used to identify where waste occurs within a production system.

venture capital firms
Companies that invest in start-up businesses with high growth potential in exchange for a share of ownership.

vertical integration
Performance of processes internally that were previously performed by other organizations in a supply chain.

vertical merger
A combination of firms at different stages in the production of a good or service.

vesting period
A specified period of time in which an employee must be employed in order to receive the full advantage of certain retirement benefits.

viral marketing
An Internet marketing strategy that tries to involve customers and others not employed by the seller in activities that help promote the product.

voluntary export restraints (VERs)
Limitations on the amount of specific products that one nation will export to another nation.

wages
The pay that employees receive in exchange for the number of hours or days that they work.

Web 2.0
An approach to e-commerce that emphasizes interactive and collaborative commercial websites in order to develop consumer loyalty and create more value.

wheel of retailing
A classic distribution theory that suggests that retail firms and retail categories become more upscale as they go through their life cycles.

whistle-blowers
Employees who report their employer's illegal or unethical behavior to either the authorities or the media.

wholesalers
Distributors that buy products from producers and sell them to other businesses or nonfinal users such as hospitals, nonprofits, and the government.

World Bank
An international cooperative of 186 member countries, working together to reduce poverty in the developing world.

World Trade Organization (WTO)
A permanent global institution to promote international trade and to settle international trade disputes.

World Wide Web
The service that allows computer users to easily access and share information on the Internet in the form of text, graphics, video, and animation.

media
    advertising and, 184–185
    product placement and,
        182
    promotion and, 179
memos and reports, 64
merchant wholesalers, 195
mergers, 81, 82
Mexico, 57
microeconomics, 17
middle management, 207,
    208, 212
minipreneurs, 98
minority business owners, 85
MinorityFran initiative, 85
minority groups, 235
mission, 213
missionary selling, 188
mission statements, 213
mixed economies, 28–29
modes of transportation,
    199, 200
monetary policy, 21–23
**money market mutual
    funds,** 122, 123–124
money supply, 21
monopolies, 25
monopolistic competition,
    25
mortgage loans, 17, 18
motivation, management and,
    208–212
multichannel retailing, 196
multilevel marketing (MLM),
    198
music industry, 203, 250
mutual funds, 145, 146

N

NASDAQ, 138, 139
NASDAQ Composite index,
    147
national brands, 174
national debt. *See* federal
    debt
National Minority Franchising
    Initiative (NMFI), 85
natural monopolies, 25
natural resources, 6, 56
nervousness, verbal
    presentations and, 71
Net Asset Value (NAV), 148
net income, 107
net operating income, 107
net present value (NPV),
    128
net working capital, 122
networks, 237, 238–239
**New York Stock Exchange
    (NYSE),** 138–139, 140
noise, 61
nonprofit corporations, 81
nonprofits, 6, 55–56, 81, 86,
    151–152
nonstore retailers, 197–198

nonverbal communications,
    62–63
**North American Free Trade
    Agreement (NAFTA),**
    14, 44–45
notes, to financial statements,
    110
NYSE Hybrid Market, 140

O

Obama, Barack, 7, 8, 19
observation research, 162
Occupational Safety and
    Health Act of 1970, 234
odd pricing, 205
offshoring, 38, 255–256, 262
off-the-job training, 229
older workers, 224, 255
oligopolies, 25
online retailing, 197–198, 202
online video advertising, 182
on-the-job training, 229
opening, in presentations, 69
open market operations, 22
operating activities, 108
operating budgets, 114
operating expenses, 107
operational planning, 212
operations management
    effectiveness and
        efficiency, 253–254
    integrating operational
        functions and,
        261–263
    key responsibilities,
        254–259
    lean production and,
        265–267
    quality and, 263–265
    technology of operations
        and, 260–261
operations managers, 254–
    259, 267
opportunity costs, 35, 99
order processing, 199
organizational ethics, 50–51
organization charts, 215–
    216
organizing, 215–218
orientation, 229
outsourcing, 36, 37, 223,
    233, 262
overhead costs, 111–112
over-the-counter market,
    140
owners' equity, 105–106
ownership formats, 73–74
ownership utility, 151, 194

P

packaging, 158, 175
paid search advertising, 182
participatory budgeting. *See*
    bottom-up budgeting

partnerships, 38, 39, 73, 74,
    76–77
par value (of a bond), 135
passive voice, 66–67
passwords, 249
pay for performance, 231
payments, electronic, 245
penetration pricing, 200–201
people marketing, 152
P/E ratio, 147
perceived value, 154
performance appraisals, 230
performance measures
    budgeting and, 113
    economic performance,
        29–31
    management and, 220
    performance appraisals,
        230
personal funding resources,
    92–93
personal selling, 187–188
pharming, 248
phishing, 247–248
physical distribution, 193,
    199–200
piracy, software and, 250
place marketing, 152
place utility, 151, 194
planned economies, 27–28
planned obsolescence, 54
planning
    human resource
        management and,
        225–233
    management and,
        212–215
poka-yokes, 264
political and legal environment
    entrepreneurs and, 99
    international trade and,
        41–42
    marketing environment
        and, 160
population changes, 12–13
positioning statements, 181
power, in business, 216, 219
PowerPoint, 69
preferred stocks, 78,
    134–135
premiums, 186
preemptive rights, 134
presentations. *See* verbal
    presentations
present values, 127–128
prestige pricing, 202
price competition, 25
price levels, 30–31
pricing strategies, 158,
    200–205
primary data, 162–164
primary securities markets,
    137–138
privacy
    information technology
        management and,
        249–250

radio frequency
    identification (RFID)
    tags, 197
    written communications
        and, 68
private enterprise system.
    See capitalism
private label brands, 174–175
private placements, 137,
    138
privatization, 28
proactive social responsibility,
    47
probationary periods, 228
processes, 256–257, 260–
    261
producer price index (PPI),
    31
product consistency, 171
product costing, 111–112
product development,
    175–176
    product adoption and
        diffusion, 176–178
    product life cycles,
        178–179
product differentiation,
    170–175
product features, 171
production
    factors of production, 6–7
    international trade and,
        36
    just-in-time (JIT)
        production, 266–267
    operations management
        and, 254
    process selection and,
        256–257
    quality and, 262
production budgets, 114
Production Era, 5, 153
productivity, 31, 255
product life cycles, 178–179,
    190
product lines, 172
product mix, 172
product placement, 182–183
products
    business products,
        169–170
    green products, 24, 177
    innovation and, 175–179
    operations management
        and, 254
    product differentiation,
        170–175
    promotion and, 179–190
    types of, 167–170
product-use-based
    segmentation, 157
profitability ratios, 119–120
profit margins, 204
profits, 3, 107, 133–134, 200
projects, operations
    management and,
    255–256

LO1

value
The relationship between the price of a good or a service and the benefits that it offers its customers.

business
Any activity that provides goods and services in an effort to earn a profit.

profit
The money that a business earns in sales (or revenue), minus expenses, such as the cost of goods, and the cost of salaries.
Revenue – Expenses = Profit (or Loss)

loss
When a business incurs expenses that are greater than its revenue.

entrepreneurs
People who risk their time, money, and other resources to start and manage a business.

standard of living
The quality and quantity of goods and services available to a population.

quality of life
The overall sense of well being experienced by either an individual or a group.

LO3

nonprofits
Business-*like* establishments that employ people and produce goods and services with the fundamental goal of contributing to the community rather than generating financial gain.

LO1 Define business and discuss the role of business in the economy

A business is any activity that provides goods and services in an effort to earn a profit. *Profit* is the money that a business earns in sales, minus expenses, such as the cost of goods and the cost of salaries. Profit potential provides a powerful incentive for people to start their own businesses, or to become *entrepreneurs*. Successful businesses create wealth, which increases the standard of living for virtually all members of a society.

LO2 Explain the evolution of modern business

Business historians typically divide the history of American business into five distinct eras, which overlap during the periods of transition.

- *Industrial Revolution:* From the mid-1700s to the mid-1800s, technology fueled a period of rapid industrialization. Factories sprang up in cities, leading to mass production and specialization of labor.
- *Entrepreneurship Era:* During the second half of the 1800s, large-scale entrepreneurs emerged, building business empires that created enormous wealth, but often at the expense of workers and consumers.
- *Production Era:* In the early 1900s, major businesses focused on further refining the production process, creating huge efficiencies. The assembly line, introduced in 1913, boosted productivity and lowered costs.
- *Marketing Era:* After WWII, consumers began to gain power. As goods and services flooded the market, the marketing concept emerged: a consumer-first orientation as a guide to business decision-making.
- *Relationship Era:* With the technology boom in the 1990s, businesses have begun to look beyond the immediate transaction, aiming to build a competitive edge through long-term customer relationships.

LO3 Discuss the role of nonprofit organizations in the economy

Nonprofit organizations often work hand in hand with business to improve the quality of life in our society. Nonprofits are business-like establishments that contribute to economic stability and growth. Similar to businesses, nonprofits generate revenue and incur expenses. Their goal is to use any revenue above and beyond expenses to advance the goals of the organization, rather than to make money for its owners. Some nonprofits—such as museums, schools, and theaters—can act as economic magnets for communities, attracting additional investment.

The Relationship Between Nonprofits and Businesses

Advance Goals of Organization

Generate Revenue Incur Expenses Provide Employment

Create Profit for Owners

LO4

factors of production
Four fundamental elements—natural resources, capital, human resources, and entrepreneurship—that businesses need to achieve their objectives.

LO5

business environment
The setting in which business operates. The five key components are: economic environment, competitive environment, technological environment, social environment, and global environment.

speed-to-market
The rate at which a new product moves from conception to commercialization.

business technology
Any tools—especially computers, telecommunications, and other digital products—that businesses can use to become more efficient and effective.

World Wide Web
The service that allows computer users to easily access and share information on the Internet in the form of text, graphics, video, and animation.

e-commerce
Business transactions conducted online, typically via the Internet.

demographics
The measurable characteristics of a population. Demographic factors include population size and density and specific traits such as age, gender, and race.

free trade
An international economic and political movement designed to help goods and services flow more freely across international boundaries.

General Agreement on Tariffs and Trade (GATT)
An international trade agreement that has taken bold steps to lower tariffs and promote free trade worldwide.

LO4 Outline the core factors of production and how they affect the economy

The four factors of production are the fundamental resources that both businesses and nonprofits use to achieve their objectives.

1. *Natural resources:* All inputs that offer value in their natural state, such as land, fresh water, wind, and mineral deposits. The value of natural resources tends to rise with high demand, low supply, or both.
2. *Capital:* The manmade resources that an organization needs to produce goods or services. The elements of capital include machines, tools, buildings, and technology.
3. *Human resources:* The physical, intellectual, and creative contributions of everyone who works within an economy. Education and motivation have become increasingly important as technology replaces manual labor jobs.
4. *Entrepreneurship:* Entrepreneurs take the risk of launching and operating their own businesses. Entrepreneurial enterprises can create a tidal wave of opportunity by harnessing the other factors of production.

LO5 Describe today's business environment and discuss each key dimension

Accelerating change marks every dimension of today's business environment.

- *Economic environment:* In late 2008, the U.S. economy plunged into a deep financial crisis. The value of the stock market plummeted, companies collapsed, and the unemployment rate soared. The president, Congress, and the Federal Reserve took unprecedented steps—including a massive economic stimulus package—to encourage a turnaround.
- *Competitive environment:* As global competition intensifies, leading-edge companies have focused on long-term customer satisfaction as never before.
- *Technological environment:* The recent digital technology boom has transformed business, establishing new industries and burying others.
- *Social environment:* The U.S. population continues to diversify. Consumers are gaining power, and society has higher standards for business behavior. Sustainability has become a core marketplace issue.
- *Global environment:* The U.S. economy works within the context of the global environment. The worldwide recession has dampened short-term opportunities, but China and India continue their rapid economic development.

The Business Environment

LO6 Explain how current business trends might affect your career choices

With automation picking up speed, many traditional career choices have become dead ends. But some things—including empathy, creativity, change management, and great communication—can't be digitized. Having these skills can provide you with personal and financial opportunity.

Visit **www.cengagebrain.com**
for additional study tools!

LO1

economy
A financial and social system of how resources flow through society, from production, to distribution, to consumption.

economics
The study of the choices that people, companies, and governments make in allocating society's resources.

macroeconomics
The study of a country's overall economic issues, such as the employment rate, the gross domestic product, and taxation policies.

microeconomics
The study of smaller economic units such as individual consumers, families, and individual businesses.

LO2

fiscal policy
Government efforts to influence the economy through taxation and spending.

budget surplus
Overage that occurs when revenue is higher than expenses over a given period of time.

budget deficit
Shortfall that occurs when expenses are higher than revenue over a given period of time.

federal debt
The sum of all the money that the Federal Government has borrowed over the years and not yet repaid.

monetary policy
Federal Reserve decisions that shape the economy by influencing interest rates and the supply of money.

money supply
The total amount of money within the overall economy.

M1 money supply
Includes all currency plus checking accounts and traveler's checks.

M2 money supply
Includes all of M1 money supply plus most savings accounts, money market accounts, and certificates of deposit.

open market operations
The Federal Reserve function of buying and selling government securities, which include treasury bonds, notes, and bills.

discount rate
The rate of interest that the Federal Reserve charges when it loans funds to banks.

Federal Deposit Insurance Corporation (FDIC)
A federal agency that insures deposits in banks and thrift institutions for up to $100,000 per customer, per bank.

reserve requirement
A rule set by the Fed, which specifies the minimum amount of reserves (or funds) a bank must hold, expressed as a percentage of the bank's deposits.

LO1 Define economics and discuss the global economic crisis

Economics—the study of how people, companies, and governments allocate resources—offers vital insights regarding the forces that affect every business on a daily basis. Understanding economics helps businesspeople make better decisions, which can lead to greater profitability both short-term and long-term. Macroeconomics is the study of broad economic trends. Microeconomics focuses on the choices made by smaller economic units, such as individual consumers, families, and businesses.

In September 2008, the United States economy plunged into a deep economic crisis. The banking system hovered on the edge of collapse, property values plummeted, and home foreclosure rates soared. Massive layoffs put more than a million Americans out of work. By the end of the year, the stock market had lost more than a third of its value. To prevent total financial disaster, the federal government and the Federal Reserve intervened in the economy at an unprecedented level by bailing out huge firms that faced total collapse. In early 2009, Congress passed a colossal economic stimulus package, designed to turn around the economy and position the United States for long-term economic growth. In mid-2010 the economy began a painfully slow turnaround.

LO2 Analyze the impact of fiscal and monetary policy on the economy

Fiscal policy and monetary policy refer to efforts to shape the health of the economy. Fiscal policy involves government taxation and spending decisions designed to encourage growth and boost employment. Monetary policy refers to decisions by the Federal Reserve that influence the size of the money supply and the level of interest rates. Both fiscal and monetary policies played a pivotal role in mitigating the impact of the recent financial crisis and establishing a framework for recovery. These tools can also help sustain economic expansions.

LO3 Explain and evaluate the free market system and supply and demand

Equilibrium

Capitalism, also known as the free market system, is based on private ownership, economic freedom, and fair competition. In a capitalist economy, individuals, businesses, or nonprofit organizations privately own the vast majority of enterprises. As businesses compete against each other, quality goes up, prices remain reasonable, and choices abound, raising the overall standard of living.

The interplay between the forces of supply and demand determines the selection of products and prices available in a free market economy. Supply refers to the quantity of products that producers are willing to offer for sale at different market prices at a specific time. Demand refers to the quantity of products that consumers are willing to buy at different market prices at a specific time. According to economic theory, markets will naturally move toward the point at which supply and demand are equal: the equilibrium point.

LO3

economic system
A structure for allocating limited resources.

capitalism
An economic system—also known as the private enterprise or free market system—based on private ownership, economic freedom, and fair competition.

pure competition
A market structure with many competitors selling virtually identical products.

Barriers to entry are quite low.

monopolistic competition
A market structure with many competitors selling differentiated products. Barriers to entry are low.

oligopoly
A market structure with only a handful of competitors selling products that are either similar or different. Barriers to entry are typically high.

monopoly
A market structure with one producer completely dominating the industry, leaving no room for any significant competitors. Barriers to entry tend to be virtually insurmountable.

natural monopoly
A market structure with one company as the supplier of a product because the nature of that product makes a single supplier more efficient

than multiple competing ones. Most natural monopolies are government sanctioned and regulated.

supply
The quantity of products that producers are willing to offer for sale at different market prices.

supply curve
The graphed relationship between price and quantity from a supplier standpoint.

demand
The quantity of products that consumers are willing to buy at different market prices.

demand curve
The graphed relationship between price and quantity from a customer demand stand-point.

equilibrium price
The price associated with the point at which the quantity demanded of a product equals the quantity supplied.

LO4

socialism
An economic system based on the principle that the government should own and operate key enterprises that directly affect public welfare.

communism
An economic and political system that calls for public ownership of virtually all enterprises, under the direction of a strong central government.

LO5

mixed economies
Economies that embody elements of both planned and market-based economic systems.

privatization
The process of converting government-owned businesses to private ownership.

LO6

gross domestic product (GDP)
The total value of all final goods and services produced within a nation's physical boundaries over a given period of time.

unemployment rate
The percentage of people in the labor force over age 16 who do not have jobs and are actively seeking employment.

business cycle
The periodic contraction and expansion that occur over time in virtually every economy.

contraction
A period of economic downturn, marked by rising unemployment and falling business production.

recession
An economic downturn marked by a decrease in the GDP for two consecutive quarters.

depression
An especially deep and long-lasting recession.

LO4 Explain and evaluate planned market systems

In planned economies, the government—rather than individual choice—plays a pivotal role in controlling the economy. The two main types of planned economies are socialism and communism. While planned economies are designed to create more equity among citizens, they tend to be more prone to corruption and less effective at generating wealth than market-based economies.

LO5 Describe the trend toward mixed market systems

Most of today's nations have mixed economies, falling somewhere along a spectrum that ranges from pure planned at one extreme to pure market at the other. Over the past 30 years, most major economies around the world have moved toward the market end of the spectrum, although recently—in the wake of the global financial crisis—the United States has added more planned elements to the economy.

LO6 Discuss key terms and tools to evaluate economic performance

Since economic systems are so complex, no one measure captures all the dimensions of economic performance. But each measure yields insight on overall economic health.

- *Gross domestic product (GDP):* The total value of all goods and services produced within a nation's physical boundaries over a given period of time.
- *Unemployment rate:* The percentage of the labor force reflecting those who don't have jobs and are actively seeking employment.
- *Business cycle:* The periodic expansion and contraction that occur over time in virtually every economy.
- *Inflation rate:* The rate at which prices are rising across the economy. The government tracks the consumer price index and the producer price index.
- *Productivity:* The relationship between the goods and services that an economy produces and the inputs needed to produce them.

Business Cycle

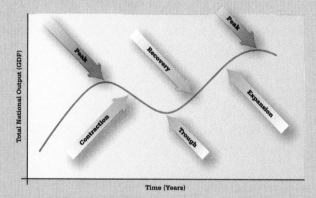

recovery
A period of rising economic growth and employment.

expansion
A period of robust economic growth and high employment.

inflation
A period of rising average prices across the economy.

hyperinflation
An average monthly inflation rate of more than 50%.

disinflation
A period of slowing average price increases across the economy.

deflation
A period of falling average prices across the economy.

consumer price index (CPI)
A measure of inflation that evaluates the change in the weighted-average price of goods and services that the average consumer buys each month.

producer price index (PPI)
A measure of inflation that evaluates the change over time in the weighted-average wholesale prices.

productivity
The basic relationship between the production of goods and services (output) and the resources needed to produce them (input), calculated via the following equation: output/input = productivity.

Visit **www.cengagebrain.com**
for additional study tools!

LO2

opportunity cost
The opportunity of giving up the second-best choice when making a decision.

absolute advantage
The benefit a country has in a given industry when it can produce more of a product than other nations using the same amount of resources.

comparative advantage
The benefit a country has in a given industry if it can make products at a lower opportunity cost than other countries.

balance of trade
A basic measure of the difference in value between a nation's exports and imports, including both goods and services.

trade surplus
Overage that occurs when the total value of a nation's exports is higher than the total value of its imports.

LO3

trade deficit
Shortfall that occurs when the total value of a nation's imports is higher than the total value of its exports.

balance of payments
A measure of the total flow of money into or out of a country.

balance of payments surplus
Overage that occurs when more money flows into a nation than out of that nation.

balance of payments deficit
Shortfall that occurs when more money flows out of a nation than into that nation.

exchange rates
A measurement of the value of one nation's currency relative to the currency of other nations.

countertrade
International trade that involves the barter of products for products rather than for currency.

LO4

foreign outsourcing
(also contract manufacturing) Contracting with foreign suppliers to produce products, usually at a fraction of the cost of domestic production.

importing
Buying products domestically that have been produced or grown in foreign nations.

exporting
Selling products in foreign nations that have been produced or grown domestically.

foreign licensing
Authority granted by a domestic firm to a foreign firm for the rights to produce and market its product or to use its trademark/patent rights in a defined geographical area.

foreign franchising
A specialized type of foreign licensing in which a firm expands by offering businesses in other countries the right to produce and market its products according to specific operating requirements.

LO1 Discuss business opportunities in the world economy

Advancing technology and falling trade barriers have created unprecedented international business opportunities. Despite the global economic crisis that began in 2008, high-population developing countries—such as China, India, Indonesia, and Brazil—continue to offer the most potential due to both their size and their relatively strong economic growth rates.

LO2 Explain the key reasons for international trade

The benefits of international trade for individual firms include access to factors of production, reduced risk, and an inflow of new ideas from foreign markets. Overall, industries tend to succeed on a global basis in countries that enjoy a competitive advantage. A country has an absolute advantage in a given industry when it can produce more of a good than other nations, using the same amount of resources, and a country has a comparative advantage when it can make products at a lower opportunity cost than other nations. Unless they face major trade barriers, the industries in any country tend to produce products for which they have a comparative advantage.

LO3 Describe the tools for measuring international trade

Measuring the impact of international trade on individual nations requires a clear understanding of balance of trade, balance of payments, and exchange rates.
- *Balance of trade:* A basic measure of the difference between a nation's exports and imports.
- *Balance of payments:* A measure of the total flow of money into or out of a country, including the balance of trade, plus other financial flows, such as foreign loans, foreign aid, and foreign investments.
- *Exchange rates:* A measure of the value of one nation's currency relative to the currency of other nations. The exchange rate has a powerful influence on how global trade affects both individual nations and their trading partners.

LO4 Analyze strategies for reaching global markets

Firms can enter global markets by developing foreign suppliers, foreign customers, or both. Two strategies for acquiring foreign suppliers are outsourcing and importing. Key strategies for developing foreign markets include exporting, licensing, franchising, and direct investment. Exporting is relatively low cost and low risk, but it offers little control over how the business unfolds. Direct investment, at the other end of the spectrum, tends to be high cost and high risk, but it offers more control and higher potential profits.

Market Development Options

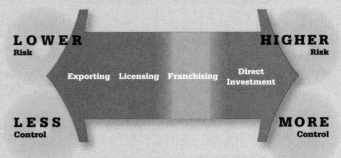

LOWER Risk — HIGHER Risk

Exporting Licensing Franchising Direct Investment

LESS Control — MORE Control

LO5 Discuss barriers to international trade and strategies to surmount them

Most barriers to trade fall into the following categories: sociocultural differences, economic differences, and legal/political differences. Each country has a different mix of barriers. Often countries with the highest barriers have the least competition, which can be a real opportunity for the first international firms to break through. The best way to surmount trade barriers is to cultivate a deep understanding of a country before beginning business. And since conditions change rapidly in many nations, learning and responding are continual processes.

direct investment
(or foreign direct investment) When firms either acquire foreign firms or develop new facilities from the ground up in foreign countries.

joint ventures
When two or more companies join forces—sharing resources, risks, and profits, but not actually merging companies—to pursue specific opportunities.

partnership
A voluntary agreement under which two or more people act as co-owners of a business for profit.

strategic alliance
An agreement between two or more firms to jointly pursue a specific opportunity without actually merging their businesses. Strategic alliances typically involve less formal, less encompassing agreements than partnerships.

LO5

sociocultural differences
Differences among cultures in language, attitudes, and values.

infrastructure
A country's physical facilities that support economic activity.

protectionism
National policies designed to restrict international trade, usually with the goal of protecting domestic businesses.

tariffs
Taxes levied against imports.

quotas
Limitations on the amount of specific products that may be imported from certain countries during a given time period.

voluntary export restraints (VERs)
Limitations on the amount of specific products that one nation will export to another nation.

embargo
A complete ban on international trade of a certain item, or a total halt in trade with a particular nation.

LO6

free trade
The unrestricted movement of goods and services across international borders.

General Agreement on Tariffs and Trade (GATT)
An international trade treaty designed to encourage worldwide trade among its members.

World Trade Organization (WTO)
A permanent global institution to promote international trade and to settle international trade disputes.

World Bank
An international cooperative of 186 member countries, working together to reduce poverty in the developing world.

LO6 Describe the free trade movement and discuss key benefits and criticisms

Over the past two decades, the emergence of regional trading blocs, common markets, and international trade agreements has moved the world economy much closer to complete free trade. Key players include:

- GATT and the WTO
- The World Bank
- The International Monetary Fund (IMF)
- The North American Free Trade Agreement (NAFTA)
- The European Union (EU)

The free trade movement has raised the global standard of living, lowered prices, and expanded choices for millions of people, but critics are troubled by the growing economic gap between the haves and the have-nots, worker abuse, large-scale pollution, and cultural homogenization.

European Union 2010

International Monetary Fund (IMF)
An international organization of 186 member nations that promote international economic cooperation and stable growth.

trading bloc
A group of countries that has reduced or even eliminated tariffs, allowing for the free flow of goods among the member nations.

common market
A group of countries that has eliminated tariffs and harmonized trading rules to facilitate the free flow of goods among the member nations.

North American Free Trade Agreement (NAFTA)
The treaty among the United States, Mexico, and Canada that eliminated trade barriers and investment restrictions over a 15-year period starting in 1994.

European Union (EU)
The world's largest common market, composed of 27 European nations.

LO1

ethics
A set of beliefs about right and wrong, good and bad.

universal ethical standards
Ethical norms that apply to all people across a broad spectrum of situations.

LO1 Define ethics and explain the concept of universal ethical standards

Ethics is a set of beliefs about right and wrong, good and bad. Who you are as a human being, your family, and your culture all play a role in shaping your ethical standards. The laws of each country usually set minimum ethical standards, but truly ethical standards typically reach beyond minimum legal requirements. Despite some significant cultural and legal differences, people around the globe tend to agree on core values, which can serve as a starting point for universal ethical standards across a wide range of situations: trustworthiness, respect, responsibility, fairness, caring, and citizenship.

Universal Ethical Standards

Trustworthiness, respect, responsibility, fairness, caring, citizenship

LO2

business ethics
The application of right and wrong, good and bad in a business setting.

ethical dilemma
A decision that involves a conflict of values; every potential course of action has some significant negative consequences.

LO2 Describe business ethics and ethical dilemmas

Business ethics is the application of right and wrong, good and bad in a business setting. Ethical dilemmas arise when you face business decisions that throw your values into conflict. These are decisions that force you to choose among less-than-ideal options because whatever choice you make will have some significant negative consequences.

Ethical Dilemma

LO3

code of ethics
A formal, written document that defines the ethical standards of an organization and gives employees the information they need to make ethical decisions across a range of situations.

whistle-blowers
Employees who report their employer's illegal or unethical behavior to either the authorities or the media.

LO3 Discuss how ethics relates to both the individual and the organization

Ethical choices begin with ethical individuals. To help people make good choices, experts have developed frameworks for reaching ethical decisions. While the specifics vary, the core principles of most decision guides are similar:

- Do you fully understand each dimension of the problem?
- Who would benefit? Who would suffer?
- Are the alternative solutions legal? Are they fair?
- Does your decision make you comfortable at a "gut feel" level?
- Could you defend your decision on the nightly TV news?
- Have you considered and reconsidered your responses to each question?

While each person is responsible for his or her own actions, the organization can also have a dramatic influence on the conduct of individual employees. An ethical culture—which includes ethical leadership from top executives, and accountability at every level of the organization—has an outsized impact on individual conduct. But formal ethics programs also play a crucial role. A written code of ethics—a document that lays out the values and priorities of the organization—is the cornerstone of a formal ethics program. Other key elements include ethics training and a clear enforcement policy for ethical violations.

LO4

social responsibility
The obligation of a business to contribute to society.

stakeholders
Any groups that have a stake—or a personal interest—in the performance and actions of an organization.

consumerism
A social movement that focuses on four key consumer rights: (1) the right to be safe, (2) the right to be informed, (3) the right to choose, and (4) the right to be heard.

planned obsolescence
The strategy of deliberately designing products to fail in order to shorten the time between purchases.

Sarbanes-Oxley Act of 2002
Federal legislation passed in 2002 that sets higher ethical standards for public corporations and accounting firms. Key provisions limit conflict-of-interest issues and require financial officers and CEOs to certify the validity of their financial statements.

corporate philanthropy
All business donations to nonprofit groups, including money, products, and employee time.

cause-related marketing
Marketing partnerships between businesses and nonprofit organizations, designed to spike sales for the company and raise money for the nonprofit.

corporate responsibility
Business contributions to the community through the actions of the business itself rather than donations of money and time.

sustainable development
Doing business to meet the needs of the current generation, without harming the ability of future generations to meet their needs.

carbon footprint
Refers to the amount of harmful greenhouse gases that a firm emits throughout its operations, both directly and indirectly.

green marketing
Developing and promoting environmentally sound products and practices to gain a competitive edge.

LO6

social audit
A systematic evaluation of how well a firm is meeting its ethics and social responsibility goals.

LO4 Define social responsibility and examine the impact on stakeholder groups

Social responsibility is the obligation of a business to contribute to society. Enlightened companies carefully consider the priorities of all stakeholders—groups who have an interest in their actions and performance—as they make key decisions. Core stakeholder groups for most businesses are listed below, along with key obligations.

- *Employees:* Treat employees with dignity, respect, and fairness. Ensure that hard work and talent pay off. Help workers balance emerging work–life priorities.
- *Customers:* Provide quality products at a fair price. Ensure that customers are safe and informed. Support consumer choice and consumer dialogue.
- *Investors:* Create an ongoing stream of profits. Manage investor dollars according to the highest legal and ethical standards. Support full disclosure.
- *Community:* Support nonprofit groups that improve the community and fit with your company. Minimize the negative environmental impact of your business.

The Spectrum of Social Responsibility

LESS Responsible

No Contribution
Some businesses do not recognize an obligation to society and do only what's legally required.

Responsive Contributions
Some businesses choose to respond on a case-by-case basis to market requests for contributions.

Proactive Contributions
Some businesses choose to integrate social responsibility into their strategic plans, contributing as part of their business goals.

MORE Responsible

LO5 Explain the role of social responsibility in the global arena

Social responsibility becomes more complex in the global arena largely due to differences in the legal and cultural environments. Bribery and corruption are key issues, along with concern for human rights and environmental standards.

Social Responsibility Issues in the Global Arena

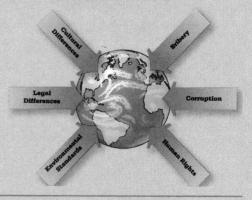

Cultural Differences

Bribery

Legal Differences

Corruption

Environmental Standards

Human Rights

LO6 Describe how companies evaluate their efforts to be socially responsible

Many companies—even some entire industries—monitor themselves. The process typically involves establishing objectives for ethics and social responsibility and then measuring achievement of those objectives on a systematic, periodic basis. Other groups play watchdog roles as well. Key players include activist customers, investors, unions, environmentalists, and community groups.

WATCHDOG GROUPS
- Activist Customers
- Investors
- Unions
- Environmentalists
- Community Groups

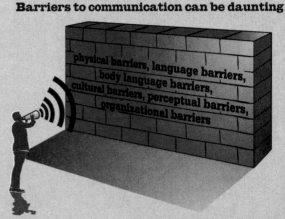

LO1

communication
The transmission of information between a sender and a recipient.

noise
Any interference that causes the message you send to be different from the message your audience understands.

communication barriers
Obstacles to effective communication, typically defined in terms of physical, language, body language, cultural, perceptual, and organizational barriers.

intercultural communication
Communication among people with differing cultural backgrounds.

LO2

nonverbal communication
Communication that does not use words. Common forms of nonverbal communication include gestures, posture, facial expressions, tone of voice, and eye contact.

active listening
Attentive listening that occurs when the listener focuses his or her complete attention on the speaker.

LO3

communication channels
The various ways in which a message can be sent, ranging from one-on-one, in-person meetings to Internet message boards.

LO1 Explain the importance of excellent business communication

Effective communication happens when *relevant meaning* is transmitted from the sender to the receiver. Skillful communicators save time and money, and develop deeper, more trusting relationships with their colleagues. Anything that interferes with the correct transmission of your message is a barrier to communication. Barriers can be physical, verbal, nonverbal, cultural, perceptual, or organizational. To communicate effectively, you should be able to identify and surmount any barriers that stand between you and your audience. The result? Greater long-term success in every aspect of business.

Barriers to communication can be daunting

physical barriers, language barriers, body language barriers, cultural barriers, perceptual barriers, organizational barriers

LO2 Describe the key elements of nonverbal communication

The key elements of nonverbal communication include eye contact, tone of voice, facial expressions, gestures, and posture. Studies suggest that on average, only 7% of meaning during face-to-face communication comes from the verbal content of the message, which magnifies the importance of every element of nonverbal communication. Active listening also plays an influential role. The starting point is empathy: a genuine attempt to understand and appreciate the speaker. You should signal your focus to the speaker through verbal cues, such as "I understand your point," and nonverbal cues such as nods, eye contact, and leaning forward. The result will be better relationships and better information for you.

eye contact
tone of voice
facial expressions
gestures
posture

93% of meaning comes from nonverbal communication

LO3 Compare, contrast, and choose effective communication channels

Communication channels differ significantly in terms of richness: the amount of information that they offer the audience. The spectrum ranges from written communication at the low end to face-to-face meetings at the high end. The best choice depends on your objective, your message, and your audience. To ensure that your communication achieves your goals, always consider the needs and expectations of your audience. If you tailor each message with the audience in mind, you'll give yourself a competitive edge in terms of the time, attention, and response of your audience.

Communication Channels Have Different Levels of Richness

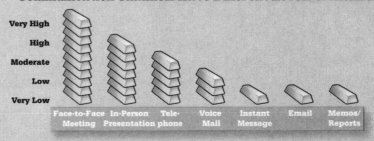

	Very High	High	Moderate	Low	Very Low

Face-to-Face Meeting · In-Person Presentation · Telephone · Voice Mail · Instant Message · Email · Memos/Reports

LO4

bias
A preconception about members of a particular group. Common forms of bias include gender bias, age bias, and race, ethnicity, or nationality bias.

active voice
Sentence construction in which the subject performs the action expressed by the verb (e.g., *My sister wrote the paper*). Active voice works better for the vast majority of business communication.

passive voice
Sentence construction in which the subject does not do the action expressed by the verb; rather the subject is acted upon (e.g., *The paper was written by my sister*). Passive voice tends to be less effective for business communication.

LO6

dynamic delivery
Vibrant, compelling presentation delivery style that grabs and holds the attention of the audience.

LO4 Choose the right words for effective communication

The right words can make the difference between a message your audience absorbs, and a message your audience ignores. Keep these considerations in mind: analyze your audience, be concise, avoid slang, avoid bias, and use active voice.

LO5 Write more effective business memos, letters, and emails

Here, too, you should begin with the needs of your audience; their anticipated response should drive the structure of your writing. Determine the "bottom line" of your communication, and be sure to deliver it up front. Your message itself should have a natural tone and must be completely free of grammatical errors.

Sample Emails: Same Message, Different Approach

If the recipient will feel positive or neutral about your message...

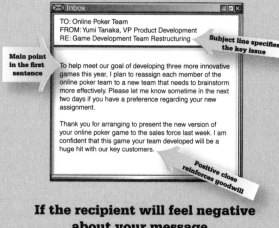

If the recipient will feel negative about your message...

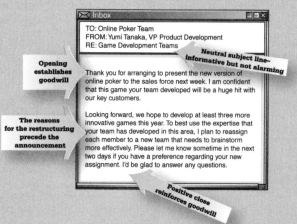

LO6 Create and deliver successful verbal presentations

A great presentation begins with a hook that draws in your audience and engages their attention. The body of the presentation typically focuses on three key points, supported by credible information and persuasive arguments. The close summarizes the key points and often refers back to the opening hook. Dynamic delivery is simply a matter of practice, with a focus on knowing your material.

LO1

sole proprietorship
A form of business ownership with a single owner who usually actively manages the company.

partnership
A voluntary agreement under which two or more people act as co-owners of a business for profit.

general partnership
A partnership in which all partners can take an active role in managing the business and have unlimited liability for any claims against the firm.

corporation
A form of business ownership in which the business is considered a legal entity that is separate and distinct from its owners.

articles of incorporation
The document filed with a state government to establish the existence of a new corporation.

limited liability
When owners are not personally liable for claims against their firm. Limited liability owners may lose their investment in the company, but their personal assets are protected.

limited liability company (LLC)
A form of business ownership that offers both limited liability to its owners and flexible tax treatment

LO3

limited partnership
A partnership that includes at least one general partner who actively manages the company and accepts unlimited liability and one limited partner who gives up the right to actively manage the company in exchange for limited liability.

limited liability partnership (LLP)
A form of partnership in which all partners have the right to participate in management and have limited liability for company debts.

LO4

C corporation
The most common type of business corporation, where ownership offers limited liability to all of its owners, also called stockholders.

corporate bylaws
The basic rules governing how a corporation is organized and how it conducts its business.

stockholder
An owner of a corporation.

institutional investor
An organization that pools contributions from investors, clients, or depositors and uses these funds to buy stocks and other securities.

board of directors
The individuals who are elected by stockholders of a corporation to represent their interests.

LO1 Describe the characteristics of the four basic forms of business ownership

A sole proprietorship is a business that is owned, and usually managed, by a single person. A partnership is a voluntary arrangement under which two or more people act as co-owners of a business for profit. A corporation is a legal entity created by filing a document (known in most states as the "articles of incorporation") with a state agency. A corporation is considered to be separate and distinct from its owners, who have limited liability for the debts of their company. A limited liability company (LLC) is a relatively new form of business ownership that, like a corporation, offers limited liability to its owners. However, LLCs offer more flexibility in tax treatment and simpler operating requirements.

LO2 Discuss the advantages and disadvantages of a sole proprietorship

A sole proprietorship is the simplest and least expensive form of ownership to establish. It offers the single owner the flexibility of running the business without having to seek the approval of other owners. If the business is successful, the sole proprietor retains all of the profits. Finally, the earnings of a sole proprietorship are taxed only as income of the owner with no separate tax levied on the business itself. A key disadvantage of a sole proprietorship is that the single owner has unlimited liability for the debts of the business. The sole owner also must often work long hours and assume heavy responsibilities. Sole proprietorships normally have difficulty raising funds for expansion. Finally, because the law views sole proprietorships as simply an extension of the person who owns the company, this form of ownership has a limited life.

LO3 Evaluate the pros and cons of the partnership as a form of ownership

The most basic type of partnership is a *general partnership,* In a general partnership, each co-owner takes an active role in management. Compared to the sole proprietorships, a general partnership offers the advantages of pooled financial resources and the benefits of a shared workload and complementary skills. The earnings of general partnerships are taxed only as income to the partners; there is no separate income tax on the business itself. A major disadvantage of a general partnership is that each owner has unlimited liability for the debts of the company. Also, disagreements among partners can complicate decision-making. Finally, the death or withdrawal of a partner can create instability and uncertainty in the management and financing of the company.

Another common type of partnership, the *limited partnership,* must have at least one general partner and at least one limited partner. The general partner actively manages the company and accepts unlimited liability for the company's debts. The limited partner invests money (and possibly other resources) in the business and shares in its profits. Limited partners have limited liability but cannot actively manage the partnership.

The newest form of partnership is the *limited liability partnership.* Under this arrangement all partners have the ability to manage their company and some degree of limited liability for the debts of their firm. In most states, this type of partnership can be formed only by professional businesses, such as law or accounting firms.

LO4 Explain why corporations have become the dominant form of business ownership

The most common form of corporation is the C corporation. All stockholders (the owners of a C corporation) have limited liability for company debts. C corporations can raise financial capital by issuing bonds or shares of stock, giving them an advantage when it comes to financing growth—a key reason most large businesses are corporations. Other advantages are unlimited life, easy transfer of ownership, and the ability to take advantage of professional management. One disadvantage of a corporation is the complexity and expense involved in its formation. Another drawback is that any profits distributed to stockholders are taxed twice—once as income to the corporation, then again as income to the stockholders. Other disadvantages are more extensive government regulation and the possibility of conflicting interests between owners and professional management.

The S corporation is another common form of corporation. Like a C corporation, all stockholders have the protection of limited liability. However, an S corporation is taxed as if it were a partnership, thus avoiding the problem of double taxation that characterizes the

© COLORBLIND IMAGES/ICONICA/GETTY IMAGES

S corporation
A form of corporation that avoids double taxation by having its income taxed as if it were a partnership.

statutory close (or closed) corporation
A corporation with a limited number of owners that operates under simpler, less formal rules than a C corporation.

nonprofit corporation
A corporation that does not seek to earn a profit and differs in several fundamental respects from C corporations.

acquisition
A corporate restructuring in which one firm buys another.

merger
A corporate restructuring that occurs when two formerly independent business entities combine to form a new organization.

divestiture
The transfer of total or partial ownership of some of a firm's assets to investors or to another company.

horizontal merger
A combination of two firms that are in the same industry.

vertical merger
A combination of firms at different stages in the production of a good or service.

conglomerate merger
A combination of two firms that are in unrelated industries.

LO6

franchise
A licensing arrangement whereby a franchisor allows franchisees to use its name, trademark, products, business methods, and other property in exchange for monetary payments and other considerations.

franchisor
The business entity in a franchise relationship that allows others to operate their business using resources it supplies in exchange for money and other considerations.

franchisee
The party in a franchise relationship that pays for the right to use resources supplied by the franchisor.

distributorship
A type of franchising arrangement in which the franchisor makes a product and licenses the franchisee to sell it.

business format franchise
A broad franchise agreement in which the franchisee pays for the right to use the name, trademark, and business and production methods of the franchisor.

franchise agreement
The contractual arrangement between a franchisor and a franchisee that spells out the duties and responsibilities of both parties.

Franchise Disclosure Document (FDD)
A detailed description of all aspects of a franchise that the franchisor must provide to the franchisee at least 14 calendar days before the franchise agreement is signed.

C corporation. One drawback of an S corporation is that ownership is limited to a maximum of 100 shareholders, all of whom must be U.S. citizens or permanent residents.

LO5 Explain why limited liability companies are becoming an increasingly popular form of ownership

Limited liability companies (LLCs) are attractive because they give owners limited liability while giving them the option of being taxed as a partnership, thus avoiding the problem of double taxation endemic to C corporations. In this sense, LLCs are similar to S corporations, but they aren't limited by the ownership restrictions placed on S corporations. LLCs also are subject to fewer regulations and give the owners the flexibility to either manage the company themselves or hire professional managers.

LO6 Evaluate the advantages and disadvantages of franchising

A franchise is a licensing arrangement under which one party (the *franchisor*) allows another party (the *franchisee*) to use its name, trademark, patents, copyrights, business methods, and other property in exchange for monetary payments and other considerations. The franchisor gains revenue without the need to invest its own money. Franchisees gain the right to use a well-known brand name and proven business methods and receive training and support from franchisors. On the downside, franchisors often find that dealing with a large number of franchisees can be complex and challenging. Also, if a few franchisees behave irresponsibly, their actions can have a negative impact on the entire organization. For franchisees, the main drawbacks are the monetary payments (fees and royalties) they must pay to the franchisor and the loss of control over management of their business. Franchisees also require franchisor approval before they can expand or sell their franchise to someone else.

Characteristics of Four Major Forms of Business Ownership

Form of Business	Number of Owners	Participation in Management	Owners' Liability	Tax Implications	State Filing Requirements
Sole Proprietorship	One	Proprietor typically manages the company.	Unlimited	Taxed only as income to the owner.	No special filing required with state.
General Partnership	Two or more (no limit on maximum)	All general partners have the right to participate in management.	Unlimited	Taxed only as income to the owners.	No special filing required with state.
General (or C) Corporation	No limit on number of stockholders	Most stockholders do not take an active role in management. Stockholders elect Board of Directors, which sets policy and appoints and oversees corporate officers who actively manage the corporation.	Limited	Earnings subject to double taxation: all earnings are taxed as income to corporation. Any dividends are also taxed as income to stockholders.	Must file articles of incorporation (or similar document) with state and pay filing fee.
Limited Liability Company (LLC)	No limit	May be member-managed, or may be manager-managed, similar to a corporation.	Limited	Has the option to be taxed either as a partnership or as a corporation. If taxed as a partnership, earnings are taxed only as income to owners.	Must file articles of organization with state and pay filing fee.

LO1

entrepreneurs
People who risk their time, money, and other resources to start and manage a business.

LO2

internal locus of control
A deep-seated sense that the individual is personally responsible for what happens in his or her life.

external locus of control
A deep-seated sense that forces other than the individual are responsible for what happens in his or her life.

LO3

angel investors
Individuals who invest in start-up companies with high growth potential in exchange for a share of ownership.

venture capital firms
Companies that invest in start-up businesses with high growth potential in exchange for a share of ownership.

LO4

market niche
A small segment of a market with fewer competitors than the market as a whole. Market niches tend to be quite attractive to small firms.

LO1 Explain the key reasons to launch a small business

Launching a business is tough, but the advantages of business ownership can far outweigh the risk and hard work. Most people who take the plunge are seeking some combination of greater financial success, independence, flexibility, and challenge. But some are seeking survival and simply have no other options.

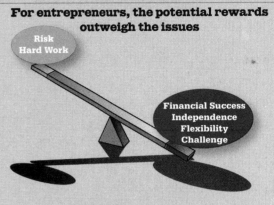

For entrepreneurs, the potential rewards outweigh the issues

LO2 Describe the typical entrepreneurial mindset and characteristics

Not all small business owners are entrepreneurs. The difference is attitude: from day one, true entrepreneurs aim to dominate their industry. The entrepreneurial personality typically includes some combination of the following characteristics: vision, self-reliance, energy, confidence, tolerance of uncertainty, and tolerance of failure. While these qualities are very helpful, they aren't essential: it's clearly possible to succeed with a number of different personality types.

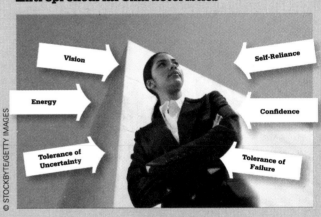

Entrepreneurial Characteristics

LO3 Discuss funding options for small business

For many entrepreneurs, finding the money to fund their business is the top challenge of their start-up year. The vast majority of new firms are funded by the personal resources of the founder, including personal accounts (e.g., credit cards), family, and friends. Other key funding sources include bank loans, angel investors, and venture capital firms.

LO4 Analyze the opportunities and threats that small businesses face

Small businesses enjoy some key advantages, but also face daunting obstacles as they fight for a foothold in the turbulent marketplace.

Opportunities:
- *Market niches:* Many small firms are uniquely positioned to exploit small but profitable market niches.
- *Personal customer service:* With a smaller customer base, small firms can develop much more personal relationships with individual customers.
- *Lower overhead costs:* Many small firms can hold down overhead costs by hiring fewer managers and fewer specialized employees.
- *Technology:* The Web has played a powerful role in opening new opportunities for small business in both local and global markets.

LO5

Small Business Administration (SBA)
An agency of the federal government designed to maintain and strengthen the nation's economy by aiding, counseling, assisting, and protecting the interests of small businesses.

Small Business Development Centers (SBDCs)
Local offices—affiliated with the Small Business Administration—that provide comprehensive management assistance to current and prospective small business owners.

SCORE (Service Corps of Retired Executives)
An organization—affiliated with the Small Business Administration—that provides free, comprehensive business counseling for small business owners from qualified volunteers.

business plan
A formal document that describes a business concept, outlines core business objectives, and details strategies and timelines for achieving those objectives.

© ZONECREATIVE/ISTOCKPHOTO.COM

Threats:

- *High risk of failure:* Starting a new business involves a lot of risk, but the odds improve significantly after the five-year mark.
- *Lack of knowledge and experience:* Entrepreneurs often have expertise in a particular area but lack the background to run a successful business.
- *Too little money:* Lack of start-up money is a major issue for most new firms, since ongoing profits don't usually begin for months, or even years.
- *Bigger regulatory burden:* Small firms spend 45% more per employee than big firms, simply complying with federal regulations.
- *Higher health insurance costs:* Small-scale health plans are much more expensive, making it harder to offer employees competitive coverage.

New Business Survival Rates

Year in Business	Survival Rate	Change vs. Prior Year (percentage points)
Year 1	81%	−19
Year 2	66%	−15
Year 3	54%	−12
Year 4	44%	−10
Year 5	38%	−6
Year 6	34%	−4
Year 7	31%	−3

LO5 Discuss ways to become a new business owner and the tools needed to facilitate success

Many people who are interested in owning their own business prefer to start from scratch and build their company from the ground up. But buying an established business, or even a franchise, can be excellent choices as well. Each choice involves a range of pros and cons, but broadly speaking, it's less risky to buy an established business or franchise, but more satisfying (at least for some people) to start a new venture from scratch. Whichever path you choose—whether you're an ambitious entrepreneur or simply a small business owner—several strategies can help you succeed over the long term: gain experience in your field, learn from others, educate yourself, access SBA resources, and develop a business plan.

BUSINESS LAUNCH OPTIONS

- Starting from scratch
- Buying an established business
- Buying a franchise

STRATEGIES FOR SUCCESS:

- Gain experience
- Learn from others
- Educate yourself
- Access SBA resources
- Develop a plan

LO6 Explain the size, scope, and economic contributions of small business

Small businesses play a vital role in the American economy, generating about half of the U.S. gross domestic product and accounting for 64% of all new jobs over the past 15 years. In addition to fueling employment growth, small businesses contribute innovations to the economy at a much higher rate than their big business counterparts. They also form the backbone of many inner-city economies, finding opportunities—and offering products and services—in places where most large firms opt not to operate. The entrepreneurship rate around the world varies dramatically from country to country, ranging from a high of 45.6% in Peru to a low of 4.4% in Japan. The differences among countries seem to depend largely on the national per capita income, the opportunity costs for entrepreneurs, and the national culture and political environment.

© JOHN ANTHONY RIZZO/BRAND X PICTURES/JUPITERIMAGES

LO1

accounting
A system for recognizing, organizing, analyzing, and reporting information about the financial transactions that affect an organization.

LO2

management accountants
Accountants who work within a business or nonprofit organization, preparing reports and analyzing financial information.

public accountants
Accountants who provide a variety of accounting services for clients on a fee basis.

government accountants
Accountants who work for a wide variety of government agencies at the local, state, and federal levels.

LO3

financial accounting
The branch of accounting that prepares financial statements for use by owners, creditors, suppliers, and other external stakeholders.

generally accepted accounting principles (GAAP)
A set of accounting standards that is used in the preparation of financial statements.

Financial Accounting Standards Board (FASB)
The private board that establishes the generally accepted accounting principles used in the practice of financial accounting.

LO4

balance sheet
A financial statement that reports the financial position of a firm by identifying and reporting the value of the firm's assets, liabilities, and owners' equity.

accounting equation
Assets = Liabilities + Owners' Equity

assets
Resources owned by a firm.

liabilities
Claims that outsiders have against a firm's assets.

owners' equity
The claims a firm's owners have against their company's assets (often called stockholders' equity on balance sheets of corporations).

income statement
The financial statement that reports the revenues, expenses, and net income that resulted from a firm's operations over an accounting period.

revenue
Increases in a firm's assets that result from the sale of goods, provision of services, or other activities intended to earn income.

LO1 Define accounting and explain how accounting information is used by a variety of stakeholders

Accounting is a system for recognizing, organizing, analyzing, and reporting information about the financial transactions that affect an organization. This information is used by virtually all of the firm's stakeholders. Owners want to know whether their firm made a profit or suffered a loss. Creditors want to make sure that the firm has the capacity to repay any loans they make. Employees want to know whether their company is performing well enough to provide job security and a good pay raise. The IRS wants to know the amount of taxable income the firm earns during each period.

LO2 Discuss the career opportunities open to accountants

Management accountants (also called private accountants) work within an organization, analyzing financial information and preparing reports and statements for that organization. Internal auditors are management accountants who are responsible for verifying the accuracy of their organization's internal records and the validity of its accounting procedures. They help a firm improve its performance by identifying areas where mismanagement, waste, and fraud may exist. Public accountants provide a broad range of accounting and consulting services to clients on a fee basis. They may help clients set up accounting systems or assist in tax preparation. Government accountants work for a variety of government agencies at the local, state, and federal levels, and perform tasks similar to those of public and private accountants.

LO3 Identify the goals of generally accepted accounting principles

Generally accepted accounting principles are rules that govern the practice of financial accounting. The goal of these rules is to ensure that the information generated by financial accounting is relevant, reliable, consistent, and comparable.

LO4 Describe the key elements of the major financial statements

The balance sheet shows the firm's financial position at a specific point in time by reporting the value of its assets, liabilities, and owners' equity. The income statement shows the net income (profit or loss) the firm earns over a stated period of time by deducting costs and expenses from revenues. The statement of cash flows shows the inflows and outflows of cash that result from a firm's operations, its financing activities, and its investing activities in a given time period and the net change in the amount of available cash the firm has over that time period.

LO5 Describe the information provided in the independent auditor's report and endnotes to financial statements

U.S. securities laws require publicly traded corporations to have an independent CPA firm perform an annual external audit of its financial statements. The purpose of the audit is to determine whether the statements were properly prepared in accordance with generally accepted accounting principles (GAAP) and fairly present the financial condition of the firm. Annual reports also include endnotes that disclose additional information about the firm's operations, accounting practices, and special circumstances that clarify and supplement the numbers reported on the financial statements. This information can provide important insights that may not be apparent from the figures presented in the financial statements.

LO6 Describe how managerial accounting can help managers with product costing, incremental analysis, and budgeting

Managers must have an accurate measure of the costs incurred to produce their firm's goods and services in order to set prices and evaluate efficiency. In recent years, managerial accountants have begun using a technique called "activity-based costing" to help assign costs more accurately. Incremental analysis helps managers evaluate and compare the impact different alternatives have on costs and revenues in a decision-making situation [Exhibits 8.5 and 8.6]. Budgeting facilitates planning by translating goals into measurable quantities and requiring managers to identify the specific resources needed to achieve them. The budgeting process involves the development of several types of budgets. The firm's master budget brings together all of these documents into a unified whole, representing the firm's overall plan of action for a specified time period.

accrual-basis accounting
The method of accounting that recognizes revenue when it is earned and matches expenses to the revenues they helped produce.

expenses
Resources that are used up as the result of business operations.

net income
The difference between the revenue a firm earns and the expenses it incurs in a given time period.

statement of cash flows
The financial statement that identifies a firm's sources and uses of cash in a given accounting period.

LO5

Sarbanes-Oxley Act of 2002
A law that created the Public Company Accounting Oversight Board and contains provisions to improve external auditing procedures.

horizontal analysis
Analysis of financial statements that compares account values reported on these statements over two or more years to identify changes and trends.

LO6

managerial (or management) accounting
The branch of accounting that provides reports and analysis to managers to help them make informed business decisions.

activity-based costing (ABC)
A technique to assign product costs based on links between activities that drive costs and the production of specific products.

incremental analysis
An evaluation of the financial impact different alternatives would have in a particular decision-making situation.

incremental costs
Costs that change as the result of a decision.

budgeting
A management tool that explicitly shows how firms will acquire and use the resources needed to achieve its goals over a specific time period.

operating budgets
Budgets that communicate an organization's sales and production goals and the resources needed to achieve these goals.

financial budgets
Budgets that focus on the firm's financial goals and identify the resources needed to achieve these goals.

master budget
A presentation of an organization's operational and financial budgets that represents the firm's overall plan of action for a specified time period.

Financial Accounting Statements

Financial Statement	Purpose	Key Components	Basic Relationship
Balance Sheet	Shows the value of a firm's assets at a particular point in time, and identifies the claims owners and outsiders have against those assets.	• Assets: things of value owned by the firm. • Liabilities: claims outsiders have against the firm's assets. • Owners' Equity: claims the owners of a firm have against its assets.	Assets = Liabilities + Owners' Equity
Income Statement	Reports the profit or loss earned by the firm over a given time period.	• Revenues: increases in cash and other assets that the firm earns from its operations. • Expenses: the cash and other resources used up to generate revenue. • Net Income: the profit or loss earned by a firm in a given time period.	Revenues – Expenses = Net Income
Statement of Cash Flows	Shows how and why the amount of cash held by the firm changed over a given period of time by identifying the cash flows from the three sources: operations, investments, and financing.	• Operations: the cash flows that arise from producing and selling goods and services. • Investments: the cash flows resulting from buying and selling fixed assets, and from buying and selling financial securities of other companies. • Financing: cash a firm receives from selling its own securities and cash the firm disburses to pay dividends and interest.	Net change in cash = Total inflow of cash – Total outflow of cash.

Comparison of Financial and Managerial Accounting

Financial Accounting	Managerial Accounting
Is primarily intended to provide information to external stakeholders such as stockholders, creditors, and government regulators	Is primarily intended to provide information to internal stakeholders such as the managers of specific divisions or departments
Prepares a standard set of financial statements	Prepares customized reports designed to deal with specific problems or issues
Presents financial statements on a predetermined schedule (usually quarterly and annually)	Creates reports upon request by management rather than according to a predetermined schedule
Is governed by a set of generally accepted accounting principles	Uses procedures developed internally and is not required to follow GAAP
Summarizes past performance and its impact on the firm's present condition	Provides reports dealing with past performance, but also involves making projections about the future when dealing with planning issues

©ANGEL HERRERO DE FRUTOS/ ISTOCKPHOTO.COM

LO2

financial ratio analysis
Computing ratios that compare values of key accounts listed on a firm's financial statements.

liquid asset
An asset that can quickly be converted into cash with little risk of loss.

liquidity ratios
Financial ratios that measure the ability of a firm to obtain the cash it needs to pay its short-term debt obligations as they come due.

asset management ratios
Financial ratios that measure how effectively a firm is using its assets to generate revenues or cash.

financial leverage
The use of debt in a firm's capital structure.

leverage ratios
Ratios that measure the extent to which a firm relies on debt financing in its capital structure.

profitability ratios
Ratios that measure the rate of return a firm is earning on various measures of investment.

LO3

budgeted income statement
A projection showing how a firm's budgeted sales and costs will affect expected net income. (Also called a *pro forma* income statement.)

budgeted balance sheet
A projected financial statement that forecasts the types and amounts of assets a firm will need to implement its future plans and how the firm will finance those assets. (Also called a *pro forma* balance sheet.)

cash budget
A detailed forecast of future cash flows that helps financial managers identify when their firm is likely to experience temporary shortages or surpluses of cash.

LO4

net working capital
The difference between a firm's current assets and its current liabilities.

cash equivalents
Safe and highly liquid assets that many firms list with their cash holdings on their balance sheet.

commercial paper
Short-term (and usually unsecured) promissory notes issued by large corporations.

U.S. Treasury bills (T-bills)
Short-term marketable IOUs issued by the U.S. federal government.

money market mutual funds
A mutual fund that pools funds from many investors and uses these funds to purchase very safe, highly liquid securities.

LO1 Explain how maximizing shareholder value relates to social responsibility

Meeting social responsibilities is often good for shareholder value. When a company treats its workers, suppliers, and customers with honesty, fairness, and respect, it builds goodwill. This can translate to lower turnover and higher motivation among workers, more customer loyalty, and other advantages that lead to a more valuable company.

LO2 Describe how financial managers use key ratios to evaluate their firm

Financial managers look at four basic types of ratios:
1. Liquidity ratios, such as the current ratio, provide insights into whether the firm will have enough cash to pay its short-term liabilities as they come due.
2. Asset management ratios tell financial managers how effectively a firm is using various assets to generate revenues for their firm.
3. Leverage ratios measure how the firm relies on debt in its capital structure.
4. Profitability ratios, such as return on assets and return on equity, measure the firm's overall success at using resources to create a profit for its owners.

LO3 Discuss how financial managers use budgeted financial statements and cash budgets

The budgeted income statement, budgeted balance sheet, and cash budget are important tools used by financial managers to develop financial plans. The budgeted income statement presents a forecast of expected revenues, expenses, and net income for the planning period. The budgeted balance sheet forecasts the types and amounts of assets a firm will need to implement its future plans. It also helps financial managers determine the amount of additional financing the firm must arrange in order to acquire those assets. The cash budget helps financial managers gain a better understanding of the *timing* of cash flows within the year. This helps financial managers determine when the firm is likely to need additional funds to meet short-term cash shortages, and when surpluses of cash will be available to pay off loans or to invest in other assets.

Major Financial Planning Tools

Tool	Purpose
Budgeted Income Statement	Forecasts the sales, expenses, and revenue for a firm in some future time period.
Budgeted Balance Sheet	Projects the types and amounts of assets a firm will need in order to carry out its plans, and shows the amount of additional financing the firm will need to acquire these assets.
Cash Budget	Projects the timing and amount of cash flows so that management can determine when it will need to arrange for external financing, and when it will have extra cash to pay off loans or invest in other assets.

LO4 Explain the significance of working cap management

Net working capital refers to the difference between a firm's current assets and its current liabilities. Current assets include cash and cash equivalents, accounts receivable, inventories, and other assets expected to be converted into cash or used up in the next year. Financial managers must weigh the costs and benefits of holding these assets to determine how much of each should be acquired. Current liabilities are debts that will come due in the next year such as accounts payable, taxes payable, and notes payable. These debts are an important source of short-term financing to the firm, and represent obligations that must be repaid in the near future.

spontaneous financing
Funds that arise as a natural result of a firm's business operations without the need for special arrangements.

trade credit
Spontaneous financing granted by sellers when they deliver goods and services to customers without requiring immediate payment.

line of credit
A financial arrangement between a firm and a bank in which the bank pre-approves credit up to a specified limit, provided that the firm maintains an acceptable credit rating.

revolving credit agreement
A guaranteed line of credit in which a bank makes a binding commitment to provide a business with funds up to a specified credit limit at any time during the term of the agreement.

factor
A company that provides short-term financing to firms by purchasing their accounts receivables at a discount.

LO5

capital budgeting
The process a firm uses to evaluate long-term investment proposals.

time value of money
The principle that a dollar received today is worth more than a dollar received in the future.

present value
The amount of money that, if invested today at a given rate of interest, would grow to become some future amount in a specified number of time periods.

net present value (NPV)
The sum of the present values of expected future cash flows from an investment minus the cost of that investment.

LO6

capital structure
The mix of equity and debt financing a firm uses to meet its permanent financing needs.

covenants
Conditions lenders place on firms that seek long-term debt financing.

retained earnings
That part of net income that a firm reinvests.

LO5 Explain how financial managers evaluate capital budgeting proposals

Capital budgeting is the process by which financial managers evaluate major long-term investment opportunities, such as proposals to build new facilities or purchase new machinery and equipment. Because capital budgeting investments are expected to generate cash flows for many years, financial managers must take the time value of money into account. The time value of money recognizes that the sooner a cash flow is received the sooner it can be re-invested to earn even more money. Thus the earlier a cash flow is received the more valuable it is. Financial managers take the time value of money into account by computing the present values of all cash flows the proposal will generate. The present value of a sum of money received in the future is the amount of money today that will grow to become that future amount if it is invested at a specified rate of interest. The net present value (NPV) of the project is the sum of the present values of all the estimated future cash flows minus the initial cost of the investment. If the NPV of a project is positive, it will increase the value of the firm. If the NPV is negative, it will decrease the value of the firm.

Decision Rule for Capital Budgeting	
NPV: the sum of the present values of all relevant cash flows resulting from a proposal including the initial cost.	
Result of NPV Calculation	Decision
NPV ≥ 0	Accept proposal ☑
NPV < 0	Reject proposal ☒

Impact of Capital Structure

LOWER Risk — Low Leverage (Mostly Equity) — HIGHER Risk

LOWER Potential Return — High Leverage (Mostly Debt) — HIGHER Potential Return

LO6 Identify the key issues involved in determining a firm's capital structure

A firm's capital structure refers to the extent to which a firm relies on debt and equity to satisfy its permanent financing needs. Debt financing offers tax advantages because interest payments on debt are tax deductible. It also offers the opportunity to use leverage to increase the return to owners during good times. However, debt is risky because the firm is required to make interest payments even when cash is tight. Also, lenders often impose covenants that can restrict the flexibility of management. Equity financing is provided by ownership. It is more flexible and is less risky than debt financing. However, existing owners might not want to dilute their share of ownership by selling additional stock. In addition, use of equity financing means that the firm is forgoing the opportunity to use financial leverage to increase the return to owners.

LO1

common stock
The basic form of ownership in a corporation.

capital gain
The return on an asset that results when its market price rises above the price the investor paid for it.

preferred stock
A type of stock that gives its holder preference over common stockholders in terms of dividends and claims on assets.

bond
A long-term debt instrument issued by a corporation or government entity.

maturity date
The date when a bond will come due.

par value (of a bond)
The value of a bond at its maturity; what the issuer promises to pay the bondholder when the bond matures.

coupon rate
The interest paid on a bond expressed as a percentage of the bond's par value.

current yield
The amount of interest earned on a bond expressed as a percentage of the bond's current market price.

secured bond
A bond backed by the pledge of specific assets.

serial bonds
A series of bonds issued at the same time but having different maturity dates to spread out the repayment of principal.

sinking fund
Funds a firm sets aside and uses to call in bonds or purchase bonds in order to assure an orderly repayment of principal.

callable bond
A bond that the issuer can redeem at a given price prior to its maturity.

convertible bond
A bond that gives its holder the right to exchange it for a stated number of shares of common stock in some specified time period.

LO2

primary securities market
The market where newly issued securities are traded. The primary market is where the firms that issue securities raise additional financial capital.

secondary securities market
The market where previously issued securities are traded.

public offering
A primary market issue in which new securities are offered to any investors who are willing and able to purchase them.

private placement
A primary market issue that is negotiated between the issuing corporation and a small group of accredited investors.

initial public offering (IPO)
The first time a company issues stock that may be bought by the general public.

LO1 Describe the three basic types of securities issued by corporations

Common stock represents basic ownership in a corporation. Common stockholders usually have voting rights and the right to receive a dividend *if* the corporation's board declares one. Some corporations also issue preferred stock. Owners of preferred stock must receive their stated dividend before *any* dividend can be paid to common stockholders. Preferred stockholders also have a preferred claim on assets over common stockholders should the company go bankrupt, but they normally do not have voting rights. Bonds are long-term IOUs issued by corporations or government entities. Firms must pay interest on the bonds they issue and must pay the face value of the bond to the bondholder when the bond matures.

Characteristics of Corporate Securities

Security	Type	Basic Return	Claim on Assets If Firm Is Liquidated	Voting Rights
Common Stock	Equity (ownership)	Dividend (distribution of profits), but only if declared by Board of Directors	Residual claim (after claims of preferred stockholders and bondholders are satisfied)	Yes
Preferred Stock	Equity (ownership)	Dividend—not guaranteed, but with preference in payment over common dividend	Claim on assets before common stockholders but after bondholders	No
Corporate Bond	Debt (long-term IOU)	Interest: legally required payment expressed as a percentage of the bond's par value	Claim on assets must be satisfied before common or preferred stockholders. Claim is sometimes secured by pledge of specific assets	No

LO2 Explain how securities are issued in the primary market and traded on secondary markets

Primary securities markets are where corporations sell newly issued securities to raise financial capital. There are two ways securities can be issued in primary markets. In public offerings, the securities are sold to the general public. In private placements, the securities are sold to a select group of accredited investors. Secondary markets are the venue for trading previously issued securities. There are two major types of secondary markets: securities exchanges and the over-the-counter market. Exchanges, such as the New York Stock Exchange (NYSE) and NASDAQ, list only stocks of corporations that satisfy their listing requirements and pay listing fees. Stocks of most large corporations are listed on one of these exchanges. Stocks of corporations not listed on an exchange are sold on the over-the-counter market through a network of securities dealers.

LO3 Discuss how the government and private organizations regulate securities markets

The securities industry is subject to both state and federal laws. All states have blue sky"laws requiring securities sold within their borders to be registered with a state authority. At the federal level the Securities Act of 1933 requires firms selling securities in the primary market to file a registration statement and prospectus, and the Securities Exchange Act of 1934, established the Securities and Exchange Commission (SEC) and gave it primary responsibility for regulating securities markets. The SEC now delegates much of its regulatory authority to a private organization known as the Financial Industry Regulatory Authority (FINRA).

investment bank
A financial intermediary that specializes in helping firms raise financial capital in primary markets.

underwriting
An arrangement under which an investment banker agrees to purchase all shares of a public offering at an agreed upon price.

accredited investors
An organization or individual investor who meets certain criteria established by the SEC and so qualifies to invest in unregistered securities.

New York Stock Exchange (NYSE)
The largest securities exchange in the United States and the world. After its 2007 merger with a large European exchange, it is formally known as NYSE Euronext.

NASDAQ
A major stock exchange that handles trades through a computerized network.

market makers
Investment companies that specialize in buying and selling specific stocks traded on the NASDAQ exchange or OTC market.

NYSE Hybrid Market
A trading system established by the NYSE in 2006 that allows investors to execute trades through the traditional floor trading or through a newer automated trading system.

over-the-counter (OTC) market
The market where securities that are not listed on exchanges are traded.

electronic communications network (ECN)
An automated, computerized securities trading system that automatically matches buyers and sellers, executing trades quickly and allowing trading when securities exchanges are closed.

LO3

Securities Act of 1933
The first major federal law regulating the securities industry.

Securities Exchange Act of 1934
A federal law dealing with securities regulation that established the Securities and Exchange Commission to oversee the securities industry.

Securities and Exchange Commission
The federal agency with primary responsibility for regulating the securities industry.

self-regulatory organizations (SROs)
Private organizations that develop and enforce standards governing the behavior of their members.

LO4

diversification
A strategy of investing in a wide variety of securities in order to reduce risk.

market order
An order telling a broker to buy or sell a specific security at the best currently available price.

limit order
An order to a broker to buy a specific stock only if its price is below a certain level, or to sell a specific stock only if its price is above a certain level.

LO4 Compare several strategies investors use to invest in securities

Income investors choose securities that tend to generate relatively steady and predictable flows of income. Market timers try to time their purchases of specific stocks to buy low and sell high on a short-term basis. Value investors try to find undervalued stocks. Growth investors often look for stocks in small companies with innovative products and the potential for exceptional growth. Investors using a buy-and-hold approach invest in a broad portfolio of securities with the intention of holding them for a long period of time.

LO5 Explain the investor appeal of mutual funds and exchange traded funds

Though created through very different processes, mutual funds and exchange traded funds (ETFs) offer similar benefits to investors. Both allow individual investors to invest in a wide "market basket of securities" at a relatively low cost. Many mutual funds and ETFs allow investors to achieve the risk-reducing benefits of diversification without having to buy a large number of stocks in separate companies. And both mutual funds and ETFs are highly liquid, meaning they can be easily converted into cash. One difference between ETFs and mutual funds is that ETFs trade just like stocks and can be bought and sold at any time. Mutual funds can only be bought or redeemed at the end of the trading day, after the major securities exchanges have closed.

LO6 Describe how investors can track the performance of their investments

Investors can track broad movements in stock prices by following stock indexes. There are several indexes; the Dow Jones Industrial Average and the Standard & Poor's 500 are two of the best-known. Many websites now provide in-depth information about actively traded securities. These websites allow investors to see current information about a stock's price, volume (number of shares traded), market capitalization (total market value of all outstanding shares), earnings per share (profit per share of stock), and other key statistics by simply typing the stock's symbol in a search box. These sites also offer information about other investments such as mutual funds and ETFs.

LO5

mutual fund
An investment vehicle that pools the contributions of many investors and buys a wide array of stocks or other securities.

exchange traded fund (ETF)
Shares traded on securities markets that represent the legal right of ownership over part of a basket of individual stock certificates or other securities.

LO6

stock index
A statistic that tracks how the prices of a specific set of stocks have changed.

Dow Jones Industrial Average
An index that tracks stock prices of 30 large, well-known U.S. corporations.

Standard & Poor's 500
A stock index based on prices of 500 major U.S. corporations in a variety of industries and market sectors.

NASDAQ Composite
A stock index based on all domestic and foreign stocks listed on the NASDAQ exchange.

Net Asset Value (NAV)
The value of a mutual fund's securities and cash holdings minus any liabilities; usually expressed on a per share basis.

© ISTOCKPHOTO.COM

LO1

marketing
An organizational function and a set of processes for creating, communicating, and delivering value to customers and for managing customer relationships in ways that benefit the organization and its stakeholders.

utility
The ability of goods and services to satisfy consumer "wants."

marketing concept
A business philosophy that makes customer satisfaction—now and in the future—the central focus of the entire organization.

LO2

customer-relationship management (CRM)
The ongoing process of acquiring, maintaining, and growing profitable customer relationships by delivering unmatched value.

value
A customer perception that a product has a better relationship than its competitors between the cost and the benefits.

customer satisfaction
When customers perceive that a good or service delivers value above and beyond their expectations.

customer loyalty
When customers buy a product from the same supplier again and again—sometimes paying even more for it than they would for a competitive product.

LO3

marketing plan
A formal document that defines marketing objectives and the specific strategies for achieving those objectives.

market segmentation
Dividing potential customers into groups of similar people, or segments.

target market
The group of people who are most likely to buy a particular product.

consumer marketers (also known as business-to-consumer or B2C)
Marketers who direct their efforts toward people who are buying products for personal consumption.

business marketers (also known as business-to-business or B2B)
Marketers who direct their efforts toward people who are buying products to use either directly or indirectly to produce other products.

demographic segmentation
Dividing the market into smaller groups based on measurable characteristics about people such as age, income, ethnicity, and gender.

LO1 Discuss the objectives, the process, and the scope of marketing

Marketing means delivering value to your customers with the goal of satisfying their needs and achieving long-term profitability for your organization. Goods and services meet customer needs by providing "utility" (or satisfaction) on an ongoing basis. Marketing has moved well beyond the scope of traditional goods and services, to include people, places, events, and ideas. Much nontraditional marketing involves both public and private not-for-profit organizations, which measure their success in nonmonetary terms. Over the last century, marketing has evolved through a number of phases. The marketing era gave birth to the marketing concept, which is still in force today: a philosophy that customer satisfaction—now and in the future—should be the central focus of the entire organization.

The Evolution of Marketing

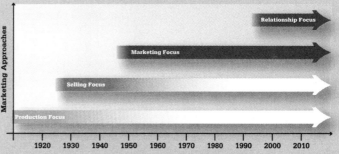

The focus of marketing has evolved over time.

Marketing Approaches (vertical axis)

Relationship Focus
Marketing Focus
Selling Focus
Production Focus

1920 1930 1940 1950 1960 1970 1980 1990 2000 2010

While individual firms differ in their approach to marketing, the prevailing view at leading-edge firms has changed over time as shown here.

LO2 Identify the role of the customer in marketing

Successful marketers always place the customer front and center, with a focus on customer relationship management: acquiring, maintaining, and growing profitable customer relationships by consistently delivering unmatched value. Effective data management and one-on-one personalization are key customer relationship tools. The result of an effective customer-first strategy is loyal customers, who may even be willing to pay more for your product.

LO3 Explain each element of marketing strategy

Marketing strategy essentially involves determining who your *target audience* is and how you will reach them. Choosing the right target begins with *market segmentation*: dividing your market into segments, or groups, of people with similar characteristics. Then you need to determine the best *marketing mix*—the most effective combination of product, pricing, distribution, and promotion strategies to reach your target market. Finally, you must continually monitor each element of the *marketing environment* to ensure that you respond quickly and effectively to change.

Consumer Decision-Making Process

Competitive
Pricing Strategy
Economic
Product Strategy
Social/Cultural
TARGET MARKET
Promotion Strategy
Distribution Strategy
Technological
Political/Legal

LO4 Describe the consumer and business decision-making process

Understanding how customers make decisions will help you meet their needs. When people buy for their own personal consumption, a number of forces influence them, including cultural, social, personal, and psychological factors. For high-risk decisions,

geographic segmentation
Dividing the market into smaller groups based on where consumers live. This process can incorporate countries, cities, or population density as key factors.

psychographic segmentation
Dividing the market into smaller groups based on consumer attitudes, interests, values, and lifestyles.

behavioral segmentation
Dividing the market based on how people behave toward various products. This category includes both the benefits that consumers seek from products and how consumers use the product.

marketing mix
The blend of marketing strategies for product, price, distribution, and promotion.

environmental scanning
The process of continually collecting information from the external marketing environment.

market share
The percentage of a market controlled by a given marketer.

LO4

consumer behavior
Description of how people act when they are buying, using, and discarding goods and services for their own personal consumption. Consumer behavior also explores the reasons behind people's actions.

cognitive dissonance
Consumer discomfort with a purchase decision, typically for a higher-priced item.

business buyer behavior
Describes how people act when they are buying products to use either directly or indirectly to produce other products.

LO5

marketing research
The process of gathering, interpreting, and applying information to uncover marketing opportunities and challenges, and to make better marketing decisions.

secondary data
Existing data that marketers gather or purchase for a research project.

primary data
New data that marketers compile for a specific research project.

observation research
Marketing research that *does not* require the researcher to interact with the research subject.

survey research
Marketing research that requires the researcher to interact with the research subject.

LO6

green marketing
The development and promotion of products with ecological benefits.

mass customization
The creation of products tailored for individual consumers on a mass basis.

they generally follow a decision process, but for low-risk decisions, they often just follow rules of thumb. When people buy for business, they typically are more methodical, driven by product specifications.

Influence	Description
Cultural	*Culture*: the values, attitudes, and customs shared by members of a society *Subculture*: a smaller division of the broader culture *Social Class*: societal position driven largely by income and occupation
Social	*Family*: a powerful force in consumption choices *Friends*: another powerful force, especially for high-profile purchases *Reference Groups*: groups that give consumers a point of comparison
Personal	*Demographics*: measurable characteristics such as age, gender, or income
Psychological	*Personality*: the mix of traits that determine who you are *Motivation*: pressing needs that tend to generate action *Attitudes*: lasting evaluations of (or feelings about) objects or ideas *Perceptions*: how people select, organize, and interpret information *Learning*: changes in behavior based on experience

LO5 Discuss the key elements of marketing research

Marketing research involves gathering, interpreting, and applying information to uncover opportunities and challenges. Primary and secondary data offer complementary strengths and weaknesses. Observation research tools involve gathering data without interacting with the research subjects, while survey tools involve asking research subjects direct questions.

Secondary Data:	Primary Data:
Existing Data That Marketers Gather or Purchase	New Data That Marketers Compile for the First Time
Tends to be lower cost	Tends to be more expensive
May not meet your specific needs	Customized to meet your needs
Frequently outdated	Fresh, new data
Available to your competitors	Proprietary—no one else has it
Examples: U.S. Census, *The Wall Street Journal*, *Time* magazine, your product sales history	Examples: Your own surveys, focus groups, customer comments, mall interviews

LO6 Explain the roles of social responsibility and technology in marketing

The surging social responsibility movement and dramatic advances in technology have had a significant influence on marketing. In addition to seeking long-term profitability, socially responsible marketers actively contribute to meeting the needs of the broader community. Key areas of concern include fair labor practices (especially in foreign markets), environmentalism, and involvement in local communities. The digital boom of the past decade has revolutionized marketing, shifting the balance of power from producers to consumers. The Internet has also created marketing opportunities, helping businesses realize new efficiencies, facilitating more customized service, and generating new promotional opportunities.

LO1 Explain "product" and identify product classifications

A product can be anything that a company offers to satisfy consumer needs and wants; the possibilities include not only physical goods, but also services and ideas. A product also includes all the attributes that consumers associate with it, such as name, image, and guarantees. Goods and services fall along a spectrum from pure goods to pure services. Most products fall somewhere between the two ends, incorporating elements of both goods and services. Products typically encompass three layers: the core benefit, the actual physical good or delivered service, and the augmented product. Customers buy consumer products for personal consumption, and business products to contribute to the production of other products.

LO2 Describe product differentiation and the key elements of product planning

Product differentiation means making your product different from—and better than—the competition. Product planning offers the opportunity to achieve differentiation through elements, such as better quality, better features and benefits, and a stronger brand. These elements are the foundation of an effective product strategy.

Differing Quality Indicators

Product Category	Some Quality Indicators
Internet search engines	Fast, relevant, and far-reaching results
Stylish blue jeans	High-profile designer, high price, and celebrity customers
TV editing equipment	Reliability, flexibility, and customer service

LO3 Discuss innovation and the product life cycle

Innovation can range from small modifications of existing products to brand-new products that change how people live. Either way, for a business to thrive over the long term, effective new product development is vital. The new product development process is meant to streamline product development. The six steps include idea generation, idea screening, analysis, development, testing, and commercialization. After introduction, successful new products move through a life cycle. During the *introduction* phase, a product first hits the market. Marketing generates awareness and trial. During the *growth* phase, sales rise rapidly and profits usually peak. Competitors enter the category. Marketing focuses on gaining new customers. During the *maturity* phase, sales usually peak, while profits fall. Competition intensifies as growth stops. Marketing aims to capture customers from competitors. During the *decline* phase, sales and profits drop. Marketers consider discontinuing products.

LO4 Analyze and explain promotion and integrated marketing communications

Promotion is marketing communication that influences consumers by informing, persuading, and reminding them about products. The most effective promotion builds strong, ongoing relationships between customers and companies. The current promotional environment is changing rapidly. Thanks to technology, consumers have more control over how, when, and even *if* they receive promotional messages. Media has splintered across entertainment options, and consumer viewing patterns have changed. In response, marketers are seeking increasingly creative means to reach their target customers. Their goal is to zero in on the right customers, at the right time, with the right message.

The goal of integrated marketing communications (IMC) is to ensure that consumers receive a unified, focused message regardless of the message source. To make this

store brands
Brands that the retailer both produces and distributes (also called private-label brands).

LO3
product life cycle
A pattern of sales and profits that typically changes over time.

LO4
promotion
Marketing communication designed to influence consumer purchase decisions through information, persuasion, and reminders.

integrated marketing communication
The coordination of marketing messages through every promotional vehicle to communicate a unified impression about a product.

LO5
positioning statement
A brief statement that articulates how the marketer would like the target market to envision a product relative to the competition.

LO6
promotional channels
Specific marketing communication vehicles, including traditional tools, such as advertising, sales promotion, direct marketing, and personal selling, and newer tools such as product placement, advergaming, and Internet minimovies.

product placement
The paid integration of branded products into movies, television, and other media.

advergaming
A relatively new promotional channel that involves integrating branded products and advertising into interactive games.

buzz marketing
The active stimulation of word of mouth via unconventional, and often relatively low-cost, tactics. Other terms for buzz marketing are "guerrilla marketing" and "viral marketing."

sponsorship
A deep association between a marketer and a partner (usually a cultural or sporting event), which involves promotion of the sponsor in exchange for either payment or the provision of goods.

advertising
Paid, nonpersonal communication, designed to influence a target audience with regard to a product, service, organization, or idea.

sales promotion
Marketing activities designed to stimulate immediate sales activity through specific short-term programs aimed at either consumers or distributors.

consumer promotion
Marketing activities designed to generate immediate consumer sales, using tools such as premiums, promotional products, samples, coupons, rebates, and displays.

trade promotion
Marketing activities designed to stimulate wholesalers and retailers to push specific products more aggressively over the short term.

happen, marketers must break through the clutter, coordinating their messages through various promotional vehicles. Everyone who manages the marketing messages must have information about the customer, the product, the competition, the market, and the strategy of the organization. And clearly, solid teamwork is crucial. The result of effective IMC is a relevant, coherent image in the minds of target customers.

LO5 Discuss the development of the promotional message

The promotional message should be a big idea—a meaningful, believable, and distinctive concept that cuts through the clutter. Finding the big idea begins with the positioning statement—a brief statement that articulates how you want your target market to envision your product relative to the competition. A creative development team—often spearheaded by advertising agency professionals—uses the positioning statement as a springboard for finding a big idea. The ideas themselves are typically based on either a rational or an emotional premise, with humor as a recurrent favorite.

LO6 Discuss the promotional mix and the various promotional tools

Buzz marketing travels along social networks

The promotional mix is the combination of promotional tools that a marketer chooses to best communicate the big idea to the target audience. In today's rapidly changing promotional environment, new promotional tools have emerged, and secondary promotional tools have burst into the mainstream. Examples include Internet advertising, product placement, advergaming, buzz marketing, and sponsorships. Yet traditional promotional tools retain enormous clout in terms of both spending and impact on the market. Mainstream advertising has split among a growing array of media options. Sales promotion, designed to stimulate immediate sales, represents a quickly growing area. Public relations, designed to generate positive, unpaid media stories about a company or its products, also aims to boost brand awareness and credibility. Personal selling, designed to close sales and build relationships, continues to play a dominant role in the promotional mix. Selecting the right mix of promotional tools poses an ongoing challenge for many marketers.

public relations (PR)
The ongoing effort to create positive relationships with all of a firm's different "publics," including customers, employees, suppliers, the community, the general public, and the government.

publicity
Unpaid stories in the media that influence perceptions about a company or its products.

personal selling
The person-to-person presentation of products to potential buyers.

push strategy
A marketing approach that involves motivating distributors to heavily promote—or "push"—a product to the final consumers, usually through heavy trade promotion and personal selling.

pull strategy
A marketing approach that involves creating demand from the ultimate consumers so that they "pull" your products through the distribution channels by actively seeking them.

LO1

distribution strategy
A plan for delivering the right product to the right person at the right place at the right time.

channel of distribution
The network of organizations and processes that links producers to consumers.

physical distribution
The actual, physical movement of products along the distribution pathway.

direct channel
A distribution process that links the producer and the customer with no intermediaries.

channel intermediaries
Distribution organizations—informally called "middlemen"—that facilitate the movement of products from the producer to the consumer.

utility
The value, or usefulness, that a good or service offers a customer.

retailers
Distributors that sell products directly to the ultimate users, typically in small quantities, that are stored and merchandised on the premises.

wholesalers
Distributors that buy products from producers and sell them to other businesses or nonfinal users such as hospitals, nonprofits, and the government.

LO2

independent wholesaling businesses
Independent distributors that buy products from a range of different businesses and sell those products to a range of different customers.

merchant wholesalers
Independent distributors who take legal possession, or title, of the goods they distribute.

agents/brokers
Independent distributors who do not take title of the goods they distribute (even though they may take physical possession on a temporary basis before distribution).

LO3

multichannel retailing
Providing multiple distribution channels for consumers to buy a product.

wheel of retailing
A classic distribution theory that suggests that retail firms and retail categories become more upscale as they go through their life cycles.

LO4

supply chain
All organizations, processes, and activities involved in the flow of goods from their raw materials to the final consumer.

LO1 Define distribution and differentiate between channels of distribution and physical distribution

Distribution is the element of the marketing mix that involves getting the right product to the right customers in the right place at the right time. A channel of distribution is the path that a product takes from the producer to the consumer, while physical distribution is the actual movement of products along that path. Distributors add value by reducing the number of transactions—and the associated costs—required for goods to flow from producers to consumers. Distributors can also add a range of different utilities:

- *Form Utility:* Provides customer satisfaction by converting inputs into finished products.
- *Time Utility:* Adds value by making products available at a convenient time for consumers.
- *Place Utility:* Satisfies customer needs by providing the right products in the right place.
- *Ownership Utility:* Adds value by making it easier for customers to actually possess the goods and services that they purchase.
- *Information Utility:* Boosts customer satisfaction by providing helpful information.
- *Service Utility:* Adds value by providing fast, friendly, personalized service.

How transactions are reduced through marketing intermediaries

| Manufacturer | Manufacturer | Manufacturer | Manufacturer |

| Customer | Customer | Customer | Customer |

| Manufacturer | Manufacturer | Manufacturer | Manufacturer |

Marketing Intermediary

| Customer | Customer | Customer | Customer |

LO2 Describe the various types of wholesale distributors

Wholesalers buy products from the producer and sell them to other businesses and organizations. The two key categories of wholesalers are:

- *Merchant wholesalers* who take legal title to the goods they distribute. Full-service merchant wholesalers provide a wide array of services, whereas limited-service merchant wholesalers offer more focused services.
- *Agents and brokers* who connect buyers and sellers in exchange for commissions, but without taking legal ownership of the goods they distribute.

LO3 Discuss strategies and trends in store and nonstore retailing

Retailers are the final stop before the consumer on the distribution path. The two main retail categories are store and nonstore, but the line between the two has blurred as more and more retailers are pursuing a multichannel approach with online and offline outlets supporting each other. Key nonstore retail approaches include online retailing, direct response retailing, direct selling, and vending. As competition intensifies, a growing segment of retailers (both store and nonstore) have distinguished themselves by offering their customers an entertainment-like experience.

Retailers Add Value for Consumers

Product Selection
Look and Feel
Customer Service
Location
Promotion
Pricing
TARGET MARKET

RETAILING

| Store | Nonstore |

supply chain management (SCM)
Planning and coordinating the movement of products along the supply chain, from the raw materials to the final consumers.

logistics
A subset of supply chain management that focuses largely on the tactics involved in moving products along the supply chain.

modes of transportation
The various transportation options—such as planes, trains, and railroads—for moving products through the supply chain.

LO5

penetration pricing
A new product pricing strategy that aims to capture as much of the market as possible through rock-bottom prices.

everyday-low-pricing (EDLP)
Long-term discount pricing, designed to achieve profitability through high sales volume.

high/low pricing
A pricing strategy designed to drive traffic to retail stores by special sales on a limited number of products, and higher everyday prices on others.

loss leader pricing
Closely related to high/low pricing, loss leader pricing means pricing a handful of items—or loss leaders—temporarily below cost to drive traffic.

skimming pricing
A new product pricing strategy that aims to maximize profitability by offering new products at a premium price.

LO6

breakeven analysis
The process of determining the number of units a firm must sell to cover all costs.

profit margin
The gap between the cost and the price of an item on a per product basis.

odd pricing
The practice of ending prices in numbers below even dollars and cents in order to create a perception of greater value.

LO4 Explain the key factors in physical distribution

As marketers manage the movement of products through the supply chain, they must make decisions regarding each of the following factors:

- *Warehousing:* How many warehouses do we need? Where should we locate our warehouses?
- *Materials handling:* How should we move products within our facilities? How can we best balance efficiency with effectiveness?
- *Inventory control:* How much inventory should we keep on hand? How should we store and distribute it? What about taxes and insurance?
- *Order processing:* How should we manage incoming and outgoing orders? What would be most efficient for our customers and suppliers?
- *Customer service:* How can we serve our customers most effectively? How can we reduce waiting times and facilitate interactions?
- *Transportation:* How can we move products most efficiently through the supply chain? What are the key trade-offs?

Elements of the Supply Chain

- Raw Materials
- Logistics (transportation, coordination, etc.)
- Warehouse/Storage
- Production
- Warehouse/Storage
- Logistics (transportation, coordination, etc.)
- Distributors–Marketing and Sales

LO5 Outline core pricing objectives and strategies

Many marketers continually evaluate and refine their pricing strategies to ensure that they meet their goals. Even the goals themselves may shift in response to the changing market. Key objectives and strategies include:

- Building profitability
- Driving volume
- Meeting the competition
- Creating prestige

Pricing Considerations

Demand, Competition, Costs, Investors, Taxes, Product Strategy, Distributors, Laws → $ PRICE $

LO6 Discuss pricing in practice, including the role of consumer perceptions

While most marketers are familiar with economics, they often don't have the information they need to apply the theories to their specific pricing strategies. Because of those limitations, most companies *consider* market-based factors—especially customer expectations and competitive prices—but they rely on cost-based pricing: what should we charge to cover our costs and make a profit? Common approaches include breakeven analysis and fixed margin pricing. Many marketers also account for consumer perceptions, especially the link between price and perceived quality, and odd pricing. If no other information is available, consumers will often assume that higher-priced products are higher quality. Odd pricing means ending prices in dollars and cents rather than round numbers (e.g., $999.99 versus $1,000) in order to create a perception of greater value.

"It's a deal!" — $29.⁹⁹

"It's higher quality!" — $30.⁰⁰

$$\text{Breakeven Point} = \frac{\text{Total Fixed Costs}}{\text{Price/Unit} - \text{Variable Cost/Unit}}$$

© PIXLAND/JUPITERIMAGES

LO1

management
Achieving the goals of an organization through planning, organizing, leading, and controlling organizational resources including people, money, and time.

planning
Determining organizational goals and action plans for how to achieve those goals.

organizing
Determining a structure for both individual jobs and the overall organization.

leading
Directing and motivating people to achieve organizational goals.

controlling
Checking performance and making adjustments as needed.

top management
Managers who set the overall direction of the firm, articulating a vision, establishing priorities, and allocating time, money, and other resources.

middle management
Managers who supervise lower-level managers and report to a higher-level manager.

first-line management
Managers who directly supervise nonmanagement employees.

technical skills
Expertise in a specific functional area or department.

human skills
The ability to work effectively with and through other people in a range of different relationships.

conceptual skills
The ability to grasp a big-picture view of the overall organization, the relationship between its various parts, and its fit in the broader competitive environment.

LO2

Maslow's hierarchy of needs theory
A motivation theory that suggests that human needs fall into a hierarchy and that as each need is met, people become motivated to meet the next highest need in the pyramid.

Theory X and Theory Y
A motivation theory that suggests that management attitudes toward workers fall into two opposing categories based on management assumptions about worker capabilities and values.

job enrichment
The creation of jobs with more meaningful content, under the assumption that challenging, creative work will motivate employees.

expectancy theory
A motivation theory that deals with the relationship among individual effort, individual performance, and individual reward.

LO1 Discuss the role of management and its importance to organizational success

The formal definition of management is to achieve the goals of an organization through planning, organizing, leading, and controlling organizational resources. Managers provide vision for their company and inspire others to follow their lead. Most medium-size and large companies have three basic management levels: top management, middle management, and first-line (or supervisory) management. Managers must draw on a wide range of skills, but most of their abilities cluster into three key categories: technical skills, human skills, and conceptual skills. All three skill sets are essential for management success, but in different proportions at each managerial level.

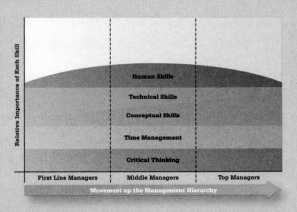

LO2 Explain key theories and current practices of motivation

Research suggests that people's thoughts and feelings play a vital role in motivation. Key theories that incorporate this perspective include Maslow's hierarchy of needs, Theory X and Theory Y, job enrichment, expectancy theory, and equity theory. In today's business environment, leading-edge firms nourish distinctive, positive cultures that tend to create productive employees who are deeply attached to both their work and their companies. Many also focus on training and education, which are especially motivating for the growing cadre of employees who identify themselves based on their field of expertise rather than their organization.

Maslow's Hierarchy of Needs

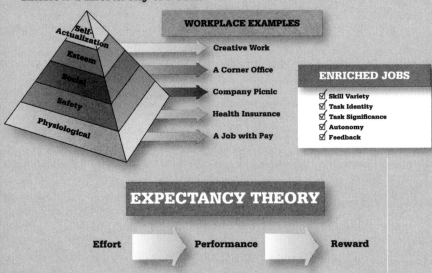

equity theory
A motivation theory that proposes that perceptions of fairness directly affect worker motivation.

LO3

strategic planning
High-level, long-term planning that establishes a vision for the company, defines long-term objectives and priorities, determines broad action steps, and allocates resources.

tactical planning
More specific, shorter-term planning that applies strategic plans to specific functional areas.

operational planning
Very specific, short-term planning that applies tactical plans to daily, weekly, and monthly operations.

contingency planning
Planning for unexpected events, usually involving a range of scenarios and assumptions that differ from the assumptions behind the core plans.

mission
The definition of an organization's purpose, values, and core goals, which provides the framework for all other plans.

SWOT analysis
A strategic planning tool that helps management evaluate an organization in terms of internal strengths and weakness, and external opportunities and threats.

strategic goals
Concrete benchmarks that managers can use to measure performance in each key area of the organization.

strategies
Action plans that help the organization achieve its goals by forging the best fit between the firm and the environment.

LO4

organization chart
A visual representation of the company's formal structure.

degree of centralization
The extent to which decision-making power is held by a small number of people at the top of the organization.

span of control
Span of management; refers to the number of people that a manager supervises.

departmentalization
The division of workers into logical groups.

line organizations
Organizations with a clear, simple chain of command from top to bottom.

line-and-staff organizations
Organizations with line managers forming the primary chain of authority in the company, and staff departments working alongside line departments.

line managers
Managers who supervise the functions that contribute directly to profitability: production and marketing.

staff managers
Managers who supervise the functions that provide advice and assistance to the line departments.

matrix organizations
Organizations with a flexible structure that brings together specialists from different areas of the company to work on individual projects on a temporary basis.

LO3 Outline the categories of business planning and explain strategic planning

The four main categories of business planning are strategic planning, tactical planning, operational planning, and contingency planning. Strategic planning, handled by top managers, sets the broad direction of the organization, typically over a five-year horizon. Strategic planning guides the entire planning process, since all other plans—and most major management decisions—stem from the strategic plan. Given fierce competition and often-unpredictable change, most large firms revise their strategic plans on a yearly basis

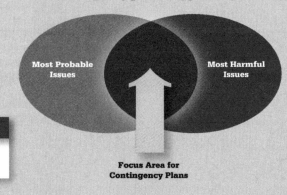

Contingency planning paradigm

Most Probable Issues

Most Harmful Issues

EFFECTIVE GOALS
- ☑ Specific and Measurable
- ☑ Tied to a Timeframe
- ☑ Realistic but Challenging

Focus Area for Contingency Plans

LO4 Discuss the organizing function of management

The organizing function of management means creating a logical structure for people, their jobs, and their patterns of interaction. In choosing the right structure for a specific company, management must consider many different factors, including the goals and strategies of the firm, its products, and its size. Management must also make decisions about the degree of centralization, the span of management control, and the type of departmentalization. Company structures tend to follow one of three different patterns: line organizations, line-and-staff organizations, and matrix organizations.

LO5 Explain the role of managerial leadership and the key leadership styles

Effective business leaders motivate others to achieve the goals of their organization. Most experts agree that true leaders are trustworthy, visionary, and inspiring. Other key leadership traits include empathy, courage, creativity, intelligence, fairness, and energy. While leaders have a range of different styles, three main approaches include autocratic, democratic, and free-rein. The best leaders tend to use all three approaches, shifting style in response to the needs of the followers and the situation.

LO6 Describe the management control process

Controlling means monitoring performance of the firm—or individuals within the firm—and making improvements when necessary. As the environment changes, plans change. And as plans change, the control process must change to ensure that the company achieves its goals. The control process has three main steps:
1. Establish clear performance standards.
2. Measure actual performance against standards.
3. Take corrective action if necessary.

LO5

autocratic leaders
Leaders who hoard decision-making power for themselves and typically issue orders without consulting their followers.

democratic leaders
Leaders who share power with their followers. While they still make final decisions, they typically solicit and incorporate input from their followers.

free-rein leaders
Leaders who set objectives for their followers but give them freedom to choose how they accomplish those goals.

© COMSTOCK IMAGES/JUPITERIMAGES

LO1

human resource management
The management function focused on maximizing the effectiveness of the workforce by recruiting world-class talent, promoting career development, and determining workforce strategies to boost organizational effectiveness.

LO4

job analysis
The examination of specific tasks that are assigned to each position, independent of who might be holding the job at any specific time.

job description
An explanation of the responsibilities for a specific position.

job specifications
The specific qualifications necessary to hold a particular position.

internal recruitment
The process of seeking employees who are currently within the firm to fill open positions.

external recruitment
The process of seeking new employees from outside the firm.

structured interviews
An interviewing approach that involves developing a list of questions beforehand and asking the same questions in the same order to each candidate.

probationary period
A specific timeframe (typically three to six months) during which a new hire can prove his or her worth on the job before the hire becomes permanent.

contingent workers
Employees who do not expect regular, full-time jobs, including temporary full-time workers, independent contractors, and temporary agency or contract agency workers.

orientation
The first step in the training and development process, designed to introduce employees to the company culture, and provide key administrative information.

on-the-job training
A training approach that requires employees to simply begin their jobs—sometimes guided by more experienced employees—and to learn as they go.

apprenticeships
Structured training programs that mandate that each beginner serve as an assistant to a fully trained worker before gaining full credentials to work in the field.

management development
Programs to help current and potential executives develop the skills they need to move into leadership positions.

LO1 Explain the importance of human resources to business success

A world-class workforce can lead straight to world-class performance. Human resource managers can directly contribute to that goal by recruiting top talent, promoting career development, and boosting organizational effectiveness. Yet human resource departments typically face numerous challenges in making this happen.

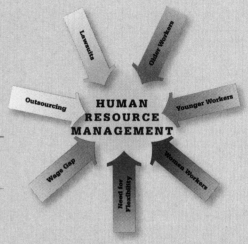

LO2 Discuss key human resource issues in today's economy

As the economy and society continue to change rapidly, a number of issues have emerged that directly affect human resources. As the recession tightened its grip in 2009, massive layoffs thrust human resources into turmoil. The growing wage gap between senior managers and the average employee has created tension for a number of stakeholders. Older workers have begun to retire, while younger workers often bring an unprecedented sense of entitlement. Many women are leaving traditional jobs. Workers are actively seeking more flexibility and a better work–life balance. And the number of costly employee lawsuits has skyrocketed in the last couple of decades.

LO3 Outline challenges and opportunities that the human resources function faces

While HR workers tend to have strong people skills, many lack the business acumen to contribute directly to broad company objectives, and other departments often view HR as either irrelevant or adversarial. HR can respond to these issues by demonstrating that they understand the strategic goals of the company, the core customers, and the competition. The best HR departments use this knowledge to raise the value of the firm's human capital, which in turn increases the value of the firm itself.

LO4 Discuss human resource planning and core human resources responsibilities

Human resource planning objectives must flow from the company's master plan, and the HR strategies must reflect company priorities. The first step should be to determine where the firm currently stands in terms of human resources and to forecast future needs. Other key areas of focus follow:

- *Recruitment:* The key to recruitment is finding *qualified* candidates who fit well with the organization. The right people can come from either internal or external labor pools.
- *Selection:* Choosing the right person from a pool of candidates typically involves applications, interviews, tests, and references. The terms of the job offer itself play a role as well.
- *Training:* The training process begins with orientation but should continue throughout each employee's tenure. Options include on-the-job training, off-the-job training, and management development.

performance appraisal
A formal feedback process that requires managers to give their subordinates feedback on a one-to-one basis, typically by comparing actual results to expected results.

compensation
The combination of pay and benefits that employees receive in exchange for their work.

wages
The pay that employees receive in exchange for the number of hours or days that they work.

salaries
The pay that employees receive over a fixed period, most often weekly or monthly.

benefits
Noncash compensation, including programs, such as health insurance, vacation, and childcare.

cafeteria-style benefits
An approach to employee benefits that gives all employees a set dollar amount that they must spend on company benefits, allocated however they wish within broad limitations.

flextime
A scheduling option that allows workers to choose when they start and finish their workdays, as long as they complete the required number of hours.

compressed workweek
A version of flextime scheduling that allows employees to work a full-time number of hours in less than the standard workweek.

telecommuting
Working remotely—most often from home—and connecting to the office via phone lines, fax machines, and broadband networks.

LO5

Civil Rights Act of 1964
Federal legislation that prohibits discrimination in hiring, firing, compensation, apprenticeships, training, terms, conditions, or privileges of employment based on race, color, religion, sex, or national origin.

Title VII
A portion of the Civil Rights Act of 1964 that prohibits discrimination in hiring, firing, compensation, apprenticeships, training, terms, conditions, or privileges of employment based on race, color, religion, sex, or national origin for employers with 15 or more workers.

Equal Employment Opportunity Commission (EEOC)
A federal agency designed to regulate and enforce the provisions of Title VII.

affirmative action
Policies meant to increase employment and educational opportunities for minority groups—especially groups defined by race, ethnicity, or gender.

sexual harassment
Workplace discrimination against a person based on his or her gender.

- *Evaluation:* Performance feedback should happen constantly. But most firms also use formal, periodic performance appraisals to make decisions about compensation, promotions, training, transfers, and terminations.
- *Compensation:* Compensation includes both pay and benefits. Interestingly, companies that offer higher compensation generally outperform their competitors in terms of total return to shareholders.
- *Separation:* Employees leave their jobs for both positive and negative reasons. When the separation is not voluntary—e.g., layoffs or termination—fairness and documentation are critical.

EMPLOYEE EVALUATION

Employee   Manager
Feedback should be continual

Considerations for Compensation

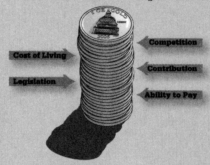

Cost of Living

Legislation

Competition

Contribution

Ability to Pay

Variable Pay System
- Commission
- Bonuses
- Profit sharing
- Stock options
- Pay for knowledge

FLEXIBLE SCHEDULING

- Flextime
- Telecommuting
- Job Sharing

LO5 Explain the key federal legislation that affects human resources

Perhaps the most influential piece of employment legislation is the Civil Rights Act of 1964. Title VII of this act prohibits discrimination in hiring, firing, compensation, apprenticeships, training, terms, conditions, or privileges of employment based on race, color, religion, sex, or national origin. Additional legislation prohibits discrimination based on pregnancy, age, and disability. The Equal Employment Opportunity Commission (EEOC) enforces the provisions of Title VII. Affirmative action programs—while controversial—have received support from the Supreme Court. And human resource managers must guard against sexual harassment in the organization, since it violates Title VII.

Visit **www.cengagebrain.com**
for additional study tools!

© DAVID & LES JACOBS/BLEND IMAGES/JUPITERIMAGES

LO1

hardware
The physical tools and equipment used to collect, input, store, organize, and process data and to distribute information.

software
Programs that provide instructions to a computer so that it can perform a desired task.

system software
Software that performs the critical functions necessary to operate the computer at the most basic level.

applications software
Software that helps a user perform a desired task.

Internet
The world's largest computer network; essentially a network of computer networks all operating under a common set of rules that allow them to communicate with each other.

Internet2 (I2)
A new high-tech Internet restricted to dues-paying members of a consortium. I2 utilizes technologies that give it a speed and capacity far exceeding the current Internet.

intranet
A network that has the look and feel of the Internet, and is navigated using a Web browser, but is confined to documents located on a single company's servers and is available only to the firm's employees.

extranet
An intranet that allows limited access to a selected group of stakeholders, such as suppliers or customers.

LO2

cloud computing
The use of Internet-based storage capacity, processing power, and computer applications to supplement or replace internally owned information technology resources.

LO3

data
Raw, unprocessed facts and figures.

information
Data that have been processed in a way that makes them meaningful to their user.

database
A file consisting of related data organized according to a logical system and stored on a hard drive or some other computer-accessible media.

decision support system (DSS)
A system that gives managers access to large amounts of data and the processing power to convert these data into high-quality information, thus improving the decision-making process.

business intelligence system
A sophisticated form of decision support system that helps decision makers discover information that was previously hidden.

LO1 Explain the basic elements of computer technology—including hardware, software, and network decisions—and analyze key trends in each area

Hardware is the physical equipment used to collect, store, organize, and process data and to distribute information. Examples include hard drives, keyboards, and printers. Software consists of computer programs that provide instructions to a computer. System software performs the critical functions necessary to operate the computer at the most basic level. Applications software helps users perform a desired task. Both hardware and software have become much more powerful, easier to use, and less expensive over the last several decades. Most firms (and many households) now use networks to enable users to communicate with each other and share both files and hardware resources. The Internet is a vast network of computer networks. The part of the Internet used most by the general public is the World Wide Web, which consists of billions of documents written and linked together using Hypertext Markup Language (HTML). In recent years, the availability of broadband connections to the Web has made it possible to share large video and audio files. A high-tech version of the Internet, known as Internet2, allows dues-paying corporations, universities, and government agencies to exchange information and collaborate with each other at much higher speeds than the fastest broadband connections currently available on the public Internet. Many organizations have developed intranets that have the same look and feel as the Internet but are limited to servers within an organization. Extranets are intranets that provide limited access to specific stakeholders, such as customers or suppliers.

LO2 Discuss the reasons for the increasing popularity of cloud computing

Cloud computing means going beyond a company's firewall to store data and run applications using Internet-based resources. Cloud computing allows firms to obtain storage space, processing power, and software without investing heavily in internally owned hardware, software, and other IT resources. Users of cloud computing can quickly adjust their computing resources as their needs change, and pay only for the resources they actually use. This can substantially reduce IT costs. Cloud computing also makes it easier for people in different organizations to collaborate since resources in the cloud are not tied to a specific type of hardware or operating system.

LO3 Describe how data become information and how decision support systems can provide high-quality information that helps managers make better decisions

Data refers to the facts and figures a firm collects. Data become information when they are processed, organized, and presented in a way that is meaningful to a decision maker. Many companies develop decision support systems (DSS) that give managers access to large amounts of data and the processing power to convert the data into high-quality information. Business intelligence systems are the newest version of DSS. These systems usually take advantage of data-mining techniques to discover information that was previously buried in masses of data. Firms sometimes develop expert systems to help decision makers when they must deal with problems beyond their expertise. To develop an expert system, programmers ask experts in the relevant area to provide step by step instructions describing how they solve a problem. The programmers then write software that mimics the expert's approach and guides the decision maker toward a good solution.

High-Quality Information Is:	
1. Accurate	Free from errors and omissions
2. Relevant	Deals with issues that are important to the decision maker
3. Timely	Available in time to make a difference to the decision maker
4. Understandable	Presented in a way that allows decision makers to grasp its meaning and significance
5. Secure	Stored and presented in a way that makes it difficult for hackers and competitors to obtain it

data warehouse
A large, organization-wide database that stores data in a centralized location.

data mining
The use of sophisticated statistical and mathematical techniques to analyze data and discover hidden patterns and relationships among data, thus creating valuable information.

expert system (ES)
A decision-support system that helps managers make better decisions in an area where they lack expertise.

LO4

e-commerce
The marketing, buying, selling, and servicing of products over a network (usually the Internet).

business-to-consumer (B2C) e-commerce
E-commerce in which businesses and final consumers interact.

business-to-business (B2B) e-commerce
E-commerce in markets where businesses buy from and sell to other businesses.

Web 2.0
An approach to e-commerce that emphasizes interactive and collaborative commercial websites in order to develop consumer loyalty and create more value.

viral marketing
An Internet marketing strategy that tries to involve customers and others not employed by the seller in activities that help promote the product.

cybermediary
An Internet-based firm that specializes in the secure electronic transfer of funds.

electronic bill presentment and payment
A method of bill payment that makes it easy for the customer to make a payment, often by simply clicking on a payment option contained in an email.

e-marketplace
A specialized Internet site where buyers and sellers engaged in business-to-business e-commerce can communicate and conduct business.

radio frequency identification (RFID)
A technology that stores information on small microchips than can transmit the information anytime they are within range of a special reader.

LO5

spyware
Software that is installed on a computer without the user's knowledge or permission for the purpose of tracking the user's behavior.

computer virus
Computer software that can be spread from one computer to another without the knowledge or permission of the computer users.

LO4 Explain how Internet-based technologies have changed business-to-consumer and business-to-business commerce

Information technology, and especially the Internet, has revolutionized the way firms interact with their customers in both the business-to-consumer (B2C) and business-to-business (B2B) markets. However, B2C and B2B have very different characteristics, so the way firms use information technology in these two types of markets tends to be quite different. In the B2C market, the Internet has enabled firms to reach broader markets, advertise in new ways, and take customer relationship marketing to a new level. In the B2B market, e-marketplaces enable firms to negotiate with suppliers or customers more effectively and share information that leads to better coordination and collaboration. Radio frequency identification (RFID) chips are another technology that has revolutionized the B2B market by making it easier to coordinate and track shipments as they move through the supply chain.

LO5 Describe the problems posed by the rapid changes in Internet-based technologies, and explain ways to deal with these problems

The rapid development of Internet-based technologies has created enormous business opportunities, but it has also created several challenges and raised some controversial issues. The Internet has made it easier for spyware and viruses to land on your computer, undermining the security and stability of your system. Regular backups of hard drives, the use of updated antivirus and antispyware software, and frequent updating of the computer's operating system can reduce (but not eliminate) these threats. Spam is unsolicited commercial email, usually sent to huge numbers of people with little regard for whether they have any interest in the message. Spam filters are available, but spammers are good at finding ways to fool the filters. Phishing and pharming are scams that use fake websites to trick people into divulging private information. Most phishing scams rely on links embedded in emails to send victims to the fake sites, so it's important to be suspicious of requests to divulge private information via email. One of the most controversial impacts of information technology has been the potential loss of personal privacy. For example, email messages are usually stored on many computers, making it possible for people to locate and view messages that their senders believed were private communications. Some personal privacy advocates are also concerned about the use of RFID chips in driver's licenses and passports, fearing they may allow the government to track individuals. A final issue involves intellectual property. The Internet makes it possible to share videos, music, and computer programs with huge numbers of people, leading to a surge in the illegal sharing of copyrighted material. Owners of copyrighted materials have developed methods to make illegal file sharing harder and have become more aggressive at prosecuting those involved in piracy.

spam
Unsolicited email advertisements usually sent to very large numbers of recipients, many of whom may have no interest in the message.

phishing
A scam in which official-looking emails are sent to individuals in an attempt to get them to divulge private information such as passwords, user names, and account numbers.

pharming
A scam that seeks to steal identities by routing Internet traffic to fake websites.

hacker
A skilled computer user who uses his or her expertise to gain unauthorized access to the computer (or computer system) of others, sometimes with malicious intent.

firewall
Software and/or hardware designed to prevent unwanted access to a computer or computer system.

intellectual property
Property that is the result of creative or intellectual effort, such as books, musical works, inventions, and computer software.

LO1

operations management
Planning, organizing, leading, and controlling the activities involved in producing goods and services and distributing them to customers.

effectiveness
Using resources to create the greatest value.

efficiency
Producing output or achieving a goal at the lowest cost.

goods
Tangible products.

services
Intangible products.

LO2

value chain
The network of relationships that channels the flow of inputs, information, and financial resources through all of the processes involved in producing and distributing goods and services.

offshoring
Moving production or support processes to foreign countries.

process
A set of activities or steps that combine inputs in order to create a desired output.

servicescape
The environment in which a customer and service provider interact.

inventory
Stocks of finished items, work in process, parts, materials, or other resources held by an organization.

Gantt chart
A chart used to track the progress of activities involved in completing a project.

critical path method (CPM)
A project management tool that illustrates the relationships among all the activities involved in completing a project and identifies the sequence of activities likely to take the longest to complete.

immediate predecessors
Activities in a project that must be completed before some other specified activity can begin.

critical path
The sequence of activities in a project that is expected to take the longest to complete.

LO3

automation
Replacing human operation and control of machinery and equipment with some form of programmed control.

robot
A reprogrammable machine that is capable of manipulating materials, tools, parts, and specialized devices in order to perform a variety of tasks.

LO1 Discuss the role of operations management in business

Operations management oversees all the activities involved in creating the right goods and services in the right quantities and distributing them to the right customers. The decisions of operations management can have a major impact on both the revenue and costs a firm incurs, and therefore on the firm's financial success. The goals of operations management center on two key concepts: effectiveness and efficiency. **Effectiveness** means completing tasks and producing products that *create value by satisfying wants*. **Efficiency** refers to completing a task or producing a product at the *lowest cost*. Both efficiency and effectiveness are important; a firm must provide customers with goods and services that satisfy their wants—otherwise customers won't buy them. But in today's competitive markets it must also keep costs under control in order to earn an attractive profit.

Differences Between Goods and Services

Goods	Services
Are tangible: they have a physical form and can be seen, touched, handled, etc.	Are intangible: they can be "experienced," but they don't have a physical form.
Can be stored in an inventory.	Must be consumed when they are produced.
Can be shipped.	Must be consumed where they are provided.
Are produced independently of the consumer.	Often require the customer to be actively involved in their production.
Can have at least some aspects of their quality determined objectively by measuring defects or deviations from desired values.	Intangible nature means quality is based mainly on customer perceptions.

LO2 Describe the key responsibilities of operations managers

Operations management is a very broad field. Operations managers often play a role in the design of products by helping designers understand the challenges and constraints involved in producing high-quality products on time and within budget. Once the design is finalized, operations managers must perform a variety of functions as they take the product from the drawing board to the final user. These tasks include (but are not limited to) selecting the best locations for facilities; determining the best production processes to convert inputs into outputs; designing a facility layout that creates an efficient flow of materials, parts, and work in process through the production process; making decisions about how much inventory to hold; and using Gantt charts, CPM networks, and other project management tools to determine how to allocate resources needed to complete complex projects.

LO3 Explain how technology has influenced operations management

Rapid changes in both machinery and equipment and in software and information technologies have revolutionized operations management. The biggest change in machinery and equipment has been the increasing use of automation, which means replacing human operation and control of machinery and equipment with programmed control. Robots, which are reprogrammable machines that can manipulate materials, tools, parts, and specialized devices in order to perform a variety of tasks, are a key example of automation. The development of software applications to allow computer-aided design (CAD), computer-aided engineering (CAE), and computer-aided manufacturing (CAM) has given firms the flexibility to design, test, and produce goods more quickly and efficiently than ever before. When these powerful software applications are integrated with robots and other automated equipment, the result is called computer integrated manufacturing. This tight integration allows firms to produce customized goods quickly and at low cost, a process called "mass customization."

computer-aided design (CAD)
Drawing and drafting software that enables users to create and edit blueprints and design drawings quickly and easily.

computer-aided engineering (CAE)
Software that enables users to test, analyze, and optimize their designs.

computer-aided manufacturing (CAM)
Software that takes the electronic design for a product and creates the programmed instructions that robots must follow to produce that product as efficiently as possible.

computer-aided design/computer-aided manufacturing (CAD/CAM)
A combination of software that can be used to design output and send instructions to automated equipment to perform the steps needed to produce this output.

computer-integrated manufacturing (CIM)
A combination of CAD/CAM software with flexible manufacturing systems to automate almost all steps involved in designing, testing, and producing a product.

LO4

vertical integration
Performance of processes internally that were previously performed by other organizations in a supply chain.

outsourcing
Arranging for other organizations to perform supply chain functions that were previously performed internally.

enterprise resource planning (ERP)
Software-based approach to integrate an organization's systems in order to improve the flow of information among all departments and operating units.

LO5

total quality management (TQM)
An approach to quality improvement that calls for everyone within an organization to take responsibility for improving quality and emphasizes the need for a long-term commitment to continuous improvement.

poka-yokes
Simple methods incorporated into a production process designed to eliminate or greatly reduce errors.

Six Sigma
An approach to quality improvement characterized by very ambitious quality goals, extensive training of employees, and a long-term commitment to working on quality-related issues.

Baldrige National Quality Program
A national program to encourage American firms to focus on quality improvement.

ISO 9000
A set of generic standards for quality management systems established by the International Organization for Standardization.

LO4 Discuss how operations managers integrate operations using supply chain management and enterprise resource planning

Two key examples of integrated operations systems are supply chain management systems and enterprise resource planning (ERP). Supply chains involve the flow of materials, goods, services, financial resources, and information among all the organizations involved in production and distribution of a good or service. From an operations management perspective, one of the most important elements of supply chain management is determining which functions to perform internally and which functions to outsource. The goal of enterprise resource planning is to integrate the information flows from *all* aspects of a business's operations—accounting, finance, sales and marketing, production, and human resources. Such systems greatly reduce the duplication of data entry and make it easier for the various departments and divisions to communicate and coordinate their actions. But ERP systems can be challenging and expensive to implement.

LO5 Discuss the ways operations managers can foster continuous quality improvement within their organizations

Quality can be defined in many ways, but operations managers usually define it in terms of how well a good or service satisfies customer preferences. Improvements in quality are a key to competitive advantage because they enable a firm to improve both its effectiveness *and* its efficiency. Better quality improves effectiveness because high quality creates value to the customer. It improves efficiency because good quality tends, in the long run, to be less expensive than poor quality. In recent years, U.S. firms have adopted programs such as total quality management (TQM) and Six Sigma to improve quality. Another approach firms have taken to improve efficiency has been to launch programs designed to achieve certification or recognition from outside authorities. Two common approaches are to participate in the Baldrige National Quality Program and to seek certification under the International Organization for Standardization's ISO 9000 standards.

The Deming Chain Reaction

- Improve quality
- Costs decrease because of less rework, fewer mistakes, fewer delays and snags, and better use of time and materials
- Productivity improves
- Capture the market with better quality and lower price
- Stay in business
- Provide jobs and more jobs

LO6 Explain the movement toward lean production

Lean production refers to a set of strategies and practices to eliminate waste and thus make organizations more efficient, responsive, and flexible. Operations managers who implement lean production often use value stream mapping to identify waste, which refers to activities or functions that use resources but don't create value. They then work to find ways to redesign processes to reduce or eliminate the waste. Inventory control is one of the key areas where waste often occurs. Many lean firms have adopted just-in-time production methods to minimize the amount of parts, work in process, and finished products they hold in inventory.

LO6

lean production
An approach to production that emphasizes the elimination of waste in all aspects of production processes.

value stream map
A tool used in lean production to show the flows of materials and information from the beginning to the end of a production process; used to identify where waste occurs within a production system.

just-in-time (JIT) production
A production system that emphasizes the production of goods to meet actual current demand, thus minimizing the need to hold inventories of finished goods and work in process at each stage of the supply chain.

REVIEW CARD
APPENDIX 1

Labor Unions and Collective Bargaining
Visit www.cengagebrain.com to find this online appendix.

LO1

labor union
A group of workers who have organized to work together to achieve common job-related goals, such as higher wages, better working conditions, and greater job security.

craft union
A union comprised of workers who share the same skill or work in the same profession.

industrial union
A union comprised of workers employed in the same industry.

LO2

employment at will
A legal doctrine that views employment as an entirely voluntary relationship that both the employee and employer are free to terminate at any time and for any reason.

National Labor Relations Act (Wagner Act)
Landmark pro-labor law enacted in 1935. This law made it illegal for firms to discriminate against union members and required employers to recognize certified unions and bargain with these unions in good faith.

Labor–Management Relations Act (Taft–Hartley Act)
Act passed in 1947 that placed limits on union activities, outlawed the closed shop, and allowed states to pass right-to-work laws that made union shops illegal.

closed shop
An employment arrangement in which the employer agrees to hire only workers who already belong to the union.

union shop
An employment arrangement in which a firm can hire nonunion workers, but these workers must join the union within a specified time period to keep their jobs.

right-to-work law
A state law that makes union shops illegal within that state's borders.

open shop
An employment arrangement in which workers who are represented by a union are not required to join the union or pay union dues.

LO3

collective bargaining
The process by which representatives of union members and employers attempt to negotiate a mutually acceptable labor agreement.

distributive bargaining
The traditional adversarial approach to collective bargaining.

interest-based bargaining
A form of collective bargaining that emphasizes cooperation and problem solving in an attempt to find a "win–win" outcome that benefits both sides.

strike
A work stoppage initiated by a union.

LO1 Describe how unions in the United States are organized

A labor union is a group of workers who have organized in order to pursue common job-related objectives, such as better wages and benefits, safer working conditions, and greater job security. Unions can be organized either as craft unions, which consist of members who share the same skill or profession, or as industrial unions, which consist of workers in the same industry. The most basic unit of a union is the local union. This is the level at which most members have an opportunity to get directly involved in union activities. Most locals belong to a national (or international) union. The national union provides training, legal support, and bargaining advice to locals; organizes new locals; and sometimes takes an active role in the collective bargaining process. Many national unions belong to the AFL-CIO, which serves as the national voice for the labor movement.

LO2 Discuss the key provisions of the laws that govern labor–management relations

Until the 1930s, no federal laws dealt specifically with the rights of workers to organize unions or the way unions could carry out their functions. During the Great Depression of the 1930s, several pro-labor laws were enacted. The most important of these was the National Labor Relations Act, often called the Wagner Act. This law prevented employers from discriminating against union members and required employers to recognize and bargain with certified unions. It also established the National Labor Relations Board to investigate charges of unfair labor practices. After World War II, Congress enacted the Labor–Management Relations Act, more commonly called the Taft–Hartley Act. This law sought to limit the power of unions. It identified several unfair labor practices by unions and declared them illegal and allowed workers to vote to decertify a union that represented them. It also made closed shops (in which employers could only hire workers who already belonged to a union) illegal. Finally, it allowed states to pass right-to-work laws that made union shops (in which all workers had to join the union within a specified time in order to keep their jobs) illegal.

Other Major Labor Legislation in the United States

Date	Law	Major Provisions
1932	Norris–LaGuardia Act	• Stated that workers had a legal right to organize • Made it more difficult to get injunctions against peaceful union activities
1935	National Labor Relations Act (or Wagner Act)	• Made it illegal for employers to discriminate based on union membership • Established the National Labor Relations Board to investigate unfair labor practices • Established a voting procedure for workers to certify a union as their bargaining agent • Required employers to recognize certified unions and bargain with them in good faith
1938	Fair Labor Standards Act	• Banned many types of child labor • Established the first federal minimum wage (25 cents per hour) • Established a standard 40-hour workweek • Required that hourly workers receive overtime pay when they work in excess of 40 hours per week.
1947	Labor–Management Relations Act	• Identified unfair labor practices by unions and declared them illegal • Allowed employers to speak against unions during organizing campaigns • Allowed union members to decertify their union, removing its right to represent them • Established provisions for dealing with emergency strikes that threatened the nation's health or security
1959	Labor–Management Reporting and Disclosure Act (or Landrum–Griffin Act)	• Guaranteed rank-and-file union members the right to participate in union meetings • Required regularly scheduled secret ballot elections of union officers • Required unions to file annual financial reports • Prohibited convicted felons and Communist Party members from holding union office

lockout
An employer-initiated work stoppage.

picketing
A union tactic during labor disputes in which union members walk near the entrance of the employer's place of business, carrying signs to publicize their position and concerns.

boycott
A tactic in which a union and its supporters and sympathizers refuse to do business with an employer with which they have a labor dispute.

mediation
A method of dealing with an impasse between labor and management by bringing in a neutral third party to help the two sides reach agreement by reducing tensions and making suggestions for possible compromises.

arbitration
A process in which a neutral third party has the authority to resolve a dispute by rendering a binding decision.

grievance
A complaint by a worker that the employer has violated the terms of the collective bargaining agreement.

LO3 Explain how labor contracts are negotiated and administered

The process by which representatives of labor and employers attempt to negotiate a mutually acceptable labor agreement is called "collective bargaining." There are two broad basic approaches to collective bargaining. In distributive bargaining, the process tends to be adversarial. The sides begin with predetermined positions and an initial set of demands. They then use persuasion, logic, and even threats to gain as much as they can. The other approach is called interest-based bargaining. In this approach, the two sides do not present initial demands. Instead, they raise issues and concerns and try to work together to develop mutually beneficial solutions.

Negotiations sometimes break down. An impasse occurs when it becomes obvious that a settlement is not possible under current conditions. When an impasse is reached, the union may call a strike, or the employer may call a lockout. However, both sides may agree to either mediation or arbitration to try to settle their differences and reach agreement without resorting to such work stoppages. Mediators can only make suggestions and encourage the two sides to settle. If one or both sides reject the mediator's efforts, then the process is likely to fail. In contrast, an arbitrator has the authority to render a binding decision. Arbitration is common in the public sector but rare in the private sector.

When workers believe they have been unfairly treated under terms of the contract, they may file a grievance. Most labor agreements contain a formal grievance procedure that identifies a specific series of steps involved in settling a complaint. The final step usually involves binding arbitration.

LO4 Evaluate the impact unions have had on their members' welfare and the economy, and explain the challenges that today's unions face

Most studies find that union workers earn higher wages and receive more benefits than nonunion workers with similar skills performing the same type of job. Union contracts and the grievance procedure also provide union members with more protection from arbitrary discipline (including firings) than nonunion workers enjoy. However, unionized industries in the private sector haven't provided much job security. Total employment in many highly unionized industries has fallen dramatically in recent years.

Many critics argue that unions undermine worker productivity by imposing rules and restrictions that reduce the ability of firms to innovate and require employers to use more labor than necessary to produce goods and services. But union supporters suggest that unions reduce worker turnover and encourage worker training, thus increasing productivity. Research on this topic has not yielded clear-cut evidence in support of either position.

One of the major problems facing unions is the continuing decline in union membership in the private sector. There are several reasons for this decline. In part, it represents a change in the structure of the U.S. economy. But another reason has been the increasing willingness of employers to use antiunion tactics to discourage union membership. The AFL-CIO and national unions have placed greater emphasis on organizing activities in recent years in an attempt to reverse this trend. Until recently, these efforts met with little success. However, between 2006 and 2007 there was a slight increase in private sector union membership for the first time in 25 years. This was followed by an even larger increase in membership between 2007 and 2008. Union membership fell in 2009 compared to its 2008 level, but this may have been due to the onset of a severe recession. The long-term trend in membership remains difficult to determine.

REVIEW CARD APPENDIX 2

Business Law
Visit www.cengagebrain.com to find this online appendix.

© COMSTOCK IMAGES/JUPITERIMAGES

LO1

laws
Rules that are enforced by the government that govern the conduct and actions of people within a society.

constitution
A code that establishes the fundamental rules and principles that govern a particular organization or entity.

statutory law
Laws that are the result of legislative action.

Uniform Commercial Code (UCC)
A uniform act governing the sale of goods, leases, warranties, transfer of funds, and a variety of other business-related activities.

administrative law
Laws that arise from regulations established by government agencies.

case law (also called common law)
Laws that result from rulings, called precedents, made by judges who initially hear a particular type of case.

tort
A private wrong that results in physical or mental harm to an individual, or damage to that person's property.

negligence
An unintentional tort that arises due to carelessness or irresponsible behavior.

crime
A wrongful act against society defined by law and prosecuted by the state.

LO2

contract
An agreement that is legally enforceable.

consideration
Something of value that one party gives another as part of a contractual agreement.

statute of frauds
A requirement that certain types of contracts must be in writing in order to be enforceable.

breach of contract
The failure of one party to a contract to perform his or her contractual obligations.

statute of limitations
The time period within which a legal action must be initiated.

compensatory damages
Monetary payments that a party who breaches a contract is ordered to pay in order to compensate the injured party for the actual harm suffered by the breach of contract.

specific performance
A remedy for breach of contract in which the court orders the party committing the breach to do exactly what the contract specifies.

LO3

sale
A transaction in which the title (legal ownership) to a good passes from one party to another in exchange for a price.

title
Legal evidence of ownership.

LO1 Explain the purposes of laws and identify the major sources of law in the United States

Laws are those rules—enforced by the government—that set parameters for the conduct and actions of people within a society. These rules promote order and stability, protect individuals from physical or mental harm, protect property from damage or theft, promote behavior that society deems desirable, and deter behavior that society deems undesirable. Laws come from several sources. Constitutional law is based on a constitution, such as the U.S. Constitution or a state constitution. Statutory law is enacted by a legislative body, such as Congress or a state legislature. Administrative laws are established and enforced by government agencies. Case law (also called common law) is law based on court decisions known as "precedents."

LO2 Describe the characteristics of a contract and explain how the terms of contracts are enforced

A contract is an agreement that is enforceable in a court of law. A valid contract must be characterized by (1) mutual assent; (2) consideration; (3) legal capacity; and (4) legal purpose. In addition, according to the statute of frauds, certain types of contracts, such as those that will take more than a year to complete or those involving the sale of goods worth more than $500, must be in writing.

A breach of contract occurs if one of the parties does not live up to the terms of the agreement. When one party breaches a contract, the other party can sue in a civil court. If the court agrees that a party breached the contract, it orders some type of remedy. The most common remedy is compensatory damages, which means the party who breached the contract must pay money to the injured party to compensate for the actual harm suffered. In cases where the contract calls for the sale of a unique good, the courts may apply a remedy known as "specific performance," which requires the party who breached the contract to do exactly what the contract says. Finally, the courts may issue injunctions (court orders) that prevent the party who breached the contract from taking some action.

Differences Between Civil and Criminal Law Cases

	Civil Law	Criminal Law
Nature of action and parties involved	Lawsuits to settle disputes between private individuals	Federal or state government prosecution of parties charged with wrongdoings against society
Examples of cases	Intentional torts such as slander, libel, invasion of privacy, wrongful death; unintentional torts arising from negligence; breach of contract	Felonies such as robbery, theft, murder, arson, identity theft, extortion, embezzlement, as well as less serious crimes called misdemeanors
Possible outcomes	Liable or not liable	Guilty or not guilty
Standard of proof (what is needed for plaintiff to win the case)	Preponderance of evidence (a much less stringent requirement than beyond reasonable doubt)	Proof beyond a reasonable doubt
Goal of remedy	Compensate injured party for harm suffered	Punish wrongdoer and deter similar behavior
Common remedies	Monetary damages (payments of money to compensate the injured party), injunctions against certain types of behavior, or requirements for specific performance	Fines and/or imprisonment; in the most serious felonies, such as premeditated murder, capital punishment (the death penalty) may be imposed.

LO4

principal–agent relationship
A relationship in which one party, called the principal, gives another party, called the agent, the authority to act in place of, and bind the principal when dealing with, third parties.

principal
A party who agrees to have someone else (called an agent) act on his or her behalf.

agent
A party who agrees to represent another party, called the principal.

scope of authority (for an agent)
The extent to which an agent has the authority to act for and represent the principal.

Chapter 7 bankruptcy
A form of bankruptcy that discharges a debtor's debts by liquidating assets and using the proceeds to pay off creditors.

Chapter 11 bankruptcy
A form of bankruptcy used by corporations and individuals that allows the debtor to reorganize operations under a court-approved plan.

Chapter 13 bankruptcy
A form of bankruptcy that allows individual debtors to set up a repayment plan to adjust their debts.

property
The legal right of an owner to exclude non-owners from having access to a particular resource.

intellectual property
Property that results from intellectual or creative efforts.

patent
A legal monopoly that gives an inventor the exclusive right over the invention for a limited time period.

trademark
A mark, symbol, word, phrase, or motto used to identify a company's goods.

copyright
The exclusive legal right of an author, artist, or other creative individual to own, use, copy, and sell their own creations and to license others to do so.

LO3 Describe how both title and risk pass from the seller to the buyer when a sale occurs

A sale occurs when the title to a good passes from one party to another in exchange for a price. Sales of goods are covered by Article 2 of the Uniform Commercial Code, which has been adopted by every state in the United States except Louisiana. Sales of services are based on precedents established by common law. A sales contract must contain the same basic elements as other contracts. However, the UCC has relaxed the requirements for some of these elements. For example, under the UCC, courts may recognize a sales contract even if certain key facts of the agreement (such as the price of the good) aren't explicitly spelled out. In such cases, the UCC provides guidelines for supplying the missing details. One key sales contract issue involves when the title actually passes from one party to another. If the contract is silent about this, the UCC generally holds that the title passes when the seller has completed all duties related to the delivery of the good. Another key issue involves which party bears the risk if the goods are lost, damaged, or destroyed during the transfer from seller to buyer. If the contract doesn't specify which party assumes the risk, the UCC normally places the risk on the party that is most likely to have insurance against a loss or on the party that is in the best position to prevent a loss.

LO4 Provide an overview of the legal principles governing agency, intellectual property, and bankruptcy

A principal–agent relationship exists when one party (the principal) gives another party (the agent) the authority to act and enter into binding agreements on the principal's behalf. As long as agents act within their scope of authority, principals are legally liable for any contracts their agents enter into while representing them. Not all employees have the authority to act as agents, but many do. A loan officer at a bank and a salesperson at a store are both employees of and agents for their companies.

Intellectual property refers to the right of inventors, innovators, authors, and artists to own their creations and prevent others from copying, distributing, or selling these creations without their permission. Patents protect the intellectual property rights of inventors. Most patents give the inventor exclusive rights to their invention for 20 years. Copyrights protect the intellectual property rights of authors, artists, and other creative individuals. Copyrights normally extend for 70 years beyond the author's or artist's life. Trademarks, which are marks, symbols, words, phrases, or mottos that identify a company's goods, are another form of intellectual property. Registered trademarks are protected for ten years, and the protection can be extended for an unlimited number of additional ten-year periods.

Bankruptcy provides a way for debtors who are unable to meet their obligations to discharge their debts and get a fresh start. There are several different types of bankruptcy procedures. In a Chapter 7 bankruptcy, the debtor's assets are liquidated and the proceeds are used to pay the creditors. Once this is done, the debtor's obligations are considered fully discharged even if (as is almost certainly the case) the proceeds are insufficient to make full payment. Chapter 11 bankruptcy occurs when a debtor reorganizes under a court-approved plan. This approach is usually used by corporations, though it is also possible for individuals to file for Chapter 11. Finally, Chapter 13 bankruptcies allow individuals to adjust their debt payments under a court-approved schedule.

REVIEW CARD
APPENDIX 3

Personal Finance
Visit www.cengagebrain.com to find this online appendix.

LO1

budget (personal)
A detailed schedule that documents your expected financial inflows (revenues earned and received) and outflows (expenses incurred and paid) in order to determine your net inflow or outflow for a given period of time.

debit card
A card issued by the bank that allows the customer to make purchases as if the transaction involved cash. In a debit card purchase, the customer's bank account is immediately reduced at the time the purchase is made.

credit card
A card issued by a bank or other finance company that allows the cardholder to make a purchase now and to pay the credit card company later.

discretionary costs
Expenditures for which the spender has significant control in terms of the amount and timing.

non-discretionary costs
Costs that the spender must incur but has little or no control over.

LO2

savings account
An interest-bearing account holding funds not needed to meet regular expenditures.

Federal Deposit Insurance Corporation (FDIC)
An independent agency created by Congress to maintain stability and public confidence in the nation's financial system, primarily by insuring bank deposits.

LO3

credit
Allows a borrower to acquire an asset or to obtain a loan and repay the balance at a later time.

credit history
A summary of a borrower's open and closed credit accounts and the manner in which those accounts have been paid.

grace period
The period of time that the credit-card holder has to pay outstanding balances before interest or fees are assessed.

annual percentage rate (APR)
The interest expense charged on a credit card expressed as an annual percentage.

LO4

investments
Reducing consumption in the current time period in order to build future wealth.

IRA
An individual retirement account that provides tax benefits to individuals who are investing for their retirement.

LO1 Apply the principles of budgeting to your personal finances

A budget is a detailed schedule that documents your expected financial inflows (revenues earned and received) and outflows (expenses incurred and paid) in order to determine your net inflow or outflow for a given period of time. You can use your budget to develop your financial plan and to monitor your progress toward achieving your financial goals. Budgeting can be as low-tech as preparing a handwritten schedule of your revenues and expenses or as automated as the latest budgeting software programs.

One key part of the budgeting process is accurately estimating revenues. After assessing your actual revenue, consider ways to increase your earnings with education, internships, and other work experience. The other key to setting up a budget is to assess your expenses by examining outflow sources, which include checkbooks, online banking statements, ATM, debit card and credit card receipts. Consideration should also be given to understanding factors that affect your spending habits. Certain types of expenditures, called discretionary costs, can be adjusted fairly easily. Other expenditures, called non-discretionary costs, are more difficult to cut—at least in the short run.

LO2 Set strategies to help build a sufficient savings and emergency fund

A savings account is an interest-bearing account that is intended to satisfy obligations that cannot be handled by a checking account. When establishing a savings account, look for reputable banks that are insured by the Federal Deposit Insurance Corporation (FDIC). To build a savings balance, set up an account that is separate from your checking account. Shop around to obtain better interest rates. In recent years, online savings banks have arisen and have been able to provide higher interest rates than traditional banks with the protection that FDIC gives to traditional banks.

A savings account is also set up for emergencies. Financial experts say that three to six months of your monthly expenses is a good savings target. In difficult financial times, six months savings is more desirable. One technique for establishing a sizable savings balance is to "pay yourself first." This technique is accomplished by automatically depositing a predetermined amount into your savings account with each paycheck.

LO3 Understand the importance of building credit history, maintaining good credit, and avoiding unwise credit decisions

The benefits of having a credit card are the obvious convenience of not having to carry cash and the opportunity to establish a credit history, which is a summary of a borrower's open and closed credit accounts and the manner in which those accounts have been paid. The downside of having a credit card are the interest fees and other charges that may be incurred if outstanding balances are not paid in a timely manner and the possible damage to your credit history if you have high or unpaid credit balances.

Before applying for your first card, make sure that you have some type of steady income. Charge small things each month, charges you know you can pay off IN FULL when you receive your credit card statement. If you cannot pay off the full amount when your credit card bill comes due then you should not make the purchase. Before you accept a credit card you should read and understand all of the main conditions for using that card. Among the major areas to consider are 1) the grace period, the period of time that you have to pay your balance before interest or fees are assessed, 2) the APR (annual interest rate on unpaid balances) as well as any other fees which may be assessed if a payment is not received within a grace period or if credit limits are exceeded when using the credit card, and 3) other fees such as those annual fees, over-the-credit-limit fees, and balance transfer fees.

The first rule when you have credit card difficulties is to just stop using the card. Then commit to setting up (and sticking to) a budget and putting a consistent amount of money toward retiring the debt on that card. Another useful tip is to use cash or a debit card instead. Many people tend to spend more when they pay with a credit card than if they pay with cash. Finally, once you have paid off the debt, don't go back to your old habits. Pay your full credit card balances at the end of each month.

401(k), 403(b), and 457 plans
Employee contribution retirement plans that offer tax benefits. The plans are named for the section of the IRS tax code where they are described.

tax deferred revenue
A portion of earnings that is not taxed now but is taxed when the employee receives the cash distribution upon retirement.

company matching
An amount contributed by the employer to an employee's retirement account that matches the employee's retirement contributions either dollar for dollar or based on a percentage of each dollar contributed by the employee.

vesting period
A specified period of time in which an employee must be employed in order to receive the full advantage of certain retirement benefits.

© SKIP ODONNELL/ISTOCKPHOTO.COM

© STOCKBYTE/GETTY IMAGES

LO4 Discuss key wealth-building principles and outline the various investments that may be part of an effective wealth-building strategy

Investments involve reducing consumption today in order to build future wealth. The time value of money tells us that a dollar invested today is worth more than a dollar invested later, because the earlier a dollar is invested, the longer it can earn a return. When it comes to investing, early is better than late—but late is better than never. It is wise to begin investing as soon as possible even if you can only invest a little at a time. Successful investing requires consistency—make it a habit to invest now and you are likely to continue investing when your income grows.

There are several different types of financial assets you might want to consider. Each has its own advantages and disadvantages. *Corporate stock* represents shares of ownership in a corporation. Investing in stock offers two possible financial benefits. The first is the possibility of receiving dividends, which are a distribution of a company's profits to its stockholders. The other return can come through capital gains, which are an increase in the market value of the stock. However, it is important to note that neither dividends nor capital gains are guaranteed. *Corporate bonds* are long-run IOUs issued by companies. Bonds typically pay a stated rate of interest until they mature. Once the bond matures the issuer is obligated to pay the bondholder an amount known as the principal (or face value) of the bond. *Government securities* are IOUs issued by a government entity. The federal government issues several types of government securities including long-term bonds and short-term T-bills. *Mutual funds* allow the buyer to obtain shares of a fund that purchases various financial securities such as stocks, corporate bonds, and government securities. These funds have managers that select the types of securities that the fund will hold. *Mutual funds* enable the owner to diversify because all of the shares are not held in any particular company. *Exchange-traded funds* are "market baskets" of securities that are traded much like individual shares of stock.

Investors have several options when it comes to building up wealth for their retirement. One approach is to open an individual retirement account (IRA). There are several types of IRAs, the most popular being the traditional IRA and the Roth IRA. A traditional IRA allows the investor to deduct any contributions from current taxable income. Contributions to a Roth IRA aren't tax deductible, but the distributions paid to retirees are tax exempt.

401(k), 403(b) and 457 employee contribution retirement plans are named for the section of the tax code where they originated. These retirement accounts are driven primarily by employee contributions toward their own retirement. One key benefit of these retirement funds is that they allow you to enjoy tax deferred income because the earnings will not be taxed until you receive the distribution upon retiring. Another possible advantage is that many companies will match (contribute) the employee contribution either dollar for dollar or a percentage of each dollar you contribute up to a limit. Finally, these funds allow you to take your contributions with you if you leave the company. However, you'll only be able to take the matching funds if you remain employed with the company for a vesting period (a period of time specified by the company). Even if you take the funds with you, under most circumstances you'll have to wait until you retire to begin receiving distributions from the funds without incurring a penalty.

Planning Your Career

Julie Griffin Levitt

Planning Your Career Planning Your

REACH YOUR FULL CAREER POTENTIAL

"A sense of purpose generates action and movement in the direction of dreams and goals, while wishes generate only half-hearted intentions. Think about it. Purpose says, 'I will do this.' Wish says, 'If only I could.'

Life is not a spectator sport. Set your sights on what you want in your career and then make it happen. Now, what are you waiting for?"

Joan C. Borgatti, R.N., M.Ed.
Editorial Director
NursingSpectrum.com

Chapter 1 provides guidelines to help you strengthen career-boosting skills, attitudes, and strategies that persuade employers to hire and promote. You will learn and apply nine strategies to give you the competitive edge in achieving career success and reaching your full potential.

❖ The Changing Workplace

The forces of technology and globalization are rapidly changing the nature of work. Savvy job seekers know that they need to prepare for these predicted workplace developments:

- Technology will continue to advance and will affect how, when, and where business is done; the pace of work; and how people communicate.

- The global economy will continue to result in some jobs being outsourced to other countries and will lead to more mergers and management changes.

Resourcefulness, adaptability, and efficiency will be essential for workers to succeed.

- International time zone differences will demand flexible hours and possibly extra hours to communicate and conduct business.

- A complex and diverse workforce will require workers to be flexible, respect differences, and work together to increase productivity.

- Workers can expect to change jobs about 10 times! Managing one's career is a must.

- Small businesses will prosper, and home-based businesses and services will multiply. Entrepreneurial skills and attitudes will be important.

- The fastest-growing occupations are in computers; preventive health care; and other health and human services, such as registered nursing, social work, teaching, police work, and security.

- Most of the fastest-growing occupations will require specific post-secondary education, on-the-job training, or a bachelor's degree. Education and training will be critical.

To gain a competitive edge, today's job seekers must know about changes like these and demonstrate a positive attitude that shows they are ready, willing, and able to take on these challenges.

❖ Get the Competitive Edge With Nine Success Strategies

Successful leaders in all fields, from business to entertainment, consistently use the nine success strategies discussed in this chapter to achieve their career goals. These strategies focus on positive attitudes and actions. Throughout the world, Olympic sports psychologists coach competitors to achieve maximum performance by learning and applying these strategies. Renowned motivational experts—such as Anthony Robbins, Brian Tracy, Denis Waitley, and Stephen Covey—teach these strategies to help business leaders, politicians, and performers reach their peak potential.

USE NINE SUCCESS STRATEGIES

Review and use the nine strategies that follow to help achieve your full career potential. They profoundly affect career success at every step.

1. Positive Thinking and Behavior

2. Visualization

3. Positive Self-Talk

4. Affirmation Statements

5. Dynamic Goal Setting

6. Positive Action

7. Assertive Behavior

8. Self-Esteem Builders

9. Proactive Habits

These nine success strategies and behaviors are major career enhancers that help transform goals into realities. Pay close attention to any that are new ideas for you. They provide wide-ranging benefits; you can use them to:

- Create and sustain your inner drive.

- Increase your confidence.

- Generate mental and physical energy.

- Guide you toward goals.

- Help you project competence, enthusiasm, and presence.

- Improve your performance.

It's shocking but true: The most qualified person is not always the one who gets the job or promotion. The person hired is the one the employer perceives to be the most qualified. Your experience, skills, resumes, and more—your entire job search package—are greatly enhanced when you practice these key success strategies.

SET UP YOUR CAREER MANAGEMENT FILES BINDER

To help you prepare for job search and career success, *Your Career: How to Make It Happen* guides you through the development of your own Career Management Files. Your Career Management Files will include career development and job search documents (self-assessments, records of experience and skills developed, resumes, cover letters, job search organizational aids, and more) that you can use throughout your career each time you seek a promotion, a new job, or a career change. Career Action 1-1 is the first step in organizing this essential career information.

IMPROVE PERFORMANCE THROUGH POSITIVE THINKING AND BEHAVIOR

Positive thinking is making a conscious effort to think with an optimistic attitude and anticipate positive outcomes. Positive behavior means purposely acting with energy and enthusiasm. When you think and behave positively, you guide your mind toward your goals and generate matching mental and physical energy.

Positive thinking and behavior are often deciding factors in landing a top job—your first job, a promotion, a change of jobs—whatever career step you are targeting. That's because the subconscious is literal; it accepts what you regard as fact.

The function of your subconscious is to support your thoughts and behaviors by triggering matching physiological responses. Research has proved that positive thinking and behavior have a powerful impact on personal performance, confidence, and even health. This chapter explains how

Success Tip

The winning job candidate is perceived to be the most qualified. Use the nine success strategies to project your competence.

SET UP YOUR CAREER MANAGEMENT FILES SYSTEM

Directions: In Appendix B, Career Management Tool 1: Career Management Files, follow the instructions to set up your own Career Management Files Binder. In this binder, store completed Career Action Assignments specified throughout the book. When you have completed all of these assignments, you will have a valuable collection of career-related information that you can use throughout your life. Your completed binder will include records of your education and work experience, summaries of job- and career-related values and skills, resumes, cover letters, and more.

you can learn to use the power of autosuggestion to enhance your performance and career development.

Positive thinking causes the brain to generate matching positive chemical and physical responses, such as increased mental alertness and physical energy, improved respiration and circulation, and increased beneficial endorphins. Thinking positively actually boosts your ability to perform and to project enthusiasm, energy, competence, and confidence—the qualities interviewers look for when they hire and promote candidates.

Negative thinking causes the brain to stimulate matching negative chemical and physical responses, such as increased blood pressure, reduced mental alertness, increased anxiety, decreased physical energy, and fight or flight reactions. These responses decrease energy, creativity, and performance and simultaneously erode self-confidence.

Follow these steps to form the habit of positive thinking and to boost your success:

1. **Deliberately motivate yourself every day.** Think of yourself as successful, and expect positive outcomes for everything you attempt.

2. **Project energy and enthusiasm.** Employers hire people who project positive energy and enthusiasm. Develop the habit of speaking, moving, and acting with these qualities.

3. **Practice this positive expectation mind-set until it becomes a habit.** Applicants who project enthusiasm and positive behavior generate a positive chemistry that rubs off. Hiring decisions are influenced largely by this positive energy. The habit will help you reach your peak potential.

4. **Dwell on past successes.** Focusing on past successes to remind yourself of your abilities will help you attain your goals. For example, no one is ever born knowing how to ride a bicycle or use a computer software program. Through training, practice, and trial and error, you master new abilities. During the trial-and-error phases of development, remind yourself of past successes; look at mistakes as part of the natural learning curve. Continue until you achieve the result you want, and remind yourself that you have succeeded in the past and can do so again. You fail only when you quit trying!

"No pessimist ever discovered the secrets of the stars, or sailed to an uncharted land, or opened a new heaven to the human spirit."
—Helen Keller

USE VISUALIZATION TO YOUR ADVANTAGE

Positive visualization is purposely forming a mental picture of your successful performance and recalling the image frequently. Visualization improves performance because the positive picture triggers your subconscious to generate matching positive physiological responses that increase performance.

Athletic champions and successful people throughout the world use positive visualization to boost their performance and achieve goals. The act of visualizing the successful performance of any skill or activity in detail actually increases learning and skill development. This is because visualization serves as a form of mental practice or rehearsal that strengthens performance. Have you used it personally or in a group to help improve performance? This is definitely a technique you should apply in all your career activities.

Apply the following visualization techniques to boost your success in job searches and interviews and in attaining your goals:

1. **Relax.** Sit in a chair, close your eyes, breathe deeply, and clear your mind.

2. **Draw a mental picture or create a mental video that shows you succeeding in your goal.** To project a positive and competent image, visualize yourself doing just that—walking and speaking with confidence, maintaining good posture, and performing optimally.

3. **Make the picture detailed and visualize success.** Do not permit any negative visions or thoughts (fear, failure, anxiety, or errors). See yourself as having already achieved your goal.

4. **Incorporate pictures, words, actions, and senses.** Mentally practice exactly what you plan to say or do. This mental rehearsal strengthens your actual performance.

5. **Dwell on the image; be able to recall it instantly.** Repeat the visual picture as often as possible before the actual event.

PRACTICE POSITIVE SELF-TALK

Positive self-talk means purposely giving yourself positive reinforcement, motivation, and recognition—just as you would do for a friend. Congratulate yourself when you do well, and remind yourself of your abilities, accomplishments, strengths, and skills. Keep a to-do list, check off accomplishments, and review your progress periodically.

Make Self-Talk Work for You. What you habitually say to yourself has a profound impact on your self-image, your self-esteem, and your performance and success. Remember, your subconscious triggers physiological responses that match the pictures and thoughts you have of yourself to make them happen. Make this work *for* you by keeping your self-talk positive. For example:

- I did a good job on that report.

- I can do this.

Stop Negative Self-Talk. You may be quick to nag yourself because you want to be perfect. However, negative self-talk is damaging because the

Figure 1.1 You project your positive self-image.

subconscious believes what you say about yourself. If you catch yourself using negative self-talk, stop and rephrase. Eliminate the negative words. Focus instead on the best course of action you can take, and *do it*.

Make positive communication a habit. Focus on the positive in goal statements, self-talk, and all communications. Compare the following phrases, and notice how the positive words convey confidence, commitment, and enthusiasm.

Negative	Positive
I'll try	I will
I should do	I will do
I must	I want to/I choose to

FOCUS WITH AFFIRMATION STATEMENTS

Affirmation statements are positive self-statements or reminders to help achieve goals. They are positive messages with a punch, "mental bumper stickers" to motivate your subconscious to work for you. The following guidelines explain how to use this powerful mental reminder technique:

1. **Make the statements personal.** Use *I*, your name, or *you*.

2. **Keep affirmations short!** If you can't remember them, how can you use them?

3. **Phrase them positively.** The mind accepts as truth the words you give it. Use positive words only. Leave out negative words. For example:

   - **Negative:** I will not be nervous during my interview.

   - **Positive:** I will be calm and self-assured during my interview.

4. **Include a positive emotion.** A phrase that triggers a positive emotion strengthens the affirmation. For example: "My goal is *valuable* and it *excites* me."

5. **Phrase affirmations as fact.** Phrase a goal as though it is happening or has happened (even if you haven't achieved it yet). Your subconscious believes mental messages and works to make them reality.

   - I am making good progress on my goal.

   - I am strengthening my speaking abilities.

6. **Say your affirmations at least once a day.** Repetition enhances self-confidence, acts as a reminder, and stimulates your subconscious to help you achieve your goal.

GET AHEAD WITH DYNAMIC GOAL SETTING

Career goal setting involves recording clear objectives and the actions required to achieve them. The main reason people don't achieve goals is that they don't

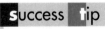

Success tip

Use positive self-talk and affirmation statements to trigger matching positive physical responses that enhance performance.

CAREER ACTION 1-2

PRACTICE POSITIVE SELF-TALK AND AFFIRMATION STATEMENTS

Directions: Access your Learner's CD or use a separate sheet of paper to write your responses.

1. Recall a goal you have been striving to achieve and on which you are making progress. Then write a positive statement about your progress.

2. Describe one or more of your work skills or abilities that fit the requirements of the job you are or will be seeking. Write complete sentences.

3. Write an affirmation statement to use as a reminder to help you achieve an important career goal.

File your affirmation statements in your Career Management Files Binder.

---

set any to begin with. Use the following steps to focus your efforts and maximize your goal achievement. You can also use this process to set team or group goals.

1. **Define your goals clearly in writing.** Writing down your goals increases your likelihood of achieving them by 80 percent! It increases your sense of commitment, clarifies required steps in the achievement process, and helps you remember important details.

2. **Identify and focus on the benefits (to you and others) of achieving goals.** This is a strong motivator.

3. **Define the purpose of your goals.** Link your goals to a practical, specific purpose. To boost your own motivation, base your goals on inspiration, not just logic.

4. **Identify your supportive forces.** Examples of supportive forces include instructors, books, training, people who encourage you to persevere, skilled coaches or mentors, and printed and online research materials.

5. **Develop an action plan, set deadlines, and act.** Establish subgoals. Divide each main goal into logical, progressive steps. Set deadlines for completing each step, and complete the steps on time.

6. **Establish priorities.** Take action in order of priority.

7. **Make a public commitment.** If appropriate, share your goals with someone who encourages you to go the extra mile. This will increase your sense of responsibility and provide motivation.

8. **Be realistic about limitations.** Don't set a short-term goal to get a job requiring more education. Set separate goals to get the education, take an interim job, and then reach the ultimate goal.

9. **Use positive self-talk and affirmation statements.** Do this every day! Write down your statements, post them prominently, and review them regularly.

10. **Use positive visualization.** This boosts goal achievement.

11. **Practice.** Practice new skills regularly. Get additional information, training, coaching, and feedback on your progress.

12. **Evaluate and revise goals as necessary.** Evaluate your progress. Experiment with new methods if you're not getting the results you want, and, if necessary, revise your goals.

13. **Persevere.** Stay the course until you succeed!

14. **Reward yourself.** Rewards are motivators. As you make progress toward your goals, do something nice for yourself.

15. **Record progress on your goals.** As simplistic as it may seem, a long series of check marks on a calendar can motivate you by providing a sense of accomplishment. Don't let missing an occasional daily goal deter you, however. Keep focusing on the ultimate goal.

TAKE POSITIVE ACTION

When you take regular positive action (no matter how small) and make progress toward goals, you create real evidence of achievement. This increases confidence and creativity and boosts your momentum. Action fuels more action! Deliberately plan and regularly work toward your goals to maximize your success.

Say you have a long-term goal of specializing in a career field. You can take momentum-building intermediate actions, as follows:

- Research to learn exactly what skills you need to qualify in the specialty. Contact specialists in your area to learn what skills they require.

- Take courses to help you develop these skills. As you complete each course, you will be a step closer to your final goal.

- Get help in arranging an internship or a work-study program with a firm noted in your target specialty area.

- Work in an entry-level position for a firm noted in your targeted specialty area. Then get additional training or education to qualify for the specialty.

> "When we set goals, the magic begins: The switch turns on, the current starts to flow, and the power to accomplish becomes a reality."
> —Wynn Davis
>   The Best of Success

CAREER ACTION 1-3

PRACTICE DYNAMIC GOAL SETTING AND POSITIVE ACTIONS

Directions: Access your Learner's CD or use a separate sheet of paper to write your responses.

1. Review and follow the guidelines for dynamic goal setting on pages 6–7. Identify a goal that is important to you.

2. Write down your goal and describe it by addressing goal-setting guidelines 1–5.

3. Identify three to five positive actions you can take in the next 10 days to achieve this goal.

4. Follow up by actually completing all 15 guidelines.

File your goal statements in your Career Management Files Binder.

DEVELOP ASSERTIVE ABILITIES

- Assertive behavior is:

- Standing up for your rights.

- Expressing yourself honestly, courteously, and comfortably.

- Observing and respecting the rights of others.

Assertive behavior promotes equality and a healthy balance in human relationships. Assertion is based on human rights—especially the right to be treated with respect in all situations. Every person has the right to be listened to and taken seriously, to say yes or no with conviction, to express his or her opinion, and to ask for what he or she wants.

Assertive Behavior Is Critical in Your Job Search. Why is assertiveness critical to a successful job search and career potential? Because it conveys self-esteem and capability.

Employers hire people who behave confidently and are able to convey their job qualifications comfortably and clearly. They want employees who strengthen human relations and project competence in the workplace through assertive behavior. They hire applicants who demonstrate assertiveness in interviews, resumes, and all communications. To reach your full career potential, be assertive and tactful in expressing yourself, and respect the rights of others.

Assertive Behavior Is Critical to Workplace Success. Personality types fall into three general categories: nonassertive, aggressive, and assertive. Employers avoid hiring nonassertive and aggressive employees because they are often detrimental in the workplace.

- **Nonassertive People.** People who are nonassertive have difficulty expressing thoughts or feelings because they lack confidence. They may become unhappy because they permit others to abuse their rights. They project their feelings of unhappiness to others.

- **Aggressive People.** People who are aggressive violate the rights of others with domineering, pushy behavior. Their goal is to dominate because they fear loss of control. Overly aggressive employees drive business away; therefore, employers avoid hiring them.

- **Assertive People.** Assertive behavior is essential to achieving career success. Assertive people are confident, express their needs and opinions comfortably, and are sensitive to the feelings and needs of others. Employers want assertive employees because assertive behavior projects capability and promotes a healthy, productive working environment.

Building Assertiveness Skills. Being assertive requires a healthy self-esteem. Therefore, a key to improving assertiveness is strengthening self-esteem. Because all the success strategies and behaviors discussed in this chapter build self-esteem, they also enhance assertiveness.

Practicing Assertiveness. Strive to deal with others in a confident, positive way without appearing boastful or overbearing. Force yourself to be more

© Getty Images/Photodisc

Employers look for people who behave confidently and respect the rights of others.

open, to express your ideas and needs, and to perform with greater confidence. At the same time, practice showing respect for others more openly. The winning combination is *assertiveness + respect.*

Techniques for Developing Assertiveness. Review the following techniques for improving assertiveness. Practice expressing your feelings and needs calmly and clearly. Also demonstrate acceptance and respect for others by praising them when they perform or behave well.

1. **Initiate a friendship.** Invite a person you don't know well to have coffee or lunch. Take time to get to know him or her.

2. **Express your opinion** in a meeting or conversation, particularly when you believe strongly about the topic. Do this even if everyone else appears to disagree with you.

3. **Join a professional or service organization or club,** and volunteer to serve on a committee. What a way to network and build your assertiveness skills!

4. **Compliment someone** on a skill, a talent, an achievement, or a positive quality.

5. **Tell someone when he or she has offended you unfairly.** Evaluate first to be certain the person was actually unfair. Being overly sensitive can impair your assertiveness.

6. **Return faulty merchandise** to get an immediate replacement or a free repair.

7. **Initiate a conversation** with a stranger before or after a class, meeting, or social event. (Just try it; you'll like it!)

ENHANCE YOUR SELF-ESTEEM

Projecting confidence requires a healthy self-esteem (belief in your abilities and your worth). Think how easy it is to project a confident, competent image when

CAREER ACTION 1-4

IMPROVE ASSERTIVENESS

Directions: Review the techniques for developing assertiveness just discussed. Select at least two activities for practicing assertiveness—exercises provided in the chapter or others more pertinent to your needs. Access your Learner's CD to write out a plan for improving your assertiveness skills

through the exercises you have chosen, and follow through with your plan.

File your assertiveness improvement plan in your Career Management Files Binder

you feel good about yourself. By developing the success habits outlined in this chapter, you will strengthen your self-esteem.

Enhancing Your Self-Esteem. Begin by describing yourself in writing. You may want to ask a friend or family member to help. Make two lists: one of your positive traits and one of your negative traits. Which list is longer? If it's your positive list, you have a good base for self-esteem. If it's your negative list, you must work harder to develop a strong sense of self-confidence. By doing so, you will strengthen your assertive abilities because having a healthy self-esteem makes behaving assertively easy.

Next, identify negative images you want to change. Begin with the trait you think you should improve first. An example of a negative trait may be a lack of initiative, expressiveness, or organization. Improving self-image often requires developing a positive habit, such as reading more to improve vocabulary or exercising to improve fitness.

After you identify the traits you want to improve, develop an Action Plan. Write your goal in positive terms, as shown in Figure 1.2. Write your Action Plan so you can evaluate it daily. This makes progress easy to evaluate and provides reinforcement. Put a check mark on your calendar each day you make progress toward your goal. This may seem simplistic, but it is surprisingly motivational.

Effects of Negative Self-Esteem and Fear. A negative self-image holds you back by promoting fear of failure. It prevents you from taking risks that

Figure 1.2 Action Plan

Action Plan

Goal: To improve my public-speaking skills by enrolling in a workshop.

Personal Action Plan for Achieving Goal: On Tuesday afternoon, I will research dates and times for public-speaking workshops offered on campus. After I have the scheduling information, I will sign up for the workshop sessions that fit my schedule. Once I have completed and participated in the sessions, I will write a summary of the skills I learned. In the summary, I will identify the three most important points to use in my public speaking. My next goal will be to practice my public speaking!

Time Frame for Action Plan: I will write the public-speaking workshop session dates and times in my planner. I will attend all sessions offered this semester.

PERSONAL BEST

Maintaining Work and Life Balance

Balancing the demands of your work and personal lives can sometimes feel like a juggling act. As you identify career goals that are important to you, consider how they affect:

- Your values. What do you consider important in your life—family, personal interests, work, education, community service, spiritual development, and so on?

- Your priorities. Based on your values, which daily tasks are most important to you? Which are the least important?

- Your physical health. With a fit body, you are better able to deal with emotional stress and physical strain.

- Your stress level. Are your goals achievable? Be realistic about what you can accomplish in one day.

Today many employers are sensitive to the importance of personal and professional balance. They know that employees who achieve a healthy balance in life are happier and more productive. Explore with employers how you can achieve a healthy life/work balance *and* deliver top-quality results at work.

can lead to growth and development. The result is stagnation, even regression, but not successful development. Have you ever avoided attempting a new activity or goal because you feared failure or rejection?

Sometimes you base your behavior on imagined fears, not on facts. You allow fear to limit your full potential. Following are tips for dealing constructively with fears and enhancing your success.

1. When working on a challenging goal, such as public speaking, avoid negative images. Concentrate on developing your skills and knowledge; then plan and act positively, and visualize your success in detail.

2. Assess the situation. Get training or additional information if necessary.

3. Seek support from those who motivate you.

4. Act with courage and conviction; be persistent.

Maintaining a Healthy Self-Esteem. Because life experiences may change your level of self-esteem, you need to work deliberately at strengthening and maintaining self-esteem. A few techniques for building self-esteem are as follows:

1. **Believe it can be done, and make a commitment.** Remember how positive suggestion positively influences your subconscious!

2. **Identify your strengths** in writing, and dwell on past successes.

3. **Set written goals** for improvement, and take action.

4. **Practice positive self-talk.**

5. **Visualize your success.**

6. **Make positive action a habit.**

7. **Surround yourself with a positive environment** (positive people and positive reading, viewing, and listening materials).

8. **Look good to feel good.** Looking your best boosts your confidence, and others respond positively to a good appearance.

9. **Stay fit.** Take care of your body, mind, and spirit. Exercise, eat properly, rest, and balance work with other life activities.

DEVELOP PROACTIVE SKILLS

In his world-acclaimed book 7 *Habits of Highly Successful People*, Stephen Covey emphasizes that the way people typically approach challenging situations and tasks is a major determinant of their career success. Many choose either a proactive or reactive approach in dealing with difficulties or challenging tasks and situations. They may also fall into the habit of using one of the approaches predominantly. One of these approaches is a consistent career booster; the other, a guaranteed detriment.

Behaviors common to approaches are outlined in Figure 1.3.

The Proactive Approach—A Synergy Booster. The proactive approach to dealing with challenges focuses on problem solution and positive action. Those who use this approach aim to resolve problems or master challenging tasks by taking full responsibility for their assignments and career growth. They actively seek resources for goal achievement. They also strive for win-win solutions that best meet the needs of all involved.

Proactive people regularly practice the nine positive success strategies emphasized in this chapter. All of these success strategies enhance your ability to take proactive steps that will boost your career success.

The Reactive Approach Is a Career Minimizer. The reactive approach focuses on problem avoidance and negative personal reactions. Those who fall into a reactive habit focus on problems, not on solutions. Their habitually negative behaviors greatly diminish their career opportunities and, in some cases, can lead to depression.

Both Approaches Are Contagious. Have you noticed how enjoyable it is to be around people who are typically proactive? Their positive, supportive, and action-oriented behaviors are energizing and motivating—they "rub off" on those they work and interact with. They motivate others to perform at their best, and they infuse a healthy aura that encourages creativity and increases productivity.

Figure 1.3 Typical Proactive and Reactive Behaviors

Typical proactive Behaviors	Typical Reactive Behaviors
Focus on problem solution/personal growth	Focus on problems/difficulties of the situation (not on solutions) and have a generally negative attitude
Take responsibility for own behavior and for personal or team assignments and productivity	Blame others or circumstances for the difficulty or try to shift responsibility for solution to others
Seek synergistic solutions through productive relationships	Procrastinate in the face of a difficult task or problem
Employ personal motivation skills based on positive expectations	Don't seek resources for problem solution (networking, researching for useful information, and so on)
Encourage/assist others	Don't strive to motivate self or others to improve or excel
Network and strive to develop mutually beneficial relationships, share information and perspectives, and get and give support	Diminish energy of others

ACCESS THE INTERNET AND DEVELOP A PROACTIVE SUCCESS ACTION PLAN

Directions: Launch your web browser and follow the steps below.

1. Access the *Your Career: How to Make It Happen* web site at *http://levitt .swlearning.com.* (You will be accessing this web site for numerous Career Action assignments, so bookmark its address in your web browser.)

2. Locate the **Proactive Success Action Plan** form.

3. Read the instructions and enter your answers on the **Proactive Success Action Plan** form.

4. Print your completed form, and file it in your Career Management Files Binder.

Rewards of Proactive Behaviors Are Great. With practice, you will increase your ability to use proactive behavior as your predominant style and enjoy greater success throughout your career. Also, by associating with other proactive people, you can mutually expand your career potential through the contagious synergy you experience. The following list summarizes the beneficial outcomes of developing good proactive skills.

- Enhance self-esteem/increase personal motivation

- Improve problem-solving skills

- Enhance self-esteem and professional reputation

- Improve ability to correct personal errors and strengthen skills

- Build positive working relationships that boost career success potential for all

- Improve performance in all endeavors

- Gain skills under the direction of mentors and in networking with others

- Increase knowledge and career resources

- Expand perspective

❖ Apply the Nine Success Strategies

Use the nine success strategies emphasized in this chapter to reach your full career potential. Apply these success strategies regularly throughout your job search and career. Throughout your life, pursue your goals with an assertive belief in yourself and your rights, and practice thinking and acting positively and proactively. Success is not a one-time destination; it's a life-long journey.

APPLYING NINE SUCCESS STRATEGIES

- Think and act positively.

- Visualize your positive performance.

- Use positive self-talk.

- Use affirmation statements.

- Write clear short-term and long-term goals, and revise them when necessary.

- Take regular action to achieve defined goals.

- Practice assertive behavior.

- Maintain self-esteem through positive thinking and actions.

- Develop proactive skills.

CRITICAL THINKING QUESTIONS

1. How can an understanding of workplace trends give you a competitive edge in a job search?

2. Which of the nine success strategies are the most useful for attaining career planning and job search success?

3. How can projecting enthusiasm and positive expectations help you in an interview?

4. What effects do positive and negative thoughts, images, and self-talk have on performance?

5. Would you rate your own assertiveness skills as excellent, good, or needing improvement? If you need improvement, what specific actions can you take to strengthen these skills?

6. What should be compiled in your Career Management Files Binder? How will the binder be useful to you throughout your career?

For convenient access to valuable career resources, activities, and job information links, vist the companion web site for this text: *http://levitt.swlearning.com*

TAKE A LOOK AT YOURSELF

"In today's job market, self-knowledge is the most important piece of a successful job search. To help you gain knowledge about different aspects of yourself, who you are, and what you want out of your life and your career, there are several types of motivational interest, workplace, and personality inventories that can be taken.

The most important result of your work is achieving personal satisfaction. The money will follow."

Henry Neils
President and Founder
Assessment.com

In Chapter 2, you take a complete inventory of your education, training, experience, accomplishments, values, work preferences, and performance traits. This personal inventory is an essential tool for developing or confirming your career target and for conveying your qualifications to potential employers.

❖ Knowing Yourself—A Must for Your Career Success

To achieve each step throughout your career—your first job, a promotion, a job or career change—throughout your career: you must sell the product: you. Just as successful salespeople must know their products, you must know your qualifications and be able to communicate them clearly to employers in a resume, in a cover letter, and in interviews.

To help ensure wise job and career choices, you need to clarify what values and work environment preferences are important to you. The Chapter 2 Career Action assignments will help you thoroughly inventory your training, education, skills, and work experience and identify your values and work preferences.

YOUR PERSONAL CAREER INVENTORY

In this chapter, all the information you compile about yourself through the Career Action assignments will form your personal career inventory. This will be an important source of information when you develop your resumes, cover letters, job applications, and more. Employers may want your inventory information when considering you for a job. Included in this career inventory are basic personal data and information about the following:

- Education and professional training
- Work experience, skills, and accomplishments
- People you can use as references

RECORD EDUCATION, TRAINING, AND ORGANIZATIONAL ACTIVITIES

The first step in compiling your personal career inventory is documenting your education and training, including dates, places, career-relevant courses and activities, skills, and accomplishments. You will also document your membership and achievements in professional and other organizations related to your job and career targets. This information will help you identify or confirm an appropriate career choice, develop resumes and cover letters, and prepare for job interviews.

Complete this section of your personal career inventory thoroughly and accurately. Put yourself under a microscope, and look at every detail carefully. Ask people who know you well to help you document your accomplishments. Consider scholarships, honors, and awards you have received and competitions in which you have participated. In describing accomplishments, be as specific as possible. For example:

- Won first place in school math competition.
- Voted president of the senior class.

When identifying the skills and accomplishments you achieved through your education, training, and organizational activities, consider two kinds of skills (or competencies) that employers are seeking: job-specific skills and transferable competencies.

Job-Specific Skills. Job-specific skills are the technical abilities that relate *specifically* to a particular job. For example, in accounting, preparing a balance sheet by using accounting software customized for a client is a job-specific skill. Relining brakes on a vehicle is a job-specific skill for an auto mechanic. Operating medical diagnostic equipment is another job-specific skill.

Transferable Competencies. Transferable competencies are abilities that can be applied in more than one work environment. For example, both accountants and auto mechanics are required to have such transferable competencies as reading, writing, doing mathematics, and using computers. Other transferable competencies include working well with others, leading, organizing work and materials, solving problems, making decisions, and managing resources.

> "It's not what you've got, it's what you use that makes a difference."
> —Zig Ziglar

EDUCATION, TRAINING, AND ORGANIZATIONAL ACTIVITIES INVENTORY

Directions: Access Career Action Worksheet 2-1 on your Learner's CD, or use the worksheet that begins on page 22 of this text. Complete each section of the worksheet that applies to you. Be thorough in providing details. When you have completed the assignment, file your worksheet in your Career Management Files Binder.

LIST EXPERIENCE AND SKILLS

In Career Action 2-2, you will document all your work and other pertinent experience and record the dates and places of these experiences. You will also list the skills and knowledge you developed and any accomplishments, achievements, or recognition you received as part of these experiences. You should include both job-specific skills and transferable competencies.

Include any paid or volunteer work (e.g., community service projects and fund-raising), internships, and cooperative education experience. Be specific about the contributions you made:

- Raised 20 percent more in contributions over previous year.

- Designed a bandwidth usage tracking tool that improved network efficiency by 45 percent.

- Suggested new file management procedures that reduced filing error rate by 25 percent.

IDENTIFY JOB REFERENCES

The final step in completing your personal career inventory is identifying job references. A job reference is someone who can and will vouch for your

> "All our dreams can come true, if we have the courage to pursue them."
> —*Walt Disney*

EXPERIENCE AND SKILLS INVENTORY

Directions: Access Career Action Worksheet 2-2 on your Learner's CD, or use the worksheet that begins on page 26 of this text. Complete each section of the worksheet that applies to you. Be as specific and thorough as possible. When you have completed the assignment, file your worksheet in your Career Management Files Binder.

capabilities, skills, and suitability for a job. References are typically people who have been your instructors and coaches in school or your supervisors or coworkers in volunteer and paid work environments. Therefore, you should review your inventory of education and work experience for potential job references.

Identify people who can *and are willing* to confirm (from firsthand observation) your good performance on the job, in school, or in other activities. Employers want at least three job references listed on application forms. Ideally, these references are supervisors, employers, or others who know your work well. Relatives or classmates are not appropriate references. The more references you have available, the better prepared you are for your current and future job campaign.

If you are qualified to work in two different fields, such as retail sales and accounting, you will get the best results by having one set of references targeted for each of the two fields, or a total of six references (three in the sales field and three in the accounting field). Some organizations ask for different types of references. For example, an employer may ask for personal references as well as professional references.

Use Career Action 2-3 to identify people you can use as references. Make note of how they know you and in what areas they can speak about your performance.

© Getty Images./Photodisc

An instructor who can attest to your strong performance in school is a valuable job reference.

❖ Self-Assessment

Also important in knowing yourself is accurate assessment of your personal values, work preferences, and job-related performance traits. Understanding the personal factors that influence your

CAREER ACTION 2-3

DEVELOP A LIST OF POTENTIAL JOB REFERENCES

Directions: Access Career Action Worksheet 2-3 on your Learner's CD, or use the Worksheet that begins on page 28. Identify at least three (but as many as possible) potential job references from your education/training and experience/skills inventories. Also consider any contacts at professional associations. Record the names of your references, their addresses, and other pertinent contact information. Plan to contact each reference and ask him or her to write you a letter of reference. When you have completed the assignment, file you worksheet in your Career Management Files Binder.

VALUES AND WORK ENVIRONMENT PREFERENCES INVENTORY

Directions: Career Action 2-4 will help you identify and prioritize the values that are important to you. It will also help you clarify the kinds of work environments you prefer. Remember, there are no wrong answers in defining what's important to you. Access Career Action Worksheet 2-4 on your Learner's CD, or use the worksheet that begins on page 30. When you have completed the assignment, file your worksheet in your career management Files Binder.

performance and job satisfaction will help you make good choices when setting job and career targets and when considering specific job offers.

PERSONAL BEST

Professional Ethics

A code of ethics is a set of principles—written or unwritten—that guides your behavior. These principles are based on your personal values. For example, if you value honesty, honesty will be part of your ethical code.

How will your behavior in the workplace reflect your personal values and ethics? If everyone else plays computer games during work hours, will you? According to Kenneth Blanchard and Norman Vincent Peale, authors of *The Power of Ethical Management,* you should ask yourself three questions when faced with an ethical dilemma.

- **Is it legal?** Will you be breaking any laws or company policies by engaging in the activity?

- **Is it balanced?** Is it fair to all parties in the short term as well as the long term? Is it a win-win situation for all those involved?

- **Is it right?** Does the action go against your conscience? How does your decision make you feel about yourself?

VALUES

Webster's New World Dictionary defines value as "that which is desirable or worthy of esteem for its own sake; the social principles, goals, or standards held or accepted by an individual." By working in a job that matches your values, you greatly increase your chances of enjoying and succeeding in the job. Career Action 2-4 will help you identify and prioritize your values.

WORK ENVIRONMENT

Most people spend a lot of time in their work environment. To maximize your success, identify the work environments you prefer and perform best in. For example, if you are an extrovert, you probably won't enjoy working in an isolated environment. Career Action 2-4 will help you clarify what is important to you in a work environment.

PERSONAL QUALITIES AND WORK PERFORMANCE TRAITS

To get the job you want, you must be able to sell your personal qualities, positive job performance traits, and enthusiasm to prospective employers. In Career Action 2-5, you will identify these qualities and traits to help you find a suitable job target match.

Identifying your personal qualities and work performance traits will also help you decide what type of work you are best suited for.

PERSONAL QUALITIES AND WORK PERFORMANCE TRAITS

Directions: Access Career Action Worksheet 2-5 on your Learner's CD, or use the worksheet that begins on page 33. Follow the instructions to complete Career Action 2-5.

When you have completed the assignment, file you worksheet in your Career Management Files Binder.

❖ Self-Assessment Resources

Many self-assessment resources speed up the process of making and confirming a successful career choice. (Note that some of these resources may have a fee attached to them.)

- **Your school's career services staff and counselors.** These specialists can provide a wide variety of aptitude and interest tests.

- **The Internet.** You can find useful information about careers and jobs on the Internet. Many sites offer online tools to help you assess your career interests and values and match the results with appropriate careers and jobs.

- **Commercial software packages.** Some commercial software packages are available on the Internet and through schools' career offices.

> **success tip**
>
> Complete self-assessments to help match your interests, values, and personality style to appropriate careers.

ONLINE SELF-ASSESSMENT TEST

Directions: Use the Internet to locate and complete two or three career-related self-assessment tests that measure your interests, values, and/or personality style. Print the results for your Career Management Files Binder. Some versions of tests to search for include The Career Key, a mini-Myers-Briggs Type Indicator quiz, and The Keirsey Temperament Sorter. Resources for this assignment include the following:

1. The *Your Career: How to Make It Happen* web site at http://levitt.swlearning.com. Access the "Links" page; then click on the "Self-assessment links" category.

From there, review the self-assessment links and select assessment tests you are most interested in completing.

Also check out the "Efficient web searching links" for more information on conducting Internet research.

2. Your favorite search engines. Conduct a search using a search string such as *self-assessment.*

When you have completed the assignment, file your worksheet in your Career Management Files Binder.

SELF-ASSESSMENT

- Check each of the actions you are currently taking to increase your career success:

- Identifying skills, abilities, work experience, values, and work preferences to achieve a good job match

- Identifying potential references—people who can *and are willing* to confirm your good performance on the job, in school, or in other activities

- Completing self-assessments to help match interests, values, and personality style to appropriate career and job targets

- Using self-assessment resources—such as school career services, career counselors, the Internet, and commercial software packages—to help validate successful career choices

CRITICAL THINKING QUESTIONS

1. Why is it important in career planning and a job search to assess and document thoroughly your education, training, work experience, and accomplishments?

2. How are job-specific skills different from transferable competencies? Give two examples of each.

3. What is the important role of references in a job campaign?

4. Why is it useful to identify your work performance traits and career-related personal qualities?

For convenient access to valuable career resources, activities, and job information links, visit the companion web site for this text: *http://levitt.swlearning.com*

EDUCATION, TRAINING, AND ORGANIZATIONAL ACTIVITIES INVENTORY

Directions: This inventory of your education and training contains three sections: (1) High School Inventory; (2) Post-Secondary Education Inventory; and (3) Seminars and Workshops Inventory. Complete each section that applies to you. List information related to your career target. Be thorough in documenting your accomplishments and achievements.

HIGH SCHOOL INVENTORY

Name of School: _____

Address: _____

_____

Dates of Attendance: _____ to _____ Date of Diploma: _____

Grade Point Average: _____ GED (Date): _____

1. **Career-Related Courses.** List the career-related courses you completed.

   _____

   _____

2. **Career-Related and Organizational Activities.** Describe your involvement in school, extracurricular, community, and other activities (examples: clubs, sports, organizations, and volunteer work).

   _____

   _____

3. **Career-Related Skills.** List the skills you developed in high school and through other activities. Include both job-specific skills and transferable competencies (examples: operating a computer, calculating numbers, persuading others, using specific tools/equipment, leading others, and working in a team).

   _____

   _____

4. **Accomplishments, Achievements, and Recognition.** List all special accomplishments, achievements, and recognition you received in high school and through other activities (examples: selected to play lead in musical production, selected to serve on state debate team, and awarded first place in math competition). List any scholarships or honors you earned. Also summarize praise you received from instructors, peers, and others.

   _____

   _____

(Continued)

POST-SECONDARY EDUCATION INVENTORY

Directions: Complete one form for each school attended. Duplicate the form if you have attended more than one post-secondary school.

Name of School: _____

Address: _____

_____

Dates of Attendance: _____ to _____ Date of Diploma: _____

Grade Point Average: _____

1. **Career-Related Courses.** List the career-related courses you completed.

_____

_____

_____

_____

_____

_____

_____

_____

2. **Career-Related and Organizational Activities.** Descibe your involvement in school and extracurricular activities, in professional or other associations or organizations, in community activities, in volunteer work, and in other activities (examples: sports, clubs, offices held, volunteer work, and community projects or programs).

_____

_____

_____

_____

_____

_____

_____

_____

(Continued)

3. **Career-Related Skills.** List the skills you developed through your classes and other activities. Include both job-specific skills and transferable competencies (examples: operating a computer, using specific software, oral and written communication, marketing, calculating numbers, persuading and leading others, working as a team member, and researching).

_____

_____

_____

_____

_____

_____

_____

_____

4. **Accomplishments, Achievements, and Recognition.** List all special accomplishments, achievements, and recognition you received for school activities. List any scholarships or honors you earned (examples: awarded second place in state business education skills competition, won scholarship, earned service award, inducted into National Technical Honor Society, prepared lesson plans that were used as model for campus, and restored two-bedroom apartment).

_____

_____

_____

_____

_____

_____

_____

_____

_____

(Continued)

SEMINARS AND WORKSHOPS INVENTORY

Directions: List the seminars and workshops you have attended. If necessary, add to the list of seminars and workshops by keying in the additional information (if you are using a computer for this activity) or by using additional paper (if you are handwriting this activity).

Name of Seminar/Workshop: _____

Offered by: _____ Date(s): _____

Career-related concepts or skills I learned: _____

Name of Seminar/Workshop: _____

Offered by: _____ Date(s): _____

Career-related concepts or skills I learned: _____

Name of Seminar/Workshop: _____

Offered by: _____ Date(s): _____

Career-related concepts or skills I learned: _____

Name of Seminar/Workshop: _____

Offered by: _____ Date(s): _____

Career-related concepts or skills I learned: _____

Name of Seminar/Workshop: _____

Offered by: _____ Date(s): _____

Career-related concepts or skills I learned: _____

EXPERIENCE AND SKILLS INVENTORY

Directions: Complete one form for each position or project you have had (cooperative work experience, internship, volunteer/paid work experience, military experience). Begin with the most recent experience, and continue in reverse chronological order. Two copies of the form are provided; duplicate the form for additional job experience.

POSITION TITLE: _____

Name of Organization: _____

Address: _____

Telephone Number: _____ Salary (if paid experience): _____

Circle Type of Experience: (1) Cooperative   (2) Volunteer   (3) Internship   (4) Paid Work

Dates of Employment or Involvement: _____

Supervisor Name/Title:

_____

1. **Career-Related Skills.** List the job-specific skills, transferable competencies, and responsibilities you developed in this position.

   _____

   _____

2. **Accomplishments and Achievements.** List your accomplishments in this position, preferably in measurable terms (examples: increased sales by 20 percent, reduced order processing time by 15 percent by developing more efficient processing methods, named employee/volunteer of the month, and supervised evening shift of eight employees).

   _____

   _____

3. **Praise Received.** Summarize praise received from employers, coworkers, and customers.

   _____

   _____

   Why did you leave? _____

   Performance rating (circle one): Excellent Very Good Good Needs Improvement Poor

   (Continued)

POSITION TITLE: _____

Name of Organization: _____

Address: _____

Telephone Number: _____ Salary (if paid experience): _____

Circle Type of Experience: (1) Cooperative (2) Volunteer (3) Internship (4) Paid Work

Dates of Employment or Involvement: _____

Supervisor Name/Title:

_____

1. **Career-Related Skills.** List the job-specific skills, transferable competencies, and responsibilities you developed in this position.

_____

_____

_____

_____

2. **Accomplishments and Achievements.** List your accomplishments in this position, preferably in measurable terms (examples: increased sales by 20 percent, reduced order processing time by 15 percent by developing more efficient processing methods, named employee/volunteer of the month, and supervised evening shift of eight employees).

_____

_____

_____

3. **Praise Received.** Summarize praise received from employers, coworkers, and customers.

_____

_____

_____

Why did you leave? _____

Performance rating (circle one): Excellent Very Good Good Needs Improvement Poor

(Continued)

DEVELOP A LIST OF POTENTIAL JOB REFERENCES

Directions: List at least three people who would recommend you to prospective employers. List more references if possible. Be sure to get their permission to use them as references during your job search.

Name: _____

Title and Organization: _____

_____

Address: _____

          Street   City   State   ZIP Code

Telephone: _____

          Home   Work   Fax

E-Mail Address: _____

How I know this reference: _____

Date I received permission to use reference: _____

Date of reference letter on file: _____

Date of last personal contact: _____

Name: _____

Title and Organization: _____

_____

Address: _____

          Street   City   State   ZIP Code

Telephone: _____

          Home   Work   Fax

E-Mail Address: _____

How I know this reference: _____

Date I received permission to use reference: _____

Date of reference letter on file: _____

Date of last personal contact: _____

(Continued)

Name: _____

Title and Organization: _____

_____

Address: _____

                Street   City   State   ZIP Code

Telephone: _____

                Home   Work   Fax

E-Mail Address: _____

How I know this reference: _____

_____

Date I received permission to use reference: _____

Date of reference letter on file: _____

Date of last personal contact: _____

Name: _____

Title and Organization: _____

_____

Address: _____

                Street   City   State   ZIP Code

Telephone: _____

                Home   Work   Fax

E-Mail Address: _____

How I know this reference: _____

_____

Date I received permission to use reference: _____

Date of reference letter on file: _____

Date of last personal contact: _____

VALUES AND WORK ENVIRONMENT PREFERENCES INVENTORY

PART 1: VALUES

Directions: Review the values listed below, and rank the importance of each as it relates to your career and job goals (H=high, M=medium, and L=low).

Value	Ranking (H, M, L)
1. Adventure (risk taking, new challenges)	_____
2. Education/Learning/Wisdom	_____
3. Social needs (need for relationships with people)	_____
4. Self-respect/Integrity/Self-discipline	_____
5. Helping/Serving	_____
6. Recognition/Respect from others	_____
7. Freedom/Independence (working independently with minimal supervision)	_____
8. Security (job, family, national, financial)	_____
9. Spiritual needs	_____
10. Expression (creative, artistic)	_____
11. Responsibility (reliability, dependability)	_____
12. Balance in work and personal life	_____

Others (List other values below and rank each one.)

_____	_____
_____	_____
_____	_____
_____	_____
_____	_____
_____	_____
_____	_____
_____	_____
_____	_____

(Continued)

PART 2: WORK ENVIRONMENT PREFERENCES

Directions: In the boxes to the right, place a check mark next to each work environment condition you prefer.

Work Environment	Check Those Preferred
1. Indoor work	☐
2. Outdoor work	☐
3. Industrial/manufacturing setting	☐
4. Office setting	☐
5. Working alone	☐
6. Working with people	☐
7. Working with things	☐
8. Working with data	☐
9. Working with ideas	☐
10. Challenging opportunities	☐
11. Predictable, orderly, structured work	☐
12. Pressures at work	☐
13. Problem solving	☐
14. Standing while working	☐
15. Sitting while working	☐
16. Busy surroundings	☐
17. Quiet surroundings	☐
18. Exciting, adventurous conditions	☐
19. Safe working conditions/environment	☐
20. Creative environment	☐
21. Opportunities for professional development and ongoing training/education	☐

(Continued)

Work Environment	Check Those Preferred
22. Flexibility in work structure	☐
23. Teamwork and work groups	☐
24. Opportunities to supervise, lead, advance	☐
25. Opportunities to make a meaningful difference or to help others	☐
26. Using cutting-edge technology or techniques	☐
27. Integrity and truth in work environment	☐
28. Stability and security	☐
29. High-level earnings potential	☐
30. Opportunities to participate in community affairs	☐

Others (List other conditions you are seeking in your job target.)

	Check Those Preferred
_____	☐
_____	☐
_____	☐
_____	☐
_____	☐
_____	☐
_____	☐
_____	☐
_____	☐

PERSONAL QUALITIES AND WORK PERFORMANCE TRAITS

Directions: Rate yourself on each of the personal qualities and work performance traits listed below by using a scale of high, average, or low (H, A, or L). For example, if you think you have a high degree of dependability, write H in the space to the right of *Dependability*. Be sure to list other qualities or traits that are important for success in your targeted career. In developing your resume and preparing to interview well, you should be able to prove that you possess these traits by giving examples of how you have used them successfully. At the end of the form, write at least five brief positive examples of how you have used these qualities or traits.

Personal Quality or Work Performance Trait	Rating (H, A, L)
1. Initiative/Resourcefulness/Motivation	_____
2. Dependability	_____
3. Punctuality	_____
4. Flexibility	_____
5. Creativity	_____
6. Patience	_____
7. Perseverance	_____
8. Humor	_____
9. Diplomacy	_____
10. Intelligence	_____
11. High energy level	_____
12. Ability to work well with a team	_____
13. Ability to set and achieve goals	_____
14. Ability to plan, organize, prioritize work	_____
15. Outgoing personality	_____
16. Ability to handle conflict	_____
17. Optimistic attitude	_____
18. Realistic attitude	_____
19. Enthusiastic attitude	_____

(Continued)

Personality Quality or Work Performance Trait	Rating (H, A, L)
20. Willingness to work	_____
21. Orderliness of work	_____
22. Attention to detail	_____
23. Ability to manage time well	_____
24. Honesty and integrity	_____
25. Ability to multitask	_____

Others (List and rank other positive personal qualities or work performance traits.)

_____   _____

_____   _____

_____   _____

_____   _____

_____   _____

_____   _____

_____   _____

_____   _____

_____   _____

_____   _____

Examples: List at least five positive examples of how you have used some of these qualities and traits in the past.

_____

_____

_____

_____

_____

_____

WHAT DO EMPLOYERS WANT?

"When hiring for any position, I look for people who have a grasp of computers and good communication skills. I also look for people who can work well with others, adapt easily to change, and be creative when looking for new ways to do things."

Debbie Bornholdt
Human Resource Project Manager
QVC, Electronic Retailer
West Chester, PA

Chapter 3 identifies the skills, work attitudes, and other qualifications that employers focus on in making hiring decisions. The chapter guides you through a self-assessment from the employer's perspective. The assessment will help you identify your most important qualifications so you will be ready to present them effectively to an employer during your job search. This chapter identifies excellent career and job planning resources to help you confirm appropriate goals. Chapter 3 also explains the importance of developing a career portfolio.

❖ What Employers Want

Employers want to hire people who will make their businesses more successful. The most desirable employees have the specific skills, transferable career competencies, work values, and personal qualities necessary to be successful in the employers' organizations. The more clearly you convey your skills as they relate to your job target, the greater your chance of landing your ideal job. Chapter 3 helps you identify these skills and qualities so you will be prepared to interview successfully.

JOB-SPECIFIC SKILLS

Employers seek employees with job-specific skills (skills and technical abilities that relate specifically to a particular job). Two examples of job-specific skills are using specialized tools and equipment and using a custom-designed software program.

TRANSFERABLE SKILLS AND ATTITUDES

Change is a constant in today's business world. Strong transferable career skills are the keys to success in managing your career through change. The most influential skills and attitudes are the abilities to:

- Work well with people.
- Plan and manage multiple tasks.
- Maintain a positive attitude.
- Show enthusiasm.

Employers need workers who have transferable career competencies—basic skills and attitudes that are important for all types of work. These skills make you highly marketable because they're needed for a wide variety of jobs and can be transferred from one task, job, or workplace to another. Examples include these:

- Planning skills
- Research skills
- Communication skills
- Human relations and interpersonal skills
- Critical thinking skills
- Management skills

Take, for example, a construction supervisor and an accountant. Both must work well with others, manage time, solve problems, read, and communicate effectively. All of these are transferable competencies. Both professionals must be competent in these areas even though framing a house and balancing a set of

CAREER ACTION 3-1

SKILLS AND COMPETENCIES PROFILE

Directions: Access Career Action Worksheet 3-1 on your Learner's CD, or use the worksheet that begins on page 43 to complete the assignment. When you have completed the assignments, file your worksheet in your Career Management Files Binder.

CAREER COMPETENCIES INVENTORY

Part A: Access Career Action Worksheet 3-2 on your Learner's CD, or use the worksheet that begins on page 47 to complete the assignment. As you read the summaries of the competencies, foundation skills, and personal qualities listed, think about and check each one you've developed.

Part B: Once you have completed Part A of this Career Action, do the following:

1. Write descriptions of at least three tasks you have carried out on a regular basis in each of the following categories:

a. Current or past jobs

b. Community, school, volunteer, or other activities

2. List as many examples as possible of both task- and job-specific skills and transferable competencies you used in each of the activities you described in number 1.

When you have completed the assignment, file your worksheet in your Career Management Files Binder

---

Success tip

Identify your job-specific skills and transferable competencies to convince employers you fit the job.

books (a job-specific skill for each field, respectively) are not related. In every occupation, transferable competencies are as important as technical expertise and job-specific skills.

ASSESSING YOURSELF FROM AN EMPLOYER'S PERSPECTIVE

In Chapter 2, you identified specific skills you developed in school, in work, and through other activities. Chapter 3 has provided you with insights into how employers view skills and competencies. Now it's time to review your inventory and self-assessment from an employer's perspective. How would an employer categorize your skills and personal qualities?

❖ Career Planning Resources

Success tip

Consult a variety of career planning resources to improve the processes of making and confirming your best career choice.

Many convenient resources are available to speed and improve the processes of making and confirming your best career choice. Review the following resources, and place a check mark next to those you could use to improve your career planning. (Note that comprehensive sources of job information are discussed in Chapter 6. You may want to review those now because some of them can also be used as career planning resources.)

- **Your school's career services staff and counselors.** These counselors specialize in assisting students with career planning. They provide aptitude and interest tests, as well as current resources for and information about the job market and occupational fields.

- **The Internet.** A wealth of career planning and job information is available through the Internet. Many sites offer online tools that assess your career interests and values and match the results with appropriate careers and jobs.

The *Your Career: How to Make It Happen* web site (http://levitt.swlearning.com) links to many of these. See your school's career services office for recommendations for helpful web sites, and check out the career center web sites of your local colleges and universities.

- **Computerized career information systems.** With these systems, users complete a computerized questionnaire regarding their personal interests and abilities. The program then provides a list of occupations consistent with a user's answers. Other information provided may include job descriptions, hiring requirements, employment prospects, and education and training requirements. Check with your school's career counselor or state department of education to locate the nearest computerized system.

- **City, county, state, and federal employment or human resources departments.** For information about government occupations, contact the employment or human resources department that manages employment in your target field.

- **Career planning publications.** Ask your school career services counselor or librarian for help in locating books, magazines, and articles about your field and current job target. (Many of these publications are now available online.)

- **People you know.** Contact people you have observed or known, people you admire, and people who have jobs just like the one you dream of. Ask them to help you explore your readiness for a similar job or career.

- **Volunteer work.** Volunteer experience can be a big asset when applying for the job you want. It demonstrates initiative and helps you get a feel for a job and a career. You can volunteer on a part-time or temporary basis or arrange an internship through your school.

PERSONAL BEST

Career Competencies

Your transferable career competencies or skills are every bit as important to your success in the workplace as your job-specific skills and training. The ability to identify, communicate, and demonstrate these skills in an interview could make the difference between you and other qualified job candidates.

The SCANS Report (Secretary's Commission on Achieving Necessary Skills), published by the U.S. Department of Labor, identified the transferable competencies essential for career and business success in the twenty-first century.

Workplace Competencies

1. **RESOURCES:** Identifies, organizes, plans, and manages resources.

2. **INTERPERSONAL:** Works well with others.

3. **INFORMATION:** Acquires, organizes, interprets, and uses information.

4. **SYSTEMS:** Understands complex social, organizational, and technological systems and interrelationships.

5. **TECHNOLOGY:** Works with a variety of technologies (tools, equipment, computers).

Foundation Skills and Personal Qualities

1. **BASIC SKILLS:** Reads, writes, and performs mathematical operations; listens; and speaks.

2. **THINKING SKILLS:** Thinks creatively, makes decisions, solves problems, visualizes, knows how to learn, and reasons.

3. **PERSONAL QUALITIES:** Displays responsibility, self-esteem, sociability, self-management, integrity, and honesty.

❖ Successful Career Planning Requires Flexibility

Changing technologies and a global economy cause some careers to become obsolete or vastly changed. Broaden your job options. Prepare to qualify for two closely related career goals (such as becoming a mathematician or a systems analyst) that require related education, training, and general capabilities. Which

INTERNET CAREER PLANNING RESOURCES

Directions: Use several of the Internet resources below to search for information about your career and job targets, including descriptions of your targeted fields and jobs, salary information, employment outlook projections, and more. Prepare a written summary of your findings, or print useful information that you find. Links can be found on the *Your Career: How to Make It Happen* Web site (http://levitt.swlearning.com).

- Bureau of Labor Statistics
- America's Career InfoNet

- JobStar
- Occupational Outlook Handbook
- collegeboard.com
- O*Net OnLine

When you have completed the assignment, file your findings in your Career Action Worksheet.

transferable career competencies do you have that qualify you for jobs within and between career clusters? Ask a knowledgeable career counselor to help you identify multicareer goals appropriate for your interests and abilities. Continually work at developing your career flexibility and pursuing lifelong learning.

❖ Set Your Career Target

success tip

Use a variety of career planning resources to help you choose and validate appropriate career and job goals.

The work you have completed in this chapter has prepared you to set your career target. You may want to use the visualization skills from Chapter 1 to help you define your personal career objectives. Together with friends and associates, brainstorm appropriate careers. Think about work, hobbies, and volunteer experiences you have enjoyed in the past. What kind of work do you want to do? Where would you like to do this work? How much do you want to get paid for your work? What is the best career match for your unique skills, experiences, values, and interests? The form for Career Action 3-4 will help you organize your thoughts.

MY CAREER TARGET

Directions: Access Career Action Worksheet 3-4 on your Learner's CD, or use the Worksheet on page 50 to complete the assignment.

When you have completed the assignment, file your worksheet in your Career Management Files Binder.

❖ Your Career Portfolio

A portfolio is a collection of documents and other items that demonstrate your skills, abilities, achievements, experience, and training. The purpose of a career portfolio is to organize relevant examples of skills and achievements that you can present during interviews as proof of your qualifications. A career portfolio provides tangible proof of your qualifications. It also demonstrates important skills that employers are seeking: critical thinking, analyzing, planning, and preparation. Examples of appropriate portfolio items include the following:

- An official copy of your transcript(s)

- Your resume

- Exemplary samples of your work, such as business writing, graphic artwork, and printed samples from software presentations

- Evidence of specialized computer usage, such as desktop publishing and web site creation

- Awards

- Work performance evaluations

- Letters of reference

A more comprehensive list of appropriate items and ideas for building your portfolio are contained in the "Career Portfolio" section of Appendix B, "Career Management and Marketing Tools." Additional activities are presented later in this text to assist you in developing an effective portfolio.

Portfolio samples can be from paid or volunteer work, internships, cooperative education, clubs, community activities, and more. Begin considering what you have done or accomplished that best demonstrates your qualifications for the job you want. For example, to demonstrate your computer skills, you could include transcripts listing related coursework or a CD or portable flash drive containing examples of multimedia presentations or programming code you have developed. To demonstrate a strong background in foreign languages, you could include transcripts listing appropriate coursework and a letter of recommendation from an instructor or employer who is familiar with your language skills.

For now, you can use a folder to store appropriate portfolio items to be used later in your job search. Begin listing appropriate items in Career Action 3-5.

> "Formulate and stamp indelibly on your mind a mental picture of yourself succeeding. Hold this picture tenaciously. Never permit it to fade. Your mind will seek to develop this picture!"
> —*Norman Vincent Peale*

success tip

Begin listing appropriate items for your career portfolio that demonstrate your job qualifications.

Presenting a portfolio to a potential employer helps you prove your qualifications for the job.

LIST APPROPRIATE PORTFOLIO ITEMS

Part A: To identify additional useful ideas for your own career portfolio, use two or more search engines to search the Internet for career portfolio information. Also check out other links available on the *Your Career: How to Make It Happen* web site (http://levitt.swlearning.com).

Part B: Access Career Action Worksheet 3-5 on your Learner's CD, or use a separate paper to complete the assignment. Take a moment now to list items that seem appropriate to include in your career portfolio. As you progress through the upcoming chapters, add other items to your list. Later you will be instructed to complete the assembly of your actual portfolio.

_____

_____

_____

_____

_____

_____

_____

_____

When you have completed the assignment, file your worksheet in your Career Management Files Binder.

C H E C K L I S T

ASSESSING YOURSELF FROM AN EMPLOYER'S PERSPECTIVE

- Check each of the actions you are currently taking to increase your career success:

- Identifying job-specific skills and transferable career competencies to convince employers of appropriateness for the job

- Using a variety of career planning resources to help in choosing and validating appropriate career and job goals

- Preparing to qualify for two closely related career goals taht require similar skills and training in order to increase your career flexibility

- Using visualization, brainstorming, personal reflection, and other techniques to set your career target

- Developing a portfolio of items to demonstrate job qualifications for prospective employers

- Collecting items that will demonstrate job qualifications for prospective employers

CRITICAL THINKING QUESTIONS

1. Why is it important to develop a broad career base that is flexible enough to encompass at least two fields?

2. What career planning resources will be most helpful in your job search and career planning activities? Why?

3. Why do employers value employees who have the career competencies and foundation skills identified in the SCANS Report?

For convenient access to valuable career resources, activities, and job information links, visit the companion Web site for this test: ***http:// levitt.swlearning.com***

CAREER ACTION WORKSHEET 3-1

SKILLS AND COMPETENCIES PROFILE

PART 1: JOB-SPECIFIC SKILLS

Directions: Review Career Actions 2-1 and 2-2 to refresh your memory regarding the job-specific skills and transferable career competencies you developed through your education, training, and experiences. Then identify and list below the 10 most important job-specific skills related to your current career target (examples: using job-specific computer software; operating specific equipment or tools; and performing specific tasks, such as mixing dental adhesives).

My Most Important Job-Specific Skills Related to My Career Target

1. _____
2. _____
3. _____
4. _____
5. _____
6. _____
7. _____
8. _____
9. _____
10. _____

In Chapter 9 (resume development) and Chapter 11 (the interview), you will be asked to prove that you have these job-specific skills by documenting examples of times you used them—providing "proof by example." Employers ask for such examples, and you need to be prepared to give them.

(Continued)

PART 2: BASIC SKILLS AND ATTITUDES

Directions: Review the following skill categories and related transferable career competencies. Check the box to the left of each skill category that applies to you in any way. Then circle each transferable competency you have developed (from those listed after each skill category). Finally, list under *Other* any additional transferable competencies you have that relate to each category.

Skill Category	Related Transferable Career Competencies
☐ **Art:**	Drawing, designing, painting, sculpting, computer graphics design
	Other: _____
	_____
☐ **Athletics:**	Physical strength, physical ability, physical coordination, coaching, physical development, agility, team sports, individual sports
	Other: _____
	_____
☐ **Communication:**	Explaining/persuading, strong grammar/vocabulary, organizing thoughts clearly, communicating logically, listening, speaking, good telephone/reception skills, writing, knowledge of foreign languages
	Other: _____
	_____
☐ **Computer Technology:**	Computer operation, researching, training, testing, workflow analysis, evaluating, writing instructions, programming
	Other: _____
	_____
☐ **Creativity:**	Innovative, imaginative, idea person, bold
	Other: _____
	_____
☐ **Engineering:**	Researching, testing, designing, constructing, analyzing, evaluating, controlling, electronic technology
	Other: _____
	_____

(Continued)

☐ **Human Relations:** Counseling, diplomacy, negotiating, patience, outgoing, teamwork ability, understanding, resolving conflict, handling complaints

Other: _____

_____

☐ **Management:** Analyzing data, directing, delegating, evaluating performance, organizing people/data/things, leading, making decisions, managing time, motivating self/others, planning, budgeting money/resources, solving problems, supervising, interviewing/hiring people, owning/operating a business

Other: _____

_____

☐ **Manual/Mechanical:** Good manual dexterity, building, operating, maintaining/ repairing, assembling, Installing, carrying, loading, lifting, cooking, driving/operating vehicles, performing precision work, assessing spatial relationships, operating heavy equipment

Other: _____

_____

☐ **Mathematical:** Mathematical computations, accuracy, analyzing data, mathematical reasoning, statistical problem solving, analyzing cost effectiveness, budgeting, applying formulas, collecting money, calculating

Other: _____

_____

☐ **Office:** Keyboarding, data entry, computer operation, text processing, data processing, office equipment operation, filing/retrieving records, recording data, computing data, record keeping, telephone skills, business writing

Other: _____

_____

☐ **Outdoor Activities:** Animal care, farming, landscaping, grounds care, boating, navigating, oceanographic studies, forestry, logging, mining, fishing, horticulture

Other: _____

_____

(Continued)

☐ **Performing:**
Speaking, acting, dancing, singing, musical ability, comedy, conducting

Other: _____

_____

☐ **Sales/Promotion:**
Persuading, negotiating, promoting, influencing, selling, projecting enthusiasm, organizing, handling rejection, following up

Other: _____

_____

☐ **Scientific Activities:**
Investigating, researching, analyzing, systematizing, observing, diagnosing

Other: _____

_____

☐ **Service/General:**
Serving, referring, receiving, billing, handling complaints, good customer relations, good listening skills, patience, managing difficult people, helping others, relating to others

Other: _____

_____

☐ **Service/Medical:**
Nursing, diagnosing, treating, rehabilitating, counseling, consoling, sympathizing, managing stress/emergencies, good interpersonal skills

Other: _____

_____

☐ **Training/Teaching:**
Teaching skills/knowledge, tutoring, researching instructional content, organizing/developing content, explaining logically/clearly, demonstrating clearly, coaching others, evaluating learning, addressing all learning styles, using instructional technology

Other: _____

_____

CAREER COMPETENCIES INVENTORY

Directions: Check the box to the left of each competency, skill, or quality you've developed, and circle the portions of the detailed descriptions that apply to you.

PART 1: WORKPLACE COMPETENCIES

RESOURCES: Identifies, organizes, plans, and manages resources

☐ **Manages Time:** Selects relevant, goal-related activities; ranks activities in order of importance; allocates time to activities; and understands, prepares, and follows schedules

☐ **Manages Money:** Uses budgets, keeps records, and makes adjustments to meet objectives

☐ **Manages Materials and Facilities:** Acquires, stores, allocates, and uses materials and/or space efficiently

☐ **Manages Human Resources:** Assesses skills and distributes work accordingly, uses coaching/mentoring skills with peers and subordinates, evaluates performance, and provides feedback

INTERPERSONAL: Works well with others

☐ **Participates as Team Member:** Contributes to group effort

☐ **Teaches Others New Skills**

☐ **Serves Clients/Customers:** Works to satisfy customers' expectations

☐ **Exercises Leadership:** Communicates ideas to justify position and persuades/convinces

☐ **Negotiates Decisions:** Works toward agreements involving exchange of resources and resolves divergent interests

☐ **Respects Cultural Diversity:** Works well with people from diverse backgrounds

INFORMATION: Acquires, organizes, interprets, and uses information

☐ **Acquires/Evaluates Information**

☐ **Organizes/Maintains Information**

☐ **Interprets/Communicates Information**

☐ **Uses Computers to Process Information**

SYSTEMS: Understands complex social, organizational, and technological systems and interrelationships

☐ **Understands Systems:** Knows how social, organizational, and technological systems work and operates effectively with them

(Continued)

☐ **Monitors/Corrects Performance:** Distinguishes trends, predicts impacts on system operations, diagnoses deviations in systems' performance, and corrects malfunctions

☐ **Improves/Designs Systems:** Suggests modifications to existing systems and develops new or alternative systems to improve performance

TECHNOLOGY: Works with a variety of technologies

☐ **Selects Technology:** Chooses procedures, tools, or equipment, including computers and related technologies

☐ **Applies Technology to Task:** Understands overall intent and proper procedures for setup and operation of equipment

☐ **Maintains/Troubleshoots Technology:** Prevents, identifies, or solves problems with equipment, including computers and other technologies

PART 2: FOUNDATION SKILLS AND PERSONAL QUALITIES

BASIC SKILLS: Reads, writes, performs arithmetic/mathematical operations, listens, and speaks

☐ **Reading:** Locates, understands, and interprets written information, including material in documents such as manuals, graphs, and schedules

☐ **Writing:** Communicates thoughts, ideas, information, and messages in writing and creates documents such as letters, directions, manuals, reports, graphs, and flowcharts

☐ **Arithmetic/Mathematics:** Performs basic computations and approaches practical problems by choosing appropriately from a variety of mathematical techniques

☐ **Listening:** Receives, attends to, interprets, and responds to verbal messages and other cues

☐ **Speaking:** Organizes ideas and communicates orally

THINKING SKILLS: Thinks creatively, makes decisions, solves problems, visualizes, knows how to learn, and reasons

☐ **Creative Thinking:** Generates new ideas

☐ **Decision Making:** Specifies goals and constraints, generates alternatives, considers risks, facilitates group decision-making processes, and evaluates and chooses best alternative

☐ **Problem Solving:** Recognizes problems, devises and implements plan of action, and facilitates problem solving and brainstorming discussions

☐ **Knowing How to Learn:** Uses efficient learning techniques to acquire and apply new knowledge and skills

☐ **Reasoning:** Discovers a rule or principle underlying the relationship between two or more objects and applies it when solving a problem

(Continued)

PERSONAL QUALITIES: Displays responsibility, self-esteem, sociability, self-management, integrity, and honesty

☐ **Responsibility:** Exerts a high level of effort, perseveres toward goal attainment, and multitasks effectively

☐ **Self-Esteem:** Believes in own self-worth and maintains a positive view of self

☐ **Sociability:** Demonstrates understanding, friendliness, adaptability, and empathy; manages conflict effectively; is polite

☐ **Self-Management:** Assesses self accurately, sets personal goals, monitors progress, works well under pressure, and exhibits self-control

☐ **Integrity/Honesty:** Chooses ethical courses

Fine-Tune Your Competencies List

Directions: Review the items you identified in Career Action 3-2. Then select the 10 strongest of these transferable career competencies and basic skills related to your current job target. List them below.

1. _____   6. _____

2. _____   7. _____

3. _____   8. _____

4. _____   9. _____

5. _____   10. _____

NOTE: You will expand on this information in Chapters 9 and 11.

MY CAREER TARGET

Directions: Answer the following questions about your current career target.

1. In what career field are you planning to seek employment? (Examples: accounting, office management, health care, teaching, administration, construction, and computer technology)

_____

_____

_____

_____

2. What specific job or jobs are you targeting in your employment search? (List every job you are qualified for and interested in pursuing. Maximize your options by listing jobs within and between career fields or clusters that require transferable competencies you have.)

_____

_____

_____

_____

_____

3. What specific activities are you most interested in performing in your ideal job? What energizes and excites you most?

_____

_____

_____

_____

_____

4. Are you willing to travel or relocate? Explain.

_____

_____

_____

_____

❖ Notes

_____

_____

_____

_____

_____

_____

_____

_____

_____

_____

_____

_____

_____

_____

_____

_____

_____

_____

_____

_____

_____

_____

_____

_____

_____

_____

_____